The Eclipse of Community Mental Health and Erich Lindemann

These volumes make new contributions to the history of psychiatry and society in three ways: First, they propose a theory of values and ideology influencing the evolution of psychiatry and society in recurring cycles and survey the history of psychiatry in recent centuries in light of this theory. Second, they review the waxing, prominence, and waning of community mental health as an example of a segment of this cyclical history of psychiatry. Third, they provide the first biography of Erich Lindemann, one of the founders of social and community psychiatry, and explore the interaction of the prominent contributor with the historical environment and the influence this has on both. We return to the issue of values and ideologies as influences on psychiatry, whether or not it is accepted as professionally proper. This is intended to stimulate self-reflection and the acceptance of the values sources of ideology, their effect on professional practice, and the effect of values-based ideology on the community in which psychiatry practices. The books will be of interest to psychiatric teachers and practitioners, health planners, and socially responsible citizens.

David G. Satin is a board-certified psychiatrist who has trained at the Massachusetts General and McLean Hospitals, has been Assistant Professor of Psychiatry at Harvard Medical School, where he also obtained his MD and taught gerontology and the history of psychiatry, and has had a clinical practice in adult and geriatric psychiatry.

The Eclipse of Community Mental Health and Erich Lindemann

Community Mental Health, Erich Lindemann, and Social Conscience in American Psychiatry, Volume 3

David G. Satin

NEW YORK AND LONDON

First published 2021
by Routledge
52 Vanderbilt Avenue, New York, NY 10017

and by Routledge
2 Park Square, Milton Park, Abingdon, Oxon, OX14 4RN

Routledge is an imprint of the Taylor & Francis Group, an informa business

© 2021 David G. Satin

The right of David G. Satin to be identified as author of this work has been asserted in accordance with sections 77 and 78 of the Copyright, Designs and Patents Act 1988.

All rights reserved. No part of this book may be reprinted or reproduced or utilised in any form or by any electronic, mechanical, or other means, now known or hereafter invented, including photocopying and recording, or in any information storage or retrieval system, without permission in writing from the publishers.

Trademark notice: Product or corporate names may be trademarks or registered trademarks, and are used only for identification and explanation without intent to infringe.

Library of Congress Cataloging-in-Publication Data
Names: Satin, David G., author.
Title: Community mental health, Erich Lindemann, and social conscience in American psychiatry / David G. Satin.
Description: New York, NY : Routledge, 2021. | Includes bibliographical references and indexes.
Identifiers: LCCN 2020026022 (print) | LCCN 2020026023 (ebook) | ISBN 9780429331350 (v. 1 ; ebook) | ISBN 9781000169805 (v. 1 ; adobe pdf) | ISBN 9781000169812 (v. 1 ; mobi) | ISBN 9781000169829 (v. 1 ; epub) | ISBN 9780429331374 (v. 2 ; ebook) | ISBN 9781000169867 (v. 2 ; adobe pdf) | ISBN 9781000169881 (v. 2 ; mobi) | ISBN 9781000169904 (v. 2 ; epub) | ISBN 9780429331367 (v. 3 ; ebook) | ISBN 9781000171280 (v. 3 ; adobe pdf) | ISBN 9781000171273 (v. 3 ; mobi) | ISBN 9781000171297 (v. 3 ; epub) | ISBN 9780367354336 (v. 1 ; hardcover) | ISBN 9780367354374 (v. 2 ; hardcover) | ISBN 9780367354350 (v. 3 ; hardcover)
Subjects: LCSH: Social psychiatry. | Community psychiatry. | Mental health services.
Classification: LCC RC455 (ebook) | LCC RC455 .S197 2021 (print) | DDC 362.2—dc23
LC record available at https://lccn.loc.gov/2020026022

ISBN: 978-0-367-35435-0 (hbk)
ISBN: 978-0-429-33136-7 (ebk)

Typeset in Sabon
by Apex CoVantage, LLC

This history is dedicated to those who created it: the people who raised and struggled with issues of social influences on mental health, the place of social responsibility in mental health professional practice, and the social conscience of society. Committed and thoughtful people took different approaches on these questions but confronted them seriously. Sometimes this brought fulfillment, sometimes despair. Often it took courage; sometimes this resulted in professional and personal injury. Such is the fate of committed people in the historical clash of values. This record and interpretation is especially dedicated to those who unearthed for the record their experiences, memories, and insights—sometimes with pain—to teach their successors about this endeavor. We trust it has been worth their efforts:

"All of us bear witness to the dissolution of our piece of creation. Only the novelist can restore to us, in the miracle of ink that pours itself like blood onto paper, the lineaments of our lost worlds, alive".[1]

Note

1. Rosen, Norma, "My Son, the Novelist", LIVES column, *The New York Times Magazine*, 8/3/1997, p. 60

Figure FM-1 Frontispiece: Erich Lindemann, Palo Alto, CA, 1960s [courtesy Lindemann Estate]

Contents

List of Figures viii
Preface for All Three Volumes x
Acknowledgments for All Three Volumes xix

1 A Sampling of Community Mental Health Programs   1

2 The Counterrevolution of Biology and Business
   and the Suppression of Community Mental Health:
   1966–1974   150

3 Continuity and Replacement: After 1974—Legacy
   and Successors of Community Mental Health   310

4 Lindemann, Social Ideology, and Social Conscience
   in Psychiatry and Society: Expectations
   and Experience   388

Appendix: Informants Interviewed 445
Index 451

Figures

FM-1	Frontispiece: Erich Lindemann, Palo Alto, CA, 1960s	vi
1.1	Hugo Biehl, M.D., Meiner, Ph.D., Jung, Ph.D., research staff, Zentralinstitut für Seelisches Gesundheit, Mannheim, West Germany	121
1.2	Wofgang Bolm, M.D. (psychiatrist), Ingmar Steinhart (psychologist), Irmeli Rotha (social worker), Social Psychiatry Department, Freie Universität Berlin	122
1.3	Hartmut Dziewas, M.D., Prof. of Social Psychiatry, University of Hamburg, new director, Im Schlosspark Klinik	122
1.4	Heinz Häfner, Direktor and E. Schramek., secretary, Zentralinstitut für Seelisches Gesundheit, Mannheim, W. Germany	123
1.5	Alfred Kraus, Dept. of Psychiatry, phenomenologist, University of Heidelberg, W. Germany	123
1.6	Prof. Christoph Mundt, Direktor, Psychiatrische Polyklinik; and Prof. Werner Janzarik, Professor (Chairman) Psychiatry, University of Heidelberg	124
1.7	Walter Ritter von Baeyer, Heidelberg University	124
1.8	Hartmut Schneider, director, Social Psychiatry Unit. Zentralinstitut für Seelisches Gesundheit, Mannheim, West Germany	125
1.9	Caspar Kulenkampff and Ulrich Hoffmann, Aktion Psychisch Kranke, Bonn, W. Germany	125
1.10	Frau Dr. Christa Meyn, German Federal Ministerium Jugend-Familie-Gesundheit, Bonn	125
1.11	Niels and Britta Pörksen, 1988	126
2.1	Budget of the National Institute of Mental Health, 1948–77	155
2.2	Erich Lindemann Mental Health Center	264
2.3	Erich Lindemann Mental Health Center	265
2.4	Erich Lindemann Mental Health Center, 1970	266
2.5	Erich Lindemann Mental Health Center	266

Figures ix

2.6 Erich Lindemann Mental Health Center 267
2.7 Jean Farrell (Erich Lindemann's administrative assistant) outside the Erich Lindemann Mental Health Center, summer 1973 268
2.8 Erich Lindemann Mental Health Center dedication, 11/22/71—Dr. Lindemann in earnest conversation 268
2.9 Erich Lindemann Mental Health Center dedication, 11/22/71—Erich and Elizabeth Lindemann 269
2.10 Erich Lindemann Mental Health Center dedication, 11/22/71—Erich Lindemann receiving applause 270
2.11 Lindau Psychotherapy Group, 1973 271
2.12 Lindau Psychotherapy Group Meeting Place, 1968 271
2.13 Erich Lindemann, Palo Alto, CA, 1960s 272
2.14 Erich Lindemann in California, 1969 272
2.15 Erich Lindemann at the piano at home, Palo Alto, CA, 1966–8 273
2.16 Erich Lindemann, terminally ill, 1972 273
2.17 Erich Lindemann death certificate, 11/16/74 274
3.1 Lindau Psychotherapy Group, 4/8/07 375
3.2 Elizabeth B. Lindemann and Brenda Lindemann, Anaheim, CA—American Public Health Association award to Erich Lindemann, 1983 376
3.3 Plainfield, VT—Ami (8), Jamin (6–1/2), and Brenda Lindemann with "Kitty Tall Tail", Fall 1996 376

Preface for All Three Volumes

One of the pitfalls of the celebration of history is "presentism"—the self-centered belief that current values and perspectives are the only or highest in history. Oliver Wendell Holmes tartly observed: "Much, therefore, which is now very commonly considered to be the result of experience, will be recognized in the next, or in some succeeding generation, as no such result at all, but as a foregone conclusion, based on some prevalent belief or fashion of the time".[1] And, further, that perspectives change: "One has to remember there's a kind of cyclical rhythm in American public affairs, cycles of intense activism succeeded by a time of exhaustion and acquiescence".[2]

Social history has a tradition of tracing historical movements through outstanding figures, the individuals exemplifying as much as determining the movements.[3] "Psychohistory" goes further, seeking to understand group movements as the cumulative effect of the psychodynamics of individuals: "Methodological individualism is the principle that group processes may be entirely explained by ... psychological laws governing the motivations and behavior of individuals".[4] Erich Lindemann's life—1900 to 1974—was contemporaneous with the origins of and developments in the community mental health (CMH) movement. He was involved in many important CMH activities and with important participants, and he contributed to and influenced CMH in important ways, both as a leader of its admirers and as a target of its critics. His personal development, the social movements and academic developments around him, the education to which he was exposed and which he chose, the sequence of his professional development, and the responses—positive and negative—which he received, paralleled at least the health promotion and illness prevention branch of CMH. We see in his person the development of the values and ideology that were mirrored in that branch and it's conflict with other psychiatric ideologies. For these reasons, he provides a useful microcosm of the history of CMH. In addition, there has never been a comprehensive biography of this important contributor to CMH and psychiatry, so that people develop their opinions of him based on only reports or fragments of his thinking and activities. A more complete understanding of the man will make him and his place in psychiatry more comprehensible.

Most emphatically this is not a work of hagiography. We subscribe to Iago Galdston's dual cautions:[5]

Medical history as it has been written during the past 100 years manifestly suffers from two corrupting biases, *progressivism* and *hero worship*. Medical history is represented as a pageant of progressive enlightenment, celebrating the labors and achievements of its medical heroes.

On the contrary, we take the social history stance of seeing people and events as the manifestations of social conditions and forces from which they arise. In this sense, Lindemann was molded by the values and ideas of the personal and public times through which he lived and contributed his values and ideas to the ideologies and movements in which he participated. In this sense, we seek to understand the interaction of the man and the social (and mental health) environment. We try to understand the special contributions of these ideologies and ideas, resisting the temptation to see some as more ideal than others, heeding Sigerest's admonition: "Nothing could be more foolish in comparing ancient theories with ours than to call progressive what corresponds to our views, and primitive what is different".[6]

This book contributes to the understanding of the roots, germination, flowering, response, overthrow, and successors of CMH. Norman Bell had proposed a similar study of the origins of social psychiatry:[7]

> It is characteristic of the United States as a nation that it pays little attention to its past. Our eyes are usually on the future . . . This is particularly true of psychiatry and of the social sciences. Only major figures are preserved in the memories of the present generation and even these memories tend to fade . . . In the field of social psychiatry, this fall-out of information works a special hardship. Although the term "social psychiatry" has been in use for half a century, it is treated as if it were a recent development. Insights which were gained decades ago are repeatedly discovered anew. The long history of engagement, uneasy marriage, annulment or divorce and remarriage between psychiatry and social science is unknown or disregarded. Thus, the lessons which the past has to offer are not available to the present generation . . . In the last ten years the phrase, social psychiatry, has been institutionalized in the titles of journals, professorships and institutes. There is little current disagreement that social factors are involved in the etiology, treatment and effects of mental illness . . . The investigators believe that the field of social psychiatry has reached the stage of maturity where it can and should examine its origins and assess its present standing.

That the neglect of important aspects of the past continues to be true of CMH at present is attested to by a comment of a reviewer who persisted in rejecting this study for publication to correct that neglect:[8]

2. Is the article/book/monograph a significant contribution to knowledge?

A. What is its relation to other works in the field? Does it offer new concepts?

I'm not actually sure how much of a field there is, since I'm unaware that there is much current writing about topics such as prevention and social psychiatry. The basic concepts it explores are old, but by no means irrelevant. The field of mental health prevention essentially has been abandoned over the past 25 years.

People often speak of organizations or institutions as influencing or leading society. While society is heterogeneous and there is ongoing dissonance and rivalry for influence among the subcultures and ideologies, they are all substantially creatures of the society within which they developed. As such, they reflect the manifold needs and values of the host society rather than being external influences on it. The life cycle of the CMH movement illustrates the contest of values in psychiatry, and we argue that this reflects the contest of values in the society. Thus, this exploration of the CMH movement contributes to an understanding of the shifting of societal values and ideologies during that era.

A "movement" is defined as "a series of actions and events taking place over a period of time and working to foster a principle or policy ... an organized effort by supporters of a common goal".[9] Few movements are so homogeneous that all actions are focused toward a single goal. Usually there are shifting and evolving ideas among people who have varying intensity, duration, and motivations of participation. It is after the fact—in historical perspective—that the commonality of ideas and character of results become apparent.

Inductively, a movement is an accumulation of activities, people, concepts, and, above all, intentions. These intentions are the action implications of the ideologies and ideas through which participants understand the participants and goals of the movement. Further, ideas and ideologies are related to values—beliefs and feelings of esteem, worth, and priority that weight these ideas and ideologies. Thus, it follows that the values that shape the ideas and ideologies that, in turn, form the intentions of those participating in a movement, all, in some sense, become embodied in the actions and programs that result from that movement. In other words, movements, even those believed to be "objective" and "scientific", are not independent of the ideas, values, and ideologies of those who participate in them. As Oliver Wendell Holmes the elder recognized:[10]

> The truth is, that medicine, professedly founded on observation, is as sensitive to outside influences, political, religious, philosophical, imaginative, as is the barometer to the changes of atmospheric density. Theoretically it ought to go on its own straightforward inductive path, without regard to changes of government or to fluctuations of public opinion. But look a moment . . . and see . . . a closer relation between the Medical Sciences and the condition of Society and the general thought of the time, than would at first be suspected. Observe the coincidences between certain great political and intellectual periods and the appearance of illustrious medical reformers and teachers.

Murray and Adeline Levine applied much the same observations to more recent mental health theory and practice:[11]

> As social scientists, and as practitioners in the mental health field, we pride ourselves on our objectivity, and upon the empirical base of our theories, our generalizations, and our practices. Let me suggest, on the contrary, that we are all creatures of our times; that our theories and practices are shaped as much, or more, by broad social forces as they are by inference from hard data . . . the set of variables which have been included in the theories is too limited . . . The forms of practice are said to be determined by whatever conceptions of personality and of psychopathology are dominant . . . vital details of practice in the mental health fields are determined by potent social forces which are reflected in the organization and delivery of services, in the forms of service which are delivered, and in conceptions of the nature of the mental health problem.

The relationship between ideology and values applies also to psychiatry. In his talk at Stanford Medical Center, Erich Lindemann hearkened back to the sociology and psychology of psychiatry:

> Karl Mannheim, in the sociology of knowledge, began to talk about ideologies. He pointed out that theories represent values which for some reason are important to an individual, and for which he feels he must fight. And about ten years ago, Melvin Sabshin together with Anselm Strauss came around to the notion that most of the convictions in psychiatry are really ideologies for which you fight; and that some of the information which you gather is collected . . . because they want to get to a particular goal.[12]

These issues certainly apply to the community mental health movement. The overriding commonality is attending to populations of functionally interrelated people ("community") in addition to individuals, problems, or techniques. There have been many studies of this movement focusing on chronology of events, personages, politics, economics, and technical theories.[13] The present history is unique in its focus on the ideas and ideologies participants brought to the movement, which motivated their participation, through which they understood CMH, and which became actualized in their plans and actions.

The CMH movement embodied several ideologies reflected in their respective definitions of CMH. One was making traditional psychiatric treatment available to a larger population. A second was developing new strategies and facilities for the treatment of mental illnesses and for bringing these treatments to mentally ill populations, with special emphasis on the severely and chronically mentally ill. A third was an interest in the prevention of mental illness; a professional role in "mental health", and human fulfillment; and often the association of these with a democratic, participatory approach to caregiving and care programs in the context of cultural settings. And a fourth was the shift of attention and effort to change and improvement in society as the source of mental illness and mental health. These all imply values that contended with one another in professional technical debate, in competition for material resources and programmatic control, and in battles for public and official recognition. These considerations will lead us to a consideration of the social values implied in the various psychiatric ideologies—biological, psychological, and social—and the mental health goals and programs that are the consequences of these values.

Three overarching issues are highlighted by this study and will be followed throughout:

A. Cycles of psychiatric ideology repeat through history, contrasting and contesting with one another.

   Biological, psychological, and social perspectives and priorities predominate sequentially. CMH represents a social psychiatry phase.[14]

B. These ideologies reflect differing societal values, which, in turn, appear in their theories and are essential constituents of their goals and programs. The interrelationship of societal values, psychiatric ideology and movements, and Lindemann's professional and personal life are mutually illuminating.

C. Any new ideology confronts attitudes toward change versus conservation. These can be expressed through growth versus tradition, or, more aggressively, overthrow versus suppression. The character and strategy of change affects its reception by the host system. In addition, the character of leadership reflects and colors the program led and the reaction of its environment. This leadership may be nurturing and convincing or threatening and attacking and may take the role of the guru or the wielder of power.

Resources on which this study is based include the following: The author has the advantage of having participated in and observed at first hand some of these events and people and thus has a technical and personal understanding of them. Important literature on social and psychiatric ideologies has been reviewed as the lens through which to understand the CMH movement. We explored the social and psychiatric climate and movements just prior to the movement (the late 19th and early 20th centuries), during the movement (roughly the middle third of the 20th century), and just after the CMH movement (the late 20th century). We have reviewed other studies of CMH. Primary sources[15] include 105 interviews (by the author or others) of people who have worked in CMH and psychiatry, both in the United States and Germany (Erich Lindemann's country of origin), participants in CMH programs, and authorities in contemporary psychiatry and society. We utilized interviews of Lindemann himself, members of his family, and those who knew him. We also reviewed all of Erich Lindemann's papers, as well as selected documents from other CMH programs and institutions. The author is solely responsible for the selection of materials and interpretations and conclusions drawn from them.

CMH touched on major social issues, such as the causes and cures of mental and social pathology, the responsibilities of private agencies and government in dealing with these problems, and priorities in the allocation of social resources—"what we can afford". It also raised considerations of professionalism: identity, scope of practice, financial support, power, and interrelationships—all sensitive issues. Therefore, it caused much debate and not a little hostility and conflict. We expect that revisiting events, persons, issues, and interpretations in this book will stimulate reaction. We hope for debate and the surfacing of further information. We expect also the resumption of old hurts and prejudices—in the past, people have accepted only information and interpretations that validated their prejudices about community mental health and Erich Lindemann. For example, Dr. Lindemann's professional files were relegated to a flooded basement in an outhouse of the Massachusetts General Hospital, and successors in the Department of Psychiatry resisted releasing them to safety and study because of resentment of Lindemann and rejection of the legitimacy of CMH.[16] We intend light as well as expecting heat from this endeavor.

Historical writing can be memoir, advocacy, or observation without conclusion. Memoir offers the most authentic data. Advocacy is always present, whether overt, covert, or unconscious. Observation without conclusions has limited usefulness. This study brings some information not heretofore published. It is a further attempt at assembling it in a coherent narrative regarding ideas and ideologies—a perspective not previously attempted. It suggests patterns and draws conclusions about values, motivations, and their effects. It is in this manner that this study contributes to a new, useful perspective on CMH with implications for the history of its social context. We offer it as a further product of the community mental health movement.

In sum, this work offers

- a theory of values and their elaboration to ideologies as motivators of history with historical documentation
- this theory demonstrated in the historical cycle of ideologies in society, medicine, and psychiatry
- a history of the CMH movement and its historical context as one manifestation of social ideology
- a biography of Erich Lindemann as an outstanding figure in social and community psychiatry
- Lindemann and CMH as an example of the interaction of personality and historical context

This work is presented in three volumes:

The Sources and Development of Social and Community Psychiatry: Community Mental Health, Erich Lindemann, and Social Conscience in American Psychiatry, Volume 1

The Challenge of Community Mental Health and Erich Lindemann: Community Mental Health, Erich Lindemann, and Social Conscience in American Psychiatry, Volume 2

The Eclipse of Community Mental Health and Erich Lindemann: Community Mental Health, Erich Lindemann, and Social Conscience in American Psychiatry, Volume 3

Notes

1. Holmes, Oliver Wendell, "Currents and Counter-Currents in Medical Science", an address delivered before the Massachusetts Medical Society Annual Meeting 5/30/1860, in Holmes, Oliver Wendell (ed.) *Medical Essays, 1842–1882* (Boston: Houghton, Mifflin, 1883), pp. 175, 177
2. Schlesinger, Arthur M., "Arthur Schlesinger Answers His Critics", *Boston Sunday Globe*, 10/1/1978
3. See, for example, Tuchman, B.W., *A Distant Mirror* (New York: Ballantine, 1978), Tuchman, B.W., *Stillwell and the American Experience in China* (New York: Ballantine, 1971), Caro, Robert A., *Robert Moses and the Fall of New York* (New York: Knopf, 1974)
4. DeMause, Lloyd, *Foundations of Psychohistory* (New York: Creative Roots, Inc., 1982). For instance, "Methodological individualism is the principle that

group processes may be entirely explained by (1) psychological laws governing the motivation and behavior of individuals and (b) descriptions of their current physical historical situation, which itself is only the outcome of prior motivations acting on physical reality . . . All group phenomena have psychological explanations; individuals in groups act differently than individuals alone only because they split their psychic conflicts differently, not because some 'social' force is acting on them . . . With the disappearance of the deathless entity 'society' all group values are revealed as tentative and subject to change each generation; what now seems problematic is not change but constancy" (Chapter 4 THE PSYCHOGENIC THEORY OF HISTORY . . . 1C., p. 134).

5. Galdston, Iago, "Preface: On Medial Historiography—By Way of Introduction", in Galdston, Iago (ed.) *Historic Derivations of Modern Psychiatry* (New York: McGraw Hill, 1967), p. 2
6. Sigerist, Henry, *A History of Medicine*, vol. I (London: Oxford University Press, 1951), p. 10
7. "2/27/63 "The Origin of Social Psychiatry", grant application to PHS, DHEW", 2/27/1963, p. 7. [folder "BELL, NORMAN W., M.D.", Box IIIB1 e 2), A–E", Erich Lindemann Collection, Center for the History of Medicine, Francis A. Countway Library of Medicine, Boston, MA]
8. Reviewer 2 comment, American Philosophical Society, 11/6/18
9. *The American Heritage Dictionary of the English Language*, Third Edition (Boston: Houghton Mifflin, 1992), p. 1182
10. Holmes, Oliver Wendell, 1883, *ibid*, p. 177
11. Levine, Murray and Levine, Adeline, "THE MORE THINGS CHANGE", Yale University-Psycho-Educational Clinic (manuscript, late 1960s), folder "LEVINE: SOCIAL FORCES + M.H.", IIIB3 d, Erich Lindemann Collection, Rare Books Department, Countway Library of Medicine, Boston, MA
12. Lindemann, Erich, "Talk Given by Erich Lindemann to Staff of Student Health Center at Stanford", 11/12/1971 (Lindemann Collection, Rare Books Department, Francis A. Countway Library of Medicine, Boston, MA), p. 13
13. Musto, David, "What Ever Happened to Community Mental Health?" *The Public Interest* 39:53–79 (1975, Spring); Greenblatt, Milton, *Psychopolitics* (New York: Grune & Stratton, 1978)
14. Almond and Astrachan identified these three competing ideological perspectives in the training of psychiatric residents, and named them "Directive-Organic", Analytic-Psychological (described in Hollingshead, A. and Redlich, F., *Social Class and Mental Illness* (New York: Wiley, 1958)), and "Sociotherapeutic" (as discussed by Sharaf, M. and Levinson, D., "The Quest for Omnipotence in Professional Training", *International Journal of Psychiatry* 4:426–442 (1967)). The overlap of these ideologies was noted by Armor, D. and Klerman, G., "From Community Mental Health to Human Service Ideology", *Journal of Health and Social Behavior* 9:243–255 (1968); and Brauer *et al.* Almond, R. and Astrachan, B., "Social System Training for Psychiatric Residents", *Psychiatry* 32:277–291 (1969)
15. Primary sources are archived in the Erich Lindemann Collection, Center for the History of Medicine, Francis A. Countway Library of Medicine, Harvard Medical School, Boston, MA
16. For instance, Francis O. Schmitt, who shared scientific values and mutual support with Lindemann, used his position as Trustee and member of Scientific Advisory Committee of the Massachusetts General Hospital to have the papers released, using a mixture of diplomatic notice and warning: "I was informed that you have been good enough to interest yourself protectively in the papers of the late Erich Lindemann. Erich, who was a very close friend

of mine, was a great scholar and a great contributor to the development of social psychiatry . . . It is a matter of great importance that his papers be preserved and it is my understanding that they now rest in the basement of the Mass General but that Countway Library has offered to take them into protective custody. Dr. Satin is working on the papers as a labor of love . . . I believe that Mr. David Crocket [Special Assistant to the General Director of the Massachusetts General Hospital] is also acquainted with the facts on the case and is also very much interested in helping . . . I intend to keep in touch with the progress of Dr. Satin and Mrs. Lindemann and to be helpful . . . I look forward to seeing you again at the time of the visitation of the Scientific Advisory Committee . . . With best personal greetings, I am . . ." (letter from Francis O. Schmitt to Dr. Thomas Hackett, [Chief] Psychiatry Department, Massachusetts General Hospital, 12/5/78; in Box XII 1 folder "Satin-Bio of E.L.", Erich Lindemann Collection, Center for the History of Medicine, Francis A. Countway Library of Medicine, Boston, MA

Acknowledgments for All Three Volumes

Elizabeth Brainerd Lindemann contributed invaluable acute observations about Erich Lindemann and his activities and associates and facilitated access to other valuable sources. However, she maintained a realistic perspective, balancing keeping faith with Lindemann and his works with having this history honest, even-handed, and constructive. She also lent the gentle impetus to bring to fruition the review of community mental health that Dr. Lindemann could not bring himself to complete.

Special appreciation is due to Richard J. Wolfe, former Joseph Garland Librarian at the Boston Medical Library, and Rare Books Librarian at the Francis A. Countway Library of Medicine, Harvard Medical School. His idea of archiving was to support all areas of scholarship and researchers, and in this service, he was most generous with advice, space, resources, and encouragement. His mentorship helped turn an idea into a completed work. The resources and support he offered were sorely missed after his departure.

The late Francis O. Schmitt, Ph.D., Chairman of the Department of Biology and Institute Professor at the Massachusetts Institute of Technology, Chairman of the Neurosciences Research Program, and Trustee and Chairman of the Committee on Research of the Massachusetts General Hospital, was crucial in obtaining Erich Lindemann's papers and transferring them to the Countway Library of Medicine for safekeeping and study.

Appreciation is due the 105 people interviewed for their insights into community mental health (CMH), Erich Lindemann, the development of psychiatry, and the influence of contemporary society. They made themselves available and took time to discuss their experiences and ideas. Not infrequently, these rearoused difficult and sometimes painful memories. We are grateful for their honesty and unique contributions.

The American Philosophical Society provided financial support via Grant No. 8224 from the Penrose Fund. Its interest in this exploration extended to the publication of a preliminary monograph, which helped structure this research. Similarly, the *Deutscher Akademischer Austauschdienst* (German Academic Exchange Service) awarded Grant

Program Area II no. 315 to support a study trip through the Federal Republic of Germany. This allowed both exploration of community mental health and the social psychiatry tradition in Germany, as well as Dr. Lindemann's learning and teaching there at various times in his career.

The National Library of Medicine, through Publication Grant Award no. 42 USC 280–9 42 CFR 52, provided limited financial support for a period during the collection and organization of interviews and records, though it denied extension of funding with the prediction that the book would not be completed—now happily disproved.

Photographs are included with permission:

> Photographs from the Lindemann family and Erich Lindemann papers retained by the Lindemann family are included with the permission of Brenda Lindemann, executrix, Lindemann Estate.
> Photographs by David G. Satin are included with his permission.

The author has the advantage of having lived through the latter part of the CMH movement, participated in and observed at first hand some of these events, and met some of those involved. He interviewed many principal contributors to CMH, those who knew Erich Lindemann, and participants in parallel programs. He also consulted others with experience of CMH and contemporary psychiatry and society, as well as written reports and reviews. He is solely responsible for the selection of materials to be included, their interpretation, and the conclusions drawn.

It is noteworthy that the Psychiatry Service of the Massachusetts General Hospital, which Lindemann had led, was not interested in or supportive of this review of his work and person. A successor Chief of the Service, Thomas Hackett, was reluctant to release his papers for adequate preservation and use until Francis O. Schmitt, a member of the MGH Board of Trustees, expressed his interest in the project. And a subsequent MGH Chief of Psychiatry, Edwin Cassem, thought community mental health and those interested in it did not represent good psychiatry and sought to eliminate them from the department. It is also noteworthy that, while professional journals outside psychiatry (*The Proceedings of the American Philosophical Society* and *The American Journal of Community Psychology*) found monographs on this topic worthy of publication, psychiatry journals (*The Archives of General Psychiatry, Hospital and Community Psychiatry, The Journal of Nervous and Mental Diseases, Social Psychiatry*) did not. This all took place in an era of biological psychiatry ideology; perhaps it is another illustration of the difference in these value systems extending beyond the theory and practice of social psychiatry even to its literature.

1 A Sampling of Community Mental Health Programs

Introduction

It will be remembered that social and professional change, in addition to the social and moral content, was an important factor in the history of community mental health. Aldous Huxley noted the resistance to change as a human characteristic:

> The vast majority of human beings dislike and even dread all notions with which they are not familiar. Hence it comes about that at their first appearance innovators have always been derided as fools and madmen.

Derek Bok, former president of Harvard University, particularized this observation to academia:

> many of the most important changes that have taken place in the University have been pushed through in the face of indifference or even opposition on the part of the faculty . . . A president who always defers to the Faculty will just as surely condemn the University to sluggish conservatism.

During various phases of the era of community mental health [CMH] there were many experiments with community mental health programs. While we do not present a comprehensive inventory of them all or a complete history of each one, we offer descriptions or vignettes of several to give the flavor of the variety of CMH concepts, practices, relationships with their environments (community, academic, governmental, etc.), and the personalities involved. The commonalities and variations are instructive.

Leonard Duhl, who championed CMH in government and academia, thought that most community mental health centers (CMHCs) repeated the old model of clinical treatment of mental illness.[1] Among the few exceptions he counted Robert Leopold's work with the West Philadelphia program, Sheppard G. Kellam's work with Woodlawn in Chicago, the Mount Zion program in San Francisco, and the West Side program—the last two which he thought had deteriorated from a CMH ideal. In contrast, Jack Ewalt judged that the CMH programs that succeeded concentrated in caring for casualties, while those that failed tried to address broad social issues such as racism, poverty, and education.[2] He thought it takes a long time for community boards to learn to be effective in meeting their goals, and that to make massive progress mental health needed to be integrated into federal comprehensive health planning rather than standing alone.

The Group for Discussion of Problems in Community Mental Health Research met several times to monitor and compare several major CMH research projects in various parts of the country.[3] They met in 1950, February 1951 in Syracuse, NY, and November 11–December 2, 1951, in Wellesley, MA. Topics discussed were:

> The Epidemiological Approach to Mental Health Problems": introduction—Dr. John Gordon; discussion initiated by—Dr. Edward J. O'Rourke (Department of Epidemiology, Harvard School of Public Health [HSPH]), Dr. F. L. W. Richardson, Jr., Dr. Johannes Ipsen
> (Associate Professor of Epidemiology, HSPH)

Reports on Progress by Members:

- "The Wellesley Project for the Study of Certain Problems in Community Mental Health"—Erich Lindemann, M.D.
- "Sterling County Project"—Alexander Leighton (Professor of Sociology, Cornell University)
- "The New Haven Project"—August Hollingshead (Professor of Sociology, Yale University), Fritz Redlich (Director, Department of Psychiatry, Yale University)
- "The Phoenix, Arizona Mental Health Center"—Dr. Robert Hewitt (Psychiatrist, Phoenix, AZ), Dr. John Clausen (Head, Social Science Division, National Institute of Mental Health [NIMH])
- "The Breakstone Village Project (University of Toronto)"—John R. Seeley (Professor of Sociology, Toronto, Canada)
- "The Yorkville Project"—Dr. Thomas Rennie (Associate Professor of Psychiatry, Cornell University)
- "The New York State Mental Health Commission Research Program"—Dr. Ernest Gruenberg (Executive Director, New York State Commission of Mental Hygiene)
- "The Social Science Approach to Community Mental Health Problems": opening—Prof. Talcott Parsons (Chairman, Department of Social Relations, Harvard University [HDSR]), discussion—Dr. Alfred Stanton (Psychiatrist, Cushing Veterans Hospital, Framingham, MA)

- "Personality Development and Community Mental Health": opening—Dr. Hubert Coffey, discussion—Dr. Benjamin Spock (Director, Children's Medical Center, University of Pittsburgh)
- "The Problems of Training Mental Health Personnel in Connection with Research Projects": Dr. Erich Lindemann

Albany Medical Center Community Psychiatry Project[4]

A biologically oriented member of the psychiatry department faculty was interested in developing a day hospital to maintain patients in the community. A psychiatry resident disciple worked on the project. He recognized the need for public funds and became interested in the emotional problems of the underserved poor, and developed working relationships with community groups and institutions. Opposition to the resident and his work developed among the senior psychiatry staff motivated by seeing a threat to private psychiatric practice and fearing the development of a new facility and staff that would constitute a power base for the resident that would eclipse the medical center's psychiatric outpatient department. Despite the psychiatry department members' derision of "grandiosity", the resident and a collaborating anthropologist won a state-managed Office of Economic Opportunity (OEO) support grant of $300,000. Plans grew into a community mental health (CMH) program, which incorporated private agencies and indigenous workers, with the collaboration of the medical center, the resident and anthropologist, and collaborating psychiatrists, and with the support of the resident's biologically oriented psychiatrist mentor. The project was delayed by county and city political agencies by setting up various committees and boards without representation of the community poor, and the OEO funds were held up.

The Medical Center Community Psychiatry Project was directed by the Medical College dean and the psychiatrist mentor. With the support of OEO administration, the project submitted a proposal to OEO for $400,000 in support for comprehensive coordination, staffing, and community support. The county psychiatrists wanted county and city involvement. The Council of Churches and local newspapers applauded this approach in contrast to past city and county mental health services that provided unsatisfactory service to the poor. The anthropologist was recommended for academic promotion. The federal government recommended an NIMH grant for a day hospital. The state department of mental health (DMH) supported both the antipoverty (community psychiatry) and day hospital programs, as did the county and medical college, the director of outpatient group psychotherapy, the director of the child guidance clinic. An English department faculty member helped edit newspaper reports.

Subsequently, the county psychiatrists, mayor, and city and county officials withdrew their support. The Medical College criticized in the newspapers the anthropologist for leftist and journalistic characteristics. The chairman of the department of psychiatry encouraged the resident to drop his relationship with the anthropologist as a bad influence and to support M.D.s over Ph.D.s. The medical college, local OEO office, and Community Chest agencies took the anthropologist to task for manipulating the resident. And pressure on the newspaper led to resignations in the program and loss of support from the Catholic community. The Protestant community and the African-American newspaper maintained support, which increased among the intelligentsia and academics. The resident and his mentor forced reluctant senior and county psychiatrists to bring the project before relevant county bodies. The Department of Psychiatry was surprised at the actions. It criticized the resident as unready to direct the day hospital and for emphasizing community psychiatry over individual psychotherapy. The mentor was angered when the resident wrote an informational letter to local authorities. The Catholic hierarchy advised no support of the project though it favored service to the poor. County psychiatrists advised cooperating with the local political machine. The state health department withdrew its support, and the county health department denied that there were mental health problems.

The university's Department of Psychiatry was divided between those who criticized the resident and anthropologist's work and sentiments and blamed them for negative newspaper reports and those who offered moral support. While the dean of the Medical College supported the project as contributing to the university's finances and demonstrating good medical practice, the Department of Psychiatry rumored that the resident and anthropologist were building their own empire and were sociopathic and pressured the dean against the project because the resident and anthropologist were unacceptable to the local political establishment. The dean conceded and did not sign off on the project, though he needed the funding.

In the end, the resident and anthropologist were terminated from the Medical College and university.

Bangor, Maine, Community Mental Health Program

Viola Bernard viewed this program as having many problems of personality clash with the director as well as political difficulties.[5] In the 1960s, there were convergences of interests, jealousies, rivalries, greediness for money, and problems around control. She thought that those who assumed control knew nothing about mental health and professional staff were not caring or understanding about community process. While many good things came out of the program, it was complex psychodynamically and sociodynamically.

Boston College Department of Psychology

The life of this program serves as a case study of the complications of academic–community relations in CMH.

Boston College adopted the CMH focus partly due to its heritage of service adapted to academic recognition.[6] Its president wanted to build a small, mediocre school into an urban university in competition with its neighbor, Boston University.[7] In its struggle to qualify as a fundable scientific institution—secular but not just "do gooders"—it needed to integrate the academic and service aspects.[8] Since it has no medical school, the Department of Psychology was the vehicle. Community psychology gave psychologists prestige that clinical psychology did not offer, with service as an outlet and psychiatrists not inevitably in control. An influx of psychologists from Erich Lindemann's projects at MGH and Wellesley Human Relations Service (HRS)—John von Felsinger, Marc Fried, Donald Klein, and William Ryan—brought CMH and social psychiatry perspectives with them and led this restructuring.

Thus was founded the Institute of Social Relations—later renamed the Institute of Human Sciences:[9]

> THE GRADUATE SCHOOL OF BOSTON COLLEGE A New Program For Research and Practice in COMMUNITY PSYCHOLOGY and PROFESSIONAL SOCIAL PSYCHOLOGY leading to the Ph.D. IN SOCIAL PSYCHOLOGY With Special Emphasis on: Research on Processes of Social Change and Social Planning; Observation and Intervention in the Natural Human Settings of Work, Education and Health; Ecological Studies of Social Conflict and Organizational Behavior Using University-Affiliated Urban Field Stations as Social Laboratories; THIS PROGRAM IS OFFERED WITH THE COOPERATION OF THE INSTITUTE OF HUMAN SCIENCES; For Further Information . . . Dr. John M. von Felsinger, Chairman, Department of Psychology, Boston College

John ["Mike"] von Felsinger, Chairman of the Psychology Department, wrote:[10] "Our new Community-University Center for [Inner city] Change in Roxbury is well under way. We have received Title I money and . . . the Ford Foundation is seriously evaluating us". There was conflict between knowledge and service.

Erich Lindemann spent part of his time at Boston College (he held an appointment 1968–1972)[11] and part at Stanford Medical Center.[12] He saw himself as an advisor to von Felsinger and Fried (without long-term commitment) in developing an interdisciplinary faculty group interested in the relationship of research and social action.[13]

> my plan to spend a longer period . . . this summer and fall to work intensively at the Boston College with John von Felsinger and Marc

Fried in their efforts to develop a program concerned with the Negro community in Roxbury and with the usefulness of mental health workers and social scientists in community development.[14]

He also supervised doctoral theses and consulted with students.

William Ryan, known for his community perspective on mental health and his liberal political leanings, joined the Boston College project partly because of Lindemann's presence. Von Felsinger joined to help the school grow. He reported that it was, with few exceptions, unable to attract big names and top-notch people even with large salaries but accepted lesser lights in order to keep the faculty positions filled.

The Institute prepared for a project of university–community cooperation in research and community action. Its initial focus was on Charlestown, a substantially white, working-class neighborhood in Boston. At the last minute, Mel King, a charismatic African-American community activist and leading light, proposed that a black Boston community be the partner, with the goal of developing black community leadership.[15] Von Felsinger jumped at this opportunity for strengthening the community, though faculty colleagues warned against involvement with a minority community in turmoil during the era of civil rights activism, and the Charlestown community was upset at being preempted. Working with downtrodden inner-city African-Americans presented the opportunity for providing service as well as academic accomplishment. The original plan for egalitarian participation saw university and community people collaborating under university leadership: Boston College would teach the black community participants leadership, and the black participants would teach Boston College students about the community. The African-Americans participating in the program would gain a good feeling (a form of "mental health") and prestige with their peer groups. They expected to gain a sense of identity by baiting whites and taking their power and regain the proud power of their African heritage as well as contributing insights to the white culture. The list of tentative field projects focused exclusively on black programs: FIRST, Highland Park Free School, Black Student Union, Operation Exodus, Negro Ring School Cabinet, Direct Service Project, Urban League, CIRS, Small Business Development Center, Bridge, Master's Program, AIM, United Community Construction Workers, Poro-Afro, CAUSE, Roxbury Library Committee, White Racism Project, and Joint Center.[16]

Lindemann cast it in terms of his conception of CMH:[17]

> Much of the field work will be in the heart of the Negro community in Boston's Roxbury section. Much of their concern will be to find ways to enable members of that community to be more effective and, it may be hoped, less belligerent in the pursuit of their social goals. As participant observer, I expect to have the opportunity to clarify some

of my notions about collective defenses and coping mechanisms and hope to return here [Stanford] with some new insights.

He tried to see a social psychiatry process in this engagement of academic professionalism with street and interest groups' politics:[18]

> The Department of Psychology has decided to take a bold new approach in creating new professional roles for psychologists... Roxbury in Boston was chosen as a field area in which to bring into close daily contact the resources of the Department of Psychology at Boston College and members of the Black community seeking for better community organization and for more effective ways of winning from the white population the prerogative of developing their own programs in business, administration and education. Graduate students find themselves immersed in frequent encounters with the Black community, and develop from direct experience appropriate psychological skills to make available to the community leaders.

The new department struggled with its internal organization and relationship to the more traditional university, balancing innovative creativity against accreditation requirements and scientific rigor.[19] This last was a concern for Lindemann, who felt that since the Joint Center focus was on action and black identity, perhaps there was a need for a traditionally oriented approach to the mental health area.[20] Murray Horwitz (research professor at the Institute of Human Sciences and professor of psychology at Boston College; involved in the Center) wanted the center to find, form, and work with community groups, some of which were concerned with mental health issues.

Almost immediately, there were problems: The community demanded control of administration (King as director, von Felsinger as assistant director) and finances. A proposed structure embodied this struggle for control and direction:[21]

1. <u>Aims of the Center</u>: The measure of success of the proposed Center is the extent to which it contributes to community action on problems of the inner city. The Center will operate on two key principles: (a) community action should be carried out by community residents; (b) such action should be informed by social-science research. Accordingly, the Center will aim to train a new type of community leader, one who can use social-science knowledge and skills, and a new type of social scientist, one who can investigate issues directly relevant to community action. In structure and function, the Center will link community leaders and social scientists in order that each group can aid the development of the other.

8   *A Sampling of Community Mental Health Programs*

2. <u>Participants in the Center</u>: The initial participants in the Center are community workers from the Boston Urban League and faculty and graduate students from the Institute of Human Sciences and Ph.D. Program in Community Social Psychology at Boston College. Both parties are committed to extending participation to other relevant groups . . . the Departments of Sociology and Economics, the Law and Business Schools, etc., as well as from other Universities in the Boston Metropolitan area. On the Community [p. 1] side . . . Community workers will include high school and college drop-outs, street corner leaders, unemployed adults, middle class parents interested in change, etc. Boston College will provide research and training facilities, although programs will be conducted in the Roxbury facility of the Urban League whenever feasible. . .
3. <u>Activities of the Center</u> . . . such activities as . . . 1) <u>Studies of the demography and community structure of Roxbury and the South End</u> . . . 2) <u>Attitude surveys of community residents</u> . . . 3) <u>Training in small groups and organizational leadership</u> . . . 4) <u>Training in the methodology of planned social change</u> . . . 5) <u>Initiating and evaluating community change projects</u> . . . [p. 2] . . .
4. <u>Structure of the Center</u> . . . the Center will be administered by two Co-Directors, one a University person, (initially from Boston College) responsible for research and training, one a Community Organization person (initially from the Urban League), responsible for community action . . . elected by an Executive Board . . . consist of all faculty and community project heads regularly working in the Center . . . graduate student trainees and community worker trainees will each elect one representative to the Executive Board. . . [p. 6] . . . policy-making should be controlled by those conducting Center projects . . . administrative authority within the Center should be maximally responsive to whatever divergent interests arise from its University and Community components . . . The success of the Center rides on the ability of the Co-Directors (and Executive Board) to develop creative integration of these differences. [p. 7] . . . 1. Co-Directors: Mr. Bryant Rollins is current Special Assistant for Community Development in the Boston Urban League. He received his B.A. in Journalism from Northeastern in 1960. . . [p. 12] Dr. Murray Horwitz [is] Research Professor at the Institute of Human Sciences and Professor of Psychology at Boston College. He received his Ph.D. in Social Psychology from the University of Michigan in 1950. . . 2. Center Faculty and Project heads . . . Prof. Marc Fried . . . Research Professor, Institute of Human Sciences. . . [p. 13] . . . Assistant Professor Harold Kellner . . . Mr. Mellvin King (M.Ed., Boston State College) Director of Urban League of Boston . . . Assistant Professor Jane Moosbruker . . . Associate Professor Ronald Nuttall . . . Professor Leslie Phillips . . . Research Professor, Institute of Human

Sciences . . . Professor John M. von Felsinger . . . Head, Department of Psychology, Assistant Professor Gunther Weil [p. 14]

In meetings, blacks vilified and degraded whites, and white graduate students were humiliated and assaulted verbally and physically so that they refused to participate. The approximately six students in the program depended on Lindemann for support. Large amounts of funds were diverted. Overall the innovations in the program exceeded the bounds of acceptance and viability. "University-affiliated field stations" included community residents and organizations coopting one another, leading to conflict and failure. Lindemann interpreted the psychodynamics of culturally and individually stored hostility and self-destructive and projective and acting-out defenses enculturated in black ghetto society.[22]

Lindemann tried to help in this turmoil of a split administration versus students and the department versus the community.[23] In the research project the project supervisors were radicalized and became hostile to the department and the establishment in general, seduced students into this fervor, and made things difficult for von Felsinger. Von Felsinger accepted Lindemann's advice for a time, but when the situation became critical, he shut Lindemann out. This stimulated Lindemann's thoughts about the need for a ritual way to change leaders when the initiator is no longer appropriate. (One wonders if he thought of his own experience in this regard.) He wrote back to his Stanford colleagues:

> During the first months of the fall when I was still able to work with the Roxbury group here at Boston College . . . Working with a negro population is a lot more difficult than I ever dreamed it would be. Some written material is coming out now.[24]
>
> I am sending you some of the material which emerged in the actual work life of the Boston College Department of Community Psychology . . . the description on the part of the faculty and the account of the experiences of one of the students, Mrs. Carol Feldman, gives a very lively sense of participation with the groupings of the academic institution for opportunities to make knowledge and skills available to the black community.[25]
>
> I thought this might be useful in some of your discussions with Peter [?Fuller] Torrey and when you are dealing with the young residents.

In retrospect, Lindemann formulated an analysis of the conflict between the academic/professional perspective and that of the community.[26] Clearly this came from his concept of CMH as understanding and reinforcing community resources and values.

> [T]he sponsoring college's department of psychology committed itself to . . . pursue mental health by helping with social action . . . a

center to facilitate change, to make poor blacks socially and politically more effective . . . they would go into the field and dirty their hands as advocates . . . as dispensers of knowledge, and consultants. White psychologists and graduate students would work with blacks in the ghetto center. Indigenous blacks would also be enrolled in the department as degree candidates, and T-groups would be a major teaching modality . . . they failed to recognize the already-existing expertise in inner-city [p. 3] strategies. The knowledge and experience of psychoanalysts, social workers, union organizers and other . . . specialists were not incorporated . . . psychodynamics were operative . . . the initially collaborative, loving culture regressed and fragmented, and there was denial and acting out, and ultimately, sacrifice of the leader . . . the whites were to get academic plaudits for helping the poor blacks. In the black ghetto culture, however, prestige was based on getting power and goods away from whites . . . The blacks began to caucus and make unilateral decisions. Staff were in a quandary. How should they accede to these personal and professional demands? Could they somehow be token slaves without loss of dignity? . . . The college had offered the blacks "Masters of Social Action". . . . They soon decided that they could learn all that was 'relevant' in four months . . . instead of in four semesters. [p. 4] T-groups mobilized tremendous aggression . . . a task-oriented . . . discussion might have been productive . . . the center social system fragmented and became paranoid . . . distrust and competitiveness emerged . . . Ideological schisms deepened, as between T-group experts and psychodynamicists. Students decided they could do it better than faculty. Dissatisfaction began to center on the project's director. He . . . instead of seeing . . . the process of change, felt betrayed and hurt . . . Ultimately, he had to leave, as have several other directors of similar enterprises . . . the cost in human suffering was considerable.

(p. 5)

Elizabeth Lindemann saw Lindemann always loyal to his institution and the professional role.[27] The Boston College case demonstrated that in some situations, the consultee may not be able to use the mental health consultation; then the consultant does not address the development of the consultee but finds resources for a worthy cause in that situation.

The Ford Foundation withdrew its funding. Questions were raised about whether King really did not want the project to work or whether he was regretfully pushed by the times and other community leaders into undermining it.

Boston College itself was in the turmoil of rebellion against injustice, tradition, and authority. Student activists demanded control; faculty members and the dean sided with them and minority advocates with minorities. Von Felsinger thought the dean experienced a values conversion stemming from talking with activist students and himself acted it out. Von Felsinger found the situation untenable, insisting on standards and procedures. He was disappointed that he never asked Lindemann for help, Lindemann did not offer it, and Elizabeth Lindemann protected Lindemann from these conflicts and stresses, perhaps in part because of his illness. (It should be remembered that Lindemann avoided conflict, though he could advise others in dealing with it.)

The prolonged crisis, the demands of the community project, and the breakup of a relationship (partly due to these stresses) led von Felsinger to resign from his position and take a year's sabbatical leave. William Ryan was listed as chairman of the department at one point.[28] Von Felsinger returned to find an absurd leadership void and makeshift program. He left CMH and community work for existential psychology and farming. A correspondent wrote to Lindemann:[29] "The news which I have received from BC is very mixed. I sense a certain 'peace at any cost' philosophy, with the cost in this case being real community relevance . . . as you suggested over the phone, there appears to be a shift away from a community base to an agency base".

Elizabeth Lindemann viewed this project as idealistic and adapting academic standards to community relations—such as offering fake academic degrees to community leaders. However, the leaders wanted real power and money, and so the project failed.[30]

Boston University School of Medicine Division of Psychiatry and Boston University/Solomon Carter Fuller Mental Health Center

Division of Psychiatry

William I. Malamud (Jr.) reviewed the history of the Division of Psychiatry:[31] In the Boston University Medical Center (BUMC), the Boston University School of Medicine (BUSM) included one psychiatrist in the Department of Medicine until his father, William I. Malamud, (Sr.), a former colleague of Lindemann's, founded the Division of Psychiatry in 1946—the beginning of locating psychiatric treatment in general hospitals. He followed a psychoanalytic approach via a Psychosomatic Clinic and recruited psychoanalysts: Bernard Bandler, Jacob Swartz, George Carter, and James Skinner. The focus was on psychosomatic disease, involving Peter Knapp and Charles Kaufman, and child development, embodied in a study of families in the adjacent South End neighborhood of Boston, staffed by Eleanor Pavenstedt and Joseph Devlin. In 1956–1957, Malamud obtained state funding to develop a psychopathic hospital similar to the Boston Psychopathic Hospital (and perhaps the Iowa Psychopathic Hospital where he had served), to provide service, research, and teaching focusing on the South End and Boston. This was not to be a state hospital, and the community would have no authority over it. This would have a larger capacity and wider scope than the inpatient psychiatry ward opened in 1956 in the University Hospital (BUSM's teaching hospital). Malamud thought he saw the direction psychiatry funding opportunities were taking in response to President Kennedy's message and the civil rights movement and developed an interest in collaboration with community professionals similar to the process of liaison psychiatry.

In 1958, Bernard Bandler was appointed to succeed Malamud as chairman of the Division of Psychiatry. His focus then was medical student teaching, liaison psychiatry, and community psychiatry in the hospital wards with joint teaching.

Bernard Bandler was one of the mid-20th-century psychoanalysts who developed a dedication to social and community psychiatry. He graduated from Harvard College, earned a master's degree in philosophy, and taught it there for two years.[32] He attended medical school at the Columbia University College of Physicians and Surgeons and served as a neurologist at the Boston City Hospital 1939–1940. At the MGH, he completed his psychiatric residency and served on the psychiatry staff,[33] as well as undergoing training at the Boston Psychoanalytic Institute. In 1947, he transferred to the University Hospital and the Division of Psychiatry of the BUSM. In the late 1950s, Bandler was appointed to chair the American Psychiatric Association's Committee on Psychoanalysis and State Hospitals. The committee was interested in the community, state hospitals, and the change to CMHCs. Bandler was more concerned with programs than buildings. Lindemann is reported to have had a cool relationship and little contact with him,[34] though they worked in parallel and struggled with the same enthusiasms for and resistances to social psychiatry.

Bandler's view of the CMHC and community psychiatry as a very important responsibility incorporating research, child psychiatry, psychiatric consultation, and psychodynamic psychiatry and his attraction of funding was thought to be part of his ambition to build the best department of psychiatry in the world. Bandler remembers developing his CMH expertise through experience and practice without reference to models.[35] In involving the Division of Psychiatry faculty (most dedicated to a psychological or biological ideology), he avoided rhetoric (eliciting positive and negative reactions) and becoming the leader of a small group practice that would distance them from the rest of the department. He attempted to involve all faculty members in experience as a reference for the theory, expanded psychiatrists' practice and responsibility, and sought continuing discussion. The staff had not been taught that consulting to another service or agency is consultation and change to a social system and thus felt that this consultation was a new practice. Bandler was drawn into mental health consultation to agencies by Gertrude Cuthbert, a member of the division's community advisory group, in 1965 director of the new Roxbury Multi-Service Center, and involved at the antipoverty agency Action for Boston Community Development (ABCD). The first psychiatric consultant, George Carter,[36] failed, but William I. Malamud increased his commitment to this program from 4 to 20 hours per week and succeeded because he worked through systems theory, attending to the agency, goals, and community. Malamud saw Bandler become excited about mental health service delivery in the community and developing the concepts of the mental health consultant and facilitator and the relation of the psychiatric institution to the community agency.

Bandler believed that psychiatry staff and trainees can learn the community perspective but need a cadre of experts to teach them; otherwise they often fail and complain that this is not real psychiatry—i.e., individual and group psychotherapy. He involved many faculty members in community meetings to hear community problems, priorities, and experience of isolation. He thought there was great interest in CMH laboratories and teaching.

Bandler's goal was to develop CMH but also research and other areas. He thought CMH was not accepted because, despite his efforts, many faculty members did not experience it. In addition, the impact of CMH on resources and institutions and a population-wide responsibility roused questioning of psychiatry's responsibility for such issues as well as advocacy, the burden of needs (10% of the population had major problems), and the need to break down barriers between disciplines. Bandler made an effort not to ask psychiatrists to assume burdens beyond their capacities or resources but still was perceived as overextending the profession and threatening the clarity of disciplinary identities—perceptions and resistances were common in CMH programs. He recognized the effect of social and health resources on mental health and the need to advocate for them by mental health practitioners and professional institutions such as the American Psychiatric Association (APA) and the American Medical Association. All this had limited influence on the Division of Psychiatry or BUSM.

In 1961–1963, he also attempted to bring other Boston University schools and departments into the CMH endeavor through each program having space in the CMHC for training leading to interdisciplinary education and an interuniversity committee consisting of four people (including the dean) each from nursing, social work, psychology, allied health professions, and medicine with enthusiasm for planning common teaching at the CMHC. Bandler was talked down, and involvement of the medical school was limited to him as an individual.

Sanford Cohen, his successor, saw Boston University as giving very little material support to psychiatry, having little use for psychiatrists except to deal with patient problems, not liking psychiatric patients, not liking the idea of a large psychiatric hospital on its grounds, and not liking the invasion by the community. Psychiatrists felt they had nothing to learn in this process, that CMH was an insubstantial furor, that it was subversive, and that it resulted in intrusion and interference by other professions. They felt CMH deprived them of control due to the self-sufficiency of other professions. CMH developed in spite of this because it was funded by the federal government when these funds were plentiful.[37] Some psychiatry faculty members were enthusiastic participants in this priority for social psychiatry and especially its associated humility, deference, and openness to self-examination and change. Some acknowledged its usefulness, but not for them, or considered it not even a proper endeavor for the medical profession. And an entrenched segment disputed, resented, and resisted it.[38]

The most senior person in the division identified with CMH was William I. Malamud (Jr.), son of the founding chairman. He traced his interest in CMH to his social worker mother.[39] He enjoyed the Home Medical Service in the BUSM and went on home visits to World War II veterans. He felt that he transmitted this enthusiasm to junior staff and accepted assignments to CMH projects and efforts to establish it formally within the division. He perceived the faculty generally treating him with respect and acceptance though not necessarily shared interest, and he seemed to stay on the acceptable side of the ideological line without being identified with extremism or threat to the social order.

In 1966, the South End Neighborhood Action Program was formed and asked Bandler for psychiatric consultation. Malamud was assigned. In 1965–1966, the division created the Section on Community Psychiatry with ten members and Malamud as chairman. It developed consultation relationships with many community agencies, providing direct services rather than Gerald Caplan's more distant consultee-centered mental health consultation. He obtained an NIMH grant to support liaison between the division and the Roxbury Multi-Service Center (a local manifestation of the Johnson-era federal encouragement of bringing human services to underserved inner city populations), and to teach CMH in the division. He perceived the division as having a positive attitude toward the Section but no involvement with it. He saw Bandler as overinvolved and not paying enough attention to other parts of the division, resulting in staff disinterest and resentment.

In 1966–1967, the state, under guidelines from the federal government, defined catchment areas to be served by CMHCs. To prepare for this development in the community and to satisfy requirements for community participation, Bandler arranged three meetings with segments of the community: mental health professionals (successful), related professionals (successful), and community residents (critical but cooperative, with complaints that this constituency was involved last and about defects in service delivery). Malamud thought that these planning groups accomplished little. To begin implementing CMH services, Bandler elected to reorient the division's clinical services to this model, putting all staffing money into a consultation and education program with the University Hospital (modeled on Malamud's liaison work), designating the University Hospital psychiatric outpatient department (which did serve local residents) as the CMH outpatient department, and designating the hospital's psychiatry inpatient ward as the CMH inpatient ward (a radical change in its culture without negotiating this change with the staff). This resulted in a block to hiring clinicians for consultation and education and for staff positions.

Peter H. Knapp, professor in the division, was interested in psychoanalysis and psychosomatic medicine. He separated himself firmly from CMH and gave the following perspective on CMH at Boston University:[40] He saw it as the product of the temper of the times and Bandler's vigorous leadership. In the 1950s, DMH commissioner Harry Solomon encouraged replication of the Boston Psychopathic Hospital/Massachusetts Mental Health Center, and planning for the BUCMHC began with an unusual, vigorous community group. Bandler's work at the NIMH Training Branch in the 1960s developed his idea for a community psychiatry training program, which he imported to Boston University as a specialty training program similar to child psychiatry and others. William I. Malamud, at the start of his career, directed this and led a Section on Community Psychiatry. Knapp saw this expand from a special concentration for those interested to an enrichment of the entire psychiatric training program and then, buoyed by the national CMHC program, fused and confused the entire Division of Psychiatry and the mental health center. In his judgment, only an infinitesimal fraction of a CMH program would have been accomplished without Bandler's commitment.

Knapp attributed Bandler's dramatic conversion from psychoanalysis to CMH to the influence of Val Hammett, Robert Leopold, Paul Fink, Les Madow, and possibly Israel Zwerling; his experiences at the NIMH Training Branch; the national scene of the Great Society decade; and stormy interactions with CMH planning groups. Bandler reported that the interaction with community people had an impact equivalent to a personal psychoanalysis: the confrontation with people, seeing the needs of the community, attitudes toward psychiatry, and collisions with racism. He became a zealot, a charismatic leader, and loaded with the causes of population area responsibility, the limited care for the community, elitism, and the immorality of private-office psychiatric practice.

The revolution in psychiatry from these new interests and the changes they implied, including catchment area service responsibility, produced conflict within the division between supporters and resisters. Bandler's strong leadership and forceful style produced resistance to CMH mixed with resistance to him personally. Psychoanalysts were threatened by these less intensive, non–personality-restructuring approaches. Researchers were threatened by community hostility to academia and the elite, and the feeling of being exploited for research excellence. The community resented funding for research rather than service: Paul Myerson, chairman of the Tufts Medical School Department of Psychiatry, observed that pre-existing strong research interests colliding with a difficult and demanding community added fuel to the struggles.[41] There was fear that traditional professional control of academic standards and professional preparation were being bypassed by senior academic appointments and CMHC hiring via joint faculty and community screening committees. For instance, the faculty endorsed a community professional, Donald Taylor, as director of the Consultation and Education Program, while the community committee rejected him in favor of Ruth Batson as a community nonprofessional. Bandler brought pressure to bear to overcome the resistance, though his retirement deprived the process of his help in working this through.

The author was a faculty member of the Division of Psychiatry and a staff member of the affiliated community mental health center from 1966 to 1978 and can report on his experiences and observations of CMH in that context. He transferred from the Harvard/MGH Department of Psychiatry because it was ridding itself of CMH after the departure of Erich Lindemann and his influence and because Bernard Bandler was leading a vigorous CMH program at Boston University. Bandler was delighted at the addition of someone with a social psychiatry ideology and committed to CMH as an implementation of it. However, my assumption that the faculty and staff shared Bandler's thinking and efforts collided with the fact that only a few identified themselves with CMH, while most firmly denied any interest and functioned beside but not within it. Thus it quickly became clear that this was not a CMH program but a chairman and junior-level minority group functioning as best they could in an institution alien to its ideology and efforts.

Bandler negotiated relationships and projects with the community, BUSM, and federal and state agencies. The Community Psychiatry Section members were interested and active in planning CMH projects, teaching, consulting, and service. The uncommitted participated in applying for CMH funding grants and their implementation for their financial benefits to the division. However, they always had an eye to the benefit and protection of the non-CMH programs: in one instance, Knapp declared that a secretary funded for a CMH program would be assigned half time to division work. Psychiatric residents were excluded from CMH and interdisciplinary training programs. Staff members at federal and state funding agencies expressed some hesitation about division grant applications because of the university's history of failure to carry through funded programs. And CMH was referred to with disdain; the addition of CMH practices—such as home visiting—to training and clinical practice was stubbornly opposed; and sabotaged—such as insisting on taking responsibility for disseminating a notice encouraging home visiting in the clinics, and then "losing" them for six months.

Bandler saw the need for change in faculty attitudes toward community psychiatry because psychiatry's tasks were being extended beyond professional competence, its responsibilities extending outside current knowledge, there was the perception that adding CMH would dilute psychiatric residency training, and the resentment that the new expertise distorted psychiatry's traditional identity. This was aggravated by community psychiatry's challenging individual psychodynamics, the dyadic therapeutic relationship, and the medical model of treatment. The retreat program evaluators found significant faculty attitudes toward value problems: role differentiation versus homogenization; treating unmotivated patients; and involvement in social action for environmental change, including concerns about selection of problems to address, ethical issues, social coercion, and struggles for political power.

One of Bandler's attempts to meet this resistance constructively was arranging a three-day retreat institute for the faculty, administered by Columbia University psychiatric faculty.[42] The rationale was that it is ineffective to teach community psychiatry as a subspecialty within the psychiatric residency training program in an environment that is ignorant, suspicious, or hostile, because this will lead to polarization with the psychoanalytic group administering the training program. In his grant application for this retreat, Bandler observed that "the disparity between the enthusiasm of a new point of view and the tenacity of a specialty's basic practices tends to force a 'polarization' between those 'committed' to the concept and practice of community psychiatry and those 'committed' to the more traditional psychoanalytic approaches".[43] The retreat was planned to prevent that polarization with a saturation experience for division faculty as a community within which to give information about community psychiatry and uncover and change those attitudes about it that dominated the faculty.

In its results, the evaluation of the Institute distinguished the issues it was presenting and testing for: Community psychiatry is the field of practice; social psychiatry is the field of inquiry; and community mental health is the goal of both. The measurement of attitudes toward CMH using the Baker and Shulberg Community Mental Health Ideology Scale found psychiatrists least favorable toward CMH (though more favorable than the average in the American Psychiatric Association) and social workers most favorable. Most faculty members agreed with comprehensive continuity of care and total community involvement; disagreed with program shift from treating individuals to treating populations; and split about changing diagnostic and treatment approaches. On the Semantic Differential Scale, 20% to 30% thought community psychiatry was weak, naïve, ineffective, and conflicting; psychiatrists were most negative and social workers most positive. More time spent in teaching correlated with a more negative attitude toward CMH, suggesting polarization in the faculty centered on loyalty to psychodynamic psychiatry and adherence to a concept of professional role and responsibility.

It was found in retrospect that participants felt they learned about community psychiatry (the amount learned correlated with their attitudes toward CMH) and liked the institute (attitudes toward the institute were independent of attitude toward CMH). Overall, 16% felt a strong or moderate positive change in attitude, 82% felt little or no change, and 4% felt a negative change. Those with strong positive and negative scores on the Community Mental Health Ideology scale tended to be unchanged, the 50% with moderate scores shifted—6% to higher and 3% to lower; and there was no significant relationship between professional groups and shifts in ideology. The author observed reluctant, forced participation on the parts of some faculty, including one member's refusal to accept the role of taking minutes and no other group member willing to replace him. The main result documented was an increase in contact and acquaintance among faculty and staff and a desire for communication and intimacy. There was a feeling that faculty and staff were not consulted, informed, or participants in the division's growth, and there was a desire for a role in reviewing and participating in the division structure.

The faculty signified an acceptance of the CMH issues of continuity of care, the integration of services, and work with other professions. There was denial that power, legitimacy, and patient rights were at issue.

> A crisis of professional identity appears to have been triggered by the emergence of pressure on mental health professions to give higher priorities to the problems of community mental health than ever before . . . It is the psychiatrist who clings most doggedly to the traditional psychotherapeutic model as the guiding frame of reference for his professional behavior. This model is not claimed to be transferable to community problems . . . but, the psychiatrist asserts, it is "what we can do" and "what we can teach". It is the hallmark of "what we are". The abstract knowledge and clinical skills of psychodynamic practice provide a coherent structure for professional identity, and it is against these secure certainties that community and social psychiatry is perceived as vague and unspecific in both basic knowledge and skill.[44]

The institute was judged successful as an intense group experience. It failed in depolarizing and may have hardened positions. It indicated the need for ongoing work on division structure. This illustrated the issue of change in an academic setting in terms of the governance in that setting. In reviewing the process, it was observed that[45] "The decision to hold the Institute and the lack of faculty preparation for it was thus a good example of benevolent leadership in which the community of the Division of

Psychiatry did not actively and democratically participate. It represented the style of leadership and an important aspect of the organizational and structural functioning of the Division". However, Malamud credited the workshop with pulling the division together over a long period of time and short-lived improvement of feelings about CMH.

> Medical schools and their departments are not notorious for democratic process and faculty power ... those who were most concerned delegated freely, and never moved toward basic change in important new departures without senior faculty consensus (which had never been achieved over four years in respect to community psychiatry.) ... However, there was no basic faculty structure, no mechanisms, and no process for faculty participation in decision—making.[46]

Thus one must ask what form of leadership is required for ideological and institutional change: responsive (to the existing satisfactions and preferences) or directive (toward new goals and motivations)?

Bandler's concept of leadership envisioned a democratic department to plan the direction and priorities in times of professional and social change but influenced by power flowing from vision, persuasion, and responsiveness. However, this faculty had little knowledge about each other's units. Bandler was surprised at their dissatisfaction with what he intended as his benevolent paternalistic leadership and at the faculty's sense of lack of input and control over the division's direction. After the institute, Bandler and the faculty developed more faculty participation via official senior faculty committees and an unofficial junior faculty group that would think out structures and mechanisms for faculty participation in decisions. This responsiveness on Bandler's part resulted in the faculty recommending that he stay on after the normal retirement age to oversee the transition into the CMHC. Batson saw him as a master administrator and manager who cared about people and maintained communication among them and was committed to service and good medical training.

As Bandler neared retirement, Malamud saw him become ever more antimedical and antipsychoanalytic in his perspective. He saw, in response, the faculty become hostile, feeling he had turned his back on traditional psychiatric approaches and other aspects of the division and predicting the failure of their CMHC enterprise and the CMH movement overall. (In this he paralleled Lindemann's fall from medical acceptability and turn more openly toward social psychiatry.)

Ruth Batson was a community resident and activist who was eventually chosen as a community nonprofessional to be director of the Consultation and Education Program of the CMHC. She overlapped Bandler and his successor, Sanford Cohen, and thus had a perspective on the evolution in CMH in the division and CMHC.[47] She thought Bandler recognized the ability of nonphysicians (professional and nonprofessional) including on joint committees and with other Boston University schools, seeing an interdisciplinary approach to health as the only effective one. He pushed any way he could for a good idea. She thought he would have fought harder for the university's continued involvement in CMH and that his retirement was a great loss. She saw Cohen as occupied with fighting Bandler's image and dealing with the psychiatry staff hostile to it. He allied with psychiatry against nonprofessionals to secure a power base. She thought he liked CMH but was not ready to fight for it and thus oversaw the waning of influence and roles by nonprofessionals like Batson.

She felt that the white Division of Psychiatry, through the division Administrative Committee, wanted Bandler to retire, resenting him as autocratic and controlling. Some expected that CMH was well enough established to continue without him. However, after Bandler's retirement, the department cleaned CMH out and returned to traditional psychiatry. It started with the search for a new chairman. Some of the reactionary senior faculty members hoped to gain this appointment in order to return the division to orthodox psychological and biological psychiatry. When this proved impossible, they took firm control of the search committee and were successful in the appointment of a chairman who had no firm program himself and could be directed by the senior faculty. Some senior faculty members withdrew—one to become dean of the Boston Psychoanalytic Institute. The Community Psychiatry Section under William Malamud did not include people with influence in the department and came into conflict with Ruth Batson. The strong voices for CMH who Bandler had recruited (David Satin, Pierre Johannet, Ann Davis of the Boston University School of Nursing, Ralph Notman, Orlando Lightfoot, and representatives of the Boston University School of Education and the Boston Public School System) were ineffective in the further development of the department and soon scattered. The successor chairman observed to the author that he was a scapegoat, cast off by both the Division of Psychiatry and the mental health center because he was a reminder of past conflict.[48] No group wanted the author, so the chairman could not offer him a position. The chairman confirmed the ideological basis for this situation as no criticism of the author's capacities, and it was not to be taken as a personal failure.

Bandler blamed himself for a failure of leadership:[49] not working hard enough to give the faculty direct experience in the intellectual climate of CMH, the time and thought needed for institutional change, recruiting the interest and understanding over two to three years, dealing with the pain of growing. He felt he had not recognized this as a crucial task, involved as he was in his own learning and experience. He knew and had taught many of the division faculty—Peter Knapp, James Skinner, George Carter, Louis Sander, Jacob Schwartz—who must have thought that he abandoned the old beliefs when he turned to CMH. CMH requires the participation of a major and critical part of the department—including academic and analytic credentials and power—in order to embody respect and function, rather than being marginalized in a few proponents (all in all, a familiar picture of a CMH casualty).

After retirement, Bandler served as acting director of the Division of Manpower and Training Programs at the NIMH. The concept of psychiatric training and practice that he had developed was expressed in his David C. Wilson Lecture:[50]

> [T]he present health and human service delivery systems are failures. They do not provide comprehensive care to our population . . . the concept of Community Mental Health Centers . . . hold certain assumptions in common . . . The first is the assumption of responsibility for the mental health of a distinct population . . . The second is the importance of demographic and epidemiologic data (p. 1) The third is the concept of mental health as optimal psychosocial functioning . . . not simply [to] be defined in terms of symptoms . . . The fourth is the importance of prevention . . . The skeptics are employing a medical diagnostic treatment disease model. The community psychiatrist is using additional models: the developmental, organizational and ecological models . . . The fifth is the importance of consultation and education . . . Health is indivisible from the conditions in which people live . . . health, education, housing, employment, human dignity, degradation, poverty and racism . . . The sixth is the importance of indirect services (p. 2) . . . The seventh is the importance of continuity of care . . . The eighth is the enlargement of the knowledge and skills of the psychiatrist . . . in addition [to traditional skills], competence in group and family therapy, and understanding and skill in group processes with groups far removed from his traditional ritualized settings . . . The ninth is an awareness of . . . community organization . . . The tenth is community participation . . . when from the beginning there is planning with the community rather than for it, when power is explicitly shared, then the community and the Center will . . . share a common identity and a common destiny. Then the community will fight for the Center rather than with it, will organize to defend the Center rather than to destroy it. (p. 3) The eleventh is the experience with new careerists. Mental health professionals . . . have as much . . . to learn from the neighbors of minority groups as to teach them . . . The minority community has developed an extraordinary new teaching device—confrontation. Confrontation is an educational process over time. (p. 4)

> Training in community psychiatry, I believe, should be an integral part of basic residency training . . . There is so much to learn about basic psychiatry, it is said, that the inclusion of community psychiatry will dilute training and leave the resident both superficial and

confused (p. 4) ... The educational continuum ... include the years of college and medical school ... the training [should] take place in a community-based comprehensive health service delivery system.

Bandler died on March 9, 1993, at age 88.[51]

Sanford I. Cohen, M.D. was Bandler's successor as Chairman of the BUSM Division of Psychiatry. Choosing him was the subject of intense though covert political and ideological pressures. Senior members of the psychiatry faculty—principally Peter Knapp and Jacob Swartz—were eager to assume leadership to guide the division back into traditional psychoanalytic and biological teaching and research and away from the threats, conflicts, and vagaries of social issues and community relationships. Knapp was a candidate for the department chairmanship but withdrew in light of the "crisis of the decision-making process".[52] Malamud reported that they approached him for the job, but he was not interested in administration. He and the conservative senior faculty members and faculty were active in the selection of an outside candidate, seeking one who would share their ideology and organizational concept and/or would be responsive to their faction's influence. Knapp assumed the role of spokesman for the division in meetings of the division, spoke many times with the search committee (which included Milton Greenblatt, Commissioner of Mental Health, and Theodore Lidz, M.D. of Yale Medical School, and chaired by a Boston University faculty member) as well as with community leaders, members of the Mental Health Area Board, and Boston University faculty members sympathetic to psychiatry; and insisted on seeing all applicants. He reported that he recruited Cohen and submitted his name to the search committee. Division faculty members were anxious and scattered in their opinions; a senior division researcher, Alan Mirsky, was interested in social and clinical psychiatry and research without Bandler's preoccupation with the community and captivated community representatives on Cohen's behalf.

Knapp claimed that Sanford Cohen was the division's choice. Cohen revealed that he had accepted the chairmanship at Louisiana State University inadvertently and was eager to return to the northeast. The impression was that his goal was diplomatic accommodation with and among the academic faculty, and he avoided challenging initiatives and conflict in the division, the medical school, and the university. Knapp saw him as having past interest in the psychodynamic and biological aspects of psychosomatic medicine (Knapp's interest) and wanting excellence without conflicts in community, clinical, behavioral, and other aspects of academic psychiatry.[53] His research interests appealed to Knapp and Louis Vachon (a middle-level faculty member who would later chair the department for a time); and his goals of departmental financial growth and making money from service to those who could pay to make up for the progressive diminution of grant funds appealed to Schwartz and

Vachon.[54] Knapp thought Cohen came into a chaotic situation and had to accept the CMH mandate and the superintendency of the CMHC. Malamud thought Cohen was ambitious to be head of the department and to focus on stress and psychophysiology as they affected illness, with the inpatient ward researching this. While he became interested in CMH activities, he hoped to shed them.

Cohen claimed that he was chosen to bring together the fractured division,[55] and Malamud thought that his promise to bring central coordination and individual freedom to the department was appealing. Cohen claimed that the choice was made by the university without involvement of the psychiatry department and based on his laboratory science background. He carried the title of community psychiatrist, learned on the job, and communicated well without racism (in fact, he developed a good relationship with Ruth Batson) because of his own background. His tolerance for multiple viewpoints may also have been seen as avoiding commitment to controversial ideologies. In fact, he thought he may have caused discomfort by bringing together the isolated researchers and clinicians.

Cohen revealed some of his feeling about CMH in his strong retrospective views of Bandler, though it is unclear what they were based on.[56] He believed that Bandler was not a real community psychiatrist but a *padrone*, patronizing the needy with psychiatric resources. His intentions were benevolence and perhaps recognition for himself. His roots were in the New England upper class, and he did not understand or communicate well with earthy, inner-city blacks. He was appointed chairman possibly because he had been the first full-time and best-known staff member under his predecessor, William Malamud (Sr.). He was liked by the teaching hospital (University Hospital) but not by the medical school. Cohen criticized Bandler for not shrewdly exploiting the growing source of funding for CMH.

Batson saw Cohen as occupied with fighting Bandler's image and dealing with the psychiatry staff hostile to it.[57] He seemed allied with psychiatry against nonprofessionals to secure a power base. She thought he liked CMH but was not ready to fight for it, and thus oversaw the waning of influence and function by nonprofessionals like Batson. She recalled that he was criticized for not making decisions (as Bandler had) and thus was pushed into decisions with which he was not comfortable or able to maintain. He was not able to implement his own style of leadership and thus vacillated under pressure. And she thought he failed to maintain communication among participants in the division, CMHC, and community.

Knapp acknowledged a continued split in the division over CMH. He claimed that a substantial number, including senior people such as James Skinner, William Malamud, the child psychiatry group, and the CMH group, did not want Bandler's work lost though not to the exclusion of all else, and opposed candidates uninterested in CMH (and psychoanalysis), such as Jonathan Cole, a researcher in psychopharmacology. Hostility to CMH grew because of conflict in the Appointments and Promotions Committee between Ruth Batson and senior researcher Conan Kornetsky over complaints of racism and elitism: It is reported that, after Batson presented at grand rounds, Kornetsky made a racist remark, they clashed over it, and Kornetsky was removed from the Division Appointments Committee. The division was polarized over this: While Malamud said he refused to participate in the executive committee's deliberations about this, his name was attached to the decision; Kornetsky was angry at him and held abiding resentment; Alan Mirsky was upset for Kornetsky, though sensitive about racism; Jack Swartz was angry and became more conservative; and positions hardened with more open conflict between the community and faculty. Ruth Batson reported that she stumbled upon several faculty members (including Robert Rose, Peter Knapp, Seymour Fisher, and Louis Vachon) in the hallway, embarrassed to be caught planning to confront Cohen against the CMH program with the threat of a mass resignation.[58] Subsequently, Rose was appointed chairman of psychiatry in Texas and planned to take the group with him. Only Fisher opted to go, and when funding failed in Texas, he found it difficult to return. In any case, without Bandler's leadership and as national fervor and funding waned, interest in CMH waned in the division.

With his separation of the Division of Psychiatry from the CMHC, Cohen felt that a new perspective on community psychiatry became an increasingly solid part of the division.[59] His definition of community psychiatry was bringing the benefits of psychiatry to the community, and CMH dealt with social nonmental illness issues. Knapp saw decreased enthusiasm for CMH in the division; the CMH component decreased in importance and was certainly not its sole mission; an acceptance of relationships with community agencies and the CMHC established but with less community input into the division; less funding for CMH; and William Malamud—chief of the CMH Section—was more preoccupied with his duties as clinical director of the CMHC and less active in CMH work.

Malamud detailed progressive conflict: The Division faculty criticized the quality of residency training at the affiliated state mental hospital (the May Unit of the Boston State Hospital) under Malamud's direction. When a junior faculty member and promising researcher, Gerald Wohlberg, was killed by a black community patient in the CMHC, faculty resentment (Malamud considered it unconscious) grew against the community population and the division's mental health program for it. Richard Kahn, director of the May Unit, resigned and refused any relationship with the CMHC. The Multidisciplinary Mental Health Training Program for minority graduate students in mental health disciplines, spending a year at the May Unit, was perceived by the staff and residents there as confrontational and addressing racism (as they felt about the

CMHC's Consultation and Education Program). Psychiatric residency training was limited to what its funding could support, and state funding for the CMHC was not considered as covering all their time at the CMHC. (Cohen thought state funding favored the competitor Massachusetts Mental Health and the Erich Lindemann Mental Health Centers). Malamud did obtain a federal grant under the Carter administration for a psychiatric resident CMH training track, which could enable him to devote himself more to his position as head of the division's Department of Community and Social Psychiatry. In 1975, the University Hospital Residency Training Committee decided to give the state only what it paid for, and, with the division's criticism of the training there, the residents were withdrawn from the May Unit.

Malamud thought that the division as a whole had little interest in community psychiatry and was glad to get out of it.[60] The federal government put pressure on the Residency Training Committee to train "inner-city psychiatrists", meaning public-sector psychiatrists rather than those focused on community sites and techniques. Malamud was funded to direct such a program, which then was beset by conflict between black psychiatrists and other staff versus Cohen, Malamud, and the Residency Training Committee regarding the degree of emphasis on black issues. Besides this program, there were only isolated programs addressing community issues: some at Boston City Hospital under James Skinner and Orlando Lightfoot, some addressing cross-cultural issues under Albert Gaw and Jackie Hoover, and the Minority Psychology Training Program at Boston City Hospital under Guy Seymour. Other black professionals were recruited: Orlando Lightfoot in the geriatric service at the Boston City Hospital, Charles Pinderhughes at the Bedford Veterans Administration Hospital, and a woman psychiatrist being recruited to direct the Department of Child Psychiatry Program.

The Boston University/Solomon Carter Fuller Community Mental Health Center (SCFMHC)

Under Bandler's chairmanship, planning for a local mental hospital continued.[61] Malamud saw Bandler's program as opportunistic: He saw the direction psychiatry was taking after President Kennedy's speech and the civil rights movement and the funding opportunities this presented and became interested in collaboration with community professionals. He saw Bandler shift from a clinical approach to an advocacy and social challenge approach. Peter Randolph, who led the Tufts-Bay Cove Mental Health Center, saw the Boston University program as very different from his:[62] He thought the Boston University community was difficult and disorganized and without the political power to obtain funding. The personality of the leader (Bandler) was much different, as was the decision to create a central building (not an uncommon choice in the state) rather than a decentralized program (Lindemann's conception of CMH). But not Roxbury professionals, who were 50% to 60% black but did not necessarily live in this community) involving Bandler, Malamud, and possibly Peter Knapp. They were angry, stormy, and confrontational, with a young black man accusing and an older black woman summarizing and confronting. Classic was a meeting at the Ecumenical Center at which Bandler pointed to Malamud as an obvious example of success as a white professional working in the black community, and Duke Nelson from the community denied that Malamud or any white could work with blacks. Byrd had been optimistic about the community and the division working out their problems but then was forced to disclaim this in front of his constituency. When Bandler invited him to speak at a session of the division's grand rounds, he kept the faculty waiting a half hour.

Bandler was surprised at the resentment, attributing it to fear of mental health "bringing nuts into the community", but was interested and ambitious enough to adjust to this reality and, seeing it in the light of the community, finally getting real power. In 1965 Malamud became involved in the CMH effort and saw the community become more supportive. However, he saw the division faculty increasingly furious that Bandler was giving in to the community as too high a price for the consultation and education program and abandoning the medical model of psychiatry in favor of a social action model. Malamud saw Bandler characteristically "running off in all directions", loading the division with more than it could handle, and neglecting its other programs.

In 1968, architectural plans for the Mental Health Center were being developed.

Bandler saw his involvement in CMH as a learning or even a conversion experience. He immersed himself in the local South End neighborhood, developing working relationships with Green of the Boston Redevelopment Authority, Liddell of the United South End Settlements, George Farrah at Boston City Hall, Fr. Gildea in the Roman Catholic Church, and the local antipoverty agency ABCD.[63] He addressed issues of the commitments to make, the nature of CMH, challenge felt to local plans and ideas, and rumors about the destruction and problems that the CMHC might bring by developing collegial relationships, sharing power, and addressing the problems of living that the CMHC could help. He established an advisory committee involving key community agency representatives and involved the state commissioner of mental health (Jack Ewalt), the president of Boston University, and the chairman of the Boston University Board of Trustees. He talked about the CMHC to hundreds of groups, including all political segments and leaders, and found them educated, responsive, and responsible. The BUMC trustees and medical and surgical department heads lobbied the legislature for funding, and community leaders approved when polled by the legislators. When a DMH official advised that mental health center funds would be wasted since the community wanted storefront offices in burned-out buildings, the black community demanded their own CMHC, and the *Bay State Banner*, the community black newspaper, editorialized about racism among the whites.

In 1966, under federal and state guidelines, a Mental Health Area Advisory Board was created and made part of the division for community participation in developing the Boston University Community Mental Health Center (BUCMHC). Bandler saw it as without ultimate authority. Ruth Batson thought that it was ineffectual and unhappy under the chairmanship of Franklin Roberts but effective under Percy Wilson, including blocking the state from undermining the CMHC, such as by locating other state offices in its building. Malamud remembers it confronting the division and questioning affiliating the CMHC with Boston University. This unsettled relationship played out in the CMHC staff appointments process. The Consultation and Education Program grant embodied a commitment to working toward community control. Personnel hiring involved a community board (which screened for sensitivity to community values) and also a faculty committee (which screened for professional competence); both, as well as the division's chairman and the CMHC director, had veto power. There were confrontations between these screening committees, especially in choosing a director of the Consultation and Education Program and a Superintendent of the CMHC. For director, the division committee chose Donald Taylor, a black social worker from the community, expecting that he would be readily accepted by the community board. Bandler was shocked but accepting when the community board rejected him on the grounds that he lacked interest in the community and because the division chose him, resulting in returning $330,000 of funding to the state, delaying appointments, and revising job descriptions (including omitting the need for a professional degree). Ruth Batson, a nonprofessional community activist, was nominated by the community board and eventually approved, resulting in uneasy relationships with her (including by Malamud and Bandler) because of her nonclinical approach to CMH and suspicion of the agenda of professionals. The division faculty had been willing to accept the CMHC, but, after these conflicts, they rejected involvement with it.

As the CMHC matured, it became the target of community interest groups with their own agendas. There was conflict—such as regarding the appointment of superintendent of the CMHC—between those seen as elitist (e.g., Ruth Batson) and those identified with the common community (e.g., Donald Taylor—who was ultimately appointed superintendent).[64] Batson reports an unsuccessful attempt by Gil Lopez and associates to take over the CMHC via unsigned letters, etc.[65] Bandler saw a "cell" of activists with various community and academic ties (Velma Hoover and her mentor Elaine Pinderhughes of Boston College, Dolores Good, Chester Pierce of Harvard Medical School, and Ted Barbour) implement a political strategy to manipulate the CMHC Area Board, administration, and staff. Batson associates this group with the "Fanon Society" (adding Floyd Barber and Hussein Abdilahi) but denied that it was efficient and influential. She thought only Pierce and Barber were truly radical but not practically active. The author was witness to a radicalized segment of the CMHC staff derailing a meeting of the total staff by obstructing a request to approve a psychiatric research project authored by Division faculty and planned to involve CMHC staff and patients; vilify the respected senior faculty member investigator; and encourage the minority and CMHC staff members to walk out of the staff meeting so that any action taken would appear to represent only the nonminority members. This group also guided Hoover (co-director of the program) to covertly train the minority students in the Multidisciplinary Mental Health Training Program to oppose the white program director (the author) and to press to refocus the training from mental health needs of the (culturally mixed) community population to minority political issues and to block a student graduation celebration. The (black) mental health center superintendent, Donald Taylor, may have been seduced into joining this group of political activists or may have come to terms with this political force. Bandler saw William Malamud, a (white) Division of Psychiatry faculty member associated with community psychiatry, try to contribute good clinical skills but, despite being personally trusted and appreciated, he was politically powerless—the "house honkey".

Malamud became discouraged about developing the CMHC in conjunction with the division and medical school. The federal grant committed the division to inpatient and outpatient community service; the university hospital, which housed these services, felt community service did not meet its needs, and the effectiveness of this community orientation was questionable.

Cohen, Bandler's successor, felt the division was relieved to be rid of Bandler versus angry at him for leaving. Bandler was asked to stay on at the CMHC for a year as a consultant but was confined to committee meetings, and his suggestions were ignored. He felt that it was not practicing community psychiatry. Despite black involvement, he missed his long hours involving board members in understanding and planning and painful learning of new perspectives, perilous but enjoyed. He saw the CMHC lose communication, interchange, and partnership with the community. Taylor had different priorities and interests, and Batson did not accept professional psychiatry. Ethnic community groups had nothing to identify with in the CMHC, and it was underutilized. This demonstrates the importance of leadership and recruiting a critical mass of support to continue CMH after the passing of the founding leader.

In retrospect, Bandler articulated a broad perspective on CMH in relation to society, profession, academia, and personal growth as the philosophical background to his administrative and clinical work.[66]

He saw CMH as part of a social revolution toward greater democracy, including the resolution of racism. In exploring the relationship between the university and CMH, he found that the classical academic perspective labels the community as ill and lends a patronizing flavor to its view of the centrality of community and university mental health centers to the community, seeing satellite offices consisting of inferior positions and indigenous workers. He felt, rather, that the endeavor should emphasize the health and coping vitality of the community and the CMHC revolving around the community with shared control. This is part of the revolution against pervasive racism (especially in the black and urban ghetto) and for the democratic participation of people in all discussions that affect their lives and in the power to control their destinies. He contended that violent confrontation of white academic professionals by black community residents was not for revenge or control but for the purpose of educating whites about issues of values, control, respect and reimbursement, the locus of illness, etc. He believed that blacks understand whites and white institutions, since this was necessary for their survival. It followed from this that they saw mental health work and CMHCs as sophisticated instruments of social control similar to police, schools, and the welfare system to promote acceptance of white dominance. Trust, hope, and relationship would lead to a more vigorous identity and autonomy, leading to control over themselves, their environment, and their destinies. Otherwise the road is to identification with the aggressor or a negative identity, applicable to the development toward health of the community as well as of the individual. This requires the sharing of power and change in institutions, individuals, and society, which is bitterly resisted via appeal to professional expertise and competence, university independence and academic freedom, and legal restrictions.

In contrast to Bandler's view of academia learning and growing from the community, Cohen, with encouragement from some others in the division, explicitly disagreed, feeling that leadership of the division and the CMHC constituted a conflict of disparate interests and should not be held by one person.[67] He sided with those who wanted the CMHC to be an independent entity rather than part of the DMH or university.[68] In a meeting with Malamud, Donald Taylor (as associate area director), and Doris Bunte (black community leader and state representative), Cohen withdrew as superintendent of the CMHC when he felt it was legally untenable and that a takeover by radicals was imminent. He treated the community and the CMHC courteously but as external to his department, with relationships only through specific agreements. The BUCMHC was seen by others as a state facility separate from the BUMC and the research group separate from both.[69] Later an agreement was reached on a general affiliation, an education agreement, and a research agreement (between Kornetsky, the Area Board, and the CMHC).

Cohen felt that this made the department's input more effective and avoided the eventual explosive conflict that engulfed institutions such as Lincoln Hospital/Albert Einstein College of Medicine. The DMH's view changed from that when Milton Greenblatt was commissioner and saw them as a joint project to that when Goldman became commissioner and saw the CMHC as solely a state responsibility. Donald Taylor, the existing CMHC director, did not want to assume the position of superintendent under those conditions of instability. Cohen thought that the new leadership was responsible (though not always honest about pushing whites out) and struggled greatly to deal with irresponsible radicals on the staff. Batson was interested in community development and using institutional resources for that purpose. Cohen insisted that a white outsider as leader or a power vacuum in leadership would ensure a radical takeover and chaired the search for a new state area director: He remembers that radical candidates were weeded out and the finalists were staid black professionals.

In contrast, Batson saw the Consultation and Education Program as having the largest staff and budget in the CMHC and division.[70] Professionals and clinical service staff resented this, felt robbed of resources, and did not understand or value the program. Nonphysician professionals lost status after Bandler's retirement and allied themselves with clinical psychiatrists. CMH physicians and other professionals were isolated from the clinical professional "club", felt loyalties divided between "the movement" (CMH) and the professional group in terms of their own interests and survival, and chose the professional group. Clinicians wanted to give community service but were put off by the community review board. Cohen identified himself with the psychiatric staff at the expense of nonprofessionals. Batson saw Donald Taylor, acting superintendent of the CMHC and never appointed permanently, as a poor administrator, not caring well for the building or staff, a conciliator, not providing strong leadership, and unable to face the pressure. The lack of support from CMH professionals and top administration at the time of waning funding hampered the program.

Batson also thought that despite committed creators (Lindemann, Bandler, Batson), the fact that people occupied state jobs suppressed freedom of action for fear of losing the job; therefore she insisted on being paid by Boston University. In contrast, the first acting superintendent, Taylor, did not make trouble, was good to negotiate through, and was appreciated by all. His successor, Charles Gibson, seemed to have good training, reputation, and courage, though he was concerned with his own status.

Knapp reported that the state required Boston University to negotiate the management of the CMHC.[71] He found it underfunded, providing poor clinical care, and with a board of trustees that was never functional and waged bitter battles with the superintendent. He saw its services improve under a contract with Boston University to administer them and with some good clinical directors. George Papanek, interested in community psychiatry, was recruited from McLean Hospital to replace Malamud as clinical director.

Viola Bernard saw many crises and setbacks under Bandler, and problems worked out and things went more smoothly long after he left.[72]

This story is one of the rise and fall of social psychiatry and CMH dependent on (1) the convictions and dedication of a strong leader—Batson felt that the outcome of CMH (or any other policy) depends on the leader and not the virtue of the policy;[73] (2) dealing with a contentious academic and community environment; and (3) the task of reconciling differing interests and ideologies of community and academia/professionalism, requiring insight, creativity, patience, and dedication. Or are these disparate interests and cultures irreconcilable?

Chicago West Side Community Mental Health Center

H. Freed, a former fellow in Gerald Caplan's community mental health training program, was director of the Chicago West Side CMHC to serve a population of 130,000: 55,000 Polish, 25,000 African American, and 50,000 Mexican users.[74] The program was to be a collaboration among the Illinois State Psychiatric Institute, the Institute for Juvenile Research, the Pediatric Institute (for retarded children), and the University of Illinois Department of Psychiatry. These sponsors did not contribute their promised support, and the situation became hot, dangerous, and fraught with rivalries.

Columbia University and the Washington Heights Community Mental Health Project

In New York City the Columbia University medical center's CMH activities were related to a social psychiatry research project on urban relocation, reminiscent of the MGH and the West End Study. The Columbia-Washington Heights Community Mental Health Project was developed in the context of contemporary studies of the relationship between the social environment and mental illness in the "new field of Social Psychiatry".[75] Reference was made to August Hollingshead and Frederick Redlich's study in New Haven (*Social Class and Mental Illness* [New York: Wiley, 1958]); Thomas Rennie and Leo Srole's Yorkville study, and Alexander Leighton's Stirling County study. In this case, the New York Port Authority relocated 1,800 families from the Washington Heights neighborhood of Manhattan (adjacent to the Columbia Medical Center) in order to increase the approach to the George Washington Bridge. Researchers studied relocated families as compared with neighboring unrelocated families as a cross section of socioeconomic status and culture. It addressed the stress of relocation and adaptive and maladaptive responses as related to psychological, duration, and location factors and was titled Columbia-Washington Heights Community Mental Health Project; Urban Relocation: A "Natural Experiment" in the Cultural, Social and Psychological Sources of Adaptive and Maladaptive Responses to Stress; Design for Part I of the Study.[76]

The Washington Heights Community Mental Health Project started in 1956[77] with a three-year grant that was subsequently renewed.[78] It was clearly an academic program: Lawrence C. Kolb, professor and chairman of the Department of Psychiatry at the Columbia University School of Physicians and Surgeons, director of the New York State Psychiatric Institute (a state research and training institute under the Columbia Department of Psychiatry), and director of the Psychiatric Service in the Presbyterian Hospital in the City of New York, was the project director; Viola Bernard, clinical professor and director of the Division of Community and Social Psychiatry in the Department of Psychiatry of the Columbia University School of Physicians and Surgeons, and Ray E. Trussell, incoming director of the School of Public Health and Administrative Medicine of Columbia University, were project co-directors. The purpose was to characterize the community in terms of the prevalence of mental health and emotional maladjustment, the adequacy of mental health resources, and community attitudes toward mental health and mental health programs. The great burden of psychiatric and social problems and care directed attention to the interrelationship of social conditions and developments, social pathology, psychopathology, and their social consequences. There was dissatisfaction with past planning based on psychiatric hospital patients without consideration of function in the community, as well as dissatisfaction with the training of mental health professionals—especially psychiatrists. The co-directors and their colleagues criticized existing medical traditions:[79]

> A series of entrenched medical traditions has been recognized as obstructive for the development of effective mental health practices and the on-going assessments of patient care. Traditional patterns of isolation within and between medical and non-medical facilities of the community's resources contribute to maintenance of weak patterns of coordination, communication and fulfillment of responsibility with consequent antitherapeutic fractionation, discontinuity and inflexibility of services. Some organizational traditions in state hospital systems, such as distance from the patient's home and poor liaison with other community facilities, impede postdischarge re-adjustment. In general hospitals the old tradition of placing those with greater professional experience on inpatient services which led to enhancement of their prestige is detrimental to the growth and strengthening of the admissions office and the outpatient

A Sampling of Community Mental Health Programs 33

departments which have major importance for community mental health programs and require high levels of professional expertness. These factors are reflected in traditional organizational features of general hospitals, and influence staffing patterns and admissions procedures and policies that are now adverse to early detection and treatment of psychiatric illness. They lead to incomplete and inaccurate recording of psychiatric diagnoses and minimal attention to outpatient charts. By identifying these traditions and the obstacles they raise, it is hoped that appropriate revisions come about which will lead to more effective patient care.

This reorientation would lead to an integrated program of mental health services for the community. There were to be consequences for professional ideology: "clinicians' acceptance of a broadened scope of psychiatric responsibility, extending beyond but not replacing one-to-one forms of psychiatric treatment".[80] There was also the wish that psychiatrists be trained to work with a more diverse population than a middle-class, educated one and with methods other than one-to-one therapy. The project was to put more social science and public health content and methodology into the training of clinical psychiatrists and more mental health training into the curriculum of the school of public health.

In the future, it was planned that the multiprofessional staff from the Division of Community Psychiatry and public health would establish a population laboratory to study the prevention of illness and preservation of health; provide education in community psychiatry practice; improve service to the mentally ill; and influence practice in the Presbyterian hospital, state hospitals (the New York State Psychiatric Institute and Rockland State Hospital), local voluntary and city hospitals, and social agencies. It is noteworthy that their concept of community psychiatry included political action:[81]

> One way of effecting social change is through legislation. Community psychiatrists can contribute to this process by making relevant clinical findings and insights available to legislators, governmental decision-makers, and the general public. Thus as community psychiatrists, whose responsibilities extend beyond the individual patient, one of the most effective ways by which we can enable hospital authorities and clinicians to interrupt pregnancies that are adjudged to be injurious to mental health, such as Alice had suffered, is through striving to help bring about more liberal abortion laws.

Viola Bernard's experience with the medical establishment's reaction to CMH paralleled Lindemann's in many ways.[82] In 1965, she worked toward the development of a community mental health center connected with the Columbia Health Center with a catchment area including the neighborhoods of Washington Heights, West Harlem, and Inwood. A CMHC would have expanded the community service program and services. Sheldon Gaylen, M.D., was made chief of program development and, funded by a private foundation, a small staff and a community group was assembled for planning. The university presented many attitudinal obstacles: There were conferences to clarify the program and allay concerns, and "convince the Department of Psychiatry that this would not dilute psychiatry in its quality". The project encountered the Presbyterian Hospital (the main teaching hospital) and other medical school departments resisting this service burden but rather seeing themselves as a citadel of science. The community board was not such a problem, though it raised questions. Good progress was made, including with the hospital, which had a different board of directors than the medical school, was much more involved with the community (though not all negative attitudes were eliminated), and worked on site selection and architecture.

Bernard Bandler thought that the Boston University concept of CMH as embodying community needs and leadership was never tried anywhere else.[83] Columbia did not have the opportunity for faculty interchange with the community as Boston University's meetings had. He thought that Viola Bernard was peripheral and not involved in processing community relationships. She and Kolb got federal and state funds for the CMHC and developed the plans for it. He recalls their first meeting with community representatives resulting in Kolb's being displaced as chairman within 30 minutes and the community voting down the CMHC plans.

Richard Abrams saw one aspect of community input as the expression of frustrated needs:[84]

> What had been a profound impatience with a political system that refused honestly to confront racial injustices, poverty and problems of personal dignity having to do with mass living, working and educational conditions has . . . turned into angry desperation. The mounting violence we are experiencing expresses that desperation (p. 13) . . . the [Vietnam] war must bear primary responsibility for the changed mood . . . has presented . . . young men with the awesome choice . . . Many of the "tough" among them have "got going" with civil disruption (p. 14) . . . what has happened at Columbia . . . the faculty's discontent with their role in the governance of the University . . . the estrangement of the faculty and students from the administration . . . remains the one outstanding explanation of the disaster that has struck.

Liebert adds:[85] "the climate at Columbia—with more than its share of moral ambiguities, insensitivity to its relationship to the community and inflexible and unresponsive top leadership".

A Sampling of Community Mental Health Programs 35

From Bernard's point of view in 1968, "all hell broke loose": The Columbia University student uprising developed; the community became more coherent, with blacks organizing, indigenous leaders appeared, and the eruption of an unrecognized rivalry between black and Hispanic populations; the perception that communists exploited the student unrest and infiltrated the training program and medical center; liaisons with outside forces that wanted to appropriate university funding; the community's mental health board promulgating separate advisory boards comprised of professional and nonprofessional recipients of services; and the process politicized and radicalized. Specific radical mental health professionals were identified as moving into the situation, becoming vehement spokesmen for the people of the area, wanting to take over and run the CMHC as a community agency, though without resources. At two community meetings, Kolb was shouted down and ceded the chairmanship of the meetings. At another planning meeting, it was proposed that only those who worked in the service area would work at the CMHC. This developed into a segregation of the population, including two entrances planned for the CMHC, the Hispanic psychologist spokesman labeled an outsider and succeeded by the black head of the Washington Heights Mental Health Council, and efforts to develop a project organization politicized and exploited by radicals through the student unrest. There was much maneuvering between these political forces, community agencies, government agencies, and the university regarding control of plans, money, and official designation (including incorporation). Monies were put in escrow, though a small amount went to the community-operated program, with little accomplished.

In 1969 Bernard developed the Division of Community Psychiatry—later the Division of Community and Social Psychiatry—a collaboration between the Department of Psychiatry and the School of Public Health. This was to be the vehicle for the development social and community psychiatry in the academic department of psychiatry and in its training and community service arms. The collaboration was good. It also had working relationships with the Columbia University Teachers College and schools of Social Work, Law, Business, and Architecture. Kolb supported this effort because of his old interest in public health, and Hugh Trussel, dean of the School of Public Health, was interested.

Though the participants were outsiders in both programs, there were positive outcomes:[86] It produced the book on social psychiatry *Urban Challenges to Psychiatry: The Case History of a Response*, edited by Kolb, Bernard, and Bruce Dohrenwend (Boston: Little Brown, 1969) and including 14 authors, among them Ernest Gruenberg on the epidemiology reflected in the Washington Heights project. Jack Ellinson, a social psychologist at the School of Public Health, worked with Dr. Webber (a psychoanalyst and later director of the New York State Psychoanalytic Institute, located in the Department of Psychiatry) to develop a program of low-fee cases at the psychoanalytic clinic and require each psychoanalytic candidate to treat at least one low-fee patient. These "analyzable" patients were mostly not of low socioeconomic status but community-based teachers, social workers, and other professionals with moderate salaries, mostly white, middle class, verbal, and educated who could not afford full-fee analysis. There was a varying number of CMH psychiatry residents who were to complete a four-year psychiatry residency training program plus an MS in public health degree to prepare for their careers. A variety of community courses and experiences was offered to other psychiatric residents, though all rotated through the community clinical facility in Presbyterian Hospital. The division was an agent for change in the curricula of the participating Columbia schools.

In 1969, Alvin Mesnikoff, director of the CMHC planning project, left to direct the Staten Island State Hospital and then become regional office director for the State Department of Mental Hygiene.

Bernard's advocacy that the Division for Community Psychiatry develop a service program in the medical center rather than in city agencies was opposed by Kolb, and she resigned as director of the division, feeling it was restricted and wanting to spend more time on research into family development, though she faced resistance in that project, too. The division was run by the remaining faculty: Kolb had little time to contribute, and Shervert Frazier was only nominally in charge, leaving junior faculty in charge. Hertz, the director of the Community Service program, and Kolb left over the next 10 years. Finally, community service through the division provided community care, with psychiatry residents rotating through it.

Again we see a dedicated leader with scattered supporting people and institutions confronted by entrenched and powerful forces of the preceding traditions.

Concord, Massachusetts, Community Mental Health Center

John Merrifield finds one of the major roots of the Concord Community Mental Health Center in Abigail Adams Eliot:[87]

> Abigail Adams Eliot, born in 1892, belonged to that WASP elite that dominated the religious, political and economic life of New England. Her father was a Unitarian minister; her uncle was a renowned head of the Unitarian-Universalist Association. Another relative served as president of Harvard, cousin Tom was a poet. Her sister, Martha, was Head of the Children's Bureau . . . Abby retired as head of the Ruggles Street School, which trained teachers, especially nursery school teachers. Abby had studied early childhood development and education in England, held a doctorate and helped found a model nursery school at Tufts University, now known as the Eliot-Pearson

School... Massachusetts was served by Henry Cabot Lodge, Leverett Saltonstall, and Francis Sargent. Almost everything in Concord assumes a colonial or transcendental connection. An Emerson gave land and endowment for a hospital. The child guidance clinic was named Walden, after the pond Thoreau made famous, and renamed Eliot. If there were a coat of arms for that generation it might have been Use the Talents God Gave You to Improve Society—in Latin, of course.[88]

Merrifield's interviews of participants revealed their training in the 1960s with passionate idealism, optimism, and belief that society needed changing and that such change was possible. The Emerson Hospital administrator saw the hospital as a change agent. CMH goals went beyond responding to patients released from state mental hospitals to the prevention of mental illness and, in extreme form, the concept that mental illness is caused by a sick society, and remediation required a change in society. "They did not perceive their goals narrowly, and were disinclined to accept limits on what could be achieved".[89]

Robert W. White, a member of the Harvard Department of Social Relations (HDSR), remembers that, as a resident of Concord in 1946, he worked with a school guidance counselor, an active older lady who was a member of the Wellesley, Massachusetts Friendly Aid Society (which collaborated with Erich Lindemann's Wellesley Human Relations Service), and several others to bring a child guidance clinic to Concord, because the one-year waiting list for Boston child guidance clinics made them irrelevant.[90] Merrifield saw Abigail Eliot as the driving force behind this effort. The team developed a Mental Health Association, then the Walden Clinic, and finally the CMHC. Her energy, experience, relentlessness, and moral authority made it difficult to refuse her.

They struggled long to open the clinic, with Chester D'Autremont, M.D., as clinic director until there was massive government funding of such CMH projects. The Walden Clinic was convinced of their goal of social change. The number of mental health professionals, the central location, the idea of comprehensive services, and salaried support contrasted with contemporary child psychiatry clinic practice.

Mentally ill people continuing to live in the community, the unfamiliarity of the project organization, the fear of further innovation, and the threat to the livelihood of local practitioners contributed to resistance. White remembers fear of bringing dangerous, sick youngsters into town, rumors that the advocates for this clinic were radicals such as White advocating mixed-sex child nude bathing, not wanting it located near them, and fearing objections to minor budget items in the town meeting.

With massive federal and state funding and regulation, the Walden Clinic was caught between the ideals of the interests of children and the DMH's determination to decrease costs and focus on "deinstitutionalization" (moving patients out of state mental hospitals, which could then be closed). A system of competitive bidding put state clinics and CMHCs in competition with many others and made its original model obsolete. Vendors with lower overhead costs (e.g., not a hospital), nonunion staff, and staff with less seniority, lower pay scales, and perhaps less professional training were favored in this system, especially if they were focused on one or another aspect of deinstitutionalization. Influences changing the CMHC included the illusion that it had no cost, economic inflation, the conservative shift in national politics, the original contract for the clinic including early funding in exchange for less funding later on, and the DMH's resentment of "rich Concord".

The CMHCs board and staff were reluctant to deal with the change in the focus of service toward deinstitutionalization and the shift of funding from federal and state grants to private health insurance and fee for service. This inevitably led toward financial failure until the CMHC accepted compensated services without mental illness prevention or responsibility for a catchment-area population. "The net result [of cost-benefit strictures] was a wrenching redirection as to what was expected of the CMHC: stop trying to 'fix the community' and get busy helping to close Met[ropolitan] State [Hospital]".[91] In the spirit of Dorothea Dix's goal of public care for the mentally ill, the proceeds of the sale of the land and buildings of Metropolitan State Hospital would be placed in a trust fund for the perpetual care of the mentally ill of Middlesex County. However, "According to the plan finally approved in 2004, the town of Waltham will get a golf course, Belmont will get some cemetery space, and Lexington will get some four hundred thirty housing units, of which a fraction, 10 percent, will be set aside for DMH clients".[92]

In this environment the job of the chief executive of a CMHC is daunting:[93]

> The job is impossible from the start. . . . "here is a job, but you cannot have adequate resources or authority, and you cannot leave without damaging your career". We were naïve, uncompromising, and disappointed . . . the instigator of rapid changes—notably in mental health—and accumulated enemies as a consequence . . . All of us chafed at having to reconcile our ideal image of a CMHC with the unfolding reality . . . inexperienced or overconfident or stubbornly uncompromising . . . boards are well advised to see that the jobs they offer are realistic, and to support a CEO with constructive criticism and defense thereafter.

Merrifield believes that the struggles for the construction and deconstruction of the mental health center have caused literal human casualties:[94]

> Wars have casualties . . . I believe the casualties were significant, an opinion shared by nearly all of the people I interviewed. . .

A Sampling of Community Mental Health Programs   39

1. Eleven people, each of whom had a significant role at Concord's CMHC, have died. Dr. George Abernethy was chair of psychiatry . . . when a merger with Walden was considered . . . he died of lung cancer at age 57. Mrs. Barbara Andrews was a social worker . . . she died of cancer in her fifties. Dr. Frederic Coplon got the child development team off to a good start and served a term as chair of psychiatry; he suffered a fatal heart attack at forty-seven. Mary Fischelis . . . psychiatric nursing director, died of a cardiac arrhythmia at fifty-seven . . . Dr. Dorr Hallenbeck . . . chair when I came to Concord, died of [p. 102] post-polio dementia at seventy. George Lussier, Walden's intake social worker and . . . acting director of Walden Clinic, died . . . in his sixties . . . with Parkinson's disease. Tovah Marion, Ph.D., died of cancer while working at Walden. Nina Melbin, M.S.W., died of cancer after leaving Walden. Dr. Robert Milstein, who worked at Walden Clinic . . . was Emerson's [Hospital] psychiatry chair for a term; he died of a metastatic brain tumor at sixty-one. Henry Mirsky, M.S.W . . . transfer from Eliot to state hospital work . . . died . . . in his seventies. Barbara Sylvia was Walden's bookkeeper; she died of cancer soon after leaving work. Ruth Tobin was evening charge nurse on Wheeler III until she died of cancer in her sixties . . . the "CMHC community" . . . suffered a disproportionate number of deaths compared to Emerson's active medical staff or its entire professional staff.
2. Diminished capacity. By the time Dr. Gerry Wacks ended his three years at the Mental Health Center, "he was not the same person he was when he started". I was sacrificed". Two program directors developed symptomatic illness, which they believed were job related . . . Dr. Charles Hersch was so ill when he left as CMHC director that he did not work for two years. Charles Hersch spent two years making relationships, then two years making needed changes. At the end he came home each night in desperate straits; when wife said he cannot stand this and wife cannot he quit. Now he has Alzheimer's disease.[95] [Hersch, Charles, 11/15/07 Interview] Leslie Brody's board sent him to the National Training Laboratory in Bethel, Maine for a week's training in "anger management". On his return . . . he was abruptly fired . . . Dr. Stern declined to talk about his years as Eliot CMHC director, so I speculate that it was not a pleasant time.
3. There were three divorces among CMHC program directors . . . Among Emerson's entire medical staff over thirty years, I count 7 divorces. Again, the proportion seems high.

4. "Ruined careers". Not until 2004 did an Emerson CEO leave Emerson for another hospital CEO job. Prior to that, none went to a hospital administrator job at any level. None reached retirement age while at Emerson. Mr. Crowdis, who . . . retired at fifty-seven, spoke of "ruined careers". Two interviewees said that Emerson's reputation for being hard on its administrators was known all across the country . . . Charles Hersch . . . in my opinion remains bitter about his Concord Experience. Dr. Leslie Brody . . . spoke of the irony that his Ph.D. thesis, "Survival Strategies for Community Mental Health Centers", was approved on the same day that he was fired as Eliot's Director. Mr. Gil Aliber left Concord as soon as he could, and retired happily after twenty-five years as director of a CMHC in Rutland, Vermont.

the pace of change has slowed . . . The CEOs of Eliot Clinic and Eliot Community Human Services. . . [are] in those positions for more than ten years each. I think a slower rate of change has brought fewer casualties. The war is over, whatever one may think about its outcome.

The year 2004 was "the first year that Eliot Clinic finished in the black". Only outpatient treatment services continue. The Therapeutic Preschool Program, Employee Assistance Program, Addictions, Partial Hospitalization, Crisis Team, Special Aftercare . . . Case Management—all of these programs are gone, as are the extensive consultation services . . . the Clinic sees a few clients from the other towns in ECHS's [Elliot Community Health Service] vast area, but "most of our clients come from the Concord-area towns . . . Most of the clients who were handed over from Emerson's [Hospital] Special Aftercare Team are still being seen, most of them by me".[96]

Contra Costa County (California) Public Health Department

Leonard Duhl, later a major proponent of CMH, was drafted after his psychiatric residency into the U.S. Public Health Service and sent to the Contra Costa County, California, Public Health Department.[97] There was his first experience of people labeled community psychiatrists (such as Sam Susselman), and he learned about psychiatric community consultation and mental health services independent of psychiatric treatment.

A National Institute of Mental Health-funded study of mental health problems was unable to encompass the multitude of variables.[98] Decreases in funding required CMH programs to retrench, shifting from extensive consultation, education, and outreach to more clinical work.[99] When Erich Lindemann moved to Stanford, he brought his experiences in the community and Stanford Medical Center. He was gentle, caring, and inspiring in his lectures to the consultation staff and consulted to the staff occasionally, and the agency hired Elizabeth Lindemann as a consultant in order to increase the agency's contact with him. He asserted that the inability to prove the impact of dynamic psychiatry did not invalidate this approach and was confident that the pendulum of psychiatric ideology would eventually swing back to it. He discussed institutional defenses—authoritarian and paranoid—to inner and outer stress. He applied this to Contra Costa County consultee agencies, some of which were controlled and authoritarian, such as one that wanted to learn psychological control of teachers and was using the Minnesota Multiphasic Personality Inventory to deny tenure to troublesome staff members. He also shared his thoughts about the need to sacrifice (symbolically rather than literally) the first leader of a program when it transitioned from initiation phase to maintenance phase.

Henrik Blum reports that in 1967–1968, one or two years after he left the directorship of the mental health program, there were major changes.[100] It became a clinical treatment program to millions of residents. It brought in irrational, pathological directors who tore the program to pieces, emphasizing the prerogatives of the program or their own needs rather than of those served and caused good staff members to leave. Leonard Duhl echoed the sentiment that this program started as a good one and then was not.[101]

Blum echoes the observation that a program is a reflection of its leader. He was dedicated to a CMH model. The chief psychiatrist, Sam Susselman, was honest, conscientious, and committed and had integrity, unlike some other psychiatrists who only fulfilled their hourly obligations. The program continued to be unconventional among public agencies, open to feedback such as from Susselman and sometimes bringing patients in for an autopsy on the program's services, to the discomfort of the staff. This is another example of a program that lost its drive and focus when it lost its leader and fell prey to traditional function and special interests.

East Palo Alto (California) Project

The Stanford Medical Center Department of Psychiatry embarked on a community mental health program (headed by David Daniels, a young faculty member interested in community mental health) for East Palo Alto—an area of the city with a large proportion of minority, lower-socioeconomic-class residents. Its black community was seen to be separate politically from Palo Alto as a whole and became increasingly assertive.[102] When tensions rose, the department chairman, David Hamburg, wanted Erich Lindemann (visiting professor of social and community psychiatry), to bail him out. Dealing with community conflict was not a role with which he was comfortable, and he saw this as an impossible project. However, his wife, Elizabeth Lindemann, was active in social work services in this community.

Albert Einstein College of Medicine

Rosenbaum and Zwerling frankly addressed the relationship between social psychiatry and its host psychoanalytically oriented academic institution.[103] Rosenbaum speaks from the perspective of a psychological and not non–social psychiatry department:

> Although practically everyone who holds a position of importance or who is a teacher and has a teaching assignment is psychoanalytically trained or at least has had a personal analysis, here are people within the group who are going off in different directions—for instance into the field of social psychiatry. The people who head our division of social psychiatry are psychoanalytically trained, but their interests have shifted to areas such as family diagnosis, group process, group dynamics, group psychotherapy. Many of these things are rather strange and foreign to me because I have not had this experience or this background. But conflicts do develop within the department in terms of which is more important. We are going through this right now.

Zwerling speaks from the perspective of the Division of Social and Community Psychiatry:

> The prevailing sentiment within the Division at the close of this academic year is of a vigorous optimism concerning its mission and direction. There is, on the other hand, a far less sanguine outlook concerning future relationships with the body of the Department of Psychiatry . . . Over the three-year history of the Division, its progressive growth has been accompanied by trends towards (a) the reduction or elimination of a required period of service in the Division by all residents; and (b) the reduction or elimination of the teaching of family and group process within the integrated core of Departmental teaching and training. Equally distressing to the Division is the recurrent obverse of "social psychiatry" not "individual psychiatry" but "psychoanalysis"—in a department in which the psychoanalytic frame of reference is of unquestioned primacy. One would hardly suspect that the most significant theoretic statement in group psychology was written by Freud; that the leading contributors to the study of family dynamics are psychoanalysts; that perhaps the leading analytic theoretician of our day authored "Childhood and

Society", and very recently commented that . . . the optimum condition of drive control coincides with a combination of ego mastery and social organization.

The groups differed in daily tasks and struggles, and stresses and strains were characteristic of their relationship, conflict was inevitable, and "it may be that entirely new administrative forms will be required". Social psychiatrists were seen as less involved in individual psychodynamics and more in family and group processes—no less legitimate and scientifically based. The focus was always defined as mental illness and recovery: social psychiatry addressed the social determinants in individuals, and community psychiatry addressed populations.

Various influences encouraged social psychiatry, including the attraction of community-based treatment, revelations from sociology, group and family studies of group influences, recognition of differences among cultural groups, and pressures for economy in treatment. These strained against resistance in individual psychiatry (and the psychoanalytically oriented department) and individualistic social philosophy.

Social and community psychiatry presented a different role hierarchy, with the psychiatrists no longer most powerful, different expertise and language, and other disciplines possessing different abilities. In this setting, the psychiatrist might feel insecure and threatened. However, it was emphasized that all kinds of data are relevant, and it is the articulation among data rather than their validity or value that is to be addressed. False conflict regarding competence and authorship of overlapping areas could obscure real differences in depth and creativity of expertise. This might also lead to disparaging alternative practices. Also, there was pressure to devote clinical resources to community service to the reduction for training and research. There was also lack of precision in defining social and community psychiatry in terms of training and practice. This contributed to prejudice and criticism in judging the adequacy of training, performance, and practitioners—for instance, in resenting the intrusion of social and community psychiatry material as competitive with that of psychoanalysis.

It was concluded that social and community psychiatry was yet to be clarified in education and application and that differences between it and individual psychoanalytic psychiatry should be collaboratively studied and not obscured as personal conflicts.

Erich Lindemann Mental Health Center

We detail here the prelude to and initiation of the Erich Lindemann Mental Health Center (ELMHC) with the interaction of the Massachusetts General Hospital (MGH), Harvard Medical School (HMS), the

Massachusetts Department of Mental Health [DMH], and the federal National Institute of Mental Health (NIMH).

The MGH was distinctly reluctant in its relationship to the ELMHC: Leon Eisenberg, Lindemann's successor, when he arrived, saw little of Lindemann's heritage remaining.[104] He reported that MGH staff feared that the ELMHC would be divisive and divert funds and energies from the MGH. He thought that it was never adequately funded for the planned MGH research. Lindemann had designated Freddie Frankel, a senior MGH psychiatrist, as liaison between the Department of Psychiatry and MGH and the DMH regarding planning of the ELMHC. Frankel observed a lack of specifics about content and method in the superficial agreement between Harry Solomon (Commissioner of Mental Health), John Knowles (general director of the MGH), and Lindemann and reported his misgivings to Eisenberg and the Metropolitan Planning Commission.[105] He had his doubts about prevention in psychiatry and, with other Lindemann-era psychiatry senior staff, left MGH for the Beth Israel Hospital, where he adhered to biological psychiatry and direct treatment of individuals.

Thought was given to having Erich Lindemann retire from the chairmanship of the MGH Department of Psychiatry to direct the ELMHC. Conflict within the MGH, evolving state politics via the DMH, and Lindemann's exhaustion with administration and politics scotched this option. As noted in the history of the Yale-Connecticut Mental Health Center (CtMHC), Gerald Klerman remembers Leon Eisenberg rescuing him from the opposition to him as the CtMHC director and being appointed director of the ELMHC.[106]

Klerman's ideology and administration at the ELMHC was diametrically opposed to his at the CtMHC and to Lindemann's, undoubtedly the result of the harsh lesson he learned in Connecticut. This shift was evident in his emphasis on medication, though he also retained interests in social psychiatry:[107]

> Dr. Klerman documented the value of compounds like the phenothiazines in restoring normal behavior and adjustment in the acute stages of schizophrenia. For this study the group won, in 1969, the Hofheimer Prize, the highest research award of the American Psychiatry Association.
>
> Like Dr. Lindemann, his studies of the evaluation of social adjustment are among his major accomplishments.

A later article in the *Psychiatric News*, a publication of the American Psychiatric Association, was titled "Klerman Urges Profession to Eschew Social Change".[108] He advised that mental health intervention should be based on scientific evidence (via controlled studies and demonstration projects), be health interventions via accepted public health concepts, and remain within the mandate of federal agencies. The focus should be on the individual alone or in aggregate, dealing with environmental risk factors (such as sex, race, power, and poverty) but only in regard to illness. Leave social change to the political system and concepts of health and happiness to social philosophy. The health care system deals with death and disability (about 30 million people or 15% of the population), not stress, distress, enjoyment, or performance (a similar proportion) in which mental health professionals are not competent. He specifically disagreed with the World Health Organization's definition of health as "A state of complete physical, mental, and social well-being and not merely the absence of disease and infirmity". He opposed diagnosing and treating a "sick society" and social action by mental health professionals. For example, when an ELMHC staff member and community resident wanted the ELMHC to protest to the municipal school system, the ELMHC Area Board decided that staff should not take political action but bring issues to the citizen board to protest.[109]

It was in this atmosphere of withdrawal from social and community psychiatry that the ELMHC was named for Dr. Lindemann, and he was the guest of honor at its dedication. This event trenchantly highlights the change in ideology from social psychiatry before to biological psychiatry after.[110]

Klerman, the superintendent, described the center: Raquel Cohen, former director of the North Suffolk Mental Health Association (a community agency with which Lindemann collaborated), became clinical director at the ELMHC and later its superintendent. He noted that the MGH was affiliated with the Bunker Hill Health Center, which provided physical and mental health and social services to its community. The ELMHC had a staff of 150, including 12 psychiatrists, 9 psychologists, 12 social workers, 24 nurses, and support personnel. He highlighted 27 local residents in a training program to prepare them for mental health practice as well as their employment alleviating poverty and unemployment in the community. The MGH's benefit lay partly in the plan to make places for 400 clinical and research trainees.

Honored guests included the wife of the Massachusetts governor, Francis Sargent, and the president of the Massachusetts senate, Mario Umana, who reminded the audience of the $11 million cost provided by the state for the construction of the building.

Milton Greenblatt, then the state commissioner of mental health, took a broader bio-psycho-social view of the Center's function, including both biological and social psychiatric ideologies. He traced the history of collaboration between the Commonwealth of Massachusetts and the Harvard Medical School (HMS) to the 1912 establishment of the Boston Psychopathic Hospital. He generously and diplomatically credited this current iteration to his predecessor commissioner, Harry C. Solomon; HMS deans George Packer Berry, Robert Ebert, and Associate Dean

Henry Meadow; MGH General Director John H. Knowles; and MGH Psychiatry Chiefs Erich Lindemann, John Nemiah (acting), and Leon Eisenberg. He foresaw and hoped for a broad functioning of the Center:

> It would have responsibility for care and treatment plus training professionals and paraprofessionals plus research into the causes and treatment of mind and brain disorders. He looked forward to ELMHC providing total care to avoid transferring patients out, end state hospital backup of patients, and receiving unsuitable patients. He looked for epidemiological research into whatever ails populations, leading to assessment techniques for rapid evaluation of patients by assistants trained in the low-cost application of these techniques. "I would hope, also, for the setting up, in '70's, in the Harbor Area [ELMHC's catchment area], of a variety of group, family, social, and environmental options for healthy growth and development, with the possibility of a preventive social prescription for some individuals whose lives we can follow during their full human careers. I would expect that at least in one parcel of your area the vast therapeutic resources of the community can be identified, mobilized, and organized into a volunteer army of gifted people who, properly supervised by professionals, can begin to meet the manpower requirements of the sick through a use of latent community resources of care. I would expect the greatest [use] of sophisticated distance monitoring systems [which have already been] developed at MGH, so that a small number of highly trained professionals can spread their contacts and effectiveness over a larger group of coordinated health technicians and assistants. I would expect the exploration of new models of integrated total health care delivery systems through collaboration basically with the Harvard Community Health Plan [a Harvard-affiliated health maintenance organization]". He expected the ELMHC to be open to reasonable new treatment approaches including psychopharmacology, new intensive confrontation and marathon techniques, behavior [modification] treatment, and family approaches. It would also provide training for management and executive leadership. It would seek the source of chronicity in illness and how to treat it "which, to my mind, is the greatest challenge for the future". It would also pursue prevention and rehabilitation programs for dependent and subdependent individuals.

Leon Eisenberg, who succeeded Lindemann as chief of psychiatry, was identified with social psychiatry in his own way and spoke of the center's ambiguity in carrying out CMH, feelings that Lindemann shared:

> I would like to point out that it provides an undoubted opportunity for collaboration between the teaching hospital and the community

and the medical school. The building itself, however, it should be noted, by virtue of its sheer beauty and its massiveness, provides a challenge of another sort, and that is to somehow overcome the tendency to centralize services here instead of to carry out the basic idea of community mental health, namely to see to it that they are each to be found in the communities that are included within the Harbor Area. The architecture, in some respects, is a challenge to the program, because it would be very easy to localize everything where it's prettiest and to avoid going to the problems where they exist.

John Knowles, former MGH general director and Lindemann supporter, reminisced on the influence Lindemann's ideas had on his professional development. As an intern at MGH in 1950, he remembered learning from Lindemann the articulation and integration of psychiatry with acute medical services, social psychiatry, comprehensive services, crisis intervention, and the fruitful combination of the social sciences with the psychiatric and biological sciences.

HMS Dean Robert Ebert, a former colleague of Lindemann's, did not attend. Henry Meadow, associate dean, did. He had been active in negotiations for the Center and understood some of the CMH intentions for it: "It . . . represents an opportunity for the [Harvard] Medical School to have a new interface with the community, and to develop new ways of teaching students as well as advancing our knowledge of mental health".

Bertram S. Brown, M.D., director of the NIMH and supporter of CMH, attended as a guest speaker with the topic "Community Mental Health: A Center of Focus". He spoke of federal policy and funding affecting CMH. He noted that CMH had come upon hard times but looked to its tenacity and vigor. He noted that the federal budget for mental health increased from $60 million to $160 million over the past year. This financing was not just more money but indicated the relationship of mental health to health reform in general, human services and welfare reform, and concern with the quality of life. The three national priorities in mental health in the past year were child mental health, the behavioral sciences and mental health aspects of law and order, and the mental health concerns of minorities. He hoped that health maintenance organizations—a new concept at the time—would include comprehensive mental health services and collaboration with CMHCs.

Erich Lindemann's speech was an extensive reminiscence of his ideals and efforts in CMH, his hopes for their continuation, an effort to diplomatically accept the mental health center and its functions that contrasted so sharply with his ideas of community-based mental health, and some uncharacteristic though muted recognition of the obstacles and conflicts in the way of CMH. It stands as an effort to comprehend the past ideological and professional conflicts with the effort to see them come to some extent of constructive resolution:

> Well, thank you all. What can one say at such a moment? It is really given to few people at the end of their life to see the growth, development, and the beautiful elaboration of many of the ideas which occurred to them, which they shared with their friends, which they fought over with their colleagues, and which finally were absorbed into a broader consensus and became public and private common property of all of us today and a great many other people. It's like a tree growing from a small root and finally becoming a substantial part of creation which gives an umbrella shade to other growth and to human beings. . .
>
> Let's look at this umbrella and my notion of a tree rendering shade and protection to a large area of people. Or with this massive building perhaps a fortress presenting refuge to a lot of poor and disturbed people like some fortresses used to do in the middle ages. And this manifest massive building, which is a source of strength. And in that way it's a source of that part of understanding human nature, and healing human nature which has to do with control, power over, keeping in line, setting limits. It's that part of psychiatry which came from the mental hospital, which was nourished and developed to very high degree in hospitals in our field, which is perfected in the good mental hospital, and some of which had to be kept, and some of this seems to be in the gravity of this building, of this very strong, stony appearance of a fortress. On the other hand, when you look at the building and would like to find the sharp corners and the limits and the place where you might bump into if you don't watch out, you might find yourself in an area where are really just suggestions of limits, and just the feeling that maybe, if you are just yourself and don't get scared, you might find your way through this after all quite friendly, charming, loving, gracious, light-hearted building that is also here. And then we were thinking about another side of psychiatry.
>
> That's the psychiatry to which Dr. Knowles referred so strongly, the one which has grown up in the general hospital. That's the psychiatry which tries to understand, see the psychological roots and origins of contemporary suffering, perhaps even of misdemeanor, and tries by empathy, sympathy, and understanding to what in other situations has to be done by control and setting limits. It's the marvelous architectural combination of these two vistas of psychiatry. And it has to arrive at the psychiatric understanding that both are necessary, and both have to be eternally kept in proper balance, which makes psychiatry what it can be now.
>
> I think the people who, in my mind, stand behind this sort of thinking are Alan Gregg . . . who, some fifty years ago, was at the

point in his life where John Knowles is now, namely taking over the Rockefeller Foundation, having tremendous resources at his command to do just the right thing, as Dr. Knowles will do now, and he created what later became the psychopathic hospital—not a hospital outside town somewhere for masses of people to be looked after and separated out from the world, but near town, in town, bringing the people together with patients and with their caretakers. Alan Gregg became a friend of mine—he picked me up in Iowa City, as a matter of fact, and brought me to Boston. We have remained great friends till the end of his life. His image was so important for me because he also was the man who supported Stanley Cobb. And Stanley Cobb then became my teacher (Gregg took me to him), and the one who taught me something else—another dichotomy which has to be integrated, namely the biological component of understanding people and explaining their behavior, and the kind of report which looks at the person from the inside, his subjective experiences, his way of seeing his life and fulfilling his destiny. And these two aspects can be combined; indeed what Cobb brought us was to put these two aspects into one department.

Now it is as though it was [done] pretty nicely: we work very hard and we talked nicely and without debate. But we forget sometimes that bringing together opposites and to enable them at a superior level [so] that they now can go together doesn't go without blood, sweat, and tears. And through the years, together with John [Knowles], at the Mass General [Hospital], in a group of people who Johnnie Knowles was said to have quoted as being a bunch of tigers, once in the newspaper, that this bunch of people—biologists and also people interested in experiences—would learn to live together. And that [produced] so much extra energy that they now could look outside the hospital, and could see that, after all, the hospital is only one of many sources of support and help and restoration for sick people, perhaps even for poor people, for people who have not found the right way. And out of that emerged later that which we now call community [mental health], that doctors and clergymen and teachers and parole officers and policemen and all the citizens themselves have the feeling we are all in the same boat.

And, Indeed, the institutions we need are not specialized institutions only—surely we need them to become experts at the top level—that we also need integration, communication, bridges. And for me this building is so exciting, and the umbrella function, the social architecture of this building, is for me so important and exciting, because it effects a bridge between various, disparate, often not-communicating, segments of the community, of the professions, of the sciences. And having this possibility of reaching a consensus and common effort at a higher level than one used to before, because one just can spend energy now that is not wasted on mutual aggression anymore, which one can spend now in mutual understanding.

That seems to be the point at which we are at now in the deep spiritual sense, in which we all are working together slightly differently, perhaps because we have been pushed into it by wars and terrible experiences, but it is there. It is signified by what you are doing, by the heartwarming reception you gave to a little fella like myself who just kicked the stone which became an avalanche, and by the warmth which I feel all around from my colleagues, from my friends, from some of my competitors. And from the sense that, perhaps, in humanity we have fights, struggles, we have competition, we have rivalry, but we also have seeking out each other and coming to a joint effort for the biggest things to which you can reach—reaching for the stars. Thanks.

The affiliation agreement (this draft after Klerman had moved on)[111] between the MGH and the Harbor Area Board (community advisory board) suggests the concept of community mental health that defined the ELMHC—traditional academic research and training, and treatment of the mentally ill:

A. <u>Health Services</u>: MGH provides services at the MGH Acute Psychiatric Service. Admit to the Emergency Ward. Maintain a log of visits and patients. Medications, laboratory studies and psychiatry ward admission per MGH criteria and the judgement of the Chief of Psychiatry. Commonwealth of Massachusetts pays standard rates and funds one full time equivalent first year Acute Psychiatric Service resident.
B. <u>Joint Training</u>: Under the direction of the MGH Chief of Psychiatry, MGH will provide and the Commonwealth pay for psychiatric residents—3 first year and 4 each second and third year. MGH makes available the Director of Residency Training and other staff. ELMHC makes available the Director of Psychology, other staff, and will seek training funds.
C. <u>Research and Professional Interchange</u>: Joint collaboration and review, complaints reviewed by MGH. MGH administers grants. MGH appointments to the Harbor Area (ELMHC) Director (and appointment to research committees) and to qualified psychiatrists, psychologists, and other doctoral level professionals in the Harbor Area program. Harbor Area suggestions and comments about any new MGH Chief of Psychiatry. The state will assign rooms on the 5th floor of the ELMHC for joint research; any grant funds for rent will be paid to the Harbor Area. MGH will make suggestions and comments about any new Harbor Area Director.
D. <u>General</u>: Accounting and annual reports will be written.

Signed: Charles A. Saunders, M.D. (MGH General Director), Thomas P. Hackett, M.D. (MGH Chief of Psychiatry), Robert L. Okin, M.D. (Massachusetts Commissioner of Mental Health), Raquel E. Cohen, M.D. (Director of the Harbor Area and Superintendent of the ELMHC).

The architecture of the ELMHC deserves comment, both because it is symbolic of the differences between Lindemann's concept of CMH and the interpretation of that term in the context of public policy and psychiatry in a later era and also because it has stimulated much debate in its own right. Building construction began in March 1967 and was completed in November 1970. Paul Rudolph was the coordinating architect, Desmond and Lord were the working architects, and Vappi Construction Co. was the builder.[112]

When Alberta Siegel, one of Lindemann's colleagues and admirers in his relocation to Stanford Medical Center, saw the ELMHC, she could not imagine naming this building for Lindemann: it was a massive repository of centralized psychiatric services, in contrast to Lindemann's modesty and philosophy of integration into the community.[113] Leonard Duhl agreed.[114] A variety of others commented from their relationships to the building and program:

> The great staircase swoops up and around in curves just circular enough to get you lost, next to columns just towering enough to make you feel small . . . this cavernously empty building in Boston's Government Center.
> (Goodman, Ellen, "One less refuge for runaways" [re before opening ELMHC was used as a runaway girls refuge], *Boston Globe* 9/12/1971)

> The unit . . . still overwhelms visitors and new patients with its towering columns and great curving staircases.
> The ins and outs of labyrinth floors and corridors, located in a building erected far from some of the residential areas it serves, can be bewildering and annoying to the uninitiated . . . in addition to being structurally out of tune with the current area center trend . . . Individuals in communities needing mental health care facilities often protest against their location.

> The Lindemann Mental Health Center . . . has been called paradise only for photographers who sneak in to study light and shadows.
> The functional problem of the radical architecture . . . is summed up by a community health worker who helps escort patients in and out.
> "The building almost programs you to feel crazy. The steps expand as you go down the stairs", says Maria Anastasi of the North End, a member of a neighborhood team who helps people overcome their fear of seeking treatment.

"Unless they wear bifocal glasses, the Lindemann professional staff finds the expanding stairs the least of many challenges". . . . Although the center was planned for years . . . to serve people in the harbor area of Boston, there is now general agreement that the time of opening, the place and the architecture were all unfortunate.

Federal funding program for staff had just been slashed. Most of the community is separated by water from the Government Center, which is not a community at all.

Aesthetically speaking the center named in honor of Dr. Erich Lindemann . . . a man of modest personal style who pioneered in neighborhood psychiatry, is a monument only to the exotic taste of its architect, Paul Rudolph.
(Dietz, Jean, "Functional problems found with Lindemann architecture", Boston Evening Globe 3/7/1974)

Some services are related to mental health only in the preventive sense. For example, the huge gymnasium and 625 square foot swimming pool . . . are used by patients . . . But they are also used by 41 different community groups . . . A wide variety of outreach programs . . . include a behavior modification course for teachers in the Winthrop school system and a predelinquent screening group for East Boston children which works with local schools and courts to provide overall treatment for multiproblem families.
(Dietz, Jean, "Functional problems found with Lindemann architecture", Boston Evening Globe 3/7/74)

A wide range of human services for families who live or work in [the Harbor Area] . . . will be provided there by the Massachusetts Department of Mental Health.

The center has teaching and research affiliations with the Massachusetts General Hospital, where Dr. Lindemann was chief of psychiatry from 1954 to 1965.

Staff . . . see it providing a "sheltering umbrella", extending help within the center and with less formal satellites developing in communities nearby.

"The building may be dramatic, but we can't see ourselves tied down to an architectural symbol", says Dr. Gerald L. Klerman, superintendent and new professor of psychiatry at Harvard Medical School.

"We believe the services should be available close to where the people live and where programs can be influenced by consumer participation. An entire floor of the center is designated for laboratories to investigate causes and treatment of mental illness . . . Programs will be defined according to community needs . . . The Lindemann Center policy will be to get away from the double standard of one kind of psychiatric service for the rich and another for the poor—with the middle economic class caught in between ... standard Department of Mental Health fees will prevail—$40 a day for hospitalization, $21 for day care, and $8 for an outpatient clinic visit ... A state of 'dynamic tension' now exists between some of the staff and the highly creative forms of the building. Dr. Raquel Cohen, who directs clinical services, believes 'some of the problems we are encountering in working with the building we find so beautiful from an esthetic view may teach us some good lessons in mental health'. The varied levels and curves which sweep the visitor from area to area may confuse some patients as well as the staff... "My impression is that how a patient feels about himself is important", says Dr. Frank Paolitto, who directs the inpatient unit... "The building discourages the idea that people are not worthwhile".

"It's so clean and beautiful", said a woman in one of the pioneering groups recently admitted. "I've begun to feel well enough to want to move outside".
>(Dietz, Jean, "Mental health unit to serve harbor area',
>Boston Sunday Globe 9/19/71)

It looks like the ruins of Machu Picchu or a Greek amphitheatre or is it really a great ocean liner with towering stacks in stark silhouette. A corner could have come from Montreal; from Habitat.

It is swirls and rises, flat slab faces, slender columns and tear drop boxes that hang in space like after thoughts. It curves and sweeps. It is very female.
>(Menzies, Ian, "The City", newspaper)

Dr. Lindemann ... compared the "strong massive" building designed by Paul Rudolph and others to a strong tree, capable of growth and spreading out roots to the many communities where the staff will serve and to a fortress to protect the troubled and the poor ... Dr. Leon Eisenberg, chief of psychiatry at Massachusetts General Hospital, called the dramatic architecture of the new Lindemann Center "a real challenge to the program because it would be very easy to localize everything in the pretty building and that's not where the problems are".
>(*Psychiatric News VI (no. 20)* 10/20/71
>[American Psychiatric Association] p. 29)

Lindemann himself participated in the ceremonies at the formal opening of the ELMHC. He continued to struggle to find a place for CMH within political, economic, and ideological strictures:[115]

> The mental health center (on the other hand), would be an agency of government and the community, where patients can be viewed as citizens in temporary discomfort, and where governors could

see these people as casualties of things that ought to be changed [p. 1].... Dr. [Gerald] Klerman: How do you build a program to serve a community that doesn't limit itself to the skin of the building? Dr. Barrett: ... We have the outlying services... [p. 2] ... Erich [Lindemann]: What we are stressing is coping with situations ... The pre-clinical services are social-system-oriented ... map out several areas and ... study how much is needed ... What kinds of roles are needed ... How much consultant service and done by whom? What does the community define as problems in contrast to what we define as problems? Should we create an army of sub professionals?

(p. 3)

institutions don't have to stay the way they are... [p. 1] ... very flexible, in respect to the careers that patients and staff could have in going through ... We need organizational inventions by which people can be persuaded to be more human.

(p. 2)

From his retirement visiting professorship at the Stanford Medical Center, Lindemann showed photographs of the ELMHC and talked of his hopes for outreach from it into the neighborhoods without a focus on psychopathology and with creative approaches to clinical issues.[116] However, he felt that he could not reach out with these ideas but had to wait to be invited. He was not. In the end, he saw it as an appalling absurdity, though he liked to think that some former HRS people carried on their work there.[117]

Philosophy of the mental health services in the new MHC varied among administrative, comprehensive, and enlarged traditional clinical treatment:[118]

> Massachusetts Commissioner of Mental Health Dr. Milton Greenblatt predicted that the concept of the old state hospital as a back-up for mental health centers will disappear in the 1970's.
> He said the Lindemann Center will be a place where new technologies in family therapy and behavioral therapy, as well as group sessions and "marathons" will be tested and evaluated... "It was through Dr. Lindemann that we found out about how to combine the social sciences with the psychiatric and biological sciences and learned the importance of crisis intervention", said Dr. John Knowles, who is leaving the directorship of Massachusetts General Hospital to become new chief executive of the Rockefeller Institute ... Dr. Gerald L. Klerman, superintendent of the new center ... said the goal of the staff is to provide comprehensive services to 200,000 people of all ages who live or work in the area.

A Sampling of Community Mental Health Programs

The post-Lindemann ELMHC programs reflect a hybrid of traditional clinical services and academic training, vague involvement with community representatives (note the advisory rather than decisive capacity), agencies, and programs; and limited, low-priority, or deferred preventive programs:

> A Harbor Mental Health and Mental Retardation Area Board, brought about by statute . . . is composed of 21 cities from the communities comprising the area and serves as the advisory group to the Lindeman Center. . . "The board", Dr. Klerman said, "represents a vehicle . . . through which the communities and consumers participate in indicating their wishes and advising the staff".[119]

PROPOSED PRIORITIES FOR GOVERNMENT CENTER AREA MENTAL HEALTH PROGRAMS (1) (1) Prepared April 28, 1970. . . Prepared By GERALD L. KLERMAN, M.D. . . . Area Director—Designate [cover page] . . . Long-Term Goals . . . 1. Community-based mental health services serving the local areas . . . It is essential that a general hospital psychiatric unit be established within the North Suffolk area . . . there will be a day hospital . . . and community mental health teams . . . consisting of . . . five professionals and five non-professionals. 2. Government Center Mental Health Center adult inpatients, children inpatients, mental retardation, drug dependence, adolescents, geriatrics, alcoholism, and legal psychiatry. [p. 1] . . . "3. Specific Clinical Programs . . . [p. 3] 1. Acute Inpatient Treatment Unit . . . 2. Selected Outpatient Services . . . 3. Mental Retardation Team . . . [p. 4] 4. Adult Community Services . . . adult services . . . complementing the Children Services . . . 5. Drug Dependence . . . 4. Training The psychiatric residency program at Massachusetts General Hospital will be expanded . . . Explorations . . . for training in social work, psychology, and nursing. . . . 5. Research . . . develop an evaluation and data system . . . programs in drug treatment evaluation, children's learning and developmental problems, and new treatments. 6. Community Relations and Planning . . . relations with the Area Board, the main representative of the constituent citizens groups . . . under the supervision of Dr. Peter Chorus [Choras] . . . provide staff functions for the Area Board, develop liaison with other community groups, and plan for grant applications. . . [p. 5] . . . a community mental health planning and coordination group . . . composed of representatives of the major mental health agencies servicing the area as well as representatives from selected educational, social welfare and health agencies . . . two member of the Area Board be designated, one of whom should be Rachel [Raquel] Cohen, M.D. [Director of the North Suffolk Mental Health Association] and the second recommended by the United Community Services [metropolitan charity coordinating agency].

(p. 6)[120]

The Lindemann Center and others are daily getting more like what they were intended to be . . . enticing community based programs dealing in every phase of mental health to come under their wing . . . coordinate the efforts of all community services and . . . channel money grants where they are needed.

It is directed to get to the heart of problems that spawn in neighborhoods and treat them at the scene before victims are confined behind bars . . . in huge forbidding institutions.

From: Evelyn L. McLean, Associate Area Director, 6 June, 1972 "Planning Information and Description of Need for Program Development for the Harbor Mental Health and Mental Retardation Area" The top priority which has been set in joint agreement by the Harbor Area Board and Staff with Region VI and the Department of Mental Health is as follows:

Mental health care for all patients from the Harbor Area within the area. . .

[p. 1] Services Now In Operation

Inpatient . . . Emergency Services. . . Day Care . . . Outpatient. . . [p. 2] . . . Developmental Disabilities—Retardation Services . . . Alcoholism . . . [p. 3] . . . Children's Services . . . At present we are able to meet only a small portion of the requests which we have received for consultation and/or education.

The Mental Health Act also provides for research programs, but it has been decided that during the fiscal emergency no staff should be added to this department.

The area of prevention is one for which we have not yet developed a program. While there is considerable concern about this, it will wait until there are funds available.

Broader preventive and community outreach functions survived as a kind of wish list:[121]

Harbor Area Program Planning

We are committed to develop a mental health system that will, hopefully, eliminate needless hospitalization by providing mental health care as close to the patients' homes as possible and as rapidly as possible . . . we have been guided by a number of principles including: . . . 6. To emphasize indirect services such as consultation and education to aid prevention and interruption of mental illness.

7. The importance of developing community participation through the Area Board, various committees and local agencies. [p. 19] 8. . . . high priority care given to those . . . most disabled by psychoses, depression,

suicide . . . 10. a public health model . . . aim at primary prevention by developing special programs for specific populations. . . [p. 20] . . . III SUMMARY OF MAJOR UNMET NEEDS . . . [p. 40] . . . One of the concerns of the NIMH has been to help citizens groups become more effective with planning. . . . The Harbor Area Board . . . appointed a group of twelve persons . . . to engage in this planning process. . . [p. 41] . . . The recommendations which follow. . . Everyday Life Problems . . . which people endure, but for which they do not usually seek professional mental health assistance has the second priority among these concerns. . . [p. 42] . . . people . . . will often seek advice from a trusted third party . . . trained para professionals be assigned as "detached workers" in health care centers, social centers, public welfare, public libraries or other settings . . . public education was seen as a large part of this responsibility, we recommend . . . a trained professional who has the capability of preparing and disseminating educational materials for community use . . . speaking to groups and conducting seminars . . . Many . . . situations into which police are asked to intervene are mental health problems . . . it is proposed to request 2 psychiatric social workers or psychologists to work directly with the police . . . 1 alcoholism specialist to work as the above. . . [p. 43]

Administrative/financial tasks, procedures, and obstacles were part of the public CMHC program:

> Lindemann, according to its Superintendent, Dr. Gerald Klerman . . . is presently under-utilized due to lack of funds for full staffing . . . Today, the center . . . is serving less than one-third of this inpatient capability . . . one-half of its day-care potential, less than one-fourth of its outpatient ability and . . . one-half occupancy in its school for the retarded . . . Across the state, area centers . . . are suffering from insufficient funds, mostly for staffing . . . Evaluation tools are seldom available to assess whether or not the programs are reaching everyone who needs them.

> At Lindemann where about 20 positions have not been filled . . . Dr. Klerman has applied to the federal government for a staffing grant of $800,000. It is expected that state money will become available in July . . . Dr. Theodore I. Anderson, state assistant commissioner for community programs . . . another $400,000 have been requested . . . However, Dr. C. S. Thomas of the National Institute of Mental Health, has stated that there is a two-year backlog of already approved area center projects seeking staffing grants.

> Dr. Anderson said, "it is doubtful we will get all we've asked for. There is only $10 million available for the entire country The Nixon administration is not enthusiastic about this program. Mental health does not have a high priority . . . Dr. Anderson stated that

Massachusetts will continue to move forward whether it gets new money or not . . . by trying to get increased flexibility . . . in the use of already appropriated money, try to get private or community money wherever we can, or, if nothing else works, put a heavier reliance on volunteer services". [Jean Cole, "Bay State Potential at $13 M Hub Center is Great . . . But Plus and Minus Marks in Mental Health Program].[122]

URGENT NOTICE To All Harbor Area Board Members 7 June, 1972 The Harbor Mental Health and Mental Retardation Area has been informed that the legislature expects to cut the 1973 State budget by 85 million dollars. This . . . will result in a loss of approximately 9 million . . . for the Department of Mental Health, which will cause . . . A cutback in funds for drugs and medical services will result in inadequate medical care for patients . . . A reduction in travel funds will reduce the number of visits to patients in the community . . . The proposed transfer of 25 Harbor Area patients from Boston State Hospital to Lindemann Center . . . will be impossible . . . 26 new staff . . . have been requested . . . These 26 positions will be eliminated . . . The Department of Corrections is taking over the Building (I) in which Harbor patients have been housed and the proposed . . . plan is to rotate the Harbor patients into other buildings. This totally destroys the possibility of a continuity of care program . . . to prevent patients from . . . become chronic. . . [p. 1] . . . Included in . . . the 1972–1973 budget were 22 positions for children . . . These positions will be eliminated". [p. 2] [Jean Cole, "Bay State Potential at $13 M Hub Center is Great . . . But Plus and Minus Marks in Mental Health Program.][123]

> The Harbor Area has received a federal "start up" grant for children's services . . . by NIMH, for a total of $298.825 in matching funds to coordinate and staff the services planned [p. 1].[124]

The imperfections, complexities, and failures of hopes for the ELMHC and CMH led to disappointment and criticism of both the building and the program:[125]

> The Erich Lindemann Mental Health Center was designed as a monument to the dream of deinstitutionalization. Today, nobody knows what to do with the building or with the people who live there . . . Tony's home, the cavernous Parker Shelter Central, in the Erich Lindemann Mental Health Center . . . is in some ways as brutal as the jumbled world inside his head. For two years now, Tony has been a guest at the shelter, living with 49 other guests on a basketball court on the ground floor . . . a gargantuan concrete fortress on the edge of Government Center.

The Lindemann is one of the strangest buildings in the world. It is . . . riddled with serpentine corridors, dark alcoves, and elaborate staircases—one of which ends in thin air.

Tony calls it . . . the strongest building he's ever seen. His friend John . . . says "all the crazy stairs" make him think of a medieval castle. Paul Rudolph, the . . . architect, describes his creation . . . as a "government building" that should be "an anchor for the city", rather than a residential space. . . "I'm glad it's being used in some way . . . The history of architecture can be written in terms of people finding uses for buildings" [p. 132] . . . He is a leading light of the school of architecture known as brutalism . . . When it was designed . . . the Erich Lindemann Mental Health Center promised to be the jewel in a three building tiara called the State Service Center . . . modeled after the famous Piazza del Campo, in Siena, Italy. The Lindemann Center also promised to be the flagship for a new and more humane system of mental health care, a system that would serve patients who would live like normal people in normal houses in normal Boston neighborhoods, rather than in state hospitals. Mental health professionals referred to this revolutionary approach as deinstitutionalization.

Today the Lindemann Mental Health Center dwells in the shadow that fell between the dreams of the Great Society and the performance of the Commonwealth. The State Service Center . . . was never finished. . . [p. 133] . . . the Erich Lindemann Mental Health Center itself, once envisioned as a gateway to one of the world's great public spaces, has decompensated into an unkempt and unlandscaped pile of concrete, a brutal citadel of despair just two blocks away from City Hall . . . It is a kind of societal DMZ, a no-man's land between the unwashed windows of the Lindemann building and the luxury high rises of Charles River Park [luxury housing in the West End] . . . the concept called deinstitutionalization has fared no better . . . when the Department of Mental Health (DMH) tried to transfer eight patients from the Lindemann Center to . . . a three decker . . . 250 Eastie [East Boston neighborhood] residents protested . . . complained to state representative . . . and city councilor . . . both of whom opposed the move. Others trashed the three-decker . . . The DMH dropped the plan . . . Paul Rudolph's symphony in concrete will never be finished. The Commonwealth has decided to get rid of it. Some members of the New Chardon Street Citizen Advisory Committee . . . suggested demolishing the Lindemann building . . . building is an architectural treasure, according to the Boston Landmarks Commission . . . the state now plans to sell or lease it. . . "What Rudolph planned was a monument", says James McNeely, who studied under Rudolph . . . and then came . . . as the project architect on the Lindemann Center construction . . . everything about the Lindemann Mental Health Center was crazy . . . its scale is frightening . . . the building has a brutal, uninviting rough concrete skin that discourages touch. And it is so confusingly laid out that even staffers have a hard time finding their way through its mazelike corridors.

Even the center's name doesn't make sense . . . Herbert J. Gans wrote *The Urban Villagers* . . . critique of the displacement . . . in Boston's West End. Lindemann wrote the book's forward. He attacked the "forced relocation of families". The Commonwealth tacked Lindemann's name onto the . . . facility it had built on the ruins of West End homes . . . Erich Lindemann visited the center. . . "He had very negative feelings about it", says Dr. Norman Bernstein, a former colleague . . . and the director of child psychology [psychiatry] at the Lindemann Center. "He said it looked like a fortress, that it did not give the appearance of reaching out into the community. He thought it looked menacing". [p. 134] . . . [Tom Piper, director, Office of Real Property, Division of Capital Planning and Operations, Commonwealth of Massachusetts] "the Lindemann just doesn't work, and probably can't be made to work. It is completely uncontrolled poetry, heroics without any boundaries".

[p. 137]

Erich Lindemann continued to receive token recognition from a waning cadre of ELMHC participants who had known or knew of him:

We wish to express our sincere appreciations to you for your generous donation of Dr. Lindemann's collection of psychiatric books . . . A special shelf area for his collection has been set aside at your request . . . We expect the books . . . will prove very useful to the Harbor Area staff as well as scholars in . . . community mental health . . . we would gladly house any further archival materials . . . any papers, correspondence, etc. of Dr. Lindemann . . . We also wish to express our conviction that Erich Lindemann will be long remembered for his contribution to community mental health, especially in this community.[126]

The books were never catalogued and were soon lost.

In 1975, Klerman finally was worn out with the administrative burdens of CMH as embodied in the ELMHC, as Lindemann had been in earlier times: "As you may have heard, I have announced my resignation as Superintendent of the Erich Lindemann Mental Health Center and Area Program Director . . . the press of administrative duties has become so difficult that I now feel the desire to resume more academic and clinical activities".[127] Elizabeth Lindemann, remembering Erich Lindemann's trials, responded sympathetically and diplomatically (considering Klerman's difference from Lindemann's concepts): "I can certainly understand, and I'm sure Erich would have, why you wish to leave Lindemann Center at this time. I have lost count of the number of Commissioners you have served under, and with an adverse fiscal situation, the road must have been uphill all the way . . . I hope that your successor will carry on in the same spirit".[128]

Klerman's successor as superintendent of thee Erich Lindemann Mental Health Center and area director of the Harbor Mental Health Area program was Raquel E. Cohen, who, as executive director of the North Suffolk Mental Health Association had been a community agency collaborator with Lindemann. For seven years she had headed a team of consultants to the Boston School System and served in various local and national organizations concerned with mental health, minorities, and training. She held a master's degree in public health from the HSPH and an M.D. from HMS. She was eventually appointed associate professor of psychiatry at Harvard Medical School.[129] Eventually she, too, was stymied and worn down by the political and academic maze and obstacles and left.

In retrospect, the MGH tried to portray a successful resolution of the differences among interest groups: the MGH fearing the burden of open-ended clinical responsibility with inadequate public funding; the state government fearing exploitation of public funding for academic aggrandizement; and the community suspicious that they were pawns in academic and governmental self-serving: "with persistent suspicions that they were again to be the victims of academic and governmental rape":[130]

> Dr. Klerman . . . set up a decentralized delivery system which from the beginning was focused on providing care in its communities rather than in the Lindemann Center building. . . [p. 6] . . . Another innovation, which followed the Psychiatry Service tradition at the Hospital, was to form a close alliance in the community between the psychiatric and medical caregivers, in this case . . . with the primary care physicians in the neighborhood health centers and community hospitals within each community subcatchment. . . [p. 7]

> The Lindemann Center, with its MGH alliance, has weathered these storms better than most . . . strong leadership, . . . developed halfway houses, cooperative apartments, day treatment programs, social clubs . . . medication monitoring in its communities for patients with chronic illness. It still provides some primary preventive services to children, consultation to a variety of caregiving agencies, and a significant amount of therapy to patients without chronic illness . . . the MGH . . . provides . . . emergency services . . . and helps Lindemann recruit superior psychiatric staff . . . because of the academic-public sector tie. Although Lindemann's superintendent is no longer a psychiatrist, there has been strong psychiatric leadership . . . How much

longer it can maintain this leadership position in the face of increasing demands and decreasing resources... [p. 12]

One wonders about the place of indigenous community agencies, caregivers, and leaders who were Lindemann's hosts, resources, collaborators, and beneficiaries, trying to function in the contemporary thicket of government and academic institutions, community health centers, and programs.

This program suggests that after the passing of Lindemann's advocacy and societal/governmental ideological and material support, traditional academic perspective and direction were reasserted. The CMH interpretation of expanded treatment of the mentally ill reigned with lip service to social psychiatry and primary prevention in the indefinite future.

University of Heidelberg-Mannheim, Germany

In the 1920s (when Lindemann studied there), the Heidelberg Psychiatrische Klinik (Department of Psychiatry) functioned in the tradition of Karl Jaspers, who lived in Heidelberg until 1948 and was associated with the Klinik 1909–1913.[131] He was firstly a physician who was friendly with physicians. In 1924, while associated with the psychiatric hospital, he published *Algemeine Psychopathologie* (General Psychopathology). He then became professor (chairman) of psychology, though later there were barriers between psychiatry, psychology, and medicine. Finally he was appointed professor of philosophy, though before 1933, psychiatry had no interest in theology. Wilmans, professor of psychiatry 1925–1927, was more influenced by von Weizsäker's person concept than by phenomenology, and later gravitated toward psychoanalysis. There was some interest in social psychiatry through family care and occupational therapy, pioneered by Simon in the hospital at Gütersloh.[132] During the Nazi era (1933–1945) psychoanalysis was rejected because it was associated with Jews, including Sigmund Freud. German psychiatry, too, distanced itself from psychoanalysis because it was not based in science, and even after the Nazi era, German psychoanalysis had difficulty rejoining the International Psychoanalytic Association.

From 1955 to 1972, Walter Johannes Adolf Ritter von Baeyer (1904–1987) was professor of psychiatry. He had been an assistant in the Psychiatrische Klinik 1929–1933, he and Kurt Schneider renewed the department's interest in theology and descriptive phenomenology (inspired by Karl Jaspers) rather than biology, and he pursued it at the Kaiser Wilhelm Institute in Munich.[133] He thought Viktor von Weizsäcker's neurology had little understanding of or connection with psychiatry, and Jaspers worked in theology. In 1933, under the National Socialist regime, von Baeyer's "undesirable" family background caused his father to be dismissed from the orthopedics faculty and von Baeyer to be removed from the University of Heidelberg; during World War II, he was sent to the eastern front to practice psychiatry and neurology. During this time, social psychiatry was set back and phenomenology was tolerated in the department. Wilmans's follower, Karl Schneider, became much involved in the Nazi euthanasia program, was imprisoned when the Americans occupied the area, and committed suicide. After the war, von Baeyer returned to the Max Planck Institute in genetics, became chief physician at the Nürnberger Neurologischen und Psychiarischen Klinik (Nuremberg Neurological and Psychiatric Hospital), and then dozent (lecturer) and professor at the Friedrich Alexander Universität Erlangen. The department's ideology was broad rather than narrowed by a special approach. The Heidelberg department's spirit was phenomenological but not focused on a certain patient group.

Social psychiatry was promoted and implemented principally by Heinz Häfner. This interest in social psychiatry with international stimulation led to Lindemann's often being invited to lecture about grief work and bereavement. Social psychiatry seemed different from phenomenology, though Kisker's approach included much interest in social psychiatry and there was similarity in practice in terms of human contact and interaction. Martin Buber in Frankfurt pioneered in these developments. Contact with the U.S., Great Britain, and other countries grew, and from 1949 von Baeyer—often with Häffner (then a Privat Dozent [senior lecturer] as was Kisker)—toured the U.S. and its CMHCs, including Boston: the Boston Psychopathic Hospital under Harry Solomon and lectured at the M.G.H. under Lindemann. This encouraged Häffner to broaden his approach in Mannheim (the neighboring city housing university programs), which also included biological psychiatry. Häffner, Kisker, and von Baeyer wrote a book on the subject.

According to Niels Pörksen, after 1970, the University of Heidelberg had two psychiatry faculties: one at the university in Heidelberg under Prof. Walter Ritter von Baeyer and one in Mannheim under Prof. Heinz Häfner.[134] He reports that Häffner visited Boston, New York, and other places to study mental health centers. He was interested in Lindemann's CMH work and returned to Mannheim intending, in collaboration with the mayor, to duplicate them there by developing a CMHC in this industrial city.[135] In 1969, Der Zentralinstitut für Seelisches Gesundheit (the Central Institute for Mental Health) was established, at first in an old mental hospital in Mannheim, separate from but near Häffner's academic headquarters in Heidelberg.[136] There was enormous enthusiasm for this therapeutic approach in contrast with the traditional ones; Werner Janzarik, subsequent professor of psychiatry, thought this was an uncritical embrace of these social psychiatry ideas.[137]

Lindemann met Häffner at a meeting in New York, where he found him spontaneous and warm (he came from southern Germany), sharing interests in epidemiology, and with a sensitive, psychodynamic outlook.[138]

He became interested in Häfner's plans to develop a social psychiatry program:[139]

> For the early summer, I have an invitation from Professor [Heinz] Hefner in Heidelberg, whom I befriended at Fritz Redlich's December meeting on social psychiatry, to help him set up a program in community psychiatry in Mannheim, an industrial town adjacent to Heidelberg. The problem there, in contrast to our concern with the Negro immigrant from rural into metropolitan areas, is the European issue of intensive use of migrant workers from Spain, Italy and Greece who participate in industry without becoming acculturated to the German style of life. I am quite eager to find out what goes on with respect to their emotional well-being and with the institutional arrangements for them.

And again:[140] "the application of our concepts in a German setting, and targeting in on the migrant workers from Spain and Yugoslavia as I hope to do with Niels Pörksen and Helmut Hefner in Heidelberg".

In 1963–1965, von Baeyer lectured at the MGH.[141] Lindemann arranged an ongoing correspondence and exchange of staff through Häffner. Häffner wanted Lindemann as a visiting professor at Heidelberg, but Lindemann's illness intervened. He did visit for one to two weeks on three occasions.

Niels Pörksen was an apostle in Germany of Lindemann's concepts of CMH. His family was involved in religiously based social action, his father a north German Protestant minister. As a young psychiatric resident in the Psychiatrische Klinik (psychiatry department) of the University of Heidelberg he knew nothing of community psychiatry but was very dissatisfied with the psychiatry he was taught.[142] He reported:[143]

> My first contact with the Harvard School of Public Health in 1962 was in northern India, at Ludhiana Medical College . . . I had been asked to write a report for the German Protestant Church, which had stopped funding the Medical College. The American president of the college has resigned. He had wanted to establish highest American standards, while the Indian government as well as the staff wanted basic community medicine for the people in India. A research team from the Harvard School of Public Health supported me in writing my report in favor of public health concepts.

In 1966, during one of Lindemann's visits to the University of Tübingen, Pörksen sought out this retired American psychiatrist in the (significantly) small, dark office at the end of a row in a cellar. Pörksen felt Lindemann was not treated properly and attended his talks at doctors' conferences on the Wellesley Human Relations Service, bereavement studies, and the Laboratory for Community Psychiatry. This resonated with his family background, and the mentorship and friendship with Lindemann integrated community psychiatry, with its flavor of dedication and moral conviction, into Pörksen's professional and personal identity. This continuing influence differed from his relationship with Gerald Caplan, though he knew Caplan better.

Pörksen initiated further training and experience in CMH:[144]

> I am very much interested in social psychiatry . . . Professor Lindemann, who is in our hospital for this term, has told us a lot about the development of community psychiatry, a subject of research still rather unknown in Germany. I would be very interested, and it would be a great help to me, to take part in your training program in community psychiatry . . . My internship I have done at the Jewish Hospital of Berlin (surgery) . . . the head of our department, Professor Schulte, would like very much if I could be able to be a trainee in your department and could use my experiences later in Tübingen.

It was arranged that Pörksen would spend a year with Gerald Caplan and Lindemann at the Laboratory for Community Psychiatry to learn about their concept of CMH. He credited Lindemann for arranging, in the fall of 1968, the fellowship with Caplan and experiences in Boston and the U.S.[145] When he then applied for a position in the newly created Social Psychiatry Department at Heidelberg University, he also credited Lindemann with giving an enthusiastic recommendation in response to Häffner's inquiry.[146]

The new department was announced—the Sozial-Medizinischen Institut (Social Medicine Institute)—which made the University of Heidelberg the first German university to establish a close cooperation between practitioners, caseworkers, ministers, clinics, etc. (Lindemann was invited to visit).[147] It included Pörksen and others in neurology, psychiatry, child psychiatry, social work, epidemiology, and nursing whom he would later identify as comrades in developing CMH.[148] He applied himself to the establishment of a large mental health center program with much experimentation to provide primary, secondary, and tertiary preventive services, and absorbing the mental health clinic in Mannheim and the small psychiatric hospital in Heidelberg.[149] He had to prepare a multidisciplinary staff, including in the small university hospital in Heidelberg and the large municipal hospital and clinic in Mannheim, agency officials, and town officials in a preventive approach. In this he and Häffner agreed. When Lindemann visited in 1970 the atmosphere was open to prevention, a community orientation, teamwork, good community contacts, concern with public policy issues, collaboration of residents with professionals, and shifting the approach from casework to problems of etiology. But Germany was oriented to the treatment of mental illness and had no concept or terminology for mental health, a social orientation, or CMH, and people did not understand Lindemann's exposition. Pörksen wanted to develop a positive working relationship with other groups to help them understand the poor population with which they worked and the anger in this population. As long as he helped these groups with this task, he was successful. To prepare the Zentralinstitut and community for a CMHC, Pörksen felt that he and his team were most knowledgeable and the only ones with a clear strategy: They contacted all psychiatric, social, and other programs and were asked by community agencies for a psychosocial and sociopolitical view of Mannheim. In 1969 Die Gemeinde Psychiatrie (Community Psychiatry) program was established, providing CMH consultation to family social workers, community social work programs for those released from prison, the chronically mentally ill, alcoholics, etc.; and saw problems through their disciplinary perspectives. Pörksen felt he had support from city and agency authorities.[150]

He described his intentions and efforts:[151]

> [O]ur multidisciplinary team ... included members trained in adult and child psychiatry, psychiatric nursing, [p. 302] public health, social work, and psychology. Young professionals and graduate students from education, administration, and medicine rotated through the different fields of the service.
>
> Idealistic notions propagated by the American Mental Health Movement led us to assume that *primary preventive principles*, infused into the health, education, and social service system, would prevent or significantly diminish vulnerability to psychiatric illness in the population ... it had the favorable effect of embedding public health philosophy in our design ... and integrate mental health consultation practice ... into the general health and social systems ... We provided consultations for the staff of the city welfare department, government subsidized housing projects, and organizations providing shelter for the homeless. We fostered neighborhood initiatives and community programs, particularly in economically disadvantaged and physically rundown areas. We developed and supported social and service clubs for individuals discharged from hospitals and for the chronically mentally ill. In cooperation with a nonprofit student organization, we established a large self-help organization for alcoholics. In sum, we "interfered in community social politics", encouraging new ways of engaging people in an improved mental health environment.

Pörksen was satisfied that the project was successful in delivering services. However, he observed growing resentment from local government against intrusion on their territory and resistance to change from traditional psychiatric care. The radical outbreaks of 1968 further stoked

A Sampling of Community Mental Health Programs 67

fears of social change.[152] The University of Heidelberg tried to avoid involvement in politics and social change in the name of scientific objectivity as well as to retain government acceptance and support.

Tension and conflict grew between the young, idealistic, assertive, and crusading Pörksen and the older, pragmatic, idealistic but less radical and circumspect Häffner, who feared for his scientific reputation and dangers to the acceptance and development of his cherished social psychiatry program. Elizabeth Lindemann saw Häffner as a good, caring clinician, unhappy if others were dissatisfied, and disliking new ideas (such as group therapy), frills, and dangerous experiments.[153] He was eager to arrange a new building in Mannheim and needed to maintain good public relations including with the federal government and Mannheim's mayor, who was offended at Pörksen's alliance with rebellious social elements in the city. Pörksen later regretted that he was too partisan in favor of the townspeople and too suspicious and resistant to the mayor and other highly placed authorities and professionals, who would hear only supporters of government policies and rejected those who disagreed. He viewed Häffner as wanting distant consultation with agencies and not involved with citizens and the politics of their living conditions. This contrasted with the socially involved approach of Pörksen and the community psychiatrists. In regard to social and medical problems, Pörksen viewed the mayor as Häffner's, who feared that Pörksen's group was coopting his role and therefore insisted that they meet for one to two hours every two weeks to inform him and give him recommendations for his final decision.

Between Häffner's social psychiatry and Pörksen's community advocacy, perspectives hardened into partisanship, discomfort into conflict, and disagreement into rejection. Pörksen thought Häffner saw him as too partisan and not academically impartial,[154] and his program illicitly mixing into politics, fraught with conflict, and dangerous. He felt Häffner was himself taking a political stand in opposing community outreach, withdrawing to distant and scientific program of epidemiology and a city case register of mental health problems, and segregating social misfits in treatment institutions. Pörksen accused Häffner of being ambitious, opportunistic in terms of psychiatric ideology, fearful of opposition, not respecting CMH and professional writing in the field, and less accepted. On the other side, Pörksen reported that "Herr Haefner . . . was not longer able to see anything positive in my work . . . either in . . . Heidelberg or in Mannheim . . . he continues to let it be known that for him I am a unique disappointment and that he had apparently greatly overestimated my ability".[155] Pörksen saw this as an insoluble conflict developing with Häffner.

Pörksen later regretted too quickly opposing Häffner rather than working to clarify their problems and integrating him in the program. Lindemann gave Pörksen much support and helped him survive. He encouraged Pörksen to publish his papers outside the university (they were published by a large German publisher) and not to struggle with the more powerful Häffner. Pörksen came to the conclusion that he could never work or survive in this environment, which made him feel lacking freedom of action and at Häffner's mercy. Lindemann acknowledged that Pörksen faced complex problems and enemies in introducing a community mental health program and was interested in how this could be implemented in a German city.[156] He encouraged Pörksen not to blame himself but to leave and keep up his hopes for success—though not saying how to accomplish this.

For Pörksen, values were an integral part of the CMH approach, including fighting the social and political causes of social problems such as the rejection of people into slums and disagreement with the stance of private psychiatrists in regard to urban renewal: "You [Elizabeth Lindemann] and Erich were the ones who brought me to Boston, to community psychiatry. Not by theory, more by the love of people who suffer in this world, who need our help. Our psychiatric belief is a part of professionalism. It was caring for people, engagement for human rights and social justice, political involvement".[157] The CMH program moved on to demands for changed policies, practices, and opinions by city agencies and private psychiatrists and the rejection of bad practices (such as urban renewal), leading to conflicts with other interests.

At this time in 1971, Lindemann visited Heidelberg for the second and last time at the time of great social upheaval in Europe, including the development of terrorist groups such as the Baader-Meinhof Group of revolutionaries in Germany. Germany feared that this communist student agitation was a prelude to Russian invasion. Janzarik noted that the social psychiatry ideas and programs became radicalized and antiauthoritarian. In Heidelberg, students occupied parts of the university. In the University Psychiatrische Polyklinik/Ambulanz (psychiatric outpatient clinic) directed by Mundt, one or two psychiatrists (including Kretz and young assistant Wolfgang Huber) became politically radical. Von Baeyer thought they were vulnerable and acted out of strong political beliefs and some psychopathic elements but not psychotic ones.[158] They collected young student patients, including those acutely schizophrenic and suicidal, and told them they were not suffering from disease but from parents, society, the university, and capitalism. They wanted acceptance by the university and financing from the university and state for self-help treatment without any need for psychiatrists. When students came to the psychiatric clinic for group therapy, they organized the Sozialistisches Patienten Kollektiv Heidelberg (Socialistic Patients Collective of Heidelberg), their therapist addressed political issues (and was fired by the university), and they joined terrorist groups. They were aggressive: members would come to the hospital at night for medications. They demonstrated and took over the Klinik building. A faculty member was forced out, and a staff member committed suicide. Social Democrats such as Häffner felt vulnerable and progressively withdrew from participation in the social psychiatry institute, sensing that this approach was not good for career development.

The faculty could not accept this and found it impossible to collaborate with this faction, though they presented an interesting subject of study. Häffner and the university president tried to squelch the group by refusing money and speaking out against it. Meetings and controversies ensued. Von Baeyer observed that the younger faculty came with a different perspective, wanting a democratization of psychiatry, engaging much with the revolutionaries, and involved a social worker but mostly psychology and politics students and not medical students. The university rector was Rentof, a theologian, who was accommodating and engaging. This, he thought, was much more constructive than the hostility of the senior faculty and administrators, which made the rebels feel isolated and radicalized them. They became ever more brutal with grandiose demands such as possession of a university building. Häffner felt under siege: the radicals attacked him, wrote "murderer" on the wall of his home because of the suicide of a halfway-house patient, and said that he was the next to be killed—though no one was killed. He feared for his life and suspected Pörksen's complicity in this crisis. An in-group of four or five strong people opted for revolution and joined the Baader-Meinhof inner circle. Shortly before his retirement as professor of the psychiatry department in 1972, von Baeyer experienced these student uprisings as very bad, annoying, fanatical, and extreme and wrote an article on the subject.[159] He thought the turmoil at Heidelberg was greater than at other universities, though there were outbursts at Berlin and elsewhere.

In this context, Pörksen's CMH approach was seen as politically revolutionary and dangerous. Elizabeth Lindemann saw a parallel with Lindemann's situation: overinvestment and enthusiasm for CMH provoked contagious loyalty or repulsion.[160]

Häffner saw this situation as ill-conceived radical idealism:[161]

> Leider haben wir derzeit an der Universität sehr grosse Sorgen. Die Universität selbst ist zu schwach, sich gegen eine radikale Gruppe von Extemisten zu wehren, die glauben, die Welt mit einem Übermass an Feindseligkeit in eine Utopie von Liebe verwandeln zu können.
>
> (Sadly we have, at present, great trouble in the university. The university is too weak to protect itself against a radical group of extremists which believes it can, with an excess of hostility, change the world into a utopia of love.)

This exacerbated problems for the social psychiatry program and the strain between Pörksen and Häffner. Pörksen declared that he was not a part of the Kollektiv but felt that speaking out against it would be using patients as part of a political conflict. He would have had to say that he understood their disagreeing with the way patients were treated, including in large mental hospitals, but disagreeing with their methods. He tried to mediate, but this increased the conflict with the department.[162]

Lindemann took the situation seriously but did not panic. He understood the traditional German authoritarian university system and sympathized with students and others who wanted change but were faced with traditionalists who populated the system after those wanting change had emigrated. He was remembered in 1971 lecturing to students ready to denigrate any professor, but, weak and sick as he was, his warmth, interest, and caring earned him more acceptance and enthusiasm than given to any other lecturer.[163] He saw this CMHC as based on his and Gerald Caplan's ideas being applied to the crisis of southern European workers in conflict with middle-class German culture.[164] Lindemann tried to be a good consultant and save the program, including holding many talks with Häffner and Pörksen, but could not calm Häffner and convince him to be less outspoken against the rebels, so that they would then focus less on him.[165] He recognized the personal, institutional, and cultural change issues intertwined. Rash young innovators were impatient to have change accepted and underestimated important factors including the need for a clear authority structure in clinical departments. The stress of the young field of social psychiatry in relating to other authorities may lead us to surround ourselves with young disciples or deny them respect. He hoped Häffner would not give up a comprehensive program after investing such effort. Häffner was understandably struck by the conflict at Lincoln Hospital in the Bronx (New York) paralleling the overwhelming conflicts in Germany.[166] Lindemann, then gravely ill, tried to respond sympathetically to the problems that followed from the assertion of a CMH approach, both to Pörksen:[167]

> the job situation at the Heidelberg Clinic can't be preserved from disintegrating. One forgets sometimes how fundamentally the values of Community Psychiatry have changed vis a vis the traditional psychiatric position, and how difficult the transition is, and above all, how slowly one must go forward in order not to be brought to a halt by the inevitable resistance. I must admit I had still hoped that a modus vivendi could be found between you and your Group on the one side and Herr Haefner and Herr Boeker on the other. What you have to give is so important that it is very sad when no use can be made of it.

and also to Häffner:[168]

> We attempt to grasp the many-layered structure of the conflict situation, so that, through social psychiatry, we can analyze the personal and motivational factors of institutional processes and the resulting relatively rash cultural change. Pörksen is one of the unsettled,

A Sampling of Community Mental Health Programs 71

innovation-seeking youth who want to realize a new principle rashly for all, while underestimating important factors and responsibilities, such as a clear authority structure in a clinical department. The stress of the still young field of psychiatry in relation to other authorities in this area leads to the tendency to surround ourselves with young disciples or deny them respect. It would be a pity to have to forsake the great efforts to develop such a comprehensive program.

Henry Mason wrote a thoughtful analysis of the roots and fruits of the political turmoil in German universities with a social-psychological-political insight into the needs of various constituencies in the academic and societal community and the aspirations and resistances to them. It was, from one perspective, a CMH issue that properly engaged and reflected upon the CMH movement.[169]

Finally, the police were called in, and there were arrests and court judgements of terrorism. Finally, the rebellion was defeated, and the Kollektiv disappeared. It relieved Häffner to see this dangerous group of terrorists quashed.[170] In response to this rebellion and turmoil, the university installed a new rector (president) and professor of psychiatry. Von Baeyer thought that the university was not changed by this activism because it was unacceptably extreme. He thought that social psychiatry was independent of this political rebellion, a parallel phenomenon, and was not (should not be?) damaged by it. He did not know of Lindemann's involvement in the student agitation and thought that the mixture of psychiatry and politics led to an irrational distortion of psychiatry, with the extremists (such as Huber) incapable of settling into a more conservative function.

After retirement, von Baeyer distanced himself from and avoided the great changes that had taken place in psychiatry, doubting he could have any influence. Instead, he developed expertise in the (not irrelevant) field of trauma and psychoses resulting from the Nazi era and other persecutions.[171] He became active in responding to the Soviet abuse of psychiatry. He was honorary president of the German society against the abuse of psychiatry and was concerned with the proper, humanistic use of psychiatry. He also collected papers on the phenomenology of delusion. He made a point of staying within his own area of work (perhaps another casualty of social and humanistic psychiatry).

In 1971 Pörksen returned to Boston to consult with Lindemann about handling the conflict over the Heidelberg CMH program and last visited with him in 1972. He appreciated Lindemann's support: "The visit with you . . . will help determine my future career . . . in spite of your serious illness, you were able to take part in our problems here in Heidelberg . . . my visit with you was a determining confirmation in establishing the goal of our work. I believe as you do that the future is on our side".[172] In 1972 and 1973, Pörksen reported that "Further work in Community

Psychiatry seems to me especially difficult. We are . . . putting together our various projects . . . to make it clear in the Clinic that one cannot neglect this work without consequences. We hope thereby to make Community Psychiatry in its broad aspect an essential part of the Socialpsychiatry Clinic and of the later Institute. However, I don't know yet whether it is possible that all the other colleagues will stay here and that new doctors will go into Community Psychiatry. Interest in the research currently in progress is not easy to estimate".[173] He reported that the clinic as a whole was affected: "in the Team Leaders conference. The colleagues feel that their point of view is hardly accepted. Leaving the department is a trend that spreads like the wind, because—as planned—the key support figures are really going: Frau Rave in the Day Clinic, Herr Orimann from Child Psychiatry and myself; thus the three most important and up to now most stable and highly regarded services are practically at an end, for part of their workers will go too . . . Thus the Clinic is facing a renewal which will certainly involve a more traditional approach".[174] They suspected that Häffner was diminishing CMH to gain peace and order in the department.[175]

In contrast, Häffner wrote of Pörksen as promising but recalcitrant in causing trouble, not fulfilling his administrative duties, and threatening to leave.[176] Feeling that Pörksen was unrelenting in his defiance including stirring up his colleagues despite limits and expectations, Häffner reported giving up the effort to integrate him into the department, perhaps conflating this issue with the radicals rampaging and reflecting on the department. He turned to repairing the department, encouraging the maturation of the remaining staff and the difficult search for someone qualified in CMH to strengthen the program.[177] It was reported that Häffner turned away from the limitations (perhaps the hazards) of social psychiatry to biological psychiatry, and the Institute changed direction toward research[178]—a flight to ideological safety also chosen by other CMH participants (another CMH casualty).

Pörksen saw that his five-year contract would not be renewed because of his continued commitment to CMH through success and failure as Lindemann had encouraged, and Lindemann acknowledges this with regret:[179] "the job situation at the Heidelberg Clinic can't be preserved from disintegrating . . . What you have to give is so important that it is very sad when no use can be made of it". Pörksen acknowledged that "I have not yet overcome the depression over the present situation . . . I hope in a new position to take full advantage of the current experiences".[180] He and his family left Heidelberg without a job or home. His wife felt that he endangered his family's security with his "heroics". He reminisced that this had been one of the most active and creative times in his professional life, and, if it were not for those who did not want him, he would still be in Mannheim. Even though it was a terrible, dirty, industrial city, its people were warm and direct, unlike those in the university.

A Sampling of Community Mental Health Programs 73

After leaving the University of Heidelberg, Pörksen wrote of this approach to social psychiatry in Pörksen, Niels: *Kommunale Psychiatrie: Das Mannheimer Modell*. (Reinbek: Rowohlt Verlag, 1974). In retrospect, he felt he had moved too fast, wanted too much, become too influential, and gotten involved with too many groups. He and Lindemann were personally as well as professionally committed to social psychiatry. In contrast, he saw Häffner not personally committed to CMH values but rather psychiatry, psychoanalysis, and existential psychiatry. To him, social psychiatry enjoyed a temporary wave of popularity which offered a route to professional advancement. One interpretation of the project's struggles was the university's fear of offending governmental and professional vested interests. Elizabeth Lindemann, who was present throughout Lindemann's consultations there, thought that Häffner felt threatened and therefore undercut Pörksen.[181] Lindemann offered empathy and insight from his own experience championing CMH.[182]

Pörksen had to accept a post as chief physician at the Psychiatrische Klinik Häcklingen (Lüneburg State Mental Hospital). In addition, he said, "I still try to continue Erich's [Lindemann] work in community mental health in several national commissions".[183] He was active in the Deutsche Gesellschaft für Soziale Psychiatrie (The German Association for Social Psychiatry—DGSP), which he described as a 2,000-strong group that integrated Lindemann's ideas more than did his Lindau psychotherapy group for medical practitioners and was dedicated to social psychiatry practice and institutional and societal support: "we are looking forward to support all political initiatives [which] will prevent the world from a next war".[184] He also supported the Green Party and other liberal political parties. Lindemann's encouragement to continue his work, even if it caused him to lose his job, gave him the strength to persist with CMH.[185]

The new professor of psychiatry at Heidelberg, Werner Janzarik, trained at the Heidelberg Psychiatrische Klinik under Kurt Schneider in 1946–1951, then at Mainz. He had no connection with social psychiatry but rather clinical psychopathology.[186] He spent his first years in office fighting to regain control of the department. He reported that he did not follow a social psychiatry approach but one of psychopathology. He thought that social psychiatry contributions remained in the form of meetings, conferences, cotherapies, day clinics, sheltered workshops, and sheltered groups. He saw this as a process of thesis, antithesis, and synthesis. Von Baeyer saw social psychiatry continuing under Häffner as an alternative approach combined with biological psychiatry, and more pragmatic, less theoretical, matured, and developed. Phenomenology and medical anthropology were separate under Kraus at Heidelberg, Blankenburg at Marburg, and Wiss at Würzburg, where it could be excessively buoyant, as opposed to sound psychotherapy for psychoses and neuroses.

Pörksen had abiding strong ties and both positive and negative emotions about Mannheim/Heidelberg. He valued the yearly two-day consultation that he provided to the Mannheim social service agencies and proudly reported that even ten years after he left, everyone thought he knew more about Mannheim than the Central Institute did. He felt that he still had more friends in Mannheim than in his subsequent posts. He was invited to the 1979 Heidelberg University Community Psychiatry Program anniversary celebration. It was attended by 250 guests, including all cooperating agencies and the city's lord mayor. He was not one of five designated speakers, though he felt all were waiting for him. He remembers Häffner speaking; though he knew almost no one. He said, "We, the people of the Central Institute, reach out our arm to help the community (with a gesture)". The new director of the program spoke. During the reception that followed, Pörksen felt that he had to speak, feeling that his period in Mannheim was the most important in his professional life. He went to the front of the room and remembered giving the following remarks:

> This day it's not possible that all of you talk and I don't . . . This is a very important day for me, therefore I want to say a few words. I know most people here; I would love to talk to everyone, but I know I will not get around so I use this occasion to say hello to everyone, and to thank them for their cooperation. And everyone knows that I had very good times in Mannheim, and everyone knows that I had bad times, and I am still suffering about it . . . There were many years—many years—maybe not now, but all the years in Lüneburg I would have moved the next day to Mannheim if I would have had the opportunity. I had to leave so I took this job in Lüneburg—I didn't want it.

The outcome for the CMH program was that it gave up a community and preventive orientation and, instead, focused on epidemiological research and providing patient-oriented services, and had no catchment area population responsibility. Hartmut Schneider came from a family of physicians but wanted to help with human problems rather than work with anatomical morphology or analysis. In 1980, he joined the Zentralinstitut, eventually directed its outpatient department, and subsequently became director of its Department of Social Psychiatry. It was small, consisting of three psychiatrists, two social workers, a secretary, and a group of lay associates. Pörksen reported that it consisted of an inpatient ward, an outpatient clinic, and some research space with almost no community orientation. Pörksen's friend, director of the large family social service agency, reported little response from the CMHC to invitations to collaboration.[187] Schneider's view was different: He reported work with individual patients in psychiatric rehabilitation clubs and maintaining contact with community services. He was interested in supervising home care teams in improving home environments. He looked forward

A Sampling of Community Mental Health Programs   75

to working with sheltered workshops for the rehabilitation of recovered psychiatric patients.

German psychiatry in general and Häffner and Heidelberg in particular appeared to follow the cycle of psychiatric ideologies from the biological one of neuroanatomy to the psychological and philosophical of phenomenology, gestalt, and psychoanalysis to the social outlook of respect and advocacy for the masses and their living conditions comprehensive services and back to the biological mindset of epidemiology and clinical care of individuals.

Other German Community Mental Health Programs

Only 20 years prior to German interest in community mental health, the Nazi government had organized the killing of more than 100,000 psychiatrically and physically handicapped citizens and forcibly sterilized more than 400,000 others. After the end of this regime a traumatized Germany recoiled from government control, social engineering, and population-wide programs that smacked of coercion. Psychiatry reverted to traditional practices of custodial care in large institutions with very limited outpatient care and limited epidemiology with avoidance of patient case registers. Community mental health was met with great hesitation, skepticism, fear, and narrowing limitations. Inspiration, encouragement, program models, and training came from foreign sources—largely the U.S. and Great Britain. It was an uphill fight to introduce it into German universities, clinical institutions, and government, but there was gradual response:[188]

> In the early 1970s, pressured by a small group of community and social psychiatrists (Deutsche Gesellschaft für Soziale Psychiatrie), the German Parliament set up a national commission to study and reorganize psychiatric services in Germany. [Pörksen became part of that commission.] We learned a lot by looking into the changes that had taken place in American and Western European psychiatric service systems. De-institutionalization and decentralization of psychiatric clinical and outpatient services evolved. Community-based services for the chronically mentally ill and for alcoholics had to be established. As a result of the work of this national commission, the government set up a national program to establish community psychiatry in all regions in 1975.
>
> ('Bericht zur Lage der Psychiatrie [Report on the Condition of Psychiatry], Aktion Psychisch Kranke [Action for Mental Illness] 1988)

Pörksen, the laborer in the field of CMH, could take an optimistic view of its implementation in German psychiatry:[189] "Public health concepts and practices have been integrated into German psychiatric care as part of a professionalization process that emphasized preventive and population-directed psychiatry".

Von Bodelschwinghsche Anstalten Bethel, Serepta und Nazareth

In the 1860s and 1870s, there was a gathering of German protestant institutions such as Bethel to minister to the poor and sick.[190] At the time, it was opposed by the official church but was later accepted as "Deaconie" or "innermission" (domestic mission).

Von Bodelschwinghsche Anstalten Bethel, Serepta und Nazareth (Bethel) is a Protestant-directed, multispecialty hospital in Germany that receives patients from all of Europe for tertiary care including in psychiatry. Its board of directors wanted to change the staff–patient relationship from authoritarian. After his conflicts and disappointments at Manheim/Heidelberg, Pörksen accepted the position of Leitende Arzt, Fachbereich Psychiatrie (head physician in the psychiatry specialty) and eventually sat on the board of directors. He wanted to develop this setting similar to Mannheim—still heeding Lindemann's encouragement to persevere in CMH. The director of psychiatry was nice but ineffective. Staff members were interested in the new ideas. To achieve a social psychiatry approach, Pörksen tried to influence the interaction among people in order to change the current system rather than establish a new program, hoping to avoid major conflicts. He then sought support by increasingly incorporating the board of directors as well as meeting with town officials of the host town, Bielefeld, who were interested in social programs independent of Bethel.

He took public stands on principle such as joining a court challenge to a judge's power to commit a sexual offender to the psychiatric unit indefinitely after he had served his criminal sentence in the interests of public safety.[191] In this case, ultimately the supreme court ruled in favor of the judge, and the president of the board of directors recommended that Pörksen resign; with the support of other board and professional staff members, he stayed.

Pörksen described establishing a large "dehospitalization" program, accompanied by a large dehospitalization research project by the Public Health Faculty of Bielefeld University. This faculty grew out of the Department of Sociology rather than Medicine. He commented that traditional, institutionally based psychiatrists were slow to join social psychiatry efforts, but wide support and active involvement came from community representatives, patients, family-organized support groups, and from departments and individuals in municipal offices, state agencies, national ministries, and a few progressive academic programs. These coalitions were nurtured and enhanced by committed, multidisciplinary colleagues who made up a strong advocacy group, such as members of the DGSP. He was disappointed, however, that in Germany, the theory and practice of community psychiatry were not part of the scientific world or the psychiatry professional associations.

Eventually, Pörksen came to enjoy his placement:[192] He found the atmosphere open and saw the institution become the source of all psychiatric services to the city. His goal was "To create a community-based, comprehensive psychiatric service... [p. 304] ... A mental health board and a city steering committee are responsible for comprehensive care in the community. After a full service program for all psychiatric patients in the community was established, it became possible to restart mental health consultation and public health oriented projects".[193] His dedication to social justice and peace inspired his work with peace groups, local and national elections, and political issues such as the funding of social services. This extracurricular activity by the Bethel director of psychiatry was accepted; in fact, the head of this institution spoke out about social services and peace groups despite opposition.

Pörksen maintained his commitment to CMH:[194] "Mental health for all, and adequate treatment and care for everyone in need, are still the best way of promoting public health". Pörksen, the CMH zealot, could finally attest "I am glad to be here".

Freie Universität Berlin

The Freie Universität Berlin [Free University of Berlin (i.e., not government administered) had two psychiatry departments: The Psychiatrische Klinik [Psychiatry Department] under Prof. Hämchen was inpatient, conservative and traditional, and biologically oriented. It sought patients fitting its clinical and research interests with outpatient research in long-term follow-up of mainly medication treatment, decreasing amount of electroconvulsive therapy, and increasing amount of psychosurgery. There was no psychoanalytic therapy.

After the experience with the Nazi era of abuse of centralized power and the1960s period of social unrest, German society was apprehensive and conservative about social programs. There was decreased interest in social psychiatry in favor of psychosomatic medicine and pro- and antipsychiatric sentiment. Previous interest in social psychiatry was channeled into efforts for peace and the ecology. Also there is less students confrontation of professors about their convictions; even the conservative professors miss the vigorous discussion. It felt as if social psychiatry had no place.

There was evidence of the need for social psychiatry: Dr. Link (formerly of the Freie Universtät) surveyed in the Charlottenburg neighborhood of Berlin psychiatric problems in old-age homes to which patients had been shifted from psychiatric hospitals without providing appropriate treatment. He found that 45% were psychiatrically ill; among the 90 residents under age 65, 89% were mentally ill with such problems as schizophrenia and alcoholism. One of the homes specialized in psychiatric illness; this home could be further developed for younger patients, or their care in existing homes could be improved via frequent psychiatric consultation and appropriate training of personnel.

At the Freie Universität, the Social Psychiatry Department originated in 1981: new and developing under Prof. Bosch. It expected a 40-bed ward dedicated to a designated population sector and specializing in functioning psychosis and neurosis. Specialized programs were developed for those unable to participate in the general treatment program without help with self-care and outside resources—drug addicts, mentally retarded, organic brain syndromes, old people, and children. Manpower was divided among the units and thus not all available for total care in the community. It had 20 to 25 staff members full- and part-time, with seven teaching appointments. There was little preventive psychiatry work with community agencies, professionals, and community residents who were not ill, though it was included in the academic definition of social psychiatry and in research. Twice a year, there was a training program for factory shop stewards about the psychiatric problems of handicapped workers. Most treatment was for chronically and severely ill outpatients, and the staff would lie to health insurers in order to have day and night hospital patients' treatment paid for. A major accomplishment was Bodenmeinschaften—communal apartments for two to ten patients with one to three staff members—that reduced inpatient confinement.

Medical students, preparing for diplomas and jobs, were randomly assigned for clinical placement. They followed a rigid, full curriculum, continued active, and is valued as more self-directed and less restricted. Training was offered also for social work, occupational therapy, and art therapy students.

There is a barrier between the development of an academic program and clinical community implementation. The department discussed solutions. Plog thought that the university should do research, treatment, and political work (which was being addressed). She said a plan to increase therapeutic homes could include the residents of old-age homes, but the traditional nursing homes would resist the loss of patient revenue.[195] Traditional psychiatric facilities resist attempts to study the effect of social approaches because they do not want to limit their traditional work—a comparison of traditional and social approaches risks traditional treatment being found inferior, thus aggravating the rivalry between biological and social psychiatry for research and staffing funds and for space. The rivalry between the chiefs of the two services blocks study of comparative long-term outcomes. Some successes with social approaches are encouraging nonpsychiatrists to refer psychiatric crises to day treatment programs rather than hospitals. The Berlin geropsychiatry inpatient unit provides consultation to the community and trains homemakers. And social workers working in therapeutic group homes get consultation from a psychiatrist and are present at departmental team meetings to share information with outpatient treatment clinics.

Associated with the social psychiatry approach is the issue of disciplinary relationships. Interdisciplinary interchange is time-consuming. The institutional hierarchy reaches into the interdisciplinary team, though it tries to avoid this, and other workers participate. Senior staff advise about problem cases though there is no formal team leader. Democracy is claimed, but longevity in the job, extent of experience, personality, and group acceptance exert their influence. While discipline is not supposed to be a determining factor, the professor's wishes or assumed wishes rule, and informally, the senior social worker and the Oberarzt (chief physician) lead. Daily treatment decisions are made by the treating physicians, while larger decisions about admission to and discharge from the institution are made by team consensus unless they are urgent. Physicians and social workers collaborate as appropriate to the situation and can choose to consult the team. Psychologists are few and can take the physician role, since there is little biological treatment. Social workers participate in group psychotherapy.

Psychiatrische Klinik Häcklingen (Lüneburg)

When he had to leave the social psychiatry program in Mannheim, Niels Pörksen had to take a position at the Häcklingen Psychiatric Klinik in Lüneburg, West Germany.[196] Despite his new problems in establishing a mental health center, he was relieved of the hopeless stress of the Mannheim situation.[197] He rejoiced in motivated colleagues and good working conditions. His proposal of a social psychiatry group in Lower Saxony was rejected.

With public support, he succeeded in separating hospital issues from doctrinal political issues. There was much political maneuvering involving funding, conservative government versus liberal staff, and local resentment of outsider professional advocates. Initial conflict turned to understanding and support. Pörksen advocated units democratically directed responsive to staff members' contributions, and community and preventive orientation. He felt that people and their community were capable of handling their psychological or social problems rather than these decisions being controlled by professionals or institutions.[198]

This federally funded group had a catchment area in which it worked with clients and the community, helping community agencies with their problems without taking them over. This stood in contrast to state services that were oriented to assigning problems to someone to solve rather than prevent them, and disappoints some referring agencies which resent the group "not doing its job". However, good clinical work with patients led to a good reputation with mental health professionals, widening support inside and outside the institutions, and then to public support when problems arose. "Since September we have been considered a model program and received from Bonn [the national capital] a team for ambulatory services to take over a district. This team will function as a mobile team providing consultation, crisis intervention, supervision, and assistance in developing projects in nearby towns . . . my wife collaborates with me in a city group for single women. We have many friends in similar work".[199] "I think . . . we are doing a quite good job in the rural area, where we have our Community Mental Health Center with in-patient and out-patient . . . programs and all kinds of community [activities]".[200]

Pörksen credited to his good relationships with staff, friends and community his being able to fight through many problems.

Eberhard Karls Universität Tübingen

This university was conflicted over social psychiatry.[201] On the one hand, projects flourished: It elected one large teaching hospital (rather than small community units with medical and nonmedical staff) for teaching purposes, though community residents had priority for admission, and included a six-week alcoholism unit with a six-week program, day hospital since 1973, and a night hospital since 1979. Without a strong leader, the social psychiatry programs successfully operated independent of the department. On the other hand, the community was resistant to welcoming back the mentally ill, and the university, frightened by the Italian experience, was resistant to change toward social psychiatry. Observation of communist movements in Germany and other bordering countries led to identifying social psychiatry with communism, which was the enemy and incompatible with the existing society.

Lindemann accepted an invitation by the Professor, W. Schulte, to serve as visiting professor in the summer semester May 1–July 31, 1966.[202] This visit reminded him of the traditional German university system:[203] The professor ordinarius (head of department) was funded for life by the federal government and therefore functioned as a monarch distant from the rest of the department. Discussion was hierarchical, with no initiative. Niels Pörksen observed that no one at the University of Tübingen knew of social psychiatry or CMH.[204] The technique of home visiting was considered malpractice.

Pörksen was critical that Lindemann was treated as an old American oddity and was little valued or attended to. He was assigned a small, dark office in a cellar at the end of a row. Lindemann's attitude was nontraditional, and he attracted the malcontents full of bitterness. In the absence of the professor, he led staff meetings for physicians in which and other conferences he presented information about the Human Relations Service, bereavement studies, and the Laboratory for Community.[205] The staff came alive, and many wanted to visit this new psychiatry in Boston. Lindemann wrote to Gerald Caplan:[206]

> about young psychiatrists who have applied for admission to the Laboratory of Community Psychiatry . . . as a result of my work as Visiting Professor at the University of Tuebingen from May to July. Professor Schulte is anxious to develop a program in community psychiatry . . . They [two applicants] are, however, both aware of the tremendous difficulties which the German culture and the prevailing patterns of community organization present to a social approach in psychiatric problems.

Through this experience, Lindemann was taken aback by what he generalized as German academia:[207] "During the Spring and Summer [5–7/1966] I was in Germany serving as Visiting Professor in Tuebingen. The encounter with the German academic culture was somewhat of a shock, and I had a difficult time developing a meaningful role as a representative of our thinking in social psychiatry. David Hamburg [Chief of Psychiatry, Stanford Medical School] told me that you had similar experiences in Vienna". Elizabeth Lindemann thought that this reaction revealed the great change that had taken place in Lindemann since he left German academia.[208]

Pörksen attended his talks at doctors' conferences and found his own ideas validated by Lindemann's, which resonated with Pörksen's family background. The mentorship and friendship that developed with Lindemann integrated community psychiatry, with its flavor of dedication and moral conviction, into Pörksen's professional and personal identity. Pörksen and his family came to Boston for a year to learn about CMH. When he returned to Tübingen, his enthusiasm was not welcome, and he transferred his work to the University of Heidelberg.

Lindemann maintained his relationship with Tübingen. In 1970, he was scheduled to speak at a psychoanalytic seminar cosponsored by the university.[209]

Verein Für Fortschritt in Psychiatrie

Lindemann remembered speaking to the Verein für Fortschritt in Psychiatrie (Association for Progress in Psychiatry) about his work at the MGH, his contention that all psychiatric treatment must become crisis intervention, and that it must include all significant community members and not isolate one person for "treatment", exclude others, and stigmatize the "patient".[210] Concern should not be confined to treatment sessions with "patients" by underpaid workers interested only in patient cleanliness [shades of his experience with his grandmother]. He remembers that the Verein did not like this perspective.

Columbia Presbyterian Medical Center-Harlem Hospital

In 1962, the City of New York and Columbia University contracted for the Department of Psychiatry at the Columbia-Presbyterian Medical Center to establish and administer a psychiatric service and residency training program in a 900-bed city general hospital.[211] This was a pioneer in comprehensive psychiatric services in a large municipal hospital.[212] From the social service viewpoint, Russell is understanding and respectful:

> When a community has so few personal and family resources, it is to the public institution that its residents must turn; and out of this circumstance flows a special kind of relationship between the community and the hospital that must be understood if comprehensive patient care is to be effective. Just as any effective preventive, diagnostic and treatment services must be offered in the context of the patients' needs and their expectations of the helping agents, so the mental health services provided by the Harlem Hospital Center must be community based.
> (p. 557)

He goes on to charge social work education with failing to prepare social workers for community-directed practice:[213]

> There appears to be a gap between the formal education of social workers and what is demanded of them in practice; the average new graduate is not equipped to assume quickly the functions called for by our setting . . . It seems imperative that the schools of social work provide field work experience for the new responsibilities that beginning workers must assume.
>
> Social work has much to offer from its knowledge of skilled administration and the creative use of community resources. Yet these vital functions are not being sufficiently developed because the social work profession (p. 559) is still not flexible enough in adapting itself to various models of practice and to new types of settings.
> (p. 560)

Elizabeth Davis outlined a program of both tertiary and primary prevention:[214]

> We must direct our efforts particularly toward tertiary prevention, i.e., treatment which is aimed at reduction of disability, maintenance of therapeutic gains achieved in active treatment, and rehabilitation where possible. This is the main clinical task of community psychiatry. In order, however, that this task become increasingly

A Sampling of Community Mental Health Programs 83

encompassable, it will be essential to address thinking and innovative efforts also to the area of primary prevention, that is pursuing (p. 1) to recognition and definition those factors in our institutional and social practices which contribute unquestionably and significantly to the production of mental illness. This task is the primary obligation of the scientist in our specialty; but it is through the clinical practice of community psychiatry that the questions will be defined, and their directional signals for the scientific effort will be found . . . 900 bed general hospital. In July, 1962, a Director [of the psychiatric service] was appointed from the faculty of Columbia and funds were made available through a contract between the City of New York and Columbia University to establish and administer a psychiatric service and residency training program (p. 2) . . . The preventive efforts . . . have necessarily been limited by the pressure for direct treatment, but have nevertheless constituted an important area of concern as well as activity. Consultation to community agencies is facilitated by the . . . Division of Community Psychiatry . . . liaison was established with neighborhood schools, day care centers, Police Youth Division Unit, and the local Health Center Well-Baby Clinic. Regular structured consultation programs are now going on . . . A seminar . . . for Department of Welfare workers . . . program to combat narcotics addiction by both health and police.

The program developed consultation projects to schools (involving guidance counselors, teacher, junior guidance classes, and the youth division of the police department. The chief of the Division of Community Psychiatry, a board member of a community support program, consulted on staff training and taught training seminars on community psychiatry for social work students.

Russell presents sympathetic collaboration without commenting on obstacles and struggles.

Italy

In 1948, in the Italian government, the left was defeated and, with it, concern with psychiatric reform, and thereafter, psychiatry received almost no funding from the national government. In the 1960s, there was concern that psychiatry in Italy was falling behind that in Europe and the U.S. This also was a time of social change and rebellion in many countries, inspiring both the activation of social ideals and fear of radical revolution. For some time, academia had been home to socialists and communists.[215] In 1968, there was a revolution in Italian universities inspired by Basil Bernstein's writing on the sociocultural bases of language, Jean Paul Sartre, Herbert Marcuse, the 1970s ideas about releasing psychiatric patients from mental hospitals (as championed by Franco

Basaglia), and the integration of children with disabilities into normal classes and the closing of special schools and classes. Inspired by university revolutionaries in Berlin (such as Rudy Deutschke) the University of Rome's Department of Philosophy and Social Sciences, followed by other departments, except engineering and business, experienced unions of students and the working class advocating the liberalization of the curriculum and open enrollment instead of numerous prerequisites including a classical education. This was retrenched to 50% open admissions and multiple-choice examinations.

In 1961, Franco Basaglia, a psychiatrist from the Veneto region, was appointed medical director of the large psychiatric hospital of Gorizia.[216] He was determined to make it a pilot experiment in reform, and attracted like-minded colleagues. Basaglia's location, far removed from public view or concern, allowed him greater leeway in the implementation of change and reform. Basaglia and his colleagues, considering diagnostic categorization to be a harmful process of labeling, endeavored to communicate with patients as they would with any other human individual instead of as a doctor to a subordinate. The question became how to care for and liberate the patients who were trapped in an environment of marginalization. He and his colleagues developed what came to be known as the Democratic Psychiatry (*Psichiatrica Democratica*) movement, providing the theoretical basis for radical change in Italian psychiatry. At the same time, the leftist government in Italy in the 1960s and early 1970s was not able to deliver the social reforms for which it had been elected. The resulting frustrations pressured radical reform legislation.

Outstanding among these was the 1978 Law 180, which established the right of psychiatric patients to be admitted to general rather than mental hospitals and sought comprehensive, integrated community mental health services instead.[217] It was directed to the 90,000 chronically mentally ill patients felt to be inhumanely warehoused in 90 often decaying mental hospitals. There were contradictory reports of the results: only 14 of the state mental hospitals closed, leaving 17,000 of the most seriously ill patients hospitalized, half of whom were geriatric or handicapped. All but 15 of the former mental hospitals were transformed into small therapeutic communities, halfway houses, private clinics, and hotels; 15,000 patients were living in the community. Prof. Pier Maria Fulan, M.D. noted that, unlike what happened with massive deinstitutionalization in the U.S. in the 1960s, Italy had created an extensive network to care for the mentally ill.

When community clinics were overwhelmed with patients discharged from hospitals, the decision was made to improve local hospitals and psychiatric units rather than reopen mental hospitals. There was also concern for the sociocultural influences on language, behavior, and the social relations of children—including from the migration from the agricultural south to the industrial north. This led to the development of

Servizio Dilgiene Profilassi Mental—CMHCs originally for research then developed into comprehensive service providers, community hospital psychiatric units, street services, and the flourishing of private psychiatric hospitals. Families and the community had a high acceptance of the mentally ill, but some were burdened. There remained concern over a disorganized network of community resources, funded by state welfare but without any government monitoring. The Italian Society of Psychiatry and other critics feared this policy shift would increase hardships without a comprehensive system of community services. The national government budgeted $1.0 billion to 1.3 billion for psychiatric care. For the first time, the national government put in place standards and penalties for regional governments: a reduction of 2% in National Health Fund support if there were no concrete plan by June 1997. It also urged universities and research centers to become involved in training mental health workers and evaluating treatment.

Bergstresser concludes:[218]

> Radical transformation of Italy's mental health care system was made possible by the interaction of two significant historical variables, neither of which would have been individually sufficient. Specifically, though Franco Basaglia and his Democratic Psychiatry (*Psichiatrica Democratica*) movement were the metaphorical seeds of transformation, they only flourished as a result of their introduction during a time of hospitable social conditions. Similarly, without a firm ideology upon which to rally, psychiatric reform would not have been a salient topic of social consciousness.

This ideological and politicoeconomic transformation did not take place without conflict, obstruction, and criticism. For instance, there was criticism of the recruitment of staff for psychiatric hospitals, complaining that the number, specialties, and funding for them were inappropriate for psychiatric institutions and represented political interference in the new psychiatric assistance program in Italy.[219]

Lincoln Hospital Mental Health Center, Bronx, New York

The Home for the Relief of Aged Indigent Black Persons was established In 1839 in Bronx, New York. In 1882, its name was changed to The Colored Home and Hospital. In 1899, its name was changed to Lincoln Hospital.[220]

The conflict and turmoil attending the attempt at CMH at the Lincoln Center in New York became an exemplar to supporters and opponents alike.[221]

In 1963, the Department of Psychiatry at Albert Einstein College of Medicine proposed a community mental health service at Lincoln

86 *A Sampling of Community Mental Health Programs*

Hospital.[222] It indicated a CMH orientation with hints of cultural sensitivity and CMH procedures but was firmly controlled by academia:

1. General Assumptions . . .

    A. Goals . . . clinical services . . . of demonstrated efficacy for the cultural, national[,] social class, community, group, family and individual illness variables extant in the area . . . optimal coordination with mental health efforts and potential efforts at, of all public, voluntary and private agencies, institutions and individuals. . .
    B. Timing;

    1. The rate at which the several steps . . . are initiated and executed will be determined at the discretion of the Chairman of the Department of Psychiatry of the Albert Einstein College of Medicine.
    2. The extent of community coverage . . . will be determined at the discretion of the Chairman of the Department of Psychiatry . . . Such provisions are not designed to place limits on the extent or scope of the services . . . rather to protect the planful unfolding of the program from (p. 1) uncontrolled pressures of unmet demands. . .

    C. Administrative Structure

    1. Psychiatric services to . . . the Lincoln Hospital district will be provided by the Lincoln Hospital Service of the Department of Psychiatry . . . under the immediate direction of the Division of Social and Community Psychiatry. . .
    3. The Director of the Lincoln Hospital Service will be responsible through the Director of the Division of Social and Community Psychiatry to the Chairman of the Department of Psychiatry. . .
    4. The Director of the Lincoln Hospital Service will be responsible to the Medical Superintendent of Lincoln Hospital for compliance with such administrative regulations and procedures as apply to the psychiatric service (p. 2) . . . The full range of services will . . . encompass the following elements:
        (a) . . . preventive services through both existing and new agencies . . . in schools, housing projects, health stations, community centers, etc.; personnel . . . will include professional mental health workers, professional mental health educators, and non-professional persons trained by the staff . . . case finding and early counseling and guidance services through the clergy, teachers, welfare investigators, the police, the courts, the Youth Board, employment agencies, etc. . . . in consulteeship or

traineeship relationships with the staff . . . early treatment services, through general practitioners, pediatricians, public health and visiting nurses, voluntary family agency workers, etc. . . . in consulteeship relationships with the staff (p. 4) . . .

    (b) No traditional treatment modality will be inaugurated merely because of its traditional place in the armamentarium of a Department of Psychiatry (e.g. . . . long-term psycho-analytically-oriented program of psychotherapy) . . .

    (c) All treatment units will be oriented to the fullest exploitation of family, small group, and community processes. . .

4. the coordination and integration of the work of the agencies and institutions . . . will be the responsibility of a community committee representing these organizations . . . the responsibilities and obligations of the committee can only be defined by the committee itself (p. 5) . . .

2. It is not planned for the Lincoln Hospital Service to engage in process research". (p. 6)

    2. During this initial phase, the Lincoln Hospital Psychiatric Service will occupy the sub-basement area of the outpatient building currently occupied by the Investigations Section, the Personnel Health Unit, and the Staff locker rooms. No structural changes will be made during this period . . . preparations will be made . . . for the optimal accommodation of services . . . including plans both for the selection of the areas . . . and for the alteration and renovation of these areas (p. 3)

Erich Lindemann's ideas were contributed,[223] he was introduced to the program in a visit on April 10, 1964,[224] and he expressed his interest,[225] though it is unclear that he knew of the complexities of its relationships with the university and community.

A change in the program from a social to a traditional mental health focus, thus changing roles of the indigenous workers, and the inadequacy of funding for the many needs of the poor population may have led to major disruptions.[226] In March 1969, the indigenous workers, supposedly representing "the community", "took over" the center, and the center was disrupted and services temporarily discontinued. This sequence of administrative events and staff reaction became infamous: It was described by Shaw and Eagle as programmed failure.[227] Viola Bernard and the American Psychoanalytic Association saw radical, antiprofessional community elements taking over the Department of Psychiatry with crazy activities including a drug addiction/treatment group.[228]

Heinz Häfner, director of the Social Psychiatry Department at the University of Heidelberg, Germany, saw in this experience a reflection of the radical attacks on and undermining of his university.[229] He wrote that he was extraordinarily interested, moved, and stimulated by the developments in the Bronx. It led him to caution and limitation in the face of the catastrophe of such an extraordinarily demanding situation. The treatment of individual patients is enormously demanding. The addition of important catastrophic living situations and institutional, financial, and political problems overwhelms human power.

In contrast to these regrets, a psychologist affiliated with the Lincoln Community Mental Health Center articulated the values and value of an assertive community program.[230]

Los Angeles, California Community Mental Health Program

The American Psychoanalytic Association's Standing Committee on Community Psychiatry and Psychoanalysis and Study Group found that Hiawatha Harris, a black psychiatrist, had developed a CMH program near the Los Angeles inner-city community of Watts.[231] It was seen as going very well and sophisticated. It was based on the belief that the community was entitled to psychotherapy rather than seeing this modality as an insult with all problems stemming from society. All staff members were active in the community and had positive functions as community citizens. A multiservice social center was next door, and social problems were addressed in close collaboration with the local CMHC. The CMHCs were being converted into centers for social welfare to help, with social and human services appropriations for the needy population. The question was raised as to whether psychiatrists at the CMHC were most appropriate to deliver these services.

Martha's Vineyard Mental Health Clinic

"I will remember Erich's [Lindemann] enthusiasm [for Community Services—CMHC on Martha's Vineyard inaugurated by Milton Mazer]—and more, his support in inviting me to come to HRS and to the M.G.H".[232]

Maryland

> A program in Maryland was cited as among the most successful . . . in bringing the quality of state hospital treatment closer to that provided in the private sector. In 1976 a group of young University of Maryland psychiatrists who hadn't lost their 1960's antiestablishment bent 'took over' the state's Mental Hygiene Administration . . .

one of these... [is] now the state's mental health commissioner... A link was forged with the University of Maryland's psychiatry department... the most respected of the senior psychiatrists at the university would... go into the hospital wards and train the university's residents... The medical school's psychiatry department had enough confidence in their colleagues... that cooperation... seemed natural... 130 U.S.-trained psychiatrists have been recruited into the state system... To lure psychiatrists into the state system, the residency training staff at the medical school, headed by training director... promised... hard work... excellent clinical supervision, and administrative protection... the state administration became more specific about appropriate care standards... the Maryland program is practical because it was carried out with no major changes in the state's mental health operation or in the way the university's psychiatry department is run.[233]

(p. 26)

Massachusetts Mental Health Center

Leon Shapiro saw the Massachusetts Mental Health Center (MMHC) as more tightly structured because it was centered in a designated building.[234] Because it was a state institution and partly state funded, it had an established spirit and organization that had to include sensitivity to community needs such as services to the poor, the very ill, and multiple services.[235] However, it was aggressively physician dominated, self-centered, and inpatient oriented.[236] Shader saw it as including many individual and group interests and projects supported by superintendents Milton Greenblatt and Jack Ewalt, though Miles Shore gave it some more integration.[237] Gerald Adler thought Jack Ewalt was not interested in CMH.[238] He thought state funds were used for research and only distantly related to CMH. Therefore, though it had a full range of community programs, it had a more difficult time orienting to a CMH perspective and integrating it into the institution (as Tufts did under Myerson)[239] and did not develop a dedicated CMH residency training track. Adler remembers that, at the Northeast Professors of Psychiatry meeting in New Haven, Connecticut, in 1963, Ewalt's claim of a CMH program at MMHC was greeted with laughter.

University of North Carolina

In 1972 the University of North Carolina began a collaboration with state mental health officials that established a training link between the university's psychiatry department and nearby Dorothea Dix State Hospital... Personnel changes at both places enabled the cooperative effort to get off the ground. Seymour Halleck, M.D., director of psychiatry training at the medical school, said . . . began to seek a merger when training funds were becoming scarcer, the Federal government was making it more difficult for foreign medical graduates to enter the U.S., the medical school was expanding its student population, and the state was threatening to sell the valuable land on which Dix sits . . . Halleck became co-director of training . . . with Dix's new training director. Dix was to contribute 15 residency positions and the medical school 30 positions . . . it took about two years for the program to be accepted by his colleagues . . . reluctant to send their trainees to . . . facilities too inferior for adequate training. Dix staff were reluctant . . . because they felt threatened by the . . . more prestigious . . . U.N.C [University of North Carolina]. Most staff now acknowledge that residency training is better . . . and Dix staff are pleased because the university has (p. 1) established a medical service at the state hospital.[240]

(p. 13)

Oregon

The Oregon Division of Mental Health and the University of Oregon's department of psychiatry began a successful collaboration in 1973. . . a required curriculum for psychiatric residents that included training at public mental health facilities . . . the chair of the psychiatry department and an interinstitutional board would administer the program . . . As much emphasis is placed on training in community mental health centers as on state hospital training. Since 1978, 70 percent [of psychiatrist graduates] have decided to work at least part time in the public sector . . . faculty role models and the nature of public sector work have had the most influence on their job choice . . . with financial consideration coming in a distant ninth on the list of such factors. Shore [chair of the psychiatry department] . . . hoped the success . . . would help convince NIMH to shift some of its emphasis . . . to the public side of the community care sector.[241]

(p. 26)

Peninsula Mental Health Center

Warren Vaughan, who had trained in community mental health at the MGH and HSPH and had started the development of CMHCs in Massachusetts, migrated back to California. At the Peninsula Hospital, he transplanted these CMH ideas, expanding primary prevention to the integration of the community in a mental health program as part of the San Mateo County (California) Mental Health program: "Peninsula Hospital Community Mental Health Center . . . It is quite amazing how many of the things we worked on in Wellesley fall right into place in this new effort to develop a model community mental health service".[242] He conceptualized this in the context of the health care system policies and financing implications:[243]

> developments in the organization and financing of mental health services . . . public agencies are purchasing medical care . . . insurance coverage of psychiatric services is increasing . . . health maintenance organizations and prepaid health plans. . . [need new planning] in the face of these developments. First, how can comprehensive mental health services be included in health-care packages for consumer groups? How can we reconceptualize primary prevention services so that we can include [them] . . . in mental health packages for consumer groups? How can we . . . focus on families and children? How can we include in our health packages programs of mental health promotion and specific prevention of emotional and mental disorders for specific population groups? . . . the Peninsula Hospital Community Mental Health Center . . . In October 1969. . . obtained a contract to provide mental health services to a catchment area . . . under a contract with the San Mateo County Department of Mental Health and Welfare . . . including emergency room services . . . inpatient services . . . day treatment programs . . . mental health consultation and education to community agencies and allied professionals (p. 503) . . . Our approach to indirect services extends the role of the mental health professional beyond the traditional roles of a mental health consultant and a resource person in educational programs for allied professions. It brings mental health professionals into contact with consumers, especially parents and children, in center programs that are health oriented, rather than illness oriented; in programs in which there are no designated patients; and in programs where no labels are affixed to those participating in them (p. 504) . . . four kinds of community service programs are being developed . . . traditional mental health consultation services, collaborative and educational programs with allied professionals; mental health information, orientation, and education programs for adults (especially parents), and youth and children; collaboration with nursery schools and elementary and high schools in counseling and educational programs for families and children with special needs; and assessment and educational therapeutic programs for preschool children and their parents. (p. 505)

A new mental health center was planned for 1969 to serve a catchment area within the county, with ideas of later enlarging it.[244] He saw this general hospital and medical center as a valuable part of the mental health center. Again he emphasized the community as a part of and not passive recipient of services: "Community organization is a vital activity of the center . . . bringing community groups into program planning . . . meet with community leaders in education, family and children's services in order to include them in program planning. A community Advisory Committee will play a vital role in the new center's program development".

University of Pennsylvania

Erich Lindemann remembered Robert Leopold as running the best CMHC in Philadelphia and then moving to community psychiatry as professor of community psychiatry and community medicine at the University of Pennsylvania, working with Albert J. ("Mickey") Stunkard.[245] He continued working despite the disability of progressive multiple sclerosis. He faced the same issues that Lindemann had with no foothold at the university and no one to talk to. He pleaded with Leonard Duhl to come and talk about CMH.

University of Rochester School of Medicine and Dentistry

In 1964, Elmer Gardner and John Romero wrote:[246] "This year we have initiated an educational program in community psychiatry for our second and third year residents and have established a unit of social psychiatry toward this end". In 1979, Haroutun Babigian, M.D., the new chairman of the university's psychiatry department, felt that the psychiatry residents needed exposure to "the rest of the world". The state ended its residency program and in 1981, his lobbying resulted in the state hospital and the medical school administration agreeing to the medical school's taking responsibility for 50 beds in the hospital for residency training purposes. The medical school staff were surprised that residents were motivated to work in the public sector, not because of salary considerations but because of faculty encouragement about the rewards of public-sector work.[247]

San Mateo County (California) Public Health Department

This county near San Francisco grew 300% from 1940 to 1950 and discovered that it had major problems involving mental illness; yet in 1948, a population of a third of a million had no psychiatrists or psychiatric clinics.[248] This was an era of economic prosperity and a sense of expansiveness. There was much support for CMH, and so an unsophisticated County Board of Supervisors could start a new program.[249] Henrik Blum of the Contra Costa County Health Department followed the San Mateo example, though some felt he was more interested in the technology of administration than in service.[250] A meeting of the county welfare, school, probation, and health departments decided that a child guidance clinic would soon be filled and unhelpful and opted for psychiatrist consultation to each agency to train workers and thus multiply services to patients. In 1946, Drs. Chope and Lamb, public health officers for San Mateo County, developed consultation and outreach mental health services that influenced federal legislation. Under the 1948 Mental Health Act, a psychiatrist from the Langley Porter Neuropsychiatric Institute's child psychiatry training program was hired for three hours per week.[251]

The program started in 1949 with a Mental Health Coordinating Committee of nine city agencies overseeing 68 hours per week of consultation from nine psychiatrists. At that time, the city hospital joined the effort and, as federal funds phased out, gradually assumed the cost of the psychiatrists and developed its own department of psychiatry. The program brought into this population dozens of psychiatrists, who gradually became more comfortable in learning, collaboration, and professional function. In 1950 to 1952 the Civil Service Department joined, as did two junior colleges and the Richmond City Health Department. In 1952 to 1954, new psychiatrists joined, and the general hospital developed a psychiatry inpatient ward for local treatment. The psychiatry program provided direct medical care. The mental health program provided indirect, nonmedical care expanding to dealing with staff problems with their jobs, work situations, office relationships, and program goals. Constituent agencies developed their own mental health programs and consultant disciplines. The mental health program turned to training nurses in case management and treatment techniques in order to increase their understanding and application of knowledge. It assigned them to emotionally ill clients in community agencies, which contributed to the program costs. It involved police departments, welfare departments, schools, departments of public health, probation departments, junior colleges, cities, etc. as well as seeing people in homes and offices. The mental health consultation focus, including under Clarice Haylett as acting chief of the consultation service, shifted from the patient to the consultee to improve their capacity to help others. Mental health nursing consultants became intermediaries between psychiatrists (assistant health officers) and nurses. The program expanded to the point of requiring district supervisors and administrators. It provided postgraduate education courses. It coordinated with the state Department of Mental Hygiene to provide follow-up treatment for discharged mental hospital patients and enriched and promoted mental health work with community agencies and state departments of Maternal and Child Health, Crippled Children, Venereal Disease, and Tuberculosis.

The guiding principles were much influenced by Erich Lindemann's community orientation. For instance, Clara Mayo, researcher at the HRS, wrote to a psychologist at San Mateo: "John Hill of the University of Minnesota and I are finishing up a book on methods and problems of

94 A Sampling of Community Mental Health Programs

screening [of children]".[252] In the Lindemann perspective, patients in the phase of exacerbation of illness are more accessible to therapeutic intervention. Wider access to these patients is gained through enlisting existing community caretakers, such as school guidance counselors, teachers, probation workers, social welfare workers, medical social workers, and public health nurses. Mental health information for these caretakers is mediated through mental health consultants: psychologists, psychiatrists, public health nurses, and psychiatric social workers. These helping agents need to appreciate the effects on patients of community problems, socioeconomic groups, cultural patterns, community organizations, and government agencies. The goals are to avoid recalcitrance and legal trouble for clients, clarify and increase acceptance of administrative organization for workers, coordinate agency relationships, improve interagency communication and knowledge, and reach clients who are resistant to psychiatry.

Clarice Haylett was a public health specialist interested in Lindemann's grief studies dealing with external events that lead to emotional and psychosomatic consequences.[253] She found that the psychoanalytically oriented training program at the Mt. Zion Hospital in San Francisco did not support this perspective. At the San Mateo County Health Department, she met (and later married) Warren Vaughan, whose fellowship in Lindemann's CMH programs prepared him to introduce her to Lindemann's literature on action research in public health mental health—a preventive approach, preventive intervention, crisis theory, and communitywide services. She saw Lindemann as happy, pleasant, caring, and a bridge to many areas. In contrast, she found Gerald Caplan's approach too formalistic, overelaborate, proprietary, authoritarian, and inclined to make recipients feel inadequate. Lindemann's interest in administration and the psychopathology of organizations echoed Haylett's interests.

In 1957, the Short-Doyle Act for Community Mental Health Services (with federal and state matching) increased mental health activities but with decreased time for sharing, planning, learning, and innovation. This confined mental health professionals to direct treatment without innovation. The CMH Association, the public health department, and a minority of psychiatrists developed a community treatment program and tried to influence the Short-Doyle program, policy, and legislation.

Both Erich and Elizabeth Lindemann contributed consultation and training to the program and local agencies.[254]

Temple University Community Mental Health Center and North Philadelphia Mental Health Consortium

The Temple University CMHC developed in the 1960s, coincident with the emerging black power and antiestablishment/student unrest movements.[255] The catchment area—North Philadelphia—was an urban problem area:[256] It included more than 200,000 persons, most of them poor and 80% of them black. The area had the city's highest rate of crime, infant mortality, substandard housing, and unemployment. It regarded the university as an indifferent and even injurious representative of the White Establishment.

The Temple University Community Mental Health Center became fully operative in October 1967. Its organizational plan included:

- The Crisis Center...
- The Psychosocial Clinic (p. 70)
- A satellite center
- The Partial Hospitalization Unit
- The Children and Family Unit worked with

    - consultation with other divisions of the Center
    - schools and the welfare department
    - groups of parents in a preschool enrichment program
    - three "incentive specialists"
    - to improving the community
    - youngsters
    - case detectors
    - a children's psychiatrist—his staff met with the incentive specialists and the teachers to discuss a school's mental health problems

- the Consultation and Education Unit mental health training programs for police, public health nurses, ministers, and voluntary, state, and city agencies (p. 71)

    The Community Organization section
    a. cooperative work with a tenants; council to withhold rent from landlords to force them to meet standards of repair and maintenance
    b. "patient's advocate service" dealing with complaints to a council of community representatives about the work either of the Center or of other community agencies
    c. an effort to foster political awareness among community residents (p. 72)

- The Social Adjustment and Rehabilitation Unit (p. 72)
- Research and Evaluation Unit (p. 73)

There was tumult and confusion, including the state hospital's administration of its ward and the university hospital refusing to make its ward available for CMH service, leaving the state hospital for community admissions though it was outside the catchment area. There was no authority over the policies of the variety of community agencies, leaving the crisis center overrun with a wide variety of patients. Paraprofessionals were assigned to expand the therapist pool without clear roles or qualifications. The involvement of indigenous workers was a good idea, but it was felt that the program did not know how to select, train, and utilize them well.[257] This led to a vagueness of role relationships among the staff and effort diverted from the mental health of residents into a fight over jobs—a great need of the indigenous people. Psychiatrists were afraid to lead interdisciplinary teams and others thought that psychiatrists should not lead since everyone should be equal in the eyes of god. This led to the retreat of professionals into guild groupings and teaching positions, and, consequently, a fragmentation rather than integration of services. The partial hospitalization service had good group cohesion and a democratic work style, which conflicted with other units' styles. The patient advocate and advisory committee provoked resistance from the staff.

The consultation and education program worked with a specific clinical focus and with specific consultee groups—police, public health nurses, clergy, schools, and social agencies. The community and funding sources urged consultation and education in nonclinical areas, leading to vague goals, methods, and consultees and turmoil and disruption in the mental health center's program. The state of skills and knowledge at the time supported only pilot programs, not large population-oriented and low-cost programs.

In light of this, in 1964, the Medical Center Department of Psychiatry decided to take a hand in federally funded CMH work and applied for a federal grant for a mental health training program for community workers:[258] "In deciding on tactics to be utilized for an all-encompassing attack on the problems of poverty, emotional and intellectual deprivation and deficit, urban decay and degeneration, a major limitation continually presents itself . . . the lack of trained personnel to implement significant programs . . . This proposal has as its basic rationale . . . that a training program can be offered to community based and community oriented professionals and para-professionals which will contribute to the effectiveness of their roles in the broad plan for social reconstruction" (p. 5). "<u>Purpose and Objectives Overall</u> To make para-professionals and professionals, participating in this program more aware of and sensitive to human behavior with a view toward making them more effective in dealing with their clients" (p. 10). In a similar vein, the department applied for a nine months training program for groups of a variety of community professionals and paraprofessionals regarding mental health problems of low income areas, the interrelation of mental health agencies, and overcoming interprofessional barriers. (Lindemann, sitting on the grant review committee, recommended approval with high priority.)

However, as a whole, the Temple department of psychiatry was jealous of the CMHC's large budget and resented paying the operating costs for service programs. On the other hand, the community resented the use of CMHC staff for university teaching. With the rise of the community control movement, it demanded a controlling voice, and battles among community factions, the university, and mental health center groups surfaced. In 1969, there was a major confrontation between management, some staff (especially paraprofessionals), and the community.[259] The center was disrupted and services temporarily discontinued when indigenous mental health workers, supposedly representing the community, "took over" the centers.

Elmer Gardner, a well-recognized leader in CMHC programs, who had established the Rochester Case Register, gave his perspective:[260]

> [He was] . . . brought in to discuss . . . an epidemiologic research unit at Temple . . . suggested . . . Since the relationship between the University and the community had been less than cordial . . . a university research team. . . [it found it] difficult to get the needed facts. [suggested] Set up a mental health center that . . . gives it something . . . then the research project can be made part of the Center and will be more likely to succeed (p. 75)
>
> [direct social activism was a planned part of this CMHC, as opposed to Lindemann's consultation and research approach]
>
> Social problems contribute to mental illness. In fact, in such a community as North Philadelphia, Gardner believes, they are usually either an important cause or the chief precipitating factor. So the (p. 75) job of the community mental health center is not only to help the sick individual but also to combat the social forces that probably helped make him sick. "And the first time that we get involved in pushing for better housing, for example . . . or get involved politically", he says, "we are going to need all the support we can get" . (p. 76)
>
> the Community Organization Section, which is staffed almost entirely by black personnel . . . A Center patient . . . reported that the building . . . and three others . . . were in bad states of disrepair. The Center asked the city for quick action. The license department posted (p. 100) the four buildings as unfit for habitation and ordered . . . to bring them to standard. Meanwhile, the rent is being paid to . . . a group that mental health assistants helped to organize, as escrow agent . . . if the repairs have not been made, the money is to be returned to the tenants. The Community Organization Section expects to take similar action in other cases . . . the Center are also working to acquire five dilapidated houses, renovate them, and sell them to low-income families . . . as one step . . . to stabilize the community . . . one of the services the residents most wanted was a day care center for children. The MHAs [mental health assistants] drew up a proposal . . . Political awareness is another goal . . . some voting machines . . . people could practice using them . . . arranged for "meet your candidates" evenings . . . unusually needy families . . .

98 A Sampling of Community Mental Health Programs

> called upon the business men of the community for donations ... To combat the apathy ... an "activity therapist" has organized a drama group ... a choral group, and a dance group (p. 101)
> **Looking Ahead** (p. 103) ... greater involvement with juvenile gangs ... A broader job-training and job-getting program.
>
> (p. 105)

He further echoed Lindemann in advocating a social rather than psychiatric diagnostic system:[261]

> outpatient psychiatry ... the patient is viewed within the larger ... framework of his environment and the groups to which he belongs ... the problems which he presents may be more a product of this framework than of his own character structure (p. 39) ... With increasing horizons he [the clinician] comes into contact with problems or disorders that are not clearly confined to one person but often represent disturbances in social interaction, sometimes a result of individual personality patterns and at other times as much attributable to the social setting in which the interaction occurs as to the intrapsychic problem.
>
> (p. 53)

The split in psychiatry was highlighted between treatment of illness and correction of social determinants of illness:[262]

> Dr. Clifford J. Bodarky, chief of Philadelphia's Hahnemann Community Mental Health Center, only a few miles from Temple [University CMHC] ... offer striking evidence of a deep split in psychiatry—one traditional and mod-(p. 346) eled on concepts of illness, the other liberal and shaped by ideas of social maladjustment ... treatment is oriented toward well-established methods of individual psychotherapy stemming from Freudian theory... "We know how to help patients. Why change?" asks Dr. Bodarky.
>
> (p. 347)

Gardner saw the lack of adequate support and incompatibility of effort obstructing CMH success.[263] Between August and December 1970, he was employed by the County Welfare Board as director of intake at North Division, the center's facility for the acutely mentally ill. "He 'didn't think the whole series of services was administered very well'. Patients, he said, simply were not getting the services they should have been getting... ' I was supposed to be a planning consultant ... But they didn't pay much attention to plans ... The whole center is chaotic, South Division is the worst of the lot".[264] It was of no help that the federal government was more concerned with spending money for the short-term political gain of direct services than with funding ongoing objective evaluation of long-term programs such as CMH.

The Temple University Department of Psychiatry forced Elmer Gardner out of his job.[265] Subsequently, he was investigated by the police. The department chairman disbanded the CMHC as "too radical". Gardner subsequently directed the North Philadelphia Mental Health Center to develop good community clinical services serving a black neighborhood. He was caught in battles over this program and reportedly had to leave Philadelphia. Following this, he administered the federal drug and alcohol program, was caught up in political maneuvering, and was pressured out of that position, too. Thereafter he left CMH work entirely and developed a successful private practice of psychiatry.

Tufts Medical School Community Mental Health Center

The Tufts Medical School had a tradition of training specialists for non-urban areas. This originated with a Mr. Bingham, brother of an early congresswoman from Cleveland, who suffered from hypochondria and schizophrenia, and was treated at the Bethel Inn in Bethel, Maine.[266] He and his internist, Samuel Proger of the Tufts Medical School, became interested in the availability of medical care in Maine, and he left money to the Tufts Medical School to bring specialists to small towns in Maine. Consequently, there was some support but also resistance to community medicine at Tufts.

Tufts Medical School originally had only a small, part-time psychiatry faculty adjunct to its Department of Neurology.[267] In 1954, the Massachusetts Department of Legal Medicine (Leon Shapiro, M.D., director) funded it to provide court clinics. Paul Myerson, M.D., shared with his father and wife liberal values and was concerned with psychological and social conditions.[268] He taught in the Tufts Department of Psychiatry since 1926 and half time at the Boston Dispensary, a teaching affiliate providing medical care to the indigent in the community. There he discussed patient issues with fourth-year medical students making home visits during their two-month home medical assignment. He saw home medical care as a way of integrating liberalism and some limited opportunities for creative teaching. In 1963, Tufts Medical School dean Heinrich appointed Paul Myerson chairman of a Department of Psychiatry because he was a long-term faculty member who was sensible, intelligent, and ethical.[269] Samuel Proger, a power in the Tufts New England Medical Center (NEMC) Department of Medicine, supported him as good quality among the "weird psychiatrists". Myerson was interested in the literature and clinical cases, not publication or administration, and had an informal administrative style but with firm control of the department. In 1964, when he took up the duties of chairman of psychiatry, Myerson wanted a full-time, good department of psychiatry applying psychoanalysis, not necessarily social psychiatry.[270] He hired Leon Shapiro, Miles Shore, and Rolf Arvidson, and reorganized the department, including involving several faculty members in teaching medical students in the outpatient department.[271] He involved Jack Ewalt, commissioner of the DMH, Shapiro, and himself in designating a psychiatry clinic in the Boston Floating Hospital (the pediatric affiliate of Tufts Medical School).

The national spirit during the Kennedy and Johnson administrations was one of confidence in doing something about social problems. In the spring of 1964 at the Northeast Professors of Psychiatry Meeting at Arden House, Stanley Yolles (director) and other staff members of the National Institute of Mental Health (NIMH) announced a plan for much money for CMHCs with catchment areas to provide coherent mental health care. It called for involvement of medical schools. Peter Randolph saw the CMHC goal as bringing the best service to the public and training to professionals—not only CMH but psychodynamic and biological psychiatry.[272]

In eras of these expanding resources, programs grew, and it was easier to mesh interest groups. When resources were withdrawn, these became more difficult. The form of the CMHC was shaped by contemporary forces—community work, state hospitals, etc.

Tufts announced itself as a CMHC because it believed in a CMH approach: Shapiro had experience working with the most difficult problems among prisoners, and he and Myerson had strong concern for psychiatric services to the poor. But also "[T]hat [CMH] was music to the ears of Paul [Myerson] and Leon [Shapiro]". because Tufts needed federal funding to support a shaky department and staff for teaching and other functions.[273] It used the grants for staff positions, training, and service programs. Among these were small units for analytic training and long-term treatment, complementing CMH by teaching when analytic treatment was useful. The source of the funds colored the nature of the department, and Myerson was happy to accept this.

Tufts received a five-year planning grant. It negotiated with DMH commissioner Harry C. Solomon and other local medical schools over the division of patients and catchment areas and was assigned the South Boston and North Dorchester neighborhoods. This was a fortunate choice: While other mental health catchment areas contended with internal conflict and turmoil in the community, the power structure in these neighborhoods was settled, clear, and effective when treated supportively.[274] Money began to flow in for provision of services and psychiatric residency training.

Myerson felt that there was no conflict between his devotion to psychoanalysis and psychotherapy and community or liaison psychiatry, whereas some analysts were totally devoted to psychoanalysis and could not accept community psychiatry. Full-time psychoanalysis was too strenuous for him; he was more comfortable with five hours per week

A Sampling of Community Mental Health Programs 101

of analysis, providing training analyses, and supervising and providing psychotherapy while also administering the community psychiatry program, running a group for school principals, consulting twice a week at the South Boston Action Center, and setting an example for the department. Judgments of Myerson's involvement in CMH varied according to the perspectives of the evaluators: In an interesting distinction, Gerald Adler thought he was deeply committed to his intellectual beliefs, including Freudian psychoanalysis and liberal political causes, but did not value CMH ideology.[275] And Myerson's successor, Richard Shader, saw him as much involved in the Boston Psychoanalytic Institute and teaching there and not involved in the CMH program.[276]

Myerson and Shapiro hired Miles Shore to carry out a formal study to evaluate the community's need for poverty programs. Shore was concerned with the lack of psychiatrists outside metropolitan Boston. In the psychiatry department at Beth Israel Hospital in Boston, he was frustrated in trying to develop in the general psychiatry residency training program preparation for practice in nonurban areas and an understanding of CMH. Peter Randolph thought Shore had an interest in program administration rather than an academic interest in social psychiatry.[277] Shore transferred to the Tufts Department of Psychiatry, where Myerson felt close to him around these ideas and in having Shore develop and direct community psychiatry in South Boston. Peter Randolph admired his talent in working with and meshing interest groups, including non–mental health agencies.[278] Shore and Leon Shapiro won evaluation and staffing grants that were used for staffing in the department.

Throughout the CMH program there was an attempt to mesh community and academic interests and a sharing of responsibilities, with the CMHC as an umbrella for working through decisions.[279] The Tufts Medical School's interests and practices differed from those of the CMHC. The CMH program had funding separate from public sources, which the hospital did not want, rather than taking funding from the hospital. The Department of Psychiatry gave consultation and referral resources to the hospital. The hospital's image and funding benefitted from its CMH.

Myerson and Shapiro, in collaboration with the group of community leaders required for the staffing grant, decided on a decentralized program and staffing, with staff jointly hired by the CMHC and community agencies for agency service (staffed by the community as well as the CMHC), resources, and administration. The grant went to the NEMC for distribution as specified. This community had strong ties to state government. The first community Area Board consisted mostly of community agency directors. One community leader, Mgr. Harry O'Connor of South Boston, helped speed the state matching grant.

CMH was built into the psychiatric residency training program: the residents spent their first year in the NEMC, the second year half time in the Austin Unit of the Boston State Hospital (which had been designated as part of the CMHC and integrated into the psychiatry department), and half time in the community and the third year either in the Medical Center or the community. Thus Tufts built a new department around a source of funding that adopted a CMH organization of services. It also had, in Paul Myerson and Leon Shapiro, leaders with a commitment to training, and, with Shore, adventurous courage, confidence, and commitment to the social movement around them and public-sector psychiatry. The medical school dean and hospital administration were very supportive because of their own convictions and their pride in the school's community focus. Staff and residents were urged to participate: some residents resisted but were required to do so, and some faculty members were unable to adapt to CMH practice or did so only in token degree. Randolph regretted missed opportunities to influence the education of medical students and medical and pediatric residents.[280]

CMH was successful in this department because it was interested in general medicine and responsive to service requests.[281] The CMH staff was good, assertive about their interests, and had vigorous interaction with nonpsychiatric colleagues rather than taking a nondirective psychotherapeutic stance of passively accepting prejudices: they went on rounds, were active, and held offices in the hospital. Myerson loved to teach. He was committed to the psychoanalytic method, psychoanalytic ideas in psychotherapy, and the application of psychoanalysis to varied interventions, leading him into new ventures. Gerald Adler thought Myerson fought to maintain the independence of the Department of Psychiatry by fending off the medical school dean's control, maintaining separation from the NEMC (teaching hospitals), and refusing to sit on its Executive Committee.[282] He was pragmatic in choosing good people to carry out programs. Peter Randolph appreciated Myerson's talent in valuing and supporting a broad range of interests, though he was "the analyst's analyst".[283] Leon Shapiro also loved to teach and was interested in classical psychoanalysis and its application to various situations. He started court clinics, applied analysis creatively to social problems, and allowed Myerson to interest him in building a CMH system. Both Myerson and Shapiro, the senior members of the faculty, were interested in such humanitarian problems as poverty, racism, and social conscience, though Myerson was thought to be more intellectual and distanced.[284]

The Department was fluid in terms of ideology, with no set factions or functions. Academic appointments were routine and not factional because the creation of the department was within the memories of existing members and was ongoing. All Tufts psychiatry faculty members were practicing psychoanalysts: It was felt that the best community psychiatrists were psychotherapists, psychoanalysts, and those with a developmental psychiatry approach. Some saw CMH as an integral part of the department, arguing for resources as other programs did,[285] while others saw it as separated ideologically and administratively.[286] Some were skeptical about overoptimism about community psychiatry, as had been the case with early psychoanalysis. There was some irreconcilable tension between CMH and non-CMH segments over sharing resources, tolerating differences, and assignment of psychiatric residents who preferred NEMC to community placements. Attempts were made to talk these out, but some were left unresolvable.[287]

Many academic departments of psychiatry were built around teaching hospitals with established referral bases and only partial acknowledgement of local community needs and established hierarchies of vested interests. In contrast, the Tufts department was new, with no ideological tradition or history of an established referral system. Myerson built his ideas, structure, appointments, and ultimate authority into this new entity.[288] The inpatient and outpatient departments developed some noncommunity orientation. In the psychiatric outpatient department, the treatment was long term, psychoanalytic, reviewed by part-time psychiatrists, and refusing "uninteresting" cases.[289] Henry Friedman, its director, felt that community residents were untreatable, and so they were underrepresented in his department.[290] In 1965, Gerald Adler was hired into and succeeded Rolf Arvidson as director of the psychiatric inpatient unit at the NEMC and helped Paul Myerson administer the psychiatric residency training program (becoming its director in 1974).[291] He was a figure of conflict regarding the CMH program. He reported that initially he was skeptical about it but, through his admiration for Miles Shore, became convinced that there were good programs. His criticisms were that it was overambitious, underresourced, too superficial, that some junior staff members were incompetent, and that Mick Gill, director of the state hospital Austin Unit and a charismatic figure in the CMH program, was responsible and a good clinician but a poor administrator and exerted a transference attraction to others.[292] Dan Bouie was a critical academician but adventurous into the community and became convinced nonpsychiatrists could be effective there.

At Tufts under Myerson, there was a distinct preventive practice.[293] Some saw CMH as distinct from other Department of Psychiatry interests. It began with an interest in inpatients, setting aside half of the beds for community residents.[294] It and Adler, its director, were resented by some CMH people, such as Michael ["Mick"] Gill, George Sigel, and, to some extent, Peter Randolph (later superintendent of the CMHC), as a resource-rich elite (a "golden cookie") that was reluctant to share these resources, and they doubted that it really made 50% of beds available to community residents. Adler was skeptical about unrealistic fantasies of more understanding for CMH and about admitting sicker patients to an inpatient unit limited by its setting in a rehabilitation institution. As an extension of these doubts by the CMH staff, Adler, as director of psychiatric residency training, was accused of avoiding exposing residents to the community, provoking their feelings of entitlement and rebellion against CMH, and of devaluing CMH. Adler claimed to be committed to getting residents into the community, insisting that they go and document any defects in structure and supervision of the training program. The residents were reluctant to go into the community but often liked the experience, though they complained about the facilities, and gained valuable training from good teachers. A group of five residents (including Paul Cotton, later active in CMH) brought a list of reasonable complaints, including the need for more teaching time and supervision, which were remedied. Randolph thought the underlying issue was whether there was interest in public-sector psychiatry and the environment in which it was practiced: less controlled, more violent, and engendering feeling of being overwhelmed. He thought the battles were manageable because Myerson respected both sides and was fair and generous, and the department felt like an extended family rather than a structured business.

The CMH program quickly decided to avoid a focus on severe, chronic illness in favor of prevention, child mental health, and other "nice things". Individuals, including Shapiro and Shore, taught, practiced, and modeled social psychiatry at various times. Myerson made a great attempt to support and model social psychiatry and hired and influenced Shore to develop programs addressing social problems. Shore was active and a good administrator, including as the first superintendent of the CMHC, though sometimes his facility in dealing with people was not appreciated.[295]

Clinic directors feared being overloaded with clinical demands and resisted participation in CMH, as Shapiro experienced in court clinics. The Tufts Mental Health Center [TMHC] was never very separate from the department but was the superstructure for funding of typical psychiatry department functions of teaching, etc., and there was a casual yearly rotation of its directorship. Myerson integrated them via full-time appointments and funding sources.

Myerson remembers developing day hospitals. In the child psychiatry program, the director, Myron Stocking, wanted a traditional psychotherapy program and struggled with Myerson and Shore until he was replaced by Arthur Mutter, who oversaw an eclectic program. Myerson remembers general agreement over separate funding, psychodynamic and community philosophy, Myerson selecting all appointments, and Myerson providing a fatherly supervision for all. The only conflict was between Adler (chief of residency training) and "Mick" Gill (chief of the Austin Unit) over the assignment of residents. The NEMC was very supportive, including Vi Spinelli sitting on the mental health Area Board, and the medical school dean was interested. There were negotiations over sources of salaries, billing for third-party reimbursement, the proportion of time residents spent in the community versus inpatient ward, and the types of patients admitted to the NEMC ward versus the Austin Unit. The Community Area Board was supportive, though the medical school

Departments of Medicine and Surgery wanted to focus on academic research rather than community work.

In the summer of 1964, Alvin Poussaint, a recent Tufts psychiatry residency graduate, was funded by Physicians for Social Responsibility to provide medical support to young people from the northern U.S. who were working for civil rights in Mississippi. This was the beginning of Tufts's social psychiatry programs (Shapiro periodically visited to provide supervision and support). Count Gibson started community health services. He was followed by H. Jack Geiger, founding member and president of Physicians for Human Rights, who chaired the Department of Community Medicine and was appointed professor of social medicine. He led the development of community health (including mental health) care programs in the North (at Columbia Point in Boston, including the largest public housing project in the city and other neighborhood health centers) and the Home Medical Program (attempting a primary care center) in the South (at Mound Bayou in Mississippi), etc. He was facile in obtaining CMHC grants. The Tufts Department of Medicine as a whole collaborated with psychiatry in community medicine but was wary and not committed.

Shore was appointed dean of community medicine and then left for a chair at Harvard Medical School. Peter Randolph had trained at the Massachusetts Mental Health Center and then worked at the NIMH. He asked Myerson for a job.[296] Myerson found that he came from a wealthy background and was bright, engaging, open to community work, and interested in program development rather than CMH concepts. In 1968, Myerson appointed him to a court clinic—the first psychiatrist hired under the Tufts CMHC staffing grant—and groomed him to direct the CMH program. Randolph threw himself into the program, whose administration and accountability processes were more demanding than Tufts had experienced in the past. He appreciated the need to mesh inherently different interests: CMHCs and academic medical centers.[297] Factors that aided the success of the Tufts program included smart decisions by Myerson and Shore, the atmosphere and personalities of individuals and departments, the good fortune of CMHC support and funding just as the department was developing, and assignment to a catchment area devoid of competing and resisting mental health facilities.

Randolph, under instruction from Myerson and Shore, was clear about the mission of the Tufts CMH program: delivery of psychiatric services. It avoided diversion by politics and institutional change. His perspective was clear:[298] There was a tradition of advocacy through effectively using conflict to achieve resolution by winning and defeating. In contrast, the mental health and health professional tradition was collaboration through finding common ground, working toward common purposes, and all parties winning or losing together. He saw mental health services striving for mutuality and being alert against bias. His view of the role of academicians was striving for objectivity and comprehensiveness; i.e., they are not advocates. Guided by this perspective, the TMHC sought collaboration, avoided situations without common ground, and blurred differences.

The catchment area community focused on resisting change, delivering services locally (not in a central building), and leaving the local power structure to deal with politics. The Chinese community alone pressed for social change. During the crisis of busing for school racial integration, both the CMHC and the community Area Board decided to focus on the impartial delivery of mental health services, not racial integration or changing racial attitudes. They worked to keep the peace, helped families with the effects of the situation, and convened meetings on community issues (including non–mental health issues). Professionals who did not live in the catchment area were not entitled to involvement in community issues. Staffing was controlled by the staff, and (unlike Boston University) they resisted pressures to emphasize hiring of community residents.

Randolph had a clear philosophy of CMH mental health services as distinct from political advocacy (in contrast e.g., to Lincoln Hospital—see earlier):[299]

> if one who's come to human services through . . . the route of health care or mental health care . . . with different assumptions of values . . . conflict is best resolved by more collaborative strategies . . . find a common ground rather than polarize . . . cooperate where we can . . . their fates are tied together . . . change occurs . . . with the voluntary participation of the changed system or people. (p. 3) . . . the underlying assumption is that conflict results from irrational forces and is not so clearly based on reality . . . an example of this our own experience in the Tufts Mental Health Center . . . consistently and assiduously making an effort to avoid confrontations . . . blur over polarizations . . . tried not to advocate any one . . . of the many conflicting causes . . . find the common ground . . . see whether that common ground could enlarge. . . . In this way the program has grown very rapidly . . . these are two very different approaches . . . advocacy being one and the other . . . collaborative. These . . . come from very different historical traditions . . . they must be kept separate (p. 4) . . . mental health types, . . . health types of human service people, have a great deal of work to do simply to learn . . . the practice of their own trade . . . we don't know anything about advocacy and perhaps we don't belong there . . . there's a lot of value also in . . . providing human services as neutrally as possible . . . I am concerned that it be lost in the current wave of searching for new and different roles in the human services.
>
> (p. 5)

In the early 1970s, the federal Nixon administration sought to reduce training grants. The department arranged to integrate with the Veterans Administration (VA), which had much money; it expected to increase CMH at Tufts by having VA psychiatry residents rotate through the Tufts CMH program as well as the VA. This was a difficult period of replacing the VA staff from the old regime, the great increase in the number of staff, the drain on the CMH program imposed by the VA clinical responsibilities, and the difficult VA administrative system. Coincidentally, there was the additional burden of the landmark Rogers versus Okin class action suit against the residents and staff at the Austin Unit regarding the involuntary administration of antipsychotic medications. Community placement was no longer required because there were too many VA trainees, residency stipends were devalued by inflation, the training program's reputation as psychoanalytically oriented, and competition with Harvard Medical School. The CMH program resented this diminution, and Adler tried (unsuccessfully) to bring mental health services to veterans in the community. The department atmosphere was no longer that of an intimate family.

Shapiro felt that all CMH projects had receded: Mound Bayou became a cooperative farm. Social medicine outweighed social psychiatry, including the "elegant duplicity" of community medicine services as a cover for meeting more basic community needs: community organization at Columbia Point and food in Mound Bayou. The Department of Community Psychiatry was eventually abolished; community programs came under the dean's office of the medical school and the hospital; and Miles Shore held an appointment in the Department of Psychiatry, became dean, and was director of the CMHC.

In retrospect, Shapiro remembered few psychiatric residents affected by CMH, community medicine, or community organization, most practicing good psychotherapy and liaison psychiatry. He wondered if CMH could be taught except in terms of intellectual knowledge. It required selection of those interested and providing a full-time program with community placements. This was not done at Tufts, whose residents learned to practice in nursing homes and "quarter-way houses", not CMH as originally conceived and not integrated into their careers. Physicians with this interest, capacity, and talent are rare; they are more often found in community organizers and YMCA directors. The model of integrating undergraduate and medical school education commits 18-year-old college students to narrow studies and high marks and tends to eliminate people with other interests from the ranks of medicine. For instance, Jack Geiger was a rarity: a science writer with strong social commitments who went to medical school to gain the skills to forward these commitments.

Medical school psychiatry training focused on difficult, chronic patients had led to a decrease in applications for psychiatric residency training. Shapiro saw medical and academic centers inhospitable to

108 *A Sampling of Community Mental Health Programs*

social medicine and psychiatry, but it was where students got their education. Preventive psychiatry could be found only in preventive medicine (e.g., as learned at Columbia Point). In his opinion, preventive psychiatry had its most immediate payoff in getting patients to take their medicines and prevent decompensation and in changing life practices, as in Eleanor Pavenstedt's project to teach mothers mothering.[300] It is complex, unproven, and hard to sell.

In 1975, Shapiro left Tufts for New York Hospital; in 1977, he became residency training director at Massachusetts Mental Health Center; and in August 1981, he left to teach. By then he felt that "the whole system has changed so radically now that preventive intervention doesn't make much sense".[301]

The continued integration of CMH in the department depended on Myerson's successor.[302] Miles Shore had worked to put community-interested people on the NEMC board of trustees and establish its community affairs committee. The board strongly supported CMH, including the community representatives arranged by Shore—Evelyn Li of the Chinese Community Health Center, John Bartholomew of the Federated Dorchester Neighborhood Houses, chairman William Saltonstall, who had grown up opposite Medfield State Hospital and was interested in public patients, and Franklin Parker, who was the interim director of the hospital and one of the founders of Erich Lindemann's Wellesley Human Relations Service. The NEMC remembered its history of interest in community medicine through the Boston Dispensary for the poor and the Boston Floating Hospital for children. The Tufts Medical School remembered its tradition of training practitioners rather than academicians.

On the other hand, in choosing a new chairman of psychiatry, the medical school (especially the Department of Medicine) wanted a psychoanalyst who was really interested in biological psychiatry, rather than what they felt was Myerson's inadequate commitment to consultation and inpatient psychiatry in favor of community and outpatient psychiatry. The devaluation of psychoanalysis after a shift to biological psychiatry was another consideration—one search committee member's depressed daughter was unresponsive to psychotherapy but helped by antidepressant medication. Finally, Myerson's lack of interest in hospital committee work was criticized. The Department of Psychiatry felt impotent and resented Myerson's refusal to intrude on the selection process.

The ultimate choice, Richard Shader, was grilled by the board about his interest in and intent to continue CMH programs. These programs were valued mediators and avoided partisan battles through their good relations with the community, such as the Chinese community's complaints about the lack of multiple-language resources in the hospital. Shader satisfied many constituencies as a psychoanalyst (appealing to Myerson), who was critical of much of psychoanalysis and interested in psychopharmacology. (Adler noted the parallels to the Massachusetts General Hospital's criticism of Lindemann and later choice of Thomas Hackett as the chairman of psychiatry.)

Shader saw himself as setting the direction of the department and having the power of hiring and firing independent of past commitments.[303] All funds were comingled with expenditures decided by the department. Services were not preventive but focused on good treatment of the mentally ill and maintaining them in the community. All units were headed by psychiatrists, which he thought alienated some nonpsychiatrists and pleased others with the improvement in the quality of care. The department was strongly involved with the NEMC, on whose Executive Committee he sat, treated patients in the hospitals (including on nonpsychiatric wards), and had good support from NEMC, including underwriting debt from psychiatry as from other departments. He sought to eliminate separate interest groups, combined practices, and involved staff in group practices that decided financial expenditures. He felt that CMH continued with the support of the department, including funding of the care of state residents when state funds were withdrawn. He expected that when state and federal funds decreased, the department would not be able to support outreach, maintenance, and consultation and education services but would aim toward inpatient, emergency, acute outpatient care, and halfway-house services. With exceptionally "soft" funding at Tufts, it would be hard to predict what the department would be like in a few years.

Worcester (Massachusetts) State Hospital

The relocation of mental health services from state hospitals to community settings was a major ideological, logistical, economic, and political adjustment. David Myerson thoughtfully described the process and dynamics at the oldest state hospital in Massachusetts and a persistent site of study and innovation:[304]

> In 1969, the WSH [Worcester State Hospital] budget (p. 99) was still under the direct control of the Superintendent. The [CMH] Regional Offices were allotted only a relatively small amount of funds; the Area Offices, none. Area Directors, however, were mandated by the Commissioner [of Mental Health and Retardation] to pry funds from the state hospitals budgets to develop their community programs which eventually would be budgeted separately and assigned directly to the Area Offices (p. 100) . . . As long as patients reside in the hospital . . . Given the severely limited budget, as well as the inflation, it was difficult to pry money from the WSH budget to establish community programs (p. 105) . . . Given his authority, any real change in the state hospital system was going to be dependent on the Superintendent. As a rule, Superintendents were conservative, loyal to the old

system, and resistant in varying degrees to change (p. 107) . . . I had to . . . learn that the hospital did not exist as an autonomous entity and to understand how dependent the community was upon WSH for the disposition of its social problems. Yet, to change this system community agencies, too, had to recognize that they could not transfer . . . maladaptive people to WSH and expect it to provide for their total care . . . The question . . . was how all of the agencies (p. 109) involved in the care . . . could pool and coordinate their wide array of resources (p. 110) . . . WSH was willing to, and did, provide facilities and staff both in and out of the hospital for such persons, but only in alliance with other agencies which provided preventive and community-based care . . . it was our responsibility to help set up alternative programs, which required, however, cooperation from the same community agencies. The pooling of resources from WSH and the other community agencies was to be the key to its successful phase-down. (p. 111) . . . a complex network of institutional and community-based services developed around WSH. Additional community clinics were established in storefronts, local churches, a neighborhood settlement house, and in the outpatient department of [Worcester] Memorial Hospital . . . Special services were created for emotionally disturbed, aggressive, acting-out students, retarded youngsters, and for disturbed adolescents. A forensic psychiatric team serviced the court and jails; a consultation-liaison program served several local general hospitals. (p. 117) Additional relationships were established with local social service agencies, the police, regional universities, the Worcester Youth Guidance Center, the Welfare Department, Massachusetts [vocational] Rehabilitation Commission, and several Worcester area hospitals . . . the WSH changed from an isolated, centralized institution which provided custodial care to about 3000 people in 1950 to the center of a mental health service system which, by 1975, provided . . . care to about 450 patients and participated . . . with many other agencies in the care of about 4000 people . . . closer to their families and communities . . . The shift . . . presented problems for the psychiatrists and nursing personnel . . . were in conflict with their training and experience . . . well-defined job descriptions and easily identified lines of authority . . . job security was protected by . . . unions, their professional associations, and civil service . . . the rank and file of staff did not understand the reorganization . . . they viewed it with apprehension . . . community assignments . . . in non medical settings . . . cooperate with non-hospital trained, but often vocally anti-hospital . . . lines of authority were confusing and unpopular (p. 118) provide . . . service for people who . . . presented a wide spectrum of situational as well as psychiatric difficulties . . . socio-psychiatric conditions which did not require hospitalization but were a source of concern to the community . . . Only the exceptional nurse and psychiatrist perceived the struggles of their patients as related primarily to social conditions . . . believed that he or she should be involved in social reform . . . community work was not popular among the rank-and-file nurses and physicians . . . Because of their training and interest, the social workers and psy- (p. 119) chologists generally found this community work more acceptable than did the medically trained personnel . . . a small group of gifted personnel from the different disciplines who willingly accepted the challenge of community work . . . The American Federation of State, County, and Municipal Employees (AFSCME) . . . contracted with several local colleges which provided . . . courses that focused on the delivery of mental health services to the community . . . WSH instituted three similar programs supported out of the hospital budget for the registered nurses . . . they did earn academic credits . . . unfilled nursing service positions were assigned to community programs . . . whose administrators were authorized to hire the personnel.

(p. 120)

Yale School of Medicine-Connecticut Mental Health Center

The Connecticut Mental Health Center (CtMHC) originated from 1950s stress on mental health manpower development and research; the 1960s civil rights and citizen participation movement, and federal health and welfare programs; and the federal plans to solve social problems via CMH, giving rise to debates about the goals of service delivery versus social change.[305]

The Yale Department of Psychiatry was a loose confederation of the Yale Psychiatric Institute (university-based, expensive, intensive, psychoanalytic, 44 beds), Yale-New Haven Hospital Psychiatry Service (intensive treatment in 25 beds plus consultation, emergency-ward, and outpatient department services), and the West Haven Veterans Administration Hospital (VAH; 100 beds and training for first-year psychiatric residents).[306] Related programs at the university included the Child Study Center, Mental Health Section of the Department of Epidemiology and Public Health, the University Health Service, and other one-man projects ("the independents").

Boris Astrachan remembered that the Yale Department of Psychiatry originally was not interested in CMH.[307] "Yale . . . was not able to decide until very late in the sixties, whether it was proper for an Ivy League school to condescend to involve itself as an institution in the affairs of the city".[308] The university had little contact with the city outside of individual faculty members' personal or professional participation and student scrapes. The psychiatry chairman, Frederick Redlich, had brought in Theodore Lidz and Stephen Fleck to build applied psychoanalysis with a family focus similar to Viola Bernard's work. Daniel Freedman and Thomas Detre came to develop psychopharmacology. These two groups were in conflict, including the objection to publishing the 1955 textbook *Modern Psychiatric Treatment* because of objection to the inclusion of psychotherapy. This impeded academic promotions. The psychoanalytic and psychotherapy group objected to the CMHC, concerned that the department was already stretched too thin and that a new facility would be a burden and threat, though the University did want to close the Yale Psychiatric Institute in order to make use of its space. Interestingly, the biological psychiatrists always wanted the CtMHC as a research laboratory and were strongly based there.

Aaron Lazare suggested another facet in these developments:[309] He thought Redlich wanted Yale to become more competitive for psychiatric residents with Albert Einstein College of Medicine and the Massachusetts Mental Health Center. Its clinical facilities—the Yale-New Haven Hospital and the West Haven VA Hospital—were insufficient, and CMH offered expanded opportunities for resident training.

From the point of view of the Yale department of psychiatry and the CtMHC, Astrachan saw the advent of CMH as follows:[310] In the late 1950s and the 1960s, political and economic forces pushed mental health institutions into relationship with their host communities and toward the employment of community residents, education of these employees, the modification of mental health care, indirect mental health services (consultation, education, and mental health through the social welfare system), and competition with the traditional tasks of treatment, education, and research. Newly aroused population groups demanded redistribution of power and new economic and political relations, and the previously enfranchised groups counteracted.

Connecticut governor Abraham Ribicoff had a general interest in state-supported research and training institutes. In 1957, the Connecticut Department of Mental Health commissioner negotiated with Yale University about a CMHC.[311] The 1961 Joint Commission report *Action for Mental Health* recommended 20,000 to 25,000 population catchment areas with acute treatment, research, and training facilities associated with general hospitals for acute care and state mental hospitals for long-term-care backup. This resulted in the Connecticut Department of Mental Health and Yale University jointly planning the Connecticut Mental Health Institute for research and training, with clinical service only to provide material for these main functions; a planning grant was awarded. This operated traditionally under the Department of Psychiatry of the Yale School of Medicine, based on the model of the Massachusetts Mental Health Center, which had a history of excellent support and protection by the state of Massachusetts while serving as a major research and training site for the Department of Psychiatry at Harvard. The NIMH changed its model and the 1963 federal CMHC Act mandated a clinical

A Sampling of Community Mental Health Programs   113

program. In 1963, a $3.24 million state and federal construction grant funded the CtMHC only for research.

The department (possibly its chairman, Frederick Redlich, and Max Pepper) decided to seek federal staffing funds, perhaps to promote research and training, with the state committed to assume funding after federal funding ended. Special state legislation in 1963 provided for unclassified civil service positions for CMH staff, including reimbursement to Yale for faculty services.[312] In 1964, a collaborative agreement between the state and Yale delegated powers from the commissioner of mental health to the director of the CtMHC, the chairman of the board overseeing the MHC, and the Yale faculty. The director was in charge of patient admissions and treatment. CtMHC oversight was via a nine-member board including the Department of Mental Health Commissioner and a Yale psychiatrist (the chairman of the psychiatry department filled this role). The MHC contracted with Yale-New Haven Hospital for food and medical services, and with the Yale powerhouse for steam supply.

Consistent with modeling after the MMHC Gerald Klerman was recruited from that institution as associate professor of psychiatry and clinical director and 1967–1969 director of the CtMHC[313] (though criticized as an interloper).[314] Lazare was chief of the inpatient and day hospital services for the Hill-West Haven part of the catchment area (the only community-oriented inpatient unit in the new CtMHC building), Max Pepper was director of the Community Programs Division, and Astrachan directed a small-group day hospital. The traditional inpatient service was directed by Herrera, and there were a research unit and an emergency service. CtMHC staff consisted of 100 full-time positions, including 40 Yale faculty members working in the MHC. In its first year of operation, the CtMHC cost the state $2 million and Yale University $330,000 to $500,000. The combined state, city, and university funding was not bound to community services, leading to tension between those with community goals and academics with research goals.

Thus the MHC was seen differently: It was exciting, and Klerman encouraged research on the culture of community treatment. Lazare saw it as vigorous: well funded, protected from political interference, and without competition,[315] as Yale was the only medical school in the state at the time. It was also resented as a new force that was not under the control of vested interests.[316]

Simultaneously, the city of New Haven embarked on urban renewal and "human renewal", leading to the creation of the city's urban renewal agency Community Progress, Inc., involving community groups and political alliances and supported by Yale.[317] Goals were vague and methods untested with the goal of bringing care to the previously unreachable, poor and deprived. In contradiction to the city's claims of progress, the agency and the university were seen as intimidating, repressing any questioning, and violating the traditional social order.[318] Transgressors were excluded from the Yale medical community; this being the only academic community in town, this meant leaving town.

This led to increasing struggle for institutional control and the target population reaching for more attention and influence. At stake were decisions on service policy; program evaluation; and staff hiring, credentials, and advancement. This in turn inflamed conflict between the community and the CtMHC. In 1968, the Hill Parents Association objected to the displacement of families by a planned expansion of the Yale Medical Center involving $50 million.[319] Blacks, Puerto Ricans, and welfare recipients objected to discriminatory treatment at the Yale-New Haven Hospital. In April 1968, Yale president Kingman Brewster declared Yale's concern with and active involvement in New Haven community social problems, leading to increased hiring of community residents; a Yale Council on Community Affairs including community participants; funds for the Black Coalition; youth summer jobs; requesting student, faculty, and staff make efforts against white racism; an increase in black students and faculty; and a black curriculum. The Hill Parent Association was ungrateful, suspicious, and hostile, while the Black Coalition was appreciative and trusting.

There was ongoing tension—shared by all ideologies—between the state's interest in providing service and the university's emphasis on research and training. Redlich was a respected social psychiatry researcher, supported social psychiatry and the CtMHC, and was its first director,[320] though Lazare recalls that he was never seen in the MHC, and there were snide remarks that he was valued for his ability to get support for the school from the black population.[321] Social psychiatry in the department included the social psychologist Kenneth Kenniston and other social scientists.[322] Fleck, a psychoanalyst, was interested in social psychiatry and, as chief of psychiatry at the Yale-New Haven Medical Center, was competitive with the CtMHC. Biological psychiatry, stronger in the CtMHC than in the department, wanted basic research, training, and epidemiology and was thriving by avoiding politics.[323]

Social psychiatry wanted social change. There were many separate, competitive individuals and interest groups. Their activist wing included Nagler, Max Pepper (who was seen to want to change the world and academia through a research laboratory and institutional structure[324] and stayed only two years), Leo Fechtenbaum (a social worker friend of Pepper's); Lazare thought these were true revolutionaries. He saw William Ryan as the quiet, scholarly, intellectual energizer of the revolutionaries, and Ryan's wife was a community organizer.[325] He thought that this wing mistrusted Klerman and the leadership as not interested in CMH but in psychopharmacology or empire building. Another wing comprised those interested in clinical and epidemiological issues: Redlich, Klerman, Claude Thomas, and Astrachan were interested in small group and institutions. Redlich and Astrachan's compromise for the Department and CtMHC was to deliver high-quality clinical services to underserved populations and not the "asinine" idealistic theory of preventive mental health, activism, and social change.[326] Lazare thought large community goals were "crap"; many modest goals were practical; the basis was science and not politics. Interestingly, there was a Department of Social Psychiatry in the Department of Psychiatry, including Jules Coleman and others, but it was not associated with the CtMHC.

O'Connor reported that when the CtMHC opened in 1967, first-year psychiatry residency training partly took place there, and residency positions increased from 42 to 60.[327] In addition, social work and psychology trainees doubled, and occupational therapy and community psychiatry fellows were newly added. An MPH program in administrative psychiatry was begun. Psychiatric residency training at the CtMHC was clinical and not community oriented, and faculty such as Pepper and Ryan were irrelevant to residency training.[328] There was an unfilled hunger for conceptual education in CMH, but Yale's interest in social and community psychiatry was academic and not clinical.

An exception was Richard Almond, a graduate of Yale College and Medical School, a psychiatry resident with the strongest interest in social psychiatry.[329] His medical school thesis was on the culture of community treatment in a general hospital. He became chief resident in the CtMHC day hospital under Astrachan and did research on community treatment under Kenniston, resulting in published papers and a book.

In this ideological, mix Lazare saw people appointed on the basis of seniority or power rather than belief, and they had to assume the ideology of the job.[330] For instance, Klerman was an efficient administrator at MMHC under Elvin Semrad but had to become a community visionary when appointed as clinical director and then director of the CtMHC. When Redlich left the chairmanship of the department and directorship of the CtMHC, his personal deals and resultant inequities were revealed. This resulted in a series of power and personnel shifts, senior staff battles, junior staff demoralization, and many staff departures (Lazare himself served only from July 1967 to June 1968). Thomas Detre was seen as aloof, antipsychoanalytic, devoted to biological psychiatry, and administratively efficient in gaining a full professorship and a new unit at the CtMHC. The CtMHC staff resented decisions not in the interests of patients, staff, or CMH ideology. Theodore Lidz succeeded Redlich but quit after one year.

Then the development of CMH in psychiatry, federal policy, and the Community Mental Health Centers Act pressured CMHCs toward treatment, mental illness prevention, and social change. The Yale program was not prepared for the massive amount of self-referral, the community involvement through demands for relevant service, and the resultant internal dissention. The CtMHC leadership was tempted to change its name to "Institute" to emphasize research and training as opposed to

116 *A Sampling of Community Mental Health Programs*

the federal mission definition. In the end, it kept its original name but identified one unit as having service responsibility for one segment of the catchment area to satisfy the community, with the hope that other CMHCs would provide the bulk of service. It applied for a staffing grant for this unit and planned to use it and its service population for research and training.

The catchment area subpopulation chosen for CMH work was called the Hill-West Haven community, and the CtMHC unit designated to serve it was named the Hill-West Haven Mental Health Center (HWHMHC). The Hill area was a black ghetto and the West Haven area middle-class Italian.[331] The Hill area had many social needs, few services or benefits from urban renewal, and impacted by Yale and its medical center expansion.[332] For instance, Yale refused to house the families dispossessed by the riots of the summer of 1967.

The resultant increase in the size and resources of the Department of Psychiatry aggravated the conflicts. A psychoanalytic group (with some social interests) dominated the faculty and opposed the CtMHC. It saw community action as social engineering, too political, and inappropriate to a treatment institution. Senior faculty members rarely involved themselves in the CtMHC, while junior members joined it and explored techniques for providing services for the community population. There was a renaissance of biological psychiatry with an interest in research in the CtMHC. There were factions among state facilities, too: State hospitals sought training from the CtMHC for inpatient treatment, while community-based services were interested in the HWHMHC and wanted citizen participation and the elimination of state hospitals.

The community organization-oriented staff group, interested in change in the social environment and increase in community self-esteem, were younger, had no department tradition, and carried less prestige. They were opposed to wasting resources and staff on individual treatment. William Ryan was an example of this group. He thought his career path was characteristic of psychologists sharing his ideology:[333] He was trained in clinical psychology and practiced it. He migrated into indirect service via mental health consultation and thence to ever-broader concerns. He was a Yale employee, considered well trained and respected, on the staff of the HWHMHC, worked with school issues and improving mothering skills, studied the relationship between mental health and social action in the community, and put this knowledge into action.[334] Powledge saw him and his wife as civil rights activists and early organizers and spokespersons for activists and considered them dangerous.[335] Klerman, as CtMHC director, was talked into establishing the Community Activities Division with no clinical responsibilities, mostly staffed with community workers, with the goal of strengthening the mental health of neighborhoods. This division organized the New Haven Welfare Rights Group, which was successful and notorious—including Ryan leading it on Feb. 5, 1967 in a march on and sit-in at the Welfare Department to assert its rights (part of Saul Alinsky's welfare rights movement), for which they were arrested. Such activities got Ryan into trouble with the state and local government establishments and the police, and his promised academic promotion was much delayed. He also helped organize a white, liberal support group (with mostly black leaders) opposing a repressive city government, whose phones were tapped, marijuana was planted on them, and they were jailed. He also participated in a civil rights suit against the city. Eventually, the state budget for the CtMHC excluded funding for the Community Action Division. Yale had a close relationship with the city of New Haven, and two-thirds of the psychiatry department budget was paid out of state funds. It did not like these relationships upset. Klerman, too, thought some of these social actions were vain and self-defeating and a betrayal of the CtMHC administration: the welfare sit-in took place while Klerman was defending the CtMHC budget and resulted in its being decreased by $1 million.

Ryan thought Frederick Redlich, chairman of the Department of Psychiatry, had a reputation as a social psychiatrist and was supportive of CMH but disapproved of social action because too little was known about it. He was also much taken up with his rising administrative responsibilities as chairman, then dean of the Medical School, and finally university provost for medical affairs. He saw Theodore Lidz as interested and open but uncommitted. He thought Gerald Klerman was supportive, curious, and willing to deal with problems: he supported the staff in legal trouble and resisted a visit from the city urban renewal department demanding that the Community Activities Division stop its activities. Ryan thought the department of psychiatry had little interest in CMH, which was practiced by newly recruited staff at the CtMHC such as Klerman. When Klerman left, Aaron Lazare came from the MGH to replace him but hated the petty bickering, did not respect the department staff, and returned to the MGH after a year.

The CtMHC comprised eight autonomous units with varying ideologies. Since there was not strong central administration the units were free to disagree in theory and practice. All agreed on the use of medication for psychosis, the delivery of services to all community residents, and the development of multiple disciplines to deliver treatment. All were unimodal in treatment delivered except the HWHMHC, which was multimodal. Unexpectedly, great demands for service elicited different responses from different ideological groups: Psychoanalysts demanded more staff, while community psychiatry recommended intake and crisis treatment. Social action advocates called for the abolition of outmoded treatment methods, the involvement of paraprofessional therapists, and redressing the root social conditions.

Astrachan estimated that the CtMHC operation was a central part (60%) of the department of psychiatry.[336] In fact, the department chairman, Redlich, had his office in the CtMHC.[337] For the first few years, the psychoanalytic group was hostile, a majority of the staff were "outsiders", and the CtMHC was isolated. Theodore Lidz succeeded to the chairmanship of the Department of Psychiatry but for one year only. Astrachan saw him as an ideologue and purist who was critical of CMH. This resulted in his conflict with Klerman over resources and theory.

In August 1967 there were riots in the Hill area. Social outbursts were seen as alien in source and mutual hostility. The social action and CMH staff, concentrated in the HWHMHC, joined the community in demanding relevant services, a change in hiring practices, and community control. Lazare thought this group welcomed this social action to implement CMH by addressing the social causes of mental illness, though their program of redress was unclear.[338] Their research seemed more intellectual than clinical. Paradoxically, Pepper's group was located in the CtMHC, with the state police control headquarters on the next floor. Another socially minded group was the American Independent Movement, led by Yale sociologist Robert Cook, which distrusted and opposed city government and offered radical solutions.[339] The Coalition of Concerned Citizens was white, less radical, and concerned about injustices and inequalities in the city, discrimination, civic nonparticipation by minorities, police harassment, and the city administration's acceptance of the current situation. Klerman tried to stay neutral—slightly more community oriented than the department and criticized by the community.

This fed tension and conflict in the MHC and the Department of Psychiatry. There was also conflict among the CtMHC, the State Department of Mental Health, and the state Department of Welfare over lack of cooperation, help, and confidentiality regarding such social activism as the "Welfare Moms" group. Eventually, the State Department of Mental Health and the Yale Department of Psychiatry asserted stricter controls over social action projects. This led to a reorganization of the CtMHC, separating community activities from all other units, and the major orientation to service delivery. The department's psychoanalytic group was outraged that none of the CtMHC directors was an analyst. There were concerns over the lack of resources allocated for the Community Activities Division and the degree of the psychiatry department's commitment and authority. Other areas of conflict between the CtMHC and department chiefs included the content, quality, and control of the training of psychiatry residents; the treatment of deprived populations; training of mental health workers in short-term treatment skills; the loss of middle-class patients in long-term treatment for purposes of training and research; fear of rejection of traditional training; and federal policy and funds for community approaches.

Klerman tried to encompass both wings of the CtMHC and Psychiatry Department axis at the same time that he was sympathetic to the social action agenda:[340]

> [T]echniques such as consultation with the schools, leadership training for neighborhood people, training for residents and field workers, and development of a welfare rights organization . . . supplement the usual community mental health services . . . It became clear that direct clinical service can only meet a fraction of the need. Consequently, increasing efforts are now being devoted to preventive and community work . . . the formation of a community services committee . . . for all health services, for educational improvement, and for community organization . . . I am increasingly impressed by the far-reaching impact of this approach as compared to clinical services which are not specifically geared to the individual neighborhood and community . . . in her neighborhood context against the background of ethnic struggles, urban renewal, and community change . . . has also brought greater awareness of the gulf which often exists between professional and client in their background and attitudes.

He talked of preventive intervention via an emergency treatment unit delivered by nurses' aides and nonprofessionals taught and advised by mental health professionals; consultation to enable community groups and institutions to be more effective in participating in community services; sensitivity groups for contending parties; "There is need for greater community participation in advisory boards and decision-making bodies of mental health centers . . . to provide a mechanism for communication with neighborhood groups, particularly the inner city ghettos . . . a useful feedback . . . from the recipients of its services . . . need to add representatives from the black and Puerto Rican communities".[341]; changes in professional training and hiring practices; and adaptation of mental health service attitudes toward patients, foci, and practices to the ghetto population.

In an understatement, Klerman recognized that "The community mental health center's involvement with community activities and social issues causes serious concern to many of our colleagues".[342] The academics saw him as a nice guy but not strong enough as an administrator and allowing the radicals to give the department a bad name. The Department of Psychiatry ordered him to tighten control over the Community Activities Division.

In 1969, Redlich moved from department chairman to medical school dean, and Morton Reiser succeeded to the chairmanship of the Department of Psychiatry. As part of a revamping of the CMH program, he told Klerman to resign so that Reiser became department chairman and director of the CtMHC.[343] Klerman refused to resign, since he had tenure and was promoted by the senior department members (Lidz, Fleck, etc.).[344] He remembers being rescued from this difficult situation by Leon Eisenberg, then chairman of the Department of Psychiatry at the MGH, with an appointment as director of the Erich Lindemann Mental Health Center. Astrachan, Yale trained and an assistant professor, was trusted as a clinician and administrator by Redlich and Stephen Fleck and was the only CtMHC staff member trusted to attend senor faculty planning meetings. He succeeded to the directorship of the CtMHC. Lazare thought he was a good administrator, shrewd in balancing competing interests and seeing to it that the community work was independent of community pressures; Reiser left the CtMHC to him.[345] The University considered dropping its affiliation with the state except for research. All but Reiser and Astrachan voted to give the CtMHC back to the state.

Ultimately, the new department chairman and CtMHC director reaffirmed this affiliation and its associated responsibility for service to the underserved, accountability to the state, and CtMHC training in community and clinical psychiatry. The Community Activities Division became the Training and Consultation Division. The social activists left—some voluntarily, some because of eroded support, and some because of blocked ambition. In Astrachan's view, clinical and epidemiological factions, in a powerful alliance with the biological psychiatry group, reshaped the CtMHC, guided by social and biological reality. He thought Klerman failed to bridge psychological, social, and biological perspectives because this required an outsider to articulate a path and then be succeeded by an insider.

Astrachan saw new institutions playing out and failing due to the same conflicts that plagued the old institutions they replaced. The resolution for the CtMHC was clinical study and training subscribed to by psychological, biological, and social psychiatry. He saw the CtMHC strong and stable with investment by psychoanalytic and biological groups, the social group absent, and strong individuals and ideologies faded or gone.

In this case, there was no dedicated, powerful CMH champion, that there was no rapprochement between CMH and academic psychiatry. Resolution was brought by the ultimate exclusion of activist CMH and the activists dedicated to it.

Summary

Violation of tradition, novelty, change, and endangerment to vested interests and security generally provoke discomfort, hostility, resistance, and counteraction.

> The vast majority of human beings dislike and even dread all notions with which they are not familiar. Hence it comes about that at their

first appearance innovators have always been derided as fools and madmen.

Aldous Huxley

Of course, curiosity, stimulation, and enthusiasm also occur. The choice must depend on the existence of openness and a sense of security.

In addition, these examples repeatedly demonstrate the influence of environmental conditions: a general ideology consonant with the innovations, the availability of material resources to support the innovation and to seduce those not convinced, and dedicated champions with significant power via position and respect. These examples also illustrate the innovation's vulnerability to loss of resources and leadership and to the evolution of the cycle of ideology so that it is anachronistic.

It is noteworthy that the value and effectiveness of the innovation is only one among these many factors influencing acceptance and endurance.

In the field under exploration, academia is a formidable, historically entrenched contender.[346]

> [M]any of the most important changes that have taken place in the University have been pushed through in the face of indifference or even opposition on the part of the faculty ... A president who always defers to the Faculty will just as surely condemn the University to sluggish conservatism.

Figure 1.1 Hugo Biehl, M.D., Meiner, Ph.D., Jung, Ph.D., research staff, Zentralinstitut für Seelisches Gesundheit, Mannheim, West Germany [courtesy David G. Satin]

122 *A Sampling of Community Mental Health Programs*

Figure 1.2 Wofgang Bolm, M.D. (psychiatrist), Ingmar Steinhart (psychologist), Irmeli Rotha (social worker), Social Psychiatry Department, Freie Universität Berlin [courtesy David G. Satin]

Figure 1.3 Hartmut Dziewas, M.D., Prof. of Social Psychiatry, University of Hamburg, new director, Im Schlosspark Klinik [courtesy David G. Satin]

A Sampling of Community Mental Health Programs 123

Figure 1.4 Heinz Häfner, Direktor and E. Schramek., secretary, Zentralinstitut für Seelisches Gesundheit, Mannheim, W. Germany [courtesy David G. Satin]

Figure 1.5 Alfred Kraus, Dept. of Psychiatry, phenomenologist, University of Heidelberg, W. Germany [courtesy David G. Satin]

124   *A Sampling of Community Mental Health Programs*

Figure 1.6 Prof. Christoph Mundt, Direktor, Psychiatrische Polyklinik; and Prof. Werner Janzarik, Professor (Chairman) Psychiatry, University of Heidelberg [courtesy David G. Satin]

Figure 1.7 Walter Ritter von Baeyer, Heidelberg University [courtesy David G. Satin]

A Sampling of Community Mental Health Programs 125

Figure 1.8 Hartmut Schneider, director, Social Psychiatry Unit. Zentralinstitut für Seelisches Gesundheit, Mannheim, West Germany [courtesy David G. Satin]

Figure 1.9 Caspar Kulenkampff and Ulrich Hoffmann, Aktion Psychisch Kranke, Bonn, W. Germany [courtesy David G. Satin]

Figure 1.10 Frau Dr. Christa Meyn, German Federal Ministerium Jugend-Familie-Gesundheit, Bonn [courtesy David G. Satin]

126 *A Sampling of Community Mental Health Programs*

Figure 1.11 Niels and Britta Pörksen, 1988 [courtesy Lindemann Estate]

A Sampling of Community Mental Health Programs 127

Notes

1. Duhl, Leonard J., M.D., Department of Public Health, University of California—San Francisco and Department of Psychiatry, University of California—Berkeley; interviewed by telephone at the University of California—Berkeley by David G. Satin, 4/2/1979, 8/16/2007. [Caddy 2, Box 4, X, Lindemann Collection, Center for the History of Medicine, Francis A. Countway Library of Medicine, Boston, MA]
2. Ewalt, Jack R., "The Birth of the Community Mental Health Movement", Ch. 2 in Barton, Walter E. and Sanborn, Charlotte J. (eds.) *An Assessment of the Community Mental Health Movement* (Lexington, MA: Lexington Books, 1977)
3. "Third Conference of the Group for Discussion of Problems in Community Mental Health Research; Wellesley Inn, Wellesley, MA, 11/30–12/2/1951". [folder "Group for Discussion of Problems in Community Mental Health Res. Dec. 1951 MS", Box V 4–8, Erich Lindemann Collection, Center for the History of Medicine, Countway Library of Medicine, Boston, MA]
4. DeSole, Daniel, Singer, Philip and Swietnicki, Edward, "A Project that Failed", Ch. VIII in Duhl, Leonard J. and Leopold, Robert L. (eds.) *Mental Health and Urban Social Policy* (San Francisco: Jossey-Bass, 1968)
5. Bernard, Viola W., Chief, Division of CMH, College of Physicians & Surgeons, Columbia University: CMHCs, studies by the Standing Committee on Community Psychiatry and Psychoanalysis of the American Pschoanalytic Association Study Group. Interviewed by David G. Satin at her home in New York City, 4/26/1979. [Caddy 1, Box 4, X, Lindemann Collection, Center for the History of Medicine, Francis A. Countway Library of Medicine, Boston, MA]
6. Lindemann, Erich, Consultation Training Seminar, Mental health Unit, San Mateo County Health Department, California, 3/17/1970. [Caddy 1, Box 4, X, Erich Lindemann Collection, Center for the History of Medicine, Francis A. Countway Library of Medicine, Harvard Medical Area, Boston, MA]
7. von Felsinger, John M., Ph.D., interview by David G. Satin at McGuinn Hall, Boston College, 9/8/1978. [Caddy 2, Box 4, X, Lindemann Collection, Center for the History of Medicine, Francis A. Countway Library of Medicine, Boston, MA]
8. Lindemann, Erich, 3/17/1970, *ibid*
9. Undated Manuscript. [folder "Boston College—Administration", Box IV 3+4+5, Erich Lindemann Collection, Center for the History of Medicine, Francis A. Countway Library of Medicine, Boston, MA]
10. von Felsinger, John M., letter to Erich Lindemann, 11/22/1967. [folder "Correspondence Boston College", Box IV 3+4+5, Erich Lindemann Collection, Center for the History of Medicine, Francis A. Countway Library of Medicine, Boston, MA]
11. Lindemann, Elizabeth B., interview at her home in Wellesley, MA by David G. Satin, 1/18/1980. [Caddy 4, Box 4, X, Lindemann Collection, Center for the History of Medicine, Francis A. Countway Library of Medicine, Boston, MA]
12. Ryan, William, interview by David G. Satin in Ryan's office at Boston College, 12/14/1979. [Caddy 5, Box 5, X, Lindemann Collection, Center for the History of Medicine, Francis A. Countway Library of Medicine, Boston, MA]
13. Lindemann, Erich, letter to David A. Hamburg, 3/19/1968. [folder "Correspondence—David Hamburg", Box IV 1+2, Erich Lindemann Collection, Center for the History of Medicine, Countway Library of Medicine, Boston, MA]

14. Lindemann, Erich, letter to Hazard, Sprague W., M.D., [chairman] Mental Health Planning Committee of Metropolitan Boston, 3/19/1968. [folder "Correspondence 1968", Box IV 1+2, Erich Lindemann Collection, Center for the History of Medicine, Countway Library of Medicine, Boston, MA]
15. von Felsinger, John M., 9/8/1978, *ibid*
16. Tentative Field Projects, undated. [folder "Boston College—Administration", Box IV 3+4+5, Erich Lindemann Collection, Center for the History of Medicine, Francis A. Countway Library of Medicine, Boston, MA]
17. Lindemann, Erich, 3/19/1968, *ibid*
18. Lindemann, Erich, letter to the Danforth Foundation in pursuit of a Kent Fellowship for Carol Proudfoot, undated (possibly 12/1968). [folder "Correspondence Boston College", Box IV 3+4+5, Erich Lindemann Collection, Center for the History of Medicine, Francis A. Countway Library of Medicine, Boston, MA]
19. Psychology Department Open Faculty Meeting, 11/5/1968. [folder "Boston College—Administration", Box IV 3+4+5, Erich Lindemann Collection, Center for the History of Medicine, Francis A. Countway Library of Medicine, Boston, MA]
20. Psychology Department Open Faculty Meeting, 11/19/1968. [folder "Boston College—Administration", Box IV 3+4+5, Erich Lindemann Collection, Center for the History of Medicine, Francis A. Countway Library of Medicine, Boston, MA]
21. Joint Community-University Center for Inner-City Chane sponsored by Boson College and Urban League, undated. [folder "B.C. Center for Inner City Change", Box IV 3+4+5, Erich Lindemann Collection, Center for the History of Medicine, Francis A. Countway Library of Medicine, Boston, MA]
22. Lindemann, Erich, "Institutional Crises", Talk to San Mateo County, CA Mental Health Services Course Taught by Dr. Clarice Haylett [MH dir.]; notes by Dr. Haylett, edited by EBL, 3/17/1970. [folder Box XII 2 "Lindemann Reflections on Community Mental Health, March '70", Erich Lindemann Collection, Center for the History of Medicine, Francis A. Countway Library of Medicine, Boston, MA]
23. Lindemann, Elizabeth B., 1/18/1980, *ibid*
24. Lindemann, Erich, letter to Torey, Dr. Fuller, Stanford University Medical Center, 2/22/1969. [folder "Correspondence 1969", Box IV 1+2, Erich Lindemann Collection, Center for the History of Medicine, Countway Library of Medicine, Boston, MA]
25. Lindemann, Erich, letter to Golde, Dr. Peggy, Assistant Professor of Psychiatry, Stanford Medical Center, 3/29/1969. [folder "Correspondence 1969", Box IV 1+2, Erich Lindemann Collection, Center for the History of Medicine, Countway Library of Medicine, Boston, MA]
26. Lindemann, Erich, "Institutional Crises", pp. 3–5—talk to San Mateo County California Mental Health Services Course Taught by Dr. Clarise Haylett (Director); notes by Dr. Haylett, edited by Elizabeth B. Lindemann. [Box XII 2 folder "Lindemann Reflections on Community Mental Health, March '70", Erich Lindemann Collection, Center for the History of Medicine, Francis A. Countway Library of Medicine, Boston, MA]
27. Lindemann, Elizabeth B., 1/18/1980, *ibid*
28. Lindemann, Erich, letter addressed to Ryan, William, Chairman, Department of Psychology, Boston College, 11/11/1971. [folder "Correspondence—1971", Box IV 1+2, Erich Lindemann Collection, Center for the History of Medicine, Countway Library of Medicine, Boston, MA]

A Sampling of Community Mental Health Programs   129

29. Ed, San Fernando Valley State College, Northbridge, CA, letter to Lindemann, Erich, undated. [folder "Correspondence—1970", Box IV 1 + 2, Erich Lindemann Collection, Center for the History of Medicine, Francis A. Countway Library of Medicine, Boston, MA]
30. Lindemann, Elizabeth, Brainerd, 4/20/2004 telephone interview with David G. Satin. [David G. Satin files, Newton, MA]
31. Malamud, William I. (jr.), interviews by David G. Satin at the Solomon Carter Fuller Mental Health Center, 12/15/1980, 2/2/1981. [Box XIII Erich Lindemann Collection, Center for the History of Medicine, Francis A. Countway Library of Medicine, Harvard Medical Area, Boston, MA]
32. *The Boston Globe*, 3/16/1993 p. 21
33. Bandler, Bernard, interview by David G. Satin, 8/11/1978. [Erich Lindemann Collection, Center for the History of Medicine, Francis A. Countway Library of Medicine, Harvard Medical Area, Boston, MA]
34. Lindemann, Elizabeth B., interviews by David G. Satin 6/27/1978–10/4/1979
35. Bandler, Bernard, interview by David G. Satin at his office at 250 Beacon Street, Boston, MA, home in Swampscott, MA, 11/16/1978. [Box XIII, Erich Lindemann Collection, Center for the History of Medicine, Francis A. Countway Library of Medicine, Harvard Medical Area, Boston, MA]
36. Malamud, William I., 1980, 1981, *ibid*
37. Cohen, Sanford I., interview by David G. Satin, 12/1/1978. [Box XIII, Erich Lindemann Collection, Center for the History of Medicine, Francis A. Countway Library of Medicine, Harvard Medical Area, Boston, MA]
38. Cohen, Sanford I., 12/1/1978, *ibid*
39. Malamud, William I., 1980, 1981, *ibid*
40. Knapp, Peter H., interview by David G. Satin at the Solomon Carter Fuller Mental Health Center, 6/12/1981. It is noteworthy that in the interview, Knapp was unenthusiastic, barely polite, and allowed many phone interruptions. [Box XIII, Erich Lindemann Collection, Center for the History of Medicine, Francis A. Countway Library of Medicine, Harvard Medical Area, Boston, MA]
41. Myereson, Paul, M.D.l, Chairman of the Department of Psychiatry at Tufts Medical School. Interview at Dr. Myerson's home in Newton, MA by David G. Satin, 6/19/1981. [Box XIII, Erich Lindemann Collection, Center for the History of Medicine, Francis A. Countway Library of Medicine, Harvard Medical Area, Boston, MA]
42. Foley, Archie R., *Challenge to Community Psychiatry* (New York: Behavioral Publications, 1972)
43. Foley, Archie R., 1972, *ibid*, Ch. 6. The Evaluation, p. 123
44. Foley, Archie R., 1972, *ibid*, Ch. 6. The Evaluation, p. 656
45. Foley, Archie R., 1972, *ibid*, Ch. 5. The Aftermath: Faculty Process, Faculty Power, and Democracy", p. 101
46. Foley, Archie R., 1972, *ibid*, Ch. 5. The Aftermath: Faculty Process, Faculty Power, and Democracy", p. 101
47. Batson, Ruth, interview by David G. Satin at Massachusetts General Hospital, 1/5/1979. [Box XIII, Erich Lindemann Collection, Center for the History of Medicine, Francis A. Countway Library of Medicine, Harvard Medical Area, Boston, MA]
48. Cohen, Sanford I., M.D., interview by David G. Satin, 6/29/1978. [Box XIII, Erich Lindemann Collection, Center for the History of Medicine, Francis A. Countway Library of Medicine, Harvard Medical Area, Boston, MA]
49. Bandler, Bernard, 11/16/1978, *ibid*
50. Bandler, Bernard, Acting Director of the Division of Manpower and Training Programs at the National Institute of Mental Health, "Psychiatric Training

130 A Sampling of Community Mental Health Programs

and the Role of Psychiatry in Comprehensive Health and Human Services", in *Selected Papers on Mental Health Manpower and Training*, David C. Wilson Lecture, University of Virginia, 4/23/1971, Charlottesville, Virginia (Rockville, MD: U.S. Department of Health, Education, and Welfare, Public Health Service, Health Services and Mental Health Administration); to be published in Proceedings of the Inter-University Forum for Educators in Community Psychiatry.

51. *The Boston Globe*, 3/16/1993, p. 21
52. Knapp, Peter H., 6/12/1981, *ibid*
53. Knapp, Peter H., 6/12/1981, *ibid*
54. Malamud, William I., 1980, 1981, *ibid*
55. Cohen, Sanford I., 12/1/1978, *ibid*
56. Cohen, Sanford I., 12/1/1978, *ibid*
57. Batson, Ruth, 1/5/1979, *ibid*
58. Batson, Ruth, 1/5/1979, *ibid*
59. Cohen, Sanford I., 12/1/1978, *ibid*
60. Malamud, William I., 1980, 1981, *ibid*
61. Malamud, William I., 1980, 1981, *ibid*
62. Randolph, Peter, M.D., Superintendent and Area Director of the Tufts-Bay Cover Mental Health Center. Interview by David G. Satin at the Tufts-Bay Cove Mental Health Center, 6/26/1981. [Box XIII, Erich Lindemann Collection, Center for the History of Medicine, Francis A. Countway Library of Medicine, Harvard Medical Area, Boston, MA]
63. Bandler, Bernard, interview by David G. Satin at his summer home in Swampscott, MA, 8/11/1978. [Box XIII, Erich Lindemann Collection, Center for the History of Medicine, Francis A. Countway Library of Medicine, Harvard Medical Area, Boston, MA]
64. Cohen, Sanford I., 12/1/1978, *ibid*
65. Batson, Ruth, 1/5/1979, *ibid*
66. Bandler, Bernard, "The Reciprocal Roles of the University and the Community in the Development of Community Mental Health Centers", in Atkins, Robert W. (ed.) *How the University Can Aid Community Mental Health*, Proceedings of the Scientific Conference, 9/1969, Community Mental Health Center Division of the University of Rochester School of Medicine.
67. Cohen, Sanford I., 6/29/1978, *ibid*
68. Cohen, Sanford I., 12/1/1978, *ibid*
69. Shader, Richard, M.D., Chairman of the Department of Psychiatry at Tufts Medical School, interviewed at the Tufts Department of Psychiatry by David G. Satin, 1/29/1982. [Box XIII, Erich Lindemann Collection, Center for the History of Medicine, Francis A. Countway Library of Medicine, Harvard Medical Area, Boston, MA]
70. Batson, Ruth, 1/5/1979, *ibid*
71. Knapp, Peter H., 6/12/1981, *ibid*
72. Bernard, Viola W., 4/26/1979, *ibid*
73. Batson, Ruth, 1/5/1979, *ibid*
74. Bernard, Viola W., 4/26/1979, *ibid*
75. Dohrenwend, Bruce P., "Columbia—Washington Heights Community Mental Health Project; Urban Relocation: A 'Natural Experiment' in the Cultural, Social and Psychological Sources of Adaptive and Maladaptive Responses to Stress; Design for Part I of the Study", manuscript, 5/1958. [folder "NIMH", Box III A6, Erich Lindemann Collection, Center for the History of Medicine, Francis A. Countway Library of Medicine, Harvard Medical Area, Boston, MA]

A Sampling of Community Mental Health Programs 131

76. Dohrenwend, Bruce P., Mental Health Project, Columbia University, 722 West 168th Street, New York, 32, NY, 5/1958. [folder "Columbia-Washington Heights Community Mental Health Project", Box IIIA6 Da GAP, Erich Lindemann Collection, Center for the History of Medicine, Francis A. Countway Library of Medicine, Boston, MA]
77. Kolb, Lawrence C., Bernard, Viola W. and Dohrenwend, Bruce P., *Urban Challenges to Psychiatry: The Case History of a Response* (Boston: Little Brown, 1969)
78. Bernard, Viola W., 4/26/1979, *ibid*
79. Kolb, Lawrence C., Bernard, Viola W., Trussell, Ray E., Bernard, N.W., Dohrenwendt, Bruce P., Kohlsaat, Barbara and Weiss, Robert, "Limitations of Medical Traditions on Community Mental Health Traditions", *American Journal of Psychiatry* 117 no. 11:972–979 (May 1961)
80. Kolb, Lawrence C., Bernard, Viola W. and Dohrenwend, Bruce P., 1969, *ibid*, p. xvi
81. Kolb, Lawrence C., Bernard, Viola W. and Dohrenwend, Bruce P., 1969, *ibid*, pp. 130–131
82. Bernard, Viola W., Chief of the Division of Community Mental Health, College of Physicians and Surgeons, Columbia University, interviewed at her home by David G. Satin, 4/26/1979. [Box XIII, Erich Lindemann Collection, Center for the History of Medicine, Francis A. Countway Library of Medicine, Harvard Medical Area, Boston, MA]
    [videotape, Erich Lindemann Collection, Center for the History of Medicine, Francis A. Countway Library of Medicine, Harvard Medical Area, Boston, MA]
83. Bandler, Bernard, 11/16/1978, *ibid*
84. Abrams, Rochard M., "Associate Professor of History, University of California—Berkeley: When the Tough Get Going", *Psychiatry and Social Science Review* 2 no. 7:13–15 (7/1968); part of a volume on student political activity at Columbia University.
85. Liebert, Robert S., M.D., "Psychiatric Consultant to the Columbia College Counseling Service: Plantation Politics", *Psychiatry and Social Science Review* 2 no. 7:19–21 (7/1968).
86. Bernard, Viola W., 4/26/1979, *ibid*
87. Merrifield, John F., M.D., *Abby's Deal: A History of the Concord, Massachusetts Community Mental Health Center* (Portsmouth, NH: Peter E. Randall, 2006)
88. Merrifield, John F., 2006, *ibid*, p. 11
89. Merrifield, John F., 2006, *ibid*, p. 8
90. White, Robert W., Ph.D., interview in his apartment in Brookline, MA by David G. Satin, 11/24/1978
91. Merrifield, John F., 2006, *ibid*, p. 183
92. Merrifield, John F., 2006, *ibid*, pp. 146–147
93. Merrifield, John F., 2006, *ibid*, pp. 104–105
94. Merrifield, John F., 2006, *ibid*, pp. 102–107
95. Hersch, Charles, interviewed by John Merrifield, 11/15/2007
96. Merrifield, John F., 2006, *ibid*, p. 233
97. Duhl, Leonard J., M.D., Department of Public Health of the University of California—San Francisco, interviewed by telephone at the University of California—Berkeley by David G. Satin, 8/16/1979. [Caddy 2, Box 4, X, Lindemann Collection, Center for the History of Medicine, Francis A. Countway Library of Medicine, Boston, MA]

132 *A Sampling of Community Mental Health Programs*

98. Haylett, Clarice, Division of Mental Health of the San Mateo County Health Department, interview by David G. Satin at her home in Palo Alto, CA, 12/17/1979. [Box 4, X, Lindemann Collection, Center for the History of Medicine, Francis A. Countway Library of Medicine, Boston, MA]
99. Haylett, Clarice, 12/17/1979, *ibid*
100. Blum, Henrik L., telephone interview by David G. Satin, 3/23/1979. [Caddy 1, Box 4, X, Lindemann Collection, Center for the History of Medicine, Francis A. Countway Library of Medicine, Boston, MA]
101. Duhl, Leonard J., 4/2/1979, 8/16/2007, *ibid*
102. Lindemann, Elizabeth, Brainerd, 8/17/2004 telephone interview with David G. Satin. [David G. Satin files, Newton, MA]
103. Rosenbaum, Milton and Zwerling, Israel, "Impact of Social Psychiatry: Effect on a Psychoanalytically Oriented Department of Psychiatry", *Archives of General Psychiatry ll* no. 1:31–39 (1964)
104. Eisenberg, Leon, interviewed at Children's Hospital Medical Center by David G. Satin, 11/27/1978. [Box X, Erich Lindemann Collection, Center for the History of Medicine, Francis A. Countway Library of Medicine, Boston, MA]
105. Frankel, Freddie, interview at the Beth Israel Hospital Department of Psychiatry by David G. Satin, 11/24/1978. [Box X, Erich Lindemann Collection, Center for the History of Medicine, Francis A. Countway Library of Medicine, Boston, MA]
106. Astrachan, Boris, Professor of Psychiatry at the Yale University School of Medicine, and Director of the Connecticut Mental Health Center. Interview by David G. Satin by telephone at his office in the Connecticut Mental Health Center, 7/22/1982. [Box X, Erich Lindemann Collection, Center for the History of Medicine, Francis A. Countway Library of Medicine, Boston, MA]
107. *MGH News 31* no. 3: (3/1972)
108. Klerman, Gerald L., "Klerman Urges Profession to Eschew Social Change", *Psychiatric News*, 9/7/1979, p. 3
109. Klerman, Gerald L., interview by David G. Satin at the Institute of Medicine, Washington, DC, 1/26/1979. [Box X, Erich Lindemann Collection, Center for the History of Medicine, Francis A. Countway Library of Medicine, Boston, MA]
110. Dedication of the Erich Lindemann Mental Health Center, ELMHC Auditorium, 9/22/1971. [audio tape in the personal collection of Elizabeth B. Lindemann]
111. Affiliation Agreement between the Psychiatric Service of the MGH and the Erich Lindemann Mental Health Center Harbor Area Board, draft 9/25/1978. [Erich Lindemann Collection, Center for the History of Medicine, Francis A. Countway Library of Medicine, Boston, MA]
112. Kay, Jane Holtz, "New Lindemann Center: A Review", *Boston Globe*, 9/22/1971; "Erich Lindemann Mental Health Center Fat Sheet", 9/22/1971. [Box XII 1 folder 110b, Erich Lindemann Collection, Center for the History of Medicine, Francis A. Countway Library of Medicine, Boston, MA]
113. Siegel, Alberta, Department of Psychiatry, Stanford Medical Center, interview at Stanford Medical Center by David G. Satin, 12/20/1979. [Caddy 6, Box X, Erich Lindemann Collection, Center for the History of Medicine, Francis A. Countway Library of Medicine, Boston, MA]
114. Duhl, Leonard J., interviewed by phone at the University of California-Berkeley, 4/2/1979, 8/16/2007. [Box X, Erich Lindemann Collection, Center for the History of Medicine, Francis A. Countway Library of Medicine, Boston, MA]

A Sampling of Community Mental Health Programs 133

115. Lindemann, Erich, "Notes on Erich Lindemann's Talk at Lindemann Mental Health Center, April 13, 1971". [Box XII 2 folder "Discussion with Colleagues re Lindemann Mental Health Center April 13, 1971", Erich Lindemann Collection, Center for the History of Medicine, Francis A. Countway Library of Medicine, Boston, MA]
116. Eulau, Cleo, Chief Social, Child Psychiatry Section, Stanford Medical School. Interviewed at the Stanford Medical Center by David G. Satin, 12/19/1979. [Caddy 2, Box 4, X, Lindemann Collection, Center for the History of Medicine, Francis A. Countway Library of Medicine, Boston, MA]
117. Lindemann, Erich, Duhl, Leonard J., an Seeley, John, interview of Lindemann by Duhl at Lindemann's home in Palo Alto, CA, 6/15/74, 6/22/74. [Caddy 4, Tape 3A, 4B; 7, Erich Lindemann Collection, Center for the History of Medicine, Francis A. Countway Library of Medicine, Boston, MA]
118. *Psychiatric News* VI no. 20:29 (10/20/1971). [Box XII 1 folder 110b, Erich Lindemann Collection, Center for the History of Medicine, Francis A. Countway Library of Medicine, Boston, MA]
119. *MGH News* 31 no. 3:6 (3/1972). [Box XII 1 folder 110b, Erich Lindemann Collection, Center for the History of Medicine, Francis A. Countway Library of Medicine, Boston, MA]
120. Box XII 1 folder 110c Lindemann M.H. Center, Erich Lindemann Collection, Center for the History of Medicine, Francis A. Countway Library of Medicine, Boston, MA
121. HARBOR MENTAL HEALTH AND MENTAL RETARDATION AREA ERICH LINDEMANN MENTAL HEALTH CENTER AREA PLAN 1973–1974. . . July, 1973 Revised-August, 1973. [Box XII 1 folder 110c Lindemann M.H. Center, Erich Lindemann Collection, Center for the History of Medicine, Francis A. Countway Library of Medicine, Boston, MA]
122. *Boston Sunday Advertiser*, 5/14/1972
123. *Boston Sunday Advertiser*, 5/14/1972
124. "QUARTER MILLION DOLLAR CHILDREN'S GRANT AWARDED HARBOR AREA", *Harbor Times*, 9/1974
125. Jahnke, Art, "Mad House", *Boston*, 9/1987. [Box XII 1 folder E101, Erich Lindemann Collection, Center for the History of Medicine, Francis A. Countway Library of Medicine, Boston, MA]
126. Klerman, Gerald L., M.D., Superintendent of the ELMHC, letter to Mrs. Erich Lindemann at her home in Wellesley, MA, 2/7/1975. Elizabeth Lindemann remained loyal to the facility named for her husband, the superintendent paid lip service to him and his disease, and the books were soon lost. [Box XII 1 folder 110c Lindemann M.H. Center, Erich Lindemann Collection, Center for the History of Medicine, Francis A. Countway Library of Medicine, Boston, MA]
127. Klerman, Gerald L., letter to Elizabeth B. Lindemann, 12/30/1975. [Box XII 1 folder E101, Erich Lindemann Collection, Center for the History of Medicine, Francis A. Countway Library of Medicine, Boston, MA]
128. Lindemann, Elizabeth B., letter to Gerald Klerman, 1/10/1976. [Box XII 1 folder E101, Erich Lindemann Collection, Center for the History of Medicine, Francis A. Countway Library of Medicine, Boston, MA]
129. Unknown source and date. [Box XII 1 folder 110c Lindemann M.H. Center, Erich Lindemann Collection, Center for the History of Medicine, Francis A. Countway Library of Medicine, Boston, MA]
130. Borus, Jonathan F., M.D. "Community Psychiatry at the MGH", presented at the Colloquium "Psychiatry at the Massachusetts General Hospital" celebrating the Fiftieth Anniversary of the founding of the MGH Psychiatry

134 A Sampling of Community Mental Health Programs

Service, October 13,1984. [file "Borus—Community Psychiatry at MGH 1984", Box XII #3, Lindemann Collection, Center for the History of Medicine, Francis A. Countway Library of Medicine, Harvard Medical School, Boston, MA]

131. Janzarik, Werner, Psychiatrishe Klinik, Universität Heidelberg, West Germany, interview at the Klinik by David G. Satin, 10/29/1984. [Tape 148, Caddy 7, Box X, Erich Lindemann Collection, Center for the History of Medicine, Francis A. Countway Library of Medicine, Boston, MA]
132. von Baeyer, Walter Ritter, former Professor, Psychiatrishe Klinik, Universität Heidelberg, West Germany. Interview by David G. Satin at his office in the University 10/30/1984. [Tape 148, Caddy 7, Box X, Erich Lindemann Collection, Center for the History of Medicine, Francis A. Countway Library of Medicine, Boston, MA]
133. von Baeyer, Walter Ritter, 10/30/1984, *ibid*
134. Pörksen, Niels, Leitende Arzt, Fachbereich Psychiatrie, von Bodelschwinghsche Anstalten Bethel, Serepta und Nazareth, Bielefeld, West Germany: interview by David G. Satin at Pörksen's house, Bielefeld, West Germany, 10/13/1984. [Caddy 7, Tape 11A+12B, Box XI, Lindemann Collection, Center for the History of Medicine, Francis A. Countway Library of Medicine, Boston, MA]
135. Lindemann, Elizabeth B., interviewed by David G. Satin 6/27/1978–10/4/1979. [Erich Lindemann Collection, Center for the History of Medicine, Francis A. Countway Library of Medicine, Boston, MA]
136. Lindemann, Elizabeth B., interview by David G. Satin, 7/14/1978. [Caddy 4, Box 4, X, Lindemann Collection, Center for the History of Medicine, Francis A. Countway Library of Medicine, Boston, MA]
137. Janzarik, Werner, 10/29/1984, *ibid*
138. Lindemann, Elizabeth B., 7/14/1978, *ibid*
139. Lindemann, Erich, 3/19/1968, *ibid*, p. 1
140. Lindemann, Erich (writing from his sick bed at MGH), letter to Caplan, Gerald, 2/22/1969. [folder "Correspondence 1969", Box IV 1+2, Erich Lindemann Collection, Center for the History of Medicine, Countway Library of Medicine, Boston, MA]
141. Folder "Ebert, Dr. Robert", Box IIIA 4 (A-E), Erich Lindemann Collection, Center for the History of Medicine, Francis A. Countway Library of Medicine, Boston, MA.
142. Pörksen, Niels, University of Heidelberg. Interview with Elizabeth and Brenda Lindemann by David G. Satin at Elizabeth Lindemann's house in Wellesley, MA, 9/9/1978. [Caddy 5, Box 5, X, Lindemann Collection, Center for the History of Medicine, Francis A. Countway Library of Medicine, Boston, MA]
143. Pörksen, Niels, "Community Mental Health: The German Experience", Ch. 17 in Rohde, Jon and Wyon, John (eds.) *Community-Based Health Care: Lessons from Bangladesh to Boston* (Boston: Management Sciences for Health, 2002), pp. 301–308.
144. Pörksen, Niels, letter to David Hamburg (head of the department which hosted Lindemann after his retirement from MGH), 7/20/1966, pp. 1–2. [folder "Dr. Pörksen", Box IV 1+2, Erich Lindemann Collection, Center for the History of Medicine, Francis A. Countway Library of Medicine, Boston, MA]
145. Pörksen, Niels, 2002, *ibid*

> "During my one-year [sic] stay at the Laboratory of Community Psychiatry at [sic] Harvard Medical School in 1967–68, I was influenced by the concepts of preventive psychiatry and mental health consultation emerging from the work of Lindemann, Erich, "Mental Health and the

A Sampling of Community Mental Health Programs   135

Environment", in Duhl, Leonard J. (ed.) *The Urban Condition* (New York: Basic Books, 1963), pp. 3–10; and Caplan, Gerald, *Principles of Preventive Psychiatry* (New York: Basic Books, 1964). Caplan's *Principles of Preventive Psychiatry* became our guide".

146. Pörksen, Niels, letter to Erich Lindemann in Brighton, MA, 6/8/1969. [folder "Dr. Pörksen", Box IV 1+2, Erich Lindemann Collection, Center for the History of Medicine, Francis A. Countway Library of Medicine, Boston, MA]
    Dr. Dr. H.[einz] Häffner, Direktor, Universität Heidelberg, Sozialpsychiatrische Klinik. Mannheim, West Germany letter to Erich Lindemann 8/19/1968, p. 1:

    > Herr Dr. Pörksen, der gegenwärtig in Boston ist, hat mir kürzlich geschrieben, dass er sehr interessiert sei, eine Stelle bei uns zu übernehmen, die mit Planung und Koordination beim Aufbau unseres Community Mental Health Centers in Mannheim verknüpft ist . . . Ich wäre Ihnen sehr dankbar, wenn Sie mich gelengentlich wissen lassen könnten, ob Sie ihn empfehlen [recommend] würden. . .

    Lindemann, Erich, letter to Herrn Prof Dr. Haefner, Heidelberg 1/1/1969, p. 2:

    > Noch ein Wort ueber Herrn Pörksen. I mag ihn sehr gern, und betrachtete es als eine der schoensten Folgen meiner Tuebinger Taetigkeit dass er sich fuer unsere Arbeit so interessierte . . . Es wuerde fuer mich schoen sein, die gelegenheit zu haben mit ihm wieder zu arbeiten. Auch wuerde es wohl wichtig fuer ihn sein in einer schon entwickelten sozialpsychiatrischen Abteilung in der Grossstadt seine Kenntnisse und Methoden zu konsolidieren bevor er sein eigenes Program unternimmt. . . . Es waere wirklich schoen wenn er zu Ihnen kommen koennte. . . [folder "Heidelberg", Box IV 1+2, Erich Lindemann Collection, Center for the History of Medicine, Francis A. Countway Library of Medicine, Boston, MA]

147. Fink-Eitel, Dr. letter to Lindemann, Elizabeth B., 12/4/1962, and to Lindemann, Erich 1/17/1963. [folder "Correspondence—Europe 1960–65", Box IIIA5 1), Erich Lindemann Collection, Center for the History of Medicine, Francis A. Countway Library of Medicine, Boston, MA]

148. "GEMEINDEPSYCHIATRIE":

    > Seit dem 1. April 1969 gibt es in der Socialpsychiatrischen Klinik der Universität Heidelberg/Mannhiem eine Arbeitsgruppe 'Gemeindepsychiatrie'. ¶Dieser Arbeitsgruppe gehörten vorerst 7 Mitglieder an und zwar: Dr. Niels Pörksen . . . Dr. Anneliese Spinner . . . Fachärzte für Neurologie und Psychiatrie . . . Dr. Sebastian Drömann . . . Kinderpsychiatrie . . . Dr. Ulrich Rogal . . . Suchtbekämpfung . . . Fräulein Ingrid Rauch . . . Socialarbeiterin . . . Frau Margarete Krzossok . . . Krankenschwester . . . Fräulein Gabriele Koch . . . Sekretärin.

    Undated [folder "Heidelberg", Box IV 1+2, Erich Lindemann Collection, Center for the History of Medicine, Francis A. Countway Library of Medicine, Boston, MA]

149. Pörksen, Niels, with Elizabeth and Brenda Lindemann, interview by David G. Satin at Elizabeth Lindemann's home in Wellesley, MA, 9/9/1978; also Pörksen, Niels, interview in Wellesely, MA by David G. Satin, 9/9/1978. [Caddy 5, Box 5, X, Lindemann Collection, Center for the History of Medicine, Francis A. Countway Library of Medicine, Boston, MA]

150. Pörksen, Niels, 10/13/1984, *ibid*

151. Pörksen, Niels, *Kommunale Psychiatrie: Das Mannheimer Modell* (Reinbek: Rowohlt Verlag, 1974)

136   A Sampling of Community Mental Health Programs

152. Pörksen, Niels, 2002, *ibid*
153. Lindemann, Elizabeth B., 7/14/1978, *ibid*
154. Pörksen, Niels, Leitende Arzt, Fachberich Psychiatrie, von Bodelschwinghsche Anstalten Bethel, Serepta und Nazareth, Bielefeld, West Germany, interview by David G. Satin 7/3/2004. [Box 5, X, Lindemann Collection, Center for the History of Medicine, Francis A. Countway Library of Medicine, Boston, MA]
155. Pörksen, Niels, letter to Elizabeth B. and Erich Lindemann, 11/8/1972, p. 1. [Box XII 1 folder E107 Pörksen, Erich Lindemann Collection, Center for the History of Medicine, Francis A. Countway Library of Medicine, Boston, MA]
156. Lindemann, Erich, letter to Pörksen, Neils, 3/4/1970. [folder "Dr. Pörksen", Box IV 1+2, Erich Lindemann Collection, Center for the History of Medicine, Francis A. Countway Library of Medicine, Boston, MA]
157. Pörksen, Niels, card to Elizabeth B. Lindemann, 12/18/1995. [Box XII 1 folder E107 Pörksen, Erich Lindemann Collection, Center for the History of Medicine, Francis A. Countway Library of Medicine, Boston, MA]
158. von Baeyer, Walter Ritter, 10/30/1984, *ibid*
159. von Baeyer, Walter Ritter, 10/30/1984, *ibid*
160. Lindemann, Elizabeth B., 7/14/1978, *ibid*
161. Häffner, Dr. Dr. H.[einz], Der Direktor Der Socialpsychiatrischen Klinik Der Universität Heidelberg, letter to Lindemann, Erich, Stanford Medical Center, 2/27/1970. [folder "Heidelberg", Box IV 1+2, Erich Lindemann Collection, Center for the History of Medicine, Francis A. Countway Library of Medicine, Boston, MA]
162. Pörksen, Niels, 9/9/1978, *ibid*
163. Kraus, Alfred, Psychitrische Klinik, Universität Heidelberg, Germany: interview by David G. Satin, M.D. in tavern, Heidelberg, West Germany 10/29/84. [David G. Satin, M.D. notes, Newton, MA]
164. Lindemann, Erich, 3/17/1970, *ibid*
165. Lindemann, Erich, letter to Heinz Häfner, Der Direktor Der Socialpsychiatrischen Klinik Der Universität Heidelberg, 11/10/1972, p. 1 1. [folder "Heidelberg", Box IV 1+2, Erich Lindemann Collection, Center for the History of Medicine, Francis A. Countway Library of Medicine, Boston, MABoston, Massachusetts]:
. . .

> die vielschichtige Struktur der Konfliktsituation klar zu erfassen, sodass wir persoenliche und Motivationsfaktoren von institutionellen Prozessen und von den Resultaten eines relativ raschen Kulturwandels im Gebiet der Sozialpsychiatrie trennen konneten. Er [Niels Pörksen] . . . zu der Zahl der unruhigen innovationssuchenden jungen Leuten gehoert, die oft ein neues Prinzip wie etwa das der verantwortlichen Anteilnahme aller Mitglieder einer Sozialgruppe überhastig bewerklichen moechten, und dabei sehr wichtige Faktoren untershaetzen, die in besonderen Bereichen wie etwa eine klinishche Abteilung die Praesenze eine klare autoritative Struktur notwendig machen.
> Die Gemeinde Psychiatrie ist noch so jung, und die Begegnung mit vielen Autoritaetspersonen in diesem Gebiet so stressvoll, dass die Neigung, sich mit juengeren gleichgesinnten Leuten zu umgeben und sich auf ihrer anerkennung zu verlassen sehr verstaendlich ist. . . . Jedenfalls wuerde es sehr schade sein, wenn dieser Versuch [attempt] ein umfassendes Programm zu entfalten nach so viel Bemuehungen aufgeben werden muesste. . . . .
> [We attempt to grasp the many-layered structure of the conflict situation, so that, through social psychiatry, we can analyze the personal and

motivational factors of institutional processes and the resulting relatively rash cultural change. Pörksen is one of the unsettled, innovation-seeking youth who want to realize a new principle rashly for all, while underestimating important factors and responsibilities, such as a clear authority structure in a clinical department.

The stress of the still young field of psychiatry in relation to other authorities in this area leads to the tendency to surround ourselves with young disciples or deny them respect. It would be a pity to have to forsake the great efforts to develop such a comprehensive program.]

166. Häfner, Heinz, letter to Erich Lindemann Lindemann, 6/6/1974, p. 1. [folder "Heidelberg", Box IV 1+2, Erich Lindemann Collection, Center for the History of Medicine, Francis A. Countway Library of Medicine, Boston, MABoston, Massachusetts]:

...

den auserordentlich interessanten Bericht über die Entwicklung des Lincoln-Centers . . . Die Darstellung der Entwicklung in der Bronx hat mich sehr bewegt und beschäftigt . . . Ich habe das aussergewöhnliche Engagement der dort tätigen Leute . . . und die für usere Verhältnisse kaum vorstellbaren Scwierigkeiten kennegelernt. Ich habe auch einige Vorboten der Katastrophe miterlebt. Es war eine katastrophale Überforderungssitutation . . . die Therapie eines einselnen Patienten ist . . . eine mitunter enorme Belastung. Wenn dazu die Sorge um eine in jeder Hinsicht katastrophale Lebensituation, um institutionelle, finaziellle und politische Problem kommen, dann wächst dies über die Kraft von Menschen hinaus. Eines der grossen Probleme unseres Faches ist, dass viele unserer Kollegen ihre Fähigkeiten, zu helfen und zu ertragen, in eifernder Blindheit grenzenlos überschätzen, und viele anderer sich im Abwehr aus dem direkten Kontakt mit ihren Aufgaben und den Pastienten zurückziehen. Wir haben damit auch in Deutschland wachsende Schwierigkeiten, und die Tendenz vieler unserer Kollegen, aus der Reform unseres Faches eiene Glaubensbewegung zu machen, wächst, obwohl die Schwierigkeiten, dadurch entstehen, mit Händen zu greifen sind. Wir bräuchten dringed jemanden, der mit dem grossen Mass Ihrer Erfahrung und Lebensweisheit Einsicht in die eigenen Grenzen zu vermitteln vermag. . . .

[I followed with interest Lincoln Center in the Bronx's growing catastrophe, presaging growing problems in Germany. It is difficult to deal with individual patients; adding environmental catastrophes regarding institutions, finance, and politics overwhelms human capacities. In Germany there is a great problem with many colleagues blindly overreaching in their task of helping and taking on burdens of others. There are increasing problems with the tendency of many colleagues to make reform of the profession into an ideological change. We need someone with the experience and life wisdom to establish boundaries.]

167. Lindemann, Erich, letter to Niels Poerken 3/22/1973. [Box XII 1 folder E107 Pörksen, Erich Lindemann Collection, Center for the History of Medicine, Francis A. Countway Library of Medicine, Boston, MA]

168. Lindemann, Erich, 11/10/1972, *ibid*

"die vielschichtige [many layered] Struktur der Konfliktsituation klar zu erfassen, sodass wir persoenlich und Motivationsfaktoren von institutionellen Prozessen und von den Resultaten eines relativ raschen Kulturwandels im Gebiet der Sozialpsychiatrie trennen [separate] konneten. Er [Niels Pörksen] . . . zu der Zahl der unruhigen innovationssuchenden jungen Leuten gehoert, die oft ein neues Prinzip wie etwa das der verantwortlichen [responsible] Anteilnahme [?acceptance] aller Mitglieder einer Sozialgruppe überhastig [rashly] bewerklichen [bring about] moechten, und dabei sehr wichtige Faktoren untershaetzen [underestimate], die in besonderen Bereichen wie etwa eine klinishche Abteilung die Praesenze eine klare autoritative Struktur notwendig machen.

Die Gemeinde Psychiatrie ist noch so jung, und die Begegnung mit vielen Autoritaetspersonen in diesem Gebiet so stressvoll, dass die Neigung [tendency], sich mit juengeren gleichgesinnten Leuten zu umgeben [surround] und sich auf ihrer anerkennung [recognition] zu verlassen [deny] sehr verstaendlich ist. . . . Jedenfalls wuerde es sehr schade [a pity] sein, wenn dieser Versuch [attempt] ein umfassendes [comprehensive] Programm zu entfalten [develop] nach so viel Bemuehungen [efforts] aufgeben [forsake] werden muesste".

Also: Lindemann, Erich, handwritten note to Heinz Häfner written at the bottom of his 6/6/1974 letter to Lindemann. [folder "Heidelberg", Box IV 1+2, Erich Lindemann Collection, Center for the History of Medicine, Francis A. Countway Library of Medicine, Boston, MA]:

"Bald hoffe ich einen [?]Paüperen Gedankenaustausch über die Probleme, die in der neunen [?]Berigsleistung des Psychiaters in Community Mental Health an uns herantreten zu Papier bringen zu können".

169. Mason, Henry L., "Reflections on the Politicized University: 1. The Academic Crisis in the Federal Republic of Germany", *AAUP Bulletin*: 299–312 (Autumn, 1974),

"Some universities are traditionally calm: e.g., Cologne, Tuebingen, and Mainz; others, decidedly not: e.g., Heidelberg, Berlin, Bremen, Marburg, and Frankfurt. . . [p. 300]

"What is the nature of the crisis which has afflicted universities in Western Europe, and particularly in Germany? . . . The [West German Federal] Constitutional Court's basic model for current academic governance is the *Gruppen-Universitaet*, the university of the groups or components, where each component . . . is represented on each decision-making organ . . . My conclusion is that the applicable model today is . . . the Politicized University . . . The politicized milieu provides challenges and problems for various participants—particularly the professors, the newly established presidents or full-time *Rektors*, the nonprofessorial scientific staff, and the students. Moreover, a special kind of politicization, that of the "Left", prevails among the latter two groups . . . the future of the German universities cannot be ignored, including the prospects of a take-over by the Left in the current political atmosphere of the Federal Republic. . . [p. 299] . . . There was an urgent need for reform, and in 1965 or so a reform-minded coalition of professors, scientific staff, and perhaps students should have managed some kind of integration of the greater part of the scientific staff [lower-level teachers] into the professoriate . . . Unfortunately, this kind of reform-minded coalition did not, as a rule, materialize in German universities, perhaps because the full professors still did not care to admit that their traditional privileges would have to be curtailed, or because the professors happened to be bad campus politicians without the talent for coalitions with other components. Instead, the need for reform tended to be exploited by those for whom reform meant much more than integration of the scientific staff—by the Left which believed that meaningful reform of the university required the struggle against bourgeois society off-campus as well as against the scientific establishment on the campus which is its tool". [p. 303] . . . work in 'remote' disciplines or at 'backward' universities, colleges, or departments where the effects of politicization, or even group-structuring, are minimal. Orientalists, veterinarians, business administrationists, or lawyers in the Saarland or at Bavarian campuses cannot be compared with their harassed colleagues in education, psychology, sociology, philosophy, or German literature at such locales as Berlin or Heidelberg—to cite a few extreme examples. . . [p. 305] . . . Many of the Marxist professors belong to the Association of Democratic Scientists . . . this Association's basic principles are revealed in policy points drafted in 1973 by, for example, its Giessen and Heidelberg sections. Thus, an academician is labeled antidemocratic, which is the worst of offenses, if his work does not reflect the 'social relationships' of his science and draws the 'appropriate political consequences' from them . . . Teaching is worthwhile only if it contributes to democratization; the students' political consciousness must be turned in the democratic direction. All good science must be politicized along democratic lines; the only free science is that which reflects the right kind of 'political mandate'. The academician may not be politically neutral in a society like the Federal Republic where privileged minorities rule over the exploited masses of workers. . . [p. 311]

"Supposedly the students of the early sixties were pragmatic, admired President Kennedy, and had no basic disagreement with the Bonn brand of democracy; they still remembered World War II and the Nazis. Durng the late sixties radicalization began, but the early radicals wre democrats and their leaders showed willingness to engage in rational dialogue with the opponents. Today's generation of students is seen . . . as radical in an orthodox, rigid sense; they are unwilling to debate but determined to destroy the 'bourgeois' academic establishment. Born into the consumer society and often from well-to-do parents, they have no faith in Western democracy; Vietnam, multinational corporations, and the treacherous German major parties and their coalitions are among their horrors . . . the current radicals claim strongly to disapprove of the few Maoists or 'Chaoten' who wallow in disruptive and violent tactics; the current leaders are . . . tough, doctrinaire functionaries of the East German type who demand, and obtain, disciplined behavior . . . Financial aid from East Germany and orientation courses there are openly acknowledged . . . On political scientist suspects a 'typically German' inclination toward closed doctrines, totalitarian fanaticism, and '*Sturheit* (rigidity)'; other Communist students, for example the Czechs, are reportedly frightened by theiri rigid West German comrades . . . Are these . . . really representative of the people who now control a considerable part of the power in the official organs of the Politicized University as a result of free elections among the student component? ¶A Berlin sociologist [Ahlberg, René, *Ursachen der Revolte* (Kohlhammer: Stuttgart, 1972), pp. 79–81] has noted feelings of profound insecurity and alienation among many of the first-year students today. These feelings . . . reflect their loneliness in the mass university, but also th explosion of knowledge in the introductory courses . . . formerly the fraternities ('corporations') had provided some kind of security . . . so the Marxist student association has become the place of refuge today . . . it seems to offer 'spiritual safety (*geistige Geborgenheit*)' and answers to all questions. Marxism is popular not as an intellectuall daring adventure but rather as an avoidance of adventure. . . [.307] . . . Habermas [Habermas, J., *Protestbewegung und Hochschulreform* (Suhrkamp: Frankfurt,

140 *A Sampling of Community Mental Health Programs*

1969), pp. 29, 48, 197–200] has written of the grandiose self-deception on the part of the Leftist students; their movement has not become revolutionary just because they call it revolutionary. The student revolution is a pseudo-revolution, with pseudo-successes by a pseudo-class. The Leftist students overrate their own power, and underrate the state's power, to a ridiculous extent. The occupation of a university is confused with a real takeover; the symbol is seen as reality The students' 'new' techniques have by no means proved successful against the 'capitalists'; they merely reflect the cheap exploitation of unsuspected attitudes in the liberal system of the West German state". [310]

170. Häfner, Heinz, letter to Erich Lindemann, 10/1/1971. [folder "Heidelberg", Box IV 1+2, Erich Lindemann Collection, Center for the History of Medicine, Francis A. Countway Library of Medicine, Boston, MA]:

P.S. Ich bin persönlich enorm erleichtert, seit die Gruppe um das Sozialistische Patientenkollektiv, die mich so lange unter schweren Druck gesetzt hatte, von der Polezei aufgelöst worden ist. Man hat bei ihnen Sprengstoff, Zeitzünder, Dum-Dum Munition und Pläne für verschiedene 'Aktionen' mit Waffengewalt gefunded. Zwei Brandstiftungen soll die Gruppe bereits unternomen haben. Auch angeschossene Polizisten gehen auf das Konto der Mitglieder dieser Gruppe..

171. von Baeyer, Walter Ritter, Häfner, Heinz and Kisker, *Psychiatrie der Verfolgt* (Springer, 1982), and a book on the psychoses for the persecuted (Springer)
172. Pörksen, Niels, 11/8/1972, *Ibid*, p. 2
173. Pörksen, Niels, 11/8/1972, *Ibid*, p. 2
174. Pörksen, Niels, letter to Elizabeth B. and Erich Lindemann, 12/19/1972. [Box XII 1 folder E107 Pörksen, Erich Lindemann Collection, Center for the History of Medicine, Francis A. Countway Library of Medicine, Boston, MA]
175. Pörksen, Niels, letter to Elizabeth B. and Erich Lindemann, 12/19/1972 translated by Elizabeth Lindemann. [folder "Dr. Pörksen", Box IV 1+2, Erich Lindemann Collection, Center for the History of Medicine, Francis A. Countway Library of Medicine, Boston, MA]:

The visit with you constitutes one of the high points of the year just past and also of the high points of my life. My life's direction has received its stamp from you . . . Leaving the department is a trend that spreads like the wind, because—as planned—the key support figures are really going: Frau Rave in the Day Clinic, Herr Orimann from Child Psychiatry and myself; thus the three most important and up to now most stable and highly regarded services are practically at an end, for part of their workers will go too. ¶Thus the Clinic is facing a renewal which will certainly involve a more traditional approach.

Pörksen, Niels, letter to Elizabeth and Erich Lindemann, 4/5/1973, p. 2:

"In der Sozialpsychiatrischen Klinik . . . scheiden die gewichtigsten und fähigsten Vertreter an den klinischen und sozialpsychiatrischen Programme aus. Am 1. Juli velässt Dr. Drömann, der das kinder- und jugendpsychiatrische Programm aufgebaut hat und in der Stadt, in Heimen, im Jugendamt und im Drogenprogramm Beratungshilfe geleistet hat, aus der Klinik aus. Frau Dr. Rave, die Lieterin der Tagesklinik, wird ebenfalls aus der Klinik ausscheiden. Andere Mitarbeiter, Schwetern und Sozialarbeiterinnen, habe auch ihre Absicht zum Ausscheiden kundgetan . . .

A Sampling of Community Mental Health Programs 141

> Herr Häffner . . . versucht mich um jeden Preis so schnell wie möglich los zu werden, weil er hofft, nach meinem Ausscheiden wieder Ruhe und Ordnung in seine Klinik zu bekommen . . . Trotzdem ist mir noch nicht ganz sicher, wie weit es geingt, der Gemeindepsychiatrie auch später einem wichtigen Platz einzuräumen".

Pörksen, Niels, letter to Erich Lindemann, 5/27/1974, p. 2:

> "aus Mannheim höre ich . . . Viele alte Freunde sind ausgeschieden, der Forschungsaspekt [research] wächt und wächst . . . Schweren Herzens verlassen wir die Gegend [area] und die vielen Freunde, auch die schöne Arbeit in Mannheim . . . Das alles wird jetzt neu aufzubauen sein".

[folder "Dr. Pörksen", Box IV 1+2, Erich Lindemann Collection, Center for the History of Medicine, Francis A. Countway Library of Medicine, Boston, MA]

176. Häfner, Heinz, Der Direktor Der Socialpsychiatrischen Klinik Der Universität Heidelberg, to Erich Lindemann, 8/29/1972, summarized by David G. Satin. [folder "Heidelberg", Box IV 1+2, Erich Lindemann Collection, Center for the History of Medicine, Francis A. Countway Library of Medicine, Boston, MABoston, Massachusetts]:

> Many problems with Neils Pörksen—valued assistant left, Pörksen threatens to/relieved at leaving, problems with Mannheim community that P. works with, they are reserved with him but also Häfner and the Clinic. Primarily the problem is the working relationship between Häffner and Pörksen; Pörksen does not fulfill/make time for his responsibilities as clinical chief physician but wants a written assurance that he will retain this position; Häffner feels that Pörksen can fulfill a chief physician role but not in a demanding position. This lead to protracted conflict. Häffner has dissuaded Pörksen from leaving, but now it appears this may be best for him. These days one can no longer stick a colleague in the corner and be a clinic authority. Will not presume to expect Lindemann to counsel Pörksen about this when he visits, but would be thankful if Lindemann wants to. Would not blame him for not wanting to be burdened with this.

177. Häffner, Heinz, letter to Erich Lindemann, 12/22/1972, p. 3. [folder "Heidelberg", Box IV 1+2, Erich Lindemann Collection, Center for the History of Medicine, Francis A. Countway Library of Medicine, Boston, MA]

> Die Vorgänge [process] an der Universität Heidelberg, an der es in den letzten Wochen wieder zu dramatischen Zuspitsungen [climaxes] politischer Auseinandersetzungen [conflict] kam, strahlen [radiates] natürlich auch in die Kliniken aus und machen es ganz besonders [espeically] schwierig [difficult], das zu praktizieren, was die Sozialipsychologien eine demokratische Autorität neannen.

178. Schneider, Hartmut, Director of the Department of Social Psyciatry, Zentralinstitut für Zeelisches Gesundheit, Mannheim, West Germany. Interviewed by David G. Satin at the Zentralinstitut, 10/26/1984. [Tape 8B, Caddy 6, Box X, Erich Lindemann Collection, Center for the History of Medicine, Francis A. Countway Library of Medicine, Boston, MA]
179. Lindemann, Erich, letter to Niels Pörksen, 3/22/1973, translated by Elizabeth Lindemann. [folder "Dr. Pörksen", Box IV 1+2, Erich Lindemann Collection, Center for the History of Medicine, Francis A. Countway Library of Medicine, Boston, MA]
180. Pörksen, Niels, 11/8/1972, *ibid*, p. 2.
181. Lindemann, Elizabeth B., 6/27/1978–10/4/1979, *ibid*

142   A Sampling of Community Mental Health Programs

182. Lindemann, Erich, 3/22/1973, *ibid*
183. Pörksen, Neils, letter to Elizabeth B. Lindemann, 12/2/2002. [Box XII 1 folder E107 Pörksen, Erich Lindemann Collection, Center for the History of Medicine, Francis A. Countway Library of Medicine, Boston, MA]
184. Pörksen, Neils, note to Elizabeth B. Lindemann, 8/18/2002. [Box XII 1 folder E107 Pörksen, Erich Lindemann Collection, Center for the History of Medicine, Francis A. Countway Library of Medicine, Boston, MA]
185. Pörksen, Niels, letter to Erich Lindemann, 8/30/1974:

> "Sie wissen, dass Sie einen wesentlichen Anteil [substantial portion] an dem Zustandekommen [success] dieses Buches haben und ich weiss, dass ich Ihnen dafür viel zu danken habe. Sie haben mir in den vergangenen Jahren in all den Schwierigkeiten viel von dem Vertrauen [faith] gegeben, was für die Weiterarbeit notwendig war. Ihre Aussage 'Eines Tages werden wir es schaffen [create/build]' hat mir viel Kraft gegeben".

[folder "Dr. Pörksen", Box IV 1+2, Erich Lindemann Collection, Center for the History of Medicine, Francis A. Countway Library of Medicine, Boston, MA]
186. Janzarik, Werner, 10/29/1984, *ibid*
187. Pörksen, Niels, 10/13/1984, *ibid*
188. Pörksen, Niels, 2002, *ibid*
189. Pörksen, Niels, 2002, *ibid*, pp. 306–307
190. Pörksen, Niels, 10/13/1984, *ibid*
191. Pörksen, Niels, 7/3/2004, *ibid*
192. Pörksen, Niels, letter to Elizabeth B. Lindemann, 1/2/1986. [Box XII 1 folder E107 Pörksen, Erich Lindemann Collection, Center for the History of Medicine, Francis A. Countway Library of Medicine, Boston, MA]
193. Pörksen, Niels, 2002, *ibid*, pp. 304–305
194. Pörksen, Niels, 2002, *ibid*, p. 306
195. Plog, Ursula, Department of Social Psychiatry, Freie Universität Berlin, West Germany, interview by David Satin 10/11/84
196. Pörksen, Niels, 10/13/1984, *ibid*
197. Pörksen, Neils, letter to Elizabeth B. Lindemann, 10/7/1976. [Box XII 1 folder E107 Pörksen, Erich Lindemann Collection, Center for the History of Medicine, Francis A. Countway Library of Medicine, Boston, MA]
198. Pörksen, Niels (University of Heidelberg, West Germany), Lindemann, Elizabeth B. and Lindemann, Brenda, interview by David G. Satin, M.D. in EBL's house, Wellesley, MA, 9/9/1978. [Caddy 5, Box 5, X, Lindemann Collection, Center for the History of Medicine, Francis A. Countway Library of Medicine, Boston, MA]
199. Pörksen, Neils, 10/7/1976, *ibid*
200. Pörksen, Neils, letter to Elizbeth B. Lindemnn, 12/3/1981. [Box XII 1 folder E107 Pörksen, Erich Lindemann Collection, Center for the History of Medicine, Francis A. Countway Library of Medicine, Boston, MA]
201. Keyes, Edward, *Coconut Grove* (New York: Atheneum Press, 1984)
202. Lindemann, Erich, letter to Schulte, Dr. W. Tübinen, 6/28/1965, and Unviersitäts-Nervenklinik Tübingen letter to Lindemann, Erich, 12/23/1965. [folder "Correspondence—Europe 1960–65", Box IIIA5 1), Erich Lindemann Collection, Center for the History of Medicine, Francis A. Countway Library of Medicine, Boston, MA]
203. Lindemann, Elizabeth B., 6/27/1978–10/4/1979, *ibid*
204. Pörksen, Neils, 10/13/1984, *ibid*
205. Pörksen, Neils, 9/9/1978, *ibid*

A Sampling of Community Mental Health Programs 143

206. Lindemann, Erich, letter to Caplan, Gerald, Clinical Professor of Psychiatry, Director, Laboratory of Community Psychiatry, Department of Psychiatry, HMS, 10/21/1966. [folder "GENERAL CORRESPONDENCE—A,B,C 1966", Box IV 1+2, Erich Lindemann Collection, Center for the History of Medicine, Countway Library of Medicine, Boston, MA]
207. Lindemann, Erich, letter to Redlich, Frederick C., Director, The Connecticut Mental Health Center, New Haven, Connecticut, 10/21/1966, p. 3. [folder "GENERAL CORRESPONDENCE R-S 1966", Box IV 1+2, Erich Lindemann Collection, Center for the History of Medicine, Countway Library of Medicine, Boston, MA]
208. Lindemann, Elizabeth B., phone interview with David G. Satin, 3/30/2004. [folder "GENERAL CORRESPONDENCE R-S 1966", Box IV 1+2, Erich Lindemann Collection, Center for the History of Medicine, Countway Library of Medicine, Boston, MA]
209. Psychoanalytisches Seminar Stuttgart—Tübingen, Ausbildungsprogramm für das Sommersemester 1970, Leitung: Prof. Dr. W. Loch, p. 3: "Gastvorträge: . . . Prof. E. Lindemann (Stanford University, Palo Alto, U.S.A.), Thema, Zeit und Ort werden noch bekanntgegeben". [p. 3] [Topic, time and place to be announced] [folder "Correspondence—1970", Box IV 1+2, Erich Lindemann Collection, Center for the History of Medicine, Francis A. Countway Library of Medicine, Boston, MA]
210. Lindemann, Erich with Duhl, Leonard J., Seeley, John, and Lindemann, Elizabeth B., interview at his home in Palo Alto, CA by Leonard Duhl, 7/15/1974. [Caddy 4, Tape 8A,9B; 7, Erich Lindemann Collection, Center for the History of Medicine, Francis A. Countway Library of Medicine, Boston, MA]
211. Davis, Elizabeth, M.D., "THE CLNICAL PRACTICE OF COMMUNITY PSYCHIATRY AT HARLEM HOSPITAL". [folder "Harlem Hospital/Lincoln Hospital", David G. Satin files, Newton, MA]
212. Russell, Maurice V., Ed.D., "A Community Mental Health Program in a Municipal Hospital", *Social Casework* 11/65, pp. 557–560
213. Russell, Maurice V., Ed.D.: "A Community Mental Health Program in a Municipal Hospital", *Social Casework* 11/65; pp. 557–560
214. Davis, Elizabeth, M.D.: "THE CLNICAL PRACTICE OF COMMUNITY PSYCHIATRY AT HARLEM HOSPITAL". [folder "Harlem Hospital/Lincoln Hospital", David G. Satin files, Newton, MA]
215. Keyes, Edward, 1984, *ibid*, p. 277
216. Bergstresser, Sara May, *Therapies of the Mundane: Community Mental Health Care and Everyday Life in an Italian Town* (Doctoral dissertation, Department of Anthropology, Brown University, 5/2004)
217. R.B.K., "Italy Approves Law To Deinstitutionalize Mentally Ill, Provide Community Care", *Psychiatric News* 32:9,58 (4/18/1997); reported from Ballmaier, Martina, *Nature Medicine* 3/1997
    Mollica, A., Nitti, C., Dalseno, M. and Zilioli, N., "Nuove figure di operatori psichiatrici nelle institutzioni manicomiali. Parte I. Nuoli professionale e funzioni sociali ('New Kinds of Psychiatric Professionals in the Mental Insitutions: Part I. Professional Roles and Social Functions')", *Rivista Sperimentale di Freniatria* (Reggio Emilia) *100* no. 5:1163–1171 (1976): . . . Psychiatric hospitals will eventually be replaced with more adequate community health units.
218. Bergstresser, Sara May, 5/2004, *ibid*, p. 33
219. Mollica, A., Nitti, C., Dalseno, M. and Zilioli, N., 1976, *ibid*
220. Wikipedia

144   A Sampling of Community Mental Health Programs

221. More detailed explorations of the Lincoln Mental Health Center events is presented by Riesman, Frank (psychologist at Lincoln Hospital), *Mental Health of the Poor*, New York University Graduate School, 42nd Street, New York City
    Kaplan, S.R. and Roman, M., *The Organization and Delivery of Mental Health Services in the Ghetto: The Lincoln Hospital Experience* (New York: Prager, 1973)
222. "Proposal for the Establishment of a Lincoln Hospital Service by the Department of Psychiatry, Albert Einstein College of Medicine", draft 4/1/1963. [folder "Harlem Hospital/Lincoln Hospital", David G. Satin files, Newton, MA]
223. Rosenberg, Pearl, Ph.D., letter to Lindemann, Erich, 2/28/1964, requesting his material on crisis intervention "that you feel would be useful to Harris's [Peck, M.D.] [and] Lincoln Project staff. . . ". [folder "R Miscellaneous", Box IIIA 4 (P-S), Lindemann Collection, Center for the History of Medicine, Countway Library of Medicine, Boston, MA]
224. Rosenbaum, Milton, M.D., Professor and Chairman, Department of Psychiatry, Albert Einstein College of Medicine, Yeshiva University, letter to Lindemann, Erich, 3/20/1964: "you will be able to visit the Department on April 10,1964, especially to discuss the program of our Division of Social and Community Psychiatry. . . ". [folder "R Miscellaneous", Box IIIA 4 (P-S), Lindemann Collection, Center for the History of Medicine, Countway Library of Medicine, Boston, MA]
225. Lindemann, Erich, letter to Rosenberg, Pearl, Ph.D., 4/16/1964: "I enjoyed the whole group involved in the Lincoln plans very much indeed and had a fine time all day long. . . ". [folder "R Miscellaneous", Box IIIA 4 (P-S), Lindemann Collection, Center for the History of Medicine, Countway Library of Medicine, Boston, MA]
226. Ozarin, Lucy D., M.D., M.P.H., "Community Mental Health: Does it Work? Review of the Evaluation Literature", Ch. 9 in Barton, Walter E. and Sanborn, Charlotte (eds.) *An Assessment of the Community Mental Health Movement* (Lexington, MA: Lexington Books, 1977), pp. 21–34, based on the Dartmouth Continuing Education Institute, Department of Psychiatry, Dartmouth Medical School, 1975. [folder "Civil Rights/Minorities", David G. Satin files, Newton, MA]
227. Shaw, R. (formerly Assistant Professor of Psychiatry (Child), Albert Einstein College of Medicine, Director of Child Psychiatry, Lincoln Hospital, New York, then Associate Director Herrick-Berkeley Mental Health Center, Berkeley, CA), and Eagle, C. J. (formerly Assistant Director of Child Psychiatry, Lincoln Hospital, then Assistant Professor of Psychiatry (Child) and Director of the Evaluation Unit, Department of Psychiatry, Lincoln Hospital, Bronx, New York), "Programmed Failure: The Lincoln Hospital Story", *Community Mental Health Journal*, 7 no. 4:225–263 (12/1971)
228. Bernard, Viola, 4/26/1979, *ibid*
229. Häffner, Heinz, 6/6/1974, *ibid*

> den auserordentlich interessanten Bericht über die Entwicklung des Lincoln-Centers . . . Die Darstellung [exemplar] der Entwicklung in der Bronx hat mich sehr bewegt [moved] und beschäftigt [busy] . . . Ich habe das aussergewöhnliche Engagement der dort tätigen [involved] Leute . . . und die für usere Verhältnisse [reluctance] kaum [hardly] vorstellbaren [conceivable] Scwierigkeiten kennegelernt. Ich habe auch einige Vorboten [prohibition] der Katastrophe miterlebt [seen]. Es war eine katastrophale Überforderungsitutation [ex essively demanding situation] . . . die

Therapie eines einselnen Patienten ist . . . eine mitunter enorme Belastung. Wenn dazu die Sorge um eine in vieler Hinsicht[respect] katastrophale Lebensituation, um institutionelle, finazielle und politische Problem kommen, dann wächst dies über die Kraft von Menschen hinaus.

230. Miller, Bruce Nils, Ph.D., Lincoln Community Mental Health Center, Bronx, New York City: "A Concept of Advocacy", Presented at Mental Health Service For The 70's: Neighborhood Psychiatry Conference, Cambridge, MA, 6/8/1973 1973. [folder "CMH—Social Action", David G. Satin files, Newton, MA]
231. Bernard, Viola W., Chief, Division of Community Mental HealthH, College of Physicians and Surgeons, Columbia University, interviewed by David G. Satin at her home in New York City, 4/26/1979. This report was based on CMHCs studies by the Standing Committee on Community Psychiatry and Psychoanalysis and Study Group of the American Psychoanalytic Association. [Caddy 1, Box 4, X, Lindemann Collection, Center for the History of Medicine, Francis A. Countway Library of Medicine, Boston, MA]
232. Mazer, Milton, letter to Elizabeth B. Lindemann, 11/13/1986. [Box XII 1 folder E101, Erich Lindemann Collection, Center for the History of Medicine, Francis A. Countway Library of Medicine, Boston, MA]
233. Hausman, Kenneth, "Cooperation Needed Between Universities, State Institutions", *Psychiatric News* 19:1, 26 (7/6/1984)
234. Shapiro, Leon, Tufts Departent of Psychiatry and Community Mental Health Center, interviewed by David G. Satin in Shapiro's office in Newton, MA, 6/11/1981. [Box X, Erich Lindemann Collection, Center for the History of Medicine, Francis A. Countway Library of Medicine, Boston, MA]
235. Shore, Miles, interview by David G. Satin at the Massachusetts Mental Health Center, 8/6/1981. [Box X, Erich Lindemann Collection, Center for the History of Medicine, Francis A. Countway Library of Medicine, Boston, MA]
236. Shore, Miles, 8/6/1981, *ibid*
237. Shader, Richard, 1/29/1982, *ibid*
238. Adler, Gerald, M.D., interviewed by David G. Satin at the Massachusetts General Hospital, 3/15,22/1982. [Box X, Erich Lindemann Collection, Center for the History of Medicine, Francis A. Countway Library of Medicine, Boston, MA]
239. Myerson, Paul, interviewed by David G. Satin at his home in Newton, MA, 6/19/1981. [Box X, Erich Lindemann Collection, Center for the History of Medicine, Francis A. Countway Library of Medicine, Boston, MA]
240. Hausman, Kenneth, "Benefits of University, State Hospital Cooperation Lauded", *Psychiatric News* 19:1, 13 (7/20/1984)
241. Hausman, Kenneth, 7/6/1984, *ibid*
242. Vaughan, Warren T., Jr., M.D., Chief of Community Services, Community Mental Health Center, Peninsula Hospital and Medical Center, Burlingame, CA, letter to Lindemann, Erich, 5/15/1969. [folder "Correspondence 1969", Box IV 1 + 2, Erich Lindemann Collection, Center for the History of Medicine, Countway Library of Medicine, Boston, MA]
243. Vaughan, Warren T., Jr. M.D., Chief of Community Services; Huntington, Dorothy S., Ph.D., Coordinator of Preschool Community Services; Samuels, Thomas E., Ph.D., Youth Development Specialist; Bilmes, Murray, Ph.D., Director of Youth Services; Shapiro, Marvin, M.D., Director of Children's Services; Peninsula Hospital Community Mental Health Center, Burlingame, CA: "Family Mental Health Maintenance: A New Approach

to Primary Prevention", *Hospital and Community Psychiatry* 26:8 (8/1975) pp. 503–508
244. Vaughan, Waren T., Jr., M.D., "An Expansion of Remarks Concerning The New Peninsula Mental Health Center, presented by Warren T. Vaugan, Jr., M.D. before the Executive Committee Peninsula Hospital and Medical Center June 2, 1968". [folder"Peninsula Hospital. . . ", David G. Satin files, Newton, MA]
245. Lindemann, Erich with Duhl, Leonard J., interviewed by Leonard Duhl at Lindemann's home in Palo Alto, CA, 7/13/1974. [Caddy 4, Tape 7A; 7, Erich Lindemann Collection, Center for the History of Medicine, Francis A. Countway Library of Medicine, Boston, MA]
246. Gardner, Elmer A., M.D., Assistant Professor and Director of the Division of Preventive Psychiatry, and Romano, John, MD, Professor and Chairman, Department of Psychiatry, University of Rochester School of Medicine and Dentistry, letter to Lindemann, Erich, 1/15/1964. [folder "R Miscellaneous", Box IIIA 4 (P-S), Lindemann Collection, Center for the History of Medicine, Countway Library of Medicine, Boston, MA]
247. Housman, Kenneth, 7/20/1984, *ibid*
248. Blum, Henrik L. and Ketterer, W.A., *Public Health Reports* 73:619–626 (1958)
249. Blum, Henrik L., 3/23/1979, *ibid*.
250. Haylett, Clarice, 12/17/1979, *ibid*
251. Susselman, Samuel and Blum, Henrik L., "Origins and Progress of a Mental Health Program", Ch. II in Duhl, Leonard J. and Leopold, Robert L. (eds.) *Mental Health and Urban Social Policy* (San Francisco: Jossey-Bass, 1968)
252. Mayo, Clara, Ph.D., Director of the CMH Training Program for Psychologists at HRS, letter to Signell, Karen, Ph.D. Clinical Psychologist, County of San Mateo Department, of Public Health and Welfare. [folder "SAN MATEO", IIIB3 d, Erich Lindemann Collection, Center for the History of Medicine, Countway Library of Medicine, Boston, MA]
253. Haylett, Clarice, 12/17/1979, *ibid*
254. 1967–1968 Elizabeth B. Lindemann was consultant to the Continuation School of the San Mateo Union District, and to the San Mateo Division of Mental Health Head Start Program. [file Human Relations Service via Elizabeth Lindemann; David G. Satin files, Newton, MA]
255. Bernard, Viola W., 4/26/1979, *ibid*
256. Gardner, Elmer A., M.D., Director, "Serving an Urban Ghetto Through a Community Mental Health Center: Temple University Community Mental Health Center, Philadelphia, PA", in *Mental Health Program Reports—4, National Institute of Mental Health* (Washington, DC: U.S. Government Printing Office, 1970), pp. 69–106
257. Bernard, Viola W., 4/26/1979, *ibid*
258. O. Spurgeon English MD Professor and Chief, Stanton B. Felzer Ph.D. Program Director, "Mental Health Training Program for Community Workers", application to the Pilot and Special Grants Section, Training Branch, NIMH, 7/22/1964. [folder "NIMH Study Section 1964–65", Box IIIA 4 (Mb-O), Erich Lindemann Collection, Center for the History of Medicine, Francis A. Countway Library of Medicine, Boston, MA]
259. Ozarin, Lucy D., 1977, *ibid*, based on a Dartmouth Continuing Education Institute, Department of Psychiatry, Dartmouth Medical School, 1975.
260. Gardner, Elmer A., 1970, *ibid*
261. Gardner, Elmer A., M.D., "The Role of the Classification System in Outpatient Psychiatry", in Katz, Martin M., Cole, Jonathan O. and Barton,

A Sampling of Community Mental Health Programs 147

Walter E., *The Role and Methodology of Classification in Psychiatry and Psychopathology* (Washington, DC: National Institute of Mental Health, 1968), publication no.1584; pp. 35–53
262. McBroom, Patricia, "Psychiatry Without Doctors: Community-based Techniques Open the Doors to Innovators Challenging Basic Psychiatric Concepts", *Science News* 94:345–347 (10/5/1968)
263. Gardner, Elmer, "The Community Mental Health Center Movement: Learning from Failure", Ch. 8 in Barton, Walter E. and Sanborn, Charlotte W., *An Assessment of the Community Mental Health Movement* (Lexington, MA: Lexington Books, 1977)
264. *The Milwaukee Sentinel*, 9/10/1971, p. 3.
265. Klerman, Gerald L., Director of the Connecticut Mental Health Center and faculty member in the Yale Medical School Department of Psychiatry; Director of the Erich Lindemann Mental Health Center and faculty member in the Harvard Medical School and staff member in the Massachusetts General Hospital; and subsequently Director of the Alcohol, Drug and Mental Health Administration of the U.S. Public Health Service. Interviewed by David G. Satin at the Institute of Medicine in Washington, DC, 1/26/1979 and 8/17/1982. [Box X, Erich Lindemann Collection, Center for the History of Medicine, Francis A. Countway Library of Medicine, Boston, MA]
266. Shore, Miles, 8/6/1981, *ibid*
267. Shapiro, Leon, 6/11/1981, *ibid*
268. Myerson, Paul, 6/19/1981, *ibid*
269. Adler, Gerald, 3/15,22/1982, *ibid*
270. Randolph, Peter, Superintendent and Area Director of the Tufts-Bay Cove MHC, interview by David G. Satin at the MHC, 6/26/1981. [Box X, Erich Lindemann Collection, Center for the History of Medicine, Francis A. Countway Library of Medicine, Boston, MA]
271. Shore, Miles, 8/6/1981, *Ibid*
272. Randolph, Peter, 6/26/1981, *ibid*
273. Randolph, Peter, 6/26/1981, *ibid*
274. Randolph, Peter, 6/26/1981, *ibid*
275. Adler, Gerald, 3/15,22/1982, *ibid*
276. Shader, Richard, Chairman of the Tufts Medical School Department of Psychiatry, interviewed by David G. Satin 1/29/1982. [Box X, Erich Lindemann Collection, Center for the History of Medicine, Francis A. Countway Library of Medicine, Boston, MA]
277. Randolph, Peter, 6/26/1981, *ibid*
278. Randolph, Peter, 6/26/1981, *ibid*
279. Randolph, Peter, 6/26/1981, *ibid*
280. Randolph, Peter, 6/26/1981, *ibid*
281. Shore, Miles, 8/6/1981, *Ibid*
282. Shader, Richard, 1/29/1982, *ibid*
283. Randolph, Peter, 6/26/1981, *ibid*
284. Adler, Gerald, 3/15,22/1982, *ibid*
285. Shapiro, Leon, 6/11/1981, *ibid*
286. Shader, Richard, 1/29/1982, *ibid*
287. Randolph, Peter, 6/26/1981, *ibid*
288. Myerson, Paul, 6/19/1981, *ibid*
289. Shader, Richard, 1/29/1982, *ibid*
290. Adler, Gerald, 3/15,22/1982, *ibid*
291. Adler, Gerald, 3/15,22/1982, *ibid*
292. Adler, Gerald, 3/15,22/1982, *ibid*

148 *A Sampling of Community Mental Health Programs*

293. Shader, Richard, 1/29/1982, *ibid*
294. Adler, Gerald, 3/15,22/1982, *ibid*
295. Adler, Gerald, 3/15,22/1982, *ibid*
296. Myerson, Paul, 6/19/1981, *ibid*
297. Randolph, Peter, 6/26/1981, *ibid*
298. Randolph, Peter B., M.D., "Response to Working with Neighborhood Organizations", in *Mental Health Services for the 70is: Neighborhood Psychiatry Conference* (Cambridge, MA, 6/8/1973)
299. Randolph, Peter B., M.D., Director, Tufts Mental Health Center, Boston, MA, "Response to Working With Neighborhood Organizations", response to Miller, Bruce Nils, "A Concept of Advocacy", Presented at Mental Health Service For The 70's: Neighborhood Psychiatry Conference, Cambridge, MA, 6/8/1973. [folder "CMH—Social Action", David G. Satin files, Newton, MA]
300. Eleanor, Pavenstedt, ed., *The Drifters: Children of Disorganized Lower-Class Families* (Boston: Little Brown, 1967)
301. Shapiro, Leon, 6/11/1981, *ibid*
302. Randolph, Peter, 6/26/1981, *ibid*
303. Shader, Richard, 1/29/1982, *ibid*
304. Myerson, David J., "4. Deinstitutionalization and Decentralization: 1969–1977", in Morrissey, Joseph P., Ph.D., Goldman, Howard H., M.D., M.P.H., Ph.D. and Klerman, Lorraine V., Dr. P.H. (eds.) *The Enduring Asylum: Cycles of Institutional Reform at Worcester State Hospital* (New York: Grune & Stratton, Inc., 1980)
305. Astrachan, Boris M., "Changing Institutional Direction: The Connecticut Mental Health Center", in Nelson, Richard R. and Yates, Douglas (eds.) *Innovation and Implementation in Public Organizations* (Lexington, MA: Lexington Books, 1978).
306. O'Connor, John F., Administrator, "Financing and Administration", Chapter VII in Southern Regional Education Board and National Institute of Mental Health (eds.) *The Medical School and the Community Mental Health Center*, Public Health Service Publication no. 1858 (Washington, D.C.: U.S. Government Printing Office, 1968).
307. Astrachan, Boris, 7/22/1982, *ibid*
308. Powledge, Fred, *Model City. A Test of American Liberalism: One Town's Efforts to Rebuild Itself* (New York: Simon and Schuster, 1970), pp. 24–25
309. Lazare, Aaron, interviewed at the Massachusetts General Hospital by David G. Satin, 1/20/1981. [Box X, Erich Lindemann Collection, Center for the History of Medicine, Francis A. Countway Library of Medicine, Boston, MA]
310. Astrachan, Boris M., "Many Modes and Goals: The Pragmatics of Health Delivery", *Connecticut Medicine 37*: 174–180 (1973). [Box X, Erich Lindemann Collection, Center for the History of Medicine, Francis A. Countway Library of Medicine, Boston, MA]
311. O'Connor, John F., 1968, *ibid*
312. O'Connor, John F., 1968, *ibid*
313. *MGH News 31* no. 3: (3/1972)
314. Almond, Richard and Barbara, interviewed at their home in Palo Alto, CA by David G. Satin, 12/19/1979. [Box X, Erich Lindemann Collection, Center for the History of Medicine, Francis A. Countway Library of Medicine, Boston, MA]
315. Lazare, Aaron, 1/20/1981, *Ibid*
316. Almond, Richard and Barbara, 12/19/1979, *ibid*

317. Powledge, Fred, 1970, *ibid*
318. Powledge, Fred, 1970, *ibid*
319. Powledge, Fred, 1970, *ibid*
320. Astrachan, Boris, 7/22/1982, *ibid*
321. Lazare, Aaron, 1/20/1981, *Ibid*
322. Almond, Richard and Barbara, 12/19/1979, *Ibid*
323. Biological psychiatrists included Daniel Freedman established laboratories. Others included Jack Flynn, George Aghajamian (electrophoresis), Haringer and Bowers. Jean Redmond, and Stephen Bunny. Astrachan, Boris, 7/22/1982, *ibid*
324. Astrachan, Boris, 7/22/1982, *ibid*
325. Lazare, Aaron, 1/20/1981, *Ibid*
326. Astrachan, Boris, 7/22/1982, *ibid*
327. O'Connor, John F., 1968, *ibid*
328. Lazare, Aaron, 1/20/1981, *Ibid*
329. Almond, Richard and Barbara, 12/19/1979, *Ibid*
330. Lazare, Aaron, 1/20/1981, *Ibid*
331. O'Connor, John F., 1968, *ibid*
332. Powledge, Fred, 1970, *ibid*
333. Ryan, William, interviewed in his office in Boston College by David G. Satin, 12/14/1979. [Box X, Erich Lindemann Collection, Center for the History of Medicine, Francis A. Countway Library of Medicine, Boston, MA]
334. Klerman, Gerald L., 1/26/1979, *ibid*
335. Powledge, Fred, 1970, *ibid*
336. Astrachan, Boris, 7/22/1982, *ibid*
337. Lazare, Aaron, 1/20/1981, *Ibid*
338. Lazare, Aaron, 1/20/1981, *Ibid*
339. Powledge, Fred, 1970, *ibid*
340. Klerman, Gerald L, Associate Professor of Psyciatry, Yale School of Medicine and Director of the Connecticut Mental lth Center, "Mental Health and the Urban Crisis", *American Journal of Orthopsychiatry* 39 no.5:818–826 (10/1969)
341. Klerman, Gerald, 10/1969, *ibid*, p. 824
342. Klerman, Gerald, 10/1969, *ibid*, p. 824
343. Astrachan, Boris, 7/22/1982, *ibid*
344. Klerman, Gerald, 1/26/1979, *ibid*
345. Lazare, Aaron, 1/20/1981, *Ibid*
346. Bok, Derek, "The Conant Legacy", in *James Bryant Conant: A Remembrance* (Cambridge, MA: Harvard U., 1978), p. 30

2 The Counterrevolution of Biology and Business and the Suppression of Community Mental Health 1966–1974

Bertram Brown, later director of the National Institute of Mental Health, said: "mental health is perhaps the ultimate in applied humanism". Attitudes toward and implementation of it were shaped by social values and their politicoeconomic manifestations. Many of those devoted to social psychiatry felt betrayed and abandoned by the triumphant history they expected:

> People who came of age thinking history was on their side had a serious problem, because when bad times came, they thought history was judging their ideas. The long-distance runner knows that reform doesn't happen with a dramatic vote of confidence.

Peter's Inversion states the reinstatement of traditions: "the superior ... will probably rate his subordinate in terms of institutional values: he will see competence as the behavior that supports the rules, rituals and forms of the status quo. Promptness, neatness, courtesy to superiors, internal paperwork ... such an official *evaluates input ... internal consistency is valued more highly than efficient services*".[1]

Shift in Ideology

The latter 1960s and 1970s was a period of transition in ideology from social to biological psychiatry and medicine. While social psychiatry and community mental health ideology and programs continued and were, in some ways, elaborated, criticism, objection, countereffort, and alternative direction grew to replace them. Rothman reviewed the Progressive Era, 1900–1965, as emphasizing individualization and flexibility, and contrasted it with the 1965–1980 Post-/Antiprogressive Era of anti-institutionalism (and antiorganized programs).[2]

Barton and Sanborn, in their broad review of the CMH movement, described roiling forces:[3] Economic troubles and disenchantment with government and big business was interpreted by the Republican administration as a conservative public mood, leading them to reduce health funding, which was then restored by the Democratic congress. There were broken promises, disillusionment, and unfulfilled expectation, but also pressure for and appreciation of services. Medical service and education emphasis shifted from inpatient to ambulatory care and then to health maintenance. The recognition that social stress is an important contributor to mental disorder promoted locally accessible services and thence to citizen advisory and governing boards. Social critics were critical of all social institutions. Suspected CMH treated the "worried well" rather than the sick; they shunned professional medical care, rejected the medical/biological model of health and illness, and advocated a social model.

Navarro has summarized this shift:[4]

"Like American politics more generally, the politics of health care passed through three phases in the 1970's: (1) a period of agitation and reform in the first half of the decade when broader entitlements in social welfare and stricter regulation of industry gained ground in public opinion and law, (2) a prolonged stalemate, beginning around 1975. . . and (3) a growing reaction against liberalism and government, culminating in the election of President Reagan in 1980 and the reversal of many earlier regulatory programs". [Starr, P., *The Social Transformation of American Medicine* (Basic Books, New York, 1983)]; (p. 380) (p. 416) when the decade began, reformers were criticizing the inefficiency of the health care industry and they were able to persuade Americans of the need for government intervention; when the decade ended, the industry was criticizing the inefficiency of reform and was able to persuade Americans of the need to curtail government intervention . . . In his [Starr's] history, the social transformation of medicine is reduced to the ideological transformation of American beliefs and wants expressed either through the market or through their representative public institutions (p. 514) . . . Starr concludes . . . that the future of American medicine will depend primarily on what Americans want to happen . . . The last sentence of the book. . .: The future of American medicine depends on 'choices that Americans have still to make'. (p. 515)

Americans have been . . . divided into classes, races, genders and other power groupings, each with its own interests, set of beliefs and wants (p. 515) . . . Conflict and struggle continuously take place; and it is this struggle and conflict . . . that determines change in U.S. society and in American medicine.

(p. 516)

Musto reviewed shifts in social, political, and medical attitudes.[5] After community rebellion energized CMH with demands that CMHCs find answers to community needs, followed in the late 1960s by a sense that they had failed and, in the early 1970s, were attacked for trying to intervene in community disorders, financial viability, coordination and organization of services, lack of evaluation, effectiveness, accountability, respect for patients and community and civil rights, and control of treatment. Paradoxically, this came both from a reactionary ideology, including mental health professions' eagerness to return to their traditional power in expertise and practice, and also from the civil rights and anti–Vietnam War rebellion against government, authority, and traditions, with recourse to conflict and the legal system.[6] There were debates over professional egalitarianism versus advocacy for the predominance of psychiatrists. There followed recommendations of retrenchment to the integration of CMHCs with other medical and social services, more modest expectations, and shift of interest to individual and biochemical treatments. (Note that Musto recognized the cyclical course of history in his expectation of the future return of the temptation to grandiose social reform.)

After the shift away from social programs and social psychiatry, George Will retrospectively judged programs of social change, such as Model Cities and the Great Society, as unrealistic because we don't know how to build them.[7] He saw disappointments such as the Vietnam War and the Watergate affair leading to disillusionment with and hostility toward government and its grand social programs.

Social and Community Psychiatry

In the 1960s and into the 1970s, the institutionalization of the Community Mental Health Centers program proceeded in Massachusetts as in ACTS, EXTRA SESSION, 1966; Senate No. 889 Chap. 735. AN ACT ESTABLISHING A COMPREHENSIVE PROGRAM OF MENTAL HEALTH AND MENTAL RETARDATION SERVICES,[8] a law revising the structure and function of the state's Department of Mental Health (DMH), incorporating catchment areas, advisory boards, etc. On the federal level, relevant legislation and funding included:[9]

- National Mental Health Act 7/3/46 P.L. 487–79th Congress "research relating to psychiatric disorders and to aid in . . . more effective methods of prevention, diagnosis, and treatment"
- P.L. 182–84th Congress "Mental Health Study Act of 1955 . . . nationwide analysis . . . of the human and economic problems of mental illness"
- Mental Retardation Facilities and Community Mental Health Centers [CMHC] Construction Act of 1963 P.L. 88–164, 88th Congress 10/31/63 "grants for construction of research centers and . . . community mental health centers"

- Mental Retardation Facilities and Community Mental Health Centers Construction Act Amendment of 1965 P.L. 89–105–89th Congress, 8/4/65 "meeting the initial cost of professional and technical personnel for comprehensive community mental health centers"
- 1967 P.L. 90–32—staffing and construction extended through FY 1970
- Alcoholics and Narcotics Addict Rehabilitation Amendments of 1968 P.L. 90–574 new construction programs, initial staffing assistance, specialized facilities for treatment of alcoholism and narcotic addiction, program administration.
- CMHC Amendments of 1970 P.L. 91–211 increased the federal share of construction and administration costs, new poverty areas, children's mental health programs, addiction programs, consultation; 8 years

  P.L. 91–513 CMHC Act amended—funding for drug abuse

  P.L. 91–515 CMHC Act amended—staffing

  P.L. 91–616 CMHC Act amended—alcoholism prevention & treatment

- 1972 P.L. 92–255 CMHC Act amended—drug abuse funds
- 1973 P.L. 93–405 CMHC construction and staffing through 6/74
- Health Revenue Sharing and Health Service Act of 1975 P.L. 94–63 requirements for organization and operation of CMHCs, coordination and integration of staff and services within CMHCs and with other entities; new centers and services, monitoring
- 1977 P.L. 95–83 CMHC Act amendment—extended through 9/78
- Community Mental Health Centers Extension Act of 1978 P.L. 95–622 11/9/78 95th Congress "revise and extend the programs under that Act; 2 year extension, can carry over 5% of funds
- 1979 P.L. 96–32 CMHC Act amendment—technical clarification
- 1980 P.L. 96–398 Mental Health Systems Act—reauthorizes CMHC through FY 81, 84.
  - 1981 P.L. 97–35 Omnibus Budget Reconciliation Act—consolidates funding in block grants FY82–4; repeals CMHC Act & grants under Mental Health Systems Act

Funding

- AUTHORIZATIONS—CMHC ACT AS AMENDED. FY 1965–1981... TOTALS $1,608,710,000
- AUTHORIZATIONS (NEW grants only)—MENTAL HEALTH SYSTEMS ACT P.L. 96–398... TOTALS

  TOTAL AUTHORIZATIONS, APPROPRIATIONS, OBLIGATIONS CMHC ACT AS AMENDED... Total [1965–1981]

- Authorization. . . $1,535,716,000. . . Appropriation. . . $2,659,340,000. . . Obligation. . . $2,844,909.00
- TOTAL FEDERAL OBLIGATIONS FOR CMHCS—BY STATE FISCAL YEARS 1965 THROUGH 1981. . . STATE TOTAL

    [range] CALIFORNIA. . . $243,577,639. . . ALASKA. . . $5,031,664. . . GUAM. . . $3,657,823

- FY 1982 $204,500,000. . . FY 1983. . . $236,500,000. . . FY 1984. . . $270,000.000

The budget of the NIMH rose exponentially, from about $10 million in 1960 to $861.8 million in 1977.

Extramural research grant awards escalated $3.3 million in 1948, $12.3 million in 1958, $66.9 million in 1968, and $82.9 million in 1973.

Note that in addition to federal funding, the major source of services and funding for mental health worldwide comes from state and county governments, estimated at between $6 billion and $7 billion.[10] States and counties support (and complement) formula grants, which give them administrative authority over the monies.

These policies and funds contributed to "the dramatic reduction in the number of persons in mental health hospitals. From 1960, with a hospital population of 20,000, the number as of the end of last year [1971] had been almost cut in half [about 10,500]".[11] In terms of CMHC services[12] "statistics for 1973 show that nearly 600 mental health centers have been organized in . . . ten years. . . [though] more than half the country is still denied . . . the program . . . more than one million people receive care at community mental health centers. . . [that is] *one quarter of all mental patient care* in the United States. . . [in] 1972. . . 325 community mental health centers were in operation" (p. 179). Financially[13] "As of July 1975, 603 centers had received federal financial assistance . . . about 507 [were] operational. When all 603 are operational, services will be available to 41 percent of the population . . . Over half the centers are in designated poverty areas . . . 48 percent in cities with 25,000 to 500,000 population . . . for 1973. . . federal funds provide 35.2 percent of center funding, state funds . . . 30.7 percent, and reimbursements for services . . . less than 25 percent" (p. 125)" Ozarin reviewed many aspects of CMH in this time period.[14]

There was consideration of primary prevention of mental illness and enhancement of mental health as compared with secondary prevention in the treatment of the mentally ill:

> primary prevention applied to mental disorder is often impossible because of lack of knowledge about etiology . . . and a number of basic social functions or facilities that will not easily be modified . . . Despite vagueness of concepts and lack of research, much knowledge and experience is available, but it is not being used . . .

Counterrevolution of Biology and Business 155

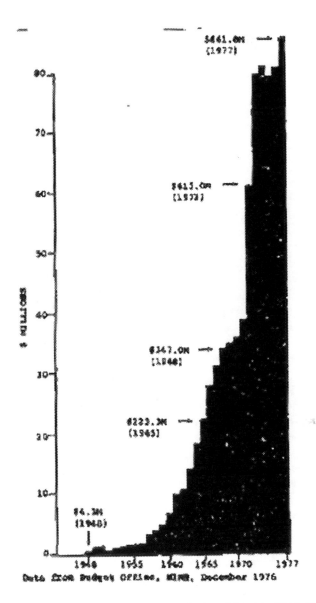

Figure 2.1 Budget of the National Institute of Mental Health, 1948–77

In February 1974, 5.7 percent of all staff hours in federally supported centers were allocated to extramural consultation. Schools receive 39 percent . . . 45 percent of all C&E effort was case oriented, 30 percent was program oriented, and a quarter went to staff development (p. 136) . . . little effort has gone into evaluating preventive

techniques . . . community psychiatry has been busy elaborating techniques theoretically . . . research dealing with consultation from 1958–72. . . . consultation as a technique . . . does have a positive effect . . . in group behavior, client functioning or client behavior.
(Mannino, F.V., McLennan, B.W., Shore, M.F., *The Practice of Mental Health Consultation*, DHEW Publication [ADM] 74-112, #1724–00395 [Washington, D.C.: U.S. Government Printing Office, 1975], pp. 43, 137)

Klerman makes a plea for more evaluative research on CMHC programs, citing the paucity of data and predicting that without adequate research findings the CMH movement will follow the path of earlier mental health reforms, with enthusiasm peaking rapidly, followed by criticism and retrenchment leading to reorganization of the contract between the professions and society [Klerman, Gerald, "Current Evaluative Research in Mental Health services", *American Journal of Psychiatry* 131,7:783–7 (July 1974)] . . . Burt S. Brown, director of NIMH, writes, "my personal and professional belief, as a physician, is that the primary responsibility of the CMHC staff is to treat those men, women, and children who are sick. This belief in no way derogates the responsibility to improve the social quality of life for individuals within the CMHC's jurisdiction" [Brown, Burt S., "Foreword", in Beigel, Allan and Levenson, Alan I. (eds.), *Community Mental Health Center: Strategies and Programs* (NY: Basic Books, 1972)]. He says that people may expect an increasing range of services to improve the environment and mitigate social pressures, but these expectations must be fused with the operational program of the center. While both treatment (p. 144) and social reform components of the CMHC programs are designed to effect change, the CMHC cannot assume the responsibility for the total reform of society.

Ochberg . . . expresses the hope that the "current and necessary preoccupation with law, politics, economics and administration does not drown the dream of better care for all people" [Ochberg, F.M., "CMHC Legislation: Flight of the Phoenix", *American Journal of Psychiatry* 133:56–61 (1976), p. 61]. [David A.] Musto writes, "psychiatry and the allied professions offer essential services not only to troubled individuals but to our general society as well . . . the CMHC's most enduring contribution may have been to lead the professions to a clearer sense of reality to its own areas of greater competence" (p. 78).
(Musto, David A., "What Ever Happened to Community Mental Health?", *Public Interest* 39 [Spring 1975]:53–79, 145)

A project sought to continue the model of collaboration among community resources and recognized the disparity in psychiatric emphasis on prevention:[15]

> Multi-agency community mental health centers consisting of two or more member organizations (affiliates) comprise 85 percent of all federally funded community mental health centers ... In general ... the Community Mental Health Centers Program has had a profound impact on the present mental health care system, in some communities, both in terms of the establishment of agencies, facilities, and services where none existed previously, and the augmentation of and improvement in existing agency programs and services (p. 157) ... the basic concept of (p. 158) integrating autonomous, local agencies into a cooperative organizational structure for the purpose of delivering coordinated services to a specific community appears to be an effective and viable approach with potential for expansion into areas beyond mental health (p. 159).
>
> Changing professional practices, i.e., a shift ... toward prevention of mental disorder and the promotion of mental health ... there is a lack of consensus within the mental health profession on what centers are and what they should do ... an underlying schism between those who felt the centers should keep their focus narrow, with traditional areas of expertise, and those who favored a more action oriented approach based on prevention and directed at the community at large ... centers have contributed substantially to the development of community concerns and involvement in mental health (p. 158).

There was consideration of serving the poor and societal factors underlying poverty:

> [T]he poor benefited most when principles of community mental health were emphasized, and when centers had a human service orientation (i.e., employment, housing) and need enhancement of the quality of life (p. 138) ... the social ills of poverty, crime, poor education, racism, and segregation cannot be met with the inadequate tools of mental health, that the concept of treatment close to home will bow to economic necessity and that a larger bureaucratic model will take over. Quality of service will have a lower priority.
> (Panzetta, A.F., *Community Mental Health, Myth and Reality* (Philadelphia: Lea & Febiger, 1971) (p. 138)

There was consideration of mental health manpower:

> psychiatric residency programs ... information from eighty ... fifty-six had an association with a CMH center, and sixteen were direct CMHC sponsors. Training in CMH is part of the residency program

> in most programs but has rarely found its way into curricula for medical students. The department chairmen consider the CMHC a federal creation but expressed little hostility. Research investment in community psychiatry was marginal (p. 142).
>
> New manpower resources have been mobilized, particularly the mental health worker . . . The CMH movement has influenced the private practice of psychiatry to broaden its treatment methods . . . embody community mental health principles and provide service to greater numbers of people. Multidisciplinary . . . groups . . . group therapies . . . Daycare programs (p. 142) . . . more mental health services are available on a local basis . . . decentralization of service . . . viable satellites . . . Stigma related to mental illness seems to have lessened and public knowledge has increased . . . influenced state mental health codes, especially . . . commitment laws and rights of patients (p. 143).

Note also that the NIMH funded the New Careers project, seeking a place for non–professionally trained community residents as a mental health resource.[16]

There was continued federal advocacy for broadened community-based mental health:[17]

> the President's (Jimmy Carter) Commission on Mental Health . . . final report urging expansion of the community mental health movement and . . . shoring up of federal financing for mental health . . . with First Lady Rosalynn Carter as Honorary Chairperson . . . the 12 percent of general health revenues now spent on mental health are not commensurate with the problem . . . since over half the dollars for mental health care are still spent in large state institutions and mental health related nursing homes . . . [need to] alter the current balance of mental health expenditures . . . to develop needed community resources (p. 1) . . . Community Mental Health Centers have been criticized for a range of things including not using traditional psychiatric concepts and not having preventive services . . . treating the chronically mentally ill . . . one of the harshest criticisms of the community mental health movement . . . Encouragement of the natural community support systems and linkage between them and the formal mental health system (p. 5).

There was also evaluation and reconsideration of CMH and CMHCs:[18]

> During the 1960's . . . new approaches to the governance of large organizations . . . exemplified by "management by objective" to secure accountability for expenditures of public funds and . . . evidence of effectiveness . . . In fiscal year (FY) 1969, 1 percent of

the appropriated operating center funds became available for evaluation purposes . . . The new mental health center legislation just enacted . . . requires that every center . . . utilize at least 2 percent of its operating funds for evaluation (p. 117).

On August 29, 1973, the U.S. Comptroller General (General Accounting Office, GAO) . . . noted that. . . "The centers have increased the accessibility, quantity and type of community services available and have enhanced the responsiveness of mental health services . . . Some success . . . in mobilizing State and local resources" . . . recommends that NIMH needs to improve performance in some program areas . . . in 1975. . . The Committee on Labor and Public Welfare . . . concludes "it is clear that the CMHC Act and the program . . . has been a success in creating community alternatives to State inpatient facilities . . . the preponderance of evidence received by the Committee attests to the fact that the CMHC program has been highly effective . . . The Administration agrees with the Congressional finding that the program is successful" . . . The report also notes the shortcomings of the centers (p. 122) . . . The Nader Report presents a different evaluation. . . [CMHCS] have not been accountable . . . windfalls for psychiatrists . . . ignored the directives to serve the poor and . . . blue collar workers . . . reduce the number of admissions to State mental hospitals . . . critical of . . . the catchment area requirement, the lack of citizen participation, and the lack of evaluation . . . Zusman has listed . . . the successes and failures of community psychiatry practice (p. 123) . . . An interesting project . . . with NIMH contract funds to determine the effect of the CMHC program on . . . mental health resources in two pairs of matched counties . . . in 1958 and 1970. . . in all four . . . substantial progress in developing mental health resources, but greater progress . . . in those counties with the CMHCs, especially in . . . indirect services such as consultation, public education, and vocational rehabilitation. All . . . decreased use of the state hospital despite population increases. . . "the results . . . suggests that the CMHC concept and movement may well be the outstanding or at least one of the major 'success stories' of this generation . . . the CMHC movement is an example of the forward steps this nation can take when its leaders and its people decide to make a major national and state effort and financial investment". (p. 124)

Bernard Holland had many questions and concerns about the CMHC program:[19] unclear concepts; conflicting goals and authority or deficiency thereof among levels of government, community, facilities, and professions; lack of coordination and fragmentation among resources and authorities; regret that CMHCs could not have supplemented mental hospitals and practitioners; inadequate funding; absence of accountability and quality measures; responsibility for psychiatric versus social problems; unclear and inappropriate role of consumers and intrusion on professional practice; lack of preparation of psychiatrists for community practice; and downgrading of psychiatrists and loss of their medical expertise, resulting in lower quality of care of community residents. He concluded that CMHC ideals were good, implementation slow and erratic in a democracy, and the inadequacy of data to monitor and help the program.

Philip Hallen, director of the Maurice Falk Foundation in Washington, saw CMHCs continuing to pursue the spirit of CMH while adapting to changing circumstances.[20] Their responsibilities included expanding the reach of services, minimizing hospitalization, and offering preventive services. He saw the contemporary President's Commission on Mental Health embodying these principles but given low priority. Their essential elements were an organizational-administrative model embodying alignment of political relationships, coordination of services, reassessment of professional roles and capabilities, citizen participation, and provision of a contact point between social change and administration of services. Contemporary critical issues were deinstitutionalization, preventive services, equity in provision of services, financial accountability and economy, innovation, the balance between promises and performance, consumer participation, and recognition of mental health care as a right. They faced the issues of manpower needs; services to minorities, children, and the aged; financing; and links to other human service systems. Dilemmas were the relation between the need for innovation and fiscal restraints, the conflict between human services and biomedical priorities, and the relation between science, ethics, and politics.

Erich Lindemann, too, was concerned about the relation of theory, scientific evidence, and program implementation. He appreciated the expansion of community mental health but nevertheless recognized ways in which this movement stumbled:[21]

> The community mental health centers are the expression of a powerful ideological thrust, which had its origins in psychiatry and public health, and was fostered by the intellectual climate of the Kennedy period. Overextension of goals, improvised planning, collision with existing power structures, [p. 1] and inevitable retrenchment ... are recurrent themes ... It was wise and courageous to take stock in this form of the almost chaotic features of the developing community mental health program, while making abundantly clear the encouraging discoveries and methodological advances which ... are continuing to appear.

Further, he wondered about the place of CMH in medicine versus in the social sciences:[22]

> Much emphasis is placed on the overexpansion of the range of problems for which the psychiatrists consider themselves competent. There is also the feeling that the concepts and orientations stemming from the psychoanalytic period of psychotherapy are unsuitable for meeting the new challenges and should be replaced by concepts developed in the field of learning theory and behavioral approaches to human distress.
>
> A plea is made that psychiatrists should return to the narrower field of clinical concerns and restrict their efforts to established disease, leaving the field of prevention to those who deal with human behavior on a broader basis, who consider social deviance not in medical but in legal, societal, and value terms, and who concern themselves with disturbed states as categories of *social* disturbance often labeled with the term "alienation". Such a plan would require the invention and implementation of patterns of social organization and community participation, which require primarily, if not exclusively, the services of the social scientists and the social action experts.

The quest for and contest among definitions of social psychiatry and community mental health continued, with various commitments to primary, secondary, and tertiary prevention:

> "the terms community mental health and social psychiatry are used differently and inconsistently...
>
> - [primary + secondary + tertiary prevention] ... Daniels says community psychiatry is a developing body of knowledge and practice which relates psychiatric and social principles to large population groups. "Its body of theory is known as social psychiatry and is derived from ecology and epidemiology, public health and preventive medicine, social systems theory, and community organization. It is also based on the psychologic insight of individual and small group dynamics and an understanding of family structure and organization". (Daniels, R.S., "Community Psychiatry—A New Profession, A Developing Subspecialty, or Effective Clinical Psychiatry?", *Community Mental Health Journal*, 2(1966):47–54; p. 48).
> - [primary + secondary + tertiary prevention] "Sabshin defines community psychiatry as 'the utilization of techniques, methods and theories of social psychiatry and other behavioral sciences to investigate and to meet the needs of a functionally

or geographically defined population over a significant period of time and the feeding back of information to modify the central body of social psychiatric and other behavioral science knowledge' ". (Sabshin, Melvin, "Theoretical Models in Community and Social Psychiatry", in L.M. Roberts, S.L. Halleck, and M.B. Loeb (eds.), *Community Psychiatry* (University of Wisconsin Press, 1966), pp. 15–30).

- [primary + secondary + tertiary prevention] "community mental health is a field of action . . . including psychiatrists, nonphysician mental health professionals, politicians, managers, . . . a wide variety of social service institutions, social scientists, citizens, and lay consumers of mental health services. 'The common general interest . . . is to change society itself . . . alter the ways in which society promotes the mental health of all its citizens and responds to mental illness in some of them' " (Karno, M and Schwartz, D.A., *Community Mental Health, Reflections and Explorations* (NY: Spectrum Publications, 1974), p. 2, 119).
- [secondary + tertiary prevention] "The report of the Joint Commission on Mental Illness and Health (1961) recommended local emergency services, community outpatient clinics, and general hospital psychiatric beds" (p. 120).
- [secondary + tertiary + primary prevention] In 1962, the NIMH . . . proposal for a community mental health program . . . the overall objective is to "increase the humanizing aspect of care and treatment of the mentally ill and the maximum integration and deployment of all possible resources for prevention of mental illness . . . prevention of mental illness . . . protection and promotion of mental health . . . appraisal of community needs, appropriate planning . . . reparative services to the mentally ill, . . . identify, correct, and control conditions inimical to mental health . . . mental health consultation . . . and educate the public about mental health . . . the goal is . . . a coordinated network of community based mental health services" (p. 120).
- [secondary + tertiary prevention] "P.L.88–164, the Community Mental Health Center Act of 1963 (Sec. 205D), says, "comprehensive mental health services for mentally ill persons". "The Regulations to P.L. 88–164, promulgated May 6, 1974, and having the force of law . . . using the objectives of the congressional mandate.
- [secondary + tertiary prevention] [Lawrence C.] Kolb says that the centers were intended . . . to the community treatment and rehabilitation of . . . severely impairing psychiatric disabilities—the psychoses.

- [secondary + tertiary + primary prevention] [H.] Diamond and [A.] Santore write, "the CMHC is to deliver readily accessible treatment and prevention services. . . [Jack] Ewalt agrees". Its purpose is to coordinate efforts to improve the community . . . that will enhance mental well being, decrease . . . the occurrence of personal and social stress, relieve troubled persons, prevent mental illness when possible and treat and rehabilitate those who become ill or disturbed" (p. 121).
- [secondary + tertiary prevention] Feldman and Windle say "the CMHC Program is an instrument of national health policy" program process goals: . . . organization and delivery of mental health services . . . increasing the accessibility of mental health services . . . Increasing the quality and range of . . . health services; . . . Enhancing the responsiveness . . . to community and individual needs (p. 121) . . . high quality standards of community care . . . Decreasing the utilization of state mental hospitals . . . increasing the participation . . . of state and local groups" (p. 122).
- [primary prevention] Stanley Yolles clearly saw social conditions as a part of the new CMH, but wondered at its limits:[23] "in the past decade society in the United States began to add . . . a further concern for mental health as a positive force and a human right . . . This dimension of the concept *Is* new" (p. 171).

"each community mental health center has resolved its own pattern of operation and program priorities . . . Some emphasize . . . to treat those already ill . . . Others—especially in . . . 1966–1970—take the social activist road . . . involved themselves in [everything from] . . . landlord boycotts to anything else they perceived as a community injustice . . . at what point . . . to improve the root causes of emotional disturbances . . . decide that it cannot be all things to all people? . . . who shall be considered therapists and in what disciplines. Is a helping grandmother, an ex-addict, a 'socially conscious activist' . . . equated with psychiatrists, psychologists, social workers, nurses" (p. 180).

"the *essence* of the [community mental health centers] program has always been . . . to remove the locus of the care and treatment of the mentally ill from large, custodial institutions to acute treatment in community-based facilities that are responsible for and responsive to the needs of the people who live in those communities" (p. 184).

While this large-scale federal involvement augmented mental health services, it cut the support for voluntary community efforts and agencies. See, for example, the disbanding of the Mental Health Planning

Committee of Metropolitan Boston[24] after the publication of its survey of Boston's mental health needs and services.[25] This shift from a community-based to a federal government–based approach to meeting health and welfare needs was acknowledged and juxtaposed with the evolution of the civil rights movement:[26]

> in the 1967. . . the community action program . . . may well have reached the end of its brief period of expansion . . . Model cities programs are now in their planning phases . . . The Urban Coalition is in the process of defining its role and organizing itself . . . the President's new JOBS program, which will reimburse employers for the extra expenses involved in training the hard-core unemployed, is only in its very beginning . . . the history of community action from the initial pilot projects supported by the Ford Foundation and the President's Committee on Juvenile Delinquency through the passage of the Economic Opportunity Act of 1964 (p. 2).
>
> community action and the anti-poverty program are largely by-products of the civil rights movement. At the time the War on Poverty was conceived and approved . . . the thrust of the civil rights movement was still basically to achieve access to opportunity—in housing, education, employment and so on . . . But as the OEO [Office of Economic Opportunity] program got under way, the civil rights movement was already shifting its emphasis from opportunity to the attainment of power (p. 5).
>
> [Paul] Ylvisaker [then head of the Ford Foundation's Public Affairs Program] and his colleagues . . . intent was to mount an effective challenge and start the process of reform in the institutions of society (p. 7).

Shift from Community to Individual, Social to Biological

The 1970s saw a shift from the post–World War II optimism and campaigns for improvement of society as a whole to a conservative, noninterventionist, and self-service social, political, and economic ideology. "He [Erich Lindemann] lived long enough to sense that the flood tide of optimism and new funding for innovation had peaked and was receding".[27]

In part, this was reaction to the civil rights and anti–Vietnam War movements, which were often challenging and sometimes violent and provoked counteraction:[28]

> "That the consumer activism of the late 1960's in the mental health movement reflected the anger and anguish of racial tensions, the drug scene, the antiwar scene, and the expressed contempt for the Establishment, for professionalism and for merit based on knowledge of substance should not have surprised . . . the mental health

community. But even thoughtful men resist change and resent a diminution of the power to which they have become accustomed" (p. 181). Historically it was recalled that "[Woodrow] Wilson failed to understand that after two decades of idealism and reform, the American people were not in the mood to be rallied—they wanted the 'normalcy' that Warren G. Harding and the Republicans promised, and they reaffirmed that demand in the elections of 1924 and 1928".[29]

One is reminded of David Rothman's highlighting of the influence of society's need for order in structuring mental health systems:[30]

> the idea of the asylum took form in the perception, in fact the fear, that once-stable social relationships were now in the process of unraveling, threatening to subvert the social order and social cohesion (p. xxix) . . . Jacksonian Americans experienced a crisis of confidence in the social organization of the new republic, fearful that the ties that once bound citizens together—the ties of community, church, and family—were loosening and that, as a consequence, social disorganization appeared imminent . . . The good order of the asylum, its routine of punctuality and steady labor, would act as both a cure and a preventive—reforming its charges and serving as a model to the community (p. xxx).

This trend was also described in psychological terms regarding the rise of narcissism:[31]

> Long before social critic Tom Wolfe labeled the '70s "The 'Me' Decade", scholars were exploring narcissism as a new—and perhaps even dominant—psychological pattern of both individual and social behavior. . . [characterized by] cannot return anyone's affection . . . grandiose expectation of himself . . . For social historian Christopher Lasch. . . "self-preservation and psychic survival" pervade the moral climate of contemporary society . . . some social scientists have adopted . . . narcissism to help explain the declining interest in politics, social action and child-rearing, and the corresponding rise of an individualistic survival ethic . . . psychoanalyst Otto F. Kernberg . . . Much as they crave admiration . . . narcissists systematically exploit and devalue others . . . enjoy only fleeting emotional contacts, rather than genuine, long-term intimacy . . . often highly successful in business, bureaucracies, or other impersonal organizations. . . [which] reward those who can manipulate others, while discouraging personal attachments and providing enough emotional feedback to satisfy self-esteem . . . unable to identify with the happiness of others or with any on-going human enterprise (p. 70).

Politically, the federal administration of Richard Nixon (1969–1974) was hostile to federal programs including mental health and undermined confidence, planning, and funding, which was demoralizing.[32] It took place in the context of ideological conflicts and rifts in the mental health community and fueled a societal mood of hostility to authority, intellectualism, and science. Opportunists among special interest groups took advantage of this turmoil to advance their programs and personal ambitions. The administration of Ronald Reagan (1981–1989) implemented these reactionary policies more concretely.

From 1972, psychiatry's criticism of the CMH movement's ideals became more open:[33] It was deemed impractical and grandiose idealism, CMHCs were seen as arms of social revolution, boundaries of practice of psychiatrists and mental health were expanded to include social revolutionary redress, team approaches blurred or abolished professional boundaries, advocacy for consumer and public regulation of the mental health system were espoused, and CMH threatened the drift of psychiatry away from medicine (including the abolition of the medical internship in favor of early psychiatric training). Organized psychiatry opted for the return of its association with medicine, focus on individual patient care, critical oversight of the control of and treatment in CMHCs, and psychiatric leadership's active participation in political decisions affecting mental health and psychiatry. Daniel X. Friedman, president of the American Psychiatric Association (APA), authored an article accusing CMH of trivializing psychiatry.[34] As an example, in social psychiatry, Alexander Leighton complained:[35] "The counterculture of the 1960s and the offshoots of the present manifest a strong antiscientific bias as part of the condemnation of 'the establishment'. Instead, the emphasis is on quick solutions to human problems by adversary and advocacy procedures".

Taking the student activism and rebellion at Columbia University as an example, there were analyses and evaluations from several points of view: Seymour Halleck explored the psychological and social motivations of student activism:[36]

> Student unrest was not out of personal defect but a justified response to oppression. "The more objective observers of student unrest seek its causes in the psychological changes that have taken place in man as he is forced to adapt to technological growth and a constantly accelerating rate of change in the everyday conditions of life . . . young people distrust the past, fear the future and are driven to live in the present. They seek immediate gratification (p. 2) . . . The following factors seem to be especially relevant to the new and more disturbing wave of unrest and violence on our campuses (p. 3) . . . All of the issues . . . become more intense as the [Vietnam] war continues . . . a few have found their masculinity . . . through defiant obstruction . . . The death of Martin Luther King has increased

everyone's desperation . . . Many white students feel that they must risk a great deal to salve their consciences . . . an almost geometric increase in the use of marijuana . . . students become contemptuous of the society that imposes such unreasonable drug control laws and begin to doubt the validity of many other rules . . . many more students . . . feel deeply about the war, the impersonality of the university, the university's failure to become involved in helping the Negro, and the need for students to have more power to direct their own lives . . . a hard core of students . . . are determined to destroy this society and its universities . . . compassionate faculty . . . are usually sympathetic . . . they are also committed to the pursuit of intellectual values in . . . peacefulness and stability. When (p. 4) a major confrontation occurs their . . . ambivalence is paralyzing . . . There is a climate of anticipation and excitement . . . it is exhilarating . . . Students who have attempted to bring about . . . changes through legitimate forms . . . have been rebuffed . . . they are learning that the establishment is surprisingly vulnerable to attack . . . University administrators have not been able to cope effectively with student protest . . . administrators and faculty must not cave in to threats of disruption . . . they must reexamine the nature of the university and must be prepared to . . . implementing much needed changes" (p. 5).

Robert S. Liebert, M.D., went further in analyzing the psychodynamics of the students coming to terms with political action.[37]

Richard Abrams saw a political reaction to unacceptable conditions:[38]

> What had been a profound impatience with a political system that refused honestly to confront racial injustices, poverty and problems of personal dignity having to do with mass living, working and educational conditions has . . . turned into angry desperation. The mounting violence we are experiencing expresses that desperation (p. 13) . . . the [Vietnam] war must bear primary responsibility for the changed mood. . . [It] has presented . . . young men with the awesome choice . . . Many of the "tough" among them have "got going" with civil disruption (p. 14) . . . what has happened at Columbia [is that] . . . the faculty's discontent with their role in the governance of the University. . . [and] the estrangement of the faculty and students from the administration . . . remains the one outstanding explanation of the disaster that has struck (p. 15).

Amitai Etzioni saw a social process with some justification:[39]

> temperaments do not find slow progress congenial and who are attracted by the drama and excitement of confrontation . . . civil disobedience is for the liberal a court of last resort, for the confronting

students it is a short-cut, and for the radical it is an attempt to destroy institutionalized channels not merely because they do not work but to insure that they will not work (p. 10) . . . if Columbia had responded earlier and more actively to the students' legitimate demands, and provided for authentic student and faculty participation in several key decision-making sectors, most of the present difficulties could have been prevented . . . The danger of excessive student power . . . cannot be ignored . . . But some significant sharing of power is considerably overdue . . . the current New Left confrontations may have been the only means of bringing about the reforms necessary for *liberal* processes to work effectively (p. 12).

Erich Fromm addressed the philosophical and moral motivation for this unrest:[40]

one of the essential features of that society which we are approaching is a state of chronic low-grade schizophrenia . . . the split between thought and feeling, truth and passion, mind and heart is becoming complete in our time (p. 6) . . . one speaks about human affairs without any corresponding emotion . . . People are taught concepts but they are not taught or confronted with the experience which corresponds to these concepts . . . The vitality of a culture depends on a tradition which inspires men, which gives them courage to live, which gives them, most of all, hope (p. 7).

John Seeley was one of the faculty and administration members who justified and joined the rebellion using sociological concepts:[41]

The university administration and mass media are duplicitous in complaints, charges, and characterizations with pre-formed criticisms of the students. The university is responsible for and guilty of what goes on inside it. It should have learned from previous experience at the University of California–Berkeley, and in Montgomery and Selma Alabama: "to make just and generous settlements with its own black students, or with Harlem. . . [It should be] fully informed . . . as to the criminality . . . of the [Vietnam] war, the evils of the draft and selective service, and the adverse effect on education of. . . 'man power channeling'—[and be] moved . . . to clear its skirts . . . of all involvement in . . . crimes against humanity. [It should] rid itself of its administration and board, go to the students it proposes to impugn, not merely with amnesty and guarantee of safe passage, but with . . . its highest accolades, its gratitude forever, its most honorary degree. . . [Then it will show it] deserves the tentative support of those who love what a university ought to be".

Bernard Steinzor did likewise using psychiatric concepts:[42]

> Obviously we cannot explain these events as mere manifestations of a phase of growth or of some sort of intrapsychic upheaval we label an identity crisis (p. 24) . . . people who have . . . outdistanced their elders in sensibility and understanding of the vital issues of the times . . . the sharp confrontation grew out of two major issues of the modern university, issues which the responsible authorities were essentially trying to avoid: the accelerating expansion into the surrounding community . . . and the university's dependence on government research grants (symbolized by the IDA [Institute for Defense Analysis]). If the students' activities bring about a serious analysis of these questions, they . . . will have been worth much more than the price paid so far (p. 26).
>
> We in the established healing professions have in the last few years found ourselves mobilizing under an apparently new banner, community psychology. This . . . came about largely from pressures outside our providence . . . to articulate . . . two related ways of perceiving and interpreting our field . . . the individual self is social . . . a relation to indeterminate time, uncertainty and the unknown. And . . . our therapeutic stance always had been a moral one. . . [leaving] our political and religious selves outside our office door . . . no more. One's life as a citizen affects one's life as a therapist . . . groups organized to achieve social equality and to implement . . . the pursuit of liberty, equality, fraternity [slogan of the French revolution] and happiness, and led by others than our professional selves, might be therapeutic agencies . . . therapy groups meeting . . . in the streets, the churches and the university dormitories . . . any group trying to reform ritualized, hierarchical relations is therapeutic, whether it is led by ourselves or by indigenous leaders . . . The students have been doing our thing . . . a progressive order ever expanding the coordinates of love and justice (p. 26).

Sidney Hook was a member of a philosophy faculty and administration who rejected the rebellion:[43]

> The unspoken allegiance of the community of scholars has been to civility of mind. Respect for the rights of teacher and students to differ with each other and among themselves has been taken for granted . . . All this has been fractured at Columbia by violence, obscenity and hysterical insult . . . as a consequence of a new concept of the university held by the students—and some faculty members, of the New Left . . . The task . . . is to expose and destroy its current role of stooge for the establishment . . . The campaign of educational disruption is to be carried from campus to campus until the universities

are radicalized, and become part of a united front for this new society (p. 22) . . . The demands made by the New Left on the universities would destroy them . . . as centers of intellectual freedom, and therefore of intellectual authority and objectivity (p. 23).

The university as an institution cannot commit itself to any partisan or non-educational cause. It must leave its teachers free to follow their own bent, subject only to the controls of the logic and ethics of honest inquiry. It cannot as such espouse any ideology, any orthodoxy, any controversial program of social action or reaction without betraying its mission, sacrificing its relative autonomy, and subjecting itself to reprisals from any power group, or coalition of such groups, that holds the dominant position for the moment in society.

Where the goal is basically educational or involves universal values such as health, or the defense of academic freedom, the university as such can take a stand. But as an institution, it cannot commit itself to . . . a campaign for this or that program of social welfare . . . or what not, without becoming in effect a political action group. Individuals within it . . . are free to engage in such activities as citizens (p. 23).

Clay Risen focused on the assassination of Martin Luther King and the civil disobedience that followed.[44] In 1968, following Martin Luther King's assassination, increased, prolonged, destructive rioting undermined white support of the civil rights movement, Lyndon Johnson's Great Society programs, and liberalism; this coalesced political opposition to government social programs and spawned a conservative backlash. It was expressed by Vice President Spiro Agnew, President Richard Nixon, and the suburban white political powers in the form of hopelessness and disinterest in the urban poor and minorities, and the conclusion that the call for solution of social problems was wasteful and extortionate: "The 1968 riots provided an entrée for conservatives to finally, fully assert law and order as a national political issue".

John Powers commented thus more broadly on the process:[45]

It's the disillusioned residue of the thwarted optimism of the 60's, which ended with John and Robert Kennedy and Martin Luther King Jr. assassinated, Lyndon Johnson's Great Society in tatters, and the country torn apart by an unpopular war, Watergate, with its sordid tales of wiretaps and hush money and a president insisting he was "not a crook", dashed what little innocence was left about government (p. 31–2) . . . If Americans aren't as fixated on societal issues as they once were, it may be because they've learned that many of the issues are complex, contradictory, and costly (p. 33) . . . the voters, who had supported the idea, rebelled at the reality (p. 33) . . . people were concerned about these things [e.g., health care] but unwilling and unprepared to pay much of a price to solve them (p. 33) . . . they either are conflicted about what to do or won't pay the price (p. 33).

Another force was the shift of public support from larger social policy reform, such as community mental health, to support for specific interest groups and their needs and rejection of traditional governmental, organizational, intellectual, and professional establishments as sources of this support:[46]

> The [Vietnam] war dramatically escalated in cost, feeding inflationary pressures and reducing the resources available for domestic problems. And the protests . . . helped turn policy makers' attention toward issues of equity for disadvantaged Americans . . . helped intensify . . . concern by newly formed public interest legal organizations for the basic constitutional rights of disabled Americans. As a result, the rights of mental patients began to be defined through major court decisions rather than by clinicians and public policy makers. When this trend was joined with the already powerful effort to secure equal opportunities for blacks and women, the product was a massive and new civil rights movement affecting every organization receiving federal monies.

Of course, adherents to the ideology of the individual as the locus of sickness and the priority of treatment (secondary prevention) reasserted themselves. Robert Glaser, who had served in the office of the deans of several medical schools—including Harvard and Stanford—was skeptical of primary prevention: it would be good to do but questioned whether it were possible.[47] He also questioned the allocation of mental health resources to social problems such as parenting and sexuality versus mental illness. And he expressed his mistrust of mental health professionals other than psychiatrists in terms of their expertise, motivation, and potential for doing damage if they intruded into social issues. Zusman and Lamb, too, maintained that the original, tested, central, and enduring function of psychiatry and CMH is the care in the community of severely mentally ill patients, otherwise currently or potentially confined in state mental hospitals.[48] They saw prevention—dealing with a sociocultural milieu relevant to mental illness—as employing little-trained but patient-matched workers to deal with the sociocultural background, prevention, mental health consultation, and the relevance of deplorable social conditions; these were recently appearing interests tangential to CMH. They regretted psychiatry's turning away from populationwide, psychiatrist-led treatment of the severely mentally ill in the conflictful community and toward private practice, academics, research, and biological approaches. Mandell decried communities, political activists, and minority cadres becoming demanding and in conflict with academics, institutions, and professionals.[49] The pressure for unorthodox roles and service agencies, and the conflict in the mental health field destroys serviceable institutions. It leads to empty and wasteful expenditures and the withdrawal of support for both good and bad services.

It is interesting that this shift away from social concerns and toward the individual as the locus of problems and their remediation drew support from psychological as well as biological ideologies.

Redlich and Kellert ruefully noted the change in psychiatric treatment methods and goals between 1950 (when psychoanalysis and psychodynamic therapy were broadly espoused) and 1975 (when social-shifting-to-biological therapy came to the fore and the psychoanalytic basis for treatment was recognized by only 45% of mental health professionals and programs).[50] They saw this psychiatric change reflecting changes in societal goals and values. They reported that in 1950, treatment was 32% psychotherapy, 32% organic therapies, and 36% custodial. In comparison, in 1975, most treatment was individual and group milieu therapy and much use of drugs—25% psychotherapy, 25% drugs, 20% group therapy, and 15% family therapy. The goals then were reduction of symptoms and increase in function rather than insight and personality change—which they thought only apparently beneficial without learning about or changing the true causes of mental illness. In fact, they were concerned that some community care could be less effective as well as detrimental to other family members. There was complaint that the distinction among disciplinary roles was lost and that psychiatrists tended to be relegated to physical examination, drug prescription, and administration and devalued. This led to psychiatrists choosing to focus on the treatment of upper-class, white, younger patients and being less involved with lower class, alcoholic, old, and nonwhite patients.

The psychoanalyst Norman Brill was most direct:[51]

> the current thesis that attributes mental illness to social stress and emphasizes social action as the mainstay of preventive psychiatry [is challenged] . . . [There is] increasing evidence for the role of genetic factors in mental illness . . . greater recognition of differences in personality characteristics . . . apparent very early in life and that persist . . . the interaction of this personality and stress to which the developing individual is exposed is a crucial determinant of late adult personality adjustment and behavior . . . there has been a turning away from the investigation of the intrapsychic factors in emotional illness and the elements of an individual's personality that contribute to maladjustment, and in its place there is an emphasis on the more obvious current societal stresses that had been ignored for so long. . . . [This] has two unfortunate potential consequences: a deterioration in the individual treatment of patients, and frustrated expectations that mental and emotional illness will

be eliminated . . . Some mental health centers, under the guise of providing psychiatric treatment, seem to be more interested in solving problems of unemployment, welfare, poverty, racial prejudice, housing, etc., than in exploring the elements of an individual's personality and life pattern that contributed to his maladjustment or illness. There is a tendency to belittle intensive individual treatment as old-fashioned, wasteful, ineffective and impractical and to offer instead crisis treatment, shortcuts, brief therapy and all sorts of innovation as panaceas.

More and more the goal of treatment seems to be merely improvement of symptoms *not* improved understanding, change in attitudes, modulation of unrealistic expectations or altered interpersonal relationships.

Closing state hospitals and returning patients to their communities is considered a great advance in the treatment of the mentally ill. However, many patients end up . . . provide[d] poorer treatment, less adequate facilities. . . [that] are far less humane than the so-called "back wards" of the state hospitals . . . Another development is the rejection of traditional standards of normality and the expectation that communities will tolerate . . . deviant behavior . . . I wonder to what extent these alternative facilities were developed because they cost less . . . not necessarily better or even sound . . . all of this has been accompanied by no visible improvement in the mental health of the community (p. 30) . . . it is unscientific to say that poverty breeds mental illness as it is to say that wealth prevents it . . . There are still vast differences of opinion among sociologists concerning the magnitude of the roles played in the development of mental disorders by low socioeconomic status or other concomitant variables of poverty. . . [Although the] incidence rates for mental disorders . . . are highest in . . . groups of low socioeconomic status, it has not yet been clearly established whether this is the result of excessive stress . . . of the poverty condition or of downward drifting of mentally disturbed persons . . . all the poor and all those who are victims of . . . prejudice do not end up with disabling emotional disorders.

While those who assume that the elimination of these stresses is the answer are to be praised for their humanitarian concerns. . . [s]kepticism is warranted in the face of the increasing demand for immediate gratification and the decreasing tolerance of compromise and self-denial that is so prevalent in the world today.

prevention of mental illness was of major importance in the Soviet Union . . . to eliminate or reduce anxiety . . . full employment, material security in case of illness or old age, free medical care for all and free higher education . . . the major goal of treatment is to maximize individual effectiveness . . . there are many parents who are not capable of rearing mentally healthy children, and that massive programs of rearing future citizens by professionals are needed (p. 31) . . . some mental health workers entertain the myth that if people are to be mentally healthy there should be no unhappiness, no anxiety, no conflict, no struggle, no emotional discomfort, and possibly no unsatisfied need, and that if any of these exist it is because of some defect in society . . . Emphasis has shifted from helping individuals adjust to society to having society adjust to individuals, and social reform has to be justified on the basis of health reasons . . . one may wonder if gratifying insatiable demands and catering to infinite expectations is, in the long run, going to advance the mental health of our nation . . . over the past 25 years . . . impressive social advances have been made . . . These have not been accompanied by any visible decrease in mental illness, crime, human unhappiness or world tension which seem to be getting worse . . . a society protected from stress might end up being more vulnerable to stress, since every spectrum of life from birth to death is accompanied by stress (p. 32) . . . I wonder if the current trend of expecting the government to cater to every individual's desires and encouraging people to believe this is their right is stimulating a massive regression of our society to an oral dependent state from which there may be no recovery without a radical, painful change in the entire sociopolitical system (p. 33) . . . A preventive psychiatry that focuses entirely on eliminating all stress and on gratifying human desires is bound to fail. While we must strive to improve the quality of life for all we cannot lose sight of the fact that man . . . must . . . learn to tolerate the frustration, anxiety, conflict, disappointment, and irrationality that inevitably is part of everyone's life . . . expectations of Utopia . . . lead to inevitable and massive disappointments . . . Margaret Mead criticized psychiatrists . . . she pointed out "The profession may be placing too much emphasis on a social consciousness . . . it might better attempt to bring out . . . sacrifice, loyalty, and unselfishness".

This is a far cry from what many mental health workers are advocating today (p. 34).

There was also a reassertion of hospital care of the mentally ill:[52]

This report was written to call attention to a major dilemma facing American psychiatry . . . We believe that psychiatric hospitals serve a unique function for many patients. The extension of mental health services from hospital and clinic into the community is (p. 88) progressive, and we support this long-overdue direction in psychiatry. But we protest against the view that psychiatric hospitalization is a sign of failure of alternate methods of therapeutic care . . . These functions can complement the community mental health programs and thus meet the needs of the troubled people to whom this report is dedicated (p. 89).

Yet another influence was the abiding competition among disciplines for benefit from the mental health system. As psychiatrists benefitted less from CMH, their support shifted to medical-controlled mental health programs. They could assert primacy under a biological ideology and chose to ally themselves with medicine rather than nonmedical mental health disciplines:[53]

> When the first [CMH] centers came into being in the late 1960's, NIMH permitted only psychiatrists to be their directors . . . By 1976 only 30% were psychiatrists, 21% were psychologists, 31% were social workers, and 18% were from other disciplines. Now only 19% are psychiatrists . . . of 43 states in 1979. . . only 17 required the state mental health commissioner to have a medical degree. Only 9 of 32 states . . . required a medical degree of the mental hospital director . . . the zeitgeist of the 1960's, an egalitarianism . . . in the community mental health centers movement . . . mental health professionals became almost indistinguishable from each other. . . [This] extended to the leadership positions as well . . . The authoritarian leadership style . . . in mental health administration . . . with which the training and professional socialization of physicians was so compatible was no longer as viable . . . Paternalism was out, replaced by citizen participation, staff involvement . . . unionization, and other characteristics of "participatory management" (p. 1149) . . . psychiatrists, with greater mobility, more options, and therefore less tolerance for the frustrations of administration, became less interested in administrative jobs. For the other mental health professionals, the financial and power rewards of administration were either greater than or at least more competitive with their other alternatives. Their options were fewer, and . . . private practice . . . was less accessible (p. 1150).

Politically, in the 1970s, a Republican federal administration tried to end the CMHC program.[54] In 1972, a budget request claimed "demonstrated success" and sought to shift funding to state and local governments, impounded funds (it took a year of litigation to overturn this), blocked renewal legislation with vetoes, and proposed shifting the funding of CMHCs to block grants to the states—as was proposed for Medicaid and ten other programs. Stanley Yolles, director of the NIMH, observed:[55]

> by 1970 a president and 'his men' would actively seek to terminate federal support—of both the community mental health centers program and the training of psychiatric manpower (p. 169) . . . [While] the intent of the Congress that this was to be a continuing program, rather than a pilot demonstration . . . the administration wanted to kill the program—or 'phase it out' . . . In 1973–74, the president

> chose *not to allocate* community mental health funds for the next fiscal year . . . the directors of the community mental health centers had formed a national organization . . . went to court. . . [with] the contention that the president does not have the power to impound funds that have been appropriated by the Congress and allocated in the Budget. The center directors won . . . and the funds were belatedly restored (p. 177) . . . they were successful enough to slow the momentum (p. 169) . . . political pressures and governmental concepts that have nothing to do with the care of the mentally ill . . . will continue to affect the national mental health program (p. 170).

Local response was observed to be reduction in services (day hospitals, children's services, etc.) and return to hospital treatment with an increase in state hospital census.[56]

In psychiatry, this manifested as a counterrevolution against social and community psychiatry and toward a reduced federal role, a business focus, and a biological ideology. The combination of financial economizing and ideological shift had a major impact on CMHCs and was sold in part under the slogan of "deinstitutionalization"—the undermining of CMH under cover of claims of its implementation and blaming it for the consequences:[57]

> the infusion of both federal and state matching dollars in the mid 60s . . . engendered great expectations for the community mental health movement. However public and political sentiment changed with the election of more conservative Administrations and resources for community mental health were curtailed . . . large expansive buildings built in flush times had to be staffed, and services provided, in times of greatly decreased financial support . . . inadequate support and unmet expectations have led to. . . <u>deinstitutionalization, disintegration</u> of the care network for the chronically ill, psychiatric <u>disenfranchisement</u> of citizens with non-chronic illness, and <u>demedicalization</u> of public psychiatry.
>
> By the early 1970s community mental health had collided . . . with . . . the deinstitutionalization movement to shift the care of the chronically mentally ill from state hospitals to the community. Deinstitutionalization was propelled by the states' hopes that they could save money in fiscally strapped times by closing down expensive . . . institutions. Community mental health centers . . . became overwhelmed with chronically mentally ill patients.

Satin, reviewing cycles of psychiatric ideology, noted this shift in the cycle:[58]

> This . . . counterrevolution of political and economic conservatism . . . contributed to the retreat to the "safe" biological study

of individual pathology; conservative and nihilistic expectations; and anatomical, biochemical, and genetic studies distant from social responsibility and involvement. A conscious political decision was made by psychiatry to ally itself with non-psychiatric medicine rather than non-medical mental health professions in order to distance itself from social conflict and preserve its competitive advantage.

These changes of course are epitomized in a petition by members of the MGH staff after Dr. Lindemann's retirement, stating their opinions that "We . . . are greatly concerned over the choice of a new Chief of Psychiatry at the M.G.H. We have the following opinions: . . . That acutely ill psychiatric patients should be cared for in a general hospital . . . psychiatric leadership must be provided to . . . establish an environment in which intensive treatment and responsibility for the welfare of patients, rather than inquiries into the hypothetical cause or causes of psychiatric illness is made the paramount function of the Psychiatric Service . . . encourage the use of physical and chemical methods in the treatment of psychiatric illness . . . To accomplish these desiderata we believe that Dr. Lindemann's successor should . . . not be a member of, nor lend his support to, any school or cult of psychiatry which substitutes 'faith' for the scientific method of diagnosing, treating and evaluating the results of treatment of mental illness". This at the MGH, dedicated since its founding to basic research in all other medical specialties, and written by adherents of the school of biological psychiatry!

And so entered the era of biological psychiatry, distanced from social responsibility and very much like the one that held sway during the latter part of the nineteenth century. Then, too, the state provided custodial care by largely untrained attendants for the severely and chronically mentally ill. Psychiatric ideology held that insanity was of biological origin (constitutional degenerate psychopathy), amenable only to palliative care until laboratory science had unraveled the neuroanatomical and neurophysiological causes. This achievement was expected to result in the prevention, cure, and eradication of insanity.

Allen reviewed the consequent reemergence of biological medicine:[59]

> During the past seventy years . . . we have become progressively more preoccupied with the biological mechanisms of disease—a preoccupation best understood as a consequence of a model of medicine that has contributed much to our therapeutic powers, and has therefore come to dominate our professional ideology (Engel, 1971, 1977) . . . Flexner (1910) advocated a mastery of the scientific method . . . his recommendations have been interpreted in a way that has emphasized unifactorial etiology, physiochemical explanations, and mind-body dualism (p. 565) . . . Current biomedical dogma has

assumed that disease is best understood in terms of deviation from measurable, biological variables, and the diagnosis of disease has preempted medical attention (p. 566).

Lamb and Zusman articulated the contemporary skepticism in psychiatry about unjustified concern with unhappiness and basic social problems, the connections between social conditions and mental illness, psychiatrists' lack of skills and professional purview in this area, the lack of evidence of effectiveness of primary prevention, and the inadequate knowledge about the genetics and biochemistry which are primary to an understanding of the causes of mental illness.[60] Alexander Leighton, known as a social psychiatrist, joined in the criticism of tying psychiatry too closely to social issues, adulterating it with social scientists, and losing core ideology and goals:[61]

> science is for humanity's sake, and scientists must be highly responsible and responsive to the needs and values of humanity. This is where we get our direction as well as our support.
>
> On the other hand, within its perimeters science has to remain science; otherwise it becomes a delusion, if not a hallucination. It must be protected from interference and influence, just as a compass must be protected from magnets. If you don't like the information the compass gives you . . . you can easily deflect the needle. But that alters no facts—it just hinders navigation (p. 54).
>
> During the Sixties . . . Psychoanalysis lost much of its prestige and authority, and diverse schools of psychotherapy emerged—transactionalists, existentialists, gestaltists, and so forth. The behavior therapists, the sex therapists, the family therapists, and the group therapists all staked out new claims. . . [Stone, Alan A., "Psychiatry: Dead or alive? *Harvard Magazine*, December, 1976] . . . among the mental health professions—psychiatry, psychology, social work, and nursing. There came to be more independence but also more antagonism. Increased participation by sociologists and social psychologists brought further uncertainties and tensions (p. 51) . . . The counterculture of the 1960's and its offshoots of the present manifest a strong anti-scientific bias as part of the condemnation of "the establishment". Instead, the emphasis is on quick solutions to human problems by adversary and advocacy procedures . . . theories are apt to lose their tentative character, to appear as scientific findings, and then to become . . . ideologies and articles of faith . . . and have become instead word packages for propaganda . . . the compass [scientific inquiry] is now in heightened danger because of reactions people have when the social and emotional seas [environment] become rough (p. 54).

the fear many people have of a "therapeutic state", a clockwork orange vision of citizens drugged and bugged by the psychiatric establishment.

there is great compassion abroad in the land, indeed on the whole earth, with perhaps unparalleled talk of caring for the handicapped and the deprived (p. 43).

Leonard Duhl thought no worthwhile CMH programs were developed in this period.

It was noted that CMH was not robust in the U.S.:[62]

In visiting some 18 major psychiatric teaching and training centers around the country, I was struck by the relative newness of programs in community psychiatry, by the paucity of programs with an actively operating full range of services, and by the relatively small amount of research into the questions raised by the vast social experiment in the reorganization of psychiatric services and concepts which is the community psychiatry movement . . . I was surprised by the number and quality of research projects in community or social psychiatry being conducted at a number of centers in Great Britain . . . partially due to the fact that experience with . . . the community approach to psychiatry has been lengthier than in this country.

Psychiatry professional organizations avoided commitment, though there were believers among their membership:[63]

the questions involving social responsibility of psychiatrists . . . As you know, the *American Journal of Psychiatry* and the APA Council have avoided, on the whole, entering into questions with political implications in order to maintain a judicial neutrality . . . major positions could be presented without official [p. 1] sanction so that our members would not be ignorant of the enormous changes which will occur with the new Federal legislation . . . yourself, and men working actively in the manpower field like Dan Blain and the commissioners of mental health in the various states, who do you think of as being good students and expositors.

(p. 2)

There was resistance to biological ("medical") psychiatry, though with limited power and influence. Some came from advocates for social psychiatry:[64]

Last June Boston University and the South Shore Mental Health Center received an NIMH grant for a four day national conference on the training of psychologists in community mental health. The conference was held in Swampscott and the 40 psychologists assembled promptly decided that restricting our efforts to the health-sickness model would yield no important preventive gains. Instead they opted for an as yet undefined field of community psychology, with mental health-illness as . . . only one part, of a large area which ought to involve the traditional disciplines in government processes, urban planning processes, educational planning, etc. The conference proceedings will be published shortly . . . chapter on Community Psychology which I wrote.

And Lindemann himself persisted in his belief in the shift to social psychiatry:[65]

> mental health . . . goals are no longer limited to health and disease, but include guiding each person to the most acceptable and achievable lifestyle of which he might be capable. Instead of dealing mainly with patients . . . the most significant interaction takes place with persons in the community who make decisions about mental health arrangements, and . . . new roles . . . required by preventive programs.

Some resistance to biological ideology came from advocates for non-medical professions who found a greater voice in CMH. George Albee was an assertive and articulate spokesman for this point of view. He, like social psychiatry, looked to social and societal sources of mental illness, though he did not focus on mental health. And he was one of those competing with psychiatry and medicine.[66]

> current and prospective manpower shortages in the mental health field derive from a set of interacting considerations . . . Disturbed and disturbing human behavior currently is "explained" by a conceptual model which attributes causation to "disease" or to some form of "illness". The content of the explanatory model accounting for these sorts of human deviation dictates the specific kind of institutional structure which society must support for the delivery of care or intervention. And the nature of the institution in turn dictates the kind of manpower required for its staffing. So we are confronted with a desperate shortage of medical and paramedical professionals required to staff hospitals, clinics, and centers.
>
> Because of the primacy of the disease explanation for disturbed behavior, the largest share of available funds for training and for research is funneled into biomedical programs . . . producing professionals who, after being trained at public expense, do not work primarily with the serious, chronically disturbed people who are the responsibility of tax-supported institutions . . . And, further, the biomedically oriented research programs demanded by the disease

model support complex laboratory research studies that have little relevance to the real etiological problems of disturbed people.

There is a current, popular platitude which says that the social and behavioral sciences seriously lag the physical and biological sciences in knowledge. If only, it is opined, we could make faster progress in behavioral science, if only we could learn as much about the human being as we know already about germs and atoms, then more effective programs could be developed to deal with man's problems with himself and with his fellows.

This reading of the knowledge situation is far from accurate. We *do* know a great deal in the behavioral sciences, but many of the things we know are threatening to the mental health Establishment and therefore to the status quo. For example, we know very well that *the nature of the social world of the infant and child in the family* are of primary importance as determinants of subsequent rates of disturbed behavior . . . Efforts at prevention of mental disorder should be directed to those social institutions that affect family stability directly or indirectly, positively or negatively . . . When eventually alternative explanatory models for disturbed behavior are widely tolerated, and institutions based on them supported with public funds are available, there will still be real mental illness to keep busy the organically oriented psychiatrist. All of the emotional problems associated with serious central nervous system malfunctioning, seizure states, toxic and endocrinologically induced psychoses, and the problems of organically induced behavioral disturbances in general will be left. . . [p. 317] . . . The illness model is supported by powerful forces . . . The model was developed, and it has persisted, because it was more convincing than the sin, taint, or demonic explanations. Also, the early success in finding the spirochete to be the cause of paresis led to hopes that other mental "illnesses" also had similar causes. Further, it seemed more and more as though genetic factors were important. The illness explanation also supported the practice of putting victims out of sight in plague houses until "a cure" was found. Money could be spent on chemical and biological research, without upsetting the value hierarchy in the society. Finally, both family and society could avoid personal responsibility for mental disorder. They could blame *Fate* . . . A scientific model will persist until a more valid and more convincing model appears.

Over the past 20 years there have begun to emerge out of psychotherapy, experimental work in the learning laboratory, cultural anthropology, and social work, to name just a few sources, elements of an explanatory model for disturbed behavior which might be called the *social learning theory*. This theory argues that most disturbed behavior consists of learned operant anxiety-avoiding responses . . .

> Psychology must create its own institutional structure for developing methods for the delivery of service, because only in its own structure can it begin to elaborate this new conceptual model . . . together with the language and the intervention methods that eventually will permit people with a bachelor's degree (or even less education) to be the line workers in the field of behavioral disorders . . . this model will not be built until [p. 319] psychology develops it in its own service delivery setting from which we can also go out into those community agencies where the real problems are . . . Unless psychology assumes leadership in developing alternatives to the illness model . . . we cannot . . . deal with the pressing problems of our urbanized, automated antihuman existence.
>
> (p. 320)

Lindemann regretted these rivalries among colleagues:[67] "I was impressed in your lecture last week by your emphasis upon the conflicts, rivalries, status-seeking, power operations, et al of the members of the care-taking professions".

Deinstitutionalization

The relationship of CMH to programs of "deinstitutionalization" (moving people out of mental hospitals) was of significance:[68]

> The CMH movement has also been emerging . . . when a vigorous deinstitutionalization process, begun in 1955, has been gaining strength . . . influenced and supported by . . . psychopharmacologic drugs, strong civil rights and patients' rights movements, changes in state mental health codes and political and economic factors. However, comprehensive planning for released . . . patients has not always been worked out, nor are comprehensive services always available (p. 143) . . . The new centers legislation (94–63) mandates that centers take responsibility for these patients through aftercare services . . . the aged . . . may be discharged from mental hospitals to nursing homes . . . without assurance . . . that adequate standards of facilities, staffing, and treatment programs exist. Again the new legislation mandates that the center offer a program of services to the elderly . . . There are those who believe that hospitalization, rather than nonresidential care, may better meet the treatment needs of psychiatric patients (p. 144).

David Rothman gave a historical perspective on the evolution of politicoeconomic conditions and policies:[69]

> after World War II, hospital-based custodial care was extremely expensive and growing in cost far more rapidly than inflation . . . from

1939 to 1949. . . . capital expenditures for state hospitals increased by 432 percent, and maintenance cost by 201 percent . . . federal policy soon intervened to provide a powerful impetus [to deinstitutionalization]. With the 1965 passage of Medicare and Medicaid, the federal government assumed between half and three-quarters of the cost of nursing home (p. 122) care for the elderly, thereby giving the states every incentive to discharge aged inpatients (some 30 percent of the total) to nursing homes. Then, in 1972, Congress enacted Supplemental Social Security Income (SSI), providing the disabled with a monthly stipend, with no requirement that the states match the funds, or cover the cost of administration, or, most important, provide ancillary programs . . . state hospitals saw a nationwide decrease in population of 13.3 percent, the largest decrease ever . . . No one built residences for them [discharged mental patients] in the community because the regulations did not require anyone to do so . . . The community mental health clinics . . . were supposed to serve as the alternatives to state hospitals, but . . . devoted themselves to acute rather than chronic patients . . . the worried well from the middle class . . . captured their concern . . . state dollars appropriated for mental hospital care did not follow . . . patients into the community . . . funds for the facilities held steady or even increased . . . employee unions . . . lobbying campaigns to protect their jobs [In another approach to the problem states phased out mental health services and expenditures and sold off institutional property] . . . community services . . . advocates were. . . [not] adept at building political constituencies . . . marshal competing political support . . . unprepared for . . . resistance to new expenditures . . . failed to appreciate . . . bias against chronic care is in psychiatry and medicine (p. 123) . . . [there are] links among homelessness, mental disability, and deinstitutionalization . . . complexities of cause and (p. 124) effect (p. 125).

Gerald Klerman explored the many contributions to deinstitutionalization from an administrative point of view. He was in the process of shifting his ideology from CMH to psychopharmacology, as is reflected in his ambivalence about the value of social psychiatry:[70]

policies of deinstitutionalization that were embodied in the community mental health movement and Federal legislation initiated under the Kennedy administration in the mid-1960's . . . The appropriateness, efficacy, and morality of treatment of schizophrenics and other seriously mentally ill persons in community settings rank very high among the many controversial issues generated by public mental health policies . . . considerable controversy now revolves around the wisdom of community mental health policies and the adequacy of resources available for community treatment programs (p. 617) . . . In the 1950's . . . The introduction of rauwolfia and the phenothiazines . . . contributed to the effective treatment and symptomatic management of many severely psychotic patients . . . At the same time, new psychosocial methods of treatment . . . and revised attitudes toward the milieu treatment of schizophrenia appeared in Britain and were later brought to the United States . . . Immediately before the drugs' introduction, the California state mental health system began the "total push" policy of intensive treatment for new admissions . . . the tranquilizing drugs were "facilitators" of attitude changes through the renewed optimism spurred by their effects on patients previously considered hopeless . . . reduction of the populations of chronic patients had been initiated by social psychiatric reforms before the introduction of tranquilizing agents (p. 618) . . . The widespread use of these . . . compounds [psychoactive drugs] has greatly contributed to . . . the shift in the focus of treatment from hospital care to community-based programs. . . [at the same time] new psychosocial technologies . . . included group dynamics, . . . non restraint, open-door policies, . . . new professions . . . They were psychosocial . . . related to social science and historical research and theory. . . . Their goals included. . . [to] reform and reconstruct the social organization and political dynamics within the mental hospital. . . [introduced] "social psychiatry" "therapeutic community"(p. 620).

In the mid-1960's, the social psychiatric reformers, radical critics, civil libertarians, and conservative budget advisors united to support deinstitutionalization . . . while earlier research efforts had documented the value of short-term hospitalization and alternatives to hospitalization for acute episodes, the most far-reaching public policy implications dealt with chronically hospitalized patients in large mental institutions . . . Yet there is little research evidence to support this policy . . . a major proportion of the reduction in the number of resident patients in public mental hospitals is accounted for by the movement of elderly mentally ill patients . . . into nursing homes. This clearly accomplishes an improvement in mental health statistics . . . It also probably contributes to an improvement in the fiscal condition of the budgets of state departments of mental health since the burden of care is shifted to Medicare and other Federally supported programs [Social Security Disability Insurance, Medicaid]. Whether community placement contributes to the quality of life and longevity . . . is not clear. There are even suggestions that . . . mentally ill patients transferred to nursing homes have fared poorly due to fewer opportunities for socialization and recreation, less sophisticated use of medication, a possible increase in mortality due to the . . . trauma of transfer itself, and the uneven if not poor quality of medical care . . . a large proportion of the population decrease was accounted for by administrative actions leading to discharge . . . into the community. This policy . . . has generated the most controversy (p. 623) . . . Deinstitutionalization . . . became a slogan and a de facto policy decision based on limited research evidence . . . Mental institutional census did drop . . . because the . . . rapid discharges shortened hospital stays even faster than the unfavorable consequences of deinstitutionalization raised admission and readmission rates . . . encouraged the romantic notion that all chronic deterioration was the product of institutional life . . . There seems to have been an interesting alliance among right-wing fiscal conservatives such as former California Governor Ronald Reagan, civil libertarians, and other critics of mental hospitals. The right-wing fiscal conservatives were interested in reducing the budgets of state government. If they could shift the fiscal burden of responsibility to the Federal level, they did so. Transferring a patient into a nursing home meant that the cost was borne by Medicare [and Medicaid], and discharging patients into the community, even if they were sent to state-subsidized boarding homes, was still less expensive per diem. If the patients could be certified as disabled, they were eligible for Social Security [Social Security Disability Insurance], with costs being borne in large part by Federal rather than state or local funds . . . civil libertarians . . . were horrified by . . . the large institutions . . . the popular press and media depicted the public mental hospital as a snake pit . . . The relative cost-benefit ratio (fiscal or human) of deinstitutionalization is unclear . . . At a minimum, 50 percent of these patients are living in . . . markedly socially isolated and disabled states. They require fiscal subsidy . . . and they . . . have minimum opportunities for socialization . . . serious questions as to the adequacy of . . . safety and . . . protection of their financial resources and personal security. Followup care is often inadequate, and . . . multiple readmissions and discharges is well known (p. 624).

The sum total of all these trends has been a shift from inpatient to ambulatory care, from institutional to community settings, and from the public to the private sector (Kramer, M., *Applications of Mental Health Statistics: Uses in Mental Health programs of Statistics Derived from Psychiatric Services and Selected Vital and Morbidity Records.* (Geneva, Switzerland: World Health Organization, 1969, p. 625) . . . The living conditions of ex-mental patients existing untended in such "community settings" [show that] back wards can be created in the community as well as in the "total institution" (p. 627) . . . The high promises of the community mental health program have only been partially realized. Application of available knowledge failed to materialize . . . Perhaps the mental health movement became overly ambitious . . . too quickly expanding . . . to include alcoholism, drug abuse, racism, and social unrest . . . Perhaps there has also been a failure on the part of the NIMH to assign priority and resources to this need, or perhaps . . . an overestimation of the extent . . . community attitudes have . . . changed.

Community Mental Health Casualties

The loss of support and reactionary defamation of social and community psychiatry and its adherents heavily impacted some who had committed themselves rationally and emotionally and had found personal fulfillment in this calling. These were true casualties in terms of personal doubts and suffering. Some continued to seek CMH projects, some dropped out of the public service to clinical practice, and some switched allegiance to the new dominant biological ideology—out of new conviction or for professional advancement.

A parallel example in politics provoked the search for understanding of the reactions of these and perhaps other devotees to a losing cause:[71]

> The historian Allan Nevins struggled to understand the reasons for his [John Gilbert Winant, Governor of New Hampshire and U.S. ambassador to Great Britain in World War II] suicide. . . "Was it that, like Hamlet, you found the times were hopelessly out of joint—that, as one of the best idealists and most truly humane men of your age, you were laboring in an environment that could offer you nothing but hopelessly cruel frustrations?"

Another parallel example in public education provides another poignant illustration:[72]

> [Superintendent of Cleveland public schools] Frederick (Doc) Holliday's . . . suicide note. . . [Holliday] "The fighting among school board members and what petty politics is doing to the system has sickened me" . . . it became evident how badly life had soured for the superintendent . . . the 77,000 student system noticeably improved under Holiday's stewardship . . . However, infighting with the school board led to talk that the superintendent's contract would not be renewed. . . "He didn't have the stomach for politics", says school-board member Joseph Tegreene. "He was sickened by what it took to run the system, and he saw no end to it". [Holliday] "The purpose seems to be lost . . . There is a mindlessness that has nothing to do with the education of children".

Some examples of those whose experience led them to leave the CMH field are:

- Richard Shader, chairman of the Tufts Medical School department of psychiatry, was a trained psychoanalyst who inherited a

- CMH-oriented program and adopted a biological ideology-motivated departmental focus on psychopharmacology.
- Even more striking is Gerald Klerman, who was psychoanalytically trained, represented an activist CMH program at the Connecticut Mental Health Center and Yale Department of Psychiatry, was terminated there because of this, and progressively shifted to become an outspoken advocate of biological psychiatry, including accusing of malpractice those who treated depression with psychological or social approaches and who disapproved of "social meddling". It is ironic that he started this conversion when he was appointed superintendent of the Erich Lindemann Mental Health Center (ELMHC).
- Gerald Caplan responded to the shifting institutional orthodoxies by shifting from the MGH to the HSPH, and then to the HMS, creating the Laboratory of Community Psychiatry as a mobile vehicle for his CMH work. While championing CMH while in the U.S., it is noteworthy that he began to establish relationships and credentials in the U.K. and Israel, to which he eventually moved:

the application of Professor Gerald Caplan of Boston to change his Associate Membership to full Membership in the British Psycho-Analytical Society . . . the year 1953 when he came to Boston to develop his psychoanalytic insights, both in service to patients and in research . . . in the frame of the Boston Psycho-Analytic Association.[73]

Our Laboratory [of Community Psychiatry] continues to flourish . . . Our budget is getting close to $2 million per annum . . . We hope shortly to move to new premises. . . [p. 1] This year I will be spending three two-month periods in Jerusalem where I have started a research project on problems of communication of Jews and Arabs.[74]

Eventually he also shifted his professional focus from community public health mental health to intercultural communication and support of individual resilience under stress.
- Niels Poerksen in Germany acutely felt his expulsion from the Department of Community Psychiatry (Die Gemeinde Psychiatrie) in Mannheim and the University of Heidelberg. At the Department's 10 year anniversary celebration he was invited to attend but not to speak.[75] He insisted on speaking of his feelings for the program he had initiated:

"This is a very important day for me, therefore I want to say a few words . . . everyone knows that I had very good times in Mannheim, and everyone knows that I had bad times, and I am still suffering about it . . . But the Mannheim period is the most important in my professional life. . . . There were many years—many years—, maybe not now, but all the years in Lüneburg I would have moved the next day to Mannheim if I would have had the opportunity. I had to leave so I took this job in Lüneburg —I didn't want it". He felt he still had more friends in Mannheim than in [subsequent] Lüneburg: in Mannheim he had one of his most active and creative times; if he had not had those who did not want him he would still be in Mannheim, even though it is a terrible, dirty, industrial city; it is warm, people are direct (unlike those at the University).

- David Daniels and Richard Almond experienced the Stanford Medical Center's Department of Psychiatry as uncomfortable with their social consciences and social action. There were doubts about their legitimacy and association with destructive radicalism. Daniels was marginalized in the student health services rather than tenure track faculty appointment. Almond was considered incompetent and as supporting unprofessional perspectives and was eventually evicted. Both sought ways to practice some fragments of social and community psychiatry within their spheres of function.
- Elmer A. Gardner, M.D., at the Temple University Community Mental Health Center was caught up in conflict and resistance both in the Department of Psychiatry and in the community. Despite trying to fathom the needs of the community and responding with services, he was eventually forced out by the Department of Psychiatry, investigated by the police, subsequently forced out of another Philadelphia CMH program and then from the federal drug abuse and alcoholism program, and escaped from CMH to the private practice of psychiatry.
- John Merrifield believes that the struggles for the construction and deconstruction of the Concord, Massachusetts, Community Mental Health Center caused human physical and mental health casualties. It is pertinent to recount here the history presented in Chapter 1:[76]

> Wars have casualties . . . I believe the casualties were significant, an opinion shared by nearly all of the people I interviewed. . .
> 1. Eleven people, each of whom had a significant role at Concord's CMHC, have died. Dr. George Abernethy was chair of psychiatry . . . when a merger with Walden was considered . . . he died of lung cancer at age 57. Mrs. Barbara Andrews was a social worker . . . she died of cancer in her fifties. Dr. Frederic Coplon got the child development team off to a good start and served a term as chair of psychiatry; he suffered a fatal heart attack at forty-seven. Mary Fischelis . . . psychiatric nursing director, died of a cardiac arrhythmia at fifty-seven . . . Dr. Dorr Hallenbeck . . . chair when I came to Concord, died of [p. 102] postpolio dementia at seventy. George Lussier, Walden's intake social worker and . . . acting director of Walden Clinic, died . . . in his

sixties ... with Parkinson's disease. Tovah Marion, Ph.D., died of cancer while working at Walden. Nina Melbin, M.S.W., died of cancer after leaving Walden. Dr. Robert Milstein, who worked at Walden Clinic ... was Emerson's [Hospital] psychiatry chair for a term; he died of a metastatic brain tumor at sixty-one. Henry Mirsky, M.S.W ... transfer from Eliot to state hospital work ... died ... in his seventies. Barbara Sylvia was Walden's bookkeeper; she died of cancer soon after leaving work. Ruth Tobin was evening charge nurse on Wheeler III until she died of cancer in her sixties ... the CMHC "community" ... suffered a disproportionate number of deaths compared to Emerson's active medical staff or its entire professional staff.

2. Diminished capacity. By the time Dr. Gerry Wacks ended his three years at the Mental Health Center, "he was not the same person he was when he started". "I was sacrificed". Two program directors developed symptomatic illness, which they believed were job related ... Dr. Charles Hersch was so ill when he left as CMHC director that he did not work for two years. Charles Hersch spent two years making relationships, then two years making needed changes. At the end he came home each night in desperate straits; when his wife said he cannot stand this and his wife cannot he quit. Now he has Alzheimer's disease.[77] [Hersch, Charles, 11/15/07 Interview] Leslie Brody's board sent him to the National Training Laboratory in Bethel, Maine for a week's training in "anger management". On his return ... he was abruptly fired ... Dr. Stern declined to talk about his years as Eliot CMHC director, so I speculate that it was not a pleasant time.

3. There were three divorces among CMHC program directors ... Among Emerson's entire medical staff over thirty years, I count 7 divorces. Again, the proportion seems high.

4. "Ruined careers". Not until 2004 did an Emerson CEO leave Emerson for another hospital CEO job. Prior to that, none went to a hospital administrator job at any level. None reached retirement age while at Emerson. Mr. Crowdis, who ... retired at fifty-seven, spoke of "ruined careers". Two interviewees said that Emerson's reputation for being hard on its administrators was known all across the country ... Charles Hersch ... in my opinion remains bitter about his Concord Experience. Dr. Leslie Brody ... spoke of the irony that his Ph.D. thesis, "Survival Strategies for Community Mental Health Centers", was approved on the same day that he was fired as Eliot's director. Mr. Gil Aliber left Concord as soon as he could, and retired happily after twenty-five years as director of a CMHC in Rutland, Vermont.

the pace of change has slowed . . . The CEOs of Eliot Clinic and Eliot Community Human Services. . . [have been] in those positions for more than ten years each. I think a slower rate of change has brought fewer casualties. The war is over, whatever one may think about its outcome.

- Leo Berman: He developed group mental health education as a preventive mental health intervention; he became a joke at the HMS and MGH, with people referring to being "Bermanized"; hurt, he refused to talk about his experience.
- Heinz Häfner: Based on the HRS and other U.S. CMHCs he established a central community mental health center (die Zentral Institut für Seelisches Gesundheit) in Mannheim, Germany; after battles with both social activists (like Niels Pörksen) in the Institut and the University of Heidelberg's battles with political radicals, he redirected the Institut to epidemiological and biological research.
- Walter Ritter von Baeyer: Humanistic psychiatrist disciplined by the Nazi regime, who returned eventually to chair the psychiatry department at Heidelberg University. He then was unequal to the social revolutionaries who threatened the university and nation. He fled from and did not want to know about the ideological conflicts that affected society psychiatry but addressed their corollaries by retiring to research and writing about the psychopathology of persecution and the humanistic use of psychiatry
- Michael von Felsinger: A psychologist who participated in CMH at the MGH, then tried to apply its perspectives in a mental health program seeking collaboration between Boston College Department of Psychology and the African-American community of Boston, which was savaged by political ambitions and cross-currents in the community until it expired, leaving von Felsinger to retire from professional and academic life in the country.
- Harris Peck: Led the Albert Einstein College of Medicine's project to develop a community mental health center in collaboration with the local Bronx, NY community centered on the Lincoln Hospital, and was a target and casualty of the rebellions against the white community, institutions, and professionals, and moved on to other public mental health and welfare programs and institutions.

It should be noted that some dedicated to CMH had the perseverance and opportunity to find situations in which to continue to pursue it:

- Erich Lindemann himself felt the loss of validation, including recognizing the role of suffering Christ, who brought good though he was rejected. Lindemann retired early from his positions at the MGH and HMS fearing outright rejection. However, he arranged

the opportunity to focus on teaching and consulting on CMH at the Stanford University Medical Center, other facilities in California and Boston College, and German universities.
- Niels Pörksen, in addition to being a casualty at the Mannheim/Heidelberg CMH program, was also one who persisted in his efforts at CMH: At each of the subsequent settings in which he worked, Lüneburg and Bethel, he sought to develop a program with CMH characteristics of assembling an interdisciplinary staff along democratic lines, involving community agencies and important functionaries, and addressing community social issues and populations in need. Perhaps it is also a characteristic of CMH that he regularly found himself in negotiation and conflict with traditional authority because of his CMH approach.
- Another outstanding example is Warren Vaughan, who had been a fellow in CMH at MGH and then held appointments in the DMH, negotiating the transition of the state mental health system to a community base. He left Massachusetts to return to the west, where he occupied the following positions developing CMH approaches and programs:[78]

Director, mental health programs, Western Interstate Commission for Higher Education, Boulder, CO
Special consultant, Children's Unit, Napa State Hospital, Imola, CA
Chief of community services and then chief of psychiatry, Peninsula Hospital Community Mental Health Center, Burlingame, CA
Member, American Academy of Child Psychiatry
Member, Group for the Advancement of Psychiatry
Fellow and member, Committee on Policies and Standards of Hospitals and Clinics, American Psychiatric Association
Member, American Public Health Association

The classical CMH principles upon which he developed these programs he carried from project to project:[79]

Local mental health programs and services embrace a wide range of activities which necessarily involve almost all elements of community life. Mental health is concerned with the everyday life of people throughout the community as they function in many roles in family, school, job and community life. Their living conditions, learning, work and recreational conditions; their ways of coping with sickness, and with aberrant and antisocial behavior all come within the purview of a community mental health program. The community mental health program is also concerned with research; it is interested in the extent to which psychopathology is manifested in the community, and the inadequate social and other conditions which foster such psychopathology. Finally, it is concerned with the professional and other helping resources in the community, with the recruitment and education of future mental health professionals, and with inservice training (p. 388) . . . The community mental health program . . . should involve all persons whose work and responsibilities are instrumental in affecting the life of individuals, families, groups, institutions and agencies (p. 390).

Massachusetts General Hospital

Professor of psychiatry at HMS and chief of the psychiatry service at the MGH were the positions of power for the reform of psychiatry and medicine that Erich Lindemann had sought since his youth. When he gave them up, he hoped, perhaps plaintively, that his quest would go on: "We hope, of course, that all of you will be leaders in the field five, six, ten years from (p. 12) now and that all of you will hopefully carry the torch unless by then you have found this is obsolete and that you have developed a new kind of approach to care. If you can do that, all the more power to you".[80] He continued his participation in the Metropolitan Mental Health Planning Committee through 1967.

On the contrary, HMS and MGH continued their trends away from social and community psychiatry.

Consonant with the ideological, political, and economic shift in American society, the HMS and MGH aimed at reemphasizing the biological, medical, and laboratory basis of MGH psychiatry, despite their polite acknowledgement of Lindemann's social psychiatry:[81]

> neurophysiologists, neurochemists, and electronmicroscopists are currently laying the foundation of an understanding of the function of the nervous system from the properties of the component units . . . Psychologists and psychiatrists at the other extreme are attempting to describe and analyze the behavior of the total system in all its complexity . . . The gulf separating these two approaches is indeed broad and there are those on both shores who have serious doubts that there exists a common ground (p. 1) . . . Popular expectation knows no bounds. Individual maladjustment to an increasingly complex society, family and community unrest, and failure of nations to adjust to population and economic pressures all merge in the popular mind as ailments in need of psychiatric care. How much of the mental health load should psychiatry pick up? What responsibilities does it have for this need? . . . how should a university department be organized today? What are the special problems and needs confronting psychiatry at the Massachusetts General Hospital? . . . Psychiatric problems are everywhere present on our medical, surgical and pediatric wards to say nothing of the ambulatory

clinics . . . the Psychiatric Service under Dr. Cobb took a special interest in the study of psychoneurosis in collaboration with other Services. It seems timely to reemphasize this aspect of psychiatry in the Hospital (p. 2) . . . The need for more involvement of our psychiatrists within the hospital does not mean that the activities of the Psychiatric Service in community mental health, as pioneered by Dr. Lindemann in the Wellesley Mental Health Center, need not wither. Indeed, the Hospital is just embarking on a new venture in community comprehensive medical care in which psychiatry is expected to play an important role. [Refers to community health centers as well as the CMHC.] The new State mental health program includes a mental health center at Bowdoin Square . . . and is planned to have a number of beds for in-patients as well as ample clinic facilities for ambulatory patients and considerable research space. Staffing of this center is considered both the privilege and the duty of the Psychiatric Service at the Massachusetts General Hospital (p. 3) . . . We may anticipate more emphasis on the teaching of psychiatry in the medical schools . . . and closer correlation with the teaching of other clinical disciplines. [Reversal of the recent trend at HMS?] . . . No teaching of patient care activity . . . will long sustain an impact if devoid of close association with clinical investigation and laboratory research . . . The best of knowledge in the biological sciences . . . has raised the reasonable hope of understanding many ills in terms of their molecular derangements in the foreseeable future. [The usual grandiose hope of a new ideology.] . . . Hopeful workers may be found engaged in . . . psychoanalysis, simulation of behavior on computers, or steroid chemistry. It is the hallmark of a university department that it be seriously engaged in increasing knowledge and understanding within its discipline. [Differing from the MGH staff Petition.] (p. 4).

At the MGH, Fred Frankel, designated by Lindemann to represent the department in planning its relationship with state and community organizations, was dutiful but rejected many of Lindemann's beliefs. In a memorandum to the chairman of the Metropolitan Mental Health Planning Committee, he criticized "comprehensive CMH" (promising but vague and threatening disappointment), psychoanalysis (inappropriate treatment and misunderstood), and discharge of elderly from hospitals to nursing homes (where they get worse care).[82] He was more confident in secondary than primary prevention, interpreting CMH and community psychiatry as expanding earlier diagnosis of mental illness, making treatment more accessible and closer to patients' homes, organizing better aftercare, and increasing prevention. However, he did not see this as providing new insight or treatment of mental illness and as uncertain to reduce prevalence, and he urged the preservation and increase of proven treatment of mental illness. He defined community psychiatry as bringing diagnosis and treatment to the community for early detection, effective treatment, and rehabilitation to decrease mental illness. This, he believed, was necessary in order to support CMH: health maintenance, illness prevention, involving many disciplines and community agencies, and involving community political and policy issues. He opposed training of mental health professionals by superficially borrowing skills to produce ineffectual and uniform generalists.

Upon Lindemann's retirement, John Nemiah served as acting chief of the psychiatric service. In 1966, CMH staff members listed among the clinical staff included Clemens Benda, M.D. (Fernald State School), Robert L. Bragg, M.D. (HRS), John M. von Felsinger, Ph.D., Peter B. Hagopian, M.D. (Danvers State Hospital), Helen Herzan, M.D. (HRS), and Belenden Hutcheson M.D. (DMH)—Lindemann's appointees representing collaboration with community agencies and projects.[83] The CMH research staff listed included Gerald Caplan, M.D., and Gardner C. Quarton, M.D. The CMH research projects included ten in CMH, seven involving Gerald Caplan. Through a fellowship with the department senior staff, Lindemann, as chairman, had looked forward to Nemiah directing the CMH program, including the HRS pattern of a committee of mental health–related community agencies and their exchange of information on functions and service needs.[84] He expected this to improve the care of the acutely mentally ill, an interchange with patients' homes, increased community participation in the hospital, the development of partial-care programs and vocational rehabilitation, and better outreach to the disadvantaged and involving them in the hospital. He doubted that there would be discoveries in social systems, as this was foreign the hospital which was a self-contained castle.

Nemiah badly wanted permanent appointment as chief of the psychiatry service and felt support from the department staff.[85] He was passed over.[86] He thought it was because the search committee did not think he was mature and strong enough. He also thought that other chiefs of service wanted someone devoted to biological science rather than psychoanalysis. Benjamin White thought much of the hostility toward Lindemann was because of his identification with psychoanalysis and agreed that Nemiah was tainted by the then-rejected psychoanalysis.[87]

Over a two-year search for a successor the search was deadlocked over the issue of psychoanalysis rather than CMH and the position was refused by David Hamburg and Douglas Bond (including because of limitations in department's size, space, and resources). Nemiah remembered MGH wanting Seymour Kety because of his preeminence as a biological psychiatry researcher and was unhappy at Johns Hopkins University. He accepted with a condition: since he was not a good administrator [or desired to be free of administrative burdens], he would devote himself to psychiatry research, and Leon Eisenberg would be appointed as clinical chief and administrator. From 1967 to 1974, Eisenberg, a child psychiatrist known as interested in community health and social issues, succeeded Lindemann as MGH clinical chief of psychiatry. His perspective sheds light on the new ideologies and values and what became of Lindemann's heritage after his departure.

Eisenberg was described by a close assistant and observer as an angry and destructive person, though he could change to warm and caring.[88] He always kept his door closed and started each day with a rambling philosophy and schedule of tasks. He always referred to the psychiatric residents as "those bastards", calculated a delay in seeing visitors, and needed time to prepare a smiling welcome and ushered them out with the same façade, after which he rudely turned away and abruptly dropped it, leaving his assistant to fill in. Lindemann's executive assistant and loyalist, Jean Farrell, reported that Eisenberg fired her by phone with one day's notice, though the MGH board of directors extended her tenure by two to three weeks so that she could complete the preparation of the department budget.[89] He needed his assistant, resented her absence, and was dependent on his wife. The assistant thought he was very uncomfortable as chairman and wondered if he took the job as a route to an appointment and professorship at the HMS. Nemiah thought he was not a good clinician and denigrated psychiatry. Eisenberg was seen as developing an antianalytic department in response to MGH's antipathy. It is reported that Stanley Cobb, recovering from prostate surgery at the MGH, when he heard that this person, antagonistic to psychoanalysis, was appointed to chair his department, had a gastrointestinal hemorrhage.[90]

Lindemann clung to the belief in the continuation of his CMH legacy at his alma mater:[91]

> I had an opportunity for a lengthy discussion with Dr. Eisenberg and feel quite reassured about his plans for the department . . . He does not seem to be in a hurry to make many major changes in that respect. He is quite interested, and I am pleased he is, in the further development of community mental health in close cooperation with general community health centers such as is being contemplated for Charlestown [a Boston community].

Eisenberg interpreted the petition against Lindemann as opposed to him personally, psychoanalysis, and psychiatry but not to CMH.[92] He took a very different tack as part of MGH's effort to erase Lindemann's heritage.[93] His ideas about Lindemann may have been gained from others who had strong and often negative reactions: He saw Lindemann as pleasant and gentle, someone who may have related well in the community but avoided unpleasant situations at the MGH, not attending meetings, and leaving Jack Ewalt at HMS to make decisions, thus losing MGH's position at HMS and with other psychiatry departments. He characterized him as preoccupied with CMH and HRS, ignoring MGH, and abdicating his role in HMS psychiatry teaching. He thought Lindemann treated staff poorly—disapproving of Thomas Hackett's use of hypnosis, and favoring stipends to people no longer contributing while underpaying workhorses of department (Hackett, Avery Weisman, John Nemiah). He credited Lindemann with a formulation of grief (with Gerald Caplan publicizing this) and community psychiatry and valuable findings from the West End Study contributed by Marc Fried and Herbert Gans. He thought Lindemann's interest in community psychiatry was not shared by anyone else in MGH and left no mark there or in psychiatry and medicine in general. He is reported as saying he could never stomach the new CMHC being called the Lindemann Center.[94] Eisenberg saw community medicine stimulated by the spirit of the times and not as a scientifically justified subject area. He thought its origin in Clifford Beers and Adolf Meyer's interest in prevention never realized its potential and suffered from the loss of its roots in contest between medicine and social influences. He believed that mental illness can be reduced but not eradicated.

Eisenberg thought the psychiatry department had become shit, was not respected, its research program a laughingstock, and had relatively little funding. He thought the hospital was glad to have him as someone to pull the department together. He thought the HRS was isolated, a low-status "farm team", not respected at the MGH, and having outlived its demonstration project status; he did not support it because he saw it catering to the suburban middle class rather than the inner-city disadvantaged population. Its staff moved to the Bunker Hill [Community] Health Center, which Eisenberg supported. He was sorry that the West End Study terminated when funding ended without support for its staff. He thought the ELMHC planning had been completed (including by Fred Frankel); the MGH feared that it would be divisive and a drain on resources, since it was inadequately funded for the planned research function; and the MGH had different tasks. He noted that the department staff under Lindemann (John Nemiah, Peter Sifneos, Fred Frankel, and Donald Fern) soon left to staff the psychiatry department at the Beth Israel Hospital.

Eisenberg remembered applying himself to the direction of the department, unlike Lindemann. This included building up the acute psychiatric and consultation services, which were appreciated for a less psychoanalytic approach, clearer communication, practical advice, and higher quality services with "nuts" being kept out of the way. He sought to be outspoken and active in MGH administrative affairs, making psychiatry a force in the hospital, and increasing the number and stipends of the house staff and trainees. He found a collegiality among MGH clinical services, with the wish for a good psychiatric service despite the competition for resources. He recognized differences in attitudes toward the psychiatry service: John Stoeckle in Medicine understood and appreciated psychiatry and primary care. Surgery (the most powerful of the services) did not appreciate psychiatry or share resources with medicine and psychiatry, which services made its work possible; Eisenberg remembers helping block surgery's expansion into heart transplantation. Oliver Cope in surgery was interested in shared conferences but isolated in his department (though acting chief for a period). Nathan Talbot of the children's medical service was interested in social medicine and the development of neighborhood health centers, though unclear and superficial in his ideas. Eisenberg thought the further expansion of the psychiatry department was blocked by the availability of the McLean Hospital and the hostility of a the family that endowed the Stanley Cobb professorship. Social medicine was supported by only a few at MGH—John Stoeckle of medicine interested in primary care and medical sociology, Nathan Talbot of the children's medical service, and Oliver Cope, who was approaching retirement. Eisenberg, who had this interest, was too busy managing the psychiatry Service to encourage participation in social medicine by other departments.

Eisenberg had his struggles in his position, and it was reported that he could not stand the MGH.[95] John Nemiah, who had been Lindemann's subordinate and acting successor, noted that the spirit of cooperation was quite different at the Beth Israel Hospital, where he became head of the psychiatry department:[96] "The heads of all of the major departments . . . and the spirit of cooperation among us is rather different from what you and I have both been exposed to in past years!" Eisenberg wrote to Lindemann:[97]

> [T]he department is . . . continuing the tradition of concern for the community which you established. The Charlestown Program is off to a very strong start, the Wellesley Human Relations Service continues to do well under Bob Bragg and we are negotiating with the state for the Mental Health Center. This last continues to be a serious problem. On one hand, I would much prefer a contract for professional services but the trustees are quite reserved about the risk this involves since the financing would be on a year-to-year basis and subject to reduction on very short notice. On the other hand, the security of state-hospital salary lines carries with it very serious impediments in the form of civil service requirements and enormous red tape. I have been trying, so far without success, to recruit someone willing to take on the enormous administrative responsibilities of the Mental Health Center. I . . . cannot see how I can run an additional unit much larger than the present one . . . These days I feel more like a business man than a professor.

The MGH-ELMHC psychiatric training program claimed to incorporate social psychiatry in attenuated form with behavioral and psychodynamic psychiatry:[98]

> TRAINING OBJECTIVES The fundamental aims of the resident training program are: 1. To develop competence in a) early identification of psychiatric disorders; b) their differential diagnoses by

clinical and laboratory methods; and c) their treatment by the full range of available techniques. 2. To develop understanding of normal and abnormal human responses to psychological, biological and social stress. 3. To develop an awareness of the role of social systems in the maintenance of behavior, normal and abnormal, and to transmit what is known of the amelioration of behavior disorders by modification of the social environment. 4. To transmit the basic scientific principles for the acquisition of new knowledge, with an emphasis on the critical evaluation of the literature in the behavioral sciences, clinical psychiatry and psychiatric research. 5. To enhance skills in teaching and supervision of non-psychiatric personnel as providers of primary mental health services in a wide variety of community and institutional settings. 6. To permit the acquisition of a degree of greater expertise in some one of the areas of psychiatry in recognition of the trend toward sub-specialization in this as in other medical fields... [p. 1] ... SEMINAR INSTRUCTOR ... Social Psychiatry Dr. L.[eon] Eisenberg [Chief of Psychiatric Service MGH] ... Community Psychiatry Dr. J.[onathan] Borus ... Basic Dynamic Therapy Dr. J.[ack] Schwartz ... Psychoanalytic Theory Dr. S.[amuell] Silverman ... Hypnosis Dr. T.[homas] Hackett [next successor MGH Chief of the Psychiatric Service].

In this post-CMH era at the MGH, Jonathan Borus wrote of finding in 1972 a community mental health training program without participation by psychiatry residents and claims that residents had been uninterested in CMH or the community.[99] In 1972, he reports re-initiation of psychiatric residency training in community mental health from 1971, starting with a four-month didactic seminar, then, in 1974, a six-month part-time training experience in MGH-operated community health centers and with community caregiver groups, and in 1973–82, an NIMH-funded two-year post-residency fellowship in the HSPH and community health centers.

The pre-existing CMH training program continued to occupy a limited place at the MGH.[100] During the transition under John Nemiah's acting leadership, CMH was limited in the psychiatric residency program. After Leon Eisenberg was appointed chief in 1967, Robert Bragg, coordinator of the CMH training program, suggested its integration into the Department of Psychiatry:[101]

> The Base of Operation. Should not MGH (The Department of Psychiatry and the Social Service Department) be the base of operation for the program? (In the past the role of HRS as a major field station for the program has caused the program to be viewed as an HRS based program.) With MGH as the base of operation for the

program should not certain, specific conferences common to all trainees be based at MGH?

As noted, Eisenberg was dismissive of the HRS. Bragg saw the HRS becoming a practically oriented clinical service that functioned well in a community setting with Helen Herzan, M.D., an extraordinarily warm, supportive senior staff member with a sense of humor.[102] A supervisor at the Boston University School of Social Work noted that the staff functioned as a family, Franklin Parker, a long-time member of the HRS board of directors, thought HRS reached a turning point about 1968, when it became an accepted member of the community, situated among other community institutions—the Red Cross, Friendly Aid, and a church—and no longer carrying a stigma.[103]

Eisenberg is credited with establishing a course in CMH as part of the residency program:

> The first eleven years of our work has shown that it has been difficult for some psychiatric residents to integrate Community Mental Health and Epidemiological concepts with those of basic, clinical psychiatry. Therefore, we felt that the bases of Community Mental Health needed to be introduced early to the residents in psychiatry. "Dr. John C. Nemiah ... Acting Chief, Department of Psychiatry for the period Fall, 1965 to Fall, 1967. He reorganized the Residency Training Program ... including an introduction to Community Mental Health. An inclusion of sessions on Community Mental Health did not take place ... In 1967, Dr. Leon Eisenberg was appointed Chief, Department of Psychiatry ... It was and is his intention to include the teaching of foundations of Community Mental Health principles and concepts in the basic residency program ... a seminar on Social Psychiatry given by Dr. Eisenberg and staff and ... during the academic year 1970–71 a course in Community Psychiatry given by the Community Mental Health Staff".
>
> (p. 1)

The CMH training program was described as follows:[104]

> Bragg, Robert L., M.D. Asst. Prof. Psychiatry Proj. Dir. 60% [time] Herzan, Helen M., M.D. Asst. Psych. Supervisor 40% ... [p. 1] ... <u>Basic residency training program in psychiatry</u> ... <u>Occurred</u> ... a six session (one hour and fifteen minutes each session) course in Community Psychiatry to the second year residents... [p. 2] ... <u>Planned</u> ... For the academic year 1971–72 the course in Community Psychiatry will have twice as many sessions as in the past year. This again reflects the intention of the chief of the psychiatry service and the director of clinical services ... to have more time devoted to the principles and

methods of community psychiatry in the basic residency training program... there are an increasing number of our first year residents in the basic program who have interests in community psychiatry.

(insert p. 2)

The CMH training program was integrated into one of the MGH's community health centers:[105]

> The full integration of the community mental health services into this health care delivery system provides an opportunity for psychiatric residents to acquire experience in providing coordinated and continuous family oriented health care... clinical psychiatric evaluation and treatment in a community setting... the patient's internal dynamics, but will give equal emphasis to his social and community setting... the patient and his relevant human environment... family as well as work closely with the patient's teacher, [p. 1] parole officer, clergyman, or other staff members... covers the entire life span... "sort out" the psychiatric symptomatology from the social and community forces... emphasize the "situation" of the patient in his community... modest, short-term, concrete goals around situational events... [p. 2]... short-term crisis intervention and symptomatic relief... Supervision... by Dr. Alvin Simmons, Dr. William Sack, and Dr. Pattison Esmiol... [p. 3]... experience in mental health consultation. With the public and non public schools... clergy... Headstart... other BHHC [Bunker Hill Health Center] staff... [p. 4]... observe the community dimension of health care by attending meetings of formal organizations as well as local community gatherings... weekly seminars... on the strategies and techniques of mental health consultation... administration, management and organization of mental health services.
>
> (p. 6)

Alvin Simmons, Ph.D., chief of community mental health at the Bunker Hill Health Center (and a past participant in Lindemann's CMH program), remembered Lindemann's influence: "You have been and will continue to be an inspiring force in my professional career".[106] He, too, sought to see the community health center as the new base for implementing social psychiatry in the community and HMS:[107]

> delivering high quality, personalized health care in an efficient manner. We hope to be able to make some contribution in this area and also hope to have some impact on the education of health professionals at the Medical School as well as in other schools of professional training. We are trying to bring mental health into the main stream

of health care as well as to bring behavioral science into the Medical School.

Despite these gestures of recognition, CMH inexorably declined at the MGH. The year after Lindemann retired, his acting replacement reported "the West End Project now . . . is being closed out".[108] This is clearly illustrated in the fate of the Community Psychology Training: A May 26, 1967 training grant proposal suggested (continued) support for July 1, 1968–6 June 30, 1975 in the amount of $479,226.[109] The award notice stated:[110] "5. AMOUNT OF THIS AWARD $29,338. . . Remarks . . . The National Advisory Mental Health Council recommended that support for this project should be terminated. There will be no obligation to continue support beyond June 30, 1970". Eisenberg himself recognized the NIMH criticism of the MGH's lack of support:[111]

> The impression I got from the site visitors was distinctly pessimistic about the prospect of renewal. As they saw it, the MGH has kept promising changes but the delivery has been unsatisfactory . . . I mentioned the expectation that Government Center would open next summer and thus provide an opportunity to expand and augment the program. They pointed out they had been told this two years ago.

The NIMH's explanation could not be a clearer characterization of CMH at the MGH:[112]

> your Training Program in Community Mental Health has been placed on terminal notice . . . The Review Committee noted that in recent years there has been lack of staff stability in this program, a lack of clear and sustained programmatic direction, and a lack of institutional support for the training staff and the students (e.g., inadequate space for training has been provided). . . . Clearly it agrees that strengthening of the CMH program is needed . . . If continued support is sought . . . Committee will look with particular care to determine whether appropriate full-time senior staff and leadership have been provided for this program, and whether appropriate space and arrangements for students have been provided, and whether an atmosphere more conducive to training of psychologists has, indeed, developed.

When, nevertheless, an application was made for further funding the responses were even more incisive:

> re TO1 MH07451–10 BTTBT 219. . . I regret to inform you that the National Advisory Mental Health Council did not recommend

approval of the application for mental health grant support identified above.[113]

The Psychology Training Review Committee . . . requested that a communication be sent to you regarding some of the reasons for its action.

The Committee was aware that this program was a pioneer effort in community psychology, and that, during its earlier years, an impressive roster of psychologists had been trained at this institution in crisis intervention, school, and agency consultation. Two years ago, the Committee placed the program on terminal notice because of lack of institutional support for key staff and the consequent attrition of the staff. Committee also felt that the substantive scope of the program remained largely unchanged and that it was no longer an innovative enterprise, and it was concerned with what at that time was the generally perceived second class status of the psychology postdoctoral fellows within the total institution.

The Committee felt that these critical, points had not been adequately addressed in the interim. It seemed especially clear that the level of institutional support which had been anticipated with the advent of a new chairman in the department of Psychiatry has not been improved. It was apparent that the hospital felt that the training of psychologists was relatively low on its list of priorities . . . it still did not provide an adequate set of field experiences in this specialty. A portion of the program is still devoted to satisfying routine service needs . . . that aspect was weak and very traditional.[114]

The psychology fellowship program was terminated June 30, 1970.

In March 1973, Robert Bragg resigned from the state DMH, HMS, and MGH, with veiled references to declining support for CMH and his position, and the impending future for both:

In our conference on September 28, 1972 I discussed . . . my decision to make a change in geographic location. This decision was based upon my careful assessment . . . of many variables including my current professional responsibilities and levels of satisfaction with these, income as well as retirement benefits . . . and anticipated changes in these . . . I now wish to submit my resignation as Associate Psychiatrist, Massachusetts General Hospital and Assistant Professor of Psychiatry, Harvard Medical School . . . to be effective as of . . . Friday, March 30, 1973. . . . I first came to the Department of Psychiatry as a Fellow in Psychiatry in July, 1957. . . . I have learned a great deal at MGH and have had many positive experiences.

On the occasion of his resignation, a social work supervisor at HRS noted that, under his guidance, the HRS staff functioned as a family.[115]

One must wonder how much such human relations were valued in the contemporary academic and professional culture.

Eisenberg eventually resigned, stating his appreciation of the people and programs with which he worked, his accomplishments, and having learned firsthand about academic administration. However, he stated that he "continue to regret the time consumed by an activity I didn't enjoy while I was doing it. . .". and "My problem. . . [was] the extent to which administrative demands displace opportunities for personal scholarship". As noted, it was reported that he could not stand the MGH.[116] Thereafter, he focused on research, consultation, and teaching.

Lindemann could not give up his long attachment to the MGH, including in reminiscence:[117]

> My own concerns fall roughly into four areas: First, to develop psychiatry as a behavioral science; I was bent on integrating the findings in biochemistry, neurophysiology, experimental psychology and psychodynamics. Second, to add to this array the integrative resources of the social sciences by an active exchange of ideas, services and research efforts with social scientists. Third, to develop psychiatric services and inquiries outside the hospital, in a public health frame of reference, concerned with the precursors of illness, the distribution of disturbances in the population, and the initiation of service agencies which could become the location for research, such as we did in Wellesley and in the West End. Fourth, we tried hard to make useful within the general hospital, particularly [p. 1] on the Emergency Ward and within the other hospital services, the type of new information and insight which had emerged from the study of reactions in crisis situations.

However, it is hard to find Lindemann's lasting contributions at the MGH. HMS dean George Packer Berry found only his creative ideas about the social arena in which psychiatry took place.[118] Oliver Cope, a sympathetic MGH surgeon, agreed that the medical and surgical services were not interested, and Nathan Talbot, chief of the children's medical service, had a good heart but incomplete understanding of mental health and was ineffectual in implementing a program.[119]

It is interesting that old, thorny relationships may have softened over the change in circumstances and the passage of time. Avery Wiseman, a bitter opponent who made several efforts to undermine Lindemann (including encouraging the petition against him and offering to replace him—see Chapter 9), now wrote (with some ambiguity):[120] "I think often about you, regretting that our paths cross so seldom and reflecting about bygone days. The new Lindemann Center here reminds us all of the lasting mark you have left on us all. Most of all, as I continue to work along in the field that you pioneered, I appreciate your legacy and influence".

204 *Counterrevolution of Biology and Business*

Harvard Medical School

Gerald Caplan sought to continue social psychiatry and CMH at Harvard through his Laboratory for Community Psychiatry in the HMS after the HSPH became inhospitable. A principle program was the visiting faculty seminar, in which senior faculty members of other universities could become knowledgeable about CMH and spread it to their institutions. His proposal was:[121]

> The Laboratory of Community Psychiatry . . . has conducted 5 two-week sessions of the Visiting Faculty Seminar in Community Psychiatry since its inception in 1964. The Seminar is supported by a three year grant from The Grant Foundation. The topics of the Seminar have been:
>
> 1. Meaning and Scope of Community Psychiatry . . .
> 2. Researches and Theories Which Form a Basis for Concepts and Methods of Community Psychiatry . . .
> 3. Studies Relating to Preventive Psychiatry . . .
> 4. Administration and Communication . . .
> 5. Consultation . . .
>
> Three more sessions will be held in the coming fiscal year:
>
> 6. Planning and Evaluation . . .
> 7. Community Organization . . .
> 8. Residency Training in Community Psychiatry . . .
>
> The Visiting Faculty Professors: These 16 [minus Moody C. Bettis, M.D., Baylor University Coll. of Med—deceased] are senior faculty persons . . . with responsibility for residency training in community psychiatry . . . plans are underway for this group . . . with the sponsorship of their departments of psychiatry, to offer, with us, an Inter-University Program for Faculty Education in Community Psychiatry to 60–70 senior psychiatrists throughout the country.
>
> (letter p. 1)

> The purpose of this seminar is to provide senior faculty members of university departments of psychiatry with an opportunity to study the core content of community psychiatry over a three-year period in order to help them in organizing training in this subject for psychiatric residents . . . two-week visits to the Laboratory of Community Psychiatry . . . on eight occasions over a three-year period . . . three hours each morning in lectures and seminars . . . early afternoon . . . visits of observation to a variety of community

mental health and other community agencies in the health, mental health, welfare and education fields in the metropolitan Boston area . . . to investigate the practical problems of implementing programs based upon the theoretical concepts (PROPOSED p. 1) . . . end of the day . . . group discussion . . . about their field observations . . . and the range of successful and unsuccessful ways . . . to deal with them . . . report on the residency training programs . . . establishing in his home university, and . . . theoretical and methodological problems.

(p. 2)

Erich Lindemann Mental Health Center

One route taken to resist the transition from social to biological psychiatry was the naming for Erich Lindemann of the new community mental health center adjacent to MGH (initially referred to as the Bowdoin Square or Government Center mental health center). The motor in this campaign was Jean Farrell, Lindemann's former executive assistant and lasting admirer: "The Area Board Executive Committee has appointed you chairman of the 'Dedication Ceremony of Lindemann Center' to be held in the Spring of 1971".[122] She marshaled former students and colleagues and influential officials and community leaders in support of this mission:

- She addressed the Massachusetts Commissioner of Mental Health, Milton Greenblatt:[123]

    I would like to suggest that the new mental health center presently being built in the Government Center complex be named in honor of Dr. Erich Lindemann, Professor of Psychiatry emeritus, at Harvard Medical School and former Chief of Psychiatry at the Massachusetts General Hospital. . . [He] was a pioneer in the development of community mental health concepts . . . formulated the initial plan for the Government Center Mental Health Center and has great hope that it will serve a truly important role in maintaining good mental health for the citizens of Massachusetts.

- Senator Edward Brooke responded:[124] "Thank you for your letter endorsing the naming of the new mental health center in honor of Dr. Erich Lindemann. I have written to Dr. [Milton] Greenblatt and favored the stand you so eloquently support. I agree that this would be a most fitting tribute to a very distinguished man".
- The president of the Massachusetts Association for Mental Health was supportive:[125] "We have received a letter from Miss Jean M. Farrell urging our support for the naming of the Government Center

Mental Health Center for Dr. Lindemann . . . if you think it's appropriate that it be named for Dr. Lindemann, we will gladly support such a proposal".

- The Area Advisory Board in the mental health center's Mental Health Area wanted Dr. Lindemann's contributions recognized in the naming:

the naming of the Government Center Mental Health Unit . . . the Area [Advisory Board] decision was already unanimously in favor of naming the place in honor of Doctor Erich Lindemann. Casual comments of area board members and some from the State Department inform me that a unit is already named after your own proposed candidate: Dr. Stanley Cobb. I am also informed that Dr. Cobb's work was mostly with neurology, and not so much in community psychiatric services . . . would you consider the auditorium as a Dr. Cobb memorial?[126]

- There was support from the MGH staff members:[127]

my wholehearted support of a bill . . . requesting that the new mental health center . . . be named in honor of Dr. Erich Lindemann . . . aware of Dr. Lindemann's remarkable efforts in the development of mental health concepts and facilities . . . the widespread benefit resulting from his life of service . . . an indication of the significance of his contribution to the field of mental health . . . and as an expression of this community's indebtedness to him.

- There was also support from MGH administration:[128] "[reports] suggesting that the new Government Center Mental Health Center be named in honor of Dr. Erich Lindemann. I think the suggestion certainly deserves consideration and should I be asked . . . I shall certainly mention that this has been suggested".
- There was support from HMS:[129] "I would be delighted to see the new government center hospital named in honor of Dr. Erich Lindemann".
- There was support from the wider Boston medical community:[130]

I would like to join . . . in urging that the Mental Health Center . . . be named in honor of Erich Lindemann, M.D . . . he not only developed these pioneer programs but he also had the ability to interest broad segments of the public in his concepts . . . naming the Health Center for Dr. Lindemann we will be not only honoring him but dramatically calling attention to the concepts in community psychiatry he stood for.

- At the state legislative hearing,

   A Representative got up holding [a] big folder of letters stating that hundreds of letters had arrived from all over the world endorsing this idea. He . . . just mentioned three letters, one from Senator Kennedy. He then read Dana Farnsworth's letter representing Harvard University which described Erich as the originator and pioneer of the Community Mental Health movement etc. . . . Mat[t] Dumont started talking . . . saying he came with the blessings of NIMH and explained how Erich was the inventor of the comprehensive community Mental Health Centers . . . inconceivable without the teaching and thoughts of Dr. Lindemann . . . The [p. 1] whole hearing room burst into a prolonged applause . . . one person after another just followed orderly. A man from the citizen's advisory board of Gov't Mental Health Center, Phil Kubzansky, Laura Morris, Mark Fried, Mike Von Felsinger, Louisa Howe, Father Moynahan, Mr. Moor from the H.R.S. Board, and Miss [Dorothy] Hickie . . . Each one had to talk about the Erich they knew, the man and the ideas. It was obvious that the tone had changed from one of asking for approval to one of "Mass. has the honor to claim as one of its own so great a figure and surely she could never let such an opportunity slip by" . . . [p. 2] . . . the committee chairman took a few minutes to express some of his own feelings. . . "I wish the press were here". Why is it when something so good as this happens the press is absent—Why couldn't something like this be shouted about instead of the kinds of things they always look for . . . I think we all felt we had a bit of you two inside of us, and in the reflection of you we had expanded.[131]

   (p. 4)

There was also resistance from various quarters:

- Some wanted to take the opportunity to further recognize Stanley Cobb:[132]

   About the naming of the center, Dr. Bloomberg of the regional director's office announced at our last session the name of a Dr. Stanley Cobb . . . the name was never referred to previously! . . . He had suggested the auditorium be named for Dr. Lindemann but the whole center for Dr. Cobb!!

- Some wanted to recognize Harry Solomon's contributions to the CMHC program:[133] "in [Jean] Dietz' [Boston] *Globe* column. . . 'Dr. Lindemann formulated the initial plan for the Government Mental Health Center'. This is not true. I needn't tell you that the plan was formulated etc., etc. and implemented and fought for by the then Commissioner of Mental Health, Dr. Harry C. Solomon".

In the end the campaign was successful:[134] "AN ACT DESIGNATING THE MENTAL HEALTH CENTER PRESENTLY BEING CONSTRUCTED IN THE GOVERNMENT CENTER, BOSTON AS THE ERICH LINDEMANN MENTAL HEALTH CENTER".

- "As you may have heard, the Legislature has passed the legislation and the mental health center is now officially designated as the <u>Erich Lindemann Mental Health Center</u>. I feel this is a fitting tribute to your pioneering work in the field".[135]

 I am sure that you already know that your great work in psychiatry over a very active professional lifetime will be recognized in the naming of the new mental health center in Government Center after you . . . It will be operated in collaboration with the Massachusetts General Hospital and Harvard as planned by you and Harry Solomon years ago. It is a great pleasure for me to send this letter and to see a distinguished colleague so honored.[136]

Klerman's experience of training in psychoanalysis, punishment for implication in social activism at the Connecticut Mental Health Center, and later responsibility for the ELMHC held in such ambivalence by the affiliated MGH psychiatry service left him acutely aware of both the conflict in the environment in which he worked and in his own ideology:[137]

 the community mental health center attempts to be rational, aggressive, and liberal. . . [It is] in danger of being attacked by both the forces of reaction and revolution . . . The revolutionaries and radicals . . . see mental health professionals as . . . part of the repressive institutions which demand conformity in order to perpetuate the status quo . . . the forces of reaction . . . identified us as "do gooders", "socialistic", permissive, and tending to apologize for violence . . . The challenge is to change rapidly enough to meet the needs while retaining our professional values and integrity.

 (p. 826)

 the crisis model . . . described by . . . Lindemann and Caplan has only a limited generalizability for an urban population . . . crisis intervention envisioned. . . [for those] temporarily overwhelmed by external stresses beyond their capacity to cope . . . in an urban area . . . the majority of our patients have chronic social and psychopathological disabilities . . . a series of crises . . . as a pattern of life . . . with their multiple social, economic, and psychological handicaps. . .

(p. 821)

He tried to see all ideological approaches, including clinical care and community involvement, in the ELMHC's program, with an attempt to tie it to Lindemann's perspective:[138]

> *The Lindemann Center: A Family Psychiatrist* . . . Dr. Gerald L. Klerman, its Superintendent, is striving to mold its role along lines sought by the man after whom the center was named. Dr. Erich Lindemann. . . [who] pioneered in community mental-health concepts.
> Dr. Klerman, who is also a Psychiatrist at the MGH and Professor of Psychiatry at Harvard Medical School, observed:
> "The old idea of the state mental hospital was that of a self-contained society . . . That only resulted in further isolating the mental patient from the rest of the community.
> "We don't attempt to do that, and I don't think we should. The patient should remain embedded in the normal community life from which he comes. Hospitalization should be as brief as possible just to help the patient get over a crisis. The stay in a hospital is only one phase in an overall treatment program".
> This philosophy grows out of Dr. Lindemann's classic work with the people displaced by Boston's early urban renewal venture in the West End. Dr. Lindemann noted the network of human resources within a community: clergymen, courts, lawyers, general practitioners, the schools system, and the like.
> "Twenty years ago psychiatrists taught the teacher and clergyman to recognize mental illness and to refer the potential patients to the psychiatric clinic . . . The attempt now is to reverse the tide", Dr. Klerman said. "Besides making these people more effective [p. 1] case finders, we want to increase their capacity to be therapeutic and helpful in the schoolroom, in the church, in the court, in the lawyer's office, on the policeman's beat, and in the general practitioner's office.
> "Because psychiatry is a very expensive service, we would rather see the psychiatric facility as a backup resource than a place where people always come initially. . . [The] Lindemann Center seeks to avoid duplicating whatever care is offered two blocks away at the MGH. With emergency aid available at the latter's Acute Psychiatric Service, Lindemann thus can concentrate on other areas. A Developmental Disabilities program . . . Seven classrooms present educational opportunities . . . used by the Boston public schools in a

collaborative program for emotionally disturbed children . . . On the drawing board is a plan for therapeutic classes that would allow adolescents to continue school . . . The Lindemann Center also maintains a day program for adult patients . . . New drugs have made day care a successful substitute for institutionalization. So has the knowledge that human behavior, in general, and mental illness, in particular, are very responsive to improvements in the social structure of the treating institution. [p. 4] For those patients requiring 24-hour care, the Lindemann Center houses 100 beds. Eventually 75 of these will provide care for adults, and the remainder will be . . . divided between children's services and a special unit for crisis intervention".

A cut in projected state funds, however, has slowed the rate at which the beds are being opened for use . . . Research is the hardest hit. Although provision exists for a large amount of research space, almost none of it is in use . . . A white-ceilinged swimming pool and a basketball court will eventually open day and night to serve both in-patients and outpatients.

(p. 5)

Klerman's experience of training in psychoanalysis, punishment for implication in social activism at the Connecticut Mental Health Center, and later responsibility for the ELMHC, which was held in such ambivalence by the affiliated MGH Psychiatry Service, left him acutely aware of the conflictful environment in which he worked and conflicted in his own ideology:[139]

the community mental health center attempts to be rational, aggressive, and liberal . . . in danger of being attacked by both the forces of reaction and revolution . . . The revolutionaries and radicals . . . see mental health professionals as . . . part of the repressive institutions which demand conformity in order to perpetuate the status quo . . . the forces of reaction . . . identified us as "do gooders", "socialistic", permissive, and tending to apologize for violence . . . The challenge is to change rapidly enough to meet the needs while retaining our professional values and integrity. . .

(p. 826)

the crisis model . . . described by . . . Lindemann and Caplan has only a limited generalizability for an urban population . . . crisis intervention envisioned. . . [people] temporarily overwhelmed by external stresses beyond their capacity to cope . . . in an urban area . . . the majority of our patients have chronic social and psychopathological disabilities . . . a series of crises . . . as a pattern of life . . . with their multiple social, economic, and psychological handicaps. . .

(p. 821)

After Lindemann's retirement there were efforts made to maintain his communication with the mental health center. One may conjecture how much of this was Lindemann's forlorn wish to maintain CMH goals, how much superficial politeness, and how much genuine mutual respect. Lindemann appeared to initiate communication, with follow-up correspondence:

> Quite apart from the fact that the institution carries my name, I have continued to have an affectionate interest in the development of the Department of Psychiatry at the M.G.H. The opportunity to carry on innovative services and research on a broad spectrum of the behavioral sciences in an adequate facility has been a deep-felt wish of mine for many years. To see the intensive planning in which all of us, but especially Gardner Quarton, John Nemiah, Frank Erwin [Ervin] and Jack Mendelsohn were involved come to fruition is indeed a great satisfaction.[140]
>
> I had hoped to have a chance to meet with you personally, together with Bill Ryan, the new director of our [BC] Community Psychology program at this time . . . If in any way at all I can be useful to you in terms of my former experience at the local scene, or in terms of the many interesting aspects of psychiatric service and research in a community setting, please let me know. I also would be most grateful if you would put me on the mailing list for your announcements.
>
> With warm greetings
> very sincerely yours.

. . . Two recent developments prompted me to contact you . . . First, we have begun to initiate activities at the new Erich Lindemann Mental Health Center . . . Second, we are beginning the planning for a Dedication Ceremony and scientific symposium . . . I would greatly appreciate the opportunity to talk with you personally, to give you a tour of the building and to explore your ideas about the mental health programming in general and about the Dedication in particular.[141]

. . . Thank you for your invitation . . . will be glad to come to the Center at a time convenient for you.[142]

. . . it was a delight to have you visit the Lindemann Center here on Tuesday, 13 April, 1971. Your presence and talk made quite an impression on the staff and employees . . . Please accept a general invitation . . . We would be delighted to have you as a standing consultant, returning on a regular basis at your convenience.[143]

Lindemann also reached out to Harry Solomon, who had been Commissioner of Mental Health when the ELMHC was being planned. Both seemed to soften their relationship in retrospect:[144]

> an invitation to . . . the dedication of two plaques honoring your name . . . for decades I have been one of your great admirers and have

over and over again been impressed with the wisdom and tenacity of your planning and of your fostering the development of a new vision and new institution in psychiatry . . . with affectionate greetings.[145]

Dear Erich—You wrote me a very touching letter for which I am greatly appreciative. Certainly we had a pleasant and happy relationship. I will be glad to know when you will be in Boston and perhaps we can get together and reminisce.
With best regards,
Harry.[146]

Psychoanalysis

Psychoanalysis maintained some momentum in incorporating a social perspective thanks to the energy of a dedicated group.

The American Psychoanalytic Association's Committee on Social Issues was concerned with sociopolitical issues. It held a Vulnerable Child Workshop at each annual meeting of the Association for Child Analysis and the American Psychoanalytic Association, and the fourth issue of the IUP (International Universities Press) of June 1997 addressed the vulnerable child.[147] Out of this interest in children at high risk of social trauma evolved the 20-year Vulnerable Child Study of the late 1960s, chaired by Eleanor Pavenstedt and then Ted Cohen.[148] The committee developed a position paper objecting to changes in the federal welfare law ending guaranteed support for AFDC (Aid to Families with Dependent Children), which might lead to increased child abuse, neglect, pathology, and delinquency. It noted the high rate of children without health insurance and at risk for child abuse. Stricter federal disability standards would lead to loss of Medicaid coverage, and the many disabled would face decreased psychiatric personnel and services. The Chicago Psychoanalytic Institute and Society collaborated on a project dealing with parent loss. Irving B. Harris (along with Yale Medical School) pursued study and advocacy regarding children in poverty. The paper based on the workshop "Adult Analysis and Childhood Sexual Abuse", written by Alex Burland and Ray Raskin and edited by Howard Levine, was published in 1992. In 1990, the committee reissued its 1970 pro-choice statement regarding abortion and a statement opposing prejudice against homosexuality. Raskin wanted the Committee to be more active.

With effort from Viola Bernard, the New York Psychoanalytic Society and the American Psychoanalytic Society's Standing Committee on Social Problems/Issues recommended that the American Psychoanalytic Society establish a Standing Committee on Community Psychiatry.[149] It was a counterthrust by community-oriented analysts toward a synergy of concepts and practices between psychoanalysis and CMH. This led to much debate and controversy: "Even though much of the pioneering in community psychiatry was done by psychoanalysts, unfortunately, these two approaches to psychological well-being, one focused on minutia within the individual mind, the other directed toward population groups, became polarized, with consequent mutual misperceptions and derogation".[150] A consequence was analysts dissociating their community work from their analytic identity.

The Standing Committee on Community Psychiatry was established in May 1968 in collaboration with the Committee on Social Problems with "positive support" for its aims:[151]

> we believe that the explanatory power of psychoanalysis can greatly help in efforts to solve nonanalytic problems, and conversely new multiprofessional approaches to community and social psychiatry can stimulate the growth of psychoanalysis, both in scientific and technical aspects . . . we regard a psychoanalyst's work along these lines as thoroughly compatible with maintaining his identity as an analyst.

It saw itself as "interactive with concurrent developments in psychoanalysis and community psychiatry throughout the decade [since its establishment in 1968], has moved, for example, from our initial emphasis on community program dynamics to our current focus on theory and training".[152]

An example of this integration of psychoanalysis and community psychiatry was a paper by Elizabeth Davis and Jules Coleman,[153] in which they observed that in community psychiatry, a wider range of people, settings, and histories is encountered. They found understimulation, isolation, and unpredictable influences producing mottled egos with both defect and resilience. They interpreted problems with the ego ideal internalization of a hostile world and problems with trusted object relationships. Early neurological damage, low birth weight, illnesses, and discontinuous mothering balanced by support from extended family led to cognitive and emotional defects, denial, emotional constriction, present-orientation, loss of intellectual freedom and emotional depth, and distrust of authority, in turn causing withdrawal from social resources and participation. They also observed oppositional defenses, longing for belonging, and a feeling of rejection, with these fears and defenses reinforced by the reality environment. The ego struggled to adapt, reduce conflict, and establish conflict-free areas.

Another example was a paper by Louis Linn about lessons learned from his work with a CMHC in the Bronx:[154] He learned the importance of Freud's observation of the influence of social class and culture on superego development and the representation in the adult of the heritage of family, culture, and class. He found that multiple superego variants depend on culture and family structure. There also is variation in the expression of aggression via knives, guns, words, etc. Superego varies as dissolution or aggression in different social and psychological states—e.g., mob, dissociation, hypnosis, demagogy, alcoholism, and drug addiction. Benevolent forces, too, may conflict in ego development and society.

Viola Bernard was committee chairman from 1969 to 1971,[155] and there was a wide range of members.[156] It promulgated a definition of its field:[157] "Community/Social Psychiatry . . . an extension in theory and practice of the knowledge derived from clinical psychiatry and from the insights of psychoanalysis, blended with knowledge and methodologies from the social sciences and the field of public health. It seeks to foster needed research and to develop a range of practices for reducing psychiatric morbidity through an understanding of psycho-social processes". Bernard made the argument for acceptance and implementation of this unfamiliar approach to professional practice:[158]

> the soundness and value of our pronouncements and positions on matters of broad public policy depend on the results of scientific investigation and scholarship, as well as on clinical understanding and experience. But the social utility of findings about sociopsychiatric relationships depends on our making these known to the policy makers and to the general public, and in our combating, through political process, those features of society which pose serious threats to mental health.
>
> While to some of us, activity in politics seems at variance with the physician's role, it can be recognized as consistent with it if it is used as an indirect tool for the traditional psychiatric purpose in preventing and relieving mental disorder . . . the hybrid term "social psychiatry" connotes the necessity for cross-disciplinary collaboration, as well as for many other new types of working relationships and work settings. Previous unfamiliarity with these and many other aspects of social psychiatry can be anxiety arousing and thus complicate one's attitudes about its value. For both adherents and opponents of greater social involvement of psychiatry, the personal emotions and conflicts that are entailed warrant the professional safeguard of our careful and continuous self-examination as we strive to integrate clinical and societal approaches for greater psychiatric effectiveness.

Bernard remembers the committee meeting two to three times a year for intensive sharing of experience and thinking out concepts, two to three times a year for less intensive meetings with branch societies, and workshops with other members at the American Psychoanalytic Society's annual meetings. It circulated a memo to the presidents of affiliate societies and institutes inquiring about activities in community and social psychiatry and the ethnic, sociocultural, and disciplinary composition of faculty and candidates; there was a 65% to 70% return of the questionnaire. The Committee was interested in minority representation in the institutes, societies, and the American Psychoanalytic Association, and suggested future questionnaires addressing low cost clinics and the racial and ethnic backgrounds of patients in the psychoanalytic institutes. A two-day workshop was given by Moisy Shopper, suggesting a model curriculum on psychoanalytic and community psychiatry for use by institutes. There were plans for another workshop at the April 1977 meeting in Quebec City, consisting of four modules with the following possible topics: psychoanalytic consultation to agencies and institutions, psychoanalysts' participation in educational institutes, collaboration of psychoanalysts and other professionals and government at all levels, psychoanalysis and the media, psychoanalytic theory relating to community, and clinical experience with different patients, especially regarding racial and ethnic characteristics. Other workshops and seminars were planned for December 1976 in Topeka and Cincinnati. At various meetings, suggested topics included psychoanalysis and medical education and mental health, the media (Shopper, Brockman, Roy Menninger), the social sciences, ethics, literature, CMHCs, the law, public/social policy and community psychiatry (Rockland); the impact of changing social mores on psychoanalytic theory and practice, and institutional racism.[159] Its members assembled a bibliography (Tarnower, Block, and Wadeson) on and a curriculum (Shopper) in community psychiatry to be adapted by each institute.

The committee worked on a book, tentatively titled *Psychoanalysis, Psychiatry, and Social Reality*, to be edited by Viola Bernard and Jules Coleman.[160] Unpublished writings addressed the complementarity of community/social psychiatry and psychoanalysis, misconceptions and negative connotations of community application of psychoanalysis, and limitations of community psychiatry. Its main purpose was to broaden the curricula in psychoanalytic institutes.

This committee was interested in the development and success of CMH programs. In the process, it presented it's perspective on the influences within and surrounding such programs, demonstrating great commitment and sophistication regarding social and community psychiatry:[161]

> consider program goals and objectives as well as motivations—overt and covert, conscious and unconscious—for and against program participation and program success. Consider leadership-constituency factors in relation to each program component . . . The way a program functions is the result of interaction among these various components. Success or failure depends on the degree to which conflicts arising from such interactions are resolved. Breakdown occurs when central conflicts are abetted in such a way as to make resolution impossible. In the presence of crucially adverse circumstances no mental health program can succeed (p. 1).

As psychoanalysts, we ask about the underlying psychodynamic barriers which obstruct or prevent the meeting of goals (p. 3).

The committee worked to develop a research instrument to discover and describe the development of CMH programs, covering all aspects and issues (see endnotes for detailed outline of the instrument).[162] It included:

    Component #1—Social, Economic, Political, and Cultural Context
    Component #2—How and Why Programs Evolved
    Component #3—The Community
    Component #4—The Institution Providing Community Services
    Component #5—Professional Agents and Caregivers
    Component #6—Consumers
    Component #7—Funding Sources

These vigorous efforts in social psychoanalysis took place in the context of contentious debate about the relevance of social psychiatry to psychoanalytic training in consideration of the aims, needs, and responsibilities of the candidates, faculties, psychoanalytic organizations, and society.[163] The interplay of arguments in the subcommittee is interesting:

- Pro: There is a moral and professional obligation to extend psychoanalysis beyond the limited patients and segments of society treated by psychoanalysts to a public health scope. Psychoanalysis is deficient if it does not attend to social class effects on personality development, the organizational and cultural relation of symptoms and patterns of adaptation, and the varieties of external reality. Serious social problems require the attention of all disciplines—including psychoanalysis—for an understanding of individual and group behavior and treatment. Psychoanalysis needs to learn about social issues and transcend middle-class psychology, or it will be bypassed by history.
- Anti: There is a danger of dilution leading to the abandonment of traditional methods, which focus on intraindividual forces (especially unconscious ones) that determine individuals' behavior and the social organizations they form. These are distinct from external reality (interpersonal and ecological), which also influence behavior. Psychoanalytic institutions will retrench to monasteries preserving knowledge from an inimical world of "modernization" and the "in thing". The psychoanalyst is neutral, reserved, receptive, passive; the social activist and reformer is manipulative, bent on reform, seeking correction for institutional change and social management, and engaged in planning and "engineering". Overselling "community psychiatry" as a "revolution" is not helpful.

- Synthesis: Most psychoanalysts are not isolated from social issues; their patients' personal problems are interlocked with social problems. Psychoanalysts are involved with social agencies and teaching. Psychoanalytic theory contributes to research on social problems. However, social action is not integrated with psychoanalytic activities or curriculum. It is considered foreign, digressive, and minor. Faculty appointments, presentations and publications, and student role models are weighted toward "pure" psychoanalysis. Research is compartmentalized, resisting sociocultural research, though much was done in Vienna, Berlin, Moscow, Switzerland, Great Britain, and the U.S. between the 1920s and 1950s.
- Recommendations: Integrate social issues into the psychoanalytic curriculum. Strengthen it by eliminating class and cultural limitations. Make it relevant to pressing social issues. Psychoanalytic education should include relevant research and theory in class and culture, family structure and child rearing, and social history and ideology and values relevant to ego and superego formation and aggression.
- Tactics for making socio-cultural data central and the norm: Widen the range of candidates to include minorities, all disciplines (anthropology, sociology, political science, history, psychology, teaching, etc.). Offer them a full training program and make it financially accessible. Include teachers with psychological and sociocultural interests, and give them sanction and respect. Encourage guest speakers, co-teaching, and students from other disciplines. Courses should include minority cases, social agency field work integrating clinical and agency situations, and seminars on psychoanalysts as consultants. Include candidates, graduates, and continuing education for graduates. Develop faculty seminars on integrated course design and cases of the psychoanalytic perspective on social issues such as violence.

This was a familiar struggle for Lindemann, dating from his efforts to have the Boston Psychoanalytic Institute accept social psychiatry. He repeatedly argued for the consistency of social psychiatry and psychoanalysis and his investment in both:[164]

> It indicates that you and my many friends in the Society have been aware of my deep and abiding interest in the Boston Institute, and indeed in the growth and further development of psychoanalysis as a science and as a practice. My intense preoccupation with issues of the community and of the social order appeared to me always as an implementation and enrichment of the influence of psychoanalytic thought. Indeed, the community mental health development would be quite unthinkable without our understanding of unconscious

motivations, individual and collective, which determine community processes as well as individual health.

The Committee on Community Psychiatry developed a questionnaire about psychoanalysts' involvement in social psychiatry.[165] There were reports of work, consulting, and teaching in community psychiatry, mostly by individual analysts and with varying amounts of openness, support, and opposition.[166] Papers were read by Redlich, Rubin, Tarnower, Bandler, Bernard, Coleman, and Davis.

The American Academy of Psychoanalysis (AAP), too, noted that CMH legislation heralded a new pattern of psychiatric practice, including the application of psychiatry and the social sciences to large population groups.[167] Although (a minority of) psychoanalysts had participated, psychoanalysis was downplayed in this field and psychoanalysts' qualification for CMH "instead of endless individual office practice". A survey showed that 81% of psychoanalysts report community work, and most psychodynamic psychotherapists work in teams, are leaders and planners of services, work in clinics and service programs, are consultants to agencies, and are involved in research and training. It recommended that more psychoanalysts should participate. It thought that psychoanalytic training was helpful in CMH consultation, supervision, teamwork, and standards for training, though there was disagreement about its place in administration.[168] It felt that community psychiatry was desirable, for instance, as part of comprehensive mental health care. It recommended that community psychiatry be included in medical school and psychiatric residency education, training in field service and consultation, in teamwork with other mental health and helping professions, and that nonprofessionals be trained as mental health workers. Psychodynamics was seen as essential in all of this. It also recommended the training of CMH specialists with curriculum changes at all levels of training to include concepts of sociology and anthropology, exposure to community agencies, a fourth-year elective course, and psychiatry residency to include a supervised six-month CMH experience. The AAP supported finding a niche for an increased participation by psychoanalysts who have appropriate personality and work: they should be ready to learn to adapt, be familiar with the community and its agencies, recognize that they are team members and be sensitive to the needs of teammates, be able to cooperate, be dedicated to aims of service and have human sympathy, recognize cultural differences, be flexible and ingenious, and have sound judgment free of emotional involvement.

The AAP was proud of its contributions to community psychiatry, believed that psychiatric insight is uniquely valuable and that psychoanalysts should share responsibility for this approach, and encouraged this attack on the sources and varieties of mental illness. It sought changes in curriculum from premedical through residency education to increase the availability of psychoanalysts for service in CMH. Further workshops and papers on this topic were planned.

Social Psychiatry in Germany

The forbears of social psychiatry in Germany follow from the earlier phenomenological anthropology of Viktor, Erwin Strauss (in the United States), and Binswanger's *Daseinsanalyse*.[169] Heidegger and Buber's anthropological philosophy of "the other" indicates that being with another highlights the connection and is central in seeking illness not in the person but in the relationship with others. The descriptive phenomenology of Karl Jaspers and Kurt Schneider was alien to therapy.

There was no social psychiatry under National Socialism 1933–1945, and modern psychiatrists and psychoanalysts left Germany, especially to the United States.

After National Socialism, the psychiatrists remaining in Germany were traditional somaticists who continued to dominate, including occupying state hospital directorships.[170] Social psychiatry programs in post–World War II Germany started later than in the United States and were considered unusual and deviant by resistant physicians and more traditional nurses. For instance, nonphysicians took a more active and assertive role rather than being second-class professions—Poerksen, for instance, considered 60% to 70% of disciplinary roles interchangeable aside from unique disciplinary skills. Also, social and community psychiatry opposed private clinical practice as self-serving and segregating the mentally ill rather than promoting self-care capacity of individuals and communities.

Von Bayer followed the focus on the encounter with others rather than self-contained sickness. Other early protagonists were Heinz Häfner and Kisker in Heidelberg and Kuhlenkampf and Bosch in Frankfurt.[171] Since the Gütersloh conference in the 1960s, the first forays into social psychiatry involved extramural programs such as partial hospitalization, which multiplied from 20 to 80 in the 1970s and 1980s, more quickly in urban than rural areas, as community mental health programs brought to light the social context and problems behind mental illness.[172] This social psychiatry ideology was new to German psychiatry, and its adherents thought the medical ideology was properly criticized by antipsychiatry forces. Living with patients in community programs resulted in a more humanistic view than is fostered in academic psychiatry, with attraction to psychotherapy rather than custodial care; attention to family, work, and finances; and seeking the etiology of mental illness, which is not addressed in institution-based social psychiatry. Hospital clinical staff felt ineffectual in curing patients and became depressed and obstructive, withdrew within disciplinary borders, and resisted the discharge of all patients. They were conflicted between patient needs and loyalty to their superiors.[173]

Radical change without political sanction does not have many friends. Moderate social psychiatrists, such as Ursula Plog, Niels Pörksen, Klaus Dörner, and from 1970 the Deutsche Gesellschaft für Soziale Psychiatrie (German Society for Social Psychiatry—DGSP), were outside the mainstream of German psychiatry and were critical of society but continually reevaluating rather than doctrinaire. They worked for the slow evolution in decreasing state hospital census and more social and complementary programs.[174] Dörner at Gütersloh learned not to demand but to believe, express, and work with the local populace, leading to increasing cooperation, which was more successful than other contemporary attempts. Pörksen thought Franco Basaglia in Italy failed in Guritsa because he had no sanction from local political powers but succeeded in Trieste (with support from a strike of nurses), Rome, Fiorella, and Oetrso because he was supported by the local government in closing state hospitals over a year, leaving only voluntary patients. At Wundsdorf hospital, Findsen entered in with a large group, no power, and no accomplishments, retreating to a professional status and writing books. Outside psychiatry were movements of psychologists for discussion groups and radical Hilenofenziv (offensive fanatics) who were rude and critical of psychiatry. Radical claims, such as dissolving the large state hospitals, were unrealistic and grandiose.

At the University of Heidelberg, Lindemann tried (ultimately with limited success) to mediate between Hans Häfner, the head of the psychiatry department and the social psychiatry institute, and the outspoken young champions of change to social psychiatry:[175]

> We attempt to grasp the many-layered structure of the conflict situation, so that, through social psychiatry, we can analyze the personal and motivational factors of institutional processes and the resulting relatively rash cultural change. Poerksen is one of the unsettled, innovation-seeking youth who want to realize a new principle rashly for all, while underestimating important factors and responsibilities, such as a clear authority structure in a clinical department.
>
> The stress of the still-young field of psychiatry in relation to other authorities in this area leads to the tendency to surround ourselves with young disciples or deny them respect. It would be a pity to have to forsake the great efforts to develop such a comprehensive program.

Social psychiatry was a small part of institutional psychiatry, involving mostly psychiatrists and psychologists and few nurses. Its attraction to younger workers versus opposition by the chiefs of large institutions made for slow institutional change. Hospital staff members were discouraged from advocating institutional change because of concerns about job security and preserving lifetime contracts. In Italy, nurses and hospital staff members had to go outside the institutions into the community to implement the social psychiatry approach.

An example of a German social psychiatrist is Ursula Plog.[176] She reports that she was a clinical psychologist who did not like clinical testing and trained in medical psychiatry. She worked with youth in homes and education and then collaborated with Klaus Dörner in establishing a day clinic. She was a follower of Dziewas and continued his work. The first congress of social psychiatry took place in 1968–1969 and resulted in the establishment of the Deutsche Gesellschaft für Soziale Psychiatrie (DGSP—German Society for Social Psychiatry), which became the nation's premier professional society for social psychiatry. She continued training in teamwork and social psychiatry and a community viewpoint, and, with Dörner, wrote a textbook to help establish social psychiatry in Germany. Dörner then became the director of the large, old state mental hospital at Gütersloh, bringing the social psychiatry strategy of reducing the size of mental hospitals. He rented rooms in the community for patients to live in, developed private group programs for former patients, and encouraged staff to take vacations with patients to increase their sense of normality without need for institutionalization. His program found that state funds paid only for institutional treatment and not preventive services or community programs. Psychologists, nurses, social workers, occupational therapists, and teachers are not usually prepared to deal with psychiatric rehabilitation through daily coping skills, physical education, and social awareness. Health education (diet, smoking, etc.) is provided by INSURANCE companies. Pastoral counselors are few and not trained in psychotherapy, personality, and prevention; they keep to the normal population and have moved toward politics rather than mental health.

After his sampling of social and community psychiatry at Heidelberg, Tübingen, etc., Lindemann was disappointed at their reception and development of this approach and more comfortable with its place in the U.S.:[177] "The sojourn to Germany which was so important to both of us in order to test my relationship to my own past identity in another culture, turned out to be quite stressful and disheartening. All the more we will be happy to live and work where we belong".

Erich Lindemann's Postretirement Activities

Lindau Psychotherapy Week

The Lindau Psychotherapy Week in Germany was very meaningful to Lindemann. Twice a year for ten years—1963 to 1973 (when he was too ill to attend)—he led what he described as an experimental self-study group for young psychiatrists and family physicians who were interested in psychotherapy, understanding group process, and emotional self-understanding.[178]

> the Lindau Conference on Psychotherapy ... an annual affair in the last week of April ... designed for physicians in the fields of general medicine and pediatrics in Germany, with some admixture of people from Switzerland, Holland and the Scandinavian countries ... a round-up of recent developments in the psycho-social aspects of medical practice. This year, the group will try to come to grips with the effect of the aggressive advances in the so-called behavior therapies as they tend to discourage people's endeavors with the long, patient process of becoming acquainted with the patient's inner life ... the second week ... is mostly dedicated to practice in such matters as hypnosis, relaxation therapy, and also to the use of art and dancing.[179]

It became an intensely intellectually and emotionally close-knit fellowship that nourished all participants including Lindemann himself.

As Lindemann's disability progressed, he regretfully became unable to participate in the group.[180] And as his death approached, he and the group shared their grief at this mutual bereavement—Lindemann feeling it one of the high points of his professional life and the group mourning at nevermore including him.[181]

Consultation to India

One of Lindemann's fond hopes was to return to India for further consultation to his Indian colleagues and learning from their culture and philosophy:[182]

> I was indeed intending to visit you next year ... starting in December in order to follow up our long hoped for goal of working together ... in your Department and in the All India Institute. I had discussed ... it last winter with Dr. Meyer of the Rockefeller Foundation in New York. We thought there might be two visits each for about four months, the first starting at the end of '66, the second at the end of '67. My work in social psychiatry had made me all the more eager to become thoroughly familiar with the cultural differences between our two countries.
>
> There is, unfortunately, at present some doubt whether I can carry out our plan because of my somatic condition.

This plan was initially fully supported by the Rockefeller Foundation, which had a larger plan for medical education in India:[183]

> Presumably you have by now been back in Palo Alto long enough to be able to think of the possibility of again going abroad ... my hope

that it will soon be possible for you to arrange your program so as to spend several months at the All India Institute of Medical Sciences.

Since my return to Delhi both Professor Wig and Professor Satya Nand have inquired as to when you would be coming . . . You can be assured that there is a fine group of young physicians with whom you can work. As a group I believe they are interested in the general field of community psychiatry . . . It will be possible to provide accommodation for you at the Institute . . . If your plans have advanced to a stage where you are able to arrive at a definite commitment I would appreciate being informed as soon as possible. If you wish, you also may write to Dr. Maier in our New York office.

Plans and arrangements were made repeatedly but delayed and ultimately frustrated by his progressive illness.[184]

Lindemann's Other Activities

- He maintained a clinical practice to provide financial support to back up academic financing.[185]
- October 1965 Lydia Rapoport confirmed his meeting with her and Prof. Jerome Cohen at the University of California School of Social Welfare.[186]
- November 4, 1965 Even as his tenure at MGH was being closed, Lindemann applied for appointment to fellowship in the Academy of Psychoanalysis.[187]
- November 10, 1965 J. Elizabeth Jeffress, M.D., Chief of Professional Education at Agnews State Hospital in San Jose, California confirmed his talk to the professional staff on "Crisis Behavior".[188]
- November 17, 1965 Lindemann sat on the Pilot and Special Grants Section, Training and Manpower Resources Branch, NIMH where he could encourage projects outside traditional treatment of mental illness.[189]
- November 1965 Lindemann was a major speaker at the Smith College School for Social Work's Smith Benefit Lecture.[190]
- On December 16–17, 1965, Lindemann taught community psychiatry at the Arizona State Department of Health.[191]
- January 27, 1966 meeting of the Santa Clara Psychiatric Society: George Krieger, M.D., Chief of the Psychiatric Service at the Veterans Administration Hospital at Palo Alto, California invited Lindemann to speak on grief and depression.[192]
- In 1966, Lindemann prepared to give the lecture "Community Mental Health, Comments on the Social Consequences of Scientific Inquiry". In it, he clearly noted the resistance to the recognition of the effect of social process on mental health:
- March 28–April 1, 1966 a conference on mental health in Asia and the Pacific was held at the East-West Center in Honolulu. William

Caudill, Ph.D., from the Laboratory of Socio-Environmental Studies at NIMH, invited Lindemann to be a "generalist" at the meeting (along with Alexander Leighton, Wittkower, and Wynne), chairman of the conference for one day, and to present a paper (on severe, chronic mental illness versus psychodynamic and social influences on mental health)[193] to be included in a publication by the East-West Center Press.[194]

- The second Congress of Social Psychiatry took place in Wiesbaden, Germany in 1966–67. Lindemann had a major role in the planning and was scheduled to present a paper on a social psychiatry approach to adolescence as contrasted with focus on psychoneurotic and psychosomatic illness. His developing illness prevented him from continuing the planning, attending, and giving his paper. The meeting became an arena for the contest between the medical and social views of mental health.[195]

- Jurgen Ruesch . . . went to Wiesbaden and. . . [got] together with the people who were strongly dissenting from the [Joshua] Bierer approach and who insisted on the central role of psychiatry. Morri[Morris] Carstairs, who is an outspoken proponent of the view that social psychiatry should represent the study of social issues viewed from the platform of a medical model, became co-chairman for a group which evidently plans to promote social psychiatry as a sub-field of psychiatry . . . my own position . . . has been close to yours and to Eric Tryst's, to the Tavistock Clinic, to the people who are promoting social architecture emphasizing that the contribution of psychiatry is only one small segment of the several important contributions . . . to better our understanding of networks of human relations and their interplay with individual states of well being and ill health . . . this kind of [p. 1] group would now be free to go ahead with different plans, perhaps under a label other than psychiatry, with leadership not from medical men but from persons . . . who are concerned with social order and social process . . . I would be more than glad to participate . . . I doubt that much could be gained by . . . protest about the actual way in which things were handled in Wiesbaden. It reflected the problems of hierarchy which . . . are impeding so much the development of genuine collaboration in the social sciences. [p. 2]

- 1968 Lindemann spent a limited amount of time consulting with former MGH colleagues who redeveloped the Boston College Psychology Department with a CMH focus and community projects. [See Ch. 10]

- The old dream of writing a book embodying his theory and experience persisted: "Thank you very much for suggesting to Holt,

- Rinehart and Winston Publishing House that they consider a book of mine. I will be glad to discuss this further with them".[196]
- May 3, 1969 Lindemann spoke at a Massachusetts Psychological Association ceremony. His warmth and caring were fondly acknowledged:[197]

   last Saturday at the Ceremony conducted in our honor by the Massachusetts Psychological Association . . . sharing your reminiscences, your commitment, your vibrant affection for this troubled world. I hope you realize how many of the ideas you have fostered over the years have borne fruit, not always in great programs, but always in the hearts of those you have known . . . your complete involvement in a communication—your total attention and concern for the person (or group) you happened to be talking with . . . and it would apply . . . equally whether he is talking with the Queen of England or Mrs. Murphy from the south end . . . It was a joy to feel again your electric rapport with the group.

- Lindemann visited several psychiatry programs in Germany (see Ch. 10). It is reported that in 1971, he gave his last lecture at the University of Heidelberg.[198]
- It is noted that both Erich and Elizabeth Lindemann gave seminars and in-service training programs to the staff of the Peninsula Hospital Department of Psychiatry in Burlingame, CA by arrangements with its chief and Lindemann's former student, Warren Vaughan.[199]
- Even as his illness and disability progressed, Lindemann continued to teach the social epidemiology perspective on mental health and illness:[200]

   a number of psychiatrists who had become dissatisfied with the traditional clinical approach to problems of emotional disturbances have turned to public health workers, particularly to epidemiologists, and also to social scientists for assistance in developing approaches to prevention and mental health maintenance. Mindful of the great contributions which public health thinking has made towards the control of contagious disease, we believe that the basic orientation of public health workers might be useful for mental health problems also. This means turning away from the exclusive concern with individual patients for purposes of therapy. The psychiatrist had to concern himself with populations and social groupings, learn about incidence and prevalence of disorders, study the natural history of the development of typical emotional disorders from its earliest beginnings to classical cases, and what is most important had to concern himself with community-wide measures which might contribute to the maintenance of good mental health and prevent emotional disorganization.

In the search for social events or situations which could be predicted with reasonable assurance to be followed by an emotional disturbance in a considerable portion of a population we turned to the study of reactions. States of acute grief are well known to the clinician from the social histories of patients with a variety of illnesses, especially such psychosomatic disturbances as ulcerative colitis or rheumatoid arthritis . . . interfering with the recovery from severe burns . . . we made two types of observation . . . significant for the development of our thinking about reactions to crises. The first referred to the absence of grief . . . in the face of a loss . . . The second . . . was concerned with the details of . . . grief work or mourning. . . [It led us to] construct . . . the concept of an emotional crisis. . . [namely] certain inevitable events in the course of the life cycle . . . described as hazardous situations . . . like bereavement, other changes in the significant social orbit. . . [the] birth of a child or marriage . . . entrance into school or job or moving from one place to another. . . . [E]motional strain would be generated, that stress would be experienced, and that a series of adaptive mechanisms would be called into operation which might lead either to the mastery of the new situation (well-adaptive response) or to failure and more or less lasting impairment of function (maladaptive responses). While such situations create stress for all . . . they become crises for those individuals who by personality, previous experience or other factors in the present situation are especially vulnerable . . . and whose emotional resources are taxed beyond their usual adaptive resources.

Over his U.S. professional career, Lindemann's interests and commitments demonstrated a synoptic view of mental health including medicine, psychoanalysis, psychiatry, social sciences, and social and political affairs. This is demonstrated by his membership in more than 41 organizations.[201]

Stanford University Medical Center Department of Psychiatry

In 1953, Thomas Gonda joined the Division of Neurology and Psychiatry in the Department of Medicine of Stanford Medical School—a small school training clinicians for local practice in San Francisco.[202] Psychiatry established a separate department with three members, while neurology remained a division of the Department of Medicine. The university decided to move the medical school to the main university campus in Palo Alto, CA, to amalgamate it with the other arts and professional schools and appoint full-time faculty. In 1959, this move was completed, with two-thirds to three-fourths of the faculty of 80 choosing to stay in their San Francisco private practices.[203] In 1965, the faculty had grown to 300 and in 1979 to 350. It persistently sought David Hamburg as chairman until he accepted in 1961. He saw the core of the department as basic science integrated with human biology in the university. Clarice Haylett saw this as a radical change without attention to the service of human needs.[204] Lindemann remarked, with a social psychiatry perspective, upon this change and its effect on the institutional culture with mental health implications:[205]

> In . . . a medical school, the value shift was from teaching the art of medical practice to becoming a knowledge factory. Prestigious and competitive scientific performance . . . became more admired and rewarded than the delivery of excellent clinical services. . . [p. 1] . . . when values shifted, the organization began to regress from a generally collaborative culture to a mosaic of competitive enterprises . . . In [p. 6] this instance, however, there was not such a massive mobilization of aggression . . . nor did the protagonists regress to paranoid and totally irreconcilable stances. Perhaps . . . the situation was eased by the presence of a mental health consultant.

Gloria Liederman agreed that Hamburg was not warm, department members were very separate without collegiality or sharing, and the focus was on excellence of productivity and high reputation.[206] Subsequent chairmen of the department had to cope with reduced resources and struggle for support.

It was thought that the development of senior clinicians was discouraged. For enrichment, visiting emeritus professors were imported for one month to two years, including Erik Erikson, John Romano, and Lindemann. With the support of Hamburg's wife Beatrix (a child psychiatrist) and Josephine Hilgard (a senior psychoanalyst clinician who joined the department in 1963), there was an attempt to grow within the department young faculty members with a wide range of interests—David Daniels, Gig Levine (clinical psychology, endocrinology, development), Herbert Liederman (clinician), Irving Yalom (groups), William Dement (sleep), and Rosenbaum. Lindemann was recruited as a senior person to support them. Gonda, who eventually rose to be associate dean for the medical school and then executive director for the hospital and clinics, also looked to him for consultation about administration, the change to a totally elective curriculum, etc. As a department chairman, Gonda was thought to be more open, but by his time, it was suffering from reduced resources and not growing.[207]

Hamburg was seen by staff and Lindemann as acutely attuned to opportunities for advancement of his institution and himself—he "followed the lamp of power".[208] After his tenure at Stanford, he was variously chief of the National Institute of Mental Health and then President of the American Psychiatric Association, the Carnegie Corporation of New York, the Institute of Medicine, the National Academy of Sciences, and the American Association for the Advancement of Science.

Mandell saw a shifting pattern in the nature of psychiatry department chairmen generally, which may shed light on the characters of and reactions to chairmen at Stanford, MGH, and elsewhere:[209]

- Before 1950 chairmen were charismatic individuals who did their own teaching, showed humanistic clinical judgement, were not invested in research or biological psychiatry, and built personal reputations.
- Between 1950 and 1970, the influx of NIMH money supported research and scientific training and work. In these years, chairmen were respected scientists, grant getters, and consultants and speakers, especially through the federal government. There developed new programs, institutes, and techniques. Chairmen represented multidisciplinary faculty, and the chairmen were less likely to be individualists. Departments became communities of scholars protected from the real world. They developed unrealistic expectations about eliminating mental illness and poverty, which obstructed goals of individual self-development.
- Since 1970 there was disillusionment with previous goals. Community psychiatry has led to the electorate and bureaucracies causing psychiatry to be dominated by political, racial, regional, and civil liberties considerations. The department chairmen have become negotiators, targets, entrepreneurs, and placators of funding sources, community, faculty, residents, and bureaucracies. They are masters of administrative process without investment in its content.

There was conflicting opinion as to the motivation for inviting Lindemann into the department. Some thought it was at least a gesture toward building the area of social and community psychiatry.[210] Others thought that he was to address clinical issues and their relation to genetics and biology, and be a general wise man. Hamburg remembers being influenced by Lindemann's study of grief to study stress and coping, including on the Group for the Advancement of Psychiatry's Committee on Research.[211] He met Lindemann through Alfred Stanton and discovered an exciting meeting of the minds about coping, which Lindemann had taken up, e.g., through the HRS. In 1957 Lindemann invited Hamburg to join the MGH, and he met Gerald Caplan. He decided instead to accept the NIH offer to set up a research department, which included coping studies. In 1961 he moved to Stanford to build a department "from scratch", including adding visiting professors to help shape the department. He remembered getting the department to support the effort to convince Lindemann to retire as early as possible to a permanent place at Stanford.

In preparation for Lindemann's inclusion, there were extensive exploration, test visits, and preplanning with Hamburg: "It was a delight to look ahead with you into an exciting future set of activities. It was very thoughtful of you to discuss with me over the phone your plans"[212] until it was settled that Lindemann's major professional position was as visiting professor there from 1967 until his death in 1974. He was appointed for an unusually long tenure in this position—in Hamburg's words to strengthen the social and community psychiatry program, and as a mark of Hamburg's respect, friendship, and kindness in light of Lindemann's progressive illness.[213] There were mixed reports of the relationship between them: Elizabeth Lindemann thought that at the beginning, there was much harmony of interests and expectations regarding social psychiatry. Lindemann felt an underlying affection (he often personalized relationships of shared interests). And Hamburg remembered Lindemann as a stimulating visiting professor, tuning in on others' interests and values, relating his interests with theirs, not condescending or talking at people but resonating; decent and considerate. He thought Lindemann viewed his tenure as his "happiest years", stimulating interest, having a strong impact on people, a charismatic teacher, feeling appreciated, and free of the administrative demands that had distracted him from creativity more than he had expected. Hamburg showed his appreciation of Lindemann: "So many people here speak of you so often and so warmly that there is no way that I can adequately send their regard on an individual basis. I can only say that there is the greatest possible appreciation of what your presence meant to us during the past academic year and the greatest possible anticipation of your return in a few months".[214] They both strove to integrate Lindemann into the Stanford department.[215]

Lindemann and Hamburg shared an interest in the phenomenon of coping:[216]

> the coming conference on Coping and Adaptation . . . has come to mean the crowning point in a long series of efforts towards understanding of human problems . . . a few of us started just about twenty five years ago to try to apply what we had learned in psychodynamics in certain life crises rather than limiting ourselves to emotional illness . . . Breaking down the boundaries between clinic and community has made possible many new forms of helpful endeavor and also has brought about the danger of shallowness and ill-considered expansion of services.
>
> We soon began to feel the need for buttressing the new endeavor with solid academic inquiry. My discovery of your work and your ideas came as a great relief and the opportunity for continued work with you has been of great significance to me. . . [p. 1] We can indeed

build a sound basis for a whole series of helpful interventions which take little time and are open to continual evaluation . . . it will be successful in its application only if we include in the foundations the solid base of psychodynamic insight and training . . . I plan to be in touch with you . . . especially with respect to collective coping and defending. In this, for me, quite exciting area of inquiry the project at Boston College . . . has been most revealing. I think I understand now some of the baffling problems . . . in working in Palo Alto last year which . . . were much concerned with patterns of coping and defense evolving in the black population. [p. 2]

Lindemann supported Hamburg's application for funding for his projects.[217]

Lindemann came to Stanford with a rosy picture of work in social psychiatry, but there was also a pervasive feeling that there was little or no support for this or faculty work in this field. He was disappointed, including that he had not seen Hamburg in two and a half years and he did not return phone calls, though they lived one and a half blocks apart. Hilgard thought he expected to be a special advisor and assistant to Hamburg, with support and services in arranging teaching. She and others thought he was bitterly disappointed[218] and limited in his accomplishments.[219] She wondered if he and she should have spoken up more vigorously on his behalf. She remembers his wondering if he should have accepted a professorial appointment in India, where he could be powerful, respected, and effective. Lindemann's wife, too, thought he became disenchanted and disappointed and arranged his appointment at Boston College as a counterbalance.[220] Haylett thought Lindemann was disappointed at first about the lack of an active role in teaching psychiatric residents.[221]

Elizabeth Lindemann thought Hamburg was superficial and seductive when he invited Lindemann to Stanford and turned off to become only proper when he arrived;[222] she felt that he recruited Lindemann only for prestige and did not really share his interests and did not respect him adequately.[223] She thought he was afraid of CMH and became distracted by and fearful of the student rebellion in the university and the black community in East Palo Alto, where the department attempted a CMH program.[224] Daniels, too, thought Hamburg's interest in social psychiatry was more in words than in action (as demonstrated by his faculty appointments); he was a closed person, and it was hard to tell if he was hostile to this approach.[225] Hilgard saw Hamburg as an opportunist who was not close to anyone, shed his psychoanalytic identity for biological research because funding was there, expected all to accomplish on their own and demand recognition, and brought in ambitious prima donnas.[226]

Hamburg's wife Beatrix, an African-American child psychiatrist and head of child psychiatry at Stanford, was in a complicated situation. She was a peacemaker and torn between her identification with the black community and her interest in working with that community in East Palo Alto and maintaining a proper, academic character.[227] Elizabeth Lindemann wondered if she were jealous of Lindemann's work in schools and developed a well-supported program in united school districts in Palo Alto that trained adolescents for mental health work with younger children. Lindemann avoided becoming involved in Stanford's East Palo Alto CMH outreach program to avoid coming between the Hamburgs.[228] When the Stanford medical student rebellion targeted Beatrix Hamburg, Lindemann was approached to act as a mediator, but she rejected this.

Stanford Medical Center was seen as having little or no social psychiatry or social medicine program.[229] Community, social, and clinical activities were not supported though not discouraged. They developed largely outside the department and in other agencies and programs.[230] Most of the department was unreceptive to social and community psychiatry; the interest in it was transitory, and those who were involved in it were transitory—left the department, shifted to student health (David Dorosin), or died;[231] Bill Webber led the Lindemann Group for clinical discussion, and David Spiegel did outreach work with the local Veterans Administration center. Gonda thought the clinical psychologists all were diverted into other fields—e.g., Rudy Moss to social ecology (perhaps influenced by Lindemann). Moos thought,[232] "Social psychiatry was not strong in our department at that time, and there were relatively few people who shared Erich's interests, so I like to think that our interchanges made him feel more at home intellectually". The Department of Family Medicine had little importance, and it was uncertain whether Lindemann was involved with the Department of Preventive Medicine with its focus on basic laboratory research. A psychiatry faculty member interested in CMH remarked:[233] "Stanford is still perched on the edge of greatness and is also perched on the edge of the community, and does not seem to want to commit itself towards making the jump. This seems to occupy a good share of our discussions, that is, the character of our involvement with that seductive yet insatiable mistress, community need. There continues to be lots of talk, committees, but little action". And Lindemann noted:[234] "David Hamburg was reluctant to develop actual programs in a community setting because he feared overcommitment of time and funds in this area". David Daniels observed that few were interested in social psychiatry as a whole:[235] Herant Katchadourian carved out a specialty area teaching sexuality. Beatrix Hamburg consulted to schools, some provided clinical consultation in the community, and a few residents were interested. These social psychiatry people met in a few seminars but had their own projects.

Thomas Gonda, later chairman of the department, was not involved in social and community psychiatry. He consulted Lindemann about what materials to bring to students and how to attract them. He advocated knowledge of and involvement in the social environment. He occasionally invited Lindemann to talk of death and dying, the psychosomatic origins and development of his work, and thinking through his own illness and death in a new way. Lindemann functioned as a senior clinician, including participating in the planning of a new hospital psychiatry ward as a therapeutic community.

There was disagreement as to what he accomplished notwithstanding.[236] After a year or two he began to be consulted and sought after for treatment by staff and students, who had to struggle to make time for him. Just as he began to get satisfaction in his burgeoning role his illness began to be disabling.

After his struggles and withdrawal at MGH, Lindemann took up CMH again at Stanford and attracted a following of creative people who collaborated warmly with him and worked on social issues outside the official hierarchy, such as Herant Katchadourian's development of a course in sexuality, and David Dorosin leading the student mental health program.[237] Hamburg was remembered as telling Lindemann to do whatever he wanted to but not meddle in administration. Lindemann was seen (by faculty administrators, secretaries, etc.) as gentle, self-effacing, considerate, diplomatic, and warm. His personal characteristics mirrored his professional approach. He waited to be asked to contribute by those at all levels—mostly clinical questions—and allowed others (e.g., Hamburg) to initiate action, avoiding rivalry with Hamburg. He was not involved in departmental battles, had no enemies, and seemed syntonic with the department, and both Hamburgs seemed happy with him. Some suspected other senior faculty members were jealous of his attraction and role as a wise man and therefore did not invite him to lecture or supervise.[238] His wife remembers his not being assertive about the need for social psychiatry teaching, faculty, tenure, or his own role. He did not like the power position (perhaps stemming from the experience of conflict between his father and his maternal grandfather); in his concept of CMH and his Stanford appointment as visiting professional, he always assumed the position of being available to be consulted. He was seen as an older great man who became a guru for unhappy young people in the department. He did not intervene but gave perspective and encouragement and referred them to others who could take action. There were remarks that he was more comfortable in this role than as a Harvard department chairman and administrator, relieved of decision making and conflict.

Dorosin thought Lindemann had hopes of being an advisor to Hamburg to initiate a new social psychiatry direction in the department. He did not get department support in this. He sought to be a spiritual leader for the young, to share his knowledge, and to consult. He developed seminars on crisis intervention, primary and secondary prevention, the public health approach, and the physiology of stress. In the end he had limited contacts in the department, school, and university and little lasting impact on them.

In contrast to those seeing Lindemann as essentially focused on clinical issues at the Stanford department and avoiding social and community psychiatry, others thought he gradually did become a central figure in social and community psychiatry there. He brought his view of the progress of psychiatry toward CMH:[239]

> A Summary of Lecture to be given as part of the Series, "Progress in Medicine" on February 2, 1966; TITLE: Community Mental Health, Comments on the Social Consequences of Scientific Inquiry.
>
> There has been a drastic change in the care of the mentally sick during the last two decades which culminated in the development of community mental health centers. Their purpose is to provide care within the patient's community, to permit continued contact with the family and neighborhood, and to facilitate rehabilitation in occupation and social relations. They also are concerned with continuity of care, with the provision of a supportive human milieu within the center and with preventive and educational efforts outside the center.
>
> These innovations appear to originate from a number of advances in the behavioral and social sciences that have illuminated the effect of social processes on mental and emotional wellbeing. The study of group processes in small face to face groups which was started by Kurt Lewin prepared the ground for what is presently known as "therapeutic milieu". The structural-functional analysis of social events suggested by Talcott Parsons opened the way to the study and appraisal of social roles, role conflict and role transition. The extension of epidemiological demographic approach to the social order of communities provided access to ethnic, class, and social structure variables in the distribution of emotional disturbances. Finally, attention to psycho-social crises and events of rapid social change using the resources of psychodynamic observation made possible the "clinical" analysis of many forms of social pathology and deviance.
>
> Concurrent with the scientific evolution a change in attitude and increased tolerance within the community of behavior differences and different styles of conduct took place supported by new interpretations of human relations emerging from the literary elaboration of the psychoanalytic approach to understanding human behavior.
>
> These developments did not take place without numerous objections and resistances because they imply an inevitable change of the social order, of professional prerogatives and roles. The rapid evolution of new services will create problems of manpower as well as of maintaining standards in care and investigative work. They do, however, present a vast new opportunity for field observation, enriched interpretation and focused experimental study.

He outlined for interested faculty members the essentials of a CMH program:[240]

> the four indispensable aspects of community mental health programs. They concern (1) the modification of direct services to suit the existing social stratification and ethnic composition of the population; (2) the formulation of indirect services as they refer to both medical and social pathology; (3) the extension of these indirect services also to the needs for organizational and institutional advice and indeed to problems of social action which will be posed; (4) the inevitable involvement of citizens as targets for the application of existing knowledge and as participants in the acquisition of new knowledge, whether in the role of informants or in the role of collaborators in determining goals and procedures as well as limits of the inquiry.

He also acknowledges, from painful experience, the difficulty of radical change in people and institutions:[241] CMH is a struggle, visionary, with glory. And it requires participants to stick their necks out from clinical psychiatry. Dr. Denham felt it was a highly improper area for psychiatrists to address. Mental health practice in the contemporary U.S. dealt with a culture of innovation, the development of past identity, how a culture copes with rapid social change, and collective and individual defenses and coping. And there is the problem of developing a future identity that is unpredictable and anxiety producing.

He eagerly accepted participation in Stanford's review of its role in addressing social problems, though experience had taught him to restrain his optimism about academic receptivity to this endeavor:[242]

> Of course I will be delighted to participate in the seminar on the Role of the University in Current Social Problems . . . the first meeting on October 18. . . . [It calls to mind] the committee appointed by [Harvard University] President [James] Conant after the [Second World] war on the Place of Psychology in an Ideal University. Even then, the relation of action to research presented puzzling problems . . . a climate was developed in which it was possible to found the department of social relations which combined dynamic psychiatry on the one hand and experimental work on the other hand . . . As you well know, there has been some disenchantment with the so called clinical approaches. It would take much effort to justify the pursuit of social goals in an academic context but I surely believe it must be done.

The department established a Community Services Liaison Committee including Lindemann and several of those with whom he had established relationships: Herbert Liederman, David Daniels, Peggy Goldie, E. Fuller Torrey, Herant Katchadourian, Levine, and Rosenthal. Minutes of one of its meetings gives an insight into the foray into CMH by at least a cadre interested (with Lindemann's support) in developing this interest in the department:[243]

> The task of the committee was defined as (a) dealing with specific proposals for community involvement, such as the one presented by Drs. Langee and Rosenthal. (b) Outlining general departmental guidelines for such involvement in community and social psychiatry . . . The East Palo Alto OEO [federal Office of Economic Opportunity] health center . . . has created a whole new possible focus for health services in that community . . . The medical school is in the process of defining the role they will play in surrounding communities . . . there was agreement to provide some services to Alviso [one of the medical center's community health project sites] . . . Dr. Liederman is a member of that medical school committee . . . The broad issue of what the Department of Psychiatry has to give was raised. Dr. Lindemann suggested we respond to felt needs of the community (e.g., increased income, increased communication, self respect, etc.) rather than necessarily thinking in terms of formal psychiatric services. Instead of putting in a whole institution he suggested limited, high caliber services to work with already existing services.

The committee compiled a rather detailed history of social psychiatry and social medicine's part in the department's development. Perhaps it reflects the dynamic development in other academic institutions:

> . . . Since World War II the American medical school . . . is being challenged to respond to diverse and often conflicting demands. In part the pressure comes from activists who insist that the medical school more fully meet the needs of the community by reforming both training and the delivery of medical care. But another sort of pressure is exerted as a result of . . . federal support of biomedical research. As in most institutional conflicts the dispute is expressed in contests over power and money, but, at a more fundamental level, what is involved is the value and reward system of academic medicine . . . in the 1960's Stanford depended heavily on federal funds to finance expansion . . . the rapidity of the buildup and the reliance on federal funds . . . caused an unevenness in development. Then in the later years of the decade, Stanford was hit by the squeeze on federal funds and by demands on the school to exercise a greater measure of social responsibility by providing new forms of training and community service. . . [p. 551] . . . [Joshua] Lederberg [recruited to Stanford, later Nobel laureate] . . . observes that Stanford "has problems of identity and leadership which override the money problems". [p. 552][244]

... In the late 1950's Stanford medical school ... lengthening the ... course for the M.D. degree to 5 years. A decade later Stanford switched to an elective system ... This reversal was seen by many as representing a swing away from a research bias ... and toward a greater stress on clinical training and community service. The shift occurred during a period when social and political awareness was growing at Stanford and at other medical schools, but the causes of the shift were too complex to be attributed solely to a surge in medical populism ... The key to flexibility under the 5-year program was to have been a block of open time ... about half the assigned time ... learning what the department ... felt was important and the other half pursuing his [the medical student's] special medical interests. ... [p. 785] ... "The kids saw the free time as an opportunity to get out into the community; the faculty saw it as an opportunity to get the kids into the lab". By 1966 [when Lindemann arrived] it became clear that a major effort at revision of the curriculum was necessary ... A consensus developed in the committee that a totally elective system would provide the best chance of achieving the original aims of the Stanford plan ... creating a preceptor-student relationship between the faculty member and medical student and to open alternative "pathways" through medical school to fit graduates for the differing roles played by physicians today ... The changeover to the elective system was made in 1968 with less opposition than might have been anticipated ... the students have proved quite conservative in curriculum matters ... the trend is toward a heavier concentration on traditional medical school studies ... For the faculty, the elective system creates a new market situation ... faculty members are offering courses in what most interests them and what they feel is most important, and there is some indication that the quality of teaching has improved. On the other hand, as one faculty member said of his colleagues, "People are allowed to do what they damn well please without regard to what it does to total education". The elective system was adopted at a time when the demand for social relevance in medical education was growing. At a research-oriented medical school like Stanford the idea went somewhat against the grain, but during the later years of the decade a number of things were done to advance the claims of "social medicine". Probably the most significant event was the arrival in 1969 of Count Gibson who, while at Tufts, had been involved in setting up trailblazing community health centers ... Gibson came to Stanford to establish a division of community medicine in the department of preventive medicine. Stanford soon had links with three Office of Economic Opportunity–sponsored health centers. These were in [possibly East] Palo Alto, whose inhabitants are predominantly low income black people; in Alviso at the foot of San Francisco Bay with a largely Mexican-American population; and in King City in a rural area . . . The future of the program would seem to depend on how seriously the medical school pursues experimentation with the forms of delivery of medical care . . . until the Cambodia incursion last spring, few Stanford medical school students or faculty members had been actively involved in protest actions which had erupted on the Stanford campus fairly frequently. The events of last spring, however, led to the organization of a Stanford Medical Community for Peace involving students, faculty, and staff in a variety of nonviolent political activities, on and off campus, against the war.[245]

Jeff Brown, president of the medical [p. 786] school student body at the time, observed that one effect of the Cambodia crisis was to raise in a nontheoretical way the "question of the responsibility of the medical student and physician to the profession and society . . . Is it the responsibility of the physician to get involved in politics, education, mental health programs, social criticism?" organized political activity at the medical center has gone downhill since the peak period during Cambodia . . . The role of medical students in establishing goals and setting policy for the medical school has increased substantially . . . but [they] complain that they still have relatively little impact . . . medical students . . . fall into three fairly distinct categories. First . . . the "competitive" types aiming at a rather standard medical school experience . . . followed by . . . probably, careers on rather traditional lines. Next are a smaller group. . . "individualistic" [students] . . . headed for careers in research or . . . in academic medicine. Finally, there is a new breed . . . interested in community medicine and committed to entering practice as a member of a group . . . Stanford's 5-year plan, especially in the early 1960's . . . attracted a group of students who . . . lacked the conventional premedical training and . . . orientation. Many of them had particular interest in the social and behavioral sciences and social issues . . . The elective system seems to have had most effect on this group. . . "We're getting fewer social relations types from Harvard and more scientifically oriented types". A matter of real concern at the moment . . . among many faculty members, especially basic science researchers . . . is that the demand for social relevance will cause a shift in resources and emphasis away from research. [p. 787]

One of the young psychiatry faculty members at Stanford helped expressed the importance of social psychiatry in the training of new psychiatrists:[246]

> Psychiatrists are becoming increasingly aware of the importance of understanding the social and organizational framework of illness and the treatment process. Demographic variables . . . have been shown to be significantly related to incidence of illness, symptomatology, and type of treatment offered. Characteristics of the treatment setting

and its mesh with specific patients . . . influence behavior and outcome . . . the first two years of psychiatric residency—has not kept up with advances . . . that prepares him adequately . . . Psychiatric educators are realizing that training emphasizing solely psychologic or biologic aspects of the individual do not produce psychiatrists prepared to deal effectively with the ecology of illness and treatment . . . the sociotherapeutic viewpoint is not factorially independent, but is related to the psychotherapeutic view . . . the continued predominance of the psychotherapeutic orientation.

Lindemann became a gathering point for students, faculty, and staff attracted to this approach[247] and inspiring warm friendships and admiration. Hilgard saw him reach out to and be reached out to by others, his supervision especially valued by residents—he had obvious therapeutic benefit to David Dorosin, help to Fred Melges (a junior faculty member), and Marguerite (a supervised resident with obvious therapeutic needs).[248] He was in a good position to give young people the opportunity to talk about new culture and grievances.[249] He acknowledged that "You were perfectly right in suggesting that my charismatic qualities are a significant part of my influence on the students and they are in a certain sense dispensable".[250] He got into difficulty with only a few people. He taught medical students, supervised psychiatric residents in the general hospital, and was a visiting consultant. He provided supervision to the Student Health Services social workers group, commenting on cases and agency dynamics, which was much appreciated. He continued these activities even when he could travel with a wheelchair, and when he could not travel, residents came to a monthly seminar with invited speakers and visited him at home. It is significant that he refused requests to treat department members, nor did he take on patients from outside; some wondered whether this was because of his uncertainty about his future.[251]

Following are some of the special relationships Lindemann developed:

- He became a friend of David Kaplan, head of the hospital medical social service program.
- He became close to some psychiatric residents and followers of his ideas: David Dorosin came as a first-year psychiatric resident interested in general hospital psychiatry, and it was thought that Lindemann had a special bond with him and was able to plant in him the seeds of the MGH program.[252] Dorosin thought of himself as a maverick, interested in a social rather than biological approach, behavior rather than thought, and teaching this perspective.[253] He brought a social psychiatry approach to the student health services that grew. However, he was shunted to a staff rather than faculty position.[254]
- He was a friend of the director of the medical outpatient clinic, who invited Lindemann to meet with selected medical students.

- John Adams became chairman of psychiatry at the University of Florida at Gainesville.
- Lindemann supervised Frank Ochberg's psychotherapy by phone when Lindemann was in Boston recovering from surgery and wanted him to follow in Leonard Duhl's footsteps. He ultimately became an assistant to Bertram Brown, director of the NIMH.
- Lindemann had been attracted to Lois Paul when she was a graduate student in anthropology in Harvard Department of Social Relations, wrote papers at HRS, and was otherwise involved in the MGH CMH program.[255] She married the anthropologist Benjamin Paul, who Lindemann analyzed. At Lindemann's invitation, they both came to Stanford to continue their careers.
- Richard Almond, an outspoken, controversial young staff psychiatrist, asked Lindemann to read chapters of his book on charisma in psychiatry (to be published by Lindemann's beneficiary, Jason Aronson). It embodied his experiences with the Yale therapeutic environment in which he found that everyone was organized into a supportive environment, the mentally ill had lost control and needed others to add power, love, and appreciation, and this came most from nurses and psychotherapists.
- David Daniels had three or four discussions with Lindemann to explore his perspective.[256] He was a benevolent father figure who supported Daniels's work despite his lacking prospects for promotion or tenure (which were entirely in Hamburg's hands).

Daniels felt he was seen as a maverick who brought in nontraditional community activities.[257] He had a project to develop activities, industry, residence, etc. for chronically mentally ill Veterans Administration patients and study reactions to innovation and obstacles to their implementation and the need for effort and commitment for the implementation phase rather than only token effort.[258] Also, following the assassinations of Robert Kennedy and Martin Luther King, Daniels worked with a like-minded, diverse committee.

He introduced Synanon in the Clinical Forum (grand rounds) despite Hamburg's disapproval, and brought representatives of an early student movement because they raised important issues, though Daniels disagreed with them. Hamburg intensely criticized Daniels, seeing these as not appropriate to an academic setting and accusing Daniels of being not loyal or trustworthy, though others were interested and the meetings were packed.

After the assassinations of Robert Kennedy and Martin Luther King, he worked with a committee of residents (including Ochberg) interested in education and action by psychiatrists regarding violence. They developed a symposium, called in the news media, and were published in the popular media and a lead article in the April 1969 issue of the journal *Science* ("Violence and the Struggle to Adapt"), obtained a $6,000 grant from the Sytax Corporation, and felt they influenced the recommendations of the national Commission on Violence. Hamburg discouraged this activity as not a proper departmental function but did not block it.

Daniels did not seek to build a lasting social psychiatry group in the department, and this project spontaneously dissolved.

Finally, he quietly left the department, bitter that the grants he had facilitated had helped fund his and others' (including Lindemann's) salaries, seminars, clinical and environmental and institutional training, and publishing.

- Al E. Weisz wrote to Lindemann:[259] "you have been such important people in my professional life . . . I want to thank you most especially for helping me with whatever expertise I was able to develop as a clinician and as a consultant to clinicians, because I feel that nobody at Stanford gave me as much help in this area as you did . . . I want to personally acknowledge the tremendous help and interesting consultations which you provided for me. Many places in the paper will indicate sentences which are probably verbatim Lindemann.

Again thank you very much".

Lindemann wrote a revealing comment: "Erich's comment: Good illustration of the way I work—through people, not books. Martin Buber has described this type of person".

Herant Katchadourian moved from the NIMH to Lebanon, where he did social psychiatry research on the epidemiology of mental illness and culture as it contributes to psychopathology.[260] In 1966, David Hamburg invited him to Stanford with an unclear function. There he met Lindemann, who shared professional interests (not widely shared in the department) and European birth. Katchadourian, who had no close ties, was touched when Lindemann reached out to him as a mentor and developed a tutor–tutee relationship. In 1967–68, Hamburg felt the need for social psychiatry in the biologically oriented residency training program; Katchadourian, as coordinator of resident training, Lindemann, David Daniels, and Alberta Siegel developed a seminar. Katchadourian felt he "became a little like" Lindemann in developing a course in the life cycle, attention to the European–U.S. acculturation experience, the father–son relationship (Katchadourian's father was too formidable; Lindemann and his son were not close), a psychiatric identity broadened from clinical to the helping observer, attention to human conflict, philosophy, and altruism, and exceeding the "clinical straitjacket". Lindemann helped him to function as dean of Stanford University, tolerant of people and finding a place for himself. Katchadourian's heritage of the unintegrated Armenian population in Lebanon and Lindemann's scientific observer role led Katchadourian to remain uninvolved and nonpartisan in political turmoil, the civil rights struggle, and the anti–Vietnam War movement.

Katchadourian saw Hamburg as running his department via personal support to individuals and agreed with others that there were no major faculty members in social psychiatry until Lindemann came. Hamburg was a "hard-headed biologist" who had no objection to teaching social psychiatry courses but was wary of community practice, doubting its legitimacy and future developments. The junior faculty members interested in social psychiatry were not considered of high quality. By design, those interested in psychotherapy (Yalom, Rosenbaum, George Golovich) and social psychiatry constituted a group that was not weighty because it was too small without large laboratories. In this context Lindemann was a resource and not a leader.

However, David Hamburg asserted his department valued and was involved in a broad spectrum of mental health issues, with strong interests in social, community, and social science fields:[261]

> most of the field's professional manpower in 1961 was preoccupied with the less severe range of disorders . . . it seemed to me that our most distinctive contribution . . . would be to concentrate heavily . . . on a broad scientific approach to psychiatric problems, with much attention devoted to relatively severe disorders . . . In faculty development . . . we were eager to have strength in biological, psychological, and social disciplines . . . we wanted to have a reasonable sampling of strength in various areas of exceptional promise—e.g. . . . social psychology; [p. 2] anthropology, sociology, and biostatistics. . . [p. 3] . . . In connection with the national program of comprehensive community mental health centers in recent years, there has been a good deal of ferment . . . in regard to community responsibilities . . . For a department like ours, there is considerable breadth and diversity of relevant communities. . . [p. 5] . . . we had tended during the post–World War II psychiatry "boom" to neglect the poor, depreciated, and sick . . . we oriented our residency program toward preparation . . . also toward care of the less fortunate, toward public service activities . . . In our clinical commitments we took . . . a heavy responsibility for care of "marginal men", especially in . . . the Veterans Hospital . . . Stanford clinic . . . a unit at the Valley Medical Center . . . members of our faculty and of our residency program have been active in a variety of settings . . . included schools, community agencies, community lodges, employment services, neighborhood health centers, and of course community mental health centers. . .
>
> [p. 6]

He supported several projects that he saw as being CMH and saw Lindemann's role in them:[262]

> It now seems virtually certain that David Daniels will be heading up the East Palo Alto project. Also it is definite that David Dorosin will be heading up student mental health, and it is very probable that Herant Katchadourian will be undertaking a major program of research education and service on campus . . . the East Palo Alto community and the University community . . . will give us two fine models for community mental health work. Your experience, wisdom and creativity will be of enormous help . . . With deep appreciation and respect.

Lindemann developed social psychiatry seminars for medical students and psychiatric residents:

> . . . Dr. Lindemann and I will be conducting an informal seminar discussing selected issues in Social Psychiatry for some medical students".[263]
>
> [264] . . . meet with our residents . . . and present your views on . . . the nature of group experience, not only in psychotherapy but in the many life situations. . . [that] influence individual behavior and experience . . . one of the seminar sessions of a series . . . under the heading of Social Psychiatry in which we, for the first time in this department, tried to bring together relevant contributions of social scientists and psychiatric observations in a more or less coherent pattern . . . David Daniels, one of our Assistant Professors . . . has been much interested in . . . therapeutic organizational patterns which allow responsible participation by the patient . . . also has been . . . interested in the peculiar effectiveness of self-organized groups . . . in the rehabilitation of drug addicts . . . We would hope that your own remarks would deal less with pathology and more with the contributions to health and creativity.

Also education for faculty members:[265]

> There are a growing number of individuals in our department who are interested or involved in the area of social psychiatry. In discussing this with David Hamburg, we came up with the idea . . . a faculty seminar on social psychiatry during the next academic year, 1967–8. . . perhaps meeting every two weeks . . . Drs. Hamburg and [Melvin] Sabshin have already agreed to participate . . . we would like to keep the group size to about ten.

And there is evidence that he was involved in a difficult community mental health outreach effort with a disadvantaged population in East Palo Alto.[266]

Counterrevolution of Biology and Business 243

Lindemann's last CMH projects were as consultant to Warren Vaughan's psychiatry department at the Peninsula Hospital in Burlingame, California, and to Clarice Haylett at the Contra Cost County Public Health Station.[267] His wife Elizabeth drove him to these sites and herself consulted with social workers at Peninsula Hospital about the mental health of airline stewardesses who had a high casualty rate. She valued Vaughan's appreciation of and support for Lindemann:[268]

> you were probably the very first psychiatrist to take Erich's conversion to public health seriously. At the Massachusetts General Hospital, Dr. Stanley Cobb was taking a troubled, wait-and-see attitude; and the Boston Psychoanalytic Society was shocked. (You remember Ives Hendrick's response to Erich's description of the Wellesley Project: "Now I can visualize the offspring of a cat and a dog!") What a joy it was for Erich to find a colleague with your public health background . . . The final movement: Erich was very sick, and somehow you managed to extend his professional usefulness by inviting him to be a consultant at Peninsula Hospital. I would like to think that this kind of collegial loyalty and compassion is the norm; but I'm afraid it isn't; it can only happen between people who share deep beliefs and common goals; and when one of them, in this case you, is willing to go the extra mile.

There was much civil right activism, student rebellion, and conflict on campus. Gonda recounts 1969–72 as a period for young mavericks (psychiatry residents during Lindemann's time) who were gadfly activists interested in social violence and who developed a rumor-squelching network, Daniels and Ochberg (junior faculty members) were co-chairmen of a departmental Committee on Violence and wrote a book on this subject. DeLuca (another junior faculty member) directed a project on how CMH was "extruded from the main line of the department" (while Gonda thought this was not Hamburg's attitude). All ultimately left the department except David Spiegel and residents Peter Bowen and Chris Gillen, who were interested in social psychiatry but pursued it elsewhere. Lindemann never pushed his ideas openly and may have been in Boston most of 1971, including when Gonda's office was destroyed. He was never mentioned in any social psychiatry project reports or books at Stanford.

All this took up much of Hamburg's attention, including via his vulnerability through his children and African-American wife.[269] He consulted Lindemann and incorporated his ideas and trusted Lindemann to present the student revolt in historical perspective and attempt to smooth the issue over at Hamburg's Jewish community meeting. Lindemann was not an acting-out radical,[270] and the Lindemanns, too, had considerable problems with their own children in reaction to the political unrest on campus. He was opposed to the Vietnam War, and there is evidence that he was involved with both medical students and faculty speaking out about it:[271]

> GROUP COHESIVENESS HYPOTHESIS OR "WHERE HAVE ALL THE FLOWERS GONE" Debbie [photocopied, handwritten flyer]: Reviews [possibly] child psychiatry residents' meeting, encounter with faculty, criticism of faculty resistance to aggressive action leading to loss of resident activism. "COME AND TALK ABOUT ALL THIS AND MORE WITH DR. LINDEMANN AND FELLOW RESIDENTS WED 9 AM".
>
> (undated) "FACULTY STATEMENT" [dittoed]: "We, the undersigned members of the faculty of Stanford Medical School wish to express our support for a group of medical students who have stated their unwillingness to participate in the war in Vietnam". [handwritten notation] "Signed by Erich—April 1967".
>
> We, the undersigned members of the faculty of Stanford Medical School, wish to express our support for a group of medical students who have stated their unwillingness to participate in the war in Vietnam . . . We agree that patriotism and morality require opposition to the war. Active opposition to oppressive or immoral actions of government is in the finest tradition of our history, stemming from . . . the campaigns for abolition, universal suffrage, and civil rights. Opposition . . . is consonant with, indeed is required by, the code of responsibilities of citizens as established . . . at the Nuremburg Tribunal . . . Our Government is brutalizing its citizens by using violence as an instrument of foreign policy . . . We admire the initiative and courage of these students . . . We intend to support them and their position in whatever way becomes necessary and appropriate . . . Signed by Erich—April 1967.[272]

Soo Borson, one of the participating medical students, recalled:[273]

> there were many demonstrations, some occurring on the medical school campus, against the war, and of course many of us registered protests in different ways. I have no distinct recollection of dr. lindemann's participation, so can't help you there. the issue at the time was not only the war itself but the mandatory draft—as you probably know, men (5 of the 7 medical student signers) were draftable; the 2 women who signed, myself and Ann Lanzerotti, did so in principled support of objecting men.

Hamburg's wife, Beatrix Hamburg, was a child psychiatrist and black but evaded the pressures of minority group rebellion.

Lindemann was not a revolutionary but ever the medical and social scientist. He elucidated and taught the facilitating role of the mental health professional:[274]

> A psychiatrist is one who, by training and experience, in an encounter with another person can encourage him or her to be their best self . . . He is concerned with the direction in which our culture of technology and democracy is moving, seemingly toward setting a high priority on behavior control in the interests of those in power; and he would like to protect the opportunities for being a psychiatrist in this sense of being an enabling person *vis a vis* other individuals.
>
> His interest in collectivities is not primary, but derives from his concern for human beings embedded in a social system which places them under pressure. He may be perceived, and may actually become, a spokesman for people in trouble . . . Hence he risks being identified by the Establishment with the cause of the underdog. And he himself may be tempted to assume the role of advocate for persons or groups who are trying legitimately or illegitimately to manipulate the Establishment. [p. 1] This temptation may be seen as similar to . . . young therapists [who] go through periods of overidentification with a patient or client rather than helping him to be more effective in using his legitimate resources . . . the psychiatrist is required . . . to reaffirm his professional role . . . preserving social anonymity or reasserting his own position in the social order . . . even though he may sympathize with the person who wishes it to be different . . . if he recognizes, however, that some of the . . . patients or clients . . . have some very valid statements to make about the Establishment . . . we still restrict our conscience to the particular predicament in which our patient finds himself . . . We cannot, in our professional role, become the promoters or enforcers of social action because . . . we do not have the competence upon which to rely in making decisions. We are not trained as agitators or union organizers, or . . . community development experts. Hence we are not able to be effective allies in social action . . . What we <u>can</u> do is help you to [p. 2] use your very best selves . . . so that you will be less impeded by impulsive reactions which are surely going to spoil the game for you . . . If we do only that—help people preserve the ability to function in their social roles—we help them . . . far more than becoming one more person on the picket line . . . The psychiatrist who assumes this mediator function . . . has to be an expert in group behavior. . . [p. 3] . . . he will not go as a group therapist . . . he will easily recognize the phenomenon of collective transference—and will also see that there are collective, constructive coping arrangements. He will be . . . alerted to group processes, and will be . . . a trusted arbiter . . . based not only on psychiatric theory and practice, but also on the other social sciences . . .

the theory of culture change as it affects populations . . . looking at basic forms of social pathology. [p. 4] . . . one wishes to become a spokesman against social evil and for these people . . . not in the sense of social action, but . . . anticipating the untoward psychological consequences, the byproducts of certain ways of behaving, by which the free enterprise society brings about these disasters . . . in situations of confrontation . . . pointing out the emotions being activated, and the limits which people . . . must set . . . if the process is not to end in anger and chaos . . . search out the original contributing factors which result in a rising casualty rate, and become concerned . . . with planning and innovation. . . [p. 5] . . . Could communities be built which would give . . . opportunity to preserve their cultural values and their life-styles . . . could we attempt experiments in human culture?

In the preventive role, one must be able to communicate . . . with those planners and business people who possess the resources . . . to use these in health-fostering ways . . . how can the people who are despondent get enough of a voice . . . so that they can be heard, and not be perceived as destructive or revolutionary? . . . We need modulators . . . who are concerned about the human and cultural catastrophes . . . which could be studied and controlled . . . one should remind oneself. . . [p. 6] . . . that one is a mediator—please don't be seduced into the role of being a torchbearer!

[p. 7]

In commenting on a book by the young Stanford faculty member he mentored, he was critical of uncritical proposals[275]

> at a time when we are witnessing a revolution in the practice of psychiatry and psychotherapy. Old concepts are being used in a loose manner; new approaches are tried, discarded or modified without adequate description of the psychological and social processes.

and unscientific thinking:[276]

> In a time of extraordinarily rapid developments in the conceptual structure and the treatment methods of social psychiatry, in a time in which authority and tradition are suspect and a kind of pre-scientific thinking is widespread, it is a joy to find a book that allows the reader to find a surer standpoint which is ensured through the presenting of the historical development of this field.

Lindemann was seen as teaching what was asked of him, principally group interaction as the basis of psychotherapy. He always spoke at the psychiatry grand rounds. He was not involved with larger social psychiatry issues such as collaboration with other departments and schools or in local community mental health, such as the Santa Clara County Health System, with three mental health clinics providing brief treatment, which was politicized and bureaucratic. Elizabeth Lindemann thought he was uncertain how to approach the local population, which was very different from those he had experienced. He was interested in outreach to unmotivated people in need. Perhaps motivated by his own illness and treatment, he organized a small group for patients receiving radiation treatment to talk about themselves.

Those attracted by Lindemann's CMH and psychoanalytic approach and manner found him "a dream psychiatrist"—kind, warm, accessible, smart, nonjudgmental, constructive, helpful, approachable, present, and constructive in clinical conferences, loved and respected.[277]

> Lindemann's face was just a palette of colors and shades and changes; his face was constantly expressing responses . . . he was a mirror, as you were talking to him. It was also the case with David Hamburg. And those were the only two damned faces in a sea of a hundred faces that were frozen . . . His face was so much in contrast to the faces of the people around him.

"He is the kind of psychiatrist I would like my students to become", Siegel's artist daughter-in-law remarked as she sketched him: "He just looks like a doctor; he looks like your dream of what a doctor looks like". Psychologist Siegel particularly appreciated Lindemann's valuing the social sciences, "because social scientists don't have very many doctors that they feel that they're in communication with . . . there aren't many doctors of any persuasion, including psychiatrists, who know anything about social science, and Erich did". He maintained strong ties with anthropologists Lois and Benjamin Paul from their work together in Boston. Eulau, Chief Social Worker in the child psychiatry department, valued Lindemann's appreciation of social work; feeling that social workers have much to teach psychiatrists about the social context, social interaction and family systems, and work in the community; and his availability to address this relationship.[278] David Dorosin found that there were few who opened the way to talk about personal and professional issues.[279] He found Lindemann opened up human possibilities and was hopeful and that this resulted in bitter (e.g., Thomas Hackett, a successor at MGH) as well as sweet responses. He made a career of idealism, which became purer in his role as an older, wise mentor at Stanford, resulting in some inevitable disappointment. He saw Lindemann's lasting contributions in his style and approach: dignity of the individual, optimism about human beings, ability to synthesize patient and professional information in the service of patient care, the patient as the end and not the means, bringing the concern for the patient back into social and institutional policy; all gently and with a large perspective, and working in personal ways through supervision and personal teaching rather than writing. He did think that Lindemann had some subtle ego needs, and a Stanford faculty member from Boston interested in cognitive, quantitative psychiatry (perhaps Herbert Liederman) was skeptical of Lindemann's virtue. At Stanford, there were many expressions of appreciation and respect for him.[280] John Nemiah in Boston reported:[281] "Whenever I see people from Stanford I hear their great enthusiasm for what you are doing there, and by all accounts you are having a very happy time of it, for which I am glad". Those who appreciated him found him warm, supportive, and receptive, not distant but able to share himself with certain people—especially Josie Hilgard. He was revered by those in his orbit and enduringly missed.

In some quarters, there was regret that Lindemann did not contribute as much as he could have, and no senior staff member called on him as a resource in time of trouble. Eulau thought Lindemann felt frustrated at being peripheral and underutilized, as was social work. Lindemann felt that at first, people found his approach useful and that he helped the department develop creatively: the industrial medicine group was eager to write its first book in two years, and he encouraged laboratory work by Karl Pribram and Gig Levinson. However, when people wanted to be tough, demanding, unscrupulous, and focused on getting money, they realized he was not thus oriented, though some would approach through younger clinicians to ask for Lindemann's consultation. Dorosin thought he had a significant effect on some people such as himself and some programs such as the Stanford Student Health Service and the San Mateo County Mental Health Program.

Some in the psychiatry department were suspicious of radical implications of social psychiatry. To some extent, they associated Lindemann with this. Hamburg returned from England with concerns about CMH: it had been overdone, too many patients were discharged from mental hospitals without adequate protection in the community, doubts about group therapy, concerns about psychiatric confidentiality, and skepticism about its benefits as well as that of psychotherapy. He did, however, support the work and teaching of faculty and staff members associated with social psychiatry: Irvin Yalom (group and existential psychotherapy), Herant Katchadourian (sex education as preventive intervention for undergraduates, ombudsman and then dean of undergraduate studies), Rudy Moos, Alberta Siegal, Herbert, David Dorosin (head of the mental health program at the Student Health Service), and Hale Shirley (pioneering in child psychiatry).

Some tainted Lindemann by association with Richard Almond, a provocative young assistant professor of psychiatry on a postdoctoral fellowship, who identified with social and community psychiatry. In 1969, he came from Yale Medical School because of the Stanford department's reputation as a growing, exciting place with opportunity for independent activities, and David Hamburg said he needed Almond to help develop social psychiatry in the department.[282] On a personal level, Almond's family was in the area. It gave him the opportunity to distance from his wife's family, the income was good, and his wife Barbara was able to complete her residency part time while growing a family.

He found the department peaking in government funding, though the department and school were about to face deteriorating finances. He became disappointed that support and interest in his work were inconsistent, there was little interdisciplinary approach, and he felt isolated. He spent half time as psychiatrist to the medical students, sought to practice CMH and preventive psychiatry with student agencies, and thought the department was not interested in this application of social psychiatry. He remembers the students asking him to participate in agitation against the Cambodian (Vietnam) War, which elicited disapproval from the department in contrast with liberal sentiments at Yale and the NIMH. In consequence he was labeled as odd and radical, including for identifying with dissident students, involving an ugly demonstration in patient care areas of the medical center, the burning of the president's office, and other action taken around the university. This disapproval was extended to feeling that his treatment of medical students was irresponsible. He remembers feeling provoked to conforming to this image, including sharing with his wife interest in California nontraditional activities such as spending time on a seminar on rural collectives and giving a paper on this topic.

Almond met Lindemann at a Russell Sage conference on social psychiatry. Lindemann gave teaching conferences at the Student Health Service, they collaborated on a course in social psychiatry for psychiatric residents, and he consulted on Almond's book on clinical cases in the community in the light of Lindemann's publications. He found Lindemann always available for consultation on a supervisory, collegial, and friendship basis. He felt the department was oriented to biological psychiatry with limited support for clinical and social psychiatry. He thought Lindemann was puzzled and disappointed at his own limited role, especially since he considered psychosomatic medicine one of his areas of expertise. Almond attributed this situation partly to David Hamburg's position as the sole strong leader, limiting the roles of other senior faculty members—especially Lindemann with his stature. He regretted the limited role of the more highly altruistic social psychiatry and its withering in the department.

The department considered Almond not mature enough to carry his perspective but took an adversarial position rather than working things through; he got the impression that they considered his activities insane, and his appointment ended bitterly after one year. David Daniels considered Almond bright, more radical than Daniels, and having ultimately been evicted.[283] In 1972 Almond left the department, his wife completed her residency training. In Palo Alto, near Stanford, they established a private group interdisciplinary psychiatry practice influenced by community experience (including equal pay)—Collective Psychotherapy Center. He remembers Lindemann being supportive and meeting with the staff, though it was devalued by the psychiatry department, which considered it unsuccessful. He continued a psychoanalytic private practice and clung to some CMH practice as consultant to a psychiatric residential center.

On November 1, 1973, the American Public Health Association's Mental Health Section (perhaps with Warren Vaughan's encouragement) presented him with an award for major contributions to the field; Elizabeth Lindemann represented him at the ceremony.[284] Lindemann was in tears when Vaughan showed his motion picture of the ceremony at the discussion group that met at Lindemann's apartment. Walter Barton and the APA Board of Trustees wanted an extended videotaped interview of Lindemann and valued Edward Mason's videotape of Lindemann's lectures on a community interaction approach in the community and hospitals, given at Gerald Caplan's seminars.

At this stage in his life, Lindemann clarified his lifelong need for validation, acceptance, closeness, family, and caring relationships. This was reflected in his professional focus on the importance of the social network and the trauma of a disruption of this network. He regretted contemporary society's turning away from these values.[285] He saw, instead, business being central, loosened loyalties, emphasis on competition and impermanence, encouraging the search for self-centeredness and easy happiness (e.g., in commercials advising: just change your product), and the substitution of the occult for philosophy. He recognized the rebellion against parents' destructive world, duty, and authority. He was aware of the emphasis on individuality in the teachings of Marcuse, Fromm, Masserman, and Rogers as opposed to Goethe's concern with the relationship to God and people. Lindemann obtained self-affirmation from his relationship to intimate, significant others such as Duhl and his wife Elizabeth, but also saw significance in everyone. He saw impersonal fame as empty, without time for investment in such matters as sex or loyalty but instead only competition and mutual exploitation. Consequently, insecurity of position and relationships was the norm in business and university. For instance, he saw President Richard Nixon as concerned about loyalty and easily suspicious and rejecting. Another example was a book by a student/observer at Harvard Business School about the intense pressure, lack of loyalties, only three or four dyadic warm relationships, one suicide, and a professor teaching exploitative relationships. All this makes it harder to practice psychotherapy in an unsupportive world.

Lindemann sought a healing professional, scholarly, advisory role for CMH and social psychiatry. This kept him at a distance from the turmoil at the Boston College Department of Psychology, and he looked for a guru's haven at Stanford. However, the *zeitgeist* of rebellion and change reached also to California. Hamburg's attention was diverted to major academic problems: he chaired the search committee for the medical school dean; chaired the search committee for the university president (the preceding president had failed); was a member of the president's faculty advisory board regarding appointments and promotions; and was engaged in the six weeks process of firing (at the president's behest) a tenured black woman professor, inspiring hostile radicals and department faculty uninformed and unsympathetic to his administrative style. The university was in chaos with rebellion and vandalism. Hamburg was seen as brilliant at financial management, but, despite this, department finances were crumbling.

In 1972, Hamburg resigned as department chairman and stayed on as acting chairman, focusing more on research, until Albert J. ("Mickey") Stunkard was appointed as his successor.[286] Stunkard was seen as having creative ideas, being very complex and a little strange,[287] with strong theoretical and spiritual motivations (he was Buddhist and vacationed at a Buddhist monastery) toward humane caring rather than being pragmatic. At the University of Pennsylvania, he had been hurt in the course of a program of outreach to the Afro-American community and issues of race, and, fed up, had moved to Stanford.[288] He introduced his values in the Lindemann discussion group and made it a point to recognize and comfort the spouses of faculty members who had died—in fact, he visited Elizabeth Lindemann on the day of Erich Lindemann's death and had dinner with her, not mentioning that he had been fired from the department chairmanship that day. He was unmarried and devoted to his job. He was credited with doing some very good things but had limited social skills and was politically inept, so that he alienated many. Perhaps this rejection came in part because of his efforts to change the department from biological to psychological in emphasis. He served a stormy 14-month term, including calling on Lindemann daily, treating him and others in the department with the kind consideration with which he taught that patients should be treated. Both Lindemann and Stunkard were shy and had little contact, though they were neighbors. Stunkard was finally forced out (Elizabeth Lindemann thought it had to do with some moral crisis), to the pleasure of many. This experience was felt to be devastating to the department.

Stunkard was succeeded as chairman by Thomas Gonda, a longtime member of the department who did not have a strong focus of interest and policy. This calls to mind Housman's observation that strong department chairmen with clear interests and departmental direction arouse faculty resentment, causes them to feel pressured, and promoting organization to object on various grounds.[289] This results in eagerness for a successor who is bland, lacks strong direction, and may be a known and trusted colleague to usher in a period of peace, security, and stability. He saw examples in the University of Minnesota, MGH, and Stanford.

Alberta Siegal, a Stanford professor of psychology who espoused psychotherapy and humane relationships, especially resented the symbolism of the department's writing people off by focusing on political issues, the eviction of Stunkard almost on the same day Lindemann died, and neglecting the loss of Lindemann, a dear faculty member.

Lindemann was very modest and doubtful about his contributions, though he felt he had done valid work, referring especially to the Wellesley Human Relations Service.[290] His experience at Stanford may have been discouraging to his sense of worth and accomplishment. It must be recognized that David Hamburg never faltered in his expressions of recognition and appreciation:

- I cannot thank you enough for all you have done this year as in the past. Your impact on all of us has been very great. I am not sure you realize how important your contribution has been. I think the right word would be inspiring . . . I look forward with the greatest possible satisfaction to the prospect of your being with us again next year.[291]
- I only wish I could convey to you the warmth, devotion and deep appreciation which so many of us here feel for you. These feelings have been expressed in so many touching ways over the recent months of your illness that there is no way that I can convey anything more than the flavor of it. It seems to me that we have become something like your extended family.[292]
- set me to thinking about the contribution you have made to our department over the years and how deeply grateful I feel. I know I have spoken with you about this in the past but I do want to say once more how much I and many others here appreciate the immense value of having you with us. It was really a blessing when you decided to join us and many people's lives have been enriched.[293]

Lindemann was firm in his principles regarding proper psychotherapy and surprised and disapproving of novel, ill-founded treatment approaches; this may have reflected on the nonanalytic counseling in the Stanford department. Others found him very direct and outspoken about supervisees' problems—including settling marital conflicts or getting out of the marriages (note his own experience in his first marriage). His experience of European psychiatry may have been the basis of his reaction against law enforcement, concern about, e.g., the Drug Enforcement Administration replacing a mental health approach to social problems, and repressive policies sweeping aside liberal approaches under the administration of President Richard Nixon. He may have looked for the ebb and flow of history to bring back CMH through health maintenance organizations and health insurance programs.

His progressive illness restricted Lindemann's professional activities as reflected in his correspondence with past and contemporary colleagues:

- My friend Clemens Benda delivered our paper on obsessive neurosis in my place at the Lindau conference . . . I am looking forward hopefully to our return to Palo Alto and to the resumption of our visits.[294]
- [My] condition is improving only very slowly, and I had to give up my trip to Europe. This is one more frustration after a difficult period. I still regret that the side effects of this radiation episode interfered with my maintaining contact with my friends, especially with you, in whose life and activities I am as interested as ever.[295]
- My own activities here in the East were primarily concerned with the re-writing, together with Betty, in book form of my more important essays and addresses. The much-longed-for visit in Heidelberg had to be given up finally, after several periods of indecision. I do, however have hope to return to Palo Alto as planned, and to renew discussions with my friends there who are so meaningful to me—foremost, those with you.[296]
- Our hope to get to Europe once more unfortunately could not be fulfilled because of the protracted side effects of the radiation and the rather tenacious anemia. However, we feel confident that we can return to Palo Alto as planned.[297]
- [M]y frustration over my inability to move about and come out myself to visit you . . . In a couple of weeks we will return to Palo Alto, where the winter will be a bit more comfortable, and where we are located within a few minutes of the Medical Center, so that the residents and colleagues will find it easy to come in occasionally.[298]

Almond, too, saw him as less generative and more oriented to interest, support, and consultation to others, review of his past, and preoccupation with his impending death. He sighed with pleasure at Almond singing German lieder and recalled his family rewarding its family doctor with gold coin as a sign of respect.

The Lindemann Group

A group of young faculty members met with him to discuss clinical cases, perhaps initiated to increase faculty interest in clinical work:[299]

> At the suggestion of Dr. Erich Lindemann, a number of us got together to plan for an evening seminar centered about therapeutic issues in clinical practice. The planning group met on 13 November 1972 at Josie [Josephine] Hilgard's house . . . to invite a small group of clinicians to participate in this potentially exciting and instructive exercise . . . a meeting to be held about once a month . . . beginning at 8

p.m. and ending by 10 p.m. One person would be responsible for a presentation of 45 to 60 minutes with comments during and following . . . until about 9:30 p.m. This would be followed by an informal discussion over coffee until 10 p.m.

When Lindemann became too ill to leave home and was in danger of losing the contact and interaction with colleagues that was his source of intellectual and emotional sustenance, Hilgard arranged for a group of 10 to 12 senior colleagues to meet at his house every two to three weeks for presentations and discussion. These included David Dorosin (director of student mental health services), Robert White addressing ego, Brewster Smith addressing the development of competence, Meigus (director of a mental hospital in the nearby valley), two or three social workers, and others. Mickey Stunkard, the new chairman of psychiatry, dropped by to meet Lindemann. He attended three group meetings about conceiving psychotherapy as addressing competence and inner strength rather than removing obstacles to health and talked about Buddhism (his faith). The people in the group had a spiritual quality and capacity for insight and needed an appropriate social environment to discuss a psychoanalytic approach, and Lindemann was not technological but helped people to feel understood.[300]

The group provided support and enrichment for Lindemann: at first he participated in the discussion; as his disease progressed, he dozed, then listened in from a room next door.[301] Elizabeth Lindemann encouraged him to make the effort to participate. He noted:[302]

> In spite of the illness, it was possible here at Stanford to keep up a quite creative contact with the colleagues at the Stanford Clinic because they were entirely willing to come singly or in groups to discussions in our apartment, where I, as formerly with you, take part in an exchange of thoughts from the sofa. It would, however, have been quite hard for me to go to the Institute for seminars and lectures.

He described this re-creation of his teaching and floated the hope that Helmut Stolze (a colleague in Germany) could join him on a last visit.[303] When he became confined to his bed, the group met in the next room with the bedroom door left open and the speaker nearby, and Lindemann felt his intellectual and mental activity confined to his home.[304] The group also provided support and intellectual stimulation for Elizabeth Lindemann.

Even long after Lindemann's death, the group continued as a compatible though varied group.[305] It was one of his lasting CMH accomplishments since adult clinical meetings ceased, as the department was in financial straits.[306] Hilgard was important in maintaining it; she missed the Lindemanns as the soul of the group. After Hilgard died, it faltered.

The addition to the faculty of Bettelheim, the towering child psychiatrist, was eagerly awaited. Elizabeth Lindemann found him autocratic and thought his attempt to take over this group nearly wrecked it.

After Lindemann's death, any social psychiatry program at Stanford faded until there was no such curriculum, and psychiatric residents no longer had public health experience at the San Mateo County Mental Health Service.

Gloria Liederman thought that the weakness of CMH activities and programs left individuals rather than programs better remembered, such as Lindemann through his involvement in community programs such as the Peninsula Children's Center.[307] This is contested by the warm memories and nostalgia of various psychiatry department members and the effort to maintain the Lindemann Group.

Erich Lindemann—Personal

Though he found an academic haven at Stanford, Lindemann never seemed to entirely settle there and buy a home in the Californian dry and brown beauty.[308] He remembered Goethe's poem about the moon and evening and the happiness of withdrawal from the world to closeness with a friend to share deep secrets of the heart.[309] After his surgery, he remembered masses of Goethe's poems.

Lindemann's illness (malignant chordoma) was prolonged and progressive, starting in 1966, right after his retirement. At first it was misdiagnosed at the MGH as viral neuritis, and he was optimistic about it for some time, as were his physicians at the MGH:

- The illness . . . unfortunately has not been cleared up yet. It finally landed me here at the Massachusetts General Hospital . . . and everything is being done to stop this debilitating affair, a progressive polyneuritis with loss of sphincter control, etc.[310]
- The polyneuritis which struck me in the first days of August.[311]
- I caught a severe polyneuritis, probably a virus imported into Germany from Spain, and am just beginning to recover from an impairment in the sacral plexus.[312]
- It was distressing to hear that you had been so miserably laid up, but at the same time a relief to know that it was not basically serious + that you were definitely on the mend.[313]
- a severe polyneuritis from which I am just now recovering . . . December 14 or December 16. I have every reason to hope that I will be completely well by then.[314]
- I am delighted that things have now taken a turn for the better, and that although alarming and painful, the condition turned out to be benign. Please accept my very warmest good wishes for the smooth continuation of your convalescence.[315]

- During this fall, I have been somewhat handicapped by a rather severe polyneuritis which is only slowly receding. I do, however, hope for a complete recovery in a few months.[316]
- a virus polyneuritis . . . I have all reasons to hope that my condition will improve considerably over the next few months.[317]
- I do feel a lot better and look forward to the future with a great more confidence.[318]

When the diagnosis was reconsidered, the darker reality of the condition began to set in. He had exploratory surgery in 1968[319] and thereafter underwent radiation therapies. His outlook shifted from hope:

- I am going into the M.G.H. for another workup . . . My friends there are abandoning the diagnosis of an infectious polyneuritis and are now trying to track down the possibilities of herniated disc or tumor as a cause for the present episode. There is every prospect that by January I will be able to join you again, in a healthier condition.[320]
- I am about to leave the hospital . . . Perhaps I will be granted another period of grace to make some small creative contribution and you are the first person with whom I would like to share it.[321]
- I am receiving many promises that my condition will improve a great deal.[322]
- I am leaving the hospital today and everybody here gives me a good prognosis for a rapid build-up of strength in the next few weeks.[323]
- Today I am leaving the hospital and I am being assured . . . that I can expect to feel a great deal better within a few weeks. . . . If anything is crucial in the mastery of difficult life situations it is the active reaching out of friends who assure you of the continuity of personal bonds.[324]

Then to a progressive expectation of a prolonged illness and limitation on his professional activities:

- I am presently under treatment for an illness that is likely to be prolonged, and would not permit me to assume an active role in your program.[325]
- Due to spinal surgery and radiation therapy I have been unable for almost a half year to keep up with my scientific work and my correspondence . . . My return to Stanford from Boston has been delayed but I do hope to return to my activities there sometime in October.[326]
- I was in the midst of an intensive course of rad. ther. This is now finished, and I begin to reap the benefits from all that misery.[327]

Then to a struggle to come to terms with a bleaker future of limitation and with life review:

- Unfortunately, at the present time I am mostly coping with a resurgence of my tumor, and a lot more discomfort, which started already during the last weeks in Boston. Next week I will begin another series of radiation treatments, which will reduce my activities even further during the next two or three months . . . I had hoped to come back this week, as I did last year, for a couple of seminars with Dr. Leim and to attend the New England Psychological meetings; but I am not mobile enough now.[328]

- This year . . . has demanded from me a totally unexpected new kind of adaptation in connection with my spinal tumor. The image of the future in terms of scientific and professional activities had to be drastically revised. And my personal orientation to future hopes of fulfillment in family and personal relations had to be altered. I am by no means able to say that I have coped successfully with all these issues To write about them seems possible only after one has reached a certain sense of closure.

  Curiously, the same is true about the world of hopes and actions in the field of my life interests: Social aspects of psychiatry. Extremely rapidly new developments occur, some having taken impetus from my thinking and teaching, but many more of them expressing the cultural crisis in which "democracy" and human relations have become intertwined.

  As you may know, my commitment is to humanistic values as embodied in many ideas and actions of the Quakers . . . I do not write easily, and would find it particularly difficult to put on paper something with the sort of finality which the term "Faith" demands.[329]

- how grateful I am to have participated in a small manner in this remarkable enterprise. The unique way in which you defined my role made it possible for me to be a keenly interested observer without having to shoulder any of the burdensome aspects of administration. My contacts with the young members of the group, the opportunity to see them grow under your careful guidance, and the chance to have many stimulating and creative discussions with the members of the faculty—all that made the later years of my life rich in a way that few people are privileged to experience.[330]

- I am most fortunate that my own condition still permits frequent visits with colleagues, Residents and friends, so that I can maintain an active intellectual life in spite of discomfort and handicap.[331]

- And the next thing which I did was so important for me as an anticipatory griever, was to actually look at the places of former experiences. I went to Germany and visited the places where I had grown up; the house of my birth; tried to find some people whom I had known then; went back to Heidelberg where I started my career; and did something which I should have done if I had stayed in Heidelberg instead of coming to the United States, that is, I gave a lecture to the medical students. It seemed important to make up for this opportunity which had been missed. . . [p. 11] . . . I really became

> hypomanic, in the sense that I raced around and wanted to do all the things that would be wonderful to do once more... [p. 12] ... I guess it isn't silly to make up for the things you won't have any more of later, and token fulfillment along that line can make an enormous difference. [p. 13][332]
>
> And then to his final acknowledgement of his constricted existence:[333] "Sadly, I am now entirely confined to bed, and must accept my own home as the field for my intellectual and spiritual activity".

Lindemann recalled the effect of this shift in outlook on his treating physician:

> The neurosurgeon to whom you went is a good friend of yours. He thought he would find a very benign thing for the basis of your back pain and then they find some malignant tumor. Then he is very embarrassed about it. He practically weeps to your wife, 'Let's see—why didn't we find that out when Erich came three years ago—he might still have—'. Then he thought it was sort of infectious.[334] [p. 21]

He summarized his resignation to one of his Indian contacts in the context of the spiritual inspiration stimulated by his Indian immersion:[335]

> I often think how differently my life might have developed if I had been able to join you in 1966 in New Delhi for several years of collaboration, as I had very much wished to do. As it turned out, the pelvic tumor, a chordoma, had its beginning just about then. It was definitely diagnosed only two years later in Boston by an exploratory operation which was followed by intensive radiation; and I am just now working myself slowly out of the side-effects of another series of radiation treatments.
>
> In spite of my handicaps, I have managed to stay active in some measure as long-term visiting professor at the Stanford Department of Psychiatry ... My interest in the evolution of psychiatric thinking in India, blending the rich tradition of psychological insight in your own culture with concepts and facts of Western psychiatry has continued to be lively, and has been rather reinforced, as Elizabeth and I are now reviewing my former papers for publication ... including my report to the World Health Organization at the time of my visit to India ... You ask about our children. Brenda decided upon a career in health education, and has had a responsible position in a family planning organization ... Jeffrey has identified himself actively with the cause of the underprivileged minorities, and [p. 1] combines some political activity with a small car-repair co-operative business.
>
> [p. 2]

His wife Elizabeth was totally devoted to him to the extent that others were concerned about her welfare. Lindemann was reluctant to ask for help; David Dorosin, who shared his values, noted: "When you hear Erich talking about how you should treat the patient what he is talking about is how he wants to be treated". He discovered that people were hesitant to come to him when he became ill. He was furious and guilty that this was not helpful and had to make it very plain that they were welcome.

As his illness advanced, Lindemann tried nontraditional healing approaches: acupuncture, Laetrile (an illegal Mexican cancer treatment, which he received by mail), and a New Age physician for psychological benefit—all failures. He did not hope for cure but relief of pain: TENS treatment gave some relief, and Josephine Hilgard applied hypnosis for this purpose. It is reported that he considered suicide but decided it would be unfair to his wife.[336] In the last year of his life, a favorite depiction of himself was "schrittweise aus der Erscheinung zurück treten" (progressively backing out of the picture).[337]

He developed a special relationship (with his wife's understanding) with Lois Paul, who he had invited to become a professor of anthropology at Stanford. They talked often about forms of continued existence as part of the universe and living through friends and students. Clarice Haylett, a follower of his at the San Mateo County Health Department, hoped to curtail her job to help Elizabeth Lindemann edit Lindemann's papers, as he had much trouble reducing his clear thought and teaching to writing.[338]

His eclectic interests are demonstrated in the library he maintained at home:[339]

Benda, Clemens E., *Gewissen und Schuld: Die Psychiatrische, Religiöse und Politische Interpretation des Schuldig-Seins* (NY: F. K. Schattauer Verlag, 1970) [Benda (Lindemann's colleague at MGH) inscribed to Erich and Elizabeth Lindemann 1970]

Broom, Michael F., Ph.D., Klein, Donald C., Ph.D., *Power: The Infinite Game* (Amherst, MA: HRD Press, 1995) [Klein was Lindemann's colleague and protégé at HRS]

Grzimek, Dr. Bernhard, *Affen im Haus* (Stuttgart, Germany: Kosmos—Gesellschaft der Naturfreunde, Franckh'shce Velagshandlung, 1951) [Dr. med Constantin Kleefisch (Lindemann's patron in Germany) inscribed to EL 1952]

Haas, William S., *The Destiny of the Mind: East and West* (NY: MacMillan, 1956)

Hilgard, Josephine R., LeBaron, Samuel, *Hypnotherapy of Pain in Children with Cancer* (Los Altos, CA: William Kaufmann, Inc., 1984) [Hilgard (Lindemann's colleague in Stanford) inscribed to Erich and Elizabeth Lindemann]

Katchadourian, Herant A., Boli, John, *Careerism and Intellectualism Among College Students: Patterns of Academic and Career Choice in the Undergraduate Years* (San Francisco: Jossey-Bass, 1985) [Katchadourian (Lindemann's colleague and protégé at Stanford) inscribed to Elizabeth Lindemann]

Kelly, James G., *Becoming Ecological: An Expedition into Community Psychology* (NY: Oxford, 2006) [(Lindemann's protégé at MGH and HRS) inscribed to Elizabeth Lindemann]

Lifton, Robert Jay with Olson, Eric (eds.), *Explorations in Psychohistory: The Wellfleet Papers* (NY: Simon and Schuster, 1974)

Lindemann, Erich, *Jenseits von Trauer: Beiträge zur Krisenbewältigung und Krankheitsvorbeugung* (Göttingen, Germany: Verlag für Medizinische Psychologie im Verlag Vandenhoeck & Ruprecht, 1985)

Moos, Rudolf H. (ed.), *Coping with Physical Illness* (NY: Plenum Medical Book Company, 1977) [(Lindemann colleague and protégé at Stanford) inscribed to Elizabeth Lindemann, 1988]

Muret-Sanders Encyclopædic English-German and German-English Dictionary (Berlin-Schönberg: Langenscheidtsche Verlagsbuchhandlung, 1910) [inscribed by Elizabeth Lindemann]

Ploeger, Andreas with Bonzi, Andreas, Markovic, Aleksandar, *Die Therapeutische Gemeinschaft in der Psychotherapie und Socialpsychiatrie: Theorie und Praxis* (Stuttgart, Germany: Georg Tjieme Verlag, 1972) [Ploeger (Lindemann protégé in Germany) inscribed to Lindemann]

Pörksen, Niels, *Kommunale Psychiatrie: Das Mannheimer Modell* (Hamburg, Germany: Rowohlt Verlag, 1974) [(Lindemann's protégé Germany and MGH) inscribed to Lindemann 1974]

Schmitt, Francis O., *The Never-Ceasing Search* (Philadelphia: American Philosophical Society, 1990) [(Lindemann colleague and ally at MGH) inscribed to Elizabeth Lindemann]

Stokvis, Berthold, Wiesenhütter, Eckart, *Der Mensch in der Entspannung: Lehrbuch Autosuggestiver und Übender Verfahren der Psychotherapie und Psychosomatik* (Stuttgart, Germany: Hippokrates-Verlag, 1961)

Weizsäcker, Viktor von, *Der Gestaltkreis: Theorie der Einheit von Wahrnehmen und Bewegen, vierte Auflage* (Stuttgart, Germany: Georg Thieme Verlag, 1950) [Lindemann's teacher in Germany]

Weizsäcker, Viktor von, *Der Kranke Mensch: Eine Einführung in die Medizinische Anthropologie* (Stuttgart, Germany: K. F. Koehler Verlag, 1951], [((Lindemann's teacher in Germany) inscribed to Lindemann 1952]

White, Benjamin V., M.D., *Stanley Cobb: A Builder of the Modern Neurosciences* (Boston: Francis A. Countway Library of Medicine, 1984; distributed by Charlottesville, VA: University Press of Virginia) [Eugene Taylor inscribed to Elizabeth Lindemann 1984]

Wyatt, Gertud L., *Mother and Daughter: A Personal Biography* (Wellesley Hills, MA: The Windsor Press, 1989) [(Erich and Elizabeth Lindemann's consultee at HRS) inscribed to Elizabeth Lindemann]

"The desire of the esteem of others is as real a want of nature as hunger, and the neglect and contempt of the world as severe a pain as the gout or stone".[340] Despite his contra-conventional ideas, strong moral values, and courage and persistence in championing them, Lindemann was vulnerable to the reactions of others; an example of the emotional connection between the individual and the social context that was at the center of his concept of social psychiatry. His self-doubts, modesty, old-world courtesy, and struggle with the attacks by opponents of his efforts left him with disappointment about his accomplishments. At the same time, he tried to appreciate the limitations inherent in the process of fundamental change:[341] "One forgets sometimes how fundamentally the values of Community Psychiatry have changed vis a vis the traditional psychiatric position, and how difficult the transition is, and above all, how slowly one must go forward in order not to be brought to a halt by the inevitable resistance". He wrote:[342] "Perhaps I will be most remembered in the history of psychiatric ideas for the conception and implementation of the first community mental health center, as exemplified by the Wellesley Human Relations Service".

His wife insisted that he was never discouraged about the validity and importance of CMH and expected limited achievements of the far-reaching transformation of medicine and society it envisioned.[343] He dated the decline of CMH to President John Kennedy's assassination. Hilgard, who visited him weekly during his last illness, experienced him as proud of his work, feeling he had influenced people and the field via lectures, HRS, and other projects.[344] This was a source of strength for him. He regretted not having written books and feared that his work would be forgotten. He needed people and groups for emotional nourishment and teaching and perhaps to help think things through. Perhaps he wrote little because his learning, direction, and thought came only through interaction with people.

Hilgard, an acute psychoanalyst, saw much suppressed anger in him and suffering from childhood trauma and his relations with parents and siblings. He wondered if his malignancy was brought on by his frustration and unhappiness at Stanford. He was disappointed that his psychoanalysis by Helene Deutsch was too superficial. He was depressed and upset and never reconciled to death. He suffered from the loss of travel overseas, teaching, meeting with people. He was very gratified by the Lindemann Group, which brought stimulation and people to him.

In fact, appreciation and admiration came from many quarters, some surprising in light of past relations. These brought him some reassurance:

- Heinz Häfner, at the University of Heidelberg, informed Lindemann of his election to an honorary membership in the German Society for Psychiatric and Nervous Health Studies, with much appreciation of his stature and contributions to progress in modern German psychiatry.[345]
- During my three years at Stanford I learned twice as much from you as from any other member of the faculty. This is no exaggeration, and I tell you again because I feel you underestimate your contribution.[346]
- Whenever I see people from Stanford I hear their great enthusiasm for what you are doing there, and by all accounts you are having a very happy time of it, for which I am glad.[347]
- I would like very much to dedicate the completed work on the West End study to you and to the people of the West End. It seems most appropriate to dedicate it to the two participants who made the study possible quite apart from the fact that it would make me most happy to be able to honor your enormous contributions in this small way.[348]
- It is particularly gratifying at this stage of one's life to know that one's work has been understood and respected; and that the values for which one stood will be carried on by a new generation—although doubtless in a different form.[349]
- [Y]ou have established in social psychiatry what [W. H.] Auden once referred to as "a climate of opinion" which has inescapably affected so much of what has followed.[350]
- [You are] one of my most successful and cherished friends in the new psychiatry.[351]
- I think we all admired Erich for his courage and determination in carrying out his important work alone, in spite of obstacles, indifference, and—I suppose—professional rivals and enemies.[352]

During this period, the Lindemanns struggled with their children's needs, which occupied much of Elizabeth Lindemann's energies. Lindemann agonized over the feeling that he had not done right by his wife and children—his wife and children had vacationed in Vermont while he had been taken up with work.[353] This was not a peaceful and gratifying way to end a career.

A few days prior to his death, Lindemann was delirious, spoke mostly in German, and held Almond's hand, saying "Du bist ein Engel" ["You are an angel"]—giving to others even at the end.[354]

Erich Lindemann died November 16, 1974, attended by his physician of three years, R. J. Spiegl, M.D. The cause of death was basal pneumonia as a complication of malignant chordoma with metastases.[355]

Almond thought Lindemann was appreciated personally by many but without adequate professional reverence. At his Quaker funeral service, many came recalling warm experiences, feeling the need to repay him for all the service he gave without concern for material reward.

Lindemann's separation from contemporary psychiatry and medicine was symbolized at his death: HMS and MGH were not represented after his 30-year association. His funeral was simple, held under the auspices of the Society of Friends in Palo Alto, his last residence, and not in the Boston area where he had worked and lived. It was attended by an overflowing crowd of Quakers and members of the Stanford department of psychiatry; no one from the nation or world attended except for Leonard Duhl. (Later a memorial service was held at Harvard.) Warren Vaughan, Leonard Duhl, and Myra Keen (emerita professor of paleontology) spoke; Albert Stunkard, the chairman of the department of psychiatry did not—department relations were uncomfortable less than a week after a conflict had exploded. And he was buried in his family vacation home town of Plainfield, VT, his refuge from professional and academic troubles.

A memorial service at the Palo Alto Friends meeting on December 8, 1974, included some of the biblical quotations that were meaningful to him:

> Darum sahe ich, dass nichts bessers ist, denn dass der mensch fröhlich sei in seiner Arbeit, denn das ist sein Teil. Denn wer will ihn dahin bringen, das er sehe, was nach ihm geschehen wird?
>
> (Wherefore I perceive that there is nothing better, than that a man should rejoice in his own works; for that is his portion: for who shall bring him to see what shall happen after him?)
> (Ecclesiastes 3:19–22)

> Selig sind die Toten,
> die in dem Herren sterben,
> von nun an.
> Ja, der Geist spricht,
> Das sie ruhen von ihrer Arbeit;
> denn ihre Werke folgen ihnen nach.
> (Blessed are the dead
> who die in the Lord
> from henceforth.
> Yea, the Spirit proclaims,
> Let them rest from their labors,
> For their works shall follow them.)
> (Revelations 14:13)

Summary

The history of this period illustrates the complex tapestry of ideals, programs, and leaders. The milieu shifted unevenly: Some social and community programs and support continued growing at the same time that others withered and were replaced by the resurgence of an individualistic, biological, instrumental spirit. But, even if haltingly and disjointedly, overall the cycle of ideology moved on.

The late 1960s and 1970s saw psychiatric, medical, and societal retreat from a social ideology to one of focus on the individual and on people

Figure 2.2 Erich Lindemann Mental Health Center [courtesy Lindemann Estate]

Counterrevolution of Biology and Business   265

Figure 2.3 Erich Lindemann Mental Health Center [courtesy Lindemann Estate]

Figure 2.4 Erich Lindemann Mental Health Center, 1970 [courtesy Lindemann Estate]

Figure 2.5 Erich Lindemann Mental Health Center [courtesy Lindemann Estate]

Counterrevolution of Biology and Business 267

Figure 2.6 Erich Lindemann Mental Health Center [courtesy Lindemann Estate]

268 *Counterrevolution of Biology and Business*

Figure 2.7 Jean Farrell (Erich Lindemann's administrative assistant) outside the Erich Lindemann Mental Health Center, summer 1973 [courtesy Lindemann Estate]

Figure 2.8 Erich Lindemann Mental Health Center dedication, 11/22/71—Dr. Lindemann in earnest conversation [courtesy Lindemann Estate]

Counterrevolution of Biology and Business 269

Figure 2.9 Erich Lindemann Mental Health Center dedication, 11/22/71—Erich and Elizabeth Lindemann [courtesy Lindemann Estate]

Figure 2.10 Erich Lindemann Mental Health Center dedication, 11/22/71—Erich Lindemann receiving applause [courtesy Lindemann Estate]

Counterrevolution of Biology and Business   271

Figure 2.11 Lindau Psychotherapy Group, 1973 [courtesy Lindemann Estate]

Figure 2.12 Lindau Psychotherapy Group Meeting Place, 1968 [courtesy Lindemann Estate]

272 *Counterrevolution of Biology and Business*

Figure 2.13 Erich Lindemann, Palo Alto, CA, 1960s [courtesy Lindemann Estate]

Figure 2.14 Erich Lindemann in California, 1969 [courtesy Lindemann Estate]

Counterrevolution of Biology and Business 273

Figure 2.15 Erich Lindemann at the piano at home, Palo Alto, CA, 1966–8 [courtesy Lindemann Estate]

Figure 2.16 Erich Lindemann, terminally ill, 1972 [courtesy Lindemann Estate]

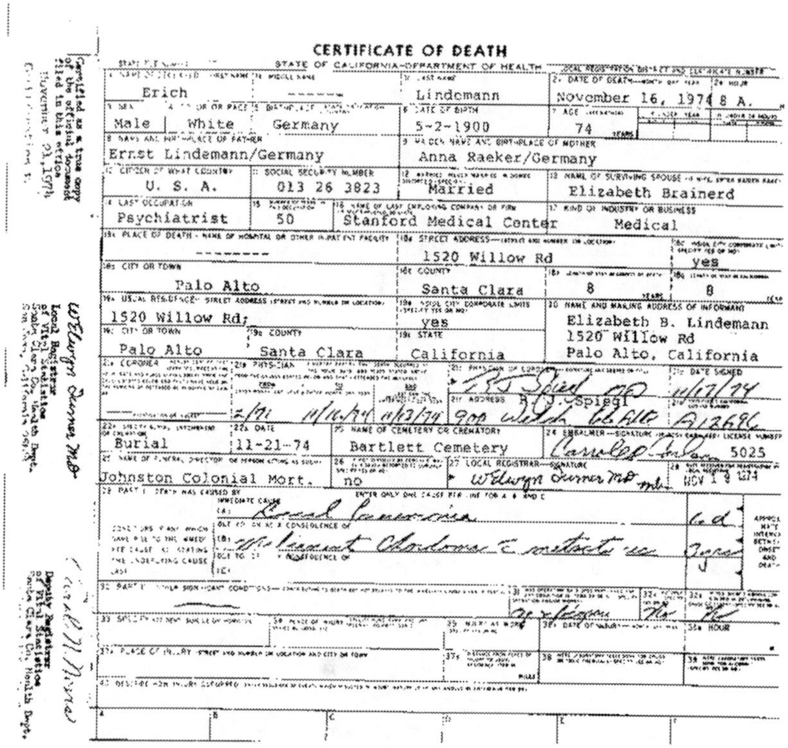

CERTIFICATE OF DEATH

STATE OF CALIFORNIA—DEPARTMENT OF HEALTH

Erich | Lindemann | November 16, 1974 | 8 A.

Male | White | Germany | 5-2-1900 | 74

Ernst Lindemann/Germany | Anna Raeker/Germany

U. S. A. | 013 26 3823 | Married | Elizabeth Brainerd

Psychiatrist | 50 | Stanford Medical Center | Medical

1520 Willow Rd | yes

Palo Alto | Santa Clara | 8 | 8

1520 Willow Rd; | yes | Elizabeth B. Lindemann, 1520 Willow Rd, Palo Alto, California

Palo Alto | Santa Clara | California

Burial | 11-21-74 | Bartlett Cemetery | 5025

Johnston Colonial Mort. | no | NOV 19 1974

Figure 2.17 Erich Lindemann death certificate, 11/16/74 [courtesy Lindemann Estate]

as elements of impersonal organizational, economic, and political policy and goals. Patients became consumers, health caregivers became providers, and cost-benefit ratio replaced responsibility for neighbors and communities. The withdrawal from and dismantling of community mental health ideals and programs progressed apace. Like a retreating glacier, it left in its wake the moraine of those professionally and spiritually devoted to the social ideology and CMH—feeling betrayed or seeking refuge in partial continuation of CMH or realistically shifting to the new ideology and its opportunities.

In a way, it cannot be said that Lindemann retired from CMH and professional life. He was steadfast in his devotion to CMH and psychoanalysis and found ways of pursuing them with some success in a new institutional context. While he was relieved of administrative burdens and distractions, he found the teaching and consulting role, too, enmired in conflicts and competitions. And he did not find the fulfillment that he sought in the total conversion of medicine and society to his ideal of a caring and healthy medicine and society. Perhaps he, like so many other idealistic leaders, ran into implacable historical dynamics.

Notes

1. Peter, Laurence J. and Hull, Raymond, *The Peter Principle* (New York: William Morrow, 1969)
2. Rothman, David J., *Conscience and Convenience: The Asylum and its Alternatives in Progressive America* (Boston: Little Brown, 1980)
3. Barton, Walter E. and Sanborn, Charlotte J., eds., "Introduction", in *An Assessment of the Community Mental Health Movement* (Lexington, MA: Lexington Books, 1977)
4. Navarro, Vicente, "MEDICAL HISTORY AS JUSTIFICATION RATHER THAN EXPLANATION: A CRITIQUE OF STARR'S *THE SOCIAL TRANSFORMATION OF AMERICAN MEDICINE*", *International Journal of Health Services*, 14 no. 4:511–528 (1984)
5. Musto, David F.: "Whatever Happened to Community Mental Health?", *The Public Interest Interest, Interest Interest* #39 39:(Spring, 1975), pp. 53–77 (Spring, 1975)
6. Musto, David F., "The Community Mental Health Center Movement in Historical Perspective", Ch. 1 in Barton, Walter E. and Sanborn, Charlotte J. (eds.) *An Assessment of the Community Mental Health Movement* (Lexington, MA: Lexington Books, 1977), pp. 1–11
7. Will, George, interview on radio station WBUR, 6/16/1983
8. June 1966. Box XII 1 folder 110c Lindemann M.H. Center, Erich Lindemann Collection, Center for the History of Medicine, Francis A. Countway Library of Medicine, Boston, MA
9. Folder "Federal U.S. Actions", David G. Satin files, Newton, MA
10. Clayton, Teddye, "The Role of State and County Governments in Funding Mental Disability Programs", *Hospital and Community Psychiatry* 28 no. 3:191–193 (1977)
11. Cole, Jean, "Bay State Potential at $13 M Hub Center is Great . . . But Plus and Minus Marks in Mental Health Program", *Boston Sunday Advertiser*, 5/14/1972]

276   *Counterrevolution of Biology and Business*

12. Yolles, Stanley F., M.D., [2nd Director of the NIMH 1964–6/2/70]: 10, "The Future of Community Psychiatry", in Barton, Walter E. and Sanborn, Charlotte J. (eds.) *An Assessment of The Community Mental Health Movement* (Lexington, MA: Lexington Books, 1977), pp. 21–34, based on Dartmouth Continuing Education Institute, Department of Psychiatry, Dartmouth Medical School, 1975
13. Ozarin, Lucy D., M.D., M.P.H., "Community Mental Health: Does it Work? Review of the Evaluation Literature", Ch. 9 in Barton, Walter E. and Sanborn, Charlotte J. (eds.) *An Assessment of The Community Mental Health Movement* (Lexington, MA: Lexington Books, 1977), pp. 21–34; based on Dartmouth Continuing Education Institute, Department of Psychiatry, Dartmouth Medical School, 1975
14. Ozarin, Lucy D., 1977, *ibid*
15. National Academy of Public Administration Contract HSM 42-70-55 August 1971, "Executive Summary; The Multi-Agency Community Mental Health Center: Administrative & Organizational Relationships", in Barton, Walter E. and Sanborn, Charlotte J. (eds.) *An Assessment of The Community Mental Health Movement* (Lexington, MA: Lexington Books, 1977), pp. 21–34, based on Dartmouth Continuing Education Institute, Department of Psychiatry, Dartmouth Medical School, 1975
16. Social Action Research Center, *Strategies for Change in Community Mental Health: New Careers* (Springfield, VA: NTIS PB-251197, 1973)
17. "Mental Health Panel Urges Community Care Expansion", *The Nation's Health*, 5/1978, p. 1, 5
18. Ozarin, Lucy D., 1977, *ibid*
19. Holland, Bernard C., "An Evaluation of the Criticisms of the Community Mental Health Movement", Ch. 7 in Barton Walter C. and Sanborn, Charlotte J. (eds.) *An Assessment of the Community Mental Health Movement* (Lexington, MA: Lexington Books, 1977)
20. Hallen, Philip, Director of the Maurice Falk Foundation, Washington, Principle Speaker at the HRS 30th Anniversary Celebration, 11/3/1978. [Erich Lindemann Collection, Center for the History of Medicine, Francis A. Countway Library of Medicine, Harvard Medical School, Boston, MA]
21. Lindemann, Erich: Preface in Bellak and Leoold, M.D., ed., *CONCISE HANDBOOK OF COMMUNITY PSYCHIATRY AND COMMUNITY MENTAL HEALTH* (Grune & Stratton, 1974). [file #104; "Preface to Bellak—Concise Handbook of Community Psychiatry—1974", Box XII #3, Erich Lindemann Collection, Center for the History of Medicine, Francis A. Countway Library of Medicine, Harvard Medical School, Boston, MA]
22. Lindemann, Erich, M.D., Ph.D., Stanford University, "Introduction", in Ryan, William (ed.) *Distress in the City: Essays on the Design and Administration of Urban Mental Health Services* (Cleveland: Case Western Reserve University, 1969), pp. xiii–xx; p. xviii
23. Yolles, Stanley F., 1977, *ibid*
24. Hazard, Sprague W., M.D., Mental Health Planning Committee of Metropolitan Boston; part of United Community Services, letter to Rhome, John O., President, United Community Services, Boston, 3/11/1968, p. 1. [folder "Correspondence 1968", Box IV 1+2, Erich Lindemann Collection, Center for the History of Medicine, Countway Library of Medicine, Boston, MA]:

> "I must advise you of my decision to resign as chairman of the Mental Health Planning Committee of Metropolitan Boston . . . the capacity to create change by the present structure of the Mental Health Planning Committee is meager, indeed. . . . the vast array of forces, some of

which are quite formidable, to be encountered are more than a part-time voluntary effort can materially influence. ¶A number of efforts . . . to obtain significant funds in order to mount a continuing program of negotiation and conversation . . . to no avail. Endorsement of the importance of continuing mental heath planning . . . was never very convincing . . . There was verbal assent that 'it was a good idea' but convincing investment of energy and recognized skills and reputation from individuals within the sponsoring organization have not been impressive . . . it is my opinion that the structure, the Mental Health Planning Committee of Metropolitan Boston should be disbanded".

25. Ryan, William, Survey Director, *Distress in the City: A Summary Report of the Boston Mental Health Survey 1968–1969* (Commonwealth of Massachusetts 3M-6-66-943307), sponsored by The Massachusetts Association for Mental Health, Inc., The Massachusetts Department of Mental Health (Division of Mental Hygiene), and the United Community Services of Metropolitan Boston, Inc. [file "Ryan, Wm. Distress in the City", Box XII #3, Lindemann Collection, Center for the History of Medicine, Francis A. Countway Library of Medicine, Harvard Medical School, Boston, MA]
26. Svirdoff, Mitchell, Vice President, Division of National Affairs, Ford Foundation, "Contradictions in Community Action", review of *Dilemmas of Social Reform: Poverty and Community Action in the United States* (Atherton Press, 1967); also in *Psychiatry and Social Science Review* 2 no. 10:2–7 (1968)
27. Lindemann, Elizabeth B., letter to Evans, Robert [Director of the Wellesley Human Relations Service], 1/4/1997. [folder "HRS—199 ff", Box Human Relations Service, via Elizabeth Lindemann, Erich Lindemann Collection, Center for the History of Medicine, Francis A. Countway Library of Medicine, Boston, MA]
28. Yolles, Stanley F., 1977, *ibid*
29. Urofsky, Melvin I., *Louis D. Brandeis: A Life* (New York: Pantheon Books 2009), p. 641
30. Rothman, David J., *The Discovery of the Asylum: Social Order and Disorder in the New Republic* (Boston: Little Brown, 1971), Introduction to the 1990 edition
31. Woodward, Kenneth, Mark, Rachel, "The New Narcissism", *Newsweek*, 1/30/1978, pp. 70,72
32. Sabshin, Melvin, "Politics and the Stalled Revolution", *Psychiatric Annals* 7:98–102 (1977)
33. Sabshin, Melvin, 1977, *ibid*
34. Smith, Steven, interview by David G. Satin at the Francis A. Countway Library of Medicine, Boston, MA, 10/23/1981. [Erich Lindemann Collection, Francis A. Countway Library of Medicine, Boston, MA]
35. Leighton, Alexander H., "The Compass and the Troubled Sea", *Psychiatric Annals* 8:43–54 (1978)
36. Halleck, Seymour L., Professor of Psychiatry, University of Wisconsin School of Medicine: "The Road to Chaos", *Psychiatry and Social Science Review* 2 no. 7:2–5 (7/1968)—volume on student political activity at Columbia University
37. Liebert, Robert S., M.D., Psychiatric Consultant to the Columbia College Counseling Service, "Plantation Politics", *Psychiatry & Social Science Review* 2 no. 7:19–21 (7/1968)—volume on student political activity at Columbia University:

> This young man had a particularly difficult time because he could not solidly ally himself with any cohesive political student body in the conflict. The group that probably adapted with least psychological cost was

the militant conservatives, who only felt outrage at the radicals and felt no conflict in identifying with administration and police positions . . . for most of the students in the 'communes' in each of the occupied buildings there was a transient sense of great purpose, commitment and connection with the future . . . a new experience of 'openness' and mutual concern (p. 19) . . . [activists] feel deep guilt and expectation of retribution . . . when the 'bust' [police action] came they received their punishment, their expiation, but in a form that also confirmed the righteousness of their cause. . . . Their need for external order and inner repression reasserted itself (p. 20) . . . the unconscious taboo against destroying the totem father . . . to endure the trial of brutality, and to survive, had . . . poof of masculinity . . . For some, out of the enormous intrapsychic upheaval, has come a crystallization of a more independent, better defined ego . . . There also were many instances in which the events causes intrapsychic turmoil . . . Transient psychotic breaks . . . in students, faculty and administration . . . the rebellion is the outgrowth of the peculiar blending of the climate of America—with its war morality, racism, and myriad hypocrises—with the climate at Columbia—with more than its share of moral ambiguities, insensitivity to its relationship to the community and inflexible and unresponsive top leadership . . . out of this common crisis, much growth, if not rebirth, will be achieved by both students and University (p. 21)

38. Abrams, Richard M., Associate Professor of History, University of California-Berkeley, "When the Tough Get Going", *Psychiatry & Social Science Review* 2 no. 7:13–15 (7/1968)—volume on student political activity at Columbia University
39. Etzioni, Amitai, Professor of Sociology, Columbia University, "Challenge to Liberalism", *Psychiatry & Social Science Review* 2 no. 7:9–12 (7/1968)—volume on student political activity at Columbia University
40. Fromm, Erich, speaker at the protest commencement at Columbia University, "In the Name of Life", *Psychiatry & Social Science Review* 2 no. 7:6–7 (7/1968)—volume on student political activity at Columbia University
41. Seeley, John R., Dean of the Center for the Study of Democratic Institutions, Santa Barbara, California, "Plantation Politics", *Psychiatry & Social Science Review* 2 no. 7:16–18 (7/1968), p. 18—volume on student political activity at Columbia University
42. Steinzor, Bernard, Ph.D., Lecturer, Department of Psychiatry, Columbia College of Physicians and Surgeons; Program in Psychiatry and Religion, Union Theological Seminary, "Symbolic Truth", *Psychiatry & Social Science Review* 2 no. 7:24–26 (7/1968)—volume on student political activity at Columbia University
43. Hook, Sidney, Chairman of the Graduate School Division of Philosophy and Psychology, New York University, "Symbolic Truth", *Psychiatry & Social Science Review* 2 no. 7:22–23 (7/1968)—volume on student political activity at Columbia University
44. Risen, Clay, *A Nation On Fire: America in the Wake of the King Assassination* (Hoboken, NJ: John Wiley & Sons, 2009)
45. Powers, John, "Running Out of Outrage", *The Boston Globe Magazine*, 10/5/1997, pp. 17, 31–33, 36–37; p. 33
46. Harshbarger, Dwight, Ph.D. [VP for Human Resources, Sealy Inc., Chicago] and Demone, Harold W., Jr, Ph.D. [Professor and Dean, Graduate School of Social Work, Rutgers—The State University of New Jersey], "Impact of Public Policy on Mental Health Services", Ch. 8 in Schulberg, Herbert C. and

Killilea, Marie (eds.) *The Modern Practice of Community Mental Health: A Volume in Honor of Gerald Caplan* (San Francisco: Jossey Bass, 1982). pp. 230–245; p. 232
47. Glaser, Robert, Director of the Kaiser Family Foundation, interviewed by David G. Satin at this office in the Kaiser Family Foundation, Palo Alto, CA, 12/18/1979. [Caddy 3, Box 4, X, Lindemann Collection, Center for the History of Medicine, Francis A. Countway Library of Medicine, Boston, MA]
48. Zusman, Jack, and Lamb, H. Richard, "In Defense of Community Mental Health", *American Journal of Psychiatry* 134:887–890 (1977)
49. Mandell, Arnold J., "The Changing Face of Chairmen of Psychiatry Departments in America", *American Journal of Psychiatry* 131:1137–1139 (1974)
50. Redlich, Fritz and Kellert, Stephen R., "Trends in American Mental Health", *American Journal of Psychiatry* 135:22–28 (1978)
51. Brill, Norman Q., M.D., Professor of Psychiatry, University of California School of Medicine in Los Angeles: "Preventive Psychiatry", *Psychiatric Opinion*, 11–12/1977, pp. 30–34
52. The Committee on Therapeutic Care, Group for the Advancement of Psychiatry, *Crisis in Psychiatric Hospitalization* (New York: Group for the Advancement of Psychiatry, 1969)
53. Feldman, Saul, D.P.A., "Leadership in Mental Health: Changing the Guard for the 1980's", *American Journal of Psychiatry* 138:9 (9/1981), pp. 1147–1153
54. Sharfstein, Steven S., M.D., "Community Mental Health Centers: Returning to Basics", *American Journal of Psychiatry* 136:8 (1979), pp. 1077–1079. [Erich Lindemann Collection, Center for the History of Medicine, Francis A. Countway Library of Medicine, Harvard Medical School, Boston, MA]
55. Yolles, Stanley F., 1977, *ibid*
56. Klerman, Gerald, Keynote speech at the Annual Meeting of the North Suffolk Mental Health Association, 6/8/1982. [Lindemann Collection, Center for the History of Medicine, Francis A. Countway Library of Medicine, Harvard Medical School, Boston, MA]
57. Borus, Jonathan F., M.D., "COMMUNITY PSYCHIATRY AT THE MGH", Presented at the Colloquium "Psychiatry at the Massachusetts General Hospital" celebrating the Fiftieth Anniversary of the founding of the MGH Psychiatry Service, 10/13/1984. [file "Borus—Community Psychiatry at MGH 1984", Box XII #3, Lindemann Collection, Center for the History of Medicine, Francis A. Countway Library of Medicine, Harvard Medical School, Boston, MA]
58. Satin, David G., "Social Psychiatry, Social Ethos, and Social Conscience: COMMUNITY MENTAL HEALTH AND THE CYCLES OF PSYCHIATRIC IDEOLOGY", Presented at the Academic Conference, McLean Hospital, Belmont, MA, 10/11/1996, pp. 11–12. [David G. Satin files, Newton, MA]
59. Allen, James R., M.D., Professor & Chairman, Department of Psychiatry and Behavioral Sciences, University of Oklahoma, Tulsa Medical College; Executive Director, Tulsa Psychiatric Center, "Social and Behavioral Sciences in Medical School Curriculum", Ch. 23 in Schulberg, Herbert C. and Killilea, Marie (eds.) *The Modern Practice of Community Mental Health: A Volume in Honor of Gerald Caplan* (San Francisco: Jossey Bass, 1982) pp. 540–564
60. Lamb, H. Richard and Zusman, Jack, "Primary Prevention in Perspective", *American Journal of Psychiatry*. 136:212–217 (1979)
61. Leighton, Alexander H.,1978, *ibid*
62. Collins, Jerome A., Captain, Medical Corps, Biomedical Stress Research Branch, U.S. Army Medical Research and Development Command,

Department of the Army, EVALUATIVE RESEARCH IN COMMUNITY PSYCHIATRY, 11/15/1967. [folder "GENERAL CORRESPONDENCE A+B 1967", Box IV 1+2, Erich Lindemann Collection, Center for the History of Medicine, Countway Library of Medicine, Boston, MA]
63. Brosin, Henry W., M.D., Center for Advanced Study in the Behavioral Sciences, Stanford, CA, letter to Lindemann, Erich, 2/7/1966. [folder "Correspondence 1966 Misc", Box IV 1+2, Erich Lindemann Collection, Center for the History of Medicine, Countway Library of Medicine, Boston, MA]
64. Hassol, Leonad Ph.D., Chief—Community Consultation Service, South Shore Mental Health Center, Quincy, MA, letter to Lindemann, Erich, 3/7/1966. [folder "Correspondence 1966 Misc", Box IV 1+2, Erich Lindemann Collection, Center for the History of Medicine, Countway Library of Medicine, Boston, MA]
65. Lindemann, Erich and Leopold, M.D., 1974, *ibid*
66. Albee, George W., Case Western Reserve University, "CONCEPTUAL MODELS AND MANPOWER REQUIREMENTS IN PSYCHOLOGY", *American Psychologist*, 23 no. 5:317–320 (5/1968)
67. Brosin, Henry W., 2/7/1966, *ibid*
68. National Academy of Public Administration Contract HSM 42–70–55 August 1971, 1977, *ibid*
69. Rothman, David J., "The Rehabilitation of the Asylum", *The American Prospect* (Fall, 1991), pp. 118–128
70. Klerman, Gerald L., "Better But Not Well: Social and Ethical Issues in the Deinstitutionalization of the Mentally Ill", *Schizophrenia Bulletin* 3 no. 4:617–631 (1977): "My participation in a number of research projects, including such NIMH Psychopharmacology Research Branch (PRB) Service research projects . . . a study of the adequacy of treatment of schizophrenics . . . patterns of utilization and follow-up of schizophrenic patients . . . My experience as director of two community mental health programs, the Connecticut Mental Health Center (1965–1968) and the Erich Lindemann Mental Health Center (1970–1976)". (p. 618)
71. Olson, Lynne, *Citizens of London: The Americans Who Stood With Britain in its Darkest, Finest Hour* (New York: Random House, 2010), p. 385
72. "'Doc' Holliday's Death", *Newsweek*, 2/11/1985, p. 33
73. Lindemann, Erich, letter to Leigh, Stanley, Honorary Business Secretary, The British Psyco-Analytic Society, 1/13/1969. [folder "Correspondence 1969", Box IV 1+2, Erich Lindemann Collection, Center for the History of Medicine, Countway Library of Medicine, Boston, MA]
74. Caplan, Gerald, letter to Lindemann, Erich and Elizabeth, 12/1/1969, p. 2. [folder "Correspondence 1969", Box IV 1+2, Erich Lindemann Collection, Center for the History of Medicine, Countway Library of Medicine, Boston, MA]
75. Poerksen, Niels, interview by David G. Satin, M.D. at Poerksen house, Bielefeld, West Germany, 10/13/1984. [Caddy 7, Tape 11A+12B, Box XI, Lindemann Collection, X, Erich Lindemann Collection, Center for the History of Medicine, Francis A. Countway Library of Medicine, Boston, MA]
76. Merrifield, John F., M.D., *Abby's Deal: A History of the Concord, Massachusetts Community Mental Health Center* (Portsmouth, NH: Peter E. Randall, 2006)
77. Hersch, Charles, interviewed by John Merrifield, 11/15/2007
78. Forlder Vaughan, Warren T., David G. Satin files, Newton, MA
79. Vaughan, Warren T., Jr., M.D., "Chapter 20: Local Mental Health Program Administration", Ch. 20 in Bellak, Leopold (ed.) *Handbook of Community*

Psychiatry and Community Mental Health (Grune & Stratton, 1964), pp. 388–408

80. Lindemann, Erich, talk to the last group of psychiatric residents entering the MGH during Lindemann's tenure as Chief; 7/1/1965, "The Role of Psychiatry at the M.G.H.", p. 13. [folder "The Role of Psychiatry at the M.G.H. July 1, 1965", IIIB3 a-c, Erich Lindemann Collection, Center for the History of Medicine, Francis A. Countway Library of Medicine, Boston, MA]

81. Report of the AD HOC COMMITTEE APPOINTED TO EXAMINE THE POSTURE OF PSYCHIATRY AT THE MASSACHUSETTS GENERAL HOSPITAL AND TO SEEK A PROFESSOR OF PSYCHIATRY

82. Frankel, Fred H., MGH observer on the steering committee and representative to the Planning Committee, Metropolitan Mental Health Planning Committee, memorandum to Hazard, Sprgue W., M.D. Chairman of the Metropolitan Mental Health Planning Committee, 3/1/1967. [Erich Lindemann Collection, Center for the History of Medicine, Countway Library of Medicine, Boston, MA]

83. "MGH Research Activities Booklet (material) Year of 1966", [folder "MGH Research Activities Booklet (material) Year of 1966", Box IIIA 4 (Mb-O), Lindemann Collection, Center for the History of Medicine, Countway Library of Medicine, Boston, MA]

84. Lindemann, Erich, "Development of Community Mental Health Centers", interview by graduate students in sociology Spivak and McGrath, 1965 (unpublished)

85. Nemiah, John, interviewed by David G. Satin at the Beth Israel Hospital, Boston, 9/21/1978. [Caddy 5, Box 5, X, Lindemann Collection, Center for the History of Medicine, Francis A. Countway Library of Medicine, Boston, MA]

86. An interesting footnote to Cobb's, Lindemann's, and Oliver Cope's interest in psychosomatic medicine was Cope's observation that Nemiah's wife's beloved father failed three times In business, and then Nemiah failed to be honored with the professorship in psychiatry at the MGH. She then suffered acute Graves' disease (hyperthyroidism) with goitre and exolphthalmos. After three sessions of insight psychotherapy with Grete Bibring her hyperthyroidism and its physical manifestations disappeared. Cope, Oliver, M.D., interview by David G. Satin, 11/21/1978. [Caddy 1, Box 4, X, Lindemann Collection, Center for the History of Medicine, Francis A. Countway Library of Medicine, Boston, MA]

87. White, Benjamin V., "Brahmin Maverick: The Struggle of Stanley Cobb to Integrate Mind and Body, MS 7/9/1980; MGH: Impact of Psychoanalysis", Ch. 9 in *Stanley Cobb: A Builder of the Modern Neurosciences* (Boston: The Francis A. Countway Library of Medicine, 1984)

88. Wanta, Lorna J. C., Executive Assistant, Department of Psychiatry, MGH. Interview by David G. Satin, 11/16/1984. [Erich Lindemann Collection, Center for the History of Medicine, Countway Library of Medicine, Boston, MA]

89. Farrell, Jean, interviews by David G. Satin at her home in Boston, 8/22/1978, and at the Countway Library, 4/25/1981. [Box 4, X, Lindemann Collection, Center for the History of Medicine, Francis A. Countway Library of Medicine, Boston, MA]

90. White, Benjamin V., *Stanley Cobb: A Builder of the Modern Neurosciences* (Boston: The Francis A. Countway Library of Medicine, 1984), Note Cobb died 2/8/1968

91. Lindemann, Erich, Visiting Professor, letter to Nemiah, Dr. John, Acting Chief, Psychiatric Service, MGH, 4/12/1967. [folder "Bodenheimer

Correspondence", Box IV 1 + 2, Erich Lindemann Collection, Center for the History of Medicine, Countway Library of Medicine, Boston, MA]
92. Eisenberg, Leon, MGH Chairman of the Psychiatry Department, interview by David G. Satin at Childrens Hospital Medical Center, Boston, 11/27/1978. [Erich Lindemann Collection, Center for the History of Medicine, Countway Library of Medicine, Boston, MA]
93. One is reminded of the pre-Columbian Mayan custom: When a new chief replaced the old the faces were chiseled off all statues from the previous era and replaced by new ones from the current era.
94. Farrell, Jean, 4/25/1981, *ibid*
95. Lindemann, Erich, M.D., Duhl, Leonard J., M.D. and Seeley, John, Ph.D., Erich Lindemann, Leonard Duhl Interviews 6/15,22/1974. [Caddy 4, Tape 3A, 4B; 7, Erich Lindemann Collection, Center for the History of Medicine, Francis A. Countway Library of Medicine, Boston, MA]
96. Nemiah, John C., M.D., HMS Professor of Psychiatry and Psychiatrist-in-Chief at Beth Israel Hospital, Boston, letter to Lindemann, Erich, Visiting Professor. of Psychiatry, Stanford University Medical Center, 4/7/1971, p. 2. [folder "Correspondence—1971", Box IV 1 + 2, Erich Lindemann Collection, Center for the History of Medicine, Countway Library of Medicine, Boston, MA]
97. Eisenberg, Leon, M.D. Professor of Psychiatry at HMS and Chief of the Psychiatry Service at MGH, letter to Lindemann, Erich, 11/17/1969. [folder "Correspondence 1969", Box IV 1 + 2, Erich Lindemann Collection, Center for the History of Medicine, Countway Library of Medicine, Boston, MA]
98. PSYCHIATRIC RESIDENCY TRAINING PROGRAM at MASSACHUSETTS GENERAL HOSPITAL and ERICH LINDEMANN MENTAL HEALTH CENTER: undated, p. 5. Box XII 1 folder 110c Lindemann M.H. Center, Erich Lindemann Collection, Center for the History of Medicine, Francis A. Countway Library of Medicine, Boston, MA
99. Borus, Jonathan F., 10/13/1984, *ibid*:

> I have been told that residents were routinely sent out to Wellesley [HRS] in the 50s, some going more willingly than others [untrue-CMH fellows] . . . there was a long-standing multidisciplinary NIMH training grant in community mental health when I arrived . . . in 1972. At that time, however, no residents were involved . . . and I found our residents neither turned-on to community psychiatry nor interested in going out into the communities served by the . . . Lindemann Center . . . the second year residents had a brief lecture series on community mental health, but there was no formal community psychiatry teaching rotation . . . I had been assigned the job of teaching the second year resident seminar. I am now in my 13th year of teaching that four month long core seminar on Social and Community Psychiatry . . . that there is both theory and data-based research in community psychiatry around which they can structure their community mental health experiences . . . in July 1974 we began the formal, six-month part-time rotation for second year residents . . . to show residents what was unique about the community psychiatrist's role . . . focused on working closely with allied professionals, para-professionals, and citizen groups; understanding the cultural and [p. 8] socio-demographic aspects of the community; seeing patients in their homes and community institutions; and consulting to the primary physicians in the neighborhood health centers as well as other community caregivers including police, the courts, probation officers, schools, and the clergy. [≈EL] . . . From 1973 through 1982 MGH sponsored an NIMH funded post-residency Fellowship in Community

Psychiatry... trained young psychiatrists to clinically and administratively plan, lead, and evaluate public mental health systems through a two year program of half-time work at the Harvard School of Public Health, leading to a Masters of Public Health degree, and concurrent half-time practical experience in one of our neighborhood health centers.

100. Bragg, Robert L., M.D., Coordinator of the CMH Training Program, MGH, letter to Levy, Bernard, M.D., 10/25/1971. [folder "CMH Tng Program Description of, for Brochure on Residency Tng": "I am enclosing a description of the Community Mental Health Training Program".

Bragg, Robert L., M.D. memorandum to Gerald Klerman, M.D. [Superintendent, ELCMHC], Helen M. Herzan, M.D. [Supervisor of CMH Project], Louisa Dierker, M.D., Kenneth M. Tardiff, M.D. [CMH fellows], William Sack, M.D., Barbara Burns, M.D. [from MGH-Bunker Hill Health Center], Jonathan Borus, M.D. [North End Health Clinic], Miss Eleanor Clark [Director of Social Service, MGH], Miss Jan LaBombard [psychiatric social service, MGH], 12/4/1972. [folder "Psychiatry-CMH. Site Visit (12/11/72) Source Materials"]:

"Site Visit, Community Mental Health Training Program—Psychiatry... The Site visitors are... John Frosch, M.D., Director Department of Psychiatry and Community Mental Health Center Brookdale Hospital... Brooklyn, New York... Henry Lederer, M.D., Professor of Psychiatry Department of Psychiatry Georgetown University... Washington, D.C.... The Project Period: 07/01/73 through 06/30/78... Trainee stipend requested:... Two stipends at the 3rd year residency level... One stipend at the 4th year residency level [p. 1]... The current grant... The number of stipends available: Two at the third year residency level. (one unfilled)". [p. 2]

Bragg, Robert L., M.D., Project Director, letter to Frosh, John, M.D., Director, Department of Psychiatry and Community Mental Health Center, The Brookdale Hospital Medical Center, Brooklyn, New York, 1/9/1973: "The psychology program was terminated as of June 30, 1970. The social work and psychiatry projects continue as of this time". [p. 1]

Bragg, Robert L., M.D., letter to Valois, Mr. Morris, Business Manger, Region V Office, Department of Mental Health, 1/9/1973

Bragg, Robert L., M.D., Project Director, CMH Fellowship, letter to Eisenberg, Leon, M.D., Chief Department of Psychiatry, MGH, 1/9/1973

[IIIB3 a-c, Erich Lindemann Collection, Center for the History of Medicine, Countway Library of Medicine, Boston, MA]

101. Bragg, Robert L., M.D., "MEMORANDUM From Robert L. Bragg, M.D., Coordinator for the [CMH] Training Program To Leon Eisenberg, M.D., Chief of Psychiatry, MGH, Eleanor Clark, M.S.W., Director, Social Services Department [MGH], Clara Mayo, Ph.D., Project Director, Psychology, Mary Kearney, M.S.W., Project Director, Social Work (7/1/69), Alvin Simmons, Ph.D., Director Community Mental Health Services, MGH-Bunker Hill Health Project", p. 1. [folder "CMH FACULTY", IIIB3 d, Erich Lindemann Collection, Center for the History of Medicine, Countway Library of Medicine, Boston, MA]

102. Bragg, Robert, M.D., interview by David G. Satin by phone from Florida, 7/13/1979. [Caddy 1, Box 4, X, Lindemann Collection, Center for the History of Medicine, Francis A. Countway Library of Medicine, Boston, MA]

103. Parker, Franklin, member of the HRS board of directors, interview at his Boston office by David G. Satin, 11/17/1978. [Caddy 5, Box 5, X, Lindemann Collection, Center for the History of Medicine, Countway Library of Medicine, Boston, MA]

104. PROGRESS REPORT Privileged Communication. [folder "Psychiatry: CMH Training Grant Application (Resource Material) Project Period: 7/1/73–6/30/78 Visit (12/11/72) [folder "Psychiatry: CMH Training Grant Application (Resource Material) Project Period: 7/1/73–6/30/78 Visit (12/11/72) Source Materials", IIIB3 a-c, Erich Lindemann Collection, Center for the History of Medicine, Countway Library of Medicine, Boston, MA] Source Materials", [IIIB3 a-c, Erich Lindemann Collection, Center for the History of Medicine, Countway Library of Medicine, Boston, MA]
105. TRAINING PROPOSAL IN COMMUNITY MENTAL HEALTH AT THE BUNKER HILL HEALTH CENTER OF THE MASSACHUSETTS GENERAL HOSPITAL 4/1972
106. Simmons, Alvin J., Ph.S., S.M.Hyg, letter to Lindemann, Erich, 5/13/1970. [folder "Correspondence—1970", Box IV 1+2, Erich Lindemann Collection, Center for the History of Medicine, Francis A. Countway Library of Medicine, Boston, MA]
107. Simmons, Alvin J., Ph.D., S.M.Hyg., Chief, Community Mental Health, Bunker Hill Health Center of the Massachusetts General Hospital, letter to Lindemann, Erich, 9/25/1969. [folder "Correspondence 1969", Box IV 1+2, Erich Lindemann Collection, Center for the History of Medicine, Countway Library of Medicine, Boston, MA]
108. Nemiah, John, letter to Lindemann, Erich, 10/12/1966, p. 3. [folder "General Correspondence L, M 1966", Box IV 1+2, Erich Lindemann Collection, Center for the History of Medicine, Countway Library of Medicine, Boston, MA]
109. 5/26/67 DHEW APPLICATION FOR TRAINING GRANT: "APPLICATION NUMBER MH-7451–98. . . 1. TITLE OF PROGRAM . . . Community Mental Health Training for Psychologists . . . 4. . . . A. PROJECT PERIOD . . . 7/1/68 6/30/75. . . 5A. TOTAL AMOUNT FOR 4A $479,226". [folder "GRANT 68–69", IIIB3 d, Erich Lindemann Collection, Center for the History of Medicine, Countway Library of Medicine, Boston, MA]
110. "6/13/68 NOTICE OF GRANT AWARDED, DHEW, PHS: "Grant Number 2 TO1 MH07451–08 PO . . . TOTAL PROJECT PERIOD 07/1/58–06/30/70. . . GRANT PERIOD 07/1/58–06/30/70. . . Title of Project or Area of Training COMMUNITY MENTAL HEALTH PSYCHOLOGY . . . Principal Investigator or Program Director MAYO, CLARA PHD DEPARTMENT OF PSYCHIATRY MASSACHUSETTS GENERAL HOSPITAL" [folder "GRANT 68–69", IIIB3 d, Erich Lindemann Collection, Center for the History of Medicine, Countway Library of Medicine, Boston, MA]
111. Eisenberg, Leon, M.D., Professor of Psychiatry and Chief of Psychiatry, MGH, letter to Mayo, Dr. Clara, Department of Psychiatry, MGH, 11/11/1969. [folder "GRANT 68–69", IIIB3 d, Erich Lindemann Collection, Center for the History of Medicine, Countway Library of Medicine, Boston, MA]
112. Tyler, Forrest B., Ph.D., Chief, Psychology Section, Behavioral Sciences Training Branch, Division of Manpower & Training Programs DHEW, PHS, letter to Mayo, Dr. Clara, Assistant Psychologist, Psychology Division, Department of Psychiatry, Massachusetts General Hospital, 7/19/1968, p. 1. [folder "GRANT 68–69", IIIB3 d, Erich Lindemann Collection, Center for the History of Medicine, Countway Library of Medicine, Boston, MA]
113. Boothe, B.E., Ph.D., Chief, Behavioral Sciences Training Branch, Division of Manpower and Training Programs, DHEW, PHS, letter to Mayo, Dr. Clara, Department of Psychiatry MGH, 3/23/1970. [folder "GRANT

68–69", IIIB3 d, Erich Lindemann Collection, Center for the History of Medicine, Countway Library of Medicine, Boston, MA]
114. Schneider, Stanley F., Ph.D., Chief, Psychology Section, Behavioral Sciences Training Branch, Division of Manpower and Training Programs, DHEW, PHS, letter to Mayo, Dr. Clara. Associate Psychologist, MGH, 4/10/1970, p. 1. [folder "GRANT 68–69", IIIB3 d, Erich Lindemann Collection, Center for the History of Medicine, Countway Library of Medicine, Boston, MA]
115. Bragg, Robert, M.D., interview by David G. Satin via telephone from his home in Florida, 7/13/1979. [Caddy 1, Box 4, X, Lindemann Collection, Center for the History of Medicine, Francis A. Countway Library of Medicine, Boston, MA]
116. Lindemann, Erich, 6/15,22/1974, *ibid*
117. Lindemann, Erich, letter to Beecher, Dr. Henry K. [MGH Chief of Anesthesia *emeritus*, 31/1971, p. 2. [folder "Correspondence—1971", Box IV 1+2, Erich Lindemann Collection, Center for the History of Medicine, Countway Library of Medicine, Boston, MA]
118. Berry, George Packer, M.D., emeritus dean of the HMS, interview by David G. Satin by phone from his home in New Jersey, 11/2/1979. [Caddy 1, Caddy 1, Box 4, X, Lindemann Collection, Center for the History of Medicine, Francis A. Countway Library of Medicine, Boston, MA]
119. Cope, Oliver, 11/21/1978, *ibid*
120. Wiseman, Avery, MGH Department of Psychiatry, letter to Lindemann, Erich, 3/17/1971. [folder "Correspondence—1971", Box IV 1+2, Erich Lindemann Collection, Center for the History of Medicine, Countway Library of Medicine, Boston, MA]
121. Caplan, Gerald M.D., Laboratory of Community Psychiatry, Clinical Professor of Psychiatry, HMS, letter to Morrison, Miss Adele, The Grant Foundation, Inc., 5/11/1966: PROPOSED PROGRAM FOR VISITING FACULTY SEMINAR IN COMMUNITY PSYCHIATRY, Laboratory of Community Psychiatry, Department of Psychiatry, Harvard Medical School. [folder "G. Caplan/Visiting Faculty Seminar on Community Psychiatry", David G. Satin files, Newton, MA]
122. Bouvier, W., S.J., Area Board President, letter to Farrell, Jean, 9/30/1969. [folder "Correspondence 1969", Box IV 1+2, Erich Lindemann Collection, Center for the History of Medicine, Countway Library of Medicine, Boston, MA]
123. Farrell, Jean M., letter to Greenblatt Dr. Milton, 6/8/1969. [folder "Correspondence 1969", Box IV 1+2, Erich Lindemann Collection, Center for the History of Medicine, Countway Library of Medicine, Boston, MA]
124. Brooke, Edward, United States Senate, letter to Farrell, Jean M., 12/2/1969. [folder "Correspondence 1969", Box IV 1+2, Erich Lindemann Collection, Center for the History of Medicine, Countway Library of Medicine, Boston, MA]
125. Chase, Irvin H., President, THE MASSACHUSETTS ASSOCIATION FOR MENTAL HEALTH, INC, letter to Greenblatt, Milton, M.D., Commissioner, Department of Mental Health, 11/13/1969. [folder "Correspondence 1969", Box IV 1+2, Erich Lindemann Collection, Center for the History of Medicine, Countway Library of Medicine, Boston, MA]
126. Bouvier, Rev. Wilfrid T., S.J., Government Center Area Board, letter to Bloomberg, Dr. Wilfred [Regional Director, Massachusetts DMH], 12/18/1969. [folder "CORRESPONDENCE RE NAMING LINDEMANN MENTAL HEALTH CENTER", Box IV 3+4+5, Erich Lindemann Collection, Center for the History of Medicine, Countway Library of Medicine, Boston, MA]

127. Sweet, William H., M.D., D.Sc. Chief, Neurosurgical Service, HMS/ MGH to Umana, Sen. Mario [Massachusetts state senate], 11/14/1969. [folder "CORRESPONDENCE RE NAMING LINDEMANN MENTAL HEALTH CENTER", Box IV 3+4+5, Erich Lindemann Collection, Center for the History of Medicine, Countway Library of Medicine, Boston, MA]
128. Knowles, John H., M.D., General Director, MGH, letter to Farrell, Miss Jean, 7/28/1969. [folder "CORRESPONDENCE RE NAMING LINDEMANN MENTAL HEALTH CENTER", Box IV 3+4+5, Erich Lindemann Collection, Center for the History of Medicine, Countway Library of Medicine, Boston, MA]
129. Ebert, Robert H. Ebert, M.D., HMS Dean, letter to Farrell, Miss Jean M., 8/14/1969. [folder "CORRESPONDENCE RE NAMING LINDEMANN MENTAL HEALTH CENTER", Box IV 3+4+5, Erich Lindemann Collection, Center for the History of Medicine, Countway Library of Medicine, Boston, MA]
130. Viguers, Richard T., Administrator, New England Medical Center Hospitals, letter to Greeenblatt, Milton, M.D., Commissioner of Mental Health, Commonwealth of Massachusetts, 8/6/1969. [folder "CORRESPONDENCE RE NAMING LINDEMANN MENTAL HEALTH CENTER", Box IV 3+4+5, Erich Lindemann Collection, Center for the History of Medicine, Countway Library of Medicine, Boston, MA]
131. Gochberg, Shayna, letter to Lindemann, Elizabeth and Erich, [undated]. [folder "Correspondence—1970", Box IV 1+2, Erich Lindemann Collection, Center for the History of Medicine, Francis A. Countway Library of Medicine, Boston, MA]
132. Bouvier, Rev. W. T., S.J., letter to Farrell, Jean, 2/26/1969. [folder "CORRESPONDENCE RE NAMING LINDEMANN MENTAL HEALTH CENTER", Box IV 3+4+5, Erich Lindemann Collection, Center for the History of Medicine, Countway Library of Medicine, Boston, MA]
133. Solomon, Maida H. [wife of Harry Solomon and consultant to the DMH], handwritten, letter to Greenblatt, Dr. Milton [DMH Commissioner], 12/1/1969. [folder "CORRESPONDENCE RE NAMING LINDEMANN MENTAL HEALTH CENTER", Box IV 3+4+5, Erich Lindemann Collection, Center for the History of Medicine, Countway Library of Medicine, Boston, MA]
134. Undated draft of legislative act. [folder "CORRESPONDENCE RE NAMING LINDEMANN MENTAL HEALTH CENTER", Box IV 3+4+5, Erich Lindemann Collection, Center for the History of Medicine, Countway Library of Medicine, Boston, MA]
135. Klerman, Gerald L., M.D., Superintendent of the ELMHC, letter to Lindemann, Erich, 5/5/1970. [folder "Correspondence—1970", Box IV 1+2, Erich Lindemann Collection, Center for the History of Medicine, Francis A. Countway Library of Medicine, Boston, MA]
136. Greenblatt, Milton, M.D., Commissioner, DMH, letter to Lindemann, Erich, 5/6/1970. [folder "Correspondence—1970", Box IV 1+2, Erich Lindemann Collection, Center for the History of Medicine, Francis A. Countway Library of Medicine, Boston, MA]
137. Klerman, Gerald L., M.D., Associate Professor of Psychiatry, Yale University School of Medicine and Director of the Connecticut Mental Health Center, New Haven, CT: "Mental Health and the Urban Crisis", *Am J. Orthopsychiatry* 39 no. 5:818–826 (10/1969)
138. *MGH News* 31 no.3: (3/1972). [folder "Correspondence—1972", Box IV 1+2, Erich Lindemann Collection, Center for the History of Medicine, Countway Library of Medicine, Boston, MA]

139. Klerman, Gerald L., 10/1969, *ibid*
140. Lindemann, Erich [letterhead Boston College Department of Psychology; Visiting Professor of Psychiatry], letter to Klerman, Dr. Gerald, Department of Psychiatry, Massachusetts General Hospital, 3/1/1971. [folder "Correspondence—1971", Box IV 1+2, Erich Lindemann Collection, Center for the History of Medicine, Countway Library of Medicine, Boston, MA]
141. Klerman, Gerald, M.D., Superintendent, Harbor Mental Health and Mental Retardation Area/Erich Lindemann Mental Health Center [typed in on DMH letterhead], letter to Lindemann, Erich, 3/9/1971
142. Lindemann, Erich, Visiting Professor of Psychiatry, letter to Klerman, Gerald L., M.D., Professor of Psychiatry, Massachusetts General Hospital, 3/22/1971
143. Klerman, Gerald, M.D., Superintendent, Harbor Mental Health and Mental Retardation Area/Erich Lindemann Mental Health Center [typed on DMH letterhead], letter to Lindemann, Erich, 5/4/1971
144. [folder "Correspondence—1971", Box IV 1+2, Erich Lindemann Collection, Center for the History of Medicine, Countway Library of Medicine, Boston, MA]
145. Lindemann, Erich, letter to Solomon, Harry C., M.D., former DMH Commissioner, 3/11/1971
146. Solomon, Harry C., letter to Lindemann, Erich, 3/19/1971
147. Committee on Social Issues—Subcommittee on The Vulnerable Child, American Psychoanalytic Association, 5/15/1997. [folders "Psychoanalysis", Research Papers, Erich Lindemann Collection, Center for the History of Medicine, Countway Library of Medicine, Boston, MA]
148. Committee on Social Issues, American Psychoanalytic Association article in *The American Psychoanalyst* 25 no. 4:17, 18 (1991) (newsletter of the American Psychoanalytic Association), folders "Psychoanalysis". [Research Papers, Lindemann Collection, Center for the History of Medicine, Francis A. Countway Library of Medicine, Boston, MA]
149. Bernard, Viola W., 4/26/1979, *ibid*
    Committee on Community Psychiatry, American Psychoanalytic Association, article in *The American Psychoanalyst* 25 no. 4:17, 18 (1991) (newsletter, American Psychoanalytic Association), [folders "Psychoanalysis", Research Papers, Lindemann Collection, Center for the History of Medicine, Francis A. Countway Library of Medicine, Boston, MA]
150. Committee on Community Psychiatry, American Psychoanalytic Association, Wadeson, Ralph W. Jr., M.D., "Psychoanalysis in Community Psychiatry: Reflections on Some Theoretical Implications", *Journal of the American Psychoanalytic Society*, 23:177–189 (1975), report of Panel (Viola Bernard, Chairman) at the Annual Meeting of the American Psychoanalytic Association, 5/1974, Denver, CO.; p. 177. [Research Papers, Lindemann Collection, Center for the History of Medicine, Countway Library of Medicine, Boston, MA]
151. Committee on Community Psychiatry, American Psychoanalytic Association, Wadeson, Ralph W., 1975, *ibid*
152. Committee on Community Psychiatry, American Psychoanalytic Association, Bernard, Viola W., "Committee on Community Psychiatry", *Newsletter, The American Psychoanalytic Association* 12 no. 2:8, 9 (7/1978), p. 8. [folder "Psychoanalysis—American Psychoanalytic Association Committee on Community Psychiatry", David G. Satin files, Newton, MA]
153. Davis, Elizabeth B. and Coleman, Jules V. "Interactions Between Community Psychiatry and Psychoanal in the Understanding of Ego Development".

[Research Papers, Erich Lindemann Collection, Center for the History of Medicine, Countway Library of Medicine, Boston, MA]
154. Linn, Louis: "Superego Variants: Lessons from Community Psychiatry", in Committee on Community Psychiatry, American Psychoanalytic Association, Wadeson, Ralph W., 1975, *ibid*
155. Kelly, Kathleen, "Viola W. Bernard, M.D., 1907–1998: Pioneer in Social Psychiatry", press release 3/25/1998
156. Committee on Community Psychiatry, American Psychoanalytic Association, "Minutes of Meeting—17 December 1976 COMMITTEE ON COMMUNITY PSYCHIATRY REPRESENTATIVES OF AFFILIATE SOCIETIES', Co-Chairmen: Viola W. Bernard, M.D., Stanley L. Block, M.D., One East Fifty-Seventh Street, New York, New York 10022; research folders "Psychoanalysis". [Research Papers, Erich Lindemann Collection, Center for the History of Medicine, Countway Library of Medicine, Boston, MA]

Members included Bernard Bandler, Elizabeth W. Davis, Louis Linn, Jules V. Coleman, Reginald Lourie, Judd Marmor, Fritz Redl, S. Mouchley Small, and Alert J. Solnit, Meyerson, Arthur—New York; Bernstein, Morris—Association for Psychoanalytic Medicine; Caldwell, John—Florida; Sabot, Lawrence—Long Island; Kritzer, Herbert—Denver; Gonzalez, R.G.—New Orleans; DeBolt, M.—New Orleans and Dallas; Ordway, John—Cincinnati (Bangor); Ross, W. Donald—Cincinnati, Berkovitz, Irv—Southern California; Parcells, F.H.—Michigan; Stump, Jacob—New Jersey; Karasic, Jerome—Los Angeles Psychoanalytic Society and Institute; Gordon, Ken—Philadelphia Psychoanalytic Society; Talbott, John—Columbia; Ocko, Felix—San Francisco; Coleman, Jules—Western New England; Schwarz, I. Gene—Denver; Shopper, Molsy—St. Louis; Tarnower, William—Topeka; Bernard, VIola—New York; Meyers, Helen—Columbia Psychoanalytic; Sklarew, B.[ruce H.]—Baltimore—D.C.; Wiedeman, George H.—Psychoanalytic of New York
157. Committee on Community Psychiatry, American Psychoanalytic Association: "The American Psychoanalytic Association Committee on Community Psychiatry; Viola W. Bernard, Chair—Stanley L. Block, Co-Chair, One East 57th Street, New York, N.Y. 10022", MEMO 11 November, 1975, p. 1. [research folders "Psychoanalysis", Research Papers, Erich Lindemann Collection, Center for the History of Medicine, Countway Library of Medicine, Boston, MA]
158. Bernard, Viola W.: "About Psychiatry, Psychiatrists, and Social Problems", *American Journal of Psychiatry 130*:2, (2/73), p. 2
159. Committee on Community Psychiatry, American Psychoanalytic Association, "MINUTES of REPS MEETING ON COMMUNITY PSYCHIATRY, Quebec City, Canada, April 29, 1977; submitted by Lawrence H. Rockland, M.D. [research folders "Psychoanalysis", Research Papers, Lindemann Collection, Center for the History of Medicine, Countway Library of Medicine, Boston, MA]
160. Committee on Community Psychiatry, American Psychoanalytic Association, Bernard, Viola W., 7/1978, *ibid*
161. Committee on Community Psychiatry, American Psychoanalytic Association: "INSTRUMENT FOR DESCRIBING THE DYNAMICS OF THE DEVELOPMENT AND COURSE OF A COMMUNITY MENTAL HEALTH SERVICE PROGRAM", ?1973; research folders "Psychoanalysis". [Research Papers, Lindemann Collection, Center for the History of Medicine, Countway Library of Medicine, Boston, MA]

162. Committee on Community Psychiatry, American Psychoanalytic Association: "E APPENDIX [to INSTRUMENT FOR DESCRIBING THE DYNAMICS OF THE DEVELOPMENT AND COURSE OF A COMMUNITY MENTAL HEALTH SERVICE PROGRAM], Corrected 11/15/1973. [research folders "Psychoanalysis", Research Papers, Lindemann Collection, Center for the History of Medicine, Countway Library of Medicine, Boston, MA]
Instrument outline:

Component #1—Social, Economic, Political, and Cultural Context
A CMH program's climate "can have a fateful impact on its effectiveness". (p. 1): The CMHCs Act of 1963 led to a favorable national climate and support from Congress and top NIMH officials, which resulted in the construction or staffing of most of the 525 CMHCs. In 1968 there was a drastic administrative alteration resulting in greater difficulties in obtaining construction and staffing grants. The "Nader Report" on the NIMH was sharply critical of aspects of CMH service programs, which may have influenced public opinion.
State and local climate is independent of the national climate: In the period 1963–1968 many governments were hostile and provided little support—for instance conservative governments cut off states' matching plans and did not support other mental health programs, which slowed the development of CMHCs. Local mayoral, councilmanic, county boards of supervisors, and directors of departments of mental health had significant impact. One example was the fact that in a majority of southern California directors of County departments of mental health were antagonistic to CMH, agreeing to only token contracts with CMHCs and providing little funding; in contrast, a majority of northern California directors of county departments of mental health were sympathetic to CMH resulting in more Short-Doyle funding and facilitating CMHCs. Fiscal stringencies and economic recession limited CMHCs funding while demands for services were increasing, resulting in untenable pressures. It was observed that cultural prejudice against mental illness was greatest where the need for services was greatest, and this prejudice needed to be overcome for CMHCs to be effective.
Component #2—How and Why Programs Evolved
a. Dynamics: development from government policy vs. professional and agency awareness, vs. community demand vs. some combination
b. Contractual and organizational arrangements.
c. Programs offered to but imposed on consumers, added to but superimposed on/substituted for preexisting services. Offered via medical institutions vs. social institutions vs. free-standing programs. Local or regional. The professional climate affects the establishment of programs.
d. The needs and problems promoting the development of programs.
Component #3—The Community:
Demography:—geography (natural boundaries vs. populations, a broad range), number of people, transportation access, housing, socioeconomic class, sex, age, marital status, national origin, generations in the U.S., rural vs. urban, religion.
Service institutions
Social interaction patterns.
Social pathology patterns
Component #4—The Institution Providing Community Services

Parent service institutions may follow medical and social models. Developing CMHCs introduces a change in orientation which is often not smooth. Issues include problems in developing mental health clinics with 24 hour per day service, medical school based CMHCs are responsible to parent educational institutions' administrations with little input from community advisory boards.

Motivation for CMH may be seeking an increased budget vs. meeting community needs, which affects the institutions' image to the service community and their own internal communities and appeal for funding.

How much is the institutional board informed and supportive of the CMHC? Are there reservations about new methods? Is there a new consumer population? How does staff respond to this program? Are there changes in parent institutions? Are sponsoring institutions organized for service delivery or coordination?

Component #5 Professional Agents and Caregivers

How adequate is support and authority? Are there appropriate skills and understanding to work with the community? Does the CMH program mesh with other staff, clinical practices, and leadership/followership roles? How much recognition and collaboration is there with representative leaders and responsible organizations? How does the program handle the stresses of community work?

Historically, how acceptable is the caregiver role to the community? (For instance, in poor areas the caseworker is anathema while the community council officer is respected.). Personal dynamics can lead to failure. Does the program work in terms of economics? Does the parent institution give moral support but not effective status? What form does "support" take?

Component #6—Consumers

What are the attitudes of individuals and groups toward mental health services and the CMHC—do they feel isolated or demeaned, prefer nonprofessionals vs. professionals? What are the external mandates, including from a community board: priorities, theoretical approaches, record-keeping and confidentiality? What are sub-group biases, utilization of various services, nature of requests, etc.?

Component #7—Funding Sources

Support vs. obstacles, determination of policies and priorities—e.g., medical schools may focus on professional and research goals, the state may focus on severe mental illness, federal authorities may be interested in innovation, community involvement, and techniques to use with ghetto populations.

The goals for the target community may be comprehensiveness, effectiveness, racism issues, outreach, or the needs of children. Priorities may be unbalanced, such as drug addiction. Do unscrupulous elements seek control of funds? Do social issues replace psychiatric issues? Are employment standards lowered in terms of quality or quantity? Do local needs conflict with state plan? Does government funding politicize the program?

163. Subcommittee for Preparatory Commission VIII in COPER [Conference on Psychoanalytic Education and Research]: "Concerning the Rationale and Strategies for Greater Inclusion of Social and Community Issues in Psychoanalytic Institute Curricula", Burnham & Dorn, 1/25/1974. [research folders "Psychoanalysis", Research Papers, Erich Lindemann Collection, Center for the History of Medicine, Francis A. Countway Library of Medicine, Boston, MA]

164. Lindemann, Erich, letter to Semrad, Elvin V., M.D., President, The Boston Psychoanalytic Society and Institute, Inc., 2/19/1970. [folder "Correspondence—1970", Box IV 1 + 2, Erich Lindemann Collection, Center for the History of Medicine, Francis A. Countway Library of Medicine, Boston, MA]
165. Committee on Community Psychiatry, American Psychoanalytic Association: "Minutes of Meeting Committee on Community Psychiatry Representatives of Affiliate Societies, 6/2/1975, Los Angeles, California Annual Meeting". [research folders "Psychoanalysis", research Papers, Erich Lindemann Collection, Center for the History of Medicine, Countway Library of Medicine, Boston, MA] Representatives on the committee included Molsy Shopper (St. Louis, MO), Arthur Meyerson (New York City), J. Hitchcock (Pittsburgh, PA), J. Spurlock (Washington, DC), R. Sokol (Los Angeles, CA), E. Davis (New York City), R. Wadeson (Washington, DC), M. Shapero (Boulder, CO), Irv Berkovitz (Los Angeles, CA), A. Coodley (Los Angeles, CA), R. Cattell (Denver, CO), John Ordway (Bangor, ME), William Tarnower (Topeka, KS), W. Donald Ross (Cincinnati, OH), R. Felix Ocko (San Francisco, CA), Viola Bernard (New York Psychoanalytic Society), G. Pollock (Chicago, IL), Stanley Block (Cincinnati, OH)
166. Committee on Community Psychiatry, American Psychoanalytic Association: "Minutes of Meeting Committee on Community Psychiatry Representatives of Affiliate Societies, 6/2/1975, Los Angeles, California Annual Meeting", research folders "Psychoanalysis". [Research Papers, Lindemann Collection, Center for the History of Medicine, Countway Library of Medicine, Boston, MA] W. Tarnower (Topeka) introduced community psychiatry into core curriculum—some resistance, general faculty support. Aging and death, hospital psychiatry and psychoanalysis, community psychiatry and psychoanalysis (fourth year, Tarnower), 2–3 hour sessions; to create positive Institute climate regarding community work; history, psychoanalysis and community psychiatry are not alien but make mutual contributions, Tarnower as a model for candidates; opposition to Tarnower teaching a course with a social worker left Tarnower to teach alone. He uses the Iowa Medical College "Teaching by Objectives". (Representatives want a copy.) George Pollock (outgoing President): alternative course is orientation and favorable faculty attitudes and then weave into many courses, field visits, community visitors. Bernard emphasized faculty orientation and acceptance to create a favorable climate.

There is a need for identity, a consort of psychoanalysts working in community psychiatry. There is resistance to community psychiatry by younger analysts and candidates. The 1972 Committee and Representatives resolution had little effect. Burnham and Dorn report is being circulated. Dr. Shopper teaches the interrelationship between individual and social psychopathology; he works as a community advocate but does not identify himself as a psychoanalyst in deference to his colleagues.
167. Lawrence, Margaret Morgan, Lief, Victor F., Millet, John A. P., M.D., "Position Paper on Community Psychiatry, The American Academy of Psychoanalysis: The Role of Psychoanalysts in Community Mental Health", *Newsletter of The American Academy of Psychoanalysis XI* no. 2:12 (10/1967). ["Psychoanalysis", Research Papers, Erich Lindemann Collection, Center for the History of Medicine, Countway Library of Medicine, Boston, MA]
168. Millet, John A. P. M.D., moderator; Lawrence, Margaret Morgan, "Workshop—The Psychoanalyst and Community Mental Health", *Newsletter*, American Academy of Psychoanalysis, p. 11. ["Psychoanalysis", Research Papers, Erich Lindemann Collection, Center for the History of Medicine, Countway Library of Med., Boston, MA]

292 Counterrevolution of Biology and Business

169. Janzarik, Werner, Professor, and Mundt, Christoph, associate professor and future professor, Psychiatrische Klinik, Universität Heidelberg, West Germany; interview by David G. Satin, M.D., 10/29/1984. [Caddy 7, Tape 14B, Box X, Lindemann Collection, Center for the History of Medicine, Francis A. Countway Library of Medicine, Boston, MA]
170. Poerksen, Niels, interviewed by David G. Satin in Wellesley, MA, 9/9/1978. [Erich Lindemann Collection, Center for the History of Medicine, Francis A. Countway Library of Medicine, Boston, MA]
171. Janzarik, Werner, 10/29/1984, *ibid*
172. Plog, Ursula, Depertent of Social Psychiatry, Freie Univeristät Berlin, West Germany, interview by David G. Satin at the Friee Universität Berlin, 10/11/1984. [Caddy 7, Tape 9A+10b, Box X, Erich Lindemann Collection, Center for the History of Medicine, Francis A. Countway Library of Medicine, Boston, MA]
173. Pörksen, Niels, Leitende Arzt, Fachbereich Psychitrie [Chief Physician, Psychiatry Department], von Bodenshwinghsche Anstalten Bethel, Serepta und Nazareth, Bielefeld, West Germany. Interviewed at his home in Bielefeld, West Germany by David G. Satin, 10/13/1984. [Tape 11 + 12B, Caddy 7, Box XI, Erich Lindemann Collection, Center for the History of Medicine, Francis A. Countway Library of Medicine, Boston, MA]
174. Schneider, Hartmut, Director, Department of Social Psychiatry, Zentralinstitüt für Zeelisches Gesundheit, Mannheim, West Germany; interview at Institüt by David G. Satin, 10/26/1984. [Tape 88, Caddy 6, Box X, Lindemann Collection, Center for the History of Medicine, Francis A. Countway Library of Medicine, Boston, MA]
175. Lindemann, Erich, letter to Heinz Häfner, Der Direktor Der Socialpsychiatrischen Klinik Der Universität Heidelberg, 11/10/1972, p. 1. [folder "Heidelberg", Box IV 1 + 2, Erich Lindemann Collection, Center for the History of Medicine, Francis A. Countway Library of Medicine, Boston, MA]:

> die vielschichtige [many layered] Struktur der Konfliktsituation klar zu erfassen, sodass wir persoenliche und Motivationsfaktoren von institutionellen Prozessen und von den Resultaten eines relativ raschen Kulturwandels im Gebiet der Sozialpsychiatrie trennen konnten. Er [Niels Pörksen] . . . zu der Zahl der unruhigen innovationssuchenden jungen Leuten gehoert, die oft ein neues Prinzip wie etwa das der verantwortlichen Anteilnahme aller Mitglieder einer Sozialgruppe überhastig bewerklichen moechten, und dabei sehr wichtige Faktoren untershaetzen, die in besonderen Bereichen wie etwa eine klinishche Abteilung die Praesenze eine klare autoritative Struktur notwendig machen.
>
> Die Gemeinde Psychiatrie ist noch so jung, und die Begegnung mit vielen Autoritaetspersonen in diesem Gebiet so stressvoll, dass die Neigung, sich mit juengeren gleichgesinnten Leuten zu umgeben und sich auf ihrer anerkennung zu verlassen sehr verstaendlich ist. . . . Jedenfalls wuerde es sehr schade sein, wenn dieser Versuch ein umfassendes Programm zu entfalten nach so viel Bemuehungen aufgeben werden muesste.

176. Plog, Ursula, 10/11/1984, *ibid*
177. Lindemann, Erich, letter to Hamburg, David, Stanford Univerity Medical Center, 8/16/1966. [folder "Correspondence—David Hamburg", Box IV 1 + 2, Erich Lindemann Collection, Center for the History of Medicine, Countway Library of Medicine, Boston, MA]
178. Lindemann, Erich, letter to Schwanenberg, Prof. Enno, University of Frankfurt, Germany, 5/30/1973. [Lindau Group Correspondence—file #106,

Erich Lindemann Collection, Center for the History of Medicine, Francis A. Countway Library of Medicine, Boston, MA] Participants included Peter Kutter, Joachim Moller, Ruth Moeller, Cornelia Schlegel, Charlotte Ruckdeschel, Olaf Martinsen-Larsen, Druckschlager, Otto Brink, Lili Schulz, Rolf Feticher, Erich Leliau, Klaus Jung, Bengt Berggren, Wolfgang Widok.

179. Lindemann, Erich, letter to Craton-Neher, Jean, M.D., Palo Alto, CA, 4/1969. [folder "Correspondence 1969", Box IV 1+2, Erich Lindemann Collection, Center for the History of Medicine, Countway Library of Medicine, Boston, MA]

180. Lindemann, Erich, letter to Stolze, Dr. med Helmuth, München, 4/10/1973: ... Lindauer Tage ... Meine Teilnahme an diesen Veranstaltungen war mir immer ein Hochpunkt der Erlebniskette im Laufe des Jahres, und es tut mir doch wieder sehr Leid nicht dabei sein su koennen". [folder "Stolze Correspondence", Box IV 1+2, Erich Lindemann Collection, Center for the History of Medicine, Countway Library of Medicine, Boston, MA]

181. Lindemann, Erich at Willow Road, Palo Alto, CA, letter to Stolze, Helmuth, 4/24/1974: "Sie und die lieben Freunde unter der Fakultaet und der Teilnehmer bereiten sich vor auf eines der schoensten Ereignisse in der aertlich-wissenschaftlichen Welt Deutschlands. Es wuerde mir viel bedeuten, wenn ich mochmal teilnehmen koennte an dieser so sorgfaeltig geplannten und so schoen ausgefuehrten Gemeinsamkeit". Stolze, Helmuth, München, letter to Lindemann, Erich, Oak Creeek Drive, Palo Alto, CA, 4/25/1974: ... Sie können sich denken, mit welchem Bedauern ich immer wider daran denke, dass Sie damals und seither nich mehr zu uns Kommen konnten.¶Sie sollen aber wissen, dass wir uns in unveränderter Weise mit Ihnen verbunden fühlen und jedes Mal, wenn wir in Lindau zusammenkommen, dankbar daran denken, wieviel wir im Laufe der Jahre an Anregungen von Ihnen bekommen haben". [folder "Stolze Correspondence", Box IV 1+2, Erich Lindemann Collection, Center for the History of Medicine, Countway Library of Medicine, Boston, MA]

182. Lindemann, Erich, letter to SatyaNand, Prof. David, All India Medical Institute, Department of Psychiatry, New Delhi, India, 8/18/1966. [folder "Correspondence—India 1966-1974", p. 1. Box IV 1+2, Erich Lindemann Collection, Center for the History of Medicine, Countway Library of Medicine, Boston, MA]

183. Churchill, Edward D., M.D., John Homans Professor of Surgery, HMS; Chief of the General Surgical Services, MGH, "Reflections on the Challenge to the Medical Profession in India", *New England Journal of Medicine* 259: 551–557 (9/18/1958), p. 1: ... [footnote] The writer spent the first three months of 1958 in India on an assignment primarily concerned with the education and training of surgeons in and for India. This was a detail of the program of far greater scope being conducted by the Rockefeller Foundation".

Allen, LeRoy R., M.D., The Rockefeller Foundation, New York, letter to Lindemann, Erich, Stanford Medical Center, 9/28/1966. [folder "Correspondence—India 1966-1974", p. 1. Box IV 1+2, Erich Lindemann Collection, Center for the History of Medicine, Countway Library of Medicine, Boston, MA]

184.
- Lindemann, Erich, letter to Galdston, Dr. Iago, Chief, Psychiatric Training, State of Connecticut, Department of Mental Health, 1/3/1966. [folder "GENERAL CORRESPONDENCE—A,B,C 1966", Box IV 1+2, Erich Lindemann Collection, Center for the History of Medicine,

294   *Counterrevolution of Biology and Business*

        Countway Library of Medicine, Boston, MA]: "about your journey to India . . . My own sojourn is now expected to take place from Stanford in the late fall of 1966 and extend to the end of their academic year sometime in May, 1967".

- Lindemann, Erich, letter to SatyaNand, Professor David, All India Medical Institute, Department of Psychiatry, New Delhi, India, 8/18/1966, p. 2. [folder "Correspondence—India 1966–1974", Box IV 1+2, Erich Lindemann Collection, Center for the History of Medicine, Countway Library of Medicine, Boston, MA]: "These developments [illness] are most frustrating as they have cast some uncertainty on my activities in the future, certainly those in distant countries with different patterns of medical care . . . I am still not reconciled to getting older and I am also basically an optimist so I hope in the near future to have a harmless explanation for all [p. 1] my symptoms".
- Lindemann, Erich, Visiting Professor, to LeRoy R. Allen, M.D., New Delhi, India, 10/28/1966. [folder "Correspondence—India 1966–1974", Box IV 1+2, Erich Lindemann Collection, Center for the History of Medicine, Countway Library of Medicine, Boston, MA]: . . . I was most unhappy that our good plans for this winter have been spoiled by the illness which I contracted . . . I wrote Professor Satya . . . that in all probability I cannot come this winter . . . I am still anxious to make good on our plans because of my keen interest in the Indian culture, in the program at New Delhi, at the New Delhi Institute, and because of my friends there . . . you might wish to consider another person to serve as consultant. . . . Dr. John Spiegel . . . now at Brandeis University at the Institute for the Study of Aggression".
- Lindemann, Erich, letter to Balbaky, Yasin, M.D., student at HSPH, 12/8/1966, p. 2. [folder "GENERAL CORRESPONDENCE A+B 1967", Box IV 1+2, Erich Lindemann Collection, Center for the History of Medicine, Countway Library of Medicine, Boston, MA]: "My plan to go to India this winter had to be delayed and perhaps even canceled because of a rather severe polyneuritis which affected me ever since last summer".
- Lindemann, Erich, Visiting Professor, letter to Teja, Dr. J.S., Assistant Professor, Department of Psychiatry, Postgraduate Institute of Medical Education and Research, Chandigarh, India, 12/11/1969. [folder "Correspondence—India 1966–1974", Box IV 1+2, Erich Lindemann Collection, Center for the History of Medicine, Countway Library of Medicine, Boston, MA]: "I have fond memories about the meeting of the [Indian Psychiatric] Society which I was privileged to attend in Calcutta in the winter of 1960".
- Lindemann, Erich, letter to Satyanand, Prof. David, New Delhi, India, 2/25/1970. [folder "Correspondence—India 1966–1974", Box IV 1+2, Erich Lindemann Collection, Center for the History of Medicine, Countway Library of Medicine, Boston, MA]: "I still regret that my condition of health did not allow me to work closely with you through a period in New Delhi".

185. Lindemann, Erich, handwritten note to Hamburg, David, 1/1/1965. [folder "Correspondence—David Hamburg", Box IV 1+2, Erich Lindemann Collection, Center for the History of Medicine, Countway Library of Medicine, Boston, MA]: "Dear David: . . . It is good of you to look into the matter of the license . . . there might be a time when I might be impeded by my state of health and age in lecturing and attending to academic matters, so that

I would be embarrassed in accepting any remuneration from the University. Yet I might still be quite able to do effective Psychotherapy".
186. Lydia Rapoport, letter to Lindemann, 10/19/1965. [folder "Correspondence 1965", Box IIIA 1-3, Lindemann Collection, Center for the History of Medicine, Francis A. Countway Library of Medicine, Boston, MA]
187. Lindemann, letter to Roy Grinker, M.D., 11/4/1965, noting that Judd Marmor sponsored him in letters dated 9/3 and 11/4 1965. [folder "Correspondence 1965", Box IIIA 1-3, Lindemann Collection, Center for the History of Medicine, Francis A. Countway Library of Medicine, Boston, MA]
188. Jeffress, J. Elizabeth, letter to Lindemann, Erich, 11/10/1965 regarding the talk on 2/16/1966. [folder "Correspondence 1965", Box IIIA 1-3, Lindemann Collection, Center for the History of Medicine, Francis A. Countway Library of Medicine, Boston, MA]
189. Goldston, Stephen E., Ed.D., Acting Chief to Lindemann regarding a site visit in New York City including the Jewish Board of Guardians, 11/17/1965. [folder "Correspondence 1965", Box IIIA 1-3, Lindemann Collection, Center for the History of Medicine, Francis A. Countway Library of Medicine, Boston, MA]
190. Parad, Howard J., Director of the Smith College School for Social Work, letter to Lindemann, 12/6/1965. [folder "Correspondence 1965", Box IIIA 1-3, Lindemann Collection, Center for the History Of Medicine, Francis A. Countway Library of Medicine, Boston, MA]
191. Stein, Sherry, letter to Lindemann, 11/9/1965. [folder "Correspondence 1965", Box IIIA 1-3, Lindemann Collection, Center for the History Of Medicine, Francis A. Countway Library of Medicine, Boston, MA]
192. Krieger, George, letter to Lindemann, 12/6/1965. [folder "Correspondence 1965", Box IIIA 1-3, Lindemann Collection, Center for the History of Medicine, Francis A. Countway Library of Medicine, Boston, MA]
193. Lindemann, Erich, "MENTAL HEALTH ASPECTS OF RAPID SOCIAL CHANGE", Conference at the East-West Institute, Honolulu, Hawaii, 3/1966 (typescript with Lindemann's hand-written editing). [file #91; "Lindemann: Mental Health Aspects of Rapid Social Change 1966", Box XII #3, Lindemann Collection, Center for the History of Medicine, Francis A. Countway Library of Medicine, Harvard Medical School, Boston, MA]:

> The sociology of knowledge has taught us to distinguish different types of professional organizations. Among psychiatrists there are at least [p. 1] two forms of interest and professional behavior. One group, working in mental hospitals where persons with disturbed behavior have been segregated for the protection of others and to some degree of themselves has been concerned with methods of case finding, prediction of case loads in order to make adequate provision of hospital facilities, and determination of the rates of return of persons who are able to reenter the community. Those psychiatrists are interested particularly in severe cases requiring maximum effort for their care and treatment. The interests characterizing the psychiatrists of the second group started from the study of the psychogenic forms of somatic disorders. Their initial interest was in hypnosis and psychotherapy, but extended to a dynamic interpretation of the social and motivational factors leading to disordered behavior. Recently their concern with the social processes influencing motivation and disturbed emotional equilibrium has developed into a study of events of social change. Those interests have also led to the study of the effect of early psychological experience on personality growth and development . . . in

the hope of finding clues to preventive measures in infant care, family organization and social planning. [p. 2]

194. Caudill, William, Ph.D., letter to Lindemann, 10/12/1965. [folder "Correspondence 1965", Box IIIA 1–3, Lindemann Collection, Center for the History Of Medicine, Francis A. Countway Library of Medicine, Boston, MA]; See Lindemann, Erich, "Mental Health Aspects of Rapid Social Change", in Caudill, William and Tsung-Yi LIn (eds.) *Mental Health Research in Asia and the Pacific* (Honolulu: East-West Center Press, 1969), pp. 478–487
195. Lindemann, Erich, letter to Seeley, Prof. John R., Center for the Study of Democratic Institutions, Santa Barbara, CA, 10/10/1967. [folder "Correspondence re Weisbaden Congress 1966–67", Box IV 1+2, Erich Lindemann Collection, Center for the History of Medicine, Countway Library of Medicine, Boston, MA]
196. Lindemann, Erich, 3/19/1968, *ibid*, p. 2
197. Bennett, Chet, Office of the Dean, Graduate School, Boston University, letter to Lindemann, Erich, 5/6/1969. [folder "Correspondence 1969", Box IV 1+2, Erich Lindemann Collection, Center for the History of Medicine, Countway Library of Medicine, Boston, MA]
198. Reported by Elizabeth B. Lindemann. [Box VIII, Erich Lindemann Collection, Center for the History of Medicine, Countway Library of Medicine, Boston, MA]
199. Folder "Vaughan Warren t.", David G. Satin files, Newton, MA:

    4/5/71 memo
    "From: Elsie Tagroff, R.N.
    Warren T. Vaughan, M.D.
    Subject: Payment to Erich Lindemann, M.D., for Professional Educational Services...
    Professional Educational Sessions at $50.00/session.
    Department of Psychiatry, professional Staff, 2 sessions December 10, January 21,28, February 4, 11, 18, 25,
    March 4, 11, 18, 25, April 1
    Community Mental Health Center In-Service Training and Education, 5 sessions
    January 28, February 11, 25, March 11, 25".
    4/5/71 memo
    "To:... Chairman: Continuing Education Committee
    Department of Psychiatry
    From: Elsie Taboroff, R.N.
    In-Service Educator
    Re: Consultation Seminar conducted by Mrs. Erich Lindemann for six (6) sessions bimontlhy from January 28th to April 1, 1971
    Sessions were open to Center staff who were actively engaged or interested in consulting work. Participants included both social work and nursing staff form partial care, alcohol, adolescent, in-patient, and referral programs...
    Recommendation: To offer consultation seminar again next year and offer Mrs. Lindemann a fee for services".

200. Lindemann, Erich, *Daystar: News Journal of Neurosis, Psychosis and Epilepsy*, 11/1971, p. 2–3. [Box XII 1 folder 110b, Erich Lindemann Collection, Center for the History of Medicine, Francis A. Countway Library of Medicine, Boston, MA]
201. Academy of Psychoanalysis (Fellow), American Academy of Arts and Sciences, American Academy of Political and Social Science, American

Anthropological Association, American Association for the Advancement of Science, American Association of Applied Anthropology, American Child Guidance Association, American Geographical Society, American Medical Association, American Neurological Association, American Orthopsychiatric Association (Fellow), American Psychiatric Association (Life Fellow, Chairman of the Committee on Preventive Psychiatry), American Psychoanalytic Association (Life Membership), American Psychological Association (Fellow and member of the Division of Community Psychology and Society for the Psychological Study of Social Issues), American Psychopathological Association, American Psychosomatic Society (Council member), American Public Health Association, American Sociological Association, Association for Research in Nervous and Mental Diseases, Boston Psychoanalytic Society and Institute (President 1943–1946, Life Membership), *Community Mental Health Journal* (Editorial Board), Delta Omega (The Honorary Public Health Society), *Family Process* (Board of Advisory Editors), Greater Boston Committee for a Sane Nuclear Policy, Group for the Advancement of Psychiatry (Chairman of the Committee on Preventive Psychiatry), Indian Psychiatric Society, Institute of Pastoral Care (member of the Board of Governors), Massachusetts Public Health Association, Massachusetts Society for Mental Hygiene, National Association for the Advancement of Colored People, National Association for the Study of Education, Neurosciences Research Foundation (Incorporator), New England Psychological Association, New England Society of Psychiatry, New York Academy of Science, *Pastoral Psychology* (Editorial Advisory Board), Physicians for Social Responsibility (Sponsor), Society for the Psychological Study of Social Issues (Institute for Social Research, University of Michigan), The Physicians Forum, World Federation for Mental Health, World Health Organization (member of the Division of Mental Health's Expert Advisory Panel on Mental Health)
202. Gonda, Thomas, interview by David G. Satin at the Stanford Department of Psychiatry, 12/17/1979. [Erich Lindemann Collection, Center for the History of Medicine, Countway Library of Medicine, Boston, MA]
203. Siegel, Alberta—Department of Psychiatry, Stanford Medical Center, Interview at Stanford Medical Center by David G. Satin, M.D., 12/20/1979. [Caddy 6, Box 4, X, Erich Lindemann Collection, Center for the History of Medicine, Countway Library of Medicine, Boston, MA]
204. Haylett, Clarice, Psychiatric Consultation and Education Administrator, Mental Health Service, San Mateo Health Department, interview by David G. Satin at her home in Palo Alto, CA, 12/17/1979. [Erich Lindemann Collection, Center for the History of Medicine, Francis A. Countway Library of Medicine, Boston, MA]
205. Lindemann, Erich, "Institutional Crises", talk in the San Mateo County, CA Mental Health Services course taught by Dr. Clarice Haylett [Director of Mental Health.]; notes by Dr. Haylett, edited by Elizabeth B. Lindemann, 3/17/1970. [Box XII 2 folder "Lindemann Reflections on Community Mental Health, March '70", Erich Lindemann Collection, Center for the History of Medicine, Francis A. Countway Library of Medicine, Boston, MA]
206. Liederman, Gloria, interview by David G. Satin at the Peninsula Chilrens Center, CA, 12/18/1979. [Caddy 4, Box 4, X, Lindemann Collection, Center for the History of Medicine, Francis A. Countway Library of Medicine, Boston, MA]
207. Liederman, Gloria, 12/18/1979, *ibid*
208. Lindemann, Erich, 6/15,22/1974, *ibid*; Siegel, Alberta, 12/20/1979, *ibid*; Daniels, David, interview by David G. Satin, Daniels office, Palo Alto, CA,

12/20/1979. [Erich Lindemann Collection, Center for the History of Medicine, Countway Library of Medicine, Boston, MA]
209. Mandell, Arnold J., 1974, *ibid*
210. Caplan, Lee, social worker in the Student Health Service, and Webber, William, psychiatrist and original member of the Lindemann Group, Stanford Medical Center, interview by David G. Satin at Stanford Medical Center, Palo Alto, CA, 12/1979. [Erich Lindemann Collection, Center for the History of Medicine, Francis A. Countway Library of Medicine, Boston, MA]
211. Hambug, David, M.D., interview by David G. Satin at the Institute of Medicine, Washington, DC., 1/26/1979. [Caddy 3, Box 4, X, Lindemann Collection, Center for the History of Medicine, Countway Library of Medicine, Boston, MA]
212. Lindemann, Erich, letter to Hamburg, Dr. David, Stanford University School of Medicine, 6/17/1965. [folder "Correspondence—David Hamburg", Box IV 1+2, Erich Lindemann Collection, Center for the History of Medicine, Countway Library of Medicine, Boston, MA]
213. Lindemann, Elizabeth B., 3/30/2004, *ibid*
214. Hamburg, David A., M.D., Professor and Executive Head, Department of Psychiatry, Stanford University School of Medicine, letter to Lindemann, Erich [in the University of Tübingen], 6/2/1966, p. 2. [folder "Correspondence 1966 Misc", Box IV 1+2, Erich Lindemann Collection, Center for the History of Medicine, Countway Library of Medicine, Boston, MA]
215. Hamburg, David A, M.D., letter to Lindemann, Erich, HMS, MGH, 7/27/1965: "I am awfully glad that it occurred to me about the Paul house and that you have worked it out with them . . . We are planning our second department retreat . . . It . . . was postponed with the primary motivation being for you to attend . . . it would be a very good occasion for the members of the full time faculty . . . to get better acquainted with you".; Lindemann, Erich, letter to Hamburg, David, M.D., Stanford University Medical Center, 8/2/1965: "of course I will be delighted to participate in the special faculty retreat and am looking forward to the opportunity of getting acquainted with the whole group . . . Both Betty and I consider our move into your orbit a most significant and rewarding new chapter in our lives. . . ". [folder "Correspondence—David Hamburg", Box IV 1+2, Erich Lindemann Collection, Center for the History of Medicine, Countway Library of Medicine, Boston, MA]
216. Lindemann, Erich (from his Boston apartment), letter to Hamburg, Davie, 3/15/1969. [folder "Correspondence—David Hamburg", Box IV 1+2, Erich Lindemann Collection, Center for the History of Medicine, Countway Library of Medicine, Boston, MA]
217. Lindemann, Erich, Professor Emeritus of Psychiatry, Harvard University, letter to Mitnick, Dr. Leonard, NIMH, 1/17/1967. [folder "Correspondence—David Hamburg", Box IV 1+2, Erich Lindemann Collection, Center for the History of Medicine, Countway Library of Medicine, Boston, MA]: "application of Professor David Hamburg . . . special fellowship . . . to carry out his plan of bringing together . . . the material . . . in the field of crisis theory and stress research . . . to buttress the practical work in the field of community mental health and psychiatric participation in social action, which is going ahead now quite without adequate theoretical qualification and discipline . . . much needed for the scientific basis of preventive psychiatry".
218. Liederman, Gloria, 12/18/1979, *ibid*
219. Hilgard, Josephine, M.D., Department of Psychiatry, Stanford Medical Center, interview by David G. Satin at Stanford Medical Center, Palo Alto,

CA, 12/17/1979. [Erich Lindemann Collection, Center for the History of Medicine, Francis A. Countway Library of Medicine, Boston, MA]
220. Lindemann, Elizabeth, interview by David G. Satin, M.D. 1/18/80 at Wellesley, MA. [Caddy 4, Box 4, X, Erich Lindemann Collection, Center for the History of Medicine, Francis A. Countway Library of Medicine, Boston, MA]
221. Haylett, Clarice, 12/17/1979, *ibid*
222. Lindemann, Elizabeth B., interviews by David G. Satin in Wellesley and Boston, MA, 6/27/1978, 11/1978, 8/1979. [Erich Lindemann Collection, Center for the History of Medicine, Countway Library of Medicine, Boston, MA]
223. Lindemann, Elizabeth Brainerd, Interviews and letters with David G. Satin, M.D., 8/14/99–8/22/06. [David G. Satin, M.D. files, Lindemann Collection, Newton, MA]
224. Lindemann, Elizabeth B., 3/30/2004, *ibid*
225. Daniels, David, 12/20/1979, *ibid*
226. Hilgard, Josephine, 12/17/1979, *ibid*
227. Lindemann, Elizabeth B., 3/30/2004, *ibid*
228. Lindemann, Elizabeth B., 6/27/1978, 11/1978, 8/1979, *ibid*
229. Haylett, Clarice, 12/17/1979, *ibid*
230. Liederman, Gloria, 12/18/1979, *ibid*
231. Gonda, Thomas, 12/17/1979, *ibid*
232. Moos, Rudolf H., Prof. of Psychology, and Director of the Social Psychology Laboratory, Stanford University School of Medicine and Veterans Administration Medical Center, Palo Alto, CA: *American Journal of Community Psychology*, 12:5 (1984), pp. 513–514
233. Dorosin, David, M.D., Assistant Professor, Department of Psychiatry, Stanford University School of Medicine, letter to Lindemann, Erich, 8/15/1967. [folder "GENERAL CORRESPONDENCE A+B 1967", Box IV 1+2, Erich Lindemann Collection, Center for the History of Medicine, Countway Library of Medicine, Boston, MA]
234. Lindemann, Erich, letter to Caplan, Gerald, M.D., Director, Laboratory of Community Psychiatry, HMS, 3/22/1971. [folder "Correspondence—1970", Box IV 1+2, Erich Lindemann Collection, Center for the History of Medicine, Francis A. Countway Library of Medicine, Boston, MA]
235. Daniels, David, 12/20/1979, *ibid*
236. Caplan, Lee, social worker in the Student Health Service, and Webber, William, psychiatrist and original member of the Lindemann Group, Stanford Medical Center, interview by David G. Satin at Stanford Medical Center, Palo Alto, CA, 12/1979. [Erich Lindemann Collection, Center for the History of Medicine, Francis A. Countway Library of Medicine, Boston, MA]
237. Lindemann, Elizabeth B., 8/14/99–8/22/06, *ibid*
238. Caplan, Lee, 12/1979, *ibid*
239. Lindemann, Erich, letter to Andreopoulos, Mr. S., Stanford University News Bureau, 2/1/1966. [folder "Correspondence 1966 Misc", Box IV 1+2, Erich Lindemann Collection, Center for the History of Medicine, Countway Library of Medicine, Boston, MA]
240. Lindemann, Erich, memo to Daniels, David with copies to Golde, Peggy and Torrey, Fuller, 11/1/1967. [folder "GENERAL CORRESPONDENCE L 1967", Box IV 1+2, Erich Lindemann Collection, Center for the History of Medicine, Countway Library of Medicine, Boston, MA]
241. Lindemann, Erich: Consultation Training Seminar, Mental healthUnit, San Mateo County Health Department, California, 3/17/1970. [videotape,

Erich Lindemann Collection, Center for the History of Medicine, Francis A. Countway Library of Medicine, Boston, MA]
242. Lindemann, Erich, letter to Golde, Dr. Peggy (Stanford anthropology professor), 11/11/1967. [folder "GENERAL CORRESPONDENCE G+H 1967", Box IV 1+2, Erich Lindemann Collection, Center for the History of Medicine, Countway Library of Medicine, Boston, MA]
243. "COMMUNITY SERVICES LIAISON COMMITTEE summary of Meeting of October 2, 1967", p. 1. [folder "Stanford Community Services Planning '61-'65", Box IV 3+4+5, Erich Lindemann Collection, Center for the History of Medicine, Francis A. Countway Library of Medicine, Boston, MA]
244. Stanford School of Medicine (1): Problems over More than Money", 2/12/1971. [folder "Stanford Community Services Planning '61-'65", Box IV 3+4+5, Erich Lindemann Collection, Center for the History of Medicine, Francis A. Countway Library of Medicine, Boston, MA]
245. Stanford School of Medicine (1): Problems over More than Money", 2/26/1971. [folder "Stanford Community Services Planning '61-'65", Box IV 3+4+5, Erich Lindemann Collection, Center for the History of Medicine, Francis A. Countway Library of Medicine, Boston, MA]
246. Almond, Richard and Astrachan, Boris, "Social System Training for Psychiatric Residents", *Psychiatry: Journal for the Study of Interpersonal Processes 32* no. 3: 277–291 (8/1969), p. 277
247. Lindemann, Erich, letter to Caplan, Gerald, M.D., 3/22/1971: "Our Residents are very much interested in community issues . . .". [folder "Correspondence—1970", Box IV 1+2, Erich Lindemann Collection, Center for the History of Medicine, Francis A. Countway Library of Medicine, Boston, MA]
248. Hilgard, Josephine ("Josie"), M.D., Department of Psychiatry, Stanford Medical Center: interview by David G. Satin at Stanford Medical Center, Palo Alto, CA, 12/18/1979. [Erich Lindemann Collection, Center for the History of Medicine, Francis A. Countway Library of Medicine, Boston, MA]
249. Lindemann, Erich, M.D. and Duhl, Leonard J., M.D., Duhl interview with Lindemann, 7/13/1974. [Caddy 4, Tape 7A; 7, Erich Lindemann Collection, Center for the History of Medicine, Francis A. Countway Library of Medicine, Boston, MA]
250. Lindemann, Erich, letter from his bed at MGH to Golde Dr. Peggy, Stanford University Medical Center, 2/22/1965. [folder "Correspondence 1969", Box IV 1+2, Erich Lindemann Collection, Center for the History of Medicine, Countway Library of Medicine, Boston, MA]
251. Caplan, Lee, 12/1979, *ibid*
252. Caplan, Lee, 12/1979, *ibid*
253. Dorosin, David, Director for the Psychotherapy Service at the Stanford Medical Health Services: interview by David G. Satin at the Stanford Medical Center, Palo Alto, CA, 12/17/1979. [Box 4, X, Erich Lindemann Collection, Center for the History of Medicine, Francis A. Countway Library of Medicine, Boston, MA]
254. Daniels, David, 12/20/1979, *ibid*
255. Lindemann, Erich and Duhl, Leonard J., 7/13/1974, *ibid*
256. Daniels, David, 12/20/1979, *ibid*
257. Daniels, David, 12/20/1979, *ibid*
258. Daniels, David, 12/20/1979, *ibid*, George Gulevich administered the project, which revealed that experimental subjects functioned better (employment, discharge from hospital and return to society, etc.), while control

subjects improved more emotionally (anxiety, sense of well-being, psychiatric symptoms). Lindemann was interested.
259. Weisz, Al E., letter to Lindemann, Erich, 6/23/1970. [folder "Correspondence—1970", Box IV 1+2, Erich Lindemann Collection, Center for the History of Medicine, Francis A. Countway Library of Medicine, Boston, MA]
260. Katchadourian, Herant, interview by David G. Satin at Katchadourian's office, Stanford Medical Center, Palo Alto, CA, 12/19/1979. [Erich Lindemann Collection, Center for the History of Medicine, Francis A. Countway Library of Medicine, Boston, MA]
261. Hamburg, David A., memo to Faculty, Staff, and Friends of the Department of Psychiatry, 8/11/1972. [folder "Hamburg—Retirement Report", box IV 3+4+5, Erich Lindemann Collection, Center for the History of Medicine, Countway Library of Medicine, Boston, MA]
262. Hamburg, David A., to Lindemann, Erich, 4/17/1968. [folder "Correspondence 1968", Box IV 1+2, Erich Lindemann Collection, Center for the History of Medicine, Francis A. Countway Library of Medicine, Boston, MA]
263. Lindemann, Erich, M.D. and Daniels, David, M.D. memo to The First-Year Residents, 2/8/1966. [folder "Stanford—Social Psychiatry Seminar 1966–1971", Box IV 3+4+5, Erich Lindemann Collection, Center for the History of Medicine, Countway Library of Medicine, Boston, MA]
264. Lindemann, Erich, letter to Coffey, Hubert S., Professor of Psychology, Psychology Clinic, University of California, Berkeley, CA [who Lindemann had brought to the MGH in the past], 3/19/1968, p. 1. [folder "Correspondence 1968", Box IV 1+2, Erich Lindemann Collection, Center for the History of Medicine, Countway Library of Medicine, Boston, MA]
265. Drs. Lindemann, Moos, Golde, and Katchadourian, memo to Dr. P. H. Leiderman, 4/18/1967. [folder "Stanford—Social Psychiatry Seminar 1966–1971", box IV 3+4+5, Erich Lindemann Collection, Center for the History of Medicine, Countway Library of Medicine, Boston, MA]
266. Lindemann, Erich, 3/19/1968, *ibid*, p. 1:
"I am looking forward happily to my involvement with . . . the East Palo Alto project [at Stanford]".
267. Lindemann, Elizabeth Brainerd, 8/17/2004 telephone interview with David G. Satin. [David G. Satin, M.D. files, Lindemann Collection, Newton, MA]
268. Lindemann, Elizabeth B. letter to Vaughan, Warren, M.D., 7/28/1990. [Elizabeth Lindemann files—file #109-B P-W A-M (EL Contemporaries), David G. Satin files, Newton, MA]
269. Lindemann, Elizabeth Brainerd, 8/20/2004 telephone interview with David G. Satin. [David G. Satin, M.D. files, Lindemann Collection, Newton, MA]
270. Lindemann, Elizabeth B., 8/14/99–8/22/06, *ibid*
271. [folder "Dissent", Box IV 3+4+5, Erich Lindemann Collection, Center for the History of Medicine, Countway Library of Medicine, Boston, MA]
272. Statement of faculty supporting medical student boycott of military service in Viet Nam, 4/1967. [CMH References & Notes (computer), Erich Lindemann Collection, Center for the History of Medicine, Countway Library of Medicine, Boston, MA]
273. Borson, Soo, MD, Professor of Psychiatry and Behavioral Sciences, Director of Geriatric and Family Services Clinic and the ADRC Satellite, University of Washington, e-mail message to David G. Satin, 1/15/2005. [CMH References and Notes (computer), Erich Lindemann Collection, Center for the History of Medicine, Countway Library of Medicine, Boston, MA]
274. Lindemann, Erich, "The Psychiatrist as Mediator", Talk and discussion at the Cowell Health Center [student-staff health center, Stanford Medical

Center], 3/20/1970. [Box XII 2 folder "The Psychiatrist as Mediator 1970", Erich Lindemann Collection, Center for the History of Medicine, Francis A. Countway Library of Medicine, Boston, MA]
275. Lindemann, Erich, publicity comment on *The Healing Community: Dynamics of the Therapeutic Milieu* by Richard Almond, M.D., undated—6–7/1974. [folder "Correspondence—1974", Box IV 1+2, Erich Lindemann Collection, Center for the History of Medicine, Countway Library of Medicine, Boston, MA]
276. Lindemann, Erich, Professor of Psychiatry, *emeritus*, Harvard University, Visiting Professor of Psychiatry, Stanford University, Foreword to Plöger, Andreas *The Therapeutic Community in Psychotherapy and Social Psychiatry—Theory and Practice*. [Satin, David G., Community Mental Health and Erich Lindemann files, Newton, MA]
277. Siegel, Alberta, 12/20/1979, *ibid*
278. Eulau, Cleo, Chief Social Worker, Child Psychiatry Unit, Stanford Medical Center: interviewed (at Stanford Med Center) by David G. Satin, M.D., 12/19/1979. [Caddy 2, Box 4, X, Erich Lindemann Collection, Center for the History of Medicine, Francis A. Countway Library of Medicine, Boston, MA]
279. Dorosin, David, 12/17/1979, *ibid*
280. "We have just gone through the annual ceremony of reappointing you as Visiting Professor and certainly look forward to having you with us for whatever portion of the academic year you feel would [p. 1] be appropriate . . . the plan of dividing the year roughly half and half between Boston and Stanford would be highly agreeable". Hamburg, David A., M.D., Professor and Executive Head, Department of Psychiatry, Stanford University School of Medicine, letter to Lindemann, Erich at his apartment in Boston, 5/2/1969, p. 2

"Interest in community and social psychiatry seems to be increasing greatly within the department [of Psychiatry, Stanford Medical School] and your contributions will be most important". Adams, John E., MD., Special Assistant to the Director, National Institute of Mental Health, letter to Lindemann, Erich, 9/16/1969

"We miss you badly here . . . the department is . . . not quiet the same—lacks the ultimate credibility that someone like you gave it". Torrey, [E.] Fuller, letter to Lindemann, Erich, 1/12/1969, p. 1

"Of course I am sorry not to have you here to learn from. I value the perspective and experience you have, and it keeps my naivite [sic] in good focus!" Torrey, [E.] Fuller, letter to Lindemann, Erich, 4/9/1969

"I am delighted at the prospect! [of your return to Stanford] Not only do I have backlog of theoretical issues to pick your brain on, but I have you as a clinical supervisor as well so I can benefit from your wisdom in that sphere too. I will keep my most difficult case to discuss with you! I would say that you now qualify as an unprecedented authority on stress + coping as well, by dint of much first-hand experience"., Torrey, [E.] Fuller, letter to Lindemann, Erich, 7/1/1969

Of course we want you back . . . Many of us miss your wisdom and wish you well. . . ", Daniels, David, letter to Lindemann, Erich, 1/12/1969

"I certainly miss your stimulation and contributions to this Department—and what is more, your friendship. Many people have said how they miss your sage comments at the clinical symposia. Indeed, many of the sessions lack that extra sparkle and insight which you gave them last year. So we all hope for your speedy recovery and are warmly anticipating your arrival out here". Melges, Fred, Los Altos, CA, letter to Lindemann, Erich, 1/11/1969, p. 1

"and hope to be back at Stanford in the near future. We need you badly"., Kaplan, David M., Division of Clinical Social Work, Department of Preventive Medicine, Stanford University School of Medicine, letter to Lindemann, Erich, 4/4/1969

"We all miss you very much and are impatient to have you back with us"., Solomon, George F., M.D., Clinical Associate Professor, Chief, Psychiatry Training and Research Section, Veterans Administration Hospital, Palo Alto/Stanford University School of Medicine, letter to Lindemann, Erich, 1/7/1969

"All of us in the department miss you a great deal and are very sorry that you had to cancel your plans to spend a few months with us"., Moos, Rudy, letter to Lindemann, Erich, 2/2/1969, p. 4

"Six students have come in to 'register' since fall . . . They chiefly are interested in a course in 'Erich Lindemann', they tell me with embarrassed smiles. A course in Charisma is what they'll really get"., Golde, Dr. Peggy, Assistant Professor of Psychiatry, Stanford University School of Medicine, letter to Lindemann, Erich, 11/18/1968.

[folder "Correspondence 1969", Box IV 1+2, Erich Lindemann Collection, Center for the History of Medicine, Countway Library of Medicine, Boston, MA]

281. Nemiah, John C., M.D., Professor of Psychiatry HMS and Psychiatrist-in-Chief, Beth Israel Hospital, Boston, letter to Lindemann, Erich, Visiting Professor of Psychiatry, Stanford University Medical Center, 4/7/1971. [folder "Correspondence—1970", Box IV 1+2, Erich Lindemann Collection, Center for the History of Medicine, Francis A. Countway Library of Medicine, Boston, MA]
282. Almond, Richard and Barbara, interview by David G. Satin at their home in Palo Alto, CA, 12/19/1979. [Erich Lindemann Collection, Center for the History of Medicine, Countway Library of Medicine, Boston, MA]
283. Daniels, David, 12/20/1979, *ibid*
284. Box X 2, Lindemann Collection, Center for the History of Medicine, Countway Library of Medicine, Boston, MA
285. Lindemann, Erich, MD, Duhl, Leonard J., M.D., Erich Lindemann, Leonard Duhl Interviews 8/6/1974. [Caddy 4, Tape 12A+13B, Erich Lindemann Collection, Center for the History of Medicine, Francis A. Countway Library of Medicine, Boston, MA]
286. Hamburg, David A., M.D., Professor of Psychiatry, Stanford University Medical Center, letter to Lindemann, Erich, Visiting Professor, Stanford University School of Medicine, 1/9/1973. [folder "Correspondence—David Hamburg", Box IV 1+2, Erich Lindemann Collection, Center for the History of Medicine, Countway Library of Medicine, Boston, MA]: "my resignation from the chairmanship . . . Now I am moving on to the research and teaching activities which I have had to neglect during the past few years when I had so much administrative responsibility . . . We have just moved into the new Laboratory of Stress and Conflict [at the Department of Psychiatry, Stanford University] . . . I feel quite lucky to have this opportunity".
287. Lindemann, Elizabeth Brainerd, 2/2/2005 phone interview with David G. Satin. [David G. Satin files, Newton, MA] She remembered a meeting at his house at which, in the absence of chairs, participants sat on pillows or the floor.

288. Lindemann, Elizabeth B., interview by David G. Satin, M.D. 1/18/1980 at Wellesley, MA. [Caddy 4, Box 4, X, Erich Lindemann Collection, Center for the History of Medicine, Francis A. Countway Library of Medicine, Boston, MA]
289. Housman, William, former Chairman of Psychiatry at the University of Minnesota, and visiting fellow at the NIMH: interviewed by David G. Satin in Newton, MA, 11/7/1980. [Erich Lindemann Collection, Center for the History of Medicine, Countway Library of Medicine, Boston, MA]
290. Lindemann, Elizabeth B., 4/20/2004, *ibid*
291. Hamburg, David A., letter to Lindemann, Erich, 6/1/1968. [folder "Correspondence—David Hamburg", Box IV 1+2, Erich Lindemann Collection, Center for the History of Medicine, Countway Library of Medicine, Boston, MA]
292. Hamburg, David A., Professor, letter to Lindemann, Erich, Lakehore Road, Boston, MA, 3/11/1969. [folder "Correspondence—David Hamburg", Box IV 1+2, Erich Lindemann Collection, Center for the History of Medicine, Countway Library of Medicine, Boston, MA]
293. Hamburg, David, Department of Psychiatry, Stanford University, letter to Lindemann, Erich, Oak Creek Drive, Palo Alto, CA, 2/25/1974, p. 1. [folder "Correspondence—David Hamburg", Box IV 1+2, Erich Lindemann Collection, Center for the History of Medicine, Countway Library of Medicine, Boston, MA]
294. Lindemann, Erich (c/o his wife's family's home in Dover, MA), letter to Almond, Dr. Richard, Palo Alto, CA, 6/3/1972. [folder "Correspondence—1972", Box IV 1+2, Erich Lindemann Collection, Center for the History of Medicine, Countway Library of Medicine, Boston, MA]
295. Lindemann, Erich, Erich (c/o his wife's family's home in Dover, MA), letter to Katchadourian, Dr. Herant, Stanford, CA, 6/13/1972, p. 1. [folder "Correspondence—1972", Box IV 1+2, Erich Lindemann Collection, Center for the History of Medicine, Countway Library of Medicine, Boston, MA]
296. Lindemann, Erich (c/o his wife's family's home in Dover, MA), letter to Adams, Dr. John, Department of Psychiatry, Stanford University Medical Center, CA, 7/27/1972. [folder "Correspondence—1972", Box IV 1+2, Erich Lindemann Collection, Center for the History of Medicine, Countway Library of Medicine, Boston, MA]
297. Lindemann, Erich (c/o Needham, MA), letter to Dorosin, David, M.D., Associate Professor of Psychiatry, Palo Alto, CA, 8/18/1972. [folder "Correspondence—1972", Box IV 1+2, Erich Lindemann Collection, Center for the History of Medicine, Countway Library of Medicine, Boston, MA]
298. Lindemann, Erich (c/o wife's family's hom, Farm Street, Dover, MA) letter to Klerman, Dr. Gerald, Superintendent, Lindemann Mental Health Center, 10/4/1972. [folder "Correspondence—1972", Box IV 1+2, Erich Lindemann Collection, Center for the History of Medicine, Countway Library of Medicine, Boston, MA]
299. Lindemann, Elizabeth Brainerd, phone interview with David Satin, 6/1/2004. [David G. Satin, M.D. files, Lindemann Collection, Newton, MA]; Leiderman, Herb memo to Lindemann, Erich, 11/15/1972. Group members were: "Dave Dorosin, Cleo Eulau, Josie [Josephine] & Jack Hilgard, Leah Kaplan, Gloria & Herb Leiderman, Erich Lindemann, Fred Melges, Mickey [Albert J.] Stunkard, William Weber, Irv [Irvin] Yalom".: Ganz, Varda P., memo to Members of the Lindemann Group, 9/7/1973. [folder "'The Lindemann Group' Clinical Meetings—1973–74", box IV 3+4+5, Erich Lindemann Collection, Center for the History of Medicine, Countway Library of Medicine, Boston, MA]

300. Lindemann, Erich, MD, Duhl, Leonard J., M.D., Leonard Duhl interviews of Lindemann at his home in Palo Alto, CA. [Caddy 4, Tape 7A; 7, Erich Lindemann Collection, Center for the History of Medicine, Francis A. Countway Library of Medicine, Boston, MA]
301. Caplan, Lee, 12/1979, *ibid*
302. Lindemann, Erich, letter to Pörkesn, Niels, University of Heidelberg Sopzialpsychiatrie Klinik, Gemeindepsychiatrie, 3/22/1973. [folder "Dr. Pörksen", Box IV 1+2, Erich Lindemann Collection, Center for the History of Medicine, Francis A. Countway Library of Medicine, Boston, MA]
303. Lindemann, Erich, 4/10/1973, *ibid*:
Zu meiner Befriedigung war es moeglich in diesem Winter nochmal an der Stanford University meine Lehrtaetigkeit weiterzufueren. Da wir nah bei der Klinik wohnen, haben meine Kollegen und die junge Aerzte zugestimmt su uns in die Wohnung zu kommen, wo wir auesserst anregende Seminare und Diskussionsgruppen durchfuehren konnten. . . . . . Zu meiner Befriedigung war es moeglich in diesem Winter nochmal an der Stanford University meine Lehrtaetigkeit weiterzufueren. Da wir nah bei der Klinik wohnen, haben meine Kollegen und die junge Aerzte zugestimmt su uns in die Wohnung zu kommen, wo wir auesserst anregende Seminare und Diskussionsgruppen durchfuehren konnten. Elizberth hilft mir bei der Korrespondenz und bei der gelegeentlichen litterarischen Arbeiten. Und so ist es nicht ein so grosse Not zu Hause bleiben zu muessen, weil das Gehen, und leider auch das Sitzen im Farhstuhl, recht schwierig geworden ist . . . Ich denke gelegentlich Sie selbst wuerden einmal den Sprung nach Amerika und besonders nach Kalifornien unternehmen. Dann koennten wir uns persoenlich noch einmal wiedersehen!. . . .
304. Lindemann, Erich, 4/10/1973, *ibid*: "Leider bin ich jetzt ganz ans Bett gefesselt, und muss mein eigenes Heim als Platz meiner intellektuellen und geistigen Taetigkeit benutzen".
305. Box XII 1 Folder EBL on EL Lindemann Discussion Group, Erich Lindemann Collection, Center for the History of Medicine, Francis A. Countway Library of Medicine, Boston, MA:

- "some of us find we dislike Bruno Bettlehim as a member of a discussion group for he tends to take over and consider himself a teacher. I compare him unfavorably with our dear Erich whose wisdom was dispensed so graciously and with such enthusiastic understanding of a subject and of his fellow members. . . ". [ltr from Josephine Hilgard to EBL July 8th]
- "The Lindemann Group—Oct 8, 1985 Present: John Beletsis, Don Ehrman, Fran Gitleson, Josie Hilgard, Lee Kaplan, Phil Stein, Bill Weber . . . secretary is Gloria Leiderman. . . [p. 1] . . . [schedule for presentations includes Phil Stein on 'The Therapeutic Process and Concepts of Safety', Josie Hilgard on 'Micropsie", John Beletsis, Randy [Randall] Weingarten, Cleo Eulau, Herbert Leiderman, Bettelheim, Lee Kaplan"] . . . [p. 2] [photocopied minutes]
- "the vicissitudes of the Lindemann group at Stanford? 'The best of times' was when you and Erich were with us . . . we have coasted on a downward course . . . We took note of members who had left or were going to leave the group and know we should elect new members. . . . Tom Anders departed, . . . Lee Kaplan resigned saying she had too many commitments . . . In as much as I will be 80 next spring, I decided to continue only through the academic year . . . My good friend, and fellow psychoanalyst Fran Gitelson is 81, severely diabetic, overweight, and blind so she is resigning. . . . Those years with you and Erich were

so meaningful to me . . . Do you see the relationship of the gifted Erich to my father. . . ". [letter from Josephine Hilgard to Elizabeth B. Lindemann attached to a family Christmas Letter, December 1985]
- "Eric D. [sic] Lindemann Seminar/Department of Psychiatry & Behavioral Sciences at Stanford/ Clinical Faculty Association of Psychiatry January 6, 1990. . . Please join us for a Sunday morning Colloquium, March 11, 1990, honoring the late Josephine Hilgard, M.D., Ph.D. . . ". [flyer]

306. Hilgard, Josephine, 12/18/1979, *ibid*
307. Liederman, Gloria, 12/18/1979, *ibid*
308. Siegel, Alberta, 12/20/1979, *ibid*
309. Lindemann, Erich and Duhl, Leonard J., 7/13/1974, *ibid*
310. Lindemann, Erich, letter to Caudill, Dr. William, NIMH, 8/16/1966. [folder "GENERAL CORRESPONDENCE—A,B,C 1966", Box IV 1+2, Erich Lindemann Collection, Center for the History of Medicine, Countway Library of Medicine, Boston, MA]
311. Lindemann, Erich, letter to Mazer, Milton, M.D., Director, The Martha's Vineyard Guidance Center, 10/21/1966
312. Lindemann, Erich, letter to Caplan, Gerald, Clinical Professor of Psychiatry, Director, Laboratory of Community Psychiatry, Department of Psychiatry, 10/21/1966. [folder "GENERAL CORRESPONDENCE—A,B,C 1966", Box IV 1+2, Erich Lindemann Collection, Center for the History of Medicine, Countway Library of Medicine, Boston, MA]
313. Nemiah, John [Acting Chief of Psychiatry, MGH] letter to Lindemann, Erich, 10/21/1966. [folder "General Correspondence L, M 1966", Box IV 1+2, Erich Lindemann Collection, Center for the History of Medicine, Countway Library of Medicine, Boston, MA]
314. Lindemann, Erich, letter to Kerner, Oliver J. B., Ph.D., Consultant in Mental Health, Illinois State Psychiatric Institute, 10/28/1966. [folder "GENERAL CORRESPONDENCE G+H 1967", Box IV 1+2, Erich Lindemann Collection, Center for the History of Medicine, Countway Library of Medicine, Boston, MA]
315. Caplan, Gerald, Clinical Prof Psychiatry, to Lindemann, Erich, M.D., Stanford University School of Medicine, 11/9/1966. [folder "GENERAL CORRESPONDENCE—A,B,C 1966", Box IV 1+2, Erich Lindemann Collection, Center for the History of Medicine, Countway Library of Medicine, Boston, MA]
316. Lindemann, Erich, letter to Addis, Mrs. Robin S., Secretary, Scientific Programme Committee, The National Association for Mental Health, UK, 12/8/1966. [folder "Correspondence 1966 Misc", Box IV 1+2, Erich Lindemann Collection, Center for the History of Medicine, Countway Library of Medicine, Boston, MA]
317. Lindemann, Erich, letter to Pfister, Dr. Maria, Division of Mental Health, World Health Organization, 7/29/1967. [folder "GENERAL CORRESPONDENCE O+P 1967", Box IV 1+2, Erich Lindemann Collection, Center for the History of Medicine, Countway Library of Medicine, Boston, MA]
318. Lindemann, Erich, letter to Schneidman, Edwin S., Ph.D., Chief, Center for Studies of Suicide Prevention, National Institute of Mental Health, 11/17/1967. [folder "GENERAL CORRESPONDENCE Q R-S 1967", Box IV 1+2, Erich Lindemann Collection, Center for the History of Medicine, Countway Library of Medicine, Boston, MA]
319. Lindemann, Erich, letter to Haylett, Clarice, Acting Chief, Consultation Service, San Mateo County Mental Health Services, 11/25/1968: "I was

quite sick again with my spinal polyneuritis. For awhile [sic] I had lost my courage; but my colleagues in neurology at Massachusetts General Hospital are considering a new tack, with some exploratory surgery, and I am in high hopes of being able to function again in a few weeks. . . ". [folder "Correspondence 1968", Box IV 1 + 2, Erich Lindemann Collection, Center for the History of Medicine, Countway Library of Medicine, Boston, MA]

320. Lindemann, Erich, letter to Hamburg, David, 11/30/1968. [folder "Correspondence—David Hamburg", Box IV 1+2, Erich Lindemann Collection, Center for the History of Medicine, Countway Library of Medicine, Boston, MA]

321. Lindemann, Erich in the MGH, letter to Caplan, Gerald, 2/22/1969. [folder "Correspondence 1969", Box IV 1 + 2, Erich Lindemann Collection, Center for the History of Medicine, Countway Library of Medicine, Boston, MA]

322. Lindemann, Erich, from the MGH, letter to Liederman, Dr. Herbert, Professor of Psychiatry, Stanford Medical School, 2/22/1969. [folder "Correspondence 1969", Box IV 1 + 2, Erich Lindemann Collection, Center for the History of Medicine, Countway Library of Medicine, Boston, MA]

323. Lindemann, Erich from the MGH, letter to Torrey, Dr. Fuller, Stanford University Medical Center, 2/22/1969. [folder "Correspondence 1969", Box IV 1 + 2, Erich Lindemann Collection, Center for the History of Medicine, Countway Library of Medicine, Boston, MA]

324. Lindemann, Erich, letter to Hamburg, Dr. David, Professor of Psychiatry, 2/22/1969. [folder "Correspondence—David Hamburg", Box IV 1+2, Erich Lindemann Collection, Center for the History of Medicine, Countway Library of Medicine, Boston, MA]

325. Lindemann, Erich, letter to Wallach, Sidney, Executive Officer, The Oliver Wendell Holmes Association, 5/5/1969. [folder "Correspondence 1969", Box IV 1 + 2, Erich Lindemann Collection, Center for the History of Medicine, Countway Library of Medicine, Boston, MA]

326. Lindemann, Erich, letter to Beals, Miss Josephine A., Executive Secretary, Northern California Psychiatric Society, 6/21/1969. [folder "Correspondence 1969", Box IV 1 + 2, Erich Lindemann Collection, Center for the History of Medicine, Countway Library of Medicine, Boston, MA]

327. Lindemann, Erich, letter to Klerman, Gerald L., M.D., Professor o Psychiatry, MGH, 11//1971. [folder "Correspondence—1971", Box IV 1+2, Erich Lindemann Collection, Center for the History of Medicine, Countway Library of Medicine, Boston, MA]

328. Lindemann, Erich, letter to Ryan, Dr. William, Chairman, Department of Psychology, Boston College, 11/11/1971, p. 1. [folder "Correspondence—1971", Box IV 1+2, Erich Lindemann Collection, Center for the History of Medicine, Countway Library of Medicine, Boston, MA]

329. Lindemann, Erich, letter to Johnson, Prof. Paul, Christian Theological Seminary, Centerville, MA, 7–8/1969. [folder "Correspondence 1969", Box IV 1 + 2, Erich Lindemann Collection, Center for the History of Medicine, Countway Library of Medicine, Boston, MA]

330. Lindemann, Erich (c/o his wife's family's home, Brainerd, Farm Street, Dover, MA), letter to Hamburg, Dr. David, Department of Psychiatry, Stanford Medical Center, 10/4/1972. [folder "Correspondence—1972", Box IV 1 + 2, Erich Lindemann Collection, Center for the History of Medicine, Countway Library of Medicine, Boston, MA]

331. Lindemann, Erich, Palo Alto, CA, letter to Hamburg, David, Department of Psychiatry, Stanford University, 3/17/1974. [folder "Correspondence—David Hamburg", Box IV 1 + 2, Erich Lindemann Collection, Center for the History of Medicine, Countway Library of Medicine, Boston, MA]

332. Lindemann, Erich, CHAPTER 13—"REACTIONS TO ONE'S OWN FATAL ILLNESS"; unpublished talk to the staff of the Radiation Department at Stanford University Medical Center, 2/25/1972. Original title: Reactions to malignancy and subjective responses of patients in life-threatening situations. [file #106; "Reactions to One's Own Fatal Illness", Box XII #3, Lindemann Collection, Center for the History of Medicine, Francis A. Countway Library of Medicine, Harvard Medical School, Boston, MA]
333. Lindemann, Erich, 4/10/1973, *ibid*: "Leider bin ich jetzt ganz ans Bett gefesselt, und muss mein eigenes Heim als Platz meiner intellektuellen und geistigen Taetigkeit benutzen".
334. Lindemann, Erich, presentation to Thomas Gonda, M.D. class on death and dying, Department of Psychiatry, Stanford Medical Center, 2/17/1972. [Box XII 2 folder "Talk on bereavement for Dr. Gonda's seminar—Feb 17, 1972", Erich Lindemann Collection, Center for the History of Medicine, Francis A. Countway Library of Medicine, Boston, MA]
335. Lindemann, Erich, Visiting Professor of Psychiatry, Stanford University Medical Center, letter to Satyanand, Dr. D.[avid], FRCP, New Delhi (India), 1/21/1972. [folder "Correspondence—1972", Box IV 1+2, Erich Lindemann Collection, Center for the History of Medicine, Countway Library of Medicine, Boston, MA]
336. Caplan, Lee, 12/1979, *ibid*
337. Lindemann, Elizabeth Brainerd, 4/1/2003 telephone interview with David G. Satin [David G. Satin files, Newton, MA]
338. Haylett, Clarice, Division of Mental Health, San Mateo Coutn Health Department: interview by David G. Satin at her home in Palo Alto, CA, 12/17/1979. [Erich Lindemann Collection, Center for the History of Medicine, Countway Library of Medicine, Boston, MA]
339. Box X2, Erich Lindemann Collection, Center for the History of Medicine, Countway Library of Medicine, Boston, MA
340. Adams, John, 9/16/1969, *ibid*
341. Lindemann, Erich, letter to Poerksen, Niels at the University of Heidelbereg, 3/22/1973. Translated by Elizabeth B. Lindemann from:
"Man vergisst manchmal, wie durchgreifend die Werthaltung der Gemeinxdepsychiatrie sich gegenueber der traditionellen psychiatrischen Enstellung geaendert haben, und wie schwierig der Uebergang ist, und vor allem wie langsam man weitergehen muss, um nicht durch die unvermeidlichen Wiederstaende zum Halt gebracht zu werden".
342. Lindemann, Erich, letter to Beecher, Dr. Henry K. [emeritus Chief of the MGH Anesthesia Service], 3/1/1971, p. 2. [folder "Correspondence—1970", Box IV 1+2, Erich Lindemann Collection, Center for the History of Medicine, Francis A. Countway Library of Medicine, Boston, MA]
343. Lindemann, Elizabeth B., 6/27/1978, 11/1978, 8/1979, *ibid*
344. Hilgard, Josephine, 12/17/1979, *ibid*
345. Häffner, Prof. Dr. Dr. H.[einz], Der Direktor Der Socialpsychiatrischen Klinik Der Universität Heidelberg, letter to Lindemann, Erich, 10/30/1970. [folder "Heidelberg", Box IV 1+2, Erich Lindemann Collection, Center for the History of Medicine, Francis A. Countway Library of Medicine, Boston, MA]: "unsere nationale Fachgesellschaft damit einen der bedeutendsten Köpfe der modernen Psychiatrie ehrt, der sich gerade in den letzten Jahren auf unschätzbare Weise den Dienst der Förderung moderner Arbeitsweisen der Deutschen Psychiatrie stellt".
346. Torrey, E. Fuller, NIMH, Health Services and Mental Health Administration, DHEW, letter to Lindemann, Erich, 11/1/1971, p. 1. [folder

"Correspondence—1971", Box IV 1+2, Erich Lindemann Collection, Center for the History of Medicine, Countway Library of Medicine, Boston, MA]
347. Nemiah, John C., 4/7/1971, *ibid*, p. 1
348. Fried, Marc, Institute of Human Sciences, Boston College, letter to Lindemann, Erich, 11/22/1971. p. 1. [folder "Correspondence—1971", Box IV 1+2, Erich Lindemann Collection, Center for the History of Medicine, Countway Library of Medicine, Boston, MA]
349. Lindemann, Erich, Palo Alto, CA, letter to Osberg, James W., M.D., Deputy Director, Mental Health Programs, State of North Carolina, 11/21/1973. [folder "Correspondence—1974", Box IV 1+2, Erich Lindemann Collection, Center for the History of Medicine, Countway Library of Medicine, Boston, MA]
350. Mazer, Milton, M.D., Edgartown, Martha's Vineyard, MA, letter to Lindemann, Erich, Palo Alto, CA, 1/14/1974. [folder "Correspondence—1974", Box IV 1+2, Erich Lindemann Collection, Center for the History of Medicine, Countway Library of Medicine, Boston, MA]
351. Lindemann, Erich, Palo Alto, CA, letter to Mazer, Dr. Milton, Edgartown, MA, 8/21/1974. [folder "Correspondence—1974", Box IV 1+2, Erich Lindemann Collection, Center for the History of Medicine, Countway Library of Medicine, Boston, MA]
352. Gifford, Sanford, M.D., Peter Bent Brigham Hospital and Librarian and Chairman of the Archives Committee, Boston Psychoanalytic Society and Institute, letter to Lindemann, Erich, Palo Alto, CA, 8/19/1974. [folder "Correspondence—1974", Box IV 1+2, Erich Lindemann Collection, Center for the History of Medicine, Countway Library of Medicine, Boston, MA]
353. Hilgard, Josephine, 12/17/1979, *ibid*
354. Almond, Richard and Barbara, interview by David G. Satin at the Almond home, Palo Alto, CA, 12/19/1977. [Erich Lindemann Collection, Center for the History of Medicine, Countway Library of Medicine, Boston, MA]
355. Death certificate 11/16/1974.

3 Continuity and Replacement

After 1974—Legacy and Successors of Community Mental Health

The struggle between conservatism and innovation is continuous, even when the innovation is in the form of reversion to some form of the status quo ante. Keyserling noted: "The taproots of the cult of truth lie in elemental aggressiveness, in the primitive vital urge to conquer new living-space, pushing others out of theirs. This is true even where alleged scientific truth seeks to supplant alleged religious error".[1] Social change is especially complex, obdurate, and potentially discouraging:

> If outrage has given way to denial, it may be because problems like racism and poverty are seen as intractable. Social recessions aren't nearly as easy to turn around as economic recessions are. They don't respond to interest-rate changes or tax cuts. They require vision, leadership, consensus, and behavioral change over a long period. In a country hooked on short-term solutions, dealing with issues that won't be solved for another generation, if ever, is seen as useless.[2]

In the 1980s, the size of the mental health issue in U.S. society was estimated at $20 billion spent per year, caring for 7 million people, and involving 4,500 mental health organizations employing more than 500,000 staff members.[3] However, in contrast with economic boom times in the mid-20th century, later economic restrictions limited expansive public policies and programs.

Shift to Biological Ideology

The societal shift away from the social body and its welfare and toward the individual and economic benefit continued in the latter part of the 20th century:[4]

> polling Princeton's [University] Class of 1982. . . to gauge how this generation will deal with each other and the problems that confront their world . . . a portrait of a group with high expectations and great confidence in themselves but with little optimism about the prospects

for most Americans . . . people from all parts of the country and a wide variety of family backgrounds (p. 10) . . . the baby boomers through student activism of the late '60's and early '70's. . . . But when political change seemed to lead nowhere the baby boomers turned inward and reemerged in the Me Decade . . . they are leery of risk-taking and experimentation because they are fundamentally frightened about the future and have little confidence in anyone's ability to change things for the better . . . they want to make the best they can for themselves.

This shift in social ideology toward the individual and his needs influenced health institutions. The social activism, civil rights movement, civil disobedience and riots, and focus by social psychiatry and CMH on social rather than individual pathology lowered the boundaries between mental health and social activism and caused a negative political reaction and retaliation by the powers that be through reestablishing previous professional role definitions.[5] "As higher education institutions respond to these policy initiatives, gerontology program administrators often find themselves faced with a restructuring of programs, a redirection of their attention toward health issues, and a decrease in their emphasis on behavioral and social science professions"[6]—i.e., health issues were not interpreted in terms of behavior or social science. David Hamburg, Lindemann's chief at Stanford, noted a strong prejudice against the social sciences in powerful groups in the U.S.[7] Psychiatry was dominated by secondary and tertiary prevention, though community psychiatry issues permeated community life.[8] Conservative academic departments, medical schools, universities, and state mental health departments ordered a stop to social activism, decreased budgets, and fired or transferred noncompliant program leaders. Contemporary conditions required tighter administrative control than during Lindemann's tenure, though it undermined energetic, independent creativity.[9] Piersma recorded several CMHCs' focus on secondary and tertiary clinical treatment dominated by psychiatry as dictated by financial reimbursement considerations.[10] A survey of CMHCs raised questions about their quality, staffing, and funding; found underfunding and use as dumping places of low quality; peaceful but not good; and not really providing comprehensive services; and they questioned whether the CMHC was the best vehicle for CMH.[11] In psychology, community psychology was considered a peripheral field and therefor focused on teaching and mentorships.[12]

It influenced ideology in the profession of psychiatry. The American Psychiatric Association was torn by this shift in ideology. There were attempts to smooth over ideological conflicts between social and biological psychiatry:[13] "Dr. Alan Stone, president of the American Psychiatric Association (APA), in his keynote address before the association's annual meeting . . . reported on the recent struggles between the four competing models in psychiatry—the biological, psychodynamic, behavioral and social—and their present peaceful coexistence within what he called 'pragmatic eclecticism' ".

Jeffrey Lieberman, past president of APA and chairman of psychiatry at Columbia University Medical Center, interpreted a history of public mental health in terms of its rescue from social psychiatry back to medical/biological psychiatry:[14]

> In 1973, the National Institute of Mental Health (NIMH) . . . was joined with the Health Services and Mental Health Administration to form the Alcohol, Drug Abuse, and Mental Health Administration (ADAMHA). However, like immiscible solutions, the medically minded researchers and socially oriented service administrators never really united and became factionalized and in some instances adversarial. As a result, in 1992, they were separated into three research institutes (NIMH, National Institute on Drug Abuse, and the National Institute on Alcohol Abuse and Alcoholism) . . . and a standalone agency, the Substance Abuse and Mental Health Services Administration (SAMHSA). This, in effect, ceded the services (as opposed to the research) component of mental health to nonmedical health care disciplines . . . As a result, for over a quarter century, SAMHSA pursued an agenda that diverged from scientifically guided evidence-based care and predominantly emphasized services and programs addressing social pathologies and promoting wellness. Over this period, the dissatisfactions of stake-holders and Congress grew, and they criticized SAMHSA for wasting money on services based on unproven theories and feel-good fads; alternatives to proven treatments that encourage patients to go off medications; wellness initiatives . . . instead of focusing efforts on programs proven to help people with severe mental illnesses. This renegade policy, which marginalized scientific influence, was exemplified by the fact that SAMHSA had only one psychiatrist on its staff, in a subordinate position . . . Several auspicious developments have recently occurred that could be game changing and signal psychiatry's reengagement in public mental health . . . culminating in Ellie's (Elinore McCance-Katz, M.D., Ph.D., a psychiatrist specializing in addiction psychiatry with a background in academic medicine and public mental health was sworn in . . . as the first Assistant Secretary of Mental Health and Substance Use) appointment which entails operational authority over all federal government agencies supporting mental health are, first and foremost SAMHSA and its $3.5 billion budget. Her appointment also calls for a close working relationship with the NIH institutes and NIMH in particular, currently led by Josh Gordon, M.D., a psychiatrist neuroscientist . . . In a way, we have come full circle to rediscover our roots in mental health care . . . the real

challenge is to use our recommitment and assumption of leadership role to fix the mental health care system and improve the quality and availability of care...

Daniel X. Freedman, another president of the APA, objected to the anti-nuclear weapons activity by some psychiatrists, emphasizing the need to concentrate on the treatment of public patients and maintaining third-party funding for psychiatric treatment.[15] H. Keith H. Brodie, another APA president, speaking for the association, was even more blunt:[16] He saw the most significant treatment advances since World War II stimulated by the serendipitous discovery of psychoactive drugs. To him, this proved the relevance of biological research to psychiatric treatment. The definition of thousands of new diagnoses of major mental illnesses insured the need for psychiatrists despite much treatment being done by nonpsychiatrist physicians and nonphysicians.

> A closer relationship between psychiatry and neuroscience research and development . . . lie in the immediate future of the profession, according to APA President H. Keith H. Brodie, speaking at the recent APA Institute on Hospital and Community Psychiatry . . . Tracing the advances in treatment from the time of World War II to today, Brodie pointed out that the most significant have been the serendipitous discoveries of psychoactive drugs . . . have demonstrated beyond a doubt the relevance of biological research to the treatment of mental illnesses, and require continued (p. 1) support of research programs (p. 32).

An interesting suggestion was that CMH opened the way for biological psychiatry:[17] "[T]he now 15 year old community psychiatry movement in the United States has moved the mental health system back into closer juxtaposition with the somatic health system. . . [T]he relative isolation of mental health . . . was broken down with the advent of community psychiatry with its emphasis on inpatient care on wards in general medical hospitals". That is, when CMH brought psychiatry into the community, psychiatry predominantly and organizationally chose to identify itself with somatic medicine rather than with social clinical professions and the social sciences.

Barton and Sanborn, in their comprehensive review of CMH, defined it as oriented to the treatment of mental illness through CMH clinics close to communities.[18] Its concerns centered on planning for meaningful catchment areas; linkage among mental health and social welfare agencies and mental hospitals; simplifying finances; and the integration of CMHCs with general hospitals and general community medical systems with emphasis on outpatient treatment. Mental health was to be separated from social issues, with CMH's main responsibility the treatment

314 Continuity and Replacement

in acute, community-based, community responsible facilities. Mental health treatment is costly and burdensome enough; prevention should be dealt with through research; social reform is not within the expertise or responsibility of a medical care system. CMH should not be guided by the "social expedience of short-term goals". Role diffusion should be offset by having each profession and paraprofession do what it is trained and able to do best; psychiatrists as physicians have a central role:[19]

> We see human service and legitimate social concerns as great problems in our society—effort at solutions, however, should be funded separately and not from the health care dollar . . . We do not believe that social reform can be accomplished by the medical care system, or that the mental health system has the talent to accomplish that objective.

Lamb and Zusman were similarly skeptical of the contemporary enthusiasm for primary prevention.[20] They insisted on distinguishing the prevention of diagnosable mental illness from unhappiness, and social incompetence from solving basic social problems. They questioned the relationship between social conditions and mental illness and felt this was not the province of mental health prevention, nor was it within the expertise of clinicians. Further, they saw no proof of the effectiveness of primary prevention, which requires knowledge of the cause of mental illness, of which little was known; and genetics and biochemistry were the important routes to such knowledge.

Allen chronicled the shift in ideology:[21]

> During the past seventy years . . . we have become progressively more preoccupied with the biological mechanisms of disease—a preoccupation best understood as a consequence of a model of medicine that has contributed much to our therapeutic powers, and has therefore come to dominate our professional ideology (Engel, 1971, 1977) . . . Flexner (1910) advocated a mastery of the scientific method . . . his recommendations have been interpreted in a way that has emphasized unifactorial etiology, physiochemical explanations, and mind-body dualism . . . Current biomedical dogma has assumed that disease is best understood in terms of deviation from measurable, biological variables, and the diagnosis of disease has preempted medical attention. . . [p. 566] . . . Two thousand years ago, Hippocrates of Cos . . . taught that no physician . . . could provide adequate treatment without an awareness of the patient's personality and interpersonal relationships as well as of the environmental precipitants of illness. In the first chapter of his *Precepts*, he attributed illness not only to organic causes, as did the exclusively organic school of Knidos, but also to "excessive indulgences or repressions

of appetites—disappointments in love and war—sustained tension in the race for fame and fortune—and fear and superstitions". The Hippocratic "medical model" was not biomedical.

[p. 567]

Gerald Caplan reviewed the evolution of psychiatry theory, practice, and support from the perspective of the latter part of his CMH career:[22] Population-oriented mental health programs were born from the shortage of sophisticated manpower since clinicians came from training programs that did not teach about social factors in mental health and from economic problems resulting in a paucity of resources. This new orientation embodied an open systems approach, and one factor/one treatment gave way to the application of all resources in a multifaceted approach.

However, too often there resulted words and intentions instead of action addressing practical complications and consequences; and overselling (as in fundraising) of the expectation of eradication of mental illness led to frustration and the disillusion of community leaders, citizens, and professionals. The refusal of mental health workers to deal with politics (including accountability and government control) resulted in poor communication with and distrust of politicians, unsatisfied patients, people in need (potential clients) not served, lack of sensitivity and response to criticism and dissent, lack of evaluation of programs, and a failure to learn from history. The 1976 CMH support of deinstitutionalization was intended to shift resources from inpatient to community mental health care and increased the expectation of results. There was also counterpressure to preserve individual- and depth-oriented psychiatric treatment and treatment centers. This led to criticism, increased administrative review, and decreased support. This trend was reinforced by the turmoil over the Vietnam War, economic inflation and depression, and the Richard Nixon administration. Caplan recalled his 1969 prediction of the ebb of interest in CMH by 1973–5 and loss of support in 1980–5.

The response to this shift in psychiatric fashion could be giving up on the population focus and retiring from practice or withdrawing to private practice. Another alternative was joining the ideological shift to the funded biological treatment of sick individuals and research. Another alternative was maintaining the CMH ideology, continuing the search for resources for this (federal funding accounted for less than 10% and came with vulnerability to political currents), protecting sanctuary institutions, and maintaining dedicated elite cadres for CMH practice, teaching, and as reference groups for those adhering to CMH. While CMH might be dying in urban, academic centers, Caplan looked to small towns and rural programs which needed the CMH approach, involving idealists who followed CMH ideas and had close community ties including the participation of professionals (who fit the local culture) in service programs (rather than teaching, research, and the occasional psychoanalytic patient as in academic centers), and supported by local funding and endowments. However, this type of setting was subject to arbitrary politics with sudden shifts, nepotism, job insecurity, and professional isolation.

Caplan saw the need for a central elite group sharing common interests and values, supporting one another and maintaining their interests, and providing mutual aid in resisting distortion of programs as through nepotism. Examples were the Peace Corps, the "Space Cadets", the Visiting Faculty Seminar in the Laboratory of Community Psychiatry at HMS, and the Inter-University Forum at the Laboratory, where university professionals shared with rural practitioners starved to hear the latest theory and practice and share problems and solutions. This built on the population-oriented skills they developed of the necessity from limited resources without concepts or training. The laboratory offered training in theory as a foundation.

Caplan predicted that even with the contemporary president, Jimmy Carter, who was supportive of mental health issues, it might take four to ten years to evolve another era of population-oriented mental health, starting from the rural reservoir of need independent of power centers and rising to academic centers.

Zwerling continued the criticism of the failings of CMH:[23]

> [T]he negative assessments are also there . . . inadequate funding, naive confusions about the role of mental health teams in effecting social change, not enough appropriately trained manpower, overly zealous prophets of the instant, society-wide elimination of mental illness. . .] N]nowhere [does it] . . . address the racism, professionalism, and elitism of the mental health professionals. . . [There are also] crucial issues about community participation, the role of paraprofessionals, the place of social activism vis-á-vis the "medical model", and the relationship between hospital and community treatment.
>
> (p. 198)

Gerald Klerman, shifting his commitment from psychoanalysis to social psychiatry to biological psychiatry, tried to straddle the social influences on mental health without social action to ameliorate them:[24]

> Mental Health professionals would do well to investigate the social risk factors that undermine mental health, but leave social change to the political system, the administrator of the Alcohol, Drug Abuse, and Mental Health Administration indicated recently . . . he advocated limits on intervening in prevention or promotion of mental health . . . the health care system . . . is being called on to relieve distress and enhance personal enjoyment and performance. Embodying this is the definition of health proposed by the World Health Organization: "A state of complete physical, mental, and social

well-being and not merely the absence of disease or infirmity". To what extent should the health care system be available to those who are distressed but not disabled? . . . how far and in what way should it delve into social, political, and economic problems? . . . There are those. . . [who] hope mental health knowledge and insights will lead the way to the "good" life and the "right" social system . . . The model he prefers . . . belongs to public health theory and separates the scientific issues from philosophical ones. Poverty, racism, unemployment, and alienation of youth are important risk factors . . . it is appropriate for us to conduct research on the relationship of the factors—even that of powerlessness—to mental health problems . . . the etiology of the mental illnesses and influences on mental health . . . They may even provide us with opportunities for preventive intervention. But the responsibility for those interventions may not rest within our mental health care system. . . [H]e disapproved of members of a community mental health center staff organizing a non-violent protest with welfare mothers they had been instructing to be better mothers [i.e., the action he had supported in the Connecticut Mental Health Center] . . . three criteria by which he determines the limits of mental health interventions: . . . based on scientific evidence and . . . controlled studies and demonstration projects; . . . within some concept of public health, leaving social change to the political system; . . . stay within the mandate of the federal agency, negotiated with society.

On the other hand, there were some individuals and groups continuing to follow CMH principles and approaches, including the involvement of federal agencies. Leopold *et al* found value in community mental health programs, especially if embedded in the community or community medical center.[25] They documented the importance of locally integrated and comprehensive service delivery as a key to effectiveness and illustrated how evaluative research can be used simultaneously for purposes of program assessment and program development. Goldston defined primary prevention and positive mental health in the context of CMH tenets, and major preventive strategies included strengthening the capacities of individuals as well as environmental modification.[26] Carver argued for the importance of preventive mental health services to more adequately prepare the population to be competent, adaptable human beings with coping skills, personal competencies, and the ability to deal with their emotions and relationships with others and thus prevent mental illness.[27] He advocated decentralizing mental health skills; recognizing schools as the central mental health agency in the lives of children; the need for the services of clergymen, physicians, teachers, and parents; training mental health professionals in consultation and education services; and community health centers as an available reservoir of skills for primary prevention.

There was some continued interest, including in the federal government, in preventive medicine and the involvement of the social sciences. The NIH's Fogarty International Center conference, The Behavioral Sciences and Preventive Medicine: Opportunities and Dilemmas, included the importance of social/psychological components in determining patient behavior, the role of the behavioral sciences in community health care, epidemiological aspect of preventive mental health care, stress theory and research, economic and political aspects of preventive medicine, and increased preventive medicine training for all health professionals.[28]

The federal government traced its conflict over its CMHC program:[29]

> a Federal commitment and investment of over $1.5 billion today [1978] in some 650 community mental health centers . . . to (p. iii) areas in which nearly 90 million Americans [some 43 percent of the total United States population (p. 1)] live. Last year, over 2 million took advantage of this opportunity . . . We estimate that to achieve the goal of total U.S. coverage, an additional 850 centers will be required . . . The previous Administration proposed phaseout and block grants, vetoed appropriations, and attempted impoundment of funds after Congress overrode the vetoes . . . The withdrawal of Federal grant support without compensating changes in Medicare and Medicaid, and without enactment of National Health Insurance, has created a critical shortfall . . . In July of 1975, the Congress demonstrated its wholehearted endorsement and commitment to the CMHC Program with passage of P.L. 94–63, overriding, overwhelmingly, the president's veto of this law (p. iv).
>
> Community mental health centers . . . have emerged from the activism and excitement of the 1960's to the sobering realities of the 1970's . . . in its enthusiasm for this species of social and medical programming the Congress may have created . . . a huge and complex organism which requires nutrients that . . . far exceed the capacity of the environment to provide . . . 860 catchment areas remaining in the United States with no CMHCs . . . the requirements and expectations of the CMHC Program must be brought into line with the fiscal realities . . . The CMHC Program, as an organized care system, publicly financed and (p. 64) accountable to a catchment area, oriented toward quality clinical care and prevention is a system worth preserving.
>
> (p. 65)

The federal commitment to CMHCs continued in the following years, though focused on treatment of individual mentally ill patients rather than amelioration of social and community pathogens:[30]

> In the 16 years since the first Community Mental Health Centers Act became law . . . Over $2 billion have been expended to fund 726 centers . . . making service available to 105 million people. In 1978 over

2 million persons received care through the centers (p. 2) ... **Congressional Intent.** It is the Committee's position that services for the mentally ill and emotionally disturbed must be provided and that CMHCs have provided an effective and economical means to provide fully comprehensive care within the patient's community ... the Federal role is one of providing construction and operational funds to new centers ... for a limited period of time on a declining basis with the ultimate goal that the centers ... become completely independent of Federal support ... to ensure that until some form of national health insurance covers the costs of care ... mental health services continue to be offered ... preamble in Title III of Public Law 94–63 [1978]: The Congress finds that (1) community mental health care is the most effective and humane form of care for a majority of mentally ill individuals; (2) the federally funded community mental health centers have had a major impact on the improvement of mental health care ... and thus are a national resource to which all Americans should enjoy access; and (3) there is currently a shortage and maldistribution of quality community mental health care resources in the United States". (p. 3)

Definition of a **Community Mental Health Center** [includes] ... A community mental health center shall ensure that persons receiving services have access to all health and social services they may require (p. 4) ... A community mental health center must have a governing body composed of individuals who reside in the center's catchment area and who, as a group, represent the residents of that catchment area. The exceptions to this requirement are centers which are operated by hospitals and Government agencies. These may be allowed to have a representative advisory board instead of a governing board". (p. 5)

The goal of CMHCs serving the entire population still was not achieved:[31]

As of October, 1980, 789 centers have received Federal funding through the Community Mental Health Center (CMHC) Program... [They] serve slightly more than half of the total number of mental health service areas in the country (1,500), approximately 53 percent of the population ... the average CMHC... [has] a budget of about $2 million, a staff of 120 people, and a clientele of 3,340 persons annually.

(p. v)

Demone, who, when an assistant commissioner in the Massachusetts Department of Mental Health, had collaborated with Lindemann, further analyzed the conflicting values impacting public CMH policies:[32]

Federal Policy Objectives ... The earlier issues were the quality, availability, accessibility, and continuity of services; removing [p. 540] the financial barriers to health care; alternative approaches to care; and subsidizing health manpower production. The focus in the 1980's is on saving money, reducing the maldistribution of health services, and enlarging the pool of minority and female mental health workers . . . Efforts to impose cost controls have been relatively consistent for more than a decade, no matter what bureaucracy, president, or political party was in power. By the late 1960's, the Nixon administration had initiated challenges to the traditional health manpower role of the federal government and sought both to phase out and reduce support for various health programs. Congress annually restored funds at varying but declining rates and also began to view manpower problems as selective rather than as absolute . . . Political ideology, mythology, and a quasi-projection science provided powerful tools for those seeking to reduce training support.

President Reagan's goal is to eliminate all training programs except for those in research. His special targets include the social and behavioral sciences and the human service professions. This negative ideology contrasts strikingly with the thinking of the 1950's and 1960's when the goal was to meet demand by expanding the supply of core mental health professionals, that is psychiatrists, clinical psychologists, psychiatric social workers . . . and psychiatric nurses. [p. 541] . . . Priorities and expenditures for human resources in the 1980's [influence] . . . professional schools and associations are playing increasingly subservient roles . . . The overriding objective is to reduce expenditures, and in this respect policy has remained unchanged since the Nixon era. The means to achieve this end are disincentives, market constraints, regulations, restructuring of the health care system, program reductions and eliminations, or some combination of the above (Zubkoff, 1977) [Zubkoff, M. (Ed). *Health: A Victim or Cause of Inflation?* NY: Rodist, 1977] . . . For example, if professionals are considered individual cost centers, the conclusion can be reached that if fewer researchers or clinicians are produced, less demand will be placed on resources, and expenditures will be reduced.

The federal bureaucracy has responded . . . in several ways. One group has joined the fray with enthusiasm, using quasi-magical formulas to legitimate the politically based conclusion that there is a surplus of human resources. A second group, new to the struggle and lacking skill in economics, has become thoroughly socialized to the surplus mentality and mouths the appropriate language. A third group . . . asserts that by controlling the number of professionals, we can anticipate reduced competition among them, higher rates for services, and income maximization for professionals. A fourth group . . . rejects the surplus theme. It continues to support maldistribution as an alternative rationale for delivering health care . . . A fifth group . . . searches for exceptions to the presidential directives.

It seeks allies in Congress, the professions, and the universities . . . this group tries to maintain low visibility in what it sees as a hostile environment. [p. 542] . . . The Health Resources Administration (Health Resources Administration, 1979a) [Health Resources Administration: *Health Professions Legislation—Areas Under Consideration.* Hyattsville, Md.] identified five objectives for 1981. The first was to remove incentives for unwarranted growth in the aggregate supply of health professionals. . . [p. 543] . . . The defunct Mental Health Systems Act (1980)[*Mental Health Systems Act,* P.L. 96–398, 1980] . . . asserted that because of the rising demand for mental health services and the wide disparity in the distribution of psychiatrists, clinical psychologists, social workers, and psychiatric nurses, there is a shortage. . .

[p. 544]

From 1974, with the National Service Research Act, funding began to be phased out for training in the forms of fellowships, training grants, and research development.[33]

The practical effects of these policies and actions were laid out by a CMH program administrator:[34]

After a brief period of optimism in the closing years of the last decade, we are now facing the certainty of dramatic, possibly traumatic, changes for community mental health services in the 1980's. The period of uncertainty regarding the federal government's role ended when Congress repealed the Mental Health Systems Act and created a single block grant for mental health, drug abuse, and alcohol abuse services. How each state will respond is still uncertain . . . Along with the demise of a categorical mechanism for funding CMHCs, we can expect a continued decline in the relative contribution of federal dollars . . . Federal leadership, evidenced by advocacy, experimentation, and demonstrations of innovations, is more likely to [p. 265] decline than are federal regulations. Already many respected professionals at the National Institute of Mental Health (NIMH) have "jumped ship", and the NIMH may yet be subsumed into the larger health bureaucracy . . . Part of the Reagan administration's rationale for a reduction in federal dollars is that monitoring and administrative costs will be reduced . . . the cynics are doubtful that citizens will support increases in local or state taxes [to make up for lost federal dollars]. [p. 266] . . . we can anticipate an increasing demand for mental health services, especially from those high-risk groups that are losing other federal entitlements or experiencing reductions in other services. In a very broad sense, the need and demand for mental health services will covary inversely with the general state of the economy.

[p. 267]

Deinstitutionalization

An important scheme for transition away from public responsibility for mental health was labeled "deinstitutionalization". It drew inspiration from the maneuver by Dr. Jerome Miller, director of the Massachusetts Department of Youth Services (DYS), to end detrimental practices in residential training schools for delinquent youth.[35] After department personnel's resistance to reform measures in 1969, he closed many of the training schools in 1970–1972, forcing the need for community programs and facilities before they had been arranged. It should be noted that upon creating this major change—the emergency need to create community programs and the outcry this caused—he felt unable to work further in this tumultuous environment, moved to a job in another state, and left the government and community to create a new care system.

Deinstitutionalization in mental health was generated by two major motives: One, similar to that in DYS, was the wish of progressives to improve the care of patients in state institutions, including strengthening their connection with their communities of origin. The other was the determination by conservative, business-oriented social forces, expressed through Massachusetts governor Edward J. King, to reduce state spending, especially on social programs. Since a major state expense was the state hospital system, he determined to implement deinstitutionalization with the goal of reducing state spending on staff and facilities, shifting the costs of institutionalized mentally ill patients to the federal government through Medicaid by placing them in nursing homes, and profiting from the sale of valuable state hospital properties. An additional influence was the 1975 the U.S. Supreme Court ruling that mentally ill people could not be institutionalized if they were not dangerous and could live with support in the community. This underlying politicoeconomic motivation of deinstitutionalization was clearly recognized:[36]

> it is not a change in the clinical characteristics of patients, nor a change in the etiology of mental disorders, nor a change in contemporary beliefs in innovative clinical interventions, nor a change in therapeutic optimism, nor even a change in the moral dilemmas for providing care that accounts for the current phenomenon of state hospital recidivism. Rather, the role of the state hospital has been altered by factors extrinsic to both the provider and the recipient of psychiatric services . . . does the current role of the state hospital—in which society refuses to permit asylum to those who are unable to function without its succor while simultaneously condoning a system of care whereby some individuals are admitted more than 100 times—make any sense?

The economic motivation for the change in socio-political policy toward mental health care is glaringly illustrated in the case of the Erich Lindemann Mental Health Center (ELMHC):[37]

> Two sprawling Government Center office buildings, constructed on the ruins of Boston's West End, would be recycled into mixed-income housing . . . the state would turn over the Lindemann Mental Health Center and the Hurley Building to developers . . . and return it to (p. 1) housing, offices and retail shops . . . the Lindemann Mental Health Center and the Hurley Building, which had been declared surplus property by the Dukakis administration . . . would enable private entrepreneurs to gain additional revenue from office and retail leases and use a substantial portion of those revenues to reduce the sale prices of at least 100 condominiums or cooperatives to be set aside as affordable housing. . . [costing] $86,000. . . or up to $110,000. . . Frank Keefe, state secretary of administration and finance, said ". . . the Lindemann and Hurley buildings are extremely inefficient . . . the developer would have to simultaneously develop a new mental health center as well as a replacement for the Parker shelter for the homeless, which now uses the Lindemann gymnasium. I think the notion of privatizing the whole block is the way to go", said Keefe. . . [He] expressed confidence that the proposal will attract substantial interest from the private sector . . . the state plans to offer a number of incentives to developers . . . as a prototype of a public-private undertaking that can be emulated in other parts of the state.

Note also the change in the socio-economic group focus of public policy from the working class of the original West End tenement housing to the upper middle class of the proposed (and later implemented) condominium housing.

The implementation of deinstitutionalization was determined and rapid:[38]

> In 1984. . . [in] all state and county mental hospitals in the United States . . . there were 118,647 patients . . . 79% below the peak census of 558,922. . . in 1955. Some states had decreased . . . census by more than 90% . . . By 1990 services for persons with serious mental illness were described as a "disaster", and deinstitutionalization was labeled a "hoax". [Isaac, R. J. and Armat, V. C: *Madness in the Streets: How Psychiatry and the Law Abandoned the Mentally Ill.* (NY: Free Press, 1990)] More persons with serious and persistent mental illness were in jails, prisons, or public shelters and on the streets than were in public mental hospitals. [Torrey, E. F.: *Nowhere to Go: The Tragic Odyssey of the Homeless Mentally Ill.* (NY:

Harper & Row, 1988)] . . . Massachusetts' expenditure for mental health and retardation services increased by $543 million, or 150%, from 1980 through 1988. . . Northampton State Hospital, being the beneficiary of a federal court consent decree mandating treatment in the least restrictive suitable alternative . . . 1978–1988. . . discharged *every* patient who had been in the hospital on the day the decree was signed . . . 1980 to 1989. . . census fell by 54%, and admissions decreased by 36% . . . the turnover rate of a bed . . . was approximately 5 times per year. Virtually all discharges were to community settings . . . the mean length of stay . . . decreased by 84% . . . The mean length of stay of all first-admission patients decreased by 98%, from 14.4 years to 87 days . . . a progressively greater percentage of them had had prior admissions. . .

Thus, deinstitutionalization was touted as CMH with the promise of community programs and blaming failures on the concept of CMH. Of course, fiscal conservatism extended to inadequate funding of the promised CMH programs. Luboff noted:[39]

large-scale federal support of community mental health systems . . . were supposed to replace outdated and inhumane state mental hospitals. But the dream of deinstitutionalization became a nightmare of underfunding and poor planning, and in many cases resulted in horror stories. . . [a] 30-year-old mentally ill daughter was discharged from a state mental hospital into a rooming house full of mentally ill residents that had [quoting her father] "no window shades, broken windows, no bed-spread, a complete horde of cockroaches in the headboard of the bed, (and) plugged-up toilet plumbing".

But if the facility was reported to the board of health it would be closed down and the result would be "more homeless people". "there are no available alternatives". "In some cases mentally ill persons receive even worse care than was available on the back wards of the state hospitals", conceded Philip Johnston, secretary of the state's executive office of human services. . . "Today I see some of the same people sleeping on the floor of the Pine Street Inn". [a shelter for the homeless] . . . Dr. Miles Shore [Superintendent] and Dr. Jon Gudeman, of the Massachusetts Mental Health Center [found that] . . . deinstitutionalization "produced a host of new problems for the 1980's". Community acceptance of former patients, adequate housing and social rehabilitation, medical care and psychiatric services in the community are often lacking or substandard . . . A number of factors fueled the deinstitutionalization movement which . . . decreased their [mental hospitals'] population from approximately 25,000 residents to roughly 2,400 residents in the past quarter century.

A growing recognition of the horrendous conditions. . . [accompanying the realization of] the right of emotionally ill patients to live near their original homes. New drugs countered many of the symptoms . . . A growing body of court decisions made it harder to commit patients . . . against their will. And a belief that deinstitutionalization would save the state money was accomplished in part because . . . many people discharged from state hospitals were offered little more than a room in a dilapidated boarding house, a drug prescription and an appointment with a therapist at a community mental center. Consequently many . . . were unable to cope and wound up wandering the streets where they aroused concern and fear among their neighbors. . . "As practiced by the department of mental health, deinstitutionalization is a negative concept and is purely quantitative", complained Benjamin Ricci, a plaintiff in a landmark suit against the state's department of mental health . . . in 1979. "It was and continues to be billed as being cheaper, an apparent appeal to those who are cost conscious".

In the mid 1970's . . . mental health advocates filed suit in federal court charging the state with violating the civil rights of mental patients in the western part of the state. In 1978 the Dukakis administration agreed to settle the case and create a court-mandated system of community-oriented mental health services in western Massachusetts . . . the administration asked mental health advocates not to file similar suits in other parts of the state . . . Instead the new system was to be a model for other parts of the state. . . [as a result] the western regions have gotten greatly increased resources for community mental health while other parts of the state lag behind. And an August 1985 study—called the Mental Health Services Equity Project—found that "services for the mentally ill are inadequate and uneven across the commonwealth". "The system has never honored its legislative mandate and political commitment to create a range of alternatives to institutions", asserts [Steven] Schwarts [director of the Coalition for the Legal Rights of the Disabled, which brought the suit] . . . researchers estimating that deinstitutionalized patients, or those who in the past would have been housed in state hospitals, constitute between 25 and 60 percent of the area's homeless population. . . [R]ising real estate prices and growing community resistance to halfway houses are making it increasingly difficult to meet that housing demand. . . [A] policy decision was made to contract out the operation of halfway houses rather than to have them staffed by the state workers. But as funding for community mental health was kept low, so were salaries—a situation that has combined to create large-scale staffing turnover. . . [T]he average salary in social services and mental health agencies is $14,602 a year. . . [I]t is still very difficult to attract new staffers and retain qualified workers . . . Dr. Benjamin

Liptzen, president of the Massachusetts Psychiatric Society, asserts that "the community system is much less likely to be the solution than it looked like it would be in the 1960's".

But many observers simply believe community mental health services were never really given the opportunity to grow to anywhere near full potential". Community mental health has been branded a failure", adds Amy Durland, the Massachusetts Association for Mental Health's (MAMH) director of public policy. "We strongly feel it isn't. It wasn't given a chance."

The dire consequences of this scenario were widely recognized. Christ noted:[40]

> ... in 1972 and 1973 ... two main ideas were pushed: dehospitalization and deprofessionalization ... after the initial push to discharge as many patients as possible from the hospitals, the "wandering crazies" were seen everywhere and outpatient facilities for them were at the time not available ... The forces at work are much larger in scope ... the decline of the liberal and humanistic treatment ideologies that were current in the mental health professions until the 1970's and the upsurge of a new conservatism and authoritarianism, manifested in politics as well as in the sciences and the medical profession.
>
> Dehospitalization and deprofessionalization in California were carried out during the administration of a governor who was a self-acknowledged conservative. Similarly in Georgia, fiscal conservatives embraced the new ideas of the reorganization that promised economies for the taxpayer. Originally, of course, it was the civil libertarians who pushed for reforms ... in the name of Constitutional freedom for ... chronically mentally ill ... The major threat to competent care or caretaking in Georgia today comes from the other side—the conservatives ... State bureaucracies and their fiscal administrators have won a limited victory: hospitals are much smaller and professionals fewer ... The commitment to training and education ... has been quietly dropped ... Psychiatrists as a group have been sharply downgraded ... in their authority for treatment planning and implementation ... no longer do the hiring and firing of their staff ... Often they are no more than glorified and expensive prescription writers.

Ruefully it was remarked:[41] "The public hospitals provide substantially lower salaries for psychiatrists than do private practice settings. They also offer less attractive work opportunities, a more restrictive image of practice, and a more highly bureaucratic environment. These issues provide an urgent agenda for a reanalysis of manpower needs and the distribution of psychiatrists to meet public health requirements". Another regret was the feeling that an anti–community psychiatry tenor of U.S. psychiatry reduced community psychiatry to individual office practice in the community setting.

The loss of interest in mental health needs was manifest on both federal and state levels:[42]

> Community mental health services appear to be eroding even further under state budgetary constraints and poor Medicaid reimbursement rates. . . . [There is] increasing incarceration and increasing use of hospital emergency departments by people with mental illness . . . fueled by the tendency of states to shift funding for mental health services to the Medicaid program. . . . [There are] pretty serious shortages in some key types of services, including residential support services . . . Psychiatric inpatient beds [are inadequate] . . . some people have had to go outside the community to get an inpatient admission. . . [Also shortages in] housing, group quarters, transitional shelters. . . . [S]tate and county psychiatric hospital capacity has been declining for several decades, . . . [P]rivate psychiatric hospitals and psychiatric units of general hospitals declined sharply during the mid and late 1990s. . . [I]ncreases in outpatient capacity have not kept pace with the decreases in inpatient capacity . . . Shortages of key outpatient care staff, especially psychiatrists, were . . . worsening in most of the communities.

Perseverance of Community Mental Health

There was resistance to this shift toward a biological ideology:[43]

> there is a strong temptation to reduce the complexity [of psychiatry] by formulating one sided explanations and applying single modes of treatment . . . he has witnessed three such cycles. The first . . . was in psychoanalysis. . . *the* basic science of psychiatry . . . Next came community psychiatry. . . [which] downplayed biological and psychological factors. The third rotation is now the embodiment of the psychiatrist as a neuroscientist.

James Kelly and associates maintained CMH's social focus:[44] "The field of community psychology is distinct . . . because of its emphasis on interdependent relationships between persons and setting, multiple levels of analysis, prevention, individual and collective resources, and social action". Those seeking to continue CMH practice had to struggle to reconcile it with contemporary values and resources. The range of interpretations of CMH and its essential elements were laid out:[45]

> The field of community mental health can be appraised from a variety of viewpoints, i.e., to emphasize the adaptation of clinical services

328 *Continuity and Replacement*

> for new clients, to evaluate community mental health services, to elaborate the role of the federal community mental health center program, to highlight the administrative and logistical issues when designing services for geographical areas with widely varying characteristics and needs . . . novel services. . . . [requiring] methods and processes when citizens and professionals work together . . . three topics, which contribute directly to the operation of these novel services: social support networks, self-help groups, and citizen participation . . . community mental health services in the U.S. . . . [embody] at least two social processes . . . the search for public support to maintain the federally initiated community mental health center program . . . struggles to create services that can meet community needs.

Leonard Duhl took note of psychiatry's waning concern for caring and the social environment, and reasserted the need for them:[46]

> There is a growing demand for the *quality* of life. Environmental concerns and shifts in the processes of governance . . . the need for *healers* . . . "community mental health" began as a dream, but . . . it quickly became a matter of pouring new wine into old wineskins. New programs were added, but the style remained unchanged. More emphasis was placed on medications than on humanistic concerns, on technicians than on healers . . . to be a healer. . . [one must] join the network of other people engaged in the healing process—other psychiatrists, physicians, religious figures, teachers, lawyers, politicians, and so on . . . pull the community together (p. 105) . . . being aware of the uniqueness of each patient and his relatedness to the many parts of the community in which he lives . . . a part of the network of health . . . Network psychiatry focuses on being aware both of the uniqueness of the individual and of his relatedness to other individuals who make up society . . . the family network, the human-service network, and the community network (p. 106) . . . that includes resource distribution (economics), power distribution (politics), autonomy and the common good, and many other factors . . . it is the mental health of the society itself . . . it is more than therapy . . . It is *educational* . . . it is political . . . we are practicing our profession as *healers*. . . . We cannot solve the problems facing us if we continue to blame the victim for his problem and deal with him outside and apart from the context of social networks (p. 109)

Considering the viability of CMH there was recognition of multiple issues:[47]

> echoes of lost ideals of social activism in older colleagues or confusion over how to negotiate the hazards of managed care, government

cutbacks, and anti medical bias in younger colleagues. The grand ideals of early pioneers for "treating communities" remain within the hearts of community psychiatrists, but our methods reflect a more realistic relationship to the field of community mental health and the priorities of service delivery. Methods such as assertive community treatment for adults and wrap-around community care for kids have been tested and proven effective for our most ill citizens.

It is seen to emphasize contextual issues, the crucial adverse influences of social factors such as poverty, discrimination, and severe mental illness. It embraces the public health model, prevention, and advocacy for vulnerable populations. Community psychiatrists are seen to work with the most severe and persistent emotional illness and the families of the most behaviorally disturbed children and adolescents. This approach seeks a community-based continuum of care and works in resource-poor environments. It requires experience in dealing with managed care's concept of the rational deployment of limited resources and shows the service population the appearance of being clinically informed and acceptable. It develops standards of practice for community psychiatrists, including education for CMH systems, an appropriate formulary, quality management, and the determination of levels of care. It involves active participation in interdisciplinary teams including other disciplines, patients, and their families. It includes the ability out of necessity of acting as team leaders, respectful collaboration, and the unique ability to relate to all parties involved in CMH.

While CMH found the going difficult in the U.S., some of its loyalists promoted its ideals in the international arena, including through the World Health Organization (WHO) of the United Nations. The Healthy Cities project was one of these:[48]

> Ultimately, we are interested not only in whether the city works well, but whether people can grow, develop, participate, and achieve their full potential.[49]
>
> WHO defines health as "a state of complete physical, mental and social well-being and not merely the absence of disease or infirmity", and... "is one of the fundamental rights of every human being".
>
> In 1977 the World Health Assembly, WHO's governing body of 166 Member States, resolved that by the end of this century people everywhere should have access to health services enabling them to lead socially and economically productive lives... known as "Health for All by the Year 2000" scheduled to last five years... The WHO Healthy Cities project... of the WHO Regional Office for Europe... toward Health for All by the Year 2000... The major aims... are:
>
> - to move health high on the agenda...
> - to better integrate health issues into city life.[50]

> health is a result of the complex interactions of people with each other and their physical and social environments . . . commonly shared parameters of a healthy city include a clean, safe, high quality physical environment and a sustainable ecosystem; a strong, supportive and participatory community; provision of basic needs; access to a wide variety of experiences and resources; a diverse, vital and innovative economy; a sense of historical, biological and cultural connectedness; a city form that makes all of these possible and a (p. i) high health status with appropriate, high quality and accessible public health and sick care services.[51]

A new focus of interest appeared:[52] "Ecopsychiatry seemed to have its heyday in the late 1970's. At that time the American Psychiatric Association (APA) convened a task force on relating the environment to mental health and illness, coining the term 'ecopsychiatry'. It produced a bibliography of resources in 1979".[53] One wonders if this "discovery" knew of its predecessors in the Space Cadets and social psychiatry.

Other continuing social psychiatry activities included the Physicians for Social Responsibility (PSR). Its 1987 annual meeting included the Third Annual Broad Street Pump Awards (for individual contributions toward the prevention of nuclear war) to Dr. Harris Peck of the Mid-Atlantic Region:[54]

> describes him as "addicted to founding institutions". Dr. Peck, a psychiatrist, was a founder of the Albert Einstein Medical College Coalition for Disarmament, the Center for Psychosocial Issues in the Nuclear Age, and the Westchester County (New York) chapter of PSR. In addition, Dr. Peck serves on the executive committee of PSR/New York City and is an active member of PSR's Psycho-Social Task Force. Since 1980, he has worked to develop model techniques for helping people move beyond a sense of helplessness about the nuclear threat to one of empowerment.

The perspective of the influence of social stresses on mental health rather than individual pathology appeared in other cultures, such as China:[55]

> while attesting to the social origins of suicide it [medicalization] emphasizes individual pathology and thereby diverts needed attention from the wider political, economic, and cultural forces that need to be targeted for intervention. And the gendered social forces in rural China are easily submerged in the homogenizing psychiatric discourse of "major depression". When psychiatric diagnostic criteria are applied to disempowered rural women, they rewrite their social experience in medical terms, and thereby destroy the moral exigencies and infra-politics of personal suffering in public life. In

Erich Lindemann's Legacy

George Packer Berry, *emeritus* dean of HMS, thought Lindemann contributed the discussion of social experience in psychiatry even if he did not permanently change the course of psychiatry, with HMS and its affiliated hospitals shifting focus to nuclear medicine and genetics.[56] The social and home medical approach cannot demonstrate quantitative results as biochemistry can, but this does not mean they do not contribute. The innovator has adherents and also opponents who do not understand or are threatened and then is forgotten while society catches up to the innovator's new ideas. For instance, Gerald Caplan had trouble getting his worthwhile social psychiatry ideas across and stirred up resistance.

It is useful to include in a survey of CMH after Erich Lindemann's death some indications of what memories of and attitudes about him were brought into this period. These will highlight the ideology and attitudes that developed thereafter. It is also relevant to note the passing of some of those who shared and supported his ideas.

Erich Lindemann Obituaries

Upon Lindemann's death, the obituaries and memorials were an illumination of the writers' grasps of and attitudes toward Lindemann and his ideas and work.[57] They are very varied, reflecting both the relationships of the writers to Lindemann and their recognition, acceptance, and appreciation of his various aspects: his sensitivity and expertise in clinical diagnosis and psychotherapy; his professional projects; his exploration of and advocacy for the influence of social relationships and the social community on mental health and illness; and his personal warmth, caring, openness, and respect. There is a striking difference between the obligatory cataloguing of his professional achievements, diplomatic words of appreciation even from those who rejected his contributions, and patronizing forgiveness for his personal shortcomings from institutional sources (see the HMS and MGH); reluctant acknowledgement of his legacy of public and personal benefits; and the heartfelt celebration of his contributions and admiration and loving remembrances of the man from those who shared his idealistic efforts (see HRS and Space Cadet colleagues).

These obituaries and memorials are useful as commentaries on attitudes toward Lindemann and on attitudes toward his concept of CMH in the period soon after his death.[58]

<u>November 17, 1974 *Boston Sunday Globe*, p. 111</u>: Harvard and MGH appointments and professional resume. ELMHC named in his

honor. Sodium amytal and recovered memory. Coconut Grove study of grief. West End relocation study "revealed that the relocation aspect was of relatively minor consideration to the uprooted families, that their major concern was being torn away from a cluster of people upon whom they could depend". HRS "Studies were made there into community conditions conducive to mental breakdowns . . . he focused the program on preventive psychiatry and preservation of mental and emotional health".

<u>November 18, 1974 *Palo Alto Times* p. 2</u>: "Stanford psychiatry professor dies at 74. . . died Saturday at his residence in the Oak Creek apartments, 1520 Willow Road, Palo Alto . . . Dr. Lindemann was a founder of the first community mental health center in Wellesley, Mass.

His professional specialty was in the changes of social structure which affect the mental well-being of individuals within the community, and he pioneered studies of how people react to loss and grief . . . At Stanford, he did clinical teaching and consulting work in mental health . . . Interment is to be in Plainfield, Vt.

The family prefers memorials be contributions to the American Friends Service Committee or CARE".

<u>November 20, 1974 *Stanford University Campus Report*</u>: "visiting professor of psychiatry at Stanford University School of Medicine and one of the world's most distinguished psychiatrists". Mentioned HRS, West End project, HMS, MGH.

<u>December 2, 1974 *Time Magazine*</u>: The application of sociological techniques to the treatment of psychological problems. The Coconut Grove fire study of grief and mourning. Directed the nation's first CMHC in Wellesley. 1957 study of the West End urban renewal and the "shattered web of ties to trusted friends and neighbors".

<u>November 20, 1974 *The New York Times*</u>:

> an experimental psychiatrist and psychologist who pioneered in applying social-science approaches to psychiatric problems . . . His interest in the effect of changes in social structure on an individual's mental well-being was stimulated while aiding victims of the Cocoanut Grove fire. . . [re West End Project] The investigators found that financial impact was far less significant than being torn from a cluster of persons on whom the exiles could depend . . . He was a member of the Cooperative Commission on the Study of Alcoholism, based at Stanford, that recommended in 1967 a national policy of promoting drinking in a family setting, and called for 'modification rather than suppression of drinking patterns.

Mentioned Stanford, Harvard University, MGH, Coconut Grove study, sodium amytal use in depression and schizophrenia.

November 29, 1974 *Wellesley Townsman* [letter from Marion H. Niles]:

> it was in Wellesley that the first community mental health center for preventative psychiatry was established . . . Dr. Linderman. . . [b]y chance, he learned that the Mental Health Committee of the Community Council of Wellesley was looking for a psychiatrist. To them he brought his new vision of a community preventive mental health clinic, and thus through his efforts and perseverance began Wellesley's Human Relations Service. Wellesley may well take pride in having shared in the pioneering demonstrations by Dr. Erich Linderman.
>
> Those of us who worked closely with Dr. Linderman in the beginning, will always remember the privilege, for he was a rare person, a gentle spirit, and a great humanitarian.

February 1975 *Northern California Psychiatric Society Newsletter* (written by Warren T. Vaughan, Jr., M.D.):

> Early memories of Erich are of an enthusiastic, warm human being with an infectious, youthful buoyancy. Even in the final year of his painful bout with cancer, these vital traits sustained him during his visits with old friends and colleagues . . . his therapeutic use of self and creative use of environmental manipulation, as he worked with difficult patients . . . he used a number of frames of reference <u>at the same time</u> as he worked with patients toward creative problem solving . . . At the Massachusetts General Hospital, he integrated the social dimension into his working armamentarium with his classical work in the 40s on ulcerative colitis, loss and grief.
>
> In late 1940s, he conceived of developing a community laboratory to study the relationships between social systems, events within them, and mental and emotional states. The Human Relations Service of Wellesley, Inc. was founded . . . the work that went on in the Wellesley Project and the Harvard School of Public Health over the next six years earned for Lindemann the unofficial title, "father of community psychiatry".
>
> Lindemann embraced the sociological concepts of role and function as they were being developed by Talcott Parsons. This provided a frame of reference for a theory of preventive psychiatry, mental health promotion, and the "mental health of organizations". Lindemann applied his theoretical insights in developing the "mental health consultation", "preventive intervention", and "crisis intervention" as new procedures in both clinical and community settings.
>
> We are still trying to absorb all of what this great teacher and humanist had to say about man and his ways . . . He built not only

conceptual bridges in the intellectual realm, but bridges of understanding and love, care and compassion. All of these made the man.

Review of his German education, analytic training, president of the Boston Psychoanalytic Society and Institute, drug research, and the West End study.

November 19, 1974 *San Francisco Chronicle* p. 22: Work at HMS, MGH, Germany, Iowa. "He was known for his original studies on loss and grief, and his relating of psychiatric symptoms to their social context". Mention Coconut Grove, West End Study.

November 13, 1975 ELMHC Memorial Tribute to Erich Lindemann, M.D., Ph.D., 1900–1974:

> Welcome—Charlyne Costin, President, Harbor Area Board. Establishment of the Annual Erich Lindemann Symposium
> Gerald Kerman M.D., Area Program Director Introduction of Dr. Matthew Dumont
> Angelo Musto, Former President of the Harbor Area Board.
> Matthew P. Dumont, M.D., Director, Chelsea Mental Health Clinic: "Reverence and Repudiation: The Uncomfortable Legacy of Erich Lindemann"
> Guy Beninati, Member, Faneuil Chapter, Massachusetts Association for Mental Health: Presentation of Gift of Film of Lindemann Center Dedication by the Faneuil Chapter to the Archives of the Lindemann Mental Health Center
> Armando Alfano, former President, Harbor Area Board: Introduction of Dr. John Nemiah
> John C. Nemiah, M.D., Psychiatrist-in-Chief, Beth Israel Hospital: Unveiling of Portrait
> Charyne Costin: Closing
> Reception.

April 29, 1976 Robert H. Ebert, Dean, HMS letter to Elizabeth B. Lindemann: "At the Faculty Meeting of March 19, 1976, Dr. John Nemiah, on behalf of a committee composed of your husband's friends and colleagues, read a beautiful memorial minute on his distinguished life. Their tribute was moving, as I am sure you will agree on reading it".

May 28, 76 *Harvard Gazette* p. 11 Memorial Minute from HMS: Written by John C. Nemiah, M.D., chairman; Gerald Caplan, M.D., Jack R. Ewalt, M.D., George E. Gardner, M.D., Elvin A. Semrad, M.D., Peter E. Sifneos, M.D.

> When Erich Lindemann died . . . he brought to a close a professional career that has profoundly shaped the course of modern American psychiatry. A masterful clinician, he could yet see beyond the

problems of the individual patient to the complexities of the social forces that help to determine illness. His talent for blending the insights of the psychological and social sciences led him to the pioneering definitions of the principles and practice of preventive psychiatry that have earned him the right to be considered among the founders of the mental health movement . . . he joined Stanley Cobb's newly created Psychiatric Service at the Massachusetts General Hospital, and in the stimulating intellectual climate of that Unit his own interests blossomed one by one—in psychoanalysis, in psychosomatic medicine, and in the social sciences. In 1948, these bore fruit when he established the Wellesley Human Relations Service, the prototype of the comprehensive community mental health centers that were the hallmark of American psychiatry in the 1960's . . . he was not always an easy person to know. Erich Lindemann was a very private man, and much of what went on inside him was hidden behind the calm, friendly, almost Buddha-like exterior that was so characteristic of him. His reserve, at times amounting almost to seclusiveness, was in part, perhaps, the result of a basic shyness and diffidence; and no doubt, too, it was a shield against the slings and arrows of departmental administration; but he had also a passionate need to be by himself for creative meditation. He was most content, he once said, on long airplane journeys, when high above the earth he could be alone with his thoughts, uninterrupted by the myriad intrusive demands of running a department.

And yet one was aware that there was far more beneath the surface distance. All who knew him caught a glimpse on occasion, for example, of his deep compassion for sick patients and his despair when they failed to respond to his treatment, of his hurt and anxiety in the face of attacks on his ideas and programs, of his acts of help and true kindness to colleagues in trouble, of his patience and courage during the course of his long and painful final illness . . . And if he made few his confidante or intimate friend in any consistent or lasting way . . . in the papers he wrote, and in the living organizations he created—are revealed many of the forces that inspired and guided him . . . he consistently went beyond the analytic focus on the internal drives and psychodynamic structures of the individual, for he had an abiding interest in the external environmental stresses and strains that, by imposing a burden on the individual human being, require him to utilize his coping mechanisms and put him at risk for the outbreak of illness . . . this led naturally and logically to the development of organized, community-based programs aimed at the detection of individuals undergoing potentially damaging human crises and at the provision of preventive interventions for individuals and their families to help them safely through their difficulties without succumbing to emotional illness. This emphasis on the role of prevention and family therapy has profoundly altered the practice of adult and child psychiatry . . . Dr. Lindemann had an unusual and remarkable effect on people when he talked about his work. He possessed a unique skill in conveying his ideas to others that enabled him to catch the understanding and imagination of laymen and professionals alike. His own enthusiasm was infectious, and it drew into his orbit a number of community leaders, and behavioral scientists from disciplines outside the conventional boundaries of psychiatry . . . It is in large part to this personal magnetism of his that one may attribute the creation of the Wellesley Human Relations Service . . . and of the West End Project, too . . . His ideas were the moving spirit in guiding and inspiring those with whom he worked, many of whom borrowed and built upon his concepts to develop a growing body of facts and practical techniques in the area of community activities that are today common knowledge. Erich Lindemann was truly the father of Community Psychiatry . . . As one sees the [ELMHC] building today, one can only repeat the words of that moving epitaph to Sir Christopher Wren in the gloomy crypt of St. Paul's Cathedral: *Si monumentum requiris, circumspice*— "If you seek my monument, look about you".

May 19, 1976 Nemiah, John C., M.D., HMS Professor of Psychiatry, and Beth Israel Hospital Psychiatrist-in-Chief, letter to Lindemann, Elizabeth B., p. 1–2: "I am glad both that you liked the Minute and felt that it caught something of the essence of Erich. I shall always treasure my association with him and the rare opportunity he provided me to grow and develop in my own professional life".

Nemiah, John C., Psychiatrist-in-Chief, Beth Israel Hospital, Professor of Psychiatry, Harvard Medical School, "The Legacy of Erich Lindemann" (delivered at the dedication of Erich Lindemann's portrait at the ELMHC, 6/1983): He knew Erich Lindemann as a medical student, resident, and staff member.

Three things stand out for me in my memory of Erich: 1) his remarkable clinical skills; 2) his receptivity to new ideas, which reflect his own inner intellectual flexibility and scientific creativity; 3) his willingness to allow younger colleagues to follow their own interests and, with his support, to develop their academic and scientific careers . . . Erich's ability to enter empathically into the patient's life and sorrows, to elicit rich an revealing clinical material as if no one else were present, and to send the patient away heartened and uplifted by the encounter, was a unique experience for all of us (p. 1) . . . Brought up in the psychoanalytic tradition, Erich was not imprisoned by psychoanalytic doctrine. He could, accordingly make and tolerate new observations that carried him beyond standard psychoanalytic formulations and theory . . . see the vital role that disruptions in human relationships and the stresses arising from their environment played in the onset and exacerbation of psychosomatic patients' illnesses. The fruits of his classical studies of grieving and of patients with ulcerative colitis are evident in the modern systematic studies of stressful life events and of family relationships in psychosomatic disorders.

Erich's awareness of the importance of environmental stress in the production of illness eventually led him to the larger concerns with defined populations at risk for psychiatric disorders and with preventive interventions designed to detect and alleviate illness early in its course as well as to modify the pathogenic influences in patients' environments. Erich's observations, his teachings, and his practical applications of his ideas in the form of prototypic community mental health organizations were the foundations of the community mental health movement that has been the central feature of American psychiatry throughout the past two decades.

Although in my own day-to-day work and interests I have remained clinically oriented and was not moved by Erich's enthusiasm for community and preventive activities to follow this line of endeavor, his ideas have inevitably had an effect on my own thinking—perhaps most evident in a developing interest in the history of social reform . . . Although this has remained for me more of an intellectual avocation than a practical activity . . . Erich's earlier work and ideas in the area of psychosomatic disorders . . . brought me to an appreciation of the possible role of environmental factors in the pathological development of both brain and psyche, and the resulting deficits in functioning that underlie somatization (p. 3–4).

3. Erich the Chief: Erich's absorbing interest in his community activities, which continued unabated after his appointment as Professor and Chief of Psychiatry at the Massachusetts General Hospital, was sometimes distressing to those of us on the Staff whose primary concern was with the functioning of the hospital service proper. We often wished that he was more available to bring his remarkable clinical talents and his brilliance as a teacher to the everyday clinical problems that faced us (p. 4) . . . Erich always respected my interests and allowed me the freedom to pursue my idiosyncratic goals without the kind of interference that so often disrupts the professional fulfillment of younger members of an academic organization. For this, and for his friendship, I shall always be grateful to Erich Lindemann (p. 4).

MGH News, undated, pp. 5–6: When the treatment of mental illness was mostly in institutions Erich Lindemann was setting up the first US CMHC in Wellesley.

> A patient must be viewed in the context of his social situation, he believed. His theory was that people function in social clusters and

that crises occur when the structure is thrown out of kilter . . . By the time of his death . . . his ideas had helped shape public policy in mental health, and he had helped launch a new field—social psychiatry . . . His interdisciplinary approach had its roots in Germany . . . To a classical education he added a degree in both psychology and psychiatry . . . After the disastrous fire at the Coconut Grove nightclub in 1942, he published what is now considered a classic paper on the effects of bereavement and the management of grief. From this study grew his interest in how changes in a person's social environment can create a crisis.

The effects of sudden loss became the key to another area of Dr. Lindemann's investigation: ulcerative colitis . . . He found that the condition began when a person important to the patient was in some way lost.

He would learn the characteristics of the essential person and begin role-playing with the patient . . . He got some very dramatic responses, with symptoms disappearing in 24 hours'. In 1948, Dr. Lindemann's interest in community psychiatry found full expression in the Wellesley Human Relations Service. While the facility offered every variety of psychiatric service to its clients, it also provided a base for studying social conditions that gave rise to mental illness.

Preventive psychiatry became the dominant theme of the center . . . The service became the prototype for numerous centers that have sprung up throughout the country, including . . . the Erich Lindemann Mental Health Center.

After Dr. Lindemann's appointment as Chief of the Department of Psychiatry [at MGH] in 1954, the department became increasingly involved in the community, adding at the MGH an acute psychiatric service and alcohol clinic and expanding the departments of psychology and social work to include community mental health programs . . . His influence had already been felt in Harvard's Department of Social Relations and School of Public Health. . . [in the West End Study of mental health effects of urban relocation] More significant than financial loss, the team of investigators learned, was the tearing away of families from a close group of people on whom they depended.

This fabric of human relationships was described in *The Urban Villagers*, a book by Herbert Gans . . . now required reading for anyone whose decisions affects city-dwellers.

Although many of Dr. Lindemann's activities were in social fields, he was a brilliant psychoanalyst and for three years a president of the Boston Psychoanalytic Society. . . "He was a very emotional and feeling person, with a high sensitivity for the predicament of people", said Dr. Clemens E. Benda, a close personal friend and psychiatrist . . . His colleagues found him warm, gentle, and generous. He gave to his staff much freedom and encouragement to pursue their special interests . . .

To Erich Lindemann, the patient always had to be viewed in the context of his environment, just as psychiatry had to reach beyond the wards.

Dr. Lindemann was also active in drug research, the effects of barbiturates releasing emotions and memories, and the emotional reactions of survivors of the Coconut Grove Nightclub fire.
Leonard Duhl:

> [while ill] He nurtured and soothed many who came to comfort and be comforted. He supported those concerned with the spiritual, psychological, and biological totality of death. Most of all, he radiated a warmth that made him a superb clinician, and a warm friend . . . He questioned himself to the end—doubted his contributions, feared his own perceptions about others—despite his many achievements.
>
> Erich felt free as, in his grief for his own death, he was confirmed by those he loved and realized that his contributions live on in his students; in community psychiatry; in the now public extensive concerns with aging and death; as well as in the lives of all he touched, both in the United States and his native Germany. Crisis theory, consultation, and a host of other theoretical issues have his deep imprint.
>
> Erich was a deeply spiritual, as well as scientific, person. His immortality rests, finally, in his ability to bridge fields and people from the many worlds of his concern.

July, 1975 Duhl, Leonard J., University of California—Berkeley "A Memorial to Erich Lindemann", *Journal of Community Psychology*, 3(3):300–302: "Somehow, spring became associated with his mother's death, and with Germany, where he went each year. . . " (p. 300)

> this gentle, kind, "Kris Kringle" (so labeled by my children) clinician was able to unfold an important issue about life; that those who did not grieve, no matter what their style, developed illnesses; and those that did regained life . . . few understand how Erich Lindemann, by his work at the Wellesley Human Relations [Service], laid the groundwork for all that crisis theory implied . . . Erich learned from his work on grief, bereavement, and crisis that mental health is really the way we live—the quality of life. (p. 301)

> deep feelings he, for so long, was afraid to express: fears of his own unworthiness . . . Erich had been grieving—down deep—for a long time. He held his pain in, while he lived and worked. Yet he shared himself with others. Each spring he went to Germany and helped to bring life to German psychiatry . . . He was a deeply religious and spiritual man. (p. 302)

340   *Continuity and Replacement*

<u>November 13, 1975 Miss Elsie Stougaard, 140 Mt. Vernon St, Boston, MA 02108, letter to Elizabeth B. Lindemann</u>: It was a privilege to know Erich Lindemann. "His warmth and compassion for people—matched his brilliance. And what he has done for people is without possible measurement". (p. 2)

<u>March, 1975 Rollin J. Fairbanks, D.D., Episcopal Divinity School, Cambridge, MA: "Erich Lindemann", *Journal of Pastoral Care* XXIX (3/1975), p. 6</u>:

> Contemporary pastoral care will long be indebted to Erich Lindemann . . . Psychologist, psychiatrist, psychoanalyst—indeed social scientist . . . this modest practitioner and teacher. . . [reviews Coconut Grove fire study] This led to an understanding of separation feelings now familiar to all of us in pastoral care.
>
> For many years Dr. Lindemann was a regular and much appreciated lecturer in the clinical pastoral training programs at the Massachusetts General Hospital. In 1947 and again in 1948 he was a valued participant in conferences on religion and psychiatry sponsored by the Institute of Pastoral Care and held at the College of Preachers in Washington, D.C.
>
> Dr. Lindemann's interest in changes in the social and environmental structure which affect a person's mental health [leading to the West End Study] . . . [HRS] sought to apply a program of preventive psychiatry to the daily emotional needs of families in a suburban community and thereby avoid subsequent mental illness.
>
> Throughout his professional career Erich Lindemann believed, taught, and practiced interprofessional cooperation with the clergy. This writer will long remember him not only as an uncanny diagnostician, kindly therapist, and responsible social scientist, but, above all, a valued personal friend.

<u>November 15, 1975 Fairbanks, Rollin J., "Reflections on Erich Lindemann's Contributions", Erich Lindemann Symposium, HMS</u>:

> Dr. Lindemann was a source of strength and encouragement during my several years of service as Protestant Chaplain to the Massachusetts General Hospital. He also was a close personal friend. I must admit, therefore, that I some times find it difficult to keep the professional and the personal dimension of our relationship in proper focus (p. 1) . . . The Symposium program is directed toward insights and skills that have grown out of the Cocoanut Grove fire. Dr. Lindemann's contributions to which I wish to address myself . . . were not restricted to that tragedy. . . [this invitation] permits me to expand the frames of reference in honoring a very dedicated, skilled and compassionate teacher and practitioner of the science and art of

helping people in trouble . . . There seems to be two strong motivating factors or forces in the whole process of transmitting knowledge. One is curiosity . . . the other strong motivating dynamic is identification. When we are drawn to a teacher, when we want to be like him, consciously or not we find ourselves identifying with him, eager to be an extension of him or her whom we admire . . . Both of these factors were operative for those of us privileged to know and to learn from Erich Lindemann . . . Dr. Lindemann's concern that all of us in the helping professions be more alert to the fact that. . . [t]he trauma of separation . . . often went unrecognized and therefore not dealt with by those of us who would assist in the emancipation and restoration process whereby individuals can be helped to understand what has happened to them. The loss of deep, close and meaningful interpersonal relationships not necessarily resulting from death but from other kinds of severance or separations—these too could incapacitate and lead to depression.

The second contribution . . . is the role of guilt or guilt feelings within the context of grief . . . Dr. Lindemann recognized that grief and genuine guilt combined could be lethal". (The third contribution is anticipatory grieving.) . . . The fourth contribution which I attribute to Dr. Lindemann probably did not originate with him . . . Reacting to what he called therapeutic imperialism, Dr. Lindemann urged his colleagues to utilize the person who was in best relationship with the patient, whether nurse, social worker, chaplain or occupational therapist. While the attending psychiatrist was to remain in charge and be responsible for treatment . . . others might be in a more advantageous position to carry out the prescribed help (p. 6) . . . Long before Dr. Kubler-Ross shared her knowledge and practice on this subject, Erich Lindemann came up with four needs he had observed [in the process of dying] . . . I have labeled the findings as the Lindemann Syndrome (p. 7) . . . I need not reiterate the important role that he brought to pastoral care. He believed that religious leaders were in an unique position to detect incipient emotional and mental illness and to interpret to their people the role of psychotherapy. He stressed again and again the importance of good pastoral care following the traditional rites of passage such as baptism, confirmation, marriage and burial (p. 7) . . . More and more Dr. Lindemann's concern moved from healing to prevention. He believed that it was poor economy to wait for trouble when it might be prevented. The Wellesley project was a natural outgrowth of his concern for a healthy society. He never forgot how the psychopathology of World War I laid the foundation for the sickness and horror that characterized World War II. He explained to me how the defeated Germany, unlike the Allies, had no resources for treating its psychiatric casualties who therefore moved back into post-war society and leadership despite their pathology . . . It is presumptuous of me to summarize the gifts of a very modest man (p. 8).

Moos, Rudolf M. Ph.D. (Associate Professor of Psychiatry, Stanford University Medical Center, Veterans Administration Hospital, Palo Alto, CA), *Coping with Physical Illness*: Dedication to Erich Lindemann "whose early descriptions of the ways in which people handle life crises influenced my thinking. He had the unusual gift of clarifying complex concepts so that others could understand them. Erich also faced his own illness, his own increasing pain and incapacitation, and the imminence of his own death better than I thought anyone could".

Fleck, Stephen, M.D. (Yale University School of Medicine), "Obituary: Erich Lindemann 1900–1974", *Social Psychiatry* 10:153 (1975):

> "With his passing our field lost one of its pioneers, possibly the most important and imaginative founder of the emerging discipline of Social and Community Psychiatry". His research in hypnosis, abreaction, one of the first to use sodium amytal interventions in psychotherapy; psychoanalysis, psychophysiological disorders, he worked with Walter Cannon on homeostasis. "he also cultivated cross-disciplinary interests and contacts with other behavioral scientists". He addressed the effects on patients and families of fire disaster. "His also was the first detailed documentation of the familial and social impact on a patient's course of ulcerative colitis, another classic study published in 1950."
>
> In 1948 Dr. Lindemann established the Wellesley project, a preventive community-wide mental health program utilizing professional and non-professional mental health workers which became a basic model for community mental health centers. . . [He] initiated studies on the psychosocial consequences of urban renewal, especially of the breaking up of neighborhood social networks and the enforced relocation of people. These findings have become guideposts no urban planner can ignore.
>
> But all these contributions are dwarfed somehow by Lindemann the clinician and clinician-teacher . . . His gifts as a teacher and clinical supervisor sustained him during his last years of painful and debilitating illness and benefitted many young colleagues. In this he was not only an educator, but a model of how to live with courage and dignity in the face of irreversible adversity.

Caplan, Gerald M.D. "Erich Lindemann: 1900–1974", *American Journal of Psychiatry 132:3* p. 196 (March 1975):

> "Erich Lindemann . . . was one of the most influential psychiatric pioneers of our time—a person who did more than almost anybody else to lay the theoretical and practical foundations of scientific community mental health". In Iowa he was a laboratory researcher and

clinician, studied abreactive techniques, pioneered the use of sodium amytal as a psychotherapeutic aid. "He later became interested in social science and was one of the first psychiatrists in this country to build working relationships with sociologists, anthropologists, and social psychologists". He worked with Walter Cannon on physiological aspects of homeostasis, the effect of drugs on neuroses, and the psychiatric sequellae of surgery. "In 1944 he published what turned out to be the most important paper of his career, 'Symptomatology and Management of Acute Grief'. In that paper he developed the groundwork of crisis theory and preventive intervention. During the following years he implemented his ideas concerning the primary prevention of mental disorders by establishing a mental health training program at the Harvard School of Public Health that included a multidisciplinary research and practice community laboratory, the Wellesley Human Relations Service."

"The Wellesley project, established in 1948, became a prototype for the comprehensive community mental health centers of the 1960's; it developed many of the basic concepts and techniques for the collaboration of mental health specialists with . . . community caregivers . . . in mental health consultation and education, community organization, and mental health epidemiology that are now standard in this field. . . . [H]e tried to introduce preventive mental health ideas into the community life of this medical school teaching hospital [MGH]. Outside the hospital he extended his researches to the field of city planning by studying the psychosocial consequences for the surrounding population of an urban renewal project. His findings concerning the harmful effects of forced relocation that ignored the consequences of widespread disruption of social ties were a major influence in persuading urban planners to pay attention to the human dimensions of their work". He was a superb diagnostic and psychotherapeutic clinical teacher. "Dr. Lindemann was also a charismatic lecturer. He rarely used notes, yet was able to cover a complicated topic completely and concisely. His forte was interweaving clinical, psychological, social science, and epidemiological material at a high level of abstraction, and yet in language understandable to his audience, who were held spellbound by his charm, his warmth, his sincerity, his command of a multitude of interlocking factors, and his intellectual clarity.

"In 1954 Erich Lindemann succeeded his former chief, Dr. Stanley Cobb, as Professor of Psychiatry of Harvard Medical School at the Massachusetts General Hospital. During the following years he tried to introduce preventive mental health ideas into the community life of this medical school teaching hospital".

In addition to these obituaries, Elizabeth Lindemann exchanged communications of mutual respect with those seeking publications (Hospice Planning and Educational Foundation of Orange, Inc., Middletown,

New York February 3, 1983; Spielberger, Charles D., Ph.D., director, Center for Research in Community Psychology, College of Social and Behavioral Sciences, University of South Florida, September 16, 1983); those with shared interests (Cath Associates, Inc./Stanley H. Cath, M.D., June 30, 1982, discussion of reluctance to face death, August 8, 1982); those contributing to public recognition of Lindemann's contributions (Ryan, William, Professor, Department of Psychology, Boston College, September 16, 1983 and Coelho, George V., NIMH, September 14, 1983 at the Community Psychology Division of the American Psychology Association meeting in Anaheim, CA, honoring Lindemann; and Gerald Caplan, M.D., for the album celebrating Lindemann); and those appreciating warm friendship (Jack Seeley, February 2, 1983).

The Passing of Others Who Shared Community Mental Health

This period included the deaths of some people important in the local and national field of social psychiatry:[59]

"Marion H.[arris] Niles" obituary, *Wellesley Townsman: 5.26/1977*: One of the respected and influential residents of Wellesley, MA, who helped develop the HRS. 1880–5/23/77 Boston College School of Social Work, then worked at girls clubs, a vacation house for working women, the Wellesley Friendly Aid Society, the Wellesley Community Chest and Council, the formation of the Wellesley Human Relations Service, and the Unitarian Service Committee, which, in 1939–40, was active in bringing European refugees to the U.S. Her niece was Mrs. Franklin Parker, wife of an HRS board member. Niles left gifts to HRS.

Manuscript: William Rice was one of the Wellesley respected figures who negotiated with Harvard University to establish what became the HRS.

> (Rev. William Brooks Rice died unexpectedly early in 1972. He had previously expressed a wish to write Erich's [Lindemann] biography. The following comments were intended by Erich to be a first draft, which has remained handwritten and unpublished.)
>
> Thanks to Bill Rice's efforts, the town of Wellesley became the home of the Human Relations Service, which was destined to be the model of the community mental health centers that now dot the country, are supported by the government and continue on a large scale the program of revolutionizing the services to the mentally sick, and preventive efforts to forestall emotional breakdown. He [Lindemann] provided impetus and wisdom for a collaborative organization in the community of professionals from Psychiatry, Psychology and the Social Sciences on the one hand and of the clergymen, educators and physicians, buttressed by outstanding citizens. They endeavored to design and demonstrate the feasibility of

a community-wide Mental Health Program. He saw to it that the foundation would be laid for the continued interest and financial support on the part of the citizens of Wellesley, and of the town administration.

He skillfully used the frequent gathering of the professional workers to enrich mutual communication between different religious bodies among each other and with other professional groups. For all those who participated there emerged new understanding and insight concerning the reactions of people to serious life crises, especially bereavement and mourning, and our skills in preventive intervention to avoid pathological consequences.

He helped in the development of a program in the schools to guard the mental health of the children from the very first contact with the educational institution.

His interest never flagged through two decades of creative effort. Just a year before his death he was concerned with writing a history of the successes and defeats, the joys and sorrows, the gradual expansion and the final victory of this absorbing and enriching experience.

"Institute Professor F[rancis]. O. Schmitt dies at 91", *MIT Tech Talk* (MIT News Office) 10/4/1995 p. 1–2): Born 1902; died 10/3/95. 1941 became MIT head of the Department of Biology, research on the molecular biology of nerves.

> At the time of his death, Dr. Schmitt was an honorary trustee of Massachusetts General Hospital and McLean Hospital. He served actively on the Massachusetts General Hospital board and the General Hospital Corporation from 1947 to 1975, when he became an honorary member. He also was for many years an active member of the Massachusetts General Hospital's Committee on Research, and for several years was its chairman . . . As professor of biology, Dr. Schmitt headed MIT's department from 1942 to 1955, when he was freed from his administrative duties so that he could devote all his attention to teaching and research. It was at this time that he was appointed Institute Professor, a distinguished academic post that recognizes outstanding achievement . . . Dr. Schmitt's standing . . . was enhanced, beginning in 1962, when he devoted much of his time to the Neurosciences Research Program (NRP), which he established with headquarters at the American Academy of Arts and Sciences. The program provided a focus, through conferences and publications, for research in neurosciences throughout the world.

It was a program in which mathematicians, physicists, chemists and engineers joined with experts in various biomedical sciences dealing with nerve, brain, and behavior to investigate the physicochemical and biophysical bases of mental processes such as long-term memory, learning, and consciousness.

An interdisciplinary, interuniversity organization, the NRP was Dr. Schmitt's means for promoting research in what he considered the last frontier of science, the brain and brain functions . . . the NRP had an academic affiliation with MIT.

Dr. Schmitt was chairman of the NRP from 1962 to 1974. In 1981 the NRP moved to Rockefeller University.

Dr. Schmitt remained at MIT.

"Faculty of Arts and Sciences—Memorial Minute, Talcott Parsons", 4/17/1981, p. 7:[60] Talcott Parsons (12/13/1902–5/7/1979) established the role theory of social relations, which attracted Lindemann and gave structure to his ideas of social psychiatry.

> Parsons' theoretical efforts throughout his life . . . unified by one great theme—the effort to develop a set of concepts of the determinants of human behavior, a 'general theory of action' as he called it, adequate to the analysis of the behavior of single individuals as well as the comparative and evolutionary analysis of complete societies.
>
> It was the desire for a truly general theory of action that led Parsons to take the lead in an important venture in interdisciplinary collaboration with his Harvard colleagues, Gordon Allport and Henry Murray, then in the Department of Psychology, and Clyde Kluckhohn, in the Department of Anthropology. Together these four broke from their traditional departmental moorings, and persuaded the faculty to establish, in 1945, the Department of Social Relations. This department became a notable landmark of interdisciplinary collaboration in the behavioral sciences, and a model for similar departments elsewhere. Parsons was its chairman for the first 10 years, and its guiding spirit until it was dissolved in 1972, with the reestablishment of the traditional departmental lines.
>
> Parsons regarded psychoanalytic theory as an important part of the general theory of action. He went through the course of training of the Boston Psychoanalytic Institute, and became an Affiliate Member of the society in 1951. . . . His intellectual contribution to the discipline was broad and profound, linking sociology in all directions to its related disciplines.
>
> (Parsons, T., *Toward a General Theory of Action*)

Reviews of Books About Lindemann

In addition to the obituaries, there were responses to two publications about Lindemann compiled by his wife, Elizabeth Lindemann:

> *Erich Lindemann: A Biographical Sketch* traced his professional life.[61] Its reviews seemed to reflect the lay friends and appreciators.

John Nemiah, who respected Lindemann, though he did not understand or share his perspective, saw the progressive expansion of his interest in social influences on health:[62] In "Symptomatology and Management of Acute Grief", *American Journal of Psychiatry*, Lindemann focused on loss and grief as significant events in human life and contributed to many subsequent studies, including Lindemann's research on ulcerative colitis as an example of the effect of stress on human physical and emotional disorders. He saw three stages in Lindemann's career:

1. Germany to the Iowa Psychopathic Hospital and the study of psychotropic drugs. "Even at that early point in his scientific development he evinced a keen interest in the psychological correlates of his subjects' physiological responses to a variety of psychotropic substances and saw the study of their human relationships as a vital dimension of their psychological functioning" (p. 545).
2. 1935 his move to MGH exposed him to Stanley Cobb's psychosomatic medicine. His concern with the human environment infused his study of ulcerative colitis as precipitated by ruptures in interpersonal relationships, and was applied to the acute grief precipitated by the Cocoanut Grove nightclub fire.
3. This perspective led him beyond intrapsychic dynamics to work with social milieu and social networks as offering potential for preventing psychiatric reactions to disruption of social relationships. The creation of the Wellesley Human Relations Service in 1948 formalized community psychiatry before the national blueprint in the 1960s. "He may with some justification be said to be the founding father of the community psychiatry movement in the United States" (p. 545–6).

Beyond Grief was a collection of some of his theretofore unpublished papers.[63] Lindemann's students and admirers were prominent among its reviewers.[64]

Bloch, Sidney, M.D. review of "Beyond Grief: Studies in Crisis Intervention by Erich Lindemann", *Psychotherapy and Social Science Review* 14:9 from *British Journal of Psychiatry* 134:3 (3/80): "In the final chapter, a 'talk' which Lindemann gave . . . on his reactions to his own fatal illness, he demonstrates his masterful capacity to combine the intimately personal and the detached scientific approaches to the study of human behavior".

Klein, Donald C., review "A Founder of Preventive Psychiatry; Erich Lindemann: Beyond Grief: Studies in Crisis Intervention", in inaugural issue of *The Journal of Prevention* (possibly 1979):

This volume . . . displays the immense richness of thought and vision about prevention by one of the most seminal thinkers in mental health ... an innovative conceptualizer and creative researcher. His work foretold much of current practice in primary prevention; it provides a framework which the field is still engaged in mastering in everyday practice ... one of the few persons who could properly be considered a founder of the preventive orientation in mental health as it is conceptualized today (ms p. 1).

The paper ["Preventive Intervention in Situational Crises", Congress of Applied Psychology, Copenhagen, 1961] concludes with ... four functions he hoped would be performed by community-oriented psychologists: (1) fostering protective measures for endangered individuals based on careful population studies; (2) serving as mental health consultants to caretaking professions; (3) serving as resource persons for city planners and others whose decisions impact on the emotional well-being of major segments of any population; and (4) turning research work and scholarly pursuits to 'a vastly expanded region of research problems and opportunities for upholding the scientific approach' afforded by public health work and preventive medicine (ms p4).

Baldwin, Bruce A, Ph.D., Department of Psychiatry, School of Medicine, University of North Carolina, Chapel Hill, "Beyond Grief: Studies in Crisis Intervention, Erich Lindemann. 1979. 274pp. $22.50. Jason Aronson, New York", *American Journal of Orthopsychiatry* 50:4;743–744 (10/1980): "one of the giants of community mental health and crisis intervention". (p. 743) Development of Erich Lindemann's work from postoperative patients, ulcerative colitis, and grief and the Coconut Grove fire.

Moving out of his hospital-based research setting, Lindemann next turned his considerable powers of observation and conceptualization to defining the basic principles of community mental health ... This work was carried out through his central role in the Wellesley project, one of the earliest community mental health centers. He took the mental health professional into the community, where clients were seen as individuals attempting to cope with change within a social system context. Through his work on this project and others, Lindemann succeeded not only in defining the basic structure and focus of community mental health as a discipline, but also created the nucleus for the systems theory of psychotherapy, particularly as currently practiced in family counseling and therapy (p. 743).

Inevitably, perhaps, his seminal work on (p. 743) a prototype community mental health center drew him to an examination of the professional's role in mental health. He emphasized the need "to train a new generation of doctors and other health professionals who would relate what they were doing to the life situations of patients as well as to disease processes". Breaking traditional patterns of training professionals brought with it a fair modicum of resistance. He anticipated it and met it well. And, in the end, he persevered. Moving back to work within the Massachusetts General Hospital, Lindemann insisted that many public health and community mental health concepts should become part of training programs there. Again he won . . . Lindemann broadens the professional's role to influencing large social systems or institutions to change adaptively. His "social therapists" would work with policy-makers to plan and implement preventive measures when a system began to change . . . Lindemann blended the tenets of psychotherapy with the principles of community mental health. Perhaps this integration was his most far-reaching accomplishment . . . Lindemann's book is also a window through which to see the man: compassionate and sensitive, a free-thinking professional, and an individual with a deeply creative energy who succeeded in shifting contemporary mental health research and practice in this country into new and productive directions . . . perhaps the original orthopsychiatrist (p. 744).

Weick, Karl E., "Erich Lindemann. *Beyond grief: Studies in crisis intervention.* New York: Aronson, 1979. Pp. xxiv+ 274. $22.50", *Contemporary Psychology 24:11*: 940 (11/1979): "Contemporary discussions of primary prevention, grieving, changes during the life cycle, aggression, and community mental health are anticipated in 11 previously published and 3 newly published studies by the social psychiatrist best known for his work with victims of the Coconut Grove fire".

Butero, Tom, Fairhaven, MA, letter in *Yankee* (3/1999), p. 8:

> Dr. Eric Lindemann, a Harvard psychiatrist, headed up much of the work that was done with survivors and families of the victims of the [Coconut Grove] fire. His book about the experience, *Beyond Grief: Studies in Crisis Intervention*, is still one of the cornerstone texts in crisis theory and its therapeutic applications. It is good to know that something positive and useful can come of such a horror.

Leonard Duhl tape recorded a series of interviews with Lindemann and other colleagues and family members. He and Elizabeth Lindemann corresponded with Jen C. Jones, Librarian to the American Psychiatric Museum Association, about depositing these recordings and editing their transcriptions. It was decided not to release these tapes until all those mentioned had died. Finally they were released to David G. Satin for inclusion in the Erich Lindemann Collection at the Francis A. Countway Library in the Harvard Medical Area.

Community Mental Health and Academic Psychiatry

Consideration and reconsideration of the uncertain relationship between CMH programs and academic psychiatry continued. This struggle was reviewed in 1994, with a focus on training and treatment rather than research, consultation, and prevention.[65] The findings were of a trend toward continued affiliation but more distant and selective involvement:

> [C]ommunity mental health centers (CMHCs) have become a vital link in our country's public mental health system . . . Considerable controversy continues, however, concerning their appropriate role within the total system, their efficacy in providing care, and their utility as sites for the training of psychiatric residents.
>
> [p. 722]
>
> surveys conducted in 1978. . . and 1987. . . revealed that a majority of medical school departments of psychiatry had incorporated CMHCs into their residency programs as training sites. Further, several successful models of collaboration between universities and community mental health programs have been described, including those at Johns Hopkins University . . . the Oregon Health Sciences University . . . the University of Maryland, and the University of Wisconsin. In addition, special public-academic initiatives funded by the National Institute of Mental Health . . . and the Pew Memorial Trust . . . have attempted to stimulate the initiation and development of other successful teaching, service, and research collaborations around the country . . . How CMHC-department relations have evolved over the past decade is the major focus of this paper. . . [p. 722] . . . Of the over 120. . . accredited medical schools in the United States, 110 have accredited psychiatric residencies . . . 76 (69%) responded to our survey. . .
>
> [p. 723]
>
> *Current Relationships Between Departments of Psychiatry and CMHCs* Of the 76 responding chairpersons, 52 (68%) reported . . . current relationships with one or more CMHCs. . . . Forty-seven (90%) indicated that their psychiatric residents trained at CMHCs. The remaining five chairpersons (10%) described . . . service delivery, teaching of CMHC staff, or research endeavors . . . 25 (27%) had been initiated within the past 5 years, 25 (27%) . . . 5 and 10 years, seven (8%) 21 and 30 years, and two (2%) more than 30 years from the date of the survey. . . [They were asked to] rate the overall quality of the relationship on a scale of 1 to 5 (with 1 meaning poor or uncooperative and 5 meaning excellent or very compatible) . . . Thirty-eight (73%) . . . ratings of 4 or higher, 45 (87%) . . . 3 or better, and

only seven (13%) . . . below 3. [T]here were no . . . rating of less than 2. . . . [T]he factors the chairpersons believed to be responsible for the quality of the CMHC-department relationships. . . [fell into] two groups: . . . ratings of 4 or higher (N = 38) and . . . ratings of 2 (N = 5). Both groups mentioned that the extent to which philosophies and goals were shared . . . and the quality of existing CMHC staff and on their relationships [determined whether] programs had substantial impact.

[p. 723]

Types of Relationships . . . Nine (17%) . . . the CMHC was totally integrated into the department . . . Twenty-two (42%) . . . on a contractual basis. . . [p. 723] . . . emergency services . . . consultation-liaison services . . . physician services . . . inpatient services . . . outpatient services . . . CMHC staffing . . . operation of a teaching unit . . . resident education in conjunction with the contract services . . . Thirty-six (69%) . . . the CMHC . . . a setting for the rotation of psychiatric residents. . . [included other services to the CMHC & indirect influence on it].

[p. 724]

Comparison of 1978 and 1990 Data [roughly similar except] . . . Departments with CMHC relationships [1978] 79% [1990] 68% . . . Types of relationships Integrated [1978] 28% [1990] 17% . . . Importance of CMHC relationship to residency Major [1978] 80% [1990] 67%, Minor [1978] 20% [1990] 33%.

[p. 725]

First . . . medical school departments still have considerable involvement with CMHCs . . . increase in number of relationships per department . . . over one-half . . . started within 10 years . . . Second . . . relationships . . . have worked out fairly well . . . Third . . . trend away from the integrated type of . . . relationship . . . more selective in their involvement . . . rather than attempting to operate an entire program . . . Fourth . . . rotation setting type of department-CMHC relationship . . . exert influence . . . to ensure . . . good educational experience . . . Fifth . . . major focus . . . residency education.

[p. 726]

medical school departments and CMHCs will continue to relate to one another for years to come. . . [p. 726] . . . advance psychiatric education but also help to meet the service needs of public programs. . . .

[p. 727]

Harvard University

At Gerald Caplan's retirement party on September 8, 1978, observers saw Harvard's involvement in CMH disbanding.[66] HMS psychiatry returned into medicine, and Caplan himself moved to Jerusalem and away from CMH to child psychiatry with a community orientation.

At the beginning of the 21st century, the Harvard president lauded the promise of the social sciences for "behavioral" health, reminiscent of the welcome Lindemann received when he was appointed MGH chairman:[67]

> research in the social sciences is expanding understanding, informing policy, and improving lives . . . New capacities that have emerged in the social sciences in recent years have rendered them increasingly valuable . . . The social sciences deploy these methods to great effect, challenging long-held assumptions and sharing knowledge in dramatic and meaningful ways.
>
> This is a time of remarkable promise for the social sciences . . . we cannot ignore unique insights into the human and behavioral [fields] that the social sciences alone can provide.

There is question as to how much this reflected contemporary ideology in the academic departments in an era heavily steeped in biological sciences, engineering, and technology and when those departments were the center of funding, growth, and a new campus.

Massachusetts General Hospital

The changing succession to Lindemann's position as chief of the psychiatry service continued after Eisenberg's term. Lindemann's associate at Stanford, Herant Katchadourian, reported:[68]

> our friend Sanford Gifford [psychiatrist at the Peter Bent Brigham Hospital and historian of the Boston Psychoanalytic Society and Institute] has suggested my name for Erich's old job at the Mass General . . . the latter seems highly unlikely at this point—Sanford says they are very divided about what they want leaving aside who . . . Stina [Katchadourian's wife] and I . . . said, "If Erich only knew ".

At the MGH—the platform from which Lindemann had sought to restructure psychiatry and medicine—Thomas Hackett, a junior staff member and one of his severest detractors during Lindemann's tenure, was appointed chief of psychiatry following the interim tenure of Leon Eisenberg. John Nemiah, former staff member and interim acting chief, recalled the department beginning with Stanley Cobb, who was accepted as a "Boston Brahmin" and neurologist and who established the department as a demonstration service; Lindemann developed it greatly but was not strong and never accepted; at Lindemann's retirement, the hostile MGH staff petition was, Nemiah thought, antipsychoanalytic rather than anti-Lindemann. It was reported that the MGH sought a clinician and not a scientist.[69] Housman observed that in a department of psychiatry, a strong chairman with clear interest and direction causes faculty resentment and feeling forced, and faculty therefore organize to object on various grounds.[70] There is pressure for and arrangement of a successor who is bland, undirected, and perhaps a colleague, and who brings security and freedom. He gave examples at the University of Minnesota, Stanford University, and MGH. One might add the Boston University School of Medicine's Division of Psychiatry, where Bernard Bandler, indefatigable in converting the program and the staff to CMH, was succeeded by a chairman carefully chosen to be manageable by the staff.[71]

Eisenberg discounted the possibility of Hackett's appointment. Gerald Klerman was an active contender but could not manage both the superintendence of the ELMHC and the chairmanship of the MGH Department of Psychiatry. Hackett fills the role of counteraction in relief from the strain and exhaustion of activism and novelty: identifying with the old staff; return to and revalidating traditional practices, roles, programs, and personnel; and avoiding unfamiliar ideals, goals, and relationships. He was seen as a good clinician, a nice guy, loyal, and one who worked well with other hospital staff despite the general demeaning of psychiatry. He was the comfortable, unexceptional, modest person who avoids threatening the status quo.[72] His executive assistant remembers that he was insecure, uncomfortable in the chairmanship, and feeling that he was appointed only because among the contenders, he came the cheapest.[73] She found Hackett not bright, prejudiced, clumsy, and avoiding decision and action until he burst out destructively. He hated Lindemann (and always said so; he was remembered as being derogatory at an APA meeting)[74] and defamed him, the executive assistant, and David Satin (a junior faculty member aligned with CMH). It was her impression that he was not held in high esteem by some members of his department and by heads of other MGH departments.

Hackett himself took pride that, under his direction, the department was well accepted, its staff the second largest in the hospital (five or six times bigger than under Lindemann but on the same budget), nonthreatening by avoiding the ambition to expand, helpful, and "played the medical game" by employing only physicians to make medical diagnoses and using medical treatments.[75] He remembered, in contrast, being ashamed of the psychiatry service under Lindemann, who he resented for not supporting the staff in battles.

Hackett was quoted as advocating the abolition of liaison psychiatry (psychiatry contributing broadly to other health services), saying that "the psychiatric consultation . . . is the cornerstone of general hospital psychiatry",[76] in direct opposition to Lindemann's perspective of treating the hospital as a community with the CMH approach of mental health consultation to its staff to recognize and prevent pathogenic environments rather than confining responsibility to consulting psychiatrists treating patients' problems. James J. Strain, M.D., director of the Psychiatric Consultation/Liaison Service at Mt. Sinai School of Medicine, New York City, echoed Lindemann: He urged liaison psychiatry in terms of spending more time with nonpsychiatrist physicians—more time to train them than to await requests for consultation about problem patients and spending only 15 minutes, with little teaching of physicians. He valued

> other approaches to augment consultation and have an impact on the system. These center on "nonconsult" patients, staff, and administration, and move more toward a public-health-based population model instead of one limiting the focus to individual patients . . . the consult model is a weak and inadequate pedagogic tool . . . In contrast . . . through the liaison models . . . several hours of formal mental health training are available to the modal internal medicine, family practice, or primary care internal medicine resident each week. . . [in analogy to a volunteer fire department] a consultation service seldom has the time or manpower to set up fire prevention programs or to educate the citizenry [nonpsychiatric clinicians] about fireproofing . . . the impediments that faced liaison psychiatry [include]—funding, resistances from medicine, and the energy to make it work . . . psychologists, social workers, sociologists, and the clergy were much more willing to be involved as teachers, team members, and researchers than were psychiatrists.

While Hackett continued his rejection of Lindemann, he showed his ambivalence in a token of respect for the previous professor and a courtesy toward Lindemann's widow through announcing a symposium in Lindemann's name:[77]

> A group of us have gotten together and organized a symposium on death and grief in honor of Erich . . . The program is being sponsored by the Harvard Medical School Department of Continuing Education . . . We would like to extend a full invitation for you [Elizabeth Lindemann] to come and participate in . . . whatever manner you would wish. I am somewhat diffident in suggesting this as I would not want to cause any distress by opening old memories. As a consequence, I must let you be the judge of whether you would prefer not to attend . . . It would be our pleasure and honor to have you in any capacity.
>
> [attached flyer] The First Annual Erich Lindemann Symposium on DEATH AND GRIEF NOVEMBER 15–16, 1975 AT THE MASSACHUSETTS GENERAL HOSPITAL UNDER THE DIRECTION OF

THOMAS P. HACKETT, M.D. AND GEORGE B. MURRAY, M.D. The late Erich Lindemann was renowned for his work on bereavement after the Cocoanut Grove Disaster, November, 1942. He left a lasting mark on the field of psychosomatic medicine. His teaching has been continued and extended by members of the Department he headed for many years. In this First Annual Erich Lindemann Symposium on Death and Grief, his influence and the work of contemporary investigators are being recognized . . . It is expected that in subsequent symposia, other topics will be studied that will better equip every professional who deals with some aspects of death and grief . . . 1. Cocoanut Grove as Remembered by Oliver Cope, M.D. [Professor of Surgery emeritus HMS, and Senior Consultant at MGH]. 2. Lindemann's Studies on Grief and Subsequent Progress by Avery D. Weisman, M.D. [Associate Professor at HMS and Psychiatrist at MGH]. 3. Grief or Depression? by Gerald L. Klerman, M.D. [Professor of Psychiatry at HMS, Psychiatrist at MGH, Superintendent of ELMHC]. 4. Counseling the Bereaved by J. William Worden, Ph.D. [Assistant Professor of Psychology at HMS, Psychologist at MGH]. 5. Special Interest Workshops on Grief: (a) Medication and Mourning by Gerald L. Klerman, M.D.; (b) The Widow by William F. McCourt, M.D. [Clinical Instructor at HMS, Assistant in Psychiatry at MGH, Chief of the Center for Problem Drinking at the West Roxbury Veterans Administration Hospital]; (c) Delayed Grief Reactions by Aaron Lazare, M.D. [Associate Professor at HMS, Director of Adult Out-Patient Psychiatry at MGH]; (d) Religious and Ethical Perspective on the Dying Patient by George B. Murray, M.D. [Clinical Fellow at HMS, Chief of the Resident Consultation Service at MGH]; (e) Sudden Death; (f) Communicating With Dying Children and Their Parents by Ned H. Cassem, M.D. [Assistant Professor at HMS, Director of Residency Training in Psychiatry at MGH]. Saturday Evening: Interview with Cocoanut Grove Survivors. 6. Encounters with Dying Patients: 1975 Perspective by Ned H. Cassem, M.D. 7. Special Interest Workshops on Grief. 8. Summary and Projections by Thomas P. Hackett, M.D. [Associate Professor at HMS, Acting Chief of Psychiatry at MGH]

At this time of the Psychiatry Service becoming more medical/biological, John Stoeckle in the MGH Medical Service, who had shared sympathies with Lindemann, decried the loss of humane interests in the doctor-patient relationship (DPR):[78]

> **Changing DPR** [doctor-patient-relationship] In the [19]50's the then paternal, often very longitudinal DPR was effectively used to gather psychosocial information for knowing the patient as a person . . . and providing helping relief. . . . [I]n the anti-authoritarian [19]60's, the . . . DPR changed so that by the [19]70's, a desubordinated DPR

that came out of the patients' rights movement was soon demanded by . . . patients seeking medical help or wanting to do their own self-help. . . [and insisting on] informed consent (p. 2) . . . with the market economy of the [19]80's, patients as "customers" have become informed from outside the DPR, in TV, magazine and newspaper ads, by drug firms on what to take, by hospitals, on where to go, and now on the Internet, on what might be their diagnosis and treatment . . . the profession itself has sought a new open "partnership" patient-doctor relationship . . . more communication of information for shared decision-making . . . behavioral change for chronic disease management, more "customer satisfaction", better outcomes, and fewer malpractice suits (p. 3) . . . The direction of psychosocial care now becomes focused on communication for medical tasks of care, less on learning about the patient as a person and psychotherapeutic helping for emotional relief (p. 4) . . . Besides health professionals so many self and group help organizations patients, informal caretakers, and information services are providing psychosocial care using communication skills (p. 5) . . . [contemporary] quick hospital work-up . . . where their speedy fact-finding checklists and body testing search for medical diagnosis, risks, and treatment that might seem body engineering . . . replace learning the patient's illness experience or about the patient as a person, and if considered, these aspects of care might be transferred to others [than physicians]. (p. 6) . . . Those changes in organization, medical work, communication, and relationships, raise questions of the doctor's role in psychosocial care . . . Scientific advance leads steadily to closer integration of medical technology, biomedical engineering, the pharmaceutical industry, and medical education (p. 7) . . . "we risk exchanging our sleep-deprived healers for a cadre of wide-awake technicians" [Drazen J.M., Epstein A.M.: "Rethinking Medical Training: The Critical Work Ahead". NEJM [*New England Journal of Medicine*] 2002 v347:1271–2] (p. 8) . . . There has been no medical educational change in the last 20 years to respond to the emerging dominance of body engineering and productivity demands. It is necessary to expand the time in medical school devoted to learning to listen to patients, their emotional lives, psychology (not just behavioral), the life cycle, language and culture (p. 9).

Nemiah recalled that the state Commissioner of Mental Health, Harry Solomon, was involved with CMH, establishing the Harry C. Solomon Mental Health Center in Lowell, MA, before the CMHC Act was passed and planning regional mental health centers by renaming the historic Boston Psychopathic Hospital as the Massachusetts Mental Health Center and looking also to the ELMHC. The MGH psychiatry staff who accepted the public CMH programs sought to add connections between the ELMHC and the MGH Psychiatry Service; Nemiah said he wanted the mental health center closer to the MGH than it was eventually situated. He remembered Solomon wanting him to direct the ELMHC as an expansion of the MGH psychiatry service—an idea Nemiah thought naïve. The MGH did continue its affiliation with the ELMHC, but only specifically for the purpose of providing health services, conducting joint training programs, and engaging in psychiatric research and professional interchange without mention of CMH services or research.[79] Franklin Parker of the HRS thought of it as a detention center, in violation of what Lindemann stood for.[80]

The MGH is an exemplar of the cycle of psychiatric ideologies: originally biological ideology with no psychiatry department but psychiatric problems seen peripherally in medical/surgical and neurology practices; then psychological ideology with the infiltration of psychoanalysis (James Jackson Putnam and Eugene Emerson) and medical social work (Ida Cannon) in the early 20th century, followed by a full-blown psychiatry service in early to mid-century (Stanley Cobb and psychosomatic medicine); followed by an intense interlude of social ideology. In the mid to latter century (with Lindemann and multidisciplinary staff he introduced in MGH and HRS); the a convulsive reorientation to biological ideology since the latter 20th century (with Hackett and his successors).

Wellesley Human Relations Service

One of the early Wellesley Human Relations Service (HRS) staff members traced its evolution on several levels:[81]

Theoretical: research → training → clinical service
Economic: private grant → federal training grants → state funding of service → community funding of service
Leadership:

- Erich Lindemann, spiritual leader; Donald Klein, practical application
- Robert Bragg, methodical practical planning of consortium with the DMH
- Frances Mervyn, leadership style of intense personal relationships
- Robert Evans, articulate spokesman and practical administrator

Lindemann's perspective remained a reference point and inspiration to the HRS and its former and contemporary staff members. They applied it to contemporary community needs:

> . . . The terrible tragedy of Oklahoma City reminded me of Erich. How proud he would be about what this nation learned + incorporated of his teachings + innovations in prevention. It seems

to me that the manner of grieving, the crisis interventions on many levels, the community reach out is all done beautifully in <u>his</u> spirit. For that we have to be grateful . . . In thoughts + prayers I felt close to him during these days + this prompted me to write you.[82]

. . . I also continue to serve as a consultant reviewing Community Mental Health Centers for the now Division of Mental Health Services Programs [NIMH] . . . The CMHC's are doing well with many managing to keep pace with the population and the rural ones stretching to serve their people. The objective of the CMHC program, i.e., to bring the mentally ill into their share of the health dollar, seems to be reaching reality.[83]

. . . As the shock of the September 11 bombings and the anxiety about terrorism continue to reverberate, we want to update you about some of the ways The Human Relations Service has responded. As the community mental health agency . . . HRS has always had a strong interest in the well-being of the towns and in preventing and reducing problems, as well as in treating them . . . HRS distributed through local schools, an article for parents, "Helping Children Cope with Tragic Loss", by HRS Director Robert Evans . . . [arranging] a number of evenings for parents to help them talk with their children and . . . how much television coverage young children should watch . . . Boston-area schools that lost parents on September 11 turned to HRS for special guidance, and our staff consulted with educators . . . to help them with students at risk. . . [prompted] Dr. Evans to write. . . "Taking Care of the Caretakers" for school personnel and other human service providers to help them manage their own personal stresses . . . HRS has also offered counseling to local residents and to students in area colleges who have found the events especially stressful.[84]

"THE GOOD GRIEF PROGRAM: Helping Schools and Community Groups Become a Base of Support for Children When a Friend Dies . . . Sandra S. Fox, Ph.D., ACSW Director . . . since the Program's establishment almost three years ago. . . [as the] FAMILY SUPPORT CENTER of Judge Baker Guidance Center, 295 Longwood Avenue . . . Program outreach and resource development activities in District III of the Boston Public Schools . . . The Family Support Center, a preventive mental health program sponsored by Judge Baker Guidance Center, serves children and families coping with the following crises:[85]

- Diagnosis of a life-threatening illness or situation
- Sudden death caused by accident, illness, murder, or suicide

- Anticipated death resulting from illness or aging
- Jailing of a family member

The goals of Family Support Center services are to promote and support the person's or family's ability to cope with these crises and to prevent the later development of emotional problems . . . It is well known that losses leave both children and adults vulnerable to ongoing distress and unresolved grief.

Robert Bragg, successor director of HRS, described its coping with its changing environment:[86] Lindemann's original ideas of life crisis intervention led HRS to be involved in crises that might lead to clearly defined psychiatric problems. The community felt some dissatisfaction with the lack of direct-service short- or long-term care. After the end of grant funding, support came from the United Way and other agencies. With the Community Mental Health Act, the Newton-Wellesley-Weston mental health area required definition of the roles of HRS, the Newton-Wellesley Hospital, and the Newton Child Guidance Center. The HRS board of directors made the decision to become part of the state mental health system despite the potential threat to the agency's decision-making independence. The state funded a psychologist, a social worker, and part of Bragg's salary. It did not fund a psychiatrist, which limited HRS's ability to deal with medications and people in danger. Bragg saw less primary prevention than was desirable, lack of federal funding for psychiatrists dissuaded them from community practice, and left more staffing by social workers and psychologists. After leaving HRS, Bragg returned to the University of Miami, FL, where he found similar meager CMH; his work consisted of collaboration with a psychologist providing mental health consultation to kindergarten teachers in two schools and case consultation with teachers. He longed for more robust CMH training for psychiatric residents in a program he developed over five to ten years.

The persistence of Lindemann's idea of prevention was combined with the practical financial necessity of providing reimbursable treatment of mental illness.[87] Practical considerations in this era of treatment of sick individuals rather than predisposing community conditions influenced HRS policy; it had to practice what would be funded—treatment of illness.[88] There was also thought that CMH requires a special environment: a stable town population of adequate size that was sophisticated about mental health issues, interested in civic welfare, and had adequate funds to support consultation and education work that does not earn money (though see HRS's viable adaptation to contemporary conditions).

In 1978, 14 years after Lindemann left his relationship with the HRS and just four years after he died, HRS thought of itself as straddling research, training, and clinical service:[89]

The Initial Objectives were:

1. To offer professional casework to individuals and families...
2. To set up collaborative relationship with such policymaking groups as...
3. To survey the extent of mild and severe emotional problems in the Wellesley community...
4. To carry out research problems of the relationship of disturbances in emotional well-being to the social system in which they occur; and
5. To operate as a team with the broad social science approach rather than a purely psychiatric one...

Our present programs include:

1. a clinical service
2. a consultation service [to education programs]...
3. an education and consultation service to the Newton-Wellesley Hospital School of Nursing
4. a mother/infant primary prevention program for Public Health Nurses, and other...
5. a pre-school check-up and
6. a training program for social work, psychology, and psychiatric interns.

As a matter of practical survival, Frances Mervyn, Bragg's successor as director of HRS, adapted to the shift in government support away from research and reform of social conditions and toward treatment of sick individuals:[90]

> while carrying on the usual high level of commitment to responsive consultation and clinical activity (Frances V. Mervyn, Ph.D., director, open letter)
> Trainees: 1978–79
> 2 psychology fellows/trainees
> 2 psychiatric residents
> 2 social work trainees
> (p. 18)
> In 1969, Massachusetts reorganized its mental health services by passing a comprehensive community mental health center act... HRS [chose to] move into a "partnership" arrangement with the State and increase its coverage to include Weston... received funding from both towns and three State funded staff positions. HRS' role was expanded to provide more extensive clinical services, including long-term treatment, to children and their families, and adult treatment was to be handled by the Newton Wellesley Hospital... Anticipating

that in the future HRS would require third-party insurance reimbursement, the agency applied for a public health license which it received in 1974... These ... developments allowed HRS to expand substantially its services to the community (p. 2).

Correspondence during the latter part of the century vividly illustrates society's and mental health's shift from a social to biological and preventive to maintenance perspective. It smacks of a return to the nontherapeutic storage of the chronically mentally ill—now not in state hospitals but in shelters, nursing homes, and jails:[91]

> 5/24/1987 letter from Lindemann, Elizabeth B. to Marsh, Robert H., Massachusetts state representative: "Now the Commonwealth's Department of Mental Health in its proposed Transition Plan, wishes to withdraw funding from all similar [to HRS] clinics and outpatient services in order to concentrate all its resources on the ... state hospital population ... Such a course would be counterproductive, even from a fiscal point of view".
>
> 7/17/1989 letter from Lindemann, Elizabeth B. to Robinson, Clifford, DMH Newton/South Norfolk Mental Health Area Director: "It is therefore a matter of deep distress to me to learn of a conflict between the H.R.S. and another badly-needed community treatment effort, the new regional day treatment center for children ... The D.M.H. contribution has been crucial to our success as an effective agency. We would be doubly crippled if two of our most experienced staff, including their stipends, were to be transferred to another treatment center".
>
> 7/18/1989 letter from Robinson, Clifford DMH Area Director, Newton/South Norfolk Area to Lindemann, Elizabeth B.: "The Department of Mental Health has as its focus and main concern, the provision of services to chronically mentally ill adults and seriously emotionally disturbed children and adolescents. This mission was first enunciated and clarified in the Governor's Special Message of 1985, which mandated the allocation of available resources to the most impaired and disturbed of the mentally ill population. The rationale for the Department's mission was clear: the chronically mentally ill adult and the seriously emotionally disturbed child had not received the attention and resources to which they were entitled. Our most vulnerable fellow citizens needed to be able to take advantage of whatever opportunities they could to improve their day to day functioning in the least restrictive environments possible ... It was and remains an expectation that all DMH funded or supported agencies adopt and incorporate the Department's mission into their overall operations. It is also a key operational principle of the Department that redeployment and reallocation of resources be

employed whenever priority client needs warrant such actions . . . The decision to transfer the social work position was made in the light of these principles and expectations . . . While HRS performs a valued and effective service, the number of DMH priority children and adolescents who are eligible for these services is very small . . . redeployment of existing resources had to occur".

3/1/1991 letter from Evans, Robert, HRS Executive Director to HRS Trustees: "The Department of Mental Health has informed us that it will soon eliminate the last two positions at HRS . . . Arnie Kerzner [psychiatrist] and Jeanne Whitehouse [psychologist]".

3/15/1991 letter from Evans, Robert, HRS Executive Director to HRS Trustees: "the Dept. of Mental Health's shrinking of its priorities to focus exclusively on the most severely impaired. Prevention, early intervention, and broad-based outpatient treatment are beyond its interest, as are very troubled clients who do not yet qualify as 'chronically mentally ill' ".

2/6/1992 Jupiter, Beryl S., "The human side: Social service agency struggles to survive tough economic times", *Wayland/Weston Town Crier*: "Since 1969 DMH had paid the salaries of one-third of the HRS staff, six half-time professionals. Now directly employing all staff members, HRS has incurred additional costs of $175,000, a 30 percent increase in total budget. Evans observed the irony of the situation. The poor economy is responsible for both the declining budget and more stress in the community. Thus, HRS has less operating funds but greater demand for services . . . In recent years, HRS has dramatically increased income from fundraising and clinical contracts".

12/16/1996 letter from Evans, Robert, HRS Executive Director to Lindemann, Elizabeth B.: "how an agency could sustain its true community mental health mission in these troubled times. I don't think it's possible. The entire field, both at the private practice level and the community non-profit level, is being destroyed by what is called 'managed care' but is really just harsh cost control and treatment-reduction. Agencies like HRS are disappearing rapidly all over Massachusetts . . . HRS is surviving . . . this is partly because we serve wealthy towns, and largely because we have developed non–mental health services outside of our communities—services like my consulting or like employee assistance plans that draw on our expertise, but that are not directed at prevention and treatment for local residents. Ever since the state took away all its funding of us, we have adapted well in terms of staying alive and remaining viable, but have lost most of our ability to undertake preventive community work and to outreach to the poor. . . [and] preservation of linkages and connections to other community caregivers. Here again, there is almost none of this left. We still consult to our local schools, but on a reduced basis, and there is now virtually no inter-agency linkage in our area: the new watchword is competition and entrepreneurship and other right-wing shibboleths. Agencies are competing against each other (as hospitals are), not cooperating. . . [Preserving a community mental health mission] expressed a worthy but vain hope. I have little to honestly present to colleagues about it except what they already know . . . I think our field is in a terrible state at the moment and getting worse. We need Lindemann-HRS approaches more than ever, but in the new dog-eat-dog, rampant-capitalism world of mental health they are not on anyone's radar screen and I can't pretend otherwise".

1/4/1997 letter from Lindemann, Elizabeth B. to Evans, Robert, HRS Executive Director: "Erich would have been the first to recognize the honesty of your appraisal of the current state of community mental health. I'm glad he isn't here to see the depth of meanness and shortsightedness uncovered now at the ebb [of optimism and new funding for innovation]".

1998 Anniversary celebration HRS at Fifty: "Conceived half a century ago as a facility for research and training in the theories and practice of community mental health, HRS is now a different organization. It no longer receives national grant money, and research and training no longer pay its bills; its emphasis is on treatment and consultation".

The HRS struggled with the effect of these forces on its character and mission. Robert Bragg, who experienced the agency in Lindemann's era and succeeded him as executive director, was deeply disappointed:[92] "I hope you can steer them towards more preventive programs. What a challenge with such focus on secondary and tertiary care. It's so disappointing. So many of the State Mental Hospitals are decreasing their bed capacities and there just are not the community programs needed to take care of these people. Measles, etc. have the top priority on Federal funds".

The agency was thought always in financial difficulties, but the staff was stable.[93]

A board member and pediatrician in the town thought contemporary medical education was much more involved in the developmental aspects of people and early intervention in mother–child relationships.[94] Practicing pediatricians varied in their interest in mental health though some physicians were. Clergymen were involved in mental health and the HRS and interested their parishioners. Police were more insightful. And schools were interested.

Another board member, a businessman, felt that conditions and the town itself had changed much. The agency and its school consultation function were much more accepted. But he did not understand the town any more: It had become a bedroom community not interested in the town itself or mental health facilities. The Italian community imposed its own social controls without need for external facilities. HRS, like any program, had to be practical and choose it's market. Other communities developed their own social structures and appropriate mental health services, as in Newport, MA and the Roxbury section of Boston.

Ten years later, HRS acknowledged the governmental and professional ideology inhospitable to social psychiatry and tried to cling to some of the community mental health objectives:[95]

> Despite a climate inimical to prevention, HRS still devotes more of its effort to this work than any agency of its kind in Massachusetts. HRS is notable for:
>
> - collaboration with local agencies and schools on preventive programs re: drugs & alcohol, AIDS, eating disorders, etc.;
> - a summer therapeutic day camp for special needs pre-school children;
> - an active community education program offering 30–40 lectures and panels each year to parent, church and civic groups.

The HRS continued in this direction of billable clinical services with the remnants of the social context of mental health and illness. It was determined to survive, adapting to a changed ideological and politico-economic environment by becoming more service-oriented and financially independent of government and foundation grants, looking to fees and contracts for service. The publicity brochure gave the span of activities:[96]

> The Human Relations Service (HRS) is a private, non-profit community mental health agency . . . provides a wide variety of clinical, consultation, community education, and employee assistance services. . . **Counseling** . . . helps children, adolescents, adults, and families cope with issues of all kinds. . . **Consultation:** HRS consults to business and education on such issues as: •communication •team building •conflict resolution •organization development **Community Education:** Staff members speak to parent groups, civic and service organizations, and businesses on topics in •mental health •child development •family and work **Employee Assistance.**

The executive director gave some of the rationale behind this:[97]

> David,
> We don't have a formal mission statement, per se. We consistently describe our mission as "to treat, reduce, and prevent mental illness, and to support the well-being of families and our community". We

phrase it in that order because it reflects the actual distribution of our work. We would doubtless prefer to move prevention forward, but in reality it remains hard to fund and though we do every bit we can, we spend much more time providing treatment. We have developed a number of hybrid programs (employee assistance plans, for instance) that combine treatment for employees and consultation to the organization. We have also developed special relationships with local pediatric practices, which has enabled us to work with many more families with young children before the presenting problems get more serious.

We still do some training of doctoral and post-doctoral psychologists, but no research at all. I have written one book (on leading change in schools) and am nearly finished [with] another (on the decline of the family as a developmental institution) and from time to time someone publishes an article somewhere, but there is no agency emphasis on (or way to afford) research.

In short, we're still as much of what we were as we can be, it still makes us very different from other clinics like us, we have, against all odds, survived as a small, high-quality place that is focused on its towns, but we're not all that we once were.

Hope this helps.
Best wishes,
Rob

In this post-CMH era, it is interesting to note that the need for CMH continued in Wellesley, MA, site of the HRS:[98]

The "Barton Road complex" is known as a source of multi-problem families and delinquency was seen (along with "Victory Village") by the Town of Wellesley as alien to the rest of town. It was one of CMH problems that brought HRS to the town and motivated research into the stress of moving to a new town. In the year 2000 this was still seen as a needy population and in need of physical renovation, and the state funded the total rehabilitation of its cement-slab housing, long road, and parking far from residences. "[In] 1949 when the complex was constructed as affordable housing for World War II veterans. . . [with] barracks-style buildings. . . [a long-time resident] said the development changed a great deal over the past three decades, developing from a place that had a reputation for being the highest crime area in town, to a safe, integral part of the Wellesley community.

"My kids went through the schools and never felt that there was a stigma or pressure from living here", she said. "I feel just as worthy as anyone else".

[p. 11]

Another local mental health organization, the North Suffolk Mental Health Association, also found ways to increase its mental health services through local initiatives, giving hope for the locally generated community mental health programs Gerald Caplan had hoped for.[99]

Stanford Medical Center

At Stanford University, Herant Katchadourian, in Lindemann's circle, reported his being considered to succeed Stunkard as chairman of psychiatry, which would have been a shift toward social psychiatry:[100]

> Around Christmas there was a sudden fuss about who would succeed [Mickey] Stunkard [as chairman of psychiatry at Stanford] . . . the choices narrowed to Tom Gonda and me. The Dean wanted me to return now [from sabbatical in England] if appointed. I could not see how that could be done . . . Anyway, Tom has just been appointed and the Dean is now after me for a position in his office and perhaps to then succeed Tom at the end of his 3 year fixed term.

Gonda was appointed, paralleling MGH's choice of a pacific insider after activists who roiled the waters.

German Psychiatry

The head of the psychiatry department at the University of Heidelberg—part of Lindemann's education and later consultation—suggested that after World War II, social psychiatry had been an exciting novelty, as usual drawing young, creative-oriented scientists and academics to new trends.[101] It had been exaggerated, overdiscussed, and the source of many meetings, and some of its tenets had not held up. Its substance had become incorporated into general psychiatry rather than its being a separate branch, and young scientists have found more interest in new themes—biological psychiatry, brain science, and physiology. Also, the politicization of social psychiatry through its leftist associations made it less palatable, leading to loss of interest, discrediting, and the distancing by legitimate psychiatry. It was thought unlikely to again attract attention and take a leadership role. Even the director of the Department of Social Psychiatry in the institute that was originally inspired by Lindemann's work distanced himself from dealing with social issues:[102] As discussed previously, Hartmut Schneider came from a family of physicians. He wanted to help people with problems rather than immerse himself in morphological, analytically oriented medicine. At the Zentralinstitut für Zeelisches Gesundheit [Central Institute for Emotional Health] in 1980, he directed the outpatient department and then succeeded to direct the Department of Social Psychiatry—a small department including three psychiatrists, two social workers, a secretary, and a group of lay associates working in clubs and with individual patients. It had contact with community services and addressed key issues. Schneider was interested in supervising home teams to improve the home environment and was contacting sheltered workshops for the rehabilitation of substantially recovered patients. He saw Klaus Dörner, Niels Pörksen, and the Deutsche Gesellschaft für Soziale Psychiatrie (German Society for Social Psychiatry) as outside the mainstream of psychiatry—protagonists in social issues, being unrealistic and mistaken in making radical claims, such as dissolving the large state hospitals. Rather than the modern trend toward social psychiatry, he was interested in practicing traditional psychiatry with the poor with social interests, leaving social issues to social workers, and decreasing use of state hospitals through slow evolution of social and complementary activities. He cited Baden-Würtemberg as incorporating many different approaches to social psychiatry.

The West Germany government commissioned a major review of mental health needs and services in the 1970s, followed by new laws providing for mental health services, much on an outpatient basis.[103]

After the German commission report, the federal government started preventive programs, but there was no legally mandated funding for them.[104] Psychiatric hospital and mental health centers were the loci of 10% to 15% of psychiatric practice, though orientation to community and prevention (e.g., helping psychiatric patients deal with their home environments) was a basic tenet. Pörksen, as an example of the community psychiatrist, was not considered a "real doctor", with his personal views more defining than his traditional psychiatrist identity. The CMH program he established at Lüneburg stands as an example [see Ch. 1].

Pörksen thought "modern" psychiatrists and psychoanalyst left Germany for the U.S. during the Nazi era because their views were forbidden. Therefore, after that era, all university psychiatry department heads were still oriented toward a traditional somatic perspective. (In addition, it should be noted that the Nazi distortion of psychiatry for political purposes left the Germans reluctant to involve psychiatry in social issues.) Therefore, social psychiatrists were not appointed to direct state hospitals. In the 1970s, there appeared young, well-trained, community-oriented psychiatrists and social workers. In Germany, nurses were not respected though they took a vigorous role in Pörksen's program, prompting an attempt by physicians to remove him and requiring his defense before the state Minister of Health. On the acute unit, he felt that in 70% of roles, disciplinary identities were interchangeable. Psychologists had no authority; a new law would empower them to engage in private practice—interestingly opposed by community psychiatrists on the grounds that this would undermine the Mental Health Commission's goals of decentralized, community-oriented prevention and service.

Psychoanalysis

One of the bastions of continuing interest in social psychiatry was the American Psychoanalytic Association (APsA)—considered a generally conservative organization, it was home to Viola Bernard, one of the more vigorous proponents of social psychiatry, who kept one of its committees active.

Committee on Social Issues

In 1975, the Committee on Social Problems's name was changed to the Committee on Social Issues,[105] and there was a question of its amalgamation with the Committee on Community and Society, including Bruce Sklarew and Irene Chradini.[106] In the late 1970s the committee proposed a consultation service to Congressional committees with analysts as consultants on vulnerable children, teenage pregnancy, foster care, maternal and child welfare, aging, drugs, etc. In the 1980s and 1990s, the committee presented workshops at the APsA's annual meetings on "Psychoanalysis of Adults Sexually Abused as Children", "The Impact of AIDS on Psychoanalytic Work", and "The Vulnerable Child". It was interested in a wide range of social phenomena considered emerging psychiatric issues:[107]

> *Social Change:*
>
> 1. war; 2. migration to cities; 3. technological explosion of knowledge; 4. breakdown of family, religious and community institutions; 5. rising expectations for one's future wellbeing; 6. expansion of government, military, and business bureaucracy; 7. instantaneous media coverage of world events; 8. threat of nuclear annihilation
>
> *Social Responsibility of Psychiatry: Case Illustration of Nuclear Issues:*
>
> 1. slow process over decades from Los Alamos, 1942 to nationwide protest movement; 2. testing numerous sites to special areas; 3. local laboratory research to massive industrial complex, 12% of USA energy; 4. origin in military to multiple uses; 5. possession of USA to worldwide distribution; 6. secret process to disseminated technology
>
> *Social Responsibility of Psychiatry: Nuclear Advances/ Technology:*
>
> Social Change to Social Conflicts to Social Responsibility of Psychiatry— 1. personnel screening—breakdown; 2. dehumanization aspects; 3. impact of chronic secrecy on public; 4. nuclear terrorism and conflict

resolution; 5. Impact of chronic tension on children and families (e.g., Three Mile Island)—sickness, cancer, genetic defects; 6. psychological aspects of accidents; 7. impact on future orientation for marriage, family formation, attitudes toward death; 8. narcissistic aspects of chronic tension in leaders ("get it over with"); 9. mass catastrophe, civil defense issues; 10. myths and phantasies about world destruction as reality or sickness; 11. ethnocentric perceptions of self and others that distort decisions; 12. medical exploitation of crises

The Committee formulated opinions about several controversial social issues:

- Alternative family structures:[108] Single-parent households lead to negative psychological and behavioral consequences in children and should not be just accepted as alternative life styles, discouraging criticism of these choices as hurtful. Individual fulfillment is king, and the middle class can afford single-parent families, with the consequences of children paying the price and long term effects on the culture. Single parenthood is supported by the elite and journalism. The committee was also critical of arguments for the acceptance of homosexuality.
- The committee sponsored a presentation by the novelist Tom Wolfe at the May 1990 APA meeting:[109] He talked about undermining the social principles of the primacy of the father/king/god, which leads to revolution, socialism, and effects on religion, the arts, and sexuality and thence to effects on aesthetics, affluence, autistic nihilism, and the abandonment of standards.

Committee on Psychoanalysis, Community, and Society

This was another of the APsA committees focusing on an aspect of social psychiatry. Chapin described its history:[110]

> Begun in 1962. . . with the idea that analysts, by virtue of their theory of human motivation and their experience with patients, might make meaningful contributions to the understanding of national and international social problems . . . early members . . . Frances Bonner, Robert Dorn, Ed Joseph, Robert Ivan, Seymour Lustman, Joseph Michaels, Burness Moore, Bernard Pacella, Calvin Settlage and Alberta Stalita . . . study of a number of social issues, including abortion, racism, and child abuse . . . studied the biographies of international political leaders in an attempt to understand their development . . . work with police departments in the selection of recruits and . . . cope with the stress and anxiety . . . Robert Dorn of the UCLA Medical School . . . study children in families at high risk for

social traumata . . . in the late 1960's . . . Vulnerable Child Study . . . first chair, Eleanor Pavenstedt, was succeeded by Ed Cohen . . . The Community Psychiatry Committee of the American [Psychoanalytic Association], originally chaired by Viola Bernard was formed at the instigation of the Social Issues Committee, with strong support from the New York Psychoanalytic Institute.

In 1975 the name of the committee was changed, the term "social problems" giving way to the broader and less controversial "social issues".

In the late seventies a consultation service for Congressional committees was proposed to:

> . . . act as consultant in the areas of the vulnerable child, teenage pregnancy, foster care, maternal and child welfare, aging, drugs and alcohol . . . the Committee has been running three workshops at the annual meeting . . . Statement of Purpose . . . 1) identify and call attention to emerging social issues; 2) clarify the current and potential impact of these issues on the psychological health and functioning of individuals; 3) . . . define the interface of these issues with our theory and clinical work; 4) encourage research and education . . . 5) recommend to the organization position statements on these issues . . . it has issued . . . statements on . . . homosexuality, the Vietnam war and abortion . . . Committee, aware of the intensity with which some analysts object to The American [Psychoanalytic Association] taking a stand on any social issue whatever . . . the Committee has engaged in . . . studies on the impact of social problems on individuals (e.g., the effect on psychic structure of being raised in a one-parent home; clinical observations on the psychology of political activism). Other positions . . . have, in fact, been made on moral or political grounds as when it opposed the war in Vietnam . . . protest of cutbacks of government spending for mental health funding for vulnerable and high risk children . . . the diagnostic status of homosexuality and the acceptance of homo- (p. 17) sexual candidates and faculty at the training institutes . . . a statement "concerning prejudice and discrimination against homosexuals. . . "the Executive Council, which approved a resolution at the May 1991 meeting (p. 18)."

The Committee's mission statement was:[111]

The mission of the Committee on Psychoanalysis, Community and Society is to focus on psychoanalytic aspects of trauma, loss, and violence in the inner city as well as in disasters and war. It is hoped that the expertise of the committee can continue to influence public policy and the legislative process on national and international levels. Through liaisons with the Committees on Social Issues and Racial and Ethnic Diversity, the committee presented a position paper that was designed to increase the visibility of community work in our meeting program. In addition, the committee sponsors open workshops at every meeting, presents our work in ongoing issues of TAP [*The American Psychoanalyst*—newsletter of the APsA], encourages courses in Institutes, and is planning a book on the psychoanalyst in the community.

(signed by Bruce Sklarew, M.D., Chairman)

The Committee addressed a role for psychiatry *vis a vis* many of the larger social issues that Lindemann's brand of CMH moved toward:[112]

> SOCIAL CHANGE [leads to] SOCIAL PROBLEMS AND CONFLICTS, [leading to] EMERGING PSYCHIATRIC ISSUES [of] (p. 1) SOCIAL CHANGE 1. War, 2. Migration to Cities, 3. Technological Explosion of Knowledge, 4. Breakdown of Family, Religious and Community Institutions, 5. Rising Expectations for One's Future Wellbeing, 6. Expansion of Government, Military, and Business Bureaucracy, 7. Instantaneous Media Coverage of World Events. 8. Threat of Nuclear Annihilation; (p. 2) <u>Social Responsibility of Psychiatry</u>: Case Illustration of Nuclear Issues (p. 3).

A position paper, "Psychoanalysis and the Community", with the concurrence of the Committees on racial and Ethnic Diversity and Social Issues, urged the association to move community psychiatry issues (the more significant illnesses of the less significant portion of society) to a more central place in the Association's work.[113] There was an opportunity to display its relevance to, e.g., sexual abuse, violence, scapegoating, prejudice, teenage pregnancy, traumatic and other losses, and the effects of various family structures.[114] The Association had not capitalized on psychoanalysts' significant roles in interventions and public policy. Community work gives understanding of ego development, resiliency, and psychopathology that enriches clinical metapsychological development theory and practice. It enhances members and offers alternative psychoanalytic careers. The association should recognize members' community activities and counter negative public images of psychoanalysis. The Association's Program Committee and the *Journal of the American Psychoanalytic Association* should focus more attention on the application of psychoanalysis to societal concerns. "The American [Psychoanalytic Association] provides scant recognition of its members' community activities internally and does not counter the image of only helping the 'worried rich' by presenting these pursuits to the public".

Community psychoanalysis struggled for respect and survival as community psychiatry had:[115] "the committee recognizes that this support [by the APsA] has been tenuous as evidenced by recent consideration of its elimination". (handwritten marginal note: "?best omitted"). In another position paper, "Psychoanalysis, Community and Society" the committee argued for a more Inclusive and integrated approach:[116]

> The mission of the recently re-organized Committee is to focus on [psychoanalytic] aspects of trauma, loss, and violence in the inner city as well as on disasters and war. [marked out] We know of at least forty members of the American [Psychoanalytic Association] who have used their psychoanalytic background in extensive "hands-on" experience that serves as a model for part-time psychoanalytic careers . . . commissioned a ten-page and continuing section in TAP [*The American Psychoanalyst*] on the Committee and Psychoanalysis in the Inner City. With the consent of the American we propose to use our involvement and expertise to influence public policy and the legislative process on a national level as has been initiated by Donald Cohen and Steven Marans. Our meeting and the workshops . . . are very well attended. . . . Viola Bernard inspired us with a twenty-five year history of the Committee that she originated at the beginning of the community mental health movement . . . We hope to have a similar liaison with the Committee on Public Information . . . extensive liaison with the Working Group on Communal Violence and War chaired by Donald Cohen, Bennett Simon, and Jim Garbarino.
>
> At the American Psychiatric Association Meeting in May, 1995 we . . . organize the American's Symposium on Intervention for Children Exposed to Violence and War . . . Examples lie in the work of Pynoos, Marans, Osofsky, Kleinman, Meyersburg, Meers, Pollen, Parens, Bernard, Simon.
>
> Psychoanalysis was beleaguered by managed care and alternative treatments, and considered marginal by the academic, literary, and artistic communities. Myerson urged the Association to make community psychiatry more central because "psychoanalysis has great opportunities to display its relevance to pressing community concerns among which are issues of sexual abuse, violence, demonization of classes and groups, prejudice, effects of family skew, etc. Many psychoanalysts play significant roles in shaping community programs of significance as well as in influencing public policy (an example is the recent crime bill), but this is not capitalized on by the Association". Psychoanalysis is relevant to public concerns, e.g., the work of Kleinman, Yale and UCLA programs in child violence, PTSD, etc. He recommended the Association's Program Committee and the *American Journal of Psychoanalysis* focus public relations more on psychoanalysis' application to community psychiatry and significant societal concerns. In 1995 the Committee reported that more than 40 of the Association's members used psychoanalysis in "hands-on" experience with the intent to influence public policy and

legislation. It was argued that community work is a natural laboratory for understanding ego development and psychopathology, as pursued by Pynoos, Marans, Osofsky, Kleinman, Meyersburg, Meers, Pollen, Parans, Bernard, and Simon.

Committee members and their work, presented in *The American Psychoanalyst*, included: Steven Maran regarding community policing in New Haven; Joy Osofsky regarding deprived mothers and infants and police in New Orleans; Alan Felix regarding intervention with homelessness in New York; Gil Kliman regarding prevention of multiple foster care placements in San Francisco; Bill Granatir regarding school consultation; Bruce Sklarew regarding a school-based mourning project in Washington, D.C.; Robert Pynoos, an international expert on the effect of loss and trauma on children, working with the UNICEF office in Bosnia; David Sachs replicating a community police project with the federal Office of Housing and Urban Development in Philadelphia; and Ruth Fuller organizing day care consultation in Denver.

Workshops at branch and national meetings included: Steven Marans: "Urban Violence: Coordinating Psychoanalytic and Law Enforcement Responses"; Gil Kliman: "Societal Problem, Clinical Breakthrough—Preventing repetitive Losses in Foster Care"; and Joy Osofsky: "The Effects of Trauma on Young Children—Developmental and Theoretical Issues". The committee explored liaison with the Committee on Social Issues via Stanley Cath, the Committee on Racial and Ethnic Diversity via Bruce Sklarew, the Working Group on Communal Violence and War—chair Donald Cohen, and Bennett Simon and Jim Garbarino; and hoped for liaison with the Committee on Public Information. In collaboration with Dr. Schachter, it organized the Symposium on Intervention for Children Exposed to Violence and War and was developing a proposal for a seminar for psychoanalysts and a panel for association meetings. Presentations through the Baltimore-Washington Psychoanalytic Institute were titled "The Psychoanalyst in the Community, A Tribute to Walter Bradshaw, M.D." These included December 7, 1996, "The School-Based Mourning Project" and consultation in inner city schools—William Granatir, M.D. and Bruce Sklarew, M.D.; January 4, 1997, "Therapeutic Schools in the Inner City"—Arthur Stein, M.D.; January 18, 1997, "Racial Aspects of Transference and Countertransference in Psychotherapy and Psychoanalysis"—Dorothy Holmes, Ph.D.; February 8, 1997, "Caring for Self-Destructive Inner-City Youth in Residential Centers", e.g., drug addiction, violence, imprisonment—Joseph Noshpitz, M.D.; and February 22, 1997, "Coordinating Psychoanalysis and Law Enforcement Responses to Community Violence, a project of the Yale Child Study Center and the New Haven Police Department"—Steven Marans, Ph.D.

Erich Lindemann—Personal

Erich Lindemann's daughter, Brenda, eventually found her way to his interest in public health:[117]

> Twenty-five years of . . . experience in public health, health education, health and human services planning and administration . . . EMPLOYMENT HISTORY . . . Prevention Planning Specialist/Director, Vermont Prevention Institute . . . 1986-present . . . EDUCATION Master's Degree in Public Health . . . 1974. . . University of Michigan—School of Public Health . . . Bachelor of Arts Degree . . . 1969. . . Major: Social Sciences, Goddard College, Plainfield, VT. Minor: Sculpture and Photography. San Francisco Art Institute.

In 2007, Elizabeth Lindemann died in a Society of Friends continuous-care community in New Hampshire: born January 4, 1913, died July 20, 2007, at age 94 years, six months, and 14 days.[118]

Summary

This period again demonstrates the coexistence of many ideologies and interpretations of them but a clear prevalence of one in general belief and focus of support. A biological ideology and focus on the individual predominated in enthusiasm and focus of resources and effort. Governments withdrew from social causes and focused on economic conservatism for the benefit of business and the taxpayer. Science and medicine chased chemical and genetic discoveries and promises—another version of the persuasion that truth had finally been found and would lead (with time, effort, and dedication) to the solution of all problems. Locally, the HMS and MGH returned to academic and professional monism and monasticism. Social and community ideology and dedication were shed as errors of the past. The succession of Thomas Hackett after Cobb, Lindemann, and Eisenberg vividly illustrated the observation of strenuous and uncomfortable activism and innovation engendering the need for bland, comfortable, familiar inertia; and the defamation and exorcism of the previous disturbing destabilization of the prior status quo.

The eulogies and memorials to Lindemann were as much farewells as appreciations of him and CMH. But, even considered as anachronistic and disdained, social and community psychiatry persisted. Ways were found to adapt and find support for fragments in programs (such as HRS under Rob Evans) and projects (such as Gerald Caplan's). It comes as a surprise that the famously orthodox field of psychoanalysis included vigorous groups, projects, and advocacy. Again, the crucial factors appear to be dedicated, independent-minded, forceful leaders and the sufficiency of resources—finding available outside sources or independence of them.

Society at large was complex in its foci. There was general focus on the individual's needs, benefits, and problems. There was also the continuation of fragmented concerns for special interests: vigorous advocacy for the rights and needs of minorities, opposition to foreign wars such as Vietnam, and assertion by subordinate groups such as students and low-status workers. But broad social problems and improvement and change were not broad societal concerns.

Society, medicine, and psychiatry had moved on from conscience about the lives of people to a technological approach to tasks, leaving people and their lives outside societal and governmental concern.

Figure 3.1 Lindau Psychotherapy Group, 4/8/07 [courtesy Lindemann Estate]

376 Continuity and Replacement

Figure 3.2 Elizabeth B. Lindemann and Brenda Lindemann, Anaheim, CA—American Public Health Association award to Erich Lindemann, 1983 [courtesy Lindemann Estate]

Figure 3.3 Plainfield, VT—Ami (8), Jamin (6–1/2), and Brenda Lindemann with "Kitty Tall Tail", Fall 1996 [courtesy Lindemann Estate]

Notes

1. Keyserling quoted by Mitscherlich, Alexander in Mitscherlich, Alexander and Mielke, Fred, translated by Norden, Heinz, *Doctors of Infamy: The Story of Nazi Medical Crimes* (New York: Henry Schuman, 1949), Appendix p. 152.
2. Powers, John, "Running Out of Outrage", *The Boston Globe Magazine*, 10/5/1997, p. 17, 31–33, 36–37
3. Feldman, Saul, D.P.A., "Leadership in Mental Health: Changing the Guard for the 1980's", *American Journal of Psychiatry* 138:9 (9/1981), pp. 1147–1153; pp. 1147–1148
4. Forman, Craig I., Princeton University class of 1982: "'A Generation of Cynics: Today's graduates have great confidence in themselves but little hope about the prospects for most Americans", *Princeton Alumni Weekly*, 6/14/1982, p. 10–11; p. 11
5. Klerman, Gerald, former Director of the Connecticut Mentl helt enter and member of the Yale University Department of Psychiatry, Superintendent of the Erich Lindemann Mental Health Center, and Director of the Alcohool, rug, an Mentl helath Administtion, U. S. Puglic Health Service (interview by David G. Satin at the Institute of Medicine, Washington, DC, 1/26/1979). [Erich Lindemann Collection, Center for the History of Medicine, Francis A. Countway Library of Medicine, Boston, MA]
6. Rich, T., Atchley, J. and Douglass, Elizabeth. "Future Trends in Gerontological Education", in Rich, T., Connelly, J. and Douglass, Elizabeth (eds.) *Standards and Guidelines for Gerontology Programs*, Second Edition (Washington DC: Association for Gerontology in Higher Education, 1990), pp. 22–24
7. Hamburg, David, M.D., former Chairman of the Stanford Medical Center Deprtment of Psychiatry: presentation at the Annual Meeting of the Massachusetts Psychiatric Society, MIT Facuty Club, Cambridge, MA, 5/3/1982. [Box 4, X, Erich Lindemann Collection, Center for the History of Medicine, Francis A. Countway Library of Medicine, Boston, MA]
8. Pörksen, Niels (University of Heidelberg, West Germany), Lindemann, Elizabeth B. and Lindemann, Brenda, interview by David G. Satin, M.D. in Elizabeth Lindemann's house, Wellesley, MA, 9/9/1978. [Caddy 5, Box 5, X, Erich Lindemann Collection, Center for the History of Medicine, Francis A. Countway Library of Medicine, Boston, MA]
9. Blum, Henrik L., interviewed by telephone by David G. Satin, MD, 3/23/1979. [Caddy 1, Box 4, X, Erich Lindemann Collection, Center for the History of Medicine, Francis A. Countway Library of Medicine, Boston, MA]
10. Piersma, Harry L., "Reflections on the Problems of a Clinical Psychologist in a Community Mental Health Center", *Clinical Psychologist* 30 no. 2:5 (1977), pp. 11–23
11. Bernard, Viola W. M.D.—Chief, Division of Community Mental Health, College of Physicians and Surgeons, Columbia University: CMHCs, studies by the Standing Committee on Community Psychiatry and Psychoanalysis, American Psychoanalytic Association Study Group., interviewed by David G. Satin, M.D., 4/26/1979. [Caddy 1, Box 4, X, Lindemann Collection, Center for the History of Medicine, Francis A. Countway Library of Medicine, Boston, MA]
12. Kelly, James, community psychologist trained under Lindemann and Caplan (interview by David G. Satin at the Francis A. Countway Library of Medicine, Boston, MA, 4/29/1983). [Erich Lindemann Collection, Center for the History of Medicine, Francis A. Countway Library of Medicine, Boston, MA]

13. "Juggling Moral Conflicts Hidden Within Psychiatry's Four Basic Paradigms", *Frontiers of Psychiatry 10* no. 9:1 (10/1/1980)
14. Lieberman, Jeffrey, "Back to the Future: Psychiatry's Re-Commitment to Public Mental Health" Inside Psychiatry, *Psychiatric News 52* no. 20:8–9 (10/20/1917)
15. Perry, Helen Swick, "Harrry Stack Sullivan", presented at the Colloquium on the History of Psychiatry and Medicine, 4/13/1982.
16. Brodie, H. and Keith H., President, American Psychiatric Association, "Brodie Predicts Closer Ties to Neurosciences", *Psychiatric News* 17:1, 32 (1982) From a talk at the American Psychiatric Association's Institute on Hospital and Community Psychiatry, 10/10–14/1982, Louisville, KY.
17. Mosher, Loren R., "Social Barriers to Innovation", Unpublished paper, NIMH, Rockville, MD, 1977, p. 5
18. Barton, Walter E. and Sanborn, Charlotte J., "Epilogue", in Barton, Walter E. and Sanborn, Charlotte J. (eds.) *An Assessment of the Community Mental Health Movement* (Lexington, MA: Heath, 1977)
19. Barton, Walter E. and Sanborn, Charlotte J., 1977, *ibid*, p. 190
20. Lamb, Richard H. and Zusman, Jack, "Primary Prevention in Perspective", *American Journal of Psychiatry 136* no. 1:12–17 (1979)
21. Allen, James R., M.D., Professor and Chairman, Department. of Psychiatry and Behavioral Sciences, University of Oklahoma, Tulsa Medical College, and Executive Director of the Tulsa Psychiatric Center, "Social and Behavioral Sciences in Medical School Curriculum", Ch. 23 in Schulberg, Herbert C. and Killilea, Marie (eds.) *The Modern Practice of Community Mental Health: A Volume in Honor of Gerald Caplan* (San Francisco: Jossey Bass, 1982), pp. 540–564
22. Caplan, Gerald, "History and Future of Community Mental Health", Erich Lindemann Memorial Lecture, Erich Lindemann Mental Health Center, 10/7/1976
23. Zwerling, Israel, M.D., Ph.D., Chairman, Department of Mental Health Sciences, Hahnemann Medical College and Hospital, Philadelphia, PA: Review of Barton, Walter E. and Sanborn, Charlotte J., eds., *An Assessment of the Community Mental Health Movement* (Lexington, MA: Lexington Books, 1977), in *Hospital and Community Psychiatry* 29 no. 3:198–199 (3/1978)
24. "Klerman Urges Profession To Eschew Social Change", *Psychiatric News*, 9/7/1979, p. 3
25. Leopold, Robert L. and Kluft, Richard D., "Evaluation of Neighborhood Mental Health Centers", in Macht, L. (ed.) *Neighborhood Psychiatry* (Lexington, MA: D.C. Heath, 1977), pp. 157–175.
26. Goldston, Stephen E., "An Overview of Primary Prevention Programming", in Klein, D. (ed.) *Primary Prevention* (Rockville, MD: NIMH, DHEW Publication No. (ADM) 77–447, 1977), pp. 23–40.
27. Carver, John, "Prevention: Begin at the Beginning; Community Based Programs for Preventing Mental Illness", *Mental Hygiene* 60:4 (1977), pp. 7–10
28. Kane, Robert L., "The Behavioral Sciences and Preventive Medicine: Opportunities and Dilemmas", Fogarty International Center Series on the Teaching of Preventive Medicine, No. 4 (Washington, DC, GPO DHEW Publication No. NIH-76-878, 1976)
29. U.S. Department of Health, Education, and Welfare, Public Health Service, Alcohol, Drug Abuse, and Mental Health Administration: "Community Mental Health Centers: The Federal Investment" (DHEW Publication No. (ADM) 78–677, 1978)
30. U.S. Department of Health, Education, and Welfare, Public Health Service, Alcohol, Drug Abuse, and Mental Health Administration: "Community

Mental Health Centers: The Federal Investment" (DHEW Publication No. (ADM) 80-397, 1977 Revised 1980)
31. U.S. Department of Health, Education, and Welfare, Public Health Service, Alcohol, Drug Abuse, and Mental Health Administration: "Community Mental Health Centers: The Federal Investment" (DHEW Publication No. (ADM) 81-1074, 1981)
32. Demone, Harold W. Jr., Ph.D., Professor and Dean, Graduate School of Social Work, Rutgers—The State University of New Jersey, "Human Resources for Mental Health Services", Ch. 22 in Schulberg, Herbert C. and Killilea, Marie (eds.) *The Modern Practice of Community Mental Health: A Volume in Honor of Gerald Caplan* (San Francisco: Jossey Bass, 1982), pp. 540-564
33. Frank, Robert G., Marshall, Louise H. and Magoun, H.W., "The Neurosciences", in Powers John Z. and Purcell, Elizabeth F. (eds.) *Advances in American Medicine: Essays at the Bicentennial*, vol. 2 (New York: Josiah Macy, Foundation, 1976), pp. 552-613
34. Broskoski, Anthony Ph.D. [psychologist], Executive Director of the Northside Community Mental Health Center, Tampa, FL: "Leading and Managing Mental Health Centers", Ch. 10 in Schulberg, Herbert C. and Killilea, Marie (eds.) *The Modern Practice of Community Mental Health: A Volume in Honor of Gerald Caplan* (San Francisco: Jossey Bass, 1982), pp. 265-288
35. www.mass.gov/eohhs/gov/departments/dys/programs-and-services/history/deinstitutionalizing-status-offenders.html, Massachusetts Department of Youth Services: "Deinstitutionalizing Status Offenders", 10/6/2016.
36. Geller, Jeffrey L., M.D., M.P.H., "A Historical Perspective on the Role of State Hospitals Viewed From the Era of the 'Revolving Door'", *Am. J. Psychiatry* 149:11, (11/1992) pp. 1526-1533; p. 1532
37. Yudis, Anthony J., "WEST END REVIVAL PLAN New housing is proposed", *The Boston Globe*, 12/9/1986, pp. 1, 66
38. Geller, Jeffrey L., 11/1992, *ibid*, p. 1530
39. Luboff, David, "The Mean Streets", *The Tab* pp. 1, 26 (11/19/1985)
40. Christ, Jacob, M.D., staff psychiatrist, Northside Community Mental Health Center in Atlanta, Clinical Associate Professor of Psychiatry, Emory University School of Medicine, "Dehospitalization in Georgia, Commentary: Dehospitalization and Deprofessionalism", *Psychiatric Annals* 8:12 (12/1978), pp. 58-64; p. 62
41. Astrachan, Boris and Sharfstein, Steven S., "The Income of Psychiatrists: Adaptation During Difficult Economic Times", *American Journal of Psychiatry* 143:885-887 (1986), p. 887
42. Moran, Mark, "Money Woes Take Toll On Local MH Services", *Psychiatric News*, 6/2/1996
43. "Psychiatrist Warns of Viewing Patients In Terms of 'Brain", *Psychiatric News*, 5/19/89, p. 17, 24. Lipowski, Zbigniew J., M.D., Distinguished Members Lecture to the Canadian Psychiatric Association's annual fall meeting; p. 17
44. Kelly, James G., Altman, David, Kahn, Robert L., Stokols, Daniel and Raush, Harold L., "Content and Process: An Ecological View of the Interdependence of Practice and Research: An Invited Address by James G. Kelly", *American Journal of Community Psychology* 14:6 (1986), pp. 573-605; p. 574
45. Gonzales, Linda R., Hayes, Robert B., Bond, Meg A. and Kelly, James G., "Community Mental Health", to be published, in Hersen, M., Kasdin, A.E. and Bellack, A.S. (eds.) *The Clinical Psychology Handbook* (Elmsford, NY: Pergamon Press, 1983), pp. 1-2
46. Duhl, Leonard J., M.D., "Mental Health: A Look Into the Future", *Psychiatric Annals* 8:5 (May, 1978), pp. 102-109

47. Huffline, Charles MD, President, American Association of Community Psychiatrists, "Community Psychiatry in the 90's", *Psychiatric News* XXXIV no. 7:3 (4/2/1999)
48. [folder "Duhl, Leonard/Healthy Cities", David G. Satin files, Newton, MA]
49. Duhl, Len, School of Public Health, Berkeley CA, and Hancock, Trevor, Public Health Consultant, Toronto, Ontario, Canada, "Community Self Evaluation: A Guide to Assessing Healthy Cities, Prepared for the Healthy Cities Project WHO--Euro", 4/1988, p. 3
50. Duhl, Leonard J., *The Healthy Cities Project Office, World Health Organization Regional Office for Europe* (Copenhagen, 4/1988), p. 2
51. Hancock, Trevor, M.B., B.S., M.H.Sc., Associate Medical Officer of Health, City of Toronto and Duhl, Leonard J., M.D., Professor of Public Health and City Planning, University of California-Berkeley, "HEALTHY CITIES: PROMOTING HEALTH IN THE URBAN CONTEXT, A Background Working Paper For The "Healthy Cities Symposium", Lisbon, Portugal, 4/7–11/1986, pp. i–ii
52. Moffic, Seven, M.D., "Is Ecopsychiatry a Specialty For the 21st Century?", *Psychiatric News* 37:37 (4/4/08)
53. APA Task Force on Ecopsychiatric Data Base: "Relating Environment to Mental Health and Illness: The Ecopsychiatric Data Base", Approved for publication 12/78; report retired to the American Psychiatric Association library and museum. [CMH history folder, Lindemann Collection, Center for the History of Medicine, Francis A. Countway Library of Medicine, Harvard Medical School, Boston, MA]
Bibliography by descriptive categories:

I. Conceptual Overview
II. Diagnosis, Treatment, and Rehabilitation
III. Level of the Social Milieu
IV. Level of the Man-Arranged and Built Environment
V. Level of the Physical Environment
VI. Psychosomatic Level
VII. Extrasystematic Events and Processes

54. "Ripping the Handle Off the Nuclear Pump", summer 1987 *PSR* [Physicians for Social Responsibility] *Reports*, p. 7
55. Lee, Sing and Kleinman, Arthur, "Suicide as Resistance in Chinese Society", in Kleinman, Arthur and Kleinman, Joan (eds.) *Moral transformations of health and suffering in Chinese society*, p. 14 in Brandt, A. and Rozin. P., eds., *Morality and Health* (New York and London: Routledge, 1997)
56. Berry, George Packer, *emeritus* dean of HMS, telephone interview by David G. Satin to his home, 11/2/1979. [Erich Lindemann Collection, Center for the History of Medicine, Francis A. Countway Library of Medicine, Boston, MA]
57. Satin, David G., letter to Lindemann, Elizabeth B., 3/21/2000. [file "Lindemann Family", David G. Satin files, Newton, MA]
58. Elizabeth Lindemann files—file #113
59. Elizabeth Lindemann files—file #109-B P-W A-M (EL Contemporaries), Erich Lindemann Collection, Center for the History of Medicine, Francis A. Countway Library of Medicine, Boston, MA
60. An interesting sidelight on Talcott Parson's work was his deerminatoin to bring to the United States respected intellects connected with Naziism:

"Talcott Parsons' Role: Bringing Nazi Sympathizers to the U.S.", Jon Wiener, *The Nation*, 3/6/1989, pp. 1, 306,8–9: "Talcott Parsons, perhaps the most influential American sociologist of the twentieth century, worked with Army Intelligence officers and State Department officials after World War II in an operation to smuggle Nazi collaborators into the country as Soviet studies experts . . . Talcott Parsons believed Harvard University needed some of them too, for its Russian Research Center". (p. 1) "Parsons advocated a value-free sociology, arguing that social science had to purge itself of political values to achieve scientific status. His theory was ahistorical and highly abstract. During the 1960's, his work came under attack by a new generation of sociologists, who argued that his claim to 'value-neutrality' masked a commitment to the status quo and to cold war ideology. . . [in archives of Harvard Russian Research Center} ten letters Parsons wrote to a colleague, Professor Clyde Kluckhohn, head of the center. The letters report on Parsons' recruiting efforts in Germany . . . Parsons made contact with [Nicholas] Poppe [Russian professor who collaborated with the Nazis including regarding the extermination of Russian Jews] a year later, and reported back to Clyde Kluckhohn the facts about 'our friend Poppe'. . . . a telegram from the State Department's policy planning staff declared they knew Harvard was 'anxious to get him'. . . . Kluckhohn, acting on Parsons' advice, put Poppe up for a Harvard appointment, which the university's officials rejected (p. 306,8) . . . Parsons reported back to Kluckhohn at Harvard that he had met not only with Poppe, Dudin and Pozdniakov but also with two U.S. Army Intelligence officers who employed them; the intelligence officers, he reported, urged that the émigrés be brought to the United States, and Parsons suggested they be given jobs at Harvard. He called the notion 'damned important'. . . . Dudin and Pozdniakov . . . were hired by Harvard's Russian Research Center to collect information about the Soviet Union from their displaced countrymen in Germany". (p. 309)

61. Lindemann, Elizabeth B., *Erich Lindemann: A Biographical Sketch* (Wellesley, MA: Elizabeth B. Lindemann, 1987)
62. Nemiah, John C., review of Lindemann, Elizabeth Brainerd, *Erich Lindemann: A Biographical Sketch* (Wellesley, MA: Elizabeth B. Lindemann, 1987), p. 90 in *American Journal of Psychiatry* 146:4 (4/1989), pp. 545–546
63. Lindemann, Erich, *Beyond Grief: Studies in Crisis Intervention*, Lindemann, Elizabeth B. (ed.) (New York: Jason Aronson, 1979)
64. Elizabeth Lindemann files—file #116 (Reviews of *Beyond Grief*)
65. Douglas, Elaine J., Faulkner, Larry R., Talbott, John A., Robinowitz, Carolyn B. and Eaton, James S. Jr., "Administrative Relationships Between Community Mental Health Centers and Academic Psychiatry Departments: A 12-Year Update", *American Journal of Psychiatry* 151:5 (5/1994), pp. 722–727
66. Pörksen, Niels (University of Heidelberg, West Germany), Lindemann, Elizabeth B. and Lindemann, Brenda, 9/9/1978, *ibid*
67. Faust, Drew Gilpin, "President, Harvard University", *Harvard Magazine ii8* no.1:3 (9–10/2015)
68. Katchadourian, Herant, letter to Lindemann, Elizabeth B., 1/22/1975. [Box XII 1 folder E104 Katchadourian, Erich Lindemann Collection, Center for the History of Medicine, Francis A. Countway Library of Medicine, Boston, MA]
69. Nemiah, John, former MGH Psychiatry Service acting chairman, then Chairman of Psychiatry Department, Beth Israel Hospital: interview by David G. Satin at Beth Israel Hospital, 9/21/1978
70. Housman, Wiliam, former chairman of psychiatry at the University of Minnesota; NIMH visiting fellow in interdisciplinary education (interview

by David G. Satin in Newton, MA) Erich Lindemann Collection, Center for the History of Medicine, Francis A. Countway Library of Medicine, Boston, MA]
71. See Ch. 7b>8b.
72. Nietzche, Friedrerich, "The Extraordinarily Excellent/Luxuriant/Powerful Individual is a Threat to Established Society and Therefore Ostracized and Exterminated. Acimon, André, Section G: Living", *The Boston Globe*, Saturday, 9/15/12: "Frequently what we look forward to is not the future but the past restored".
73. Wanta, Lorna J., former Executive Assistant in the MGH Department of Psychiatry (interview by David G. Satin, 11/16/1984)
74. Gonda, Thomas, Chairman of the Stanford Medical Center Department of Psychiatry (interview by David G. Satin at the department, 12/17/1979). Gonda interpreted Hackett's response as transference reaction to an ambivalently held father figure, part of the ambivalence of the MGH department staff—Lindemann's "children".
75. Hackett, Thomas P., Chief of Psychiatry at the MGH (interview by David G. Satin at the MGH, 4/30 and 11/30/1978). [Erich Lindemann Collection, Center for the History of Medicine, Francis A. Countway Library of Medicine, Boston, MA]
76. "Liaison Psychiatry Too Important a Field To be Dropped, Says N.Y. Psychiatrist", *Psychiatric News* XX no. 20: (9/20/1985) (newspaper of the American Psychiatric Association)
77. Hackett, Thomas P., Associate Professor of Psychiatry and Acting Chief of Psychiatry, MGH, letter to Lindemann, Elizabeth B., 10/23/1975. [Box XII 1 folder E101, Erich Lindemann Collection, Center for the History of Medicine, Francis A. Countway Library of Medicine, Boston, MA]
78. Gavin, Patricia, Project Coordinator, John D. Stoeckle Center, Massachusetts General Hospital; Stoeckle, John D.—revisions: "LEARNING TO CARE AND BODY ENGINEERING", pp. 2–9. [folder "Ideologies", Erich Lindemann Collection, files of David G. Satin, Newton, MA]
79. "AFFILIATION AGREEMENT DRAFT 9/8,25/1978". [between MGH and ELMHC].

[9/25/78 draft used] [folder" Massachusetts General Hospital", David G. Satin files, Newton, MA]

"The Massachusetts General Hospital . . . acting on behalf of its Psychiatry Service, and . . . the Commonwealth, acting through its Department of Mental Health on behalf of . . . the Area Board of the Harbor Community Mental Health and Retardation Area . . . and . . . residents of Harbor eligible for mental health and retardation services . . . signify publicly their affiliation for the purpose of providing health services, conducting joint training programs, and engaging in psychiatric research and professional interchange (p. 1)

"MGH shall . . . Make available . . . MGH"s Acute Psychiatric Service . . . admit to MGH's Emergency Ward (p. 1) . . . make available . . . medical or laboratory services . . . admit to MGH's . . . Psychiatric Ward . . . Commonwealth shall . . . reimburse MGH for the cost of all services . . . fund the equivalent of the full-time services of one First Year Resident of Acute Service . . . conduct joint professional training programs in psychiatry and psychology . . . MGH shall: . . . Make available . . . the equivalent of . . . three First Year Residents, four Second year Residents, and four Third Year Residents of MGH's Psychiatric Service . . . at Lindemann's Inpatient Psychiatric Unit, elsewhere at Lindemann, and at other facilities . . . one such Resident . . . at Acute Service . . . Make available . . . its Director of

Psychiatric Residency Training (p. 2) . . . Commonwealth shall: . . . pay MGH for such services of the said Residents . . . Make available . . . Harbor's Director of Psychology Residency Training and such other members of the professional staffs . . . Seek to obtain funding for trainees . . . The parties . . . shall collaborate in the planning and conduct of applied research . . . subject to . . . requirements of MGH, the Director, and the Research Committee of Harbor's Are Board . . . the joint direction and supervision of the Chief and the Director . . . MGH shall: . . . Act as the agent of the parties hereto in seeking (and administering. . .) grants for collaborative research projects . . . Appoint the Director to MGH's Trustees' Committee on Research and . . . Human Studies . . . consider for appointment to MGH's Professional Staff any psychiatrist, psychologist, or other doctoral level professional . . . at Harbor . . . Invite suggestions and comments from Harbor . . . the appointment of any successor to the Chief. (p. 3) . . . The Commonwealth shall: . . . Make available without charge the fifth floor at Lindemann . . . for collaborative research . . . if the funding . . . shall include any allowance for rent . . . shall be assigned to Commonwealth . . . Invite suggestions and comments from MGH if . . . appointment of any successor to the Director". (p. 4)

80. Parker, Franklin, member of the HRS Board of Directors interviewed by David G. Satin, 11/17/1978. [Erich Lindemann Collection, Center for the History of Medicine, Francis A. Countway Library of Medicine, Boston, MA]
81. Gochberg, Shayna (past HRS staff), Evans, Robert (HRS Executive Director), Lindemann, Elizabeth (past HRS staff, present HRS Board of Directors), Thoma, Lucy (past HRS staff): "Evolution of the Human Relations Service of Wellesley", Erich Lindemann Forum, 5/14/1985
82. Herzan, Helen [former HRS psychiatrist and director of the psychiatry fellowship program] letter to Lindemann, Elizabeth B., 4/26/1995. [Box XII 1 folder E101, Erich Lindemann Collection, Center for the History of Medicine, Francis A. Countway Library of Medicine, Boston, MA]
83. McNabola, Marie [former HRS researcher] letter to Lindemann, Elizabeth B., Christmas, 1993. [Box XII 1 folder E101, Erich Lindemann Collection, Center for the History of Medicine, Francis A. Countway Library of Medicine, Boston, MA]
84. Wellesley Human Relations Service flyer, 11/14/2001. [Box XII 1 folder E101, Erich Lindemann Collection, Center for the History of Medicine, Francis A. Countway Library of Medicine, Boston, MA]
85. Folder "Good Grief". [Box Human Relations Service via Elizabeth Lindemann, Erich Lindemann Collection, Center for the History of Medicine, Francis A. Countway Library of Medicine, Boston, MA]
86. Bragg, Robert, M.D., interview by David G. Satin at HRS, 7/13/1979
87. Parker, Franklin, 11/17/1978, *ibid*
88. Parker, Franklin, 11/17/1978, *ibid*
89. "History and Programs of HRS, September, 1978": Prepared for Orientation Packet for incoming Board Members. [folder "HRS 30th anniversary 1978", box Human Relations Service via Elizabeth Lindemann, Erich Lindemann Collection, Center for the History of Medicine, Francis A. Countway Library of Medicine, Boston, MA]
90. Human Relations Service, Inc., "Annual Report 1978: 30 Years of Service to the Community 1948–1978". [folder "HRS 30th anniversary 1978", box Human Relations Service via Elizabeth Lindemann, Erich Lindemann Collection, Center for the History of Medicine, Francis A. Countway Library of Medicine, Boston, MA]

91. Folder "HRS—199 ff", box Human Relations Service via Elizabeth Lindemann, Erich Lindemann Collection, Center for the History of Medicine, Francis A. Countway Library of Medicine, Boston, MA
92. Bragg, Robert, M.D., former Director of HRS, 1975 Director of Education and Training, and member of the Curriculum and Admissions Committees, Department of Psychiatry, School of Medicine, University of Miami, FL, letter to Lindemann, Elizabeth B., 3/18/1983 when she was elected Chairman of the Board of Directors of HRS. [Box XII1 folder 101, Lindemann Collection, Center for the History of Medicine, Francis A. Countway Library of Medicine, Boston, MA]
93. Brines, John K., M.D., Wellesley, MA pediatrician and HRS board member. Interview by David G. Satin at his home, 12/28/1978. [Erich Lindemann Collection, Center for the History of Medicine, Francis A. Countway Library of Medicine, Boston, MA]
94. Brines, John K., 12/28/1978, *ibid*
95. Lindemann, Elizabeth (HRS Trustee) and Evans, Robert (Executive Director of HRS), letter to friends of HRS. [folder "HRS 40th anniversary 1988", Box Human Relations Service via Elizabeth Lindemann, Erich Lindemann Collection, Center for the History of Medicine, Francis A. Countway Library of Medicine, Boston, MA]
96. *The Human Relations Service, Inc., A Private, Non-profit Community Mental Health Agency* [received 4/11/2003]
97. Evans, Robert, Ed.D., Executive Director, HRS, e-mail to Satin, David G., 3/3/2003. E-mail message reprinted with the permission of Robert Evans, Ed.D.
98. Noonan, Erica, "Getting Ready to Fix Affordable Housing", *Boston Globe-Globe West*, 11/22/2001, pp. 1, 11
99. Klerman, Gerald, Keynote speech at the Annual Meeting of the North Suffolk Mental Health Association, 6/8/1982
100. Katchadourian, Herant, 1/22/1975, *ibid*
101. Janzarik, Werner (with Mundt, Christoph)—Professor and associate (future professor), Psychiatrische Klinik, Universität Heidelberg, West Germany, interview by David G. Satin, 1984. [Box X, Lindemann Collection, Center for the History of Medicine, Francis A. Countway Library of Medicine, Boston, MA]
102. Schneider, Hartmut—Director, Department of Social Psychiatry, Zentralinstitut für Zeelisches Gesundheit, Mannheim, West Germany, interview by David G. Satin, 10/28/1984. [Caddy 6, Tape 8B, box X, Erich Lindemann Collection, Center for the History of Medicine, Francis A. Countway Library of Medicine, Boston, MA]
103. Bibliography, Box X1, Lindemann Collection, Center for the History of Medicine, Countway Library of Medicine, Boston:

   Aktion Psychisch Kranke: Kulenkampff, Caspar with Geiger, Martin, Huber, Norbert and Mutters, Tom, *Probleme der Versorgung erwachsenerer geitig Behinderter* (Köln, West Germany: Rheinland-Verlag, 1980), Tagungsberichte, Band 4
   Aktion Psychisch Kranke: Häfner, Heinz and Picard, Walter, *Psychiatrie in der Biundesrepublik Deutschland fünf Jarhe nach der Enquête* (Köln, West Germany: Rheinland-Verlag, 1980), Tagungsberichte, Band 5
   Aktion Psychisch Kranke: Bauer, Manfred and Rose, Kans K., *Ambulante Dienste für psychisch Kranke* (Köln, West Germany: Rheinland-Verlag, 1981), Tagungsberichte, Band 6
   Aktion Psychisch Kranke: Häfner, Heinz and Weiz, Rainer, *Drogenabhängigkeit und Alkoholismus* (Köln, West Germany: Rheinland-Verlag, 1984), Tagungsberichte, Band 7

Aktion Psychisch Kranke: Bosch, G. and Veltin, A., *Die Tagesklinik als Teil der psychiatrischen Versorgung* (Köln, West Germany: Rheinland-Verlag, 1983), Tagungsberichte, Band 9

Schriftenreihe des Bundesministers für Jugend, Familie und Gesundheit, Modellverbund *"Ambulante psychiatrische und psychotherapeutisch/ psychosomatische Versorgung"*: *Übergangswohnheim für psychisch Kranke, Projekt: "Elisabeth-Lutz-Haus", Mannheim (1976–1979)* (Bonn, West Germany: Der Bundesministers für Jugend, Familie und Gesundheit, 1982), Band 160

Schriftenreihe des Bundesministers für Jugend, Familie und Gesundheit, Daub, Ute, Dimmek, B., Glatzer, M., Grünewald, Eva, Haselbeck, H., Habeck, D., Schaafhausen, Chr., Simon, Hans Ulrich, Zenker, J. and Ziskoven, Manuela, Modellverbund *"Ambulante psychiatrische und psychotherapeutisch/psychosomatische Versorgung"*: *Erster gemeinsamer Erhahrungsbericht der Beteiligten am Modellverbund (1976–1979)*. (Bonn, West Germany: Der Bundesministers für Jugend, Familie und Gesundheit, 1982), Band 161

Schriftenreihe des Bundesministers für Jugend, Familie und Gesundheit, Veltin, A. and Dimmek, B., Modellverbund *"Ambulante psychiatrische und psychotherapeutisch/psychosomatische Versorgung"*: *Aufbau und Inanspruchnahme psychiatrischer Dienste eines grossstädtischen Gemeinwesens, Projekt: Mönchengladbach* (Bonn, West Germany: Der Bundesministers für Jugend, Familie und Gesundheit, 1983), Band 162

Schriftenreihe des Bundesministers für Jugend, Familie und Gesundheit, Projektleiter: Bauer, M. and Haselbeck, H., Modellverbund *"Ambulante psychiatrische und psychotherapeutisch/psychosomatische Versorgung"*: *Sozialpsychiatrische Dienste in einer Grossstadt* (Bonn, West Germany: Der Bundesministers für Jugend, Familie und Gesundheit, 1983), Band 163

Schriftenreihe des Bundesministers für Jugend, Familie und Gesundheit, Gottwald, P., Helmers, M., Hutter, A., Küttner, E., Ross, M., Stähle, R., Wigbers, W. and Ziskovern, M., Modellverbund *"Ambulante psychiatrische und psychotherapeutisch/psychosomatische Versorgung"*: *Psychosoziale Versorgung auf dem Lande* (Bonn, West Germany: Der Bundesministers für Jugend, Familie und Gesundheit, 1983), Band 164

Schriftenreihe des Bundesministers für Jugend, Familie und Gesundheit, In einer ländlicher Region Projekt: Uelzen—Friedrich Jochen; Holler, Gerhard, Melchinger, Heiner, Zenker, H.-Jochen, in einer Grossstadt Projekt: Köln—Bergener, M., Modellverbund *"Ambulante psychiatrische und psychotherapeutisch/psychosomatische Versorgung"*: *Sozialpsychiatrische Dienste* (Bonn, West Germany: Der Bundesministers für Jugend, Familie und Gesundheit, 1983), Band 165

Deutscher Bundestag, 7. Wahlperiode, Unterrichtung durch die Bundesegierung, Bericht über die Lage der Psychiatrie in der Budesrepublik Deutschland—Zur psychiatrischen und psychotherapeutisch/ psychosomatischen Versorgung der Bevölkerung; Drucksache 7/4200 (Bonner Universitäts-Buchdruckerei; verlag Dr. Hans Heger, 1975)

Deutscher Bundestag, 7. Wahlperiode, Unterrichtung durch die Bundesegierung, Bericht über die Lage der Psychiatrie in der Bundesrepublik Deutschland—Zur psychiatrischen und psychotherapeutisch/psychosomatischen Versorgung der Bevölkerung; Drucksache 7/4201 (Bonner Universitäts-Buchdruckerei; verlag Dr. Hans Heger, 1975)

104. Pörksen, Niels (University of Heidelberg, West Germany), Lindemann, Elizabeth B. and Lindemann, Brenda, 9/9/1978, *ibid*
105. "Committee on Social Issues, American Psychoanalytic Association", article in *The American Psychoanalyst* 25 no. 4:17, 18 (1991) (newsletter

of the American Psychoanalytic Association), [folders "Psychoanalysis". The Steering Committee included Kim Leary—Michigan; Mark Smaller (cochair)—Chicago, Alex Burland—Philadelphia; Joseph Coltrera (Ch)—New York University, Hossein Etezady—Philadelphia, Theodore and Millie Cohen (ch)—Philadelphia, Claire and P.T. Cath (ch), Brenda Solomon—Chicago, JoAnne Fineman (ch)—New Hampshire.

Attendance at the committee meeting during the American Psychoanalytic Association meeting in the Fall of 1994 included Stanley Cath (talking with the elderly), Theodore B. Cohen (government and the vulnerable child), Joseph T. Coltrera (black antisemitism), Hossein Etezady (volence in children), JoAnn B. Fineman (foster care in New Mexico), Milton Hollar (education and minorities), Sydney L Pomer (Children who beget children), Brenda C. Solomon (domestic violence). Carolyn, Gatto, Meeting Coordinator of the APA, memo to Raskin, Raymond A., M.D., 11/28/1994. [folder "Psychoanalysis", Research Papers, Erich Lindemann Collection, Center for the History of Medicine, Francis A. Countway Library of Medicine, Boston, MA]

Not attend: J. Alexis Burland, Phyllis Cath MD (plight of divorced women)

No response: Irma J. Bland (state of race relations), Nat Dodson (day care in America), Linda Mays (cocaine babies), Ray Raskin (sexual abuse revisited)

[folder "Research Papers", Lindemann Collection, Center for the History of Medicine, Francis A. Countway Library of Medicine, Boston, MA]

106. Schacher, Judith S., M.D., President of the American Psycholanalalytic Association, letter to Raskin, Raymond, A., M.D., Chairman of the Committee on Social Issues as of 1980, 7/11/1994. [Research Papers, Erich Lindemann Collection, Center for the History of Medicine, Francis A. Countway Library of Medicine, Boston, MA]

107. Committee on Social Issues, American Psychoanalytic Association: outlines. [folder Research Papers, Erich Lindemann Collection, Center for the History of Medicine, Francis A. Countway Library of Medicine, Boston, MA]

108. Committee on Social Issues, American Psychoanalytic Association, Notes 8/19/1992. [folder "Psychoanalysis", Research Papers, Erich Lindemann Collection, Center for the History of Medicine, Francis A. Countway Library of Medicine, Boston, MA]

109. Committee on Social Issues, American Psychoanalytic Association, Notes 9/8/1992. [folder "Psychoanalysis", Research Papers, Erich Lindemann Collection, Center for the History of Medicine, Francis A. Countway Library of Medicine, Boston, MA]

110. Chapin, Joanna, "Committee on Social Issues; The American At Work", *The American Psychoanalyst* 25:4 (1991)

111. Committee on Psychoanalysis, Community, and Society, American Psychoanalytic Association, 1995. [folder "Research Papers", folders "Psychoanalysis", Lindemann Collection, Center for the History of Medicine, Francis A. Countway Library of Medicine, Boston MA]
Committee members included:

112. Untitled. [folder "Psychoanalysis: Amer. Pschoanal. Assn—Committee on Social Issues", David G. Satin files, Newton, MA]

113. Sklarew, Bruce H., Chair, Committee on Psychoanalysis, Community, and Society of the American Psychoanalytic Society: "Psychoanalysts Help Communities in Crisis", Letters to the Editor, *The American Psychoanalyst* ?1995; repeated in "Position Paper of the Committee on Psychoanalysis,

Community and Society with the Concurrence of the Committees on Racial and Ethnic Diversity and Social Issues: Subject: Psychoanalysis and the Community" (1995) [folder "American Psychoanalytic Association: Committee on Psychoanalysis, Community and Society"", David G. Satin files]:
"Too few of the programs of The American [Psychoanalytic Association] address the importance of applying psychoanalytic understanding to vital community issues . . . The Committee on Psychoanalysis, Community, and Society, with the concurrence of the Committee on Racial and Ethnic Diversity and the Committee on Social Issues, urge the Association to move issues within the scope of community psychiatry to a more central position . . . among which are sexual abuse, violence, scapegoating of classes and groups, prejudice, teenage pregnancy, traumatic and other losses, and the effect of variations in family structure . . . the significant roles many psychoanalysts play in developing . . . major interventions as well as in influencing public policy . . . Steven Maran's model program on community policing in New Haven, Joy Osofsky's work with deprived mothers and infants and the police in New Orleans, Alan Felix's interventions with the homeless in New York, Gil Kliman's prevention of multiple foster-care placements in San Francisco, Bill Granatir's school consultation, and my School-Based Mourning Project in Washington, D.C. Robert Pynoos is considered the international expert on the effect of loss and trauma on children . . . a UNICEF office in Bosnia . . . our relevance to vital issues of public concern . . . an opportunity for the understanding of ego development, resiliency, and psychopathology . . . offer alternative psychoanalytic careers . . . counter our negative public image".

114. Letter to the Editor, *The American Psychoanlayst*, 3/31/1995. [folder "Research Papers", folders "Psychoanalysis", Lindemann Collection, Center for the History of Medicine, Francis A. Countway Library of Medicine, Boston MA]
115. Committee on Psychoanalysis, Community, and Society, American Psychoanalytic Association: "Subject: Psychoanalysis, Community and Society: A More Inclusive and Integrated Approach" (1995). [folder "American Psychoanalytic Association: Committee on Psychoanalysis, Community and Society", David G. Satin files, Newton, MA]
116. Myerson, Art, Committee on Psychoanalysis, Community, and Society, American Psychoanalytic Association: "Report of the Committee on Psychoanalysis, Community, and Society" (1995). [folders "Psychoanalysis", "Research Papers", Erich Lindemann Collection, Center for the History of Medicine, Francis A. Countway Library of Medicine, Boston, MA]; [folder "American Psychoanalytic Association: Committee on Psychoanalysis, Community and Society", David G. Satin files, Newton, MA]
117. Lindemann, Brenda, *curriculum vitæ* 3/22/1995, pp. 1–2
118. Lindemann, Jeffrey to Satin, David, copy of Elizabeth Lindemann' death celebration literature, sent 8/11/2007.

4 Lindemann, Social Ideology, and Social Conscience in Psychiatry and Society
Expectations and Experience

Cycles of Ideology and the Process of Change

The unexpected and often unpredictable shifts of conditions and events and the subjectivity of their understanding have long bedeviled mankind: " [events take] a zigzag march that takes on a discoverable direction only later, when men look back and see it as history".[1] Calvin expressed it more pointedly:

> We don't understand what really causes events to happen. History is the fiction we invent to persuade ourselves that events are knowable and that life has order and direction. That's why events are always reinterpreted when values change. We need new versions of history to allow for our current prejudices.[2]

Erich Lindemann was aware of this uncontrollable shift in history, though it did not always prevent his disappointment in his own struggles to direct history:

> A number of things which we think are happening for the first time in fact probably have happened before—they are just being reexperienced, in a kind of spiral, perhaps; or, as my friend Max Scheler used to say, there is a pendulum swinging back and forth; and the things which seem relevant now may be disappearing from the surface; but they will be back again perhaps twenty years from now. And if a person has lived long enough, and endured long enough, the old fashion will come back again—you can wear all your old clothes again![3]

This historical review demonstrates the ongoing cycle of ideologies in psychiatry, medicine, and society—biological to psychological to social and then repeat—and explores the 20th-century social segment of this cycle. Clearly ideologies and the programs that they motivate grow out of their political-economic-values milieus. These milieus and ideologies engender an emotional commitment which devalues, resists, and attacks new or alternative ideologies an the ideas and practices that they beget. This is true even in allegedly objective and innovative settings such as science and academia. And it is difficult to disentangle movements from individuals as the sources of goals and drives toward those goals, and as the sources of achievements and reactions, and as deserving of credit or blame. To Karl Marx is attributed the contention that "It is not man's consciousness that determined his social being, but rather his social being which determines his consciousness".

Levine describes the social influence on mental health ideology and practice:[4]

> As social scientists, and as practitioners in the mental health field, we pride ourselves on our objectivity, and upon the empirical base of our theories, our generalizations, and our practices. Let me suggest, on the contrary, that we are all creatures of our times; that our theories and practices are shaped as much, or more, by broad social forces as they are by inference from hard data . . . the set of variables which have been included in the theories is too limited . . . The forms of practice are said to be determined by whatever conceptions of personality and of psychopathology are dominant . . . vital details of practice in the mental health fields are determined by potent social forces which are reflected in the organization and delivery of services, in the forms of service which are delivered, and in conceptions of the nature of the mental health problem. . . [p. 1] . . . The maintenance of a method can only be seen as serving the needs of the professional and not the needs of the broader society . . . pervasive social forces shape the nature of practice [professional selection, entrenchment, and clinging to an ideology] . . . the thesis we have developed states that the conception of the mental health problem, and the form of help which is developed at any given point in time is shaped by and will reflect general social conditions. During periods of . . . reform, the dominant philosophy will be one which emphasizes the "spark of the divine" in man . . . having a potential for development which is inhibited by social conditions, and the form of help will be that of providing opportunity for the individual to develop (through changing institutions). During periods which are essentially conservative, the social world will be viewed as the best of all possible worlds, and individuals who have difficulty in living in the good social world will be viewed as "sick". The form of help will be that of removing the individual from the social setting, attempting to change him in some way, and then reintroducing him into the same setting . . . the developing helping forms will employ people who are themselves drawn into professions . . . because of social forces . . . The characteristics and social and economic needs of that group will then participate in shaping the helping forms in ways which will promote the interests

of the helping [p. 18] group . . . Our reading of history suggests the term "acute social change" may be more suitable than reform to describe what is happening in given periods. When there are major political reforms, we expect that it can be demonstrated that every one of the major institutions of society is also under pressure to change. In the period from 1890 to 1912. . . considered to be one of the great reform eras in our history, the public schools . . . courts . . . churches were under pressure to change, the relationships between men and women underwent change, and . . . even the relationship between social classes was modified . . . these gross changes in social institutions were necessitated by the shift from a rural, agricultural society, to an industrial, urban society. The introduction of the factory system led to profound changes . . . in the way of life.

It is clear that history is not linear, as some historiographers and theologians posit, in terms of inevitable progress or realization of some intelligent master plan. The world, society, institutions, and communities, like individuals, reflect many interacting forces and conditions, resulting in a more or less viable and desirable outcome. Further, there is a finite number of forces and conditions, themselves influenced by others that have impact on them. This produces a variety of more or less confluent milieus that order themselves in a recurring cycle, each with different factors more dominant. However, history does not allow for uniformity with complete domination of any ideology and its implemented practices. It always embodies variety, competition, and restless relationships. Nondominant constituents are also present as more recessive variants or alternatives and as the germs of succeeding segments in the cycle.

In the cycle of societal and psychiatric ideology, the social ideology rises to dominance from out of the preceding psychological ideology, and is, in turn, overshadowed in an upwelling of biological ideology without ceasing to flavor and provide an alternative within that ideological admixture. Lindemann recalled from his youth:[5]

> One of these [Gymnasium] teachers was a man who also was a rebel in the Establishment of those days, at the end of the First World War. This man, at a birthday celebration for Kaiser Wilhelm II made a speech before all the students and faculty and ended it "Three times hurrah"—not for Kaiser Wilhelm, but "for the representatives of the German people!" And he was fired. And that made me wonder: "here is this man, obviously a venerated teacher, who obviously said something which had to be said right now!" And I began to see that the Establishment has cracks in it—that there are critical people who won't go along any more, and who fight against it . . . when the German revolution came at the end of the War, I was just at the right age, at the end of the Gymnasium. I watched on the streets with the

people, and even gave a big talk in the Town Hall in Essen to the effect that we should all say "Du" [the familiar form of address] to our teachers and be close to them, and that we should have access to the curriculum. So what happens now has been there before—such events in the cycle of history when the conditions are ripe for these feelings to come to the surface. Well, I forgot that in the meantime, of course; for a long time what happens now seemed to me to be new; only recently these things came back to me when I reminded my self of Scheler and of some other people who say history is circular, and of Hegel, who says history is pendular, and not an advancing movement. (p. 9–10)

We are reminded of the ample evidence of the existence of differing ideologies and their cyclical dominance without the extinction of the alternatives. This forms the basis for an understanding of community mental health and of the milieu in which it and Erich Lindemann struggled, rose, and receded. We are reminded that this a temporary iteration of a recurrent reiteration which will take a leading role again . . . and again.

Social Ideology

progress and regression within . . . psychiatry have always been related to the expressed attitudes of the general population. In times of collective humanism, psychiatry has advanced; in times of political doubt, suspicion, and reaction, psychiatry has come under attack and regression. In the field of community psychiatry, especially, events of the past twelve years illustrate how closely the provision for and delivery of community mental health services is related to the national political climate.[6]

One of the formulations of conditions for social change looked to the presence of widespread dissatisfaction, a clear-cut alternative position, a core of dedicated leaders with clear vision of goals, instability in the established power structure, an overt challenge to established authority, and preparation for reactive vigorous criticism from established forces.[7]

The emergence of social psychiatry in the cycle of ideologies took place in the context of a societal sense of optimism, power, resources, and motivation to fix society and human life. In retrospect, we sharpen the appreciation of the need for a supportive liberal, philanthropic government—psychiatric ideology, like mental health, grows from nurturing soil.

Bergstresser presented the Italian example of the shift to CMH:[8]

Radical transformation of Italy's mental health care system was made possible by the interaction of two significant historical variables,

> neither of which would have been individually sufficient. Specifically, though Franco Basaglia and his Democratic Psychiatry (*Psichiatrica Democratica*) movement were the metaphorical seeds of transformation, they only flourished as a result of their introduction during a time of hospitable social conditions. Similarly, without a firm ideology upon which to rally, psychiatric reform would not have been a salient topic of social consciousness. (p. 33)

The failure of biological (including genetic) explanations of mental illness, the hunger for support for an increasingly mobile society, the inadequacy of resources available for mental health services to noninstitutionalized people in need (20% of funds was spent on inpatients versus 4% on mental health clinics) all contributed to what has been termed the fourth psychiatric revolution:[9] awareness of social conditions contributing to mental illness, proactive efforts and primary prevention, teaching early-childhood coping skills, reduction of stresses, encouraging support groups, etc.[10]

The concordance of social ethos, ideological ideal, zealous champions of it, and availability of resources (the circumstances necessary for the emergence of any movement) fueled enthusiasm, expectations, and promise for social and community psychiatry.[11] This, in turn, threatened disappointment and reconsideration. "For an idea ever to be fashionable is ominous, since it must afterwards be always old-fashioned".[12] Bergstresser saw this in Italian mental health reform, and she emphasizes the microsocial dynamics of the implementation of an ideology:[13]

> It is by now abundantly clear that oversimplification of the problem as coupled with lacunae of resources, has failed to produce meaningful solutions to overarching and systematic mental health care problems in the United States. I assert the need for mental health care to be locally meaningful and situationally relevant; standardization of the daily aspects of health care can only negate opportunities for mentally ill individuals to engage in relevant local social processes. Furthermore, a romanticized [p. 5] or teleologically ideological notion of the destination social system only serves to sabotage the real, time-consuming, often tedious, difficult, and uncertain process of effective and lasting social integration and stigma reduction. (p. 6)

Social psychiatry and community mental health may be understood either as seeking alleviation of the social vicissitudes causing mental illness to promote mental health (primary prevention) or as bringing psychiatric care to more already-sick people (secondary and tertiary prevention). Boris Astrachan reviewed the many issues and goals that might be addressed in CMH.[14] It might concern the importance of the relationship between sub-societies and the larger society. If they are in balance, they constitute democracy. If subsocieties rule, this results in anarchy, tribalism, or feudalism. If the larger society rules, this results in totalitarianism. The mental health goals at stake may be access to care, quality of care, prevention of illness, or decrease in costs. Cost control is popular; it may lead to the medical control of illness, omission of illness prevention, improvement in the quality of life, and the support of research and training.

The faction of CMH that focuses on the expansion of psychiatric treatment to more people and problems (with a nod to mental health promotion) is represented by a director of the U.S. NIMH:[15]

> Community psychiatry is based on the adaptation of public health practice to mental health service. Its objective is to provide high quality care to the population of entire communities . . . it increases the scope of mental health professionals, improves the utilization of their skills, maintains mentally ill patients in their communities, and establishes a theater for the development of a range of human services designed to improve the mental health of the consumers of those services.

Another aspect of the secondary prevention interpretation of CMH focused on the function of the mental health consultant and advocate, defined in terms of its focus, limits, and tension with the provider and recipient of mental health care:[16]

> There are three levels of intervention . . . at the individual level . . . insuring that an individual received the appropriate services and that his rights are not violated . . . at the (p. 6) institutional level . . . to see that the institution delivers its mandated services equitably and legally and. . . [the] attempt to change service delivery to be more relevant or of better quality. . . [and] at the societal level . . . to make major changes in beliefs, concepts and delivery systems. (p. 7)
> advocacy projects should only deliver those functions [organizational change] . . . They should not deliver. . . "direct services". (p. 12) [because it] produces a conflict of interest . . . it is questionable whether one can be an adversary against a system in which one has a vested interest . . . Secondly, . . . [one would] be inundated with a demand which would drain the time and energy. . . [from] change which must be his priority . . . of the advocacy projects now in existence, unfortunately most do involve the delivery of direct services . . . it was necessary to do so to gain funding. (p. 13)
> Advocacy differs from revolution in that it does not support violent overthrow of institutions . . . There is little evidence to suggest that violence on the part of the powerless in this country produces

lasting change. Advocacy is revolutionary . . . in that it suggests radical changes in power relationships . . . Advocacy is a form of consumerism but . . . not self-appointed . . . nor are they mandated by government . . . the ombudsman is an employee of the provider . . . to facilitate the working of the present system . . . the consultant provides technical (p. 14) assistance but does not involve himself with the political aspects of the group . . . and not accountable to it . . . The advocacy stance implies that one work for better service delivery for the consumer and that one works for and with the consumer to enlarge his role in delivery systems. This might mean that we become adversaries of those we most often tend to identify with and traditionally serve. (p. 15)

In a collaborative approach to secondary prevention, CMH advocacy and change were avoided:[17]

if one who's come to human services through . . . the route of health care or mental health care . . . with different assumptions of values . . . conflict is best resolved by more collaborative strategies . . . find a common ground rather than polarize . . . cooperate where we can . . . their fates are tied together . . . change occurs . . . with the voluntary participation of the changed system or people. (p. 3) . . . the underlying assumption is that conflict results from irrational forces and is not so clearly based on reality . . . an example of this [is] our own experience in the Tufts Mental Health Center. . . [We were] consistently and assiduously making an effort to avoid confrontations . . . blur over polarizations. . . [We] tried not to advocate any one . . . of the many conflicting causes . . . find the common ground . . . see whether that common ground could enlarge. . . . In this way the program has grown very rapidly . . . these are two very different approaches . . . advocacy being one and the other . . . collaborative. These . . . come from very different historical traditions . . . they must be kept separate (p. 4) . . . mental health types . . . of human service people, have a great deal of work to do simply to learn . . . the practice of their own trade . . . we don't know anything about advocacy and perhaps we don't belong there . . . there's a lot of value also in . . . providing human services as neutrally as possible . . . I am concerned that it be lost in the current wave of searching for new and different roles in the human services. (p. 5)

Within the alternative social psychiatry (primary prevention) faction in CMH, there was much debate about the need to involve psychiatry in social change and political policymaking. Some psychiatrists expect that an increase in knowledge of these social factors will lead to changing them and thus preventing mental illness. On the activist side:[18]

> Truly concerned professional and humanitarian psychiatrists can not help but become involved in and promote community psychiatry (mental health) if they do a sincere job with their clients. For the psychiatrist cannot by himself re-create each of his patients and must more often look to providing crisis assistance and thereby client growth. Psychiatrists must become aware of the need for certain social or supportive institutions and furthermore must help create them. Equally, they must realize that destructive local or socially massive environments create highly hostile, dependent, escapist personalities that would not be able to respond to psychotherapy, even if it were available. Victims of overwhelming deprivation cannot be made "normal" through the medium of psychotherapy in the unchanged and often inescapable environments such as racial ghettos invaded and surrounded by the flamboyant slogans of freedom, equality, opportunity, and wealth.

The Connecticut Community Mental Health Center, including such staff members as William Ryan, directly supported tenant rights advocacy and activity.

Community psychologists challenged their colleagues "to work harder to not just ameliorate harsh conditions but to challenge the status quo, which too often provides the underlying legitimacy of many social [influences]".[19]

Niels Pörksen at the Mannheim (Germany) community mental health center and University of Heidelberg was, like Lindemann, invested in and enthusiastic about recognizing and involving with community issues and movements. His excitement and sense of the importance of the perspective of social psychiatry/CMH gave him a sense of permission to exceed the boundaries of his agency and its tradition, a fluidity of roles, the license to uncover and interact with new issues and motivations.

Lindemann took a different tack: He accepted the political goals of CMH (policymaking, ecological improvement) but in the roles of researchers and consultants regarding the consequences of policy decisions and ecological conditions. He made the distinction of avoiding advocacy, responsibility, and leadership in policymaking for two reasons: First, he respected the community's values, decision-making right, and capacity for self-care. Second, politically he wanted to avoid destruction of this partnership and undermining cooperative relationships and acceptance as trusted consultants and educators.

CMH's involvement in politics was another of its aspects that was decried by mental health traditionalists: a source of disapproval of, counterreaction to, and withdrawal from CMH. Kingsley Davis observed that dedication to contemporary societal values prevents and forbids the recognition of the social causes of mental Illness and the need for social change that would contradict that dedication.[20] Social factors—even specific environments—are part of the social structure and therefore resistant to change. Elizabeth Lindemann raised the issue of negative identification with the sick, disadvantaged, and socially and culturally alien (echoes of William Ryan's concept of "blaming the victim"), resulting in rejecting not only these members of the community but also those who involve themselves with them: the social psychiatry and CMH workers who reach out to and mix with the community rather than using titles, uniforms, institutions, and protocols to distance from them.[21] Some in the parent institutions were interested in the idea of social psychiatry in theory but could not tolerate it in practice, fled back to traditional roles and boundaries, and reacted in fear and anger against the threatening social and community psychiatry and those who practiced them: Yale University versus Gerald Klerman, Heidelberg University versus Niels Pörksen, MGH/HMS versus Erich Lindemann.

Of course, another factor in resistance to change is vested interests. We have already noted the conflict between the mores of reformers versus traditionalists:[22] Organizational mores are the basis of social order and inevitably result in some human discomfort (misbehavior, poverty, etc.). Since society has replaced the primary group (focused on care of its own members) with the secondary group (people with instrumental function rather than being cared about as members), the undesirable results of the organizational mores are labeled "problems". This results in conflict between organizational and humanitarian mores in society but also within reformers: Reformers uphold both the society of which they are members and its mores, while also deploring some of its consequences. This may result in blunting their reform action in favor of rhetoric and understanding in order to prevent treason against their society. Those dedicated to primary-prevention social and community psychiatry may overstep the limits, accounting for their being resented as traitors and expelled.

Traditionalists have invested not only their mindsets and loyalties but also their occupational preparations, accumulated credits (including experience, expertise, accomplishments, and status), jobs and incomes, occupational supports (such as contacts, allies, appointments, seniority), etc. Tuchman notes that in government (applicable to other organizations) people acquire power over others, giving rein to passions, ambitions, ego investment, and sense of status, which stifles intelligence and common sense (and innovation).[23] These may be at hazard in a new world with its own alternative expertise, credentials, contacts, and credits. The author remembers seeking collaboration in a new education program and being accused (by those occupying existing academic empires) of wanting to develop his own empire.

Another often-mentioned criticism of social activism CMH was excessive expectations and efforts:[24]

> The subject of prevention in health policy, predictably oversimplified . . . Unrealistic expectations lead to the kinds of disillusion and backlash . . . Public health suffered a similar setback when the earlier successes with communicable diseases failed to apply so simply to the emerging concerns with chronic disease, aging, lifestyle, mental health, and injury control. Today's enthusiasm for legislative initiatives in prevention, health promotion, and health education needs tempering to avoid another cycle of disillusionment and discontinuity in programs.

Lindemann, too, was concerned about excessive promises and claims not supported by scientific evidence for fear that it would disappoint officials and the public, lead to skepticism and resentment, and endanger attitudinal and material support. Caplan's observations about the process of establishing change included community leaders' urgent needs, leading them to approach psychiatrists with irrational hopes that scientific technology would meet them and pressing the professionals to present a plan and budget for success.[25] This encourages professionals to offer inflated claims of expertise and promises of accomplishments and underestimation of both the complexity of the problem and the budget it calls for. The more urgent and complex the problem the greater the expectations of community leaders, in turn further inflating professionals' promises of success in order to justify expanded funding requests. Community leaders are often businessmen who expect concrete results, whereas professionals are used to guaranteeing only effort, this fueling the disdain for intellectual "dreamers". It is advised to recognize this difference in perspectives and language, draw up realistic contracts, and incorporate review and revision.

Caplan discusses the complexities of CMH and ways of negotiating them.[26] Participant forces include, government, which provides financial support but also monitoring and control. Professionals come with special interests: research, theory, the advancement of their professions, the advancement of personal status, and financial support. Community members come with their special interests, including the advancement of social or political groups or programs, control of patronage, and promotion of personal ambitions. Consequently, mental health professionals need to accept the political aspects of the arena in which they practice so long as they are not unethical, maintaining communication with patients, community residents, community leaders, and political actors. Unresolved, these produce escalating tension, decreasing communication, the development of stereotypes, withdrawal, political pressure on mental health professionals, and the deterioration of the mental health program.

Alternatively, professionals interacting with the other participants can obtain benefits: resources in competition with other applicants with the attendant accountability, influence on social policies through integration of central and local influence, monitoring of local needs and developing responses to meet them via building local community relationships, attending to community reaction to programs (especially criticism), and maintaining political and economic sanction through informing the public of the program. Emphasis is placed on contact with and learning from community, critics, other professional groups, and nonconformist mental health professionals.

The reactions to social and community psychiatry may be interest, puzzlement, confusion and lack of comprehension, apprehension, resistance, or frank hostility. The resistance may take the form of disagreement with the changes proposed and/or contesting the evidence supporting those changes. Leighton objected to the ideology and enthusiasm as non-/antiscientific (that is, unproven) and not only unacceptable but dangerously undermining of correct thinking:[27]

> a more diffuse, more subtle, and perhaps in the long run more dangerous current of feeling that seeks solution to our problems through magic, superstition, and faith . . . spreading even into learned societies . . . Scientists, too, have a human longing to believe in mysteries and miraculous solutions . . . its thrust is anti-intellectual and antiscientific . . . Science . . . questions dogma and hence easily comes in conflict with passionate dogmatists . . . It is frequently said that traditional hierarchies are particularly inhospitable to science because it has a potential for weakening the beliefs on which their status depends. . . [R]adical movements are equally intolerant. . . . [they bring] the social and psychologic tendencies that threaten the development and application of science in the mental health field. These can be summarized as. . . **the conviction of already knowing the truth** (p. 47) . . . **The reliance on metaphysical concepts** . . . that lead easily to explanatory legends and intuitive convictions . . . they inspire the formation of "schools"—bands of true believers who defend their convictions and practice their implications (p. 50) . . . **the Lord Ronald syndrome** . . . has led to action rather than testing. . . [and] **the Balkan wars** [among the mental health sciences]. (p. 51)

However, the resistance consists of equally irrationally committed "true believers" and strikingly often takes the form of *ad hominem* criticisms of the insurgent "school" and/or its supporters. This evades confronting the programmatic, theoretical, and ideological issues themselves and addressing them through demonstrable facts and logic and shifts the contest to personality characteristics addressed through emotional impressions and reactions. This certainly applies in Lindemann's case, with people insisting that opposition was to his personality or even appearance and denying that it was based on rejection of CMH. This contention was belied by distaste for CMH theory and practice and those affiliated with it. Examples were the HMS Curriculum Committee's rejection of Lindemann's recommendation of a social psychiatry perspective and courses as unworthy of inclusion in medical education, MGH considering HRS a poor farm team, the resentment of inclusion of social scientists and CMH professionals in the MGH Department of Psychiatry, the MGH psychiatry staff's sarcastic equating Lindemann's "cross-fertilization" with "being screwed", the rejection of the author by John Nemiah's Beth Israel Hospital Department of Psychiatry because of his association with CMH, and the denial of the author's reappointment to the MGH Psychiatry Department on the grounds of his failure to practice good (i.e., biological) psychiatry. The other contention that it was Lindemann's failure as an administrator that was disappointing and resented merits serious debate. How much was this rejection based on his failure of responsibility and being destructive of the department, and how much was it disregard of major accomplishments in a field of little interest and value to the critics though appreciated by HMS Dean George Packer Berry, administration consultant Henrik Blum, and visitors from other institutions? And criticism of Lindemann's personal characteristics (such as his high voice) and choices (such as valuing nonpsychiatrists including social scientists) seem surrogates for rejection of his ideology and programs that were disrespected, resented, and feared.

Altogether, there was remarkably little debate directly about the contending ideologies. Why not debate social and community psychiatry head on? Perhaps part of the explanation is that people—including professionals and scientists—are more focused on and motivated by values—including ideologies—than they and we recognize and thus are repelled rather than unpersuaded by alternative perspectives; and thus emotionally repel them rather than rationally disprove them. Also, perhaps the social issues dealt with and the social and political world involved in dealing with them are so far outside the traditionals' experience, skills, and identity sets and so threatening that their responses are the fight and flight of unchanged identities rather than evolving new identities, including evolved perspectives, experience, skills, and values.

Among the dissenters from CMH were the Joint Commission on Mental Illness and Health, which emphasized the secondary prevention of bringing treatment to the mentally ill; and the Boston Psychoanalytic Society and Institute, as illustrated in its reaction against the paper by Lindemann and Dawes showing the synergy between psychoanalysis and social psychiatry. MGH and HMS experienced a limited period of interest in and tolerance of social psychiatry and community medicine, including the appointment as general directors of MGH of Dean A. Clark (later dismissed) and John Knowles (struggling against the staff's disinterest) with their backgrounds and interests in community health; the choice of Lindemann to bring social science and community mental health to these bodies (and ending his tenure in the shadow of the hostile staff petition asking for a very different successor); and the brief, reluctant, and limited acceptance of the MGH Family Health Program, MGH Ambulatory Clinics Committee, and Wellesley Human Relations Service. In the case of the stubborn resistance to CMH by the Boston University Division of Psychiatry, Bernard Bandler blamed himself for a lack of leadership in developing a learning environment that would convert the division staff (see Ch. 10).

When the symbiotic social and political soil changes, liberal and socially aware ideology and programs wither:[28]

> These political events [accession of a conservative U.S. administration with Ronald Reagan as President, and social psychiatry's being associated with radical political critiques and anti-psychiatry rhetoric] demonstrate the close affiliation between community mental health programs and a liberal definition of government policy. Without continued political support at the national level, the community mental health movement has come to an end . . . There is no new "movement" on the horizon with broad goals and optimistic world view . . . such a new vision probably (p. 60) awaits a change in the political and economic climate; such visions in mental health have usually been associated with periods of social and political change, as in the Enlightenment of the late 18th century . . . the Jacksonian era . . . and the progressive era before World War I (p. 62).

Shore saw psychological issues influencing the reaction to psychiatrists espousing social and community psychiatry.[29] He thought other medical specialists were threatened by the insights of psychiatrists, respond with aggression, and psychiatrists, naturally passive and depressive, do not respond aggressively but with masochism and feeling victimized. He also saw a coterie of Boston psychiatrists who were either not interested in or had been rejected by the reigning psychoanalytic school and who counterattacked against it with a shift of focus to social issues. However, Shore saw social psychiatry as more important than as a challenge to psychoanalysis. He thought social issues had always been a part of psychoanalysis, that psychiatrists were mistaken in discrediting social and community psychiatry because they had not solved all problems, and in turning against other mental health and social science disciplines as part of a return to biological psychiatry.

Another aspect of CMH is the experiences of those who identified with it, an example of those who commit themselves to any belief system, program, or group which is under pressure from an alternative, whether the belief system, program, or group be innovative or conservative.

Note that these considerations apply both to those devoted to CMH and social psychiatry and to those devoted to resisting it in favor of biological or psychological ideology. If the commitment to CMH is a stratagem toward some practical goal those committed may be freer to accept success or failure pragmatically. If the commitment is a manifestation of some deeply felt value or important personal identity or a goal established by sacred authority, the acceptance of its success or failure is a major life event impacting the identity and values of the dedicatee. Elizabeth Lindemann saw this parallel between Lindemann and CMH: overinvestment and enthusiasm for CMH provoking contagious loyalty or repulsion,[30] and ending in self validation or discrediting. It helps account for the fierceness of the conflict and the major effect on the combatants and veterans.

When CMH was in flower, it provided validation of Lindemann's values and programs and gave the sense that his work was the inevitable future course of psychiatric history. When it fell out of favor and criticisms of Lindemann's values and efforts gained validation from the successor biological ideology, despite loyal appreciation from some quarters, Lindemann was tempted to feel a failure, a funny little foreigner, as when he retired early from his positions at HMS and MGH out of fear of being dismissed.

Some who identified with social and community psychiatry came to the conclusion that humane people were strangers in their societies. Some coped by overtly renouncing the nurturing social psychiatry and turning to covert nurturing as gurus who gradually were respected and developed networks of those who appreciated and were influenced by them—such as the "Space Cadets", Lindemann's role at Stanford Medical Center, and his work with the Lindau Group. This influence via establishing groups that espoused feelings and intuition rather than established rules and procedures could frighten authorities so that such gurus had difficulty finding jobs.[31] (Note the often contemptuous or hostile connotation of the term "humanitarian".)

An outstanding example of CMH adapting to a changed ideological environment is Lindemann's Wellesley Human Relations Service. Its later executive director, Robert Evans, described his and the agency's struggle with its heritage of CMH in the 1990s when support for it was being withdrawn:[32]

> the [Massachusetts] State Department of Mental Health . . . called me up to complete the elimination of its funding of the Human Relations Service, a process they began 18 months ago and accelerated smartly this spring. . . [I]n 1969 the Human Relations Service was already 21 years old, and joined the partnership network that the state of Massachusetts had created, which had an irony all of its own because in a sense that whole notion of community mental health

that the state was building in fact was [exactly] the kind of activity that had been created at the Human Relation Service and that is associated with the name of Erich Lindemann. And so for about 20 years, a little longer than that, we enjoyed that association, and now in the current context of things, in which not only are dollars shrinking but priorities have changed, we find that the department has eliminated its resources from us, as from many other agencies. And this, needless to say, provokes a variety of thoughts and reactions, but it made my discussion with David, and succeeding talks with him also thought-provoking for me, because we all know that history, as it's an old adage by now, history is written by the winners, and it is not clear at this point, I guess, in the end whether there will be winners or losers in this struggle, and who they will be, and whether in the long run those of us who are interested to even be here on an afternoon like this about a topic like this [Social Ethos, Social Conscience, and Social Psychiatry: Community Mental Health and the Cycles of Psychiatric Ideology], those of us who work in community mental health, whether we will look in retrospect like keepers of a precious flame, or just fossils-to-be, who didn't know that is what they were heading for.

I had . . . sort of an analogy . . . In a lot of his novels, John Le Carre writes about figures who are out of time. Very often in a lot of his books there are figures who are left over from the Second World War and the Cold War, and who cherish a dream of a certain kind of return to power or prominence or freedom, whatever it may be, which, as it happens in the course of those stories, is unrealistic and doomed. And some of his most powerful portraits of characters in his books are people who are caught, as it were, out of time, and not even really aware that that is true. And I have wondered increasingly, as the director of the Human Relations Service, whether that is true of me and my staff and the people who still labor in the community field, and whether we will turn out like that. And then I realized the other day that of course in some of those books some of the people who are most out of date are Baltic exiles who cherish a dream somehow that they will be free from Russia, and, lo and behold, we don't know what will happen, but they're still working on it. And I didn't know whether to take heart, or whether we're heading for another round of disappointment. But, in any case, I think that it is clear that whether we turn out to be fossils or not when somebody else rewrites history, it is also clear that for lots of us there is at this point not just a set of beliefs and a database and knowledge base that we are confident of, whether others pay attention to it or not. There is also a tradition at this point. For me, the Lindemann legacy actually is expressed by Betty [Lindemann], who is the one that I know and have worked with. But I think more broadly what we might think of as a Lindemann tradition or legacy, though it is one that is harder to sustain these days, is one that has inspired and animated a large number of us. Indeed, even the person in the Department of Mental Health whose job it was to call me up and tell me they had eliminated our money has worked in the field for 25 years and was reflecting on what he has seen happen in that time, and the contrast between his priorities and values and interests and the job he is currently needing to do. By chance last night I found, at the bottom of my briefcase, a scribbled piece of paper with a quote I had come across a couple years back when I was reading *Habits of the Heart*, and it is this: "Whereas tradition is the living faith of the dead, traditionalism is the dead faith of the living". And I think that it is important for us to find a way to sustain a tradition, not become traditionalists. I like to think we're here today, looking for some further perspective about our dilemma and looking for a way to sustain the living faith of Erich Lindemann.

This is a reminder of the cyclical rather than linear course of history: Values and ideologies do not appear only once and then die permanently. They remain in subdued but stubborn ideas and adherents, to arise in vigor in a later reincarnation. Caplan predicted this for community psychiatry:[33] He expected that complex historical forces would cause another eclipse of community psychiatry (optimistically expecting this to last 10–20 years). During this ebb period he recommended the retention of the theory and methodology—concepts, values, attitudes, commitment, population and historical orientation and perspective, and education and experience perpetuating practice dealing with real problems. To conserve these he looked to protected social structures and sanctuaries such as an elite cadre, gathering in a formal organization or around relevant issues, to develop and transmit CMH ideas and values, maintaining active contact with the professions and communities—perhaps through a research focus—and acting as a reference group to protect interested trainees from assimilation into the dominant ideology.

An example of this is Compton's assertion of social causes of mental illness and the responsibility for social action to address them, written in 2015 during an era of biological ideology.[34]

The social ideology is variously interpreted and followed even by those who claim it. It certainly is in contest with its alternative biological and psychological ideologies. There is limited recognition of the cycle of ideologies, much less the repeated assertion of their validity. Intolerant monism is the order of the day, so that more or less conflict and defaming is the habit. The community mental health movement presented a clear example. We regret this lack of understanding, waste of effort, and waste of potential.

The Social and Moral Implications of Mental Health Ideology and Practice

Oliver Wendell Holmes remarked:[35]

> Much, therefore, which is now very commonly considered to be the result of experience, will be recognized in the next, or in some succeeding generation, as no such result at all, but as a foregone conclusion, based on some prevalent belief or fashion of the time . . . The truth is that medicine, professedly founded on observation, is as sensitive to outside influence, political, religious, philosophical, imaginative, as is the barometer to the change of atmospheric density. Theoretically it ought to go on its straightforward and inductive path without regard to changes of government or to fluctuations of public opinion. But actually there is a closer relationship between the medical sciences and the conditions of society and the general thought of the time than would first be suspected.

The argument might be made that medicine (and psychiatry) are social institutions that are influenced by—nay, creatures of—society's values, goals, and practices. Thus, the cycles of psychiatric ideology reflect cycles in social ideology and the values, goals, and practices they embody.

Thus it follows that social and moral implications adhere to psychiatric ideologies. Certainly it is not fair to say that some ideologies or their proponents are more moral and caring about people than are others: most bolster their arguments in part as concern for their fellow man. And, in the ideal, all ideologies and practices can be helpful in some ways. Finally, in reality, no era is pure in its ideology: experience demonstrates that there is an abiding presence and intermixing of some of the products of all the psychiatric ideologies at all times despite changes in dominance. Surely virtue and vice are distributed independent of ideology, though one's intents attract one to the ideology that gives them more syntonic voice and gratifying expression.

But different social philosophies give rise to different psychiatric ideologies, and, as an extension of the relationship, these ideologies facilitate different social outcomes. This applies to the social ideology with its concern for social needs and energy for social activism for the alleviation of social and psychiatric problems. Historians have observed that societies go through periods of social ferment and creativity, and periods of inaction and retrenchment: Arthur Schlesinger noted that "there have been other times in American life when we have been willing to settle for something less than the best. One has to remember there's a kind of cyclical rhythm in American public affairs, cycles of intense activism succeeded by a time of exhaustion and acquiescence in mediocrity".[36] He recalled that after the civil rights revolution, Vietnam War agitation, turbulence on college campuses, and the Watergate affair, sights were lowered, and there was a lack of action similar to the 1920s and 1950s, followed by the accumulation of problems and return of activism in the 1980s similar to the 1930s and 1960s. Another historian, Barbara Tuchman, saw another set of influences in that when people have a sense of comprehension and mastery of social forces, they are moved to vigorous social action and great accomplishments; when social forces seem too large and beyond their control, they produce no noteworthy social accomplishments.[37]

We would argue that apprehension—the way people understand the world—is a product of their needs and cognitive vocabulary—as are their intellectual and manual tools—to serve their purposes. This complex constitutes an ideology. Also involved are values, which influence crucial aspects of the ideology as motivators of the thought and action of the believers. In the absence of overwhelmingly determining external forces—such as the ice ages, the invasion of the Roman Empire by the Asiatic tribes, or the bubonic plague—people develop apprehension and tools to implement their ideologies. Insights and technology are created and used within the context of the ideologies and are not ideology and value free. Social and community psychiatry were accelerated by values:[38]

> community psychiatrists *cared*—they tried to do something about people and problems long neglected by the mainstream group. Community psychiatry has tried too hard to do too much. It deserves credit for trying and also for some of the not insignificant successes which have been achieved. (p. 34)
>
> community psychiatry is obviously a child of the times in which it arose (or re-arose...) ... Albert Deutsch's "Shame of the States"[39] ... restated the point ... of bureaucratic man's inhumanity to man ... Maxwell Jones ... discovered that ... there was therapeutic force in ordinary human relationships ... the extraordinary vigor and enthusiasm of the generation (p. 28) of psychiatrists who came to professional maturity during World War II. They left the military services determined to ... do something about the dismal state of psychiatric treatment... [D]uring military service ... the use of a limited number of community-oriented principles by relatively untrained but dedicated mental health workers could produce miraculous improvement ... The Group for the Advancement of Psychiatry was their instrument... [as reflected in] the New Frontier of John Kennedy... [T]he community psychiatry movement achieved the national prominence and the funding without which there never could have been a community mental health movement. (p. 29)

Social psychiatry was not the only context for activism and accomplishment. The era of reflex physiology and brain anatomy and the era of psychoanalysis were also times of challenge and creativity through their respective biological and psychological ideologies. But biological ideology does not see social conditions as leading to mental health problems that are a responsibility of mental health professions and professionals. And psychological ideology tends to see social conditions as peripheral to its practice—contributions to the etiology of intrapsychic problems to be undone by the individual, and conditions to which the individual must adapt; there is little sense of professional responsibility to take action about these conditions. It can be argued that eras of biological and psychological ideology in psychiatry are correlated with more hesitation, consolidation, and conservatism in the social sphere. The corollary is that in eras of social ideology, psychiatry is involved with ferment and innovation primarily originating in and focused on the social sphere. In response social ideology has significance in terms of social philosophy: it leads psychiatry to take professional responsibility for and contribute to the sociopolitical climate of its parent society.

From this perspective, we would argue, we can relate social psychiatry and social ethos to social conscience: When society's and psychiatry's values focus on concern for the well-being of groups of people and of mankind as a whole, their ideology is likely to be a social one. And a social ideology leads psychiatry (and mental health as a whole) to efforts to understand the lives and needs of groups of people; to concern over the effects that social conditions—including economic and political policies—have on them; and to efforts to ameliorate their lives. It is thus not coincidental that a social ideology leads psychiatry toward an understanding of people's social networks, satisfactions, and the adverse consequences of disruptions in this sphere. It stimulates social therapies—group psychotherapy, the psychiatric education and sensitization of nonpsychiatric health professionals and institutions, mental health consultation to key community caregivers and agencies, and informing community policymakers of the mental health implications of their programs. It spurs efforts to retain people in their communities and move them there from restrictive environments—whether mental hospitals, wars, or oppressed social status. It propels the mental health professions into social action, including political policy, since these mightily affect community conditions, the community's mental health, and mental health resources. And it may well make them into advocates of social programs and political policies. Note again that this ideology and professional practice may be motivated not only by inductive logic but by humanistic values—not only what is but what should be.

This dynamic may also be what disaffects other psychiatric, mental health, health, and political factions from social psychiatry and the social ideology, precipitating a shift away from it in the cycle of ideologies. But it is a consequence of the value implications of social ideology and may be inescapable. As implied previously, the cycles of psychiatric ideology reflect cycles in societal social philosophy and may imply cycles in moral values.

Thus it was inevitable that the community mental health era included the study of life crises (such as bereavement)[40] that produce physical and mental illness and community conditions (such as forced urban relocation)[41] that produce social disorganization and depression. It is significant that community mental health centers close to patients' homes, a community voice in mental health programming, and the advocacy of social policies that support local institutions and cultures appeared at this time. And it is no accident that CMH appeared in the same era as the civil rights movement, broad government social programs, and radical political reform, even though they also contributed to CMH's downfall. The social psychiatry ideology begets a social conscience of humane concern with lives and social conditions and points the way to social action.

From this point of view, it is also understandable that the succeeding era of biological psychiatry is coincident with a high priority for instrumental business and self-reliance, reduced funding for human services, confining mental health services to supportive services for the severely and chronically mentally ill, control of expense including the least expensive and least capable staff, and the inexorable withdrawal of government from caregiving. It contributes directly to the numbers of mentally ill in shelters, in nursing homes, and on the streets. It contributes to the lack of programs for those not yet disabled but at risk of crippling maladjustment risk from life crisis, as well as those in acute crisis. Publicly supported programs focus resources on those already injured. Public policy has returned to the almshouse (homeless shelter) and the workhouse (requirement of work to qualify for public support) for populations with a high proportion of mentally ill. It is also consistent that psychiatry mainly avoids social issues except for concern over the funding of psychiatric research, training, and services and the status of mental health professionals. Its professional focus is on the pathology that inheres in individual patients and the biology of these problems and their solutions within the patient. Concern for the larger human condition and the condition of groups and communities is reserved for philanthropic programs and nonprofessional roles. The biological ideology in psychiatry is concerned with the impersonal mechanics of illness and treatment and does not professionally address the lives of persons individually and people as a whole; epidemiology and illness prevention is bypassed. There is some research evidence in this regard:[42]

> Clinicians who read patient vignettes using biological descriptors reported less compassion and considered psychotherapy less effective than when the same patient's illness was described in psychosocial terms. As we uncover more details about the molecular and genetic

factors that influence mental health, do we risk dehumanizing the patients who live with these conditions?

A new study from Yale University suggests . . . therapists tended to show less empathy toward people when reading case descriptions using biological explanations compared with psychosocial ones; the biological explanations also lowered the belief that psychotherapy would be an effective treatment. . . "Empathy is a critical component of the therapeutic alliance between a treatment provider and a patient, to the point that more empathy on the part of a therapist is associated with improved treatment outcomes . . . The question to address is how we take what scientific advances offer us, without running the risk of starting to view patients as malfunctioning machines".

For many in CMH and certainly Lindemann, there were philosophical and moral (with parallels in religion) implication to CMH: caring about people, families, and communities, and the obligation to ameliorate their lives and environments. While the term was not often used, this matches to the concept of humanism.[43] Community psychology reaffirmed the connections between religious beliefs and social change; between religious experience and a sense of community; and between religious practice, spirituality, and community psychology.[44] The comparison of social with biological psychiatry suggests the comparison of empathy versus objectivity and socially activist humanism versus dispassionate biological science and raises the question as to which gives a greater yield of human good.

This is not to say that biological psychiatrists are uncaring or unprincipled or even that they are not social activists in their private lives. It is to say that in their professional lives, they deemphasize social relationships and needs and avoid social causes and social change as improper professional endeavors in relation to mental health and illness. And this is the crux of the difference between social ideology and the biological and psychological ideologies: how central are social conditions to mental health and illness and how much is social concern and social action an acceptable . . . nay, essential . . . part of psychiatric professional practice. Lindemann, for instance, did not see social issues as a source of understanding of the human condition but the human condition as a reason for addressing social issues.

Is one ideology more moral than another? I think that would be hard to prove. But surely the ideologies embody different moral values that lead them to different actions with moral effects. And both financial decisions and programmatic thrusts reflect social philosophy.

It is not warranted to label social psychiatry the only ideology with a humane conscience, and certainly psychiatrists of any ideological persuasion may personally be humane and even devoted to human causes—some outstandingly. However, social psychiatry is the ideology that most clearly includes social concerns as essential to professional values and practices. Biological psychiatry may be concerned with bettering the human condition through improving or protecting the biological organism. Psychological psychiatry is concerned with development within the individual and often (but not in all its schools) with human relationship and the benefits or hurts that it causes and the need for making it more benevolent. Social psychiatry is built around the influence of human and environmental conditions on individuals and groups, and therapeutic interventions are focused on ameliorating the effect of the human condition on humans. It is in this sense that social psychiatry (and socially oriented public ideology) has the most social conscience. It is still debatable as to how much this conscience is valued.

Certainly, Lindemann and his contributions to social and community psychiatry were imbued with a strong strain of social morality. His maternal grandfather was a preacher with a sense of social responsibility to his workers and community. This grandfather adopted Lindemann and inculcated a strong sense of social responsibility and mission. Lindemann carried this mission through his education and increasingly boldly in his focus on caring for family, community, and society. His choice of courses in philosophy, his collaboration with clergymen, and his choice of the Society of Friends (Quakers) as his religious affiliation all showed this moral/religious motivation in his professional life.

The difference between social ideology and psychiatry and other ideologies is more sharply demarcated by the disapproval and rejection shown to it. Social and community psychiatry is considered "soft" and unproven; its proponents are not infrequently disrespected and rejected; and its values are considered professionally inappropriate (sociological, bleeding heart). Note that Lindemann's values and projects were disrespected: He was considered to have betrayed the values and activities of his profession and department, was personally despised and the object of anger, and his values and interests were rejected in recommendations for his successor. That is, it was not so much that he was considered *wrong* as that he was considered *bad*. Of course, during the ascendency of the social ideology, the alternative biological and psychological ideologies were demeaned. One is reminded of the Aztec custom of transitions of dynasties: The faces were chiseled off the statues of the previous dynasty, and statues of the new dynasty replaced them.

Change and Innovation

As in any challenge of previous ideology by a new one, there was a range of reaction to social psychiatry, including being inspired, interested, disinterested, puzzled, skeptical, apprehensive, and hostile.

People tend to reassert their own ideologies and doubt the legitimacy and usefulness of others. "Like a man traveling in foggy weather, those at some distance before him on the road he sees wrapped up in the fog, as well as those behind him, and also the people in the fields on each side, but near him all appears clear, though in truth he is as much in the fog as any of them".[45] Change is confusing and threatening. "The vast majority of human beings dislike and even dread all notions with which they are not familiar. Hence it comes about that at their first appearance innovators have always been derided as fools and madmen".[46]

Alongside his dedication to change, Lindemann knew of obstacles to it:[47] "These developments did not take place without numerous objections and resistances because they imply. . . [an] inevitable change of the social order, of professional prerogatives and roles". He studied the struggle for survival of innovative institutions and individuals, how they dare, what credit they get, and how to assist change without being destructive.[48] He drew parallels between institutions trying to maintain their identities through times of change, the mentally ill with problems of lost identity, and mourners who struggle to preserve their identities as opposed to identifying with those lost. He tried to rationalize this group hostility toward innovators with ideas about group development reaching a point of needing to banish/sacrifice the original leader, and wondering if an understanding of group dynamics could result in a ritual change of leadership rather than attacking the leader.[49] This raises concern about the timing of change: social psychiatry could address how to accomplish change that will bring the comfort of being stronger rather than the comfort of being inactive, and minimize violent change which would precipitate violent reaction.[50]

There are several contributors to resistance to change. One is the effort and discomfort in self-examination and reconsideration. For instance: "[T]rue to the very nature of critical reflection was the finding that some students found this reflective learning process an uncomfortable experience. This has been described as the 'disorientating dilemma' . . . which must occur for development of reflective capacity and deep learning to occur".[51] This self-reflection raises doubts about the validity of beliefs, perspectives, and values important to the sense of identity. "Old men grow rigid, and keep their shop of ideas at the same storefront; they know what goes wrong when it goes wrong, but are too brittle to fix what goes wrong. Young men grow old, too, and move from passion to politics to power soon enough".[52] It takes a strong and abiding sense of identity to accept such questioning, openness to new concepts and values, and readiness to renovate identity without feeling a loss of it. It is easier and more common to stubbornly reassert the established identity and fight against questioning and alternatives with the excuses of loyalty to the old regime, questioning the validity of the new, and attacking the capability and motivations of innovators:[53]

> Then loudly cried the bold Sir Bedivere,
> "Ah! My Lord Arthur, whither shall I go?
> Where shall I hide my forehead and my eyes?
> For now I see the true old times are dead,
> when every morning brought a noble chance,
> And every chance brought out a noble knight.
> But now the whole ROUND TABLE is dissolved
> Which was an image of the mighty world;
> And I, the last, go forth companionless,
> And the days darken round me, and the years,
> Among new men, strange faces, other minds".
> And slowly answer'd Arthur from the barge:
> "The old order changeth, yielding place to new;
> And God fulfills himself in many ways,
> Lest one good custom should corrupt the world".

And intimately involved with the process of change is the reaction to it by institutions, programs, and populations (including professions): interest, lack of understanding, and/or resistance. People and groups may be seen as entering social systems (including programs) with stores of potential for acceptance by the group—their "acceptance capital"—based on past accomplishment, reputations, characteristics, etc. They can conserve and build this capital by staying within the tolerance of the social system; they may risk this capital by attempting to expand the social system; and they may diminish or lose this capital by exceeding the tolerance and adaptability of the social system. Waller described this as a conflict of allegiance to new (e.g., humanitarian) versus established (organizational) mores:[54]

> The notion of conflict of mores enables us to understand why progress in dealing with social problems is so slow. Social problems are not solved because people do not want to solve them. Solving social problems would necessitate a change in the organizational mores from which they arise. The humanitarian, for all his allegiance to the humanitarian mores, is yet a member of our society and as such is under the sway of its organizational mores . . . Until the humanitarian is willing to give up his allegiance to the organizational mores, and in some cases to run squarely against them, he must continue to treat symptoms without removing their causes . . . any translation of humanitarianism into behavior is fenced in by restrictions which usually limit it to trivialities . . . No one loses by giving verbal expression

to humanitarianism or by the merely verbal expression of another, but many would lose by putting humanitarianism into practice . . . From the powerful someone who is certain to lose comes opposition to reform.

Gerald Caplan, drawing from his experience introducing CMH, thought new ideas and proposals are often minimally implemented due to such factors as personal idiosyncrasies of the advocates, interdisciplinary tensions, administrative and social system problems, and political and economic forces.[55] To establish enduring change, there is need for effective evaluation and quick feedback to the planning process; otherwise, an attempt is made to implement the innovations while there is enthusiasm for them, but they are dropped as fashions change. He reflected on his experience as Permanent Advisor in Mental Health to the Minister of Health of the State of Israel in 1948–1949, introducing community mental health concepts:[56]

> Without realizing it, he had been trying to impose a plan which had emerged from . . . one culture upon another culture in which there was as yet no appropriate niche for it. [p. 34] Virgin territory in human affairs is a great rarity. . . . The appearance of lack of accomplishment was not due to an absence of energy, thought and striving . . . but to the complexity of the conflicts and tensions in the socio-cultural field . . . the felt needs of the citizens and of the professional workers and politicians in regard to the type of psychiatric service which they wished to see developed . . . weighted according to the influence and power of those feeling them, represent the factors influencing the possibility of fitting any new structure into an existing cultural framework . . . In a democracy, community action takes much longer to develop . . . a stable and lasting result in terms of building a social structure can rarely come about without a process of community interaction . . . any social system has an internal set of integrating patterns to which a new institution, unless it has a protective envelope [e.g., CMHC Program's massive federal funding], must . . . conform; [p. 35] otherwise social forces will be set in motion to remove it . . . any new social institution must in its development and growth pass through a complicated series of mutual adaptive change to fit itself into the general cultural framework. This process needs time . . . some of Caplan's ideas, which were originally not acceptable . . . did eventually achieve implementation, but in a modified form which allowed them to be assimilated within the cultural setting . . . the origin of some of them was forgotten, acceptable local leaders began to "discover" the ideas for themselves, and they became part of the tradition . . . a community . . . cannot make good use of ready-made answers, but must work out its own destiny.

A helping person is most effective when he . . . is willing to give his aid in an acceptable way.

[p. 36]

Innovators, too, have ideology, mores, values, and goals varying from the established culture.[57] Conflicts can be "as passionate and pervasive within a profession or science as ideologically-based political conflicts are in society as a whole" (p. 243), though "in the case of most professions . . . there is a commitment to the scientific method of validation . . . the professional must both act and believe his action represent the 'correct' method for attaining professional goals" (p. 245).

In his talk at Stanford Medical Center, Erich Lindemann hearkened back to the sociology and psychology of psychiatry:

> Karl Mannheim, in the sociology of knowledge, began to talk about ideologies. He pointed out that theories represent values which for some reason are important to an individual, and for which he feels he must fight. And about ten years ago, Melvin Sabshin together with Anselm Strauss came around to the notion that most of the convictions in psychiatry are really ideologies for which you fight; and that some of the information which you gather is collected . . . because they want to get to a particular goal.[58]

Unconventional and boundary-crossing ideas threaten identities, disciplinary controls, and the sanctity of disciplinary doctrine.[59] Opening the new community perspective raised the potential for real or feared professional conflict, moving others to attack Lindemann. Seeley even suggested that the exemplary lives—gentle, open—of Lindemann and others like William Line in Canada presented a reproof to the biases of others. Psychoanalysis was already under such attack for being medically unconventional that many analysts did not want to stir up further reaction by delving into social issues, though we have seen that there were pioneers who did so. Of course, opportunists may enjoy participating in the abstract theory and rhetoric of a new idea, but, when the time comes for laborious creation and implementation, they shift to some safer allied or more general work or even return to the preexisting orthodoxy.[60]

It has long been recognized that nonconformists—including those who are superior—are not well tolerated by social systems:[61] "in most hierarchies *super-competence is more objectionable than incompetence . . . because it disrupts the hierarchy*, and thereby violates *the first commandment* of hierarchical life: *the hierarchy must be preserved* (p. 45) . . . It is easy to see how, in such a milieu, the advent of a genuine leader will be feared and resented" (p. 68). In Lindemann's case the moral, social, and religious principles to which he was committed lifelong and which he sought to implement through change toward social medicine and psychiatry became more nakedly apparent as his career matured and as he felt invested with the respect and resources of the exalted positions he attained. This shift from biological to psychological to social perspective contributed to his rejection by "scientific" (and class- and guild-centered) psychiatry and medicine. So, also, did his innovative advocacy and programs disturb the comfortable traditions of academia and the professions.

Innovators' counterreactions to the reaction to change is of interest: The attribution of success or failure to those who champion causes has long been critiqued. In the Psalms: "he heapeth up riches, and knoweth not who shall gather them".[62] It is recognized that people confuse the good fortune of supportive circumstances with their own triumphs. "Like all reformers, she confused her own pure conscience with the laws of nature".[63] Examples come from economic history:[64]

> It should be shown ... how much the development ... is governed by chance [i.e., external conditions], and how the ... development ... is much more dependent on chance events and inherent tendencies than on so-called consciously aimed activities of the individual. The description should be pervaded by a certain feeling of humility towards these forces. For most people suffer from exaggerated self-esteem, and ... three or six months later are inclined to adorn their actions with a degree of foresight which in reality never existed.

This was the case with a population group that was too young to suffer the Great Depression and came of age just in time to benefit from the longest sustained prosperity in history.[65]

> People who came of age thinking history was on their side had a serious problem, because when bad times came, they thought history was judging their ideas. The long-distance runner knows that reform doesn't happen with a dramatic vote of confidence.[66]

Innovators' sense of rejection could resonate with Clarence Darrow's defense of nonconformists and rebels:[67]

> When a new truth comes upon the earth, or a great idea necessary for mankind is born, where does it come from? ... It comes from the diseased, and the outcast ... it comes from men who have dared to be rebels and think their thoughts; and their fate has been the fate of rebels. This generation gives them graves while another builds them monuments; and there is no exception to it. It has been true since the world began, and it will be true no doubt forever. (p. 128–129)
>
> All through the ages, from Moses down, the men who have never followed the opinions and ideas of the people around them, are the

men who have been building for the future. They have hewn steps out of solid rock; they have worked in thorns and brambles and hard places that a stairway might be built for you and me. They are like Moses, who, defying custom and habit and giving up ease and security, and having that faith which great mortals have, could see far off something better than the world had known. They have led their people through long years of sacrifice to the Promised Land. But these poor rebels have never seen that land, for when they reached that spot their eyes were too dim to see, or they were laid in a felon's grave while the time-servers walked over their bodies to the goal. (p. 132)

[O]ther men have died before him. Whenever men have looked upward and onward, worked for the poor and the weak, they have been sacrificed.[68]

Lindemann acknowledged his struggles with the establishment as he tried to institute his approaches; he wrote to Ronald Hargreaves:[69] "As you know, the last year has been for me a very stressful one due to administrative complications but I believe the most pressing problems are solved now and I can return to the more creative aspects of my professional work". At other times, his hurt and disappointment broke through with self-doubt and discouragement.

Is it possible that some people, institutions, and ideologies are impervious to some change due to control residing in ideological, political, economic, and/or historical context rather than being accessible through individual leaders? Max Planck observed (perhaps as true in psychiatry as in physics and philosophy):[70] "An important scientific innovation rarely makes its way by gradually winning over and converting its opponents: It rarely happens that Saul becomes Paul. What does happen is that its opponents gradually die out and that the growing generation is familiarized with the idea from the beginning". And Santayana thought that "American philosophers do not refute their predecessors; they forget about them".[71]

In the case of social ideology and social and community psychiatry, several factors acted in concert. The failure of the preceding psychological ideology to solve the massive problems of the mental illness of individuals and the social problems associated with World War II combined with a sense of power from the successful prosecution of the war and international collaboration, the development of new techniques developed for the war, the availability of social psychology and other social science insights and experiments dating from before the war, and, finally, politicoeconomic wealth following the war combined to encouraged the preeminence of a social ideology in the quest for the conquest of mental and social problems. While the promise and the resources lasted, this was the theme in society and psychiatry. Biological and psychological ideology bided their time in their lairs in society. When the complexity, stubbornness, and costs of the problems obtruded, change to a new ideology overcame the inertia of its predecessor.

Change comes about as a result of societal and environmental forces that are navigated by leaders. As these forces act, they meet the inertia of the preceding *status quo*. As in geological tectonics, there is much confrontation, friction, and contention. The *status quo ante* is more or less receptive to the forces of change. There are various gains and losses from change, and the people involved may focus on and act for and against the change. Our contention is that historically, change takes place repeatedly and cyclically. This is variously understood and accepted in perspective or overlooked in the perpetual crusade for final "truth". Individuals play their participatory roles. They may feel and be seen as victorious or defeated if they are clothed with a sense of control and responsibility amidst the course of shifts in cyclical historical stages.

Leadership

There has been much interest in and exploration of leadership as it affects groups and activities. Leadership is related to the mores, gratifications and rewards, and ideologies to be led. It can be comforting and stabilizing, although also potentially frustrating of the impetus for change; or it can be assertive toward new ideologies and goals, which can result in a sense of accomplishment or can be uncomfortable and resisted by the need for stability.

As suggested previously, people come to professional and institutional networks with stores of acceptance capital. For example, John Knowles, Stanley Cobb, and Oliver Cope came from old, respected Boston families, while Lindemann came with reputation and accomplishments in biological science research and psychosomatic clinical care. People can conserve and build on their capital—including staying within the tolerance of the social system. Cobb did this well, innovating inoffensively; Cope did this within acceptable limits, being different but not unacceptable; Knowles seems to have left MGH when he reached the limits of mutual tolerance. Alternatively, people may risk this capital by confronting the social system with change. In consequence, these actors inconsistent with the social system may diminish or lose this capital by exceeding the tolerance and adaptability of the system and may thereby lose their acceptance by the system. For example, when Lindemann had gained a position of respect, authority, and tenure, he became increasingly open in shifting his interest and efforts from biological and psychological issues to social issues. Despite his insistence that his social psychiatry was based in the psychological psychiatry of psychoanalysis, he diminished acceptance by the MGH and HMS and became criticized and rejected.

An interesting example of a leader's relationship with his social system is the Arab leader Saladin:[72]

> One key to his success is that he combined two styles of leadership, exercising what modern theorists call hard and soft power . . . he mixed force with persuasion . . . It is the combination that made him so effective . . . How did he become charismatic? . . . The psychoanalyst Manfred Kets de Vries comments on business leaders:[73] "They can't be too crazy or they generally do not make it to senior positions, but they are nonetheless extremely driven people . . . I usually find that their drives spring from childhood patterns and experiences that have carried over into adulthood". The successful leader carries enough insecurity to inspire a desire to change the world, and enough of a sense of security to confront this challenge without lapsing into paranoia, criminality or any number of behavior patterns that undermine his aims . . . Security—whether provided by parents, or a wider family, or a group, or a class system, or education—gives a foundation for independence, self-confidence, and possibly leadership.

In the case of Lindemann, Pearl Rosenberg, a social psychologist with special interest in group process and an HRS staff member, offered an analysis of the group dynamics of the leader and the led in the example of the HRS as led by Lindemann, excerpted as follows:[74]

> The first task of the individuals who assembled around Dr. Lindemann in October, 1947, was to establish themselves as a group, and this was the primary group process of the first year . . . the group [members] . . . were young, intense, and . . . on the threshold of their careers. . . . [T]he only meaningful relationship in the beginning . . . was that between each member and the leader [Lindemann] . . . For most individuals . . . the eventual pull to remain with the project was a fused relationship to both the man and the idea . . . the transference relationships . . . was one of the key forces operating within the group . . . each force which helped in the formation of the group . . . contains within itself the seeds of disorganization and disruption. The preservation of a group depends on a careful balance between the cohesive and disruptive properties . . . One of the most important . . . was the character of the leadership . . . Both by nature and training, as a psychiatrist, the leader was a man with the highest respect for the individual and for the worth of his opinions and feelings. He would form a relationship with each of the staff members which was both personal and private and was able to give to each the feeling that he was on the inside of all the intimate details of the project. [Thus] each individual . . . had some of the strongest of his ego needs satisfied. . . [G]roup decision regarding important steps in the

group's work was frequently and skillfully carried out. . . . [E]ach individual contributed part of his self to the group, and the group and its life . . . became an ego-extension of the individual. . . . [T]he freedom to think was limited by a check upon the freedom to act . . . The master scheme was not clear in 1947 and . . . established only in the thinking of the leader . . . Another strong force . . . was the idea behind the formation of the study. . . [With] this concept of preventive psychiatry, they were all impressed and inspired . . . One had the feeling of pioneers. . . [T]he small group was both excited and somewhat frightened . . . This common ideology and its exciting possibilities residing mainly in the person of the leader, bound the group together and . . . still is, the key motivating force for and in the group . . . This exciting idea . . . was not received as enthusiastically by everyone concerned with the project. And this constituted another factor in producing a strong group. . . [including some] people in Wellesley. . . [O]thers did not [want to work with them on this project] . . . Fulfilling our commitments to the [funding] Grant Foundation. . . [included also] research activities [which are] . . . acceptable to a sophisticated academic executive committee . . . The common threat from the [hostiles on the] outside pulled us together. . . [W]e also had a number of excellent scapegoats (in the community, the Grant Foundation, and the executive committee) . . . What now, are the disruptive elements[:] . . . those who have been originally attracted to the project by this very appearance of intimacy with the leader and who cannot accept its limitations . . . feelings of sibling rivalry . . . the staff had soon to develop some kind of hierarchy . . . further tensions and jealousy would then develop . . . The psychiatrist's approach to administration [was] . . . [w]hile maintaining the basic attitude of attention to various opinions, he tends to act on the basis of his own judgement which he has been trained to accept as most objective and realistic. . . [E]ither phase of this problem can produce difficulties. If final action is at variance with the individual's [ideas] . . . Then] the individual has lost face and feels devalued and rejected. If no definite prohibitions on behavior are made . . . there is the danger that he will go off [with them] . . . despite their being incompatible with the total aims of the project . . . When a leader strives for consensus . . . he is . . . obligated to carry through that decision . . . If, however, he may tend to . . . act primarily according to his own re-evaluation of the consensus. . . [this] may tend to produce impatience and lack of real motivation for consensus. . . [A]n [non-psychiatrist] administrator is able to state his evaluations and decisions . . . firmly when they are at variance with those of the group's, the psychiatrist is trained to evaluate in silence, to outwardly accept but inwardly question . . . the ideology behind the project. . . [This might appear] strange and different and each member . . . had his own perception . . . The crusade-like quality of the project made each individual value his own perceptions highly, cling to them with emotional intensity, and be rather irritated with the leader and with other staff members at any difference of opinion. . . [T]he threat of our not being accepted in Wellesley was quite real . . . A hostile and manipulative orientation . . . would seriously handicap the establishment of [a] good cooperative working relationship with community agencies and individuals . . . The first year . . . might create a body of veterans who would view new members . . . coming to reap where they had sown. . . [The task of] the incorporation and orientation of new members; to give them a feeling of belongingness . . . Their youth and eagerness might make them aggressive and impatient. Their ability in their own fields might make it difficult for them to listen and accept different ideas . . . In a pater-realistic set-up, one might find it all too easy to rebel at authority. . . [With] the rapid growth intellectually and professionally. . . [they might] find the walls of the project soon too narrow. . . [M]ost of the staff members were half-time. . . [and thus] had divided loyalties . . . The first year . . . was mainly . . . becoming a group, learning a common language, and developing various intra-group relations. . . [F]requent staff meetings. . . [and] excessive verbalization . . . was priceless in fusing us into a unit. . . [T]here was an unusual and strong unwillingness to accept more members into the charmed circle . . . The process of growth . . . upset the balance previously established between the disruptive and cohesive elements. . . [This] produced a period of confusion, anxiety and frequently, much discontent. . . [With] growth in security . . . in personnel . . . in program . . . The growth in security . . . We were an accepted institution of Wellesley . . . Thus one of the strongest forces pulling us together . . . was removed. In its place . . . another cohesive force . . . the increasing success experience which the project engendered . . . by the end of the project constituted one of the strongest factors in attracting and maintaining staff . . . The growth in depth of performance of the old staff . . . led to better . . . research and service performance, but . . . aggravated sibling rivalry. . . [A] hierarchy was being established although . . . never officially outlined . . . never completely accepted . . . members of the staff would move in and take up the reins of authority . . . the staff would accept this fact outwardly. . . [but there would] inwardly be many feelings of resentment and irritation . . . Here again . . . the role of the psychiatrist clashed with that of the administrator in the position of leader. The psychiatrist views each person as an individual . . . The administrator . . . must relate to each individual in terms of . . . the general structure of the social system . . . the leader . . . must be able to delegate authority . . . support his lieutenants although still remaining available . . . The psychiatrist's interest in the . . . individual tends to undercut all other authority . . . A further result of the growing capabilities of the staff was [that it] . . . became restive in the relatively small confines of the HRS. . . . [and had a] greater desire for freedom, for position, and for financial gain. And so fewer . . . of the original group remained with the project . . . as the project's program expanded, many of the staff had an opportunity to increase the time they gave to HRS and few did so. It may be that . . . most individuals preferred to cling to the more stable, more clearly-defined [and more traditionally supported] job areas that they held outside the project . . . The growth of the project's areas of interest . . . led to an extremely varied pattern of activity. No longer was the group mutually interdependent, and . . . loss of interest and communication . . . weakened the links between members of the group. . . [T]he leader. . . [being] less available . . . in turn made the problems of the distribution of authority . . . more acute . . . The group broke up into committees . . . Clique formation . . . were noticeable and . . . in-group feelings became evident in these sub-groups . . . which ran counter to, rather than supplemented the parent group. Staff meetings fulfilled the constant need for communication and could rarely be used for group decision or group planning . . . the aims and goals of the project which seemed . . . more confused and fuzzy than ever . . . The feelings . . . found easiest expression in critical evaluation of staff meeting reports . . . More dissatisfaction . . . was expressed in this period than in any other for . . . frustrations and anxieties could only be turned back on the group . . . A great deal of discussion . . . related to the difficulties of interdisciplinary research as well as . . . the different orientations of the service and the research man . . . the project's two greatest strengths continued . . . the basic orientation and theory . . . and its leader continued to inspire, comfort and respect. Finally a relatively stable organization, quite different from the original . . . seemed to emerge . . . many of the creative ideas and theories . . . are now being tested, re-evaluated, and extended. The dependence on the leader is less evident and . . . the group is able to stand on its own . . . the basic outlines of its once hazy conceptual frame of reference appear . . . becomes verbalized and concrete, and can be passed on directly rather than absorbed though a form of osmosis. The staff . . . has worked through much of its sibling rivalry and has learned to accept the . . . difference between the leader as the psychiatrist and as the administrator . . . This in turn has contributed to the lowering of dependence upon the leader. The sub-groups . . . as successfully functioning co-existing units . . . come together predominantly . . . to make certain that they are not getting in each other's way. . . [they] rarely relate to each other functionally and the HRS family is clearly a thing of the past . . . a structure has been erected which is flexible enough to permit new members and individual expression of interest, but is solid enough to provide a pattern and plan of procedure . . . In the first period. . . [it was] mainly concerned. . . [with the] problems of the staff in becoming a group, in entering the community, in establishing a point of view . . . mainly narcissistic . . . The second period . . . reflected the needs and interests of the individual much more than . . . the project. . . . The third period's [concerns] . . . were much more related to the central theme of the project and therefore to each other . . . the period opening up new territory is over . . . and we must have a period of construction . . . The settler always follows the adventurer. . . [I]n projects of this kind . . . staff members must be young in mind if not in body, adventurous, eager and flexible; ready to try something on their own, and yet able to accept authority . . . able to accept reality of action over irreality of words . . . be ready to grow intellectually and professionally and . . . not be expected to remain with the project. . . [It can maintain] a place for training and professional development . . . Do the new group organization and . . . research and service activities require a different leader who is more the administrator and less the therapist? And should the present leader relax from the burdens of administrating and allow himself the luxury of consultation duties alone? . . . [I]t is also not difficult to suggest where the present leadership of the project could be more efficient . . . it may be impossible to combine the role of the creator with that of the administrator. Should one be first and then the other, or should both roles be held by different individuals . . . Can the psychiatrist be a business-man as well, or can we not afford to have psychiatric exuberance, trust, naiveté and self-confidence, hamstrung by earth-bound apron strings?.

Lindemann, too, addressed this issue of different types of leader. He tried to rationalize the group hostility toward innovators with ideas about group development reaching a point of needing to banish/sacrifice the original leader and wondering if an understanding of group dynamics could result in a ritual change of leadership rather than attacking the leader.[75]

Leadership is an important factor in the success of an ideology and of ideological change. There are many ideas and analyses of crucial components, as well as appropriately prepared people for the task or evolving tasks. We must remember that the leader or innovator is only one—and perhaps not the most influential one—of multiple factors that influence the state of affairs and its change: the ideology of society, availability of resources, and environmental demands and threats set directions and limits.

Social Psychiatry in Academia

Academia, supposedly dedicated to creativity through the objective search for new knowledge, is, however, often the citadel of tradition.

It is a social institution that, like most, places a high priority on self-preservation and advancement. Its members—and especially its senior members and controlling authorities—have gained their status, resources, and security through the preexisting ideology and system and therefore have a stake in maintaining it. Thomas Kuhn observed that those within a paradigm do not change it and develop but that universities and academic medical centers are exceptions to this rule—they contribute creatively even if dragged screaming into it.[76] Hausman expands on the dynamics of change and leadership in academic psychiatry:[77]

> Any changes that offer the opportunity for innovation clearly threaten the *status quo* of the existing organizational alignments and thus the security system of the best-established faculty members and groups of faculty. The resulting process is likely to represent a strong counterforce to change, with the risk of neutralizing leadership effectiveness around the very issues that call for the most critical leadership functions. The gain from maintaining the *status quo*, principally in the comfort of senior faculty and the stability of the institution, is more than offset by the loss of an element of greatest significance to the university—its freedom to experiment, to challenge and to create and test newer concepts. The consequences of this struggle between change and the *status quo* of the department are likely to be measured by its climate of inquiry, by its reputation and by its attractiveness to imaginative potential faculty and students. . . . [It is not possible to have] programmatic change . . . in the Department without redefinition and clarification of its primary task . . . with particular emphasis on the social aspects of the mental health field. The latter issue reflects recent trends in psychiatry, as well as my own principal interests, which were recognized by the university administration and Medical School faculty prior to my appointment (p. 315) . . . Another important aspect of leadership in a changing department involves the boundaries between the orientation of the new Head of the Department, the culture of the school, and the philosophies and experiences of the existing faculty. . . [It requires] the recruiting of new faculty members to . . . broaden the range of skills and interests beyond that previously existing within the department . . . the new staff members must be integrated into the existing faculty group. Their differences from the "older" faculty have had to be encouraged in order to facilitate the newer directions for the department, while at the same time the existing faculty members require well-merited support to maintain their effectiveness and the overall departmental morale (p. 316) . . . [It requires] presenting to the staff . . . the need to modify those departmental (318) activities and attitudes that have conflicted with the new definition of the primary task. . .

The contradictory argument is made to maintain safe tradition:[78]

> President [of Harvard University] Derek Bok . . . warned that major research universities today face dangers of becoming politicized . . . through efforts to exert institutional pressure to attack social evils. . . [U]niversities are tempted by the role of political activism because the evils confronting them "are often very great" and because of pressures from students, faculty, and even a portion of the alumni . . . Universities that insist on taking political positions and exerting political pressures will expose themselves to internal controversy and political diversion that will only inflame us and distract us from our real work. . . [They] will, I fear, eventually forfeit that autonomy that institutions of learning in this country have received from outside pressure to influence faculty hiring, curriculum, and other academic decisions.

Let us remember the previous discussions of periods of activism and acquiescence in society that were played out also in psychiatric ideology. In psychiatry departments, tensions during activist leadership was followed by seeking relief through the choice of conservative/traditionalist successors, e.g., Lindemann and Eisenberg followed by Hackett at MGH and Hamburg and Stunkard followed by Gonda at Stanford. This is influenced not only by the strain and discomfort of challenge but by the long tradition of the extirpation of the outstanding, extraordinarily, luxuriant, and powerful as a threat to the social structure, disturbing the normal interplay of the social forces of the ordinary:[79] "the original meaning of ostracism as it is pronounced by the Ephesians when they banished Hermodorus: 'Among us, no one shall be the best; but if someone is, then let him be elsewhere and among others . . . The individual who towers above the rest is eliminated so that the contest of forces may reawaken". Nagy tells of the Greek tyrant teaching another how to be a good tyrant by walking through a wheat field, lopping off all stalks higher than the others: trim down any extraordinary man. In the New Testament, St. Matthew is quoted:[80]

> Wherefore, behold I send unto you prophets, and wise men, and scribes; and some of them ye shall kill and crucify; and some of them ye scourge in your synagogues, and persecute them from city to city . . . O Jerusalem, thou that killest the prophets, and stonest them which are sent unto thee, how often would I have gathered thy children together, even as a hen gathereth her chickens under her wings, and ye would not! Behold, your house is left unto you desolate.

The apprehension is that if one has unchallenged superiority, this interferes with the balance of forces through rivalry and contest, and genius may degenerate into hubris, evil, cruelty, and godlessness.

Social and community psychiatry as agents of change in academia have had a variable history of the success of such relationships and the degree and nature of the collaboration (see Chapter 10). There have been some good and productive arrangements (e.g., the Tufts Community Mental Health Center), some limited to varying degrees (e.g., the Mannheim clinic-Zentralinstitut/Heidelberg Universität experience), and some more or less complete failures or outright refusals to engage (e.g., the Boston College-Roxbury, Albert Einstein-Lincoln Hospital, and Connecticut Mental Health Center-Yale University programs). Both Lindemann's experience at the MGH and Bernard Bandler's experience at the Boston University Division of Psychiatry demonstrate temporary CMH-community engagement that lasted only during the committed leadership of those champions and the temptation of external resources. In general, CMH has experienced an uphill battle in many academic settings in comparison with the responses of community settings and in political entities. This is a special case of a new ideology conflicting with an established one. Obstacles to successful collaboration were noted:[81]

> The most obvious . . . is getting a commitment from university psychiatry chairs. . . [Hausman] advised not wasting time negotiating with those who show little enthusiasm for such programs. Objectives of department chairs and state hospital superintendents frequently differ . . . Other obstacles . . . include: geographical distances between universities and state hospitals . . . quality control . . . less rigorous at state hospitals . . . well-entrenched bureaucracies at both institutions . . . physician unions, and state laws that make it a conflict of interest for an administrator in an academic psychiatry department to also have a contract with the state.
> Jerry M. Weiner, M.D., chair of the psychiatry department at George Washington University, noted. . . "It is not the responsibility of academic health centers to supply state delivery systems with their resources" . . . [John Talbott, M.D. suggested] "Lack of trust, turf issues, differing values, and fears of exploitation, control, and shrinking financial resources were likely to doom collaborative mental health efforts . . . as was the inherent human resistance to any change".
> [John] Talbott . . . was struck by several ingredients that . . . lead to success. . . [including] committed leadership at both the medical school and the state mental health administration . . . personal attributes, particularly a sense of optimism on the part of training supervisors and residents . . . flexible in orientation while . . . imposing a fairly rigid structure. . . "success seems to breed success".

It has been suggested that a CMH program can be well integrated within an academic department of psychiatry if the department starts with a CMH interest, its chairman is personally invested, and authority is centralized so warring factions do not develop. Successful collaborations were cited at Harbor-U.C.L.A. Medical Center and the Los Angeles Public Mental Health Service, the University of Colorado, the University of New Mexico, and the Virginia Department of Mental Health.

Both Erich Lindemann and Bernard Bandler attempted this programed change: They were appointed specifically to bring their social ideology and CMH programs, both sought to support traditional programs and faculty as they introduced new programs and faculty, and in both cases, this respect and valuing of the preexisting did not prevent its resentment of and resistance to the new, with ultimate extirpation of the new. A powerful institution is powerful in resistance to change.

Change is a threat and a gamble, so there is the temptation to measure new ideas and new people by traditional standards, though the judgments may be couched in terms of nonpartisan, objective, and universal verities. For example:

The MGH petition regarding the chief of the psychiatry service following Lindemann specified:[82]

- 3. c) Establish an environment in which intensive treatment and responsibility for the welfare of patients, rather than inquiries into the hypothetical cause or causes of psychiatric illness is made the paramount function of the Psychiatric Service.
- d) encourage the use of physical and chemical methods in the treatment of psychiatric illness.
- 4. He should not be a member of, nor lend his support to, any school or cult of psychiatry which substitutes "faith" for the scientific method of diagnosing, treating and evaluating the results of treatment of mental illness.

Also, when invited to support a new, interdisciplinary training program, the director of an exclusively psychiatric residency training program accused the author of trying to develop an empire, ignoring the irony of his defending his established empire.

Medical centers and psychiatry research and training departments are especially important to insight and innovation in the mental health field because they have valuable resources and expertise to apply to it. Yet they are among the most conservative and tradition-bound social institutions. While other academic entities also cling to tradition and perquisites, some have traditions of exploration and social benefit: departments of social work and occupational therapy come to mind. One would like to think of schools of public health, but their imbedding in the medical profession limits their innovation. What appears needed is the ability to call upon the medical and psychiatric tradition of committed research and humane practice and to apply it to larger social settings as has been done in social work, public health nursing, applied sociology, and the more untethered programs of public-health mental health.

The traditionalism of academia and medicine remind us that many have observed that change must come from outside the establishment:[83] "Those who govern, having much business on their hands, do not generally like to take the trouble of considering and carrying into execution new projects. The best public measures are therefore seldom adopted from previous wisdom, but forced by the occasion".

Erich Lindemann and Social and Community Psychiatry

Lindemann's experiences shaped the rationale, philosophy, and values he brought to his role in the life of the community mental health movement.

There were contending forces: On the one hand influences were his weak and unsuccessful father, whose business was ruined in the economic depression and inflation in interwar Germany, in contrast to his assertive and successful maternal grandfather, his cryptorchidism with feminizing effects, and the teasing he suffered among peers focused on his eyeglasses ("brillenschlange"—spectacled snake). These led him toward shyness, self-consciousness, and self-doubt. Even in his Harvard position, he suspected he was seen as a funny foreigner and was distant with those with whom he was not secure. He was sensitive to others' reactions, avoidant of conflict and tasks demanding assertiveness (including meetings and mail), and reluctant to commit himself strongly as in large-issue books, especially after the betrayal he felt in the affair of the textbook at the Iowa Psychopathic Hospital. He also was fearful of the disapproval of those he might write about.[84]

On the other hand, his maternal grandfather accepted and encouraged him as a disciple, in the process committing him to the religious zeal for saving people in defiance of tradition and authority. Specifically, the traumatic experience of his maternal grandmother's psychiatric illness, his grandfather's resentment of his loss of closeness and control under the authority of traditional medicine, and his grandfather's rage and helplessness at her death determined the arena in which he would pursue the mission with which his grandfather charged him: fight for the rights and the needs of people by reforming psychiatry and medicine to respect and make whole people, their families, and society. Elizabeth Lindemann learned that Lindemann's inability to save his older sister Anna from misdiagnosed tuberculosis further focused his anger at medicine and his interest in grief. He pursued studies in philosophy, psychology, and medicine toward a career in medicine and psychiatry to gain the knowledge and status that would enable him to reform these professions from within to achieve these humane and social goals.

Even as a student Lindemann was attracted to those scientific studies that emphasized human relationships and their effects on people and groups. In psychology (in which he was credentialed first) he was attracted to those schools that emphasized human relationships, especially the doctor–patient relationship—medical anthropology—and the overall pattern of the world in which the individual is embedded—gestalt psychology. Psychoanalysis gave him the theoretical and methodological structure with which to understand and remedy people and their interactions; he would later say "I am a life member of the American Psychoanalytic Society, and very happy that I am".[85] And he was drawn to the other social sciences, such as sociology and anthropology. He appreciated Talcott Parsons regarding the flexibility and adaptability of social system theory, contradicting younger people who thought him old-fashioned and status quo and supporting wealth and power. He also valued Kurt Lewin, who, he thought,[86] "in many, many ways became the model for people concerned with social action, and with social change in the direction of greater safety, and respect for more people than one had before, and a redistribution of privileges in society, for which psychological insights could be used". These larger social studies related to his concern with the effect of psychopathology on large groups (as in Nazi Germany) and with other larger social stresses and the need for "collective defenses" against them.[87]

He also pursued philosophy and theology as providing the moral authority and spiritual commitment that gave purpose to this scientific and professional calling, choosing to study at universities that included courses and teachers of theology. He recalled that his studies in medical anthropology and gestalt psychology with Viktor von Weizsäcker rearoused his boyhood religious influences regarding the limitations of natural science and that it worked through power and discipline over other people. An alternative favored bringing together the philosophies of different churches and different perspectives on the same field, and accomplishing the same improvement of behavior via giving and withholding love.[88] He emphasized the value of the person as a whole rather than focusing on functions:[89]

> the <u>uniqueness</u> of persons is particularly important just now to many people, at a time when persons are being robbed of their uniqueness by technology, which now has entered the intellectual and spiritual life ... And people are striving to recapture a sense of self, of identity, of somebody who might be venerable or lovable to somebody else—and a little bit to oneself, too! It is not surprising that self-esteem is such an important theme in your daily work, because it is so threatened in our contemporary society.

He associated these concerns with his developing interest in communes as bringing people together for investment, commitment, and promise. Later, he often looked to clergymen for support of his programs, collaboration in helping wounded spirits, and for friendship and discipleship; and he was much taken with Indian philosophy and religion as articulating and expanding the values context of the community mental health he espoused. While he did not devote himself to any established religion (though he appreciated Quaker philanthropy), there was a sense of moral values and commitment that pervaded his psychiatric interests.

Lindemann described his interests in one of his autobiographical vignettes:

> Avocational specialties: Relationships of psychological issues to religious concerns and spiritual values, especially those of Quaker organizations. I am active in community organization and promotion of mental health programs in schools, churches and social agencies. My major recreation is music.

This combination of humility and mission suggested comparison with others who had missions, such as the redeeming and suffering Jesus: see the passage from Goethe's Faust with which Lindemann empathized:[90]

> Yes, the things people claim to know!
> Who dares call the child by its true name?
> The few who know something about it,
> And foolishly do not guard their overflowing hearts, '
> But open their feelings, their responses to the mob,
> Have always been crucified and burned.

Lindemann's social psychiatry embodied moral principles: caring for people in their social lives and relationships rather than abstract science or power relationships. The juxtaposition of science and values raises questions. It was an important element in Lindemann's professional philosophy and practice and the attraction and devotion felt by his disciples. For instance, Leonard Duhl interpreted Lindemann's development from the scientific to the spiritual through the filter of his own sympathies:[91] Lindemann's success was more via influence on others and bearing witness to his beliefs via his actions and being than via reaching the heights of hierarchy. His knowledge of neurology, psychiatry, physiology, and psychoanalysis gave both insights necessary to a higher level of understanding and also the ability to deal with the real world. Without this grounding, one is mystical, unfocussed, and ineffectual. However, his progressive growth into "higher consciousness" made him poorly understood and appreciated by more secular minds, and Duhl saw Lindemann gradually turning away from mundane, pragmatic affairs. He saw Lindemann's new spiritual state as taking individuality further to interdependence dealt with through intuition rather than knowledge. This created problems for those who did not share this mentality: It left him as a leader into a new world of insight criticized by those unprepared for it and focused more on colleagues who were understanding and loving than on institutions such as his affiliated universities.[92] It helps explain his funeral at a meeting of the Society of Friends in Palo Alto and his burial in Vermont rather than as a part of the institutional formalities of Stanford or Harvard Universities.

It also contributed to the alienation of those who did not understand or accept this morality and rejected it as insubstantial dreaming or cult dogma (see the MGH petition) or who were not included in Lindemann's inner circle of confidence (see the resentment of MGH Psychiatry Service at Lindemann's retirement dinner). It undoubtedly was part of the motivation behind the petition aimed retrospectively at Lindemann and prospectively at his successor, including the passages

> Re-establish in this hospital a spirit of inquiry free of dogma which will allow for enthusiastic investigation of all avenues of approach to the cause and cure of mental illness . . . He should not be a member of, nor lend his support to, any school or cult of psychiatry which substitutes 'faith' for the scientific method of diagnosing, treating and evaluating the result of treatment of mental illness . . . encourage the use of physical and chemical methods in the treatment of psychiatric illness.

Is it possible to combine factual understanding with values-determined direction? Does factual understanding suggest another set of value-determined goals? Can commitment to values legitimately motivate marshaling facts to implement these values, as Lindemann was taught?

As discussed, values are always motivators in human endeavors—including science, medicine, and psychiatry—and influence the issues to be addressed and the use to which facts are put. This holds true in biological, psychological, and social psychiatry. The decision not to become involved with the social and societal conditions and policies that affect mental health is as much a value-driven course of action as the decision to seek out and ameliorate those social and societal conditions and policies. Can the validity of the facts discovered and marshaled in the cause and the justification of their interpretation and programs stemming from them be evaluated and confirmed independent of the values held? Lindemann tried to do this, steadfastly insisting on scientific, professional standards, and maintaining the professional role of the researcher, consultant, and educator rather than political activist or polemicist. The rejection of the factual, scientific basis of Lindemann and social and community psychiatry because of rejection of their goals is a nonfactual, unscientific, partisan attack based on the values of competing ideologies. Lindemann pursued his value-determined goals using the understanding, evidence, and methods developed through his efforts and those of other social psychiatry advocates. His values and goals can be debated by those with other values and goals in the court of psychiatry, medicine, science, and society. Sometimes they were. At other times (as in the petition), their values basis was attacked while ignoring the values basis of the attackers, and sometimes *ad hominem* rationalizations (including criticism of Lindemann's administrative style and efficacy) were substituted for addressing the social ideology and its CMH derivatives.

The result of Lindemann's contending motivations—modesty, self-doubt, avoidance of conflict versus commitment to the mission of rectifying psychiatry and medicine and society through making them appreciate and succor the coping struggles of individuals, families, and communities, and redeeming the individual and community through therapeutic intervention to aid their adaptation to the vicissitudes of life—was Lindemann's style of teaching, leading, and exemplifying rather than commanding and fighting (the *guru* rather than "following the lamp of power"). It is worth reviewing Lindemann's place in Etheridge's typology of personality and leadership styles:[93]

	Introvert	Extrovert
High dominance	bloc leaders (excluding)	world leaders (integrating)
Low dominance	maintainers	conciliators

- Bloc leaders divide the world into preferred moral values versus those who oppose them. They are stubborn, tenacious, and try to reshape the world according to their personal visions. They emphasize exclusion and are more likely to use force
- World leaders are more flexible, pragmatic, and want to lead rather than contain. They emphasize impersonal mechanisms, advocate change, cooperate, advance on many issues, and emphasize inclusion. They emphasize personal involvement and collaboration, and are more likely to employ force.
- Maintainers are less likely to use force. They employ a holding action for the status quo, and emphasize impersonal mechanisms.
- Conciliators are less likely to use force. They are egalitarian, hope to negotiate accommodations, flexible, hopeful, open to change, lack consistent and strong will power, and emphasize personal involvement and collaboration. They tend to be peripheral and ineffectual.

In this typology, Lindemann sought to be a world leader yet was seen by some as a conciliator because of unwillingness to use force in dealing with obstacles to political effectiveness.

This result is illuminated by recalling that Lindemann was influenced in his adolescence by his imposing, determined, proselytizing maternal grandfather. Later, he was drawn to a similar spiritual environment in India, where he saw Himalayan young people come not to learn surgery but to use mind and heart for brothers and neighbors. To repeat, Lindemann's approach was that of the *guru*—a wise man, teacher, persuader, and motivator for unhappy young people in the institutions where he taught rather than the "follower of the lamp of power", the course chosen by some of his contemporaries. This led to his concept of CMH mental health consultation with and reliance on key community resource people. In a discussion with his intimate colleagues, they contrasted the humanistic, social ideology approach dealing with people with the authoritarian, biotechnological ideology approach dealing with chemical and neurological factors that involved even good people in authoritarian programs and politics.[94] In psychiatry, they contrasted those who work through influencing others with those who are preoccupied with power, systems, government grants, and production to gain more power. The former teach in terms of who people are rather than what they achieve; *wirklich, nicht scheinbar* (real, not apparent).

It is helpful in an understanding of Lindemann to trace the stages of his professional development built on the foundation of his values:

- He began working psychologically with the mentally retarded in Kleefisch's sanitarium.
- He moved to Iowa to work with those brain damaged but expanded into the behavioral effects of psychotropic drugs and even further into psychological interest in psychoanalysis.
- In Boston, he was uninterested in biological brain studies and attracted to the borderland of psychosomatic medicine at MGH.
- His psychosomatic work shifted toward the influence of psychosocial experiences and losses, and he completed his training in psychoanalysis.
- The Coconut Grove fire studies shifted his gaze sharply toward the effect of social relationship on mental illness.
- At the Harvard School of Public Health and the HRS, he focused definitely on the social relationships of families and communities.
- He returned to MGH and HMS with the mandate to introduce a social ideology and social science to those institutions as a perspective both on medicine and on themselves.
- He devoted himself more openly and on an ever-larger scale to his social and humane values in his work in the Space Cadets, Lindau Psychotherapy Group, attraction to the WHO, and inspiration from Indian philosophy.

After his orthodox scientific accomplishments, Lindemann felt it was time to let loose his unorthodox creativity. He wanted to change the HMS/MGH cold atmosphere to one better for staff and community. He was unhappy and felt like a failure because people did not pay attention and follow his views but followed their own tracks without caring about service and teaching. He was involved with residents in a firm but nonpunitive way, slowly redirected the department, brought in Gerald Caplan, who was effective in organization and writing, brought visitors from around the world, expounded a new meaning for psychiatry, and HRS inspired others such as the state of California health department program.

This approach to leadership helps account for the starkly opposing reactions to him: Those who shared his values and goals felt him to be a gentle ideal and inspiration who became an abiding influence in their developments and practices. In contrast, those who saw psychiatry in terms of position, power, and impersonal practice saw Lindemann as misguided, disloyal, and ineffectual.

At Stanford Medical Center, David Hamburg, who courted Lindemann as a visiting professor, crafted an intermediate appreciation of his contributions.[95] He credited Lindemann with an understanding of the interrelationship of individual psychological and social dynamics and being one of the first to study this relationship in detail and moving mental and physical health in that direction. He especially contributed concern with prevention; the contribution of behavioral and social sciences to health; the involvement of nonmedical professions, community resources, social networks, and neighborhoods to illness; and broader concepts of and fellowship among professionals and the pooling of their useful skills. Tradition and economics supported a curative (secondary prevention) focus; primary prevention and epidemiology was more difficult to accept—the subsequent self-help movement is consistent with Lindemann's thinking. Hamburg credited Lindemann with raising concern for the disadvantaged, poor, and powerless, and the appreciation of social justice. Social activism in these areas brought with it destructiveness: "Violence in the name of peace, there was a lot of hatred in the name of love". Lindemann, an intellectual, sought intellectual exchange rather than involvement in demonstrations. Hamburg thought Lindemann shared his concern that there was little change in professional practices though now located in the community, with interest focused on geographical areas, administration, and funding. He thought the valuable contributions of CMH had to be sorted out from the disappointing and unclear results, and that Lindemann had done much useful work, including that which had yet to be mined.

Also at Stanford, Khatchadourian tried to formulate a view that would encompass Lindemann's inspirational and implementational aspects.[96] He was the biblical "man without guile", open, with integrity, benevolent, perceptive, insightful, with infectious enthusiasm that carried people with him.[97] He was not systematic or thorough, with unrealistic optimism, capable of being duped and falsely leading others. He was otherworldly, not tough and wily. Thus, he was not effective as a department chairman at Harvard but more suited to his guru role at Stanford.

Those who emphasized other aspects of psychiatry and medicine saw him as fuzzy-minded, weak, failing to forward traditional clinical and biological psychiatry, and disloyal in not fighting for and winning power, resources, and status for his department, his profession, and himself rather than as working toward the different goal of recasting psychiatry in social terms. He was not understood or valued by those who did not understand his role or convictions, resented by those who hungered for power and advancement, and caused anxiety in those who feared losing territory and perquisites to other disciplines. He and CMH were caught between those fighting for power and control of old professional institutions, disciplines, and resources (conservatives and reactionaries) and those fighting for power and control of new recognition, institutions, and resources (leftist radicals).

At the MGH, Lindemann's stance resulted in a range of opinions of him: acceptance and admiration (e.g., Laura Morris) versus mixed appreciation and disappointment (e.g., John Nemiah and Peter Sifneos) versus pockets of lack of respect or outright hostility to CMH, the social sciences, and Lindemann himself (e.g., Avery Weisman, Thomas Hackett, and Thomas Ballantine). He did not settle these factions by converting doubters, setting boundaries and expectations, or replacing dissidents. Thus, they were left as warring factions that discouraged and undermined Lindemann. These opposing perspectives were clearly expressed in formal and informal comments about him, in the evaluations of his tenure as MGH chief of psychiatry—an effective leader toward his goals (e.g., administration consultant Henrik Blum, HMS dean George Packer Berry) versus a failure, betrayer, and object of scorn (e.g., MGH petition, MGH Department of Psychiatry opponents Thomas Hackett and Avery Weisman). The experience at HMS and MGH clearly illustrates the shift in ideology: Lindemann was chosen by these bodies because of his focus on social ideology and psychiatry and promise to bring CMH and the social sciences to these bodies. A decade later, these same bodies rejected this ideology and goals, minimizing teaching time for "ineffectual" education, withdrawing support for CMH projects such as HRS, and disdaining social theory, research, and activism in favor of a biological ideology in his successor and the department (as in the MGH petition).

Lindemann had exceeded his social system's tolerance, lost "system capital", and was excluded. One may wonder if he exceeded the social tolerance with heroic boldness or was unaware that he was exceeding the social limits and felt surprised, hurt, and resentful.

Henrik Blum, as consultant on administration, accepted Lindemann's path as a choice of focus and style rather than as failure in not choosing another. He concluded that Lindemann was not a bad administrator but rather fit his organization and time. His style supported a good department: while "running a tight ship" is often equated with good administration, it would not have worked with his independent subordinates. Many of the staff members couldn't care less about his view: they did not understand or value CMH, did not get their financial support from the department, and had many interests chosen on the basis of the staff members' psychiatric rather than CMH expertise. They deferred appropriately to their great chief but did their own things. He was criticized by those who wanted him to fight for them; he was praised by those who wanted to be left alone except for consultation as needed (which was Lindemann's style) and felt supported when he appreciated their accomplishments.

Lindemann's CMH career covered several stages:

- Development of values that motivated his subsequent career
- Achievement of recognition and reward with feelings of vindication and success
- Displacement by historical shifts with feelings of failure rather than recognizing loss of synchrony with the ethos

He struggled with his experience in challenging convention with high principle:[98]

> Then the question arises: How is one so successful? What kind of self really gets you places, e.g., to be professor at Harvard? What I have just described would not off-hand be described as a success routine. It would be described as leading to a very enjoyable and intensive life, but not one in which you do the kinds of things which are bought by the environment, and for which it pays you with prestige. In speaking about myself, I'm still puzzled about that—it may be true just the same . . . It may be that in these times, when success is most clearly shown by money-making, there is a need to make a few other kinds of people important. I remember so well, when the Department of Social Relations at Harvard had its ten-year celebration (I was very soon a fringe person there, as I am here, too) that one of the speakers said, "You at Harvard in general have more crackpots than any other University—and Harvard can afford it!".

Lindemann repeatedly questioned and regretted accepting the chairmanship of the MGH psychiatry department. He had hoped that reaching for a position of power from which to implement his ideals was an unavoidable compromise during which he could maintain his purity of spirit. In retrospect, he felt guilty that he had not always chosen the humane rather than the power direction, feeling that when he chose the professorship and Cobb's position, he had let the humane role wane which should have been central, and that his relation to the HRS and West End Study was diminished because of the preoccupying battles at MGH.

It takes special insight and courage to follow Erikson's observation on self-affirmation:[99]

> Although aware of the relativity of all the various life styles which have given meaning to human striving, the possessor of integrity is ready to defend the dignity of his own lifestyle . . . For he knows that an individual life is the accidental coincidence of but one life cycle with but one segment of history; and that for him all human integrity stands and falls with the one style of integrity of which he partakes. . .

Lindemann's contributions were on several levels:

- Concrete projects: research, programs, and teaching in psychosomatic medicine, psychotherapy, mental health programs, and education curricula
- Ideology: a public health perspective on mental illness sources, vectors, and hosts; primary prevention of mental illness and strengthening of mental health; embedding in social networks underlies the personality development of individuals and social structure of communities;
- Moral values: relationship; mutual caring; a nurturing environment; the value, opportunity, and self-realization of individuals
- A psychosocial approach to helping people as an alternative to psychodynamic psychiatry in 20th century U.S.

psychiatry, with a more accepting manner through CMH outreach.

Integrated Dynamic of History: The Community Mental Health Example

Factors contributing to the synergy of the stage of social ideology and Lindemann's personality included:

- A social ethos of confidence and ideals
- Medical and psychiatric implementation of those values in their spheres of function
- Lindemann's personal experience and the values and goals they engendered
- These values and goals were further evolved by the ideas and values encountered and sought in his education and training

- These values and ambitions found opportunity for expression in contemporary syntonic ideas, values, and activities
- This formed a combination of mutually enhancing (a) societal drive and its institutionalizations and (b) a man eager for realization through them of his values and goals.

Erikson saw something akin to this in regard to Martin Luther:[100] ... Luther ... was ... beset with a syndrome of conflicts ... He found a spiritual solution ... His solution roughly bridged a political and psychological vacuum which history had created in a significant portion of Western Christendom. Such coincidence, if further coinciding with the deployment of highly specific personal gifts, makes for historical "greatness".

Later, the cycle of ideologies shifted, and among its social institutions, medicine and psychiatry incorporated this change through workers socialized in the new ideology, values, and social rewards incorporated in the new order. The persistence of previously subordinated ideologies, loyalties, and practices and the reside of resentment of the insurgence of the ideology, practices, and devotees of social psychiatry rallied to this change. The third factor—the person—does not easily change embedded values and ideology. Some of practical mind and adaptable spirit, such as Klerman and Shader, did join the new order, with varying degrees of ambivalence and admixture of practice, thus achieving success—acceptance, institutional rewards, etc. Others, such as Lindemann, did not change values and practices, were evicted by their professions and institutions, and doubted their work and worth.

The place of the individual—even the outstanding individual—in history has been hotly debated: the great person who created the direction and success of history versus historical forces giving opportunity and reward to individuals who contribute to its evolution and concrete embodiment. Our exploration of social and community psychiatry is more consistent with the latter perspective, with creative and influential individuals helping shape their local environments and gaining broader recognition for their contributions in forms determined by the larger social ideology and institutions. Successful social/community psychiatry programs clearly flourished with creative, optimistic, energetic, charismatic leaders. In a propitious context, including institutional receptivity and available resources, vital productivity can be achieved. When the committed leader leaves, equally capable successors seem uncommon, either because such people are rare or because charismatic leaders have, consciously or inadvertently, discouraged equally capable and ambitious potential successors in their orbits or because successfully driven and charismatic leaders are too uniquely fitted to their environments to be duplicated. Without such leaders, the programs lose their creativity, attractiveness, resources, and acceptance, and may become vestigial or disappear. And when the social and ideological ethos shifts, leaders and programs become anachronistic, losing enthusiasm and material support, and are criticized and rejected by successor ideologies, values, and programs. When the former ideology, values, and resources are lost, the holdover programs may make modifications that allow them to maintain some aspects of their former selves (as the human relations service of Wellesley did); become reborn in the successor ideology, goals, and procedures (as the Tufts Department of Psychiatry did); or disappear (as the Massachusetts General Hospital mental health service did).

It should be remembered that persistence of alternate ideology, ideas, practice, and people and groups committed to them remain in various forms and places, though subordinate in influence. They will reappear later in the course of the cycles of ideology. It is more likely that they will then be considered a novel discovery (people are always "finally finding the truth") than that they will be appreciated as a revitalization of past creativity, commitment, courage, and struggle.

In his era, Erich Lindemann brought a set of moral values and professional ideals honed by personal experience and focused education. How could these have the strongest influence on contemporary beliefs and practices? He was most in his element as a teacher and advocate. In that role, he was limited and shaped by the availability of people and institutions that understood, valued, and acted on what he brought. As a guru, he was free of administrative demands and distraction and could focus on his interests and advocacy, but he was curbed by the interests of his hosts and had little direct control of a program. He was less comfortable and organizationally effective as the administrator of a program but was in more control of his activities, at least to some degree) more influential on the direction of that program and its staff, and carried the added influence of the prestige of the program and his office.

On balance, could he have accomplished more as an administrator with some control and authority but also resistance, inefficiencies, and discomfort; as a teacher and advocate with recognition and respect but no burdens or control; or as an independent voice in the wilderness? His decision was to sacrifice himself to the first role and experience the second.

Thus the individual swims in and is carried by the historical milieu interacting on one another.

Notes

1. White, Theodore H., *In Search of History: A Personal Adventure* (New York: Harper & Rose/Warner Books Edition, 1978), p. 245
2. Watterson, Bill, "Calvin and Hobbes", *Boston Globe*, 7/19/1993
3. Lindemann, Erich, "TALK GIVEN BY ERICH LINDEMANN TO STAFF OF STUDENT HEALTH DEPARTMENT AT STANFORD", 11/12/1971,

p. 3. [folder "Mental Health Services of MGH a setting for Community MH", Box VII 2, Lindemann Collection, Center for the History of Medicine, Francis A. Countway Library of Medicine, Boston, MA]
4. Levine, Murray and Levine, Adeline, "THE MORE THINGS CHANGE", Yale University-Psycho-Educational Clinic, late 1960s. [folder "LEVINE: SOCIAL FORCES + M.H.", IIIB3 d, Erich Lindemann Collection, Center for the History of Medicine, Francis A. Countway Library of Medicine, Boston, MA]
5. Lindemann, Erich, 11/12/1971, *ibid*, pp. 9–10
6. Yolles, Stanley F. M.D., Second Director of the NIMH—1964–6/2/1970: 10, "The Future of Community Psychiatry", in Barton, Walter E. and Sanborn, Charlotte J. (eds.) *An Assessment of The Community Mental Health Movement* (Lexington, MA: Lexington Books, 1977), pp. 21–34, based on Dartmouth Continuing Education Institute, Department of Psychiatry, Dartmouth Medical School, 1975; p. 169
7. Albee, George, Ph.D., "Personal Change and Social Change", address at graduation ceremonies, Massachusetts School of Professional Psychology, 6/12/1983
8. Bergstresser, Sara May, *Therapies of the Mundane: Community Mental Health Care and Everyday Life in an Italian Town* (Doctoral dissertation, Department of Anthropology, Brown University, 5/2004)
9. First revolution: PInel recognizing the continuity of kind caring from normal to insane people; second revolution: Freud recognizing the continuity of understanding the mind from child to adult and from sane to insane; third revolution: John F. Kennedy recognizing the continuity of concerns for health from the healthy to the mentally ill and deficient.
10. Albee, George, 6/12/1983, *ibid*
11. Khatchadourian, Herant, M.D., interview by David G. Satin at Khatchadourian's office, Stanford Medical Center, Palo Alto, CA, 12/19/1979. [Erich Lindemann Collection, Center for the History of Medicine, Francis A. Countway Library of Medicine, Boston, MA]
12. Santayana, George:, "Flux ad Constancy in Human Nature", Ch. xii, vol. I, vol. I, *Life of Reason* (1905–1906)
13. Bergstresser, Sara May, 5/2004, *ibid*
14. Astrachan, Boris M., "Many Modest Goals: The Pragmatics of Health Delivery", *Connecticut Medicine* 37:174–180 (1973)
15. Yolles, Stanley F., 1977, *ibid*, pp. 21–34
16. Miller, Bruce Nils, Ph.D., Lincoln Community Mental Health Center, Bronx, New York City: "A Concept of Advocacy", Presented at Mental Health Service For The 70s: Neighborhood Psychiatry Conference, Cambridge, MA, 6/8/1973. [folder "CMH—Social Action", David G. Satin files, Newton, MA]
17. Randolph, Peter B., M.D., Director, Tufts Mental Health Center, Boston, MA: "Response to Working With Neighborhood Organizations", response to Miller, Bruce Nils, 6/8/1973, *ibid*, pp. 3–5
18. Susselman, Samuel and Blum, Henrik L., "Origins and Progress of a Mental Health Program", Ch. II in Duhl, Leonard J. and Leopold, Robert L. (eds.) *Mental Health and Urban Social Policy* (San Francisco: Jossey-Bass, 1968), p. 55
19. Prillentensky, Isaac and Nelson, Geoffrey, "Community Psychology: Reclaiming Social Justice", in Fox, I. and Prillentensky, Isaac (eds.) *Critical Psychology: An Introduction* (London: Sage, 1997), pp. 166–184
20. Davis, Kingsley, "Mental Hygiene and the Class Structure", *Psychiatry* 1:55–65 (1938)

21. Lindemann, Elizabeth B., interview by David G. Satin, 7/14/1978. [Caddy 4, Box 4, X, Erich Lindemann Collection, Center for the History of Medicine, Francis A. Countway Library of Medicine, Boston, MA]
22. Waller, Willard W., "Social Problems and The Mores", *American Sociology Review* 1:922–933 (1936)
23. Clark, Tim, "Barbara Tuchman: In Search of Mankind's Better Moments", *Yankee* 44:60–63, 152–156, 159 (8/1980)
24. Green, Lawrence W., Dr. PH, "The Oversimplification of Policy in Prevention", *American Journal of Public Health* 68 no. 10:953–954 (10/1978)
25. Caplan, Gerald, "Prospects for Community Psychiatry: Lessons from History", the Bertram Roberts Memorial Lecture in Social Psychiatry, Yale Medical School, 3/4/1969
26. Caplan, Gerald, 3/4/1969, *ibid*
27. Leighton, Alexander H., "The Compass and the Troubled Sea", *Psychiatric Annals* 8: 43–54, 40–51 (1978)
28. Klerman, Gerald L., M.D., George Harrington Professor of Psychiatry, HMS; Chair, Mental Health Policy Working Group, Division of Health Policy Research and Education, Harvard University; Director of Stanley Cobb Research Laboratories, Department of Psychiatry, MGH [former Superintendent, CT Mental Health Center and ELMHC]: "Community Mental Health Developments in the U.S.A.", paper at Wm. T. Grant Foundation workshop, NYC, 11/30–12/1/84; to be published in Rappaport, Robert N., ed., *Research and Action, A Collaborative Interactive Approach* (Cambridge, MA: Cambridge University Press, 1985)
29. Shore, Miles, M.D., former Superintendent of the Tufts-Bay Cove Community Mental Health Center and Area Director of the Tufts Mental Health Area: interview by David G. Satin at the Massachusetts Mental Health Center, 8/6/1981
30. Lindemann, Elizabeth B., 7/14/1978, *ibid*
31. Lindemann, Erich, Duhl, Leonard J., Seeley, John and Lindemann, Elizabeth: Erich Lindemann, Leonard Duhl Interviews by Duhl, Leonard J.—Interview, 7/15/1974. [Caddy 4, Tape 8A, 9B; 7, Erich Lindemann Collection, Center for the History of Medicine, Francis A. Countway Library of Medicine, Boston, MA]
32. Evans, Robert, Ed.D., Executive Director, Human Relations Service, Inc. of Wellesley, MA, Introduction to the Erich Lindemann Memorial Lecture #14, 4/26/1991
33. Caplan, Gerald, "Prospects for Community Psychiatry: Lessons from History", the Bertram Roberts Memorial Lecture in Social Psychiatry, Yale Medical School, 3/4/1969
34. Compton, Michael, M.D., M.P.H., Chair of Psychiatry, Department of Psychiatry at Lenox Hill Hospital, New York, and Shim, Ruth, M.D., M.P.H., Vice Chairman for Education and Faculty Development, Department of Psychiatry at Lenox Hill Hospital, New York, "Address Mental Health's Social Determinants Through Policy Change", *Psychiatric News* 50 no.3: (2/6/2015); See also *The Social Determinants of Mental Health* (American Psychiatric Publishing)
"In addition to treating mental illness, psychiatrists have a role in improving mental health and reducing risk for mental illness. Individual, patient-level opportunities exist for pursuing these prevention goals, but promoting mental health and preventing mental illness are most effectively carried out at the population level through policy changes that address the social determinants of metal health.

Defined as social and environmental factors pertaining to where and under what circumstances we grow up, go to school, work, and age that adversely impact mental well-being, the social determinants of mental health include such diverse factors as (1) adverse childhood experiences; (2) racism, social exclusion, and discrimination; (3) poor education; (4) poverty, neighborhood deprivation, and income inequality; (5) unemployment and underemployment; (6) food insecurity; (7) poor housing quality and housing instability (8) adverse features of the built environment, for example, public-works infrastructure and housing/office/school buildings; (9) poor or unequal access to health care services; and (10) exposure to natural disasters, trauma, gun violence, and war. This list artificially separates the social determinants, though they clearly overlap and interact.

Although some countries have much greater burdens of many of these adverse social and environmental factors (such as the West African nations struggling to contain Ebola virus transmission), each of the social determinants of mental health also affect people living in the United States. Furthermore, the social determinants of mental health are intimately linked to health disparities and inequalities, which are unfair differences in health risk and outcomes among specific populations groups. The social determinants of mental heath affect communities and the population as a whole, but they also affect individuals. They create psychological stress and physiological distress responses. They also constrict one's options, setting the stage for poor choices and risky health behaviors (for example, reliance on an unhealthy but inexpensive diet or substance abuse). Additionally, these social determinants increase risk of exposure to injury, pathogens, and toxins.

In these ways, the social determinants are "the causes of the causes" of both physical and mental illnesses.

Genetics undoubtedly plays a role in risk for the most mental illnesses, but the social and environmental risk factors likely interact with genetic risk through gene-by-environment interactions and epigenetic mechanisms. Although the social determinants of mental health are largely the same as those underpinning chronic physical health conditions and physical health disparities, we frame them as social determinants of mental health in order to translate existing literature to the mental heath arena and articulate specific actions that mental health professionals, policy makers, and society at large can take to improve mental health and reduce mental illness risk.

To most effectively address the social determinants of mental health, one must ask what lies beneath them at even deeper levels.

In our conceptualization, the social determinants are, for the most part, created by unequal distribution of opportunity in society—opportunity meaning safe, stable, and nurturing environments in childhood; social inclusion; political capital and the ability to participate fully in society; equal access to education, jobs, healthy food, safe housing and neighborhoods, and health care and other resources; and other dimensions of social justice.

Even deeper, the unequal distribution of opportunity is underpinned by both public policies (policies, codes, rules, and legislation pertaining to education, employment, wages, food, housing, neighborhoods, and other aspects of society) and social norms (values, attitudes, impressions, and biases that drive stigma, discrimination, and social exclusion). Thus, to act on the most fundamental causes of poor mental health and mental illness, we must address both public policies and social norms that create unequal distribution of opportunity.

Psychiatrists and other mental health professionals have a moral responsibility to shape public policies and affect social norms. To truly promote mental health, psychiatrists must consider population-level interventions on public policies and social norms with the same intensity that they carry out clinical interventions. This includes public policies that, at first glance, might not appear to be health policies at all, such as local zoning ordinances, a state college system's tuition costs, and federal minimum wage legislation. This "health in all policies" approach compliments clinical approaches at the individual patient level.

As our field pursues promotion of mental health and prevention of mental illness, we must embrace both clinical and policy approaches to addressing the social determinant of mental health. In doing so, we will move toward a more just and healthy society and better physical health and mental health for all."

35. Holmes, Oliver Wendell, "Currents And Counter-Currents In Medical Science", An Address delivered before the Massachusetts Medical Society, at the Annual Meeting, 5/30/1860, published in Holmes, Oliver Wendell, *Medical Essays 1842–1882* (Boston: Houghton, Mifflin and Company, 1883), pp. 173–208
36. Schlesinger, Arthur. "Arthur Schlesinger Answers His Critics", *Boston Sunday Globe*, 10/1/1978
37. Clark, Tim, 8/1980, *ibid*
38. Zusman, Jack, M.D., M.P.H., Professor of Psychiatry and Director, Division of Community Psychiatry, School of Medicine, State University of New York at Buffalo; then Professor, Florida Mental Health. Institute, Tampa, FL; "The Philosophic Basis for a Community and Social Psychiatry", Ch. 3 in Barton, Walter E. and Sanborn, Charlotte J. (eds.) *An Assessment of The Community Mental Health Movement* (Lexington, MA: Lexington Books, 1977), pp. 21–34, based on Dartmouth Continuing Education Institute, Department of Psychiatry, Dartmouth Medical School, 1975. [folder "CMH—Theory", David G. Satin files, Newton, MA]
39. Deutsch, Albert, *The Shame of the States: Mental Illness and Social Policy: The American Experience* (1905–1961) (Ayer vs. NY: Harcourt, Brace, 1948)
40. Lindemann, Erich, "The Meaning of Crisis in Individual and Family Living", *Teachers College Record* 57:310–315 (1956)
41. Lindemann, Erich, "Mental Health Services Relating to Crises in Urbanization", in *Die Begegnung mit dem Kranken Menschen*. (Berne: Hans Huber, 1965) pp. 75–90
42. Zagorski, Nick, "Biological Explanations for Mental Disorders Reduce Therapist Empathy", *Psychiatric News* 50 no.1:16–19 (1/2/15)
43. *The Random House Dictionary of the English Language, College Edition* (New York: Randomn House, 1968), p. 645: Humanist: . . . 1. A student of human nature or affairs. 2. A person having a strong interest in or concern for human welfare, values, and dignity.

Webster's New World Dictionary, Second Edition (Springfield, MA: G. and C. Meriam Co., 1940), p. 1212: "Humanist: . . . one whose belief consists of faith in man and devotion to human well—being . . . Humanism: . . . a system, mode, or attitude of thought or action centered upon distinctly human interests or ideals; especially as contrasted with naturalistic or religious interests".

The Oxford English Dictionary (Oxford, Great Britain: Clarendon Press, 1933), pp. 444–445: "Humanist: . . . a class of thinkers which arose in Germany toward the end of the eighteenth century, originating chiefly from the diffusion of the writings of Rouseau . . . their system—usually called humanism . . . sought to level all family distinctions, all differences of race, all nationality, all positive moral obligations, all positive religion, and to train mankind to be men, as . . . the highest accomplishment . . . Humanitarian: . . . 5b3. One who devotes himself to the welfare of mankind at large; a philanthropist. Nearly always contemptuous, connoting one who goes to excess in his human principles . . . adv. 3. Having regard to the interests of humanity or mankind at large; relating to, advocating, or practicing humanity or human action; broadly philathropic. Often contemptuous or hostile.

44. *The Community Psychologist* (1999), *Journal of Community Psychology*; referred to in Kelly, James G., "The Spirit of Community Psychology", (undated). [file "Kelly—NIMH + Founding of Community Psychology", Box XII #3, Erich Lindemann Collection, Center for the History of Medicine, Francis A. Countway Library of Medicine, Harvard Medical School, Boston, MA]
45. Franklin, Benjamin, *The Autobiography of Benjamin Franklin* (New York: Airmont Publishing Company, 1965), p. 112
46. Huxley, Aldous.
47. Lindemann, Erich, draft of a letter to Mr. S. Andereopoulos in relation to a lecture "Community Mental Health, Comments on the Social Consequences of Scientific Inquiry", to be given as part of the series "Progress in Medicine" on 2/2/1966; News Bureau, MGH, 2/1/1966. [Box XII 1 folder Satin-Bio of E.L., Erich Lindemann Collection, Center for the History of Medicine, Francis A. Countway Library of Medicine, Boston, MA]
48. Lindemann, Erich, Consultation Training Seminar, Mental Health Unit, San Mateo County Helath Department, California, 3/17/1970. [videotape, Erich Lindemann Collection, Center for the History of Medicine, Francis A. Countway Library of Medicine, Boston MA]
49. Haylett, Clarice, Director, Division of Mental Health, San Mateo County Health Department, California: interview by David G. Satin at her home, Palo Alto, CA, 12/17/1979. [Erich Lindemann Collection, Center for the History of Medicine, Francis A. Countway Library of Medicine, Boston, MA]
50. Seeley, John in Lindemann, Erich, Duhl, Leonard J., Seeley, John and Lindemann, Elizabeth, 7/15/1974, *ibid*
51. "Expanding the Caring Lens: Nursing and Medical Students Reflecting on Images of Older People." (GGE—2014–0079, Geriatrics and Gerontology Education, 2015)
52. White, Theodore H., 1978, *ibid*, p. 100
53. Tennyson, Alfred, "Morte D'Arthur", lines 226–242
54. Waller, Willard W., 1936, *ibid*, pp. 928–930
55. Caplan, Gerald, 3/4/1969, *ibid*
56. Caplan, Gerald, "ii Israel" (manuscript), [folder "Caplan, Gerald—Contrib. to proposed book on preventive psychiatry". [Box V 4–8, Erich Lindemann Collection, Center for the History of Medicine, Francis A. Countway Library of Medicine, Boston, MA]
57. Armor, David J. and Klerman, Gerald L., "Psychiatric Treatment Orientations and Professional Ideology", *Health and Social Behavior 9* no. 3:9 (1968)
58. Lindemann, Erich, 11/12/1971, *ibid*, p. 13
59. Seeley, John, interview by David G. Satin, 4/12/1979. [Caddy 5, Erich Lndemanna Collection, David G. Satin, Newton, MA]
60. Fulmer, Terry, interview by David G. Satin at the Harvard Geriatric Education Center, Boston, 5/8/1984.
61. Peter, Laurence J. and Hull, Raymond, *The Peter Principle* (New York: William Morrow, 1969)
62. Psalm 39: verse 6, Old Testament and (English) King James Version
63. White, Theodore H., 1978, *ibid*, p. 452

64. Wechsberg, Joseph, *The Merchant Bankers* (New York: Pocket Books/ Simon & Schuster, 1966), p. 145; Max M. Warburg regarding the history of M. M. Warburg & Company, Hamburg, Germany
65. Von Hoffman, Nicholas, quoted in Trudeau, Gary, address at the Harvard University commencement 1983
66. Kops, Deborah, "School is a Window on American Life . . .", interview with Joseph Featherstone, *Harvard Magazine* 81 no.4:85–86 (3–4/1979)
67. Weinberg, Arthur, ed., "The Communist Trial—Chicago, 1920, Summation to the Jury", Ch. 1 in *Attorney for the Damned: Clarence Darrow In His Own Words* (New York: Simon and Schuster, 1957)
68. Weinberg, Arthur, ed., "Haywood Trial, Boise, Idaho, 1907", Ch. 2 in *Attorney for the Damned: Clarence Darrow In His Own Words* (New York: Simon and Schuster, 1957), p. xvi
69. Lindemann, Erich, letter to Hargreaves, Dr. G. Ronald, University of Leeds, Great Britain, 5/8/1957. [folder "Oxford—July Conference on Stress (See also Hargreaves, "H")", Box IIIA7 1955–9 1 of 3, Erich Lindemann Collection, Center for the History of Medicine, Francis A. Countway Library of Medicine, Boston, MA]
70. Planck, Max, *The Philosophy of Physics* (1936)
71. Santayana, George
72. Man, John, *Saladin: The Life, The Legend and the Islamic Empire* (London: The Bantam Press, 2015); Ch 16 A Brief History of Leadership, pp. 237–248, 239–240
73. Coutu, Diane L., "Putting Leaders on the Couch: A Conversation with Manfred F. R. Ketz de Vries", *Harvard Business Review*, 1/04
74. Rosenberg, Pearl, Ph.D., "A Possible Analysis of the Group Dynamics of the Wellesley Experiment", 7/14/1953, pp. 1–17. [folder "A POSSIBLE ANALYSIS OF THE GROUP DYNAMICS OF THE WELLESLEY EXPERIMENT, July 14,1953", Box V 4–8, Erich Lindemann Collection, Center for the History of Medicine, Countway Library of Medicine, Boston, MA]
75. Haylett, Clarice, 12/17/1979, *ibid*
76. Kuhn, Thomas, "The Structure of Scientific Revolution", quoted by Trudau, Gary, address at Harvard University commencement, 1983
77. Hausman, William, "The Reorganization of a University Department of Psychiatry: A Blueprint for Change", in E. Miller (ed.) *Task and Organization* (London: Wetey, 1976)
78. "HAA 150th: Bok Cites Dangers Facing Universities" (Reprinted from 110/12/90), *Harvard Alumni Gazette*, 3/1991, p. 4
79. Nietzsche, Friederich, "Homer's Contest", in Kaufmann, Walter (trans.) *The Portable Nietzsche* (New York: Viking Press, 1954), p. 36
80. St. Matthew chapter 23, verses 34 and 38: The New Testament, Authorized (King James) Version.
81. Hausman, Kenneth, "Benefits of University, State Hospital Cooperation Lauded", *Psychiatric News* 19:1, 13 (7/20/1984)
82. Memo to MGH ad hoc committee to select a Chief of the Psychiatry Service, ?5/21–4/65
83. Franklin, Benjamin, 1965, *ibid*, pp. 126–127
84. Haylett, Clarice, 12/17/1979, *ibid*
85. Lindemann, Erich, 11/12/1971, *ibid*, in response to a request that he reconstruct some aspects of his own development as teacher and scientist
86. Lindemann, Erich, 11/12/1971, *ibid*, p. 4
87. Dorosin, David, M.D., Director of Psychological Services, Student Health Services, Stanford Medical Center, Palo Alto, CA: interview by David G.

Satin at the Student Health Services, 12/17/1979, [Erich Lindemann Collection, Center for the History of Medicine, Francis A. Countway Library of Medicine, Boston MA]
88. Lindemann, Erich, Duhl, Leonard J., Seeley, John and Lindemann, Elizabeth, 7/15/1974, *ibid*
89. Lindemann, Erich, 11/12/1971, *ibid*, p. 7
90. von Goethe, Johann Wolfgang, "Faust", translation and introduction by Kaufman, Walter (Garden City, NY: Anchor Books/Doubleday & Co., 1962), First Part of the Tragedy, pp. 108–109, lines 588–593.

"Ja, was man so erkennen heisst!
Wer darf das Kind beim rechten Namen nennen?
Die wenigen, die was davon erkannt,
Die töricht gnug ihr volles Herz nicht wahrten,
Dem Pöbel ihr Gefühl, ihr Schauen offenbarten,
Hat man von je gekreuzigt und verbrannnt".

91. Duhl, Leonard J., interviews by David G. Satin in Palo Alto and Berkeley, CA, 6/22/1974. [Erich Lindemann Collection, Center for the History of Medicine, Francis A. Countway Library of Medicine, Boston, MA]
92. One is reminded of the classification of geniuses described in "Odysseus of Ithaca" by Lem, Stanislaw, *A Perfect Vacuum* (New York: Harcourt Brace Jovanovich Publishers, 1983), pp. 103–104: "First come your run-of-the-mill and middling geniuses, that is, of the third order, whose minds are unable to go much beyond the horizon of their times. These . . . are often recognized and even come into money and fame. The geniuses of he second order are already too difficult for their contemporaries and therefore fare worse . . . the powers that be . . . compete for 'geniocide' . . . the manfold activity of exterminating geniuses . . . reognition awaits . . . in the form of a triubph beyond the grave . . . discovered by the succeeding generation or by some later one . . . the geniuses of the first order ae never known . . . for they are creators of truths so unpecedented, purveryors of proposals so revolutionary, that not a soul is capable of making head or tail of them".
93. Etheridge, Lloyd S., *A World of Men: The Private Sources of American Foreign Policy* (Cambridge, MA: The MIT Press, 1978)
94. Lindemann, Erich, Duhl, Leonard J., Seeley, John and Lindemann, Elizabeth, 7/15/1974, *ibid*
95. Hamburg, David, M.D., former Chairman of Department of Psychiatry, Stanford Medical Center; Director, National Institute of Medicine: interview by David G. Satin at the Institute, Washington, DC, 1/26/1979. [Erich Lindemann Collection, Center for the History of Medicine, Francis A. Countway Library of Medicine, Boston, MA]
96. Khatchadourian, Herant, 12/19/1979, *ibid*
97. It should be noted that some wondered if Lindemann were ambitious for recognition in the role of the wise man with answers to large questions: Dorosin, David, 12/17/1979, *ibid*
98. Lindemann, Erich, 11/12/1971, *ibid*, pp. 10–11
99. Erikson, Erik H., as quoted in Scherl, Donald J., "Lee B. Macht 1937–1981", in *Harvard Medical Alumni Bulletin* (Winter 1982), pp. 57, 58, 60
100. Erikson, Erik H., *Young Man Luther* (New York: Norton, 1962), p. 15

Appendix: Informants Interviewed

Interviewed by David G. Satin, M.D.

1. Adler, Gerald, Chairman, Psychiatry Department, Tufts Medical School, Boston, MA, 3/15,22/82
2. Almond, Richard and Barbara, Department of Psychiatry, Stanford Medical Center, Stanford University, Palo Alto, CA, 12/19/79
3. Astrachan, Boris, member, Department of Psychiatry, Yale University Medicine and Connecticut Mental Health Center, New, New Haven, CT, 7/22/82
4. Bandler, Bernard, Chairman, Division of Psychiatry, Boston University School of Medicine, MA, 8/11,11/16/78
5. Bandler, Louise, Chief Psychiatry Social Worker, Psychiatry Service, Massachusetts General Hospital, Boston, MA, 8/11/78
6. Batson, Ruth, Director, Consultation and Education Service, Boston University Community Mental Health Center, Boston, MA, 1/5/79
7. Bernard, Viola, Chief, Division of Community Mental Health, College of Physicians and Surgeons, Columbia University, New York, NY, 4/26/79
8. Berry, George Packer, *emeritus* Dean, Harvard Medical School, Boston, MA, 11/2/79
9. Blum, Henrik, consultant to the Psychiatry Service, Massachusetts General Hospital, Boston, MA, 3/23/79
10. Board of Directors, Human Relations Service of Wellesley, Inc., Wellesley, MA, 3/18/82
11. Bragg, Robert, Director, Human Relations Service of Wellesley, Wellesley, MA, 7/13/79
12. Brines, John K., Board of Directors Member, Wellesley Human Relations Service, Wellesley, MA, 12/28/78
13. Butler, Allen, Chief, Pediatrics Service, Massachusetts General Hospital and Professor of Pediatrics, Harvard Medical School, Boston, MA, 12/8/78

446 Appendix: Informants Interviewed

14. Caplan, Lee, social worker, Student Health Service, Stanford Medical Center, Stanford University, Palo Alto, CA, 12/79
15. Clark, Eleanor, former Chief Social Worker, Psychiatry Service, Massachusetts General Hospital, Boston, MA, 7/14/78
16. Cleo Eulau, Chief Social Worker, Child Psychiatry Service, Department of Psychiatry, Stanford Medical Center, Stanford University, Palo Alto, CA, 12/19/79
17. Coffey, Hugh and Franchon, group trainer and researcher (respectively), Wellesley Human Relations Service, Wellesley, MA, 12/79
18. Cohen, Sanford I., Chairman, Division of Psychiatry, Boston University School of Medicine, Boston, MA, 12/1/78
19. Cope, Oliver, Surgical Service, Massachusetts General Hospital and Professor of Surgery, Harvard Medical School, Boston, MA, 11/21/78
20. Crockett, David, Assistant to the General Director, Massachusetts General Hospital, Boston, MA, 10/17/78
21. Daniels, David, Department of Psychiatry, Stanford Medical Center, Stanford University, Palo Alto, CA, 12/20/79
22. Dawes, Lydia, staff member, Wellesley Human Relations Service, Wellesley, MA, 6/5/79
23. Deutsch, Helene, training analyst, Boston Psychoanalytic Society and Institute, Boston, MA, 10/27/78
24. Dörner, Klaus, Leitender Arzt, Westfälisches Landeskrankenhaus, West Germany, 10/15/84
25. Dorosin, David, Department of Psychiatry, Stanford Medical Center, Stanford University, Palo Alto, CA, 12/17/79
26. Duffy, Mark, Archivist, Episcopal Diocese of Massachusetts, 1/27/82
27. Duhl, Leonard, former Special Assistant and Director, Special Committee on Social and Physical Environment Variables as Determinants of Mental Health, Office of Planning, National Institute of Mental Health, National Institutes of Health, U.S. Public Health Service, Department of Health, Education and Welfare, Washington, D.C., 6/22/74, 4/2,12/17/79, 8/16/07
28. Eisenberg, Leon, Chief, Psychiatry Service, Massachusetts General Hospital, Boston, MA 11/27/78
29. Ewalt, Jack, Director, Joint Commission on Mental Illness and Health and Commissioner of Mental Health, Commonwealth of Massachusetts, Boston, MA, 1/26/79
30. Farrell, Jean, Administrative Assistant to Erich Lindemann, Psychiatry Service, Massachusetts General Hospital, Boston, MA, 8/22/78
31. Frankel, Fred, Psychiatry Service, Massachusetts General Hospital, Boston, MA, 11/24/78
32. Fried, Marc, Director, Center for Community Studies and Director, Institute of Human Sciences, Department of Psychology, Boston College, Newton, MA, 11/16/79

Appendix: Informants Interviewed 447

33. Gifford, George, Harvard Medical School, Boston, MA, 1/9/79
34. Gifford, Sanford, Librarian, Boston Psychoanalytic Society, Department of Psychiatry, Peter Bent Brigham Hospital, Boston, MA 1/16,3/29/79
35. Glaser, Robert, medical student and Associate Dean, Harvard Medical School, Boston, MA and Dean, Stanford University, Palo Alto, CA, 12/18/79
36. Gonda, Thomas, Chairman, Department of Psychiatry, Stanford Medical Center, Stanford University, Palo Alto, CA, 12/17/79
37. Hackett, Thomas, Chief of the Psychiatric Service, Massachusetts General Hospital, Boston, MA 11/30/78
38. Häfner, Heinz, Director, Zentralinstitut für Seelisches Gesundheit, Mannheim, West Germany, 10/26/84
39. Hall, Elizabeth Cobb, wife of Stanley Cobb, late Chief of the Psychiatry Service, Massachusetts General Hospital, Boston, MA, 6/6/79
40. Hamburg, Beartrix, Department of Psychiatry, Stanford Medical Center, Stanford University, Palo Alto, CA, 1/26/79
41. Hamburg, David, Chairman, Stanford Medical Center, Department of Psychiatry, Stanford University, Palo Alto, CA, 1/26/79
42. Haylett, Clarice, Public Health Officer, San Mateo County Health Department, San Mateo, CA, 12/17/79
43. Hilgard, Josephine, Department of Psychiatry, Stanford Medical Center, Stanford University, Palo Alto, CA, 12/18/79
44. Hoffmann, Ulrich, Aktien Psychisch Kranke, Bonn, West Germany, 10/22/8
45. Janzarik, Werner, Professor, Psychiatrische Klinik, Universität Heidelberg, West Germany, 10/29/84
46. Katchadourian, Herant, Department of Psychiatry, Stanford Medical Center, Stanford University, Palo Alto, CA, 2/19/79
47. Kaufmann, Franz Xaver, Professor of Sociology, Universität Bielefeld, West Germany, 10/15/84
48. Kelly, James G., Psychiatry Service, Massachusetts General Hospital, Boston, MA, 4/29/83
49. Klein, Donald C., *emeritus* Executive Director, Wellesley Human Relations Service, Wellesley, MA 11/3/78
50. Klerman, Gerald, *emeritus* Superintendent, Erich Lindemann Mental Health Center, Boston, MA, 1/26/79
51. Knapp, Peter, Division of Psychiatry, Boston University School of Medicine, Boston, MA, 6/12/81
52. Kraus, Alfred, Psychiatrische Klinik, Universität Heidelberg, West Germany, 10/29/84
53. Kulenkampff, Caspar, Aktien Psychisch Kranke, Bonn, West Germany, 10/22/84
54. Lazare, Aaron, Director, In-Patient Unit and Day Hospital, Connecticut Mental Health Center, New Haven, CT and Psychiatry Service, Massachusetts General Hospital, Boston, MA, 1/20/81

448 Appendix: Informants Interviewed

55. Liederman, Gloria, Department of Psychiatry, Stanford Medical Center, Stanford University, Palo Alto, CA, 12/18/79
56. Liederman, Herbert, Psychiatry Service, Massachusetts General Hospital, Boston, MA and Department of Psychiatry, Stanford Medical Center, Stanford University, Palo Alto, CA, 12/18/79
57. Lindemann, Brenda, daughter of Erich Lindemann, 11/22/78
58. Lindemann, Elizabeth Brainerd, wife and colleague of Erich Lindemann and social Worker, Wellesley Human Relations Service, Wellesley, MA and social work consultant, San Mateo County Health Department, CA, 12/7/77, 3,4/17,6/27,7/14,8/22,10/?,11/?, 9/9/78, 8,10/4/79, 11/18/80,12/6/85, 8/14,23,11/29/98, 8/14/05, 8/22/06
59. Lindemann, Gertrude, sister of Erich Lindemann, 10/10,11/84, 5/1,2/88
60. Lindemann, Jeffery, son of Erich Lindemann, 10/4/79
61. Malamud, William I., Division of Psychiatry, Boston University School of Medicine, Boston, MA, 12/15/80, 2/2/81
62. Malamud, William, Sr., Iowa Psychopathic Hospital, Des Moines, IA and Chairman, Division of Psychiatry, Boston University School of Medicine, Boston, MA, 10/25/79
63. Mayo, Clara, Psychologist researcher, Wellesley Human Relations Service, Wellesley, MA, 9/29/78
64. Meyn, M. Christa, Minister, Ministerium Jugend-Familie-Gesundheit, Bonn, West Germany, 10/22/84
65. Morris, Laura, Social Worker, Mental Health Service, Psychiatry Service, Massachusetts General Hospital, Boston, MA 11/19/79
66. Mundt, Christoph, Psychiatrische Klinik, Universität Heidelberg, West Germany, 10/29/84
67. Myerson, Paul, Chairman, Department of Psychiatry, Tufts Medical School, Boston, MA, 6/19/81
68. Nemiah, John, staff member and Acting Chief, Psychiatry Service, Massachusetts General Hospital, Boston, MA, 9/21/78
69. Neumann, Ellsworth, Associate Director, Massachusetts General Hospital, Boston, MA, 4/27/79
70. Newman, Henry, Department of Psychology and Department of Social Relations, Harvard University, 1/20/79
71. Parker, Franklin, Board of Directors, Wellesley Human Relations Service, Wellesley, MA, 11/17/78
72. Parsons, Talcott, Chairman, Department of Social Relations, Harvard University, Cambridge, MA, 6/29/78
73. Paul, Benjamin, Anthropologist, Department of Social Relations, Harvard University and Harvard School of Public Health, Boston, MA, 12/18/79
74. Plog, Ursula, Department of Social Psychiatry, Freie Universität Berlin, West Germany, 10/11/84

Appendix: Informants Interviewed 449

75. Pörksen, Niels, Univesität Heidelberg and Leitende Arzt, Fachbericht Psychiatrie, von Bodelschwinghsche Alstalten Bethel, Serepta und Nazareth, Bielefeld, West Germany 9/9/78, 10/3,13/84, 10/3/04
76. Randolph, Peter, Superintendent, Bay Cove Mental Health Center, Boston, MA, 6/26/81
77. Reider, Norman, Psychiatry Department, Mount Zion Hospital. San Francisco, CA 7/86
78. Ryan, William, Connecticut Community Mental Health Center, New Haven, CT, 12/14/79
79. Schmidt, Wolfram, Psychiatrische Klinik, Universität Heidelberg, West Germany, 10/29/84
80. Schmitt, Francis O., Trustee, Massachusetts General Hospital, Boston, MA, Director, Neurosciences Research Foundation, Massachusetts Institute of Technology, Cambridge, MA, 4/3/79
81. Schneider, Hartmut, Social Psychiatry Department, Zentralinstitut Seelisches Gesundheit, Mannheim, West Germany, 10/26/84
82. Seeley, John, Special Committee on Social and Physical Environment Variables as Determinants of Mental Health, Office of Planning, National Institute of Mental Health, National Institutes of Health, U.S. Public Health Service, Department of Health, Education and Welfare, Washington, D.C., 4/12/79
83. Shader, Richard, Chairman, Department of Psychiatry, Tufts Medical School, Boston, MA, 1/29/82
84. Shapiro, Leon, Department of Psychiatry, Tufts Medical School, Superintendent, Massachusetts Mental Health Center, Boston, MA, 6/11/81
85. Shore, Miles, Superintendent, Bay Cove Mental Health Center, Boston, MA, 8/6/81
86. Siegel, Alberta, Professor of Psychology, Department of Psychiatry, Stanford Medical Center, Stanford University, Palo Alto, CA, 12/20/79
87. Sifneos, Peter, Psychiatry Service, Massachusetts General Hospital, Boston, MA, 10/13,11/10/78
88. Snyder, Benson, Massachusetts Institute of Technology, Cambridge, MA, 6/16/78
89. Solomon, Harry C., Superintendent, Boston Psychopathic Hospital and Commissioner of Mental Health, Commonwealth of Massachusetts, Boston, MA, 6/22/78
90. Stoeckle, John D., Chief of the Medical Outpatient Department, Massachusetts General Hospital, Boston, MA, 2/27/03
91. Stunkard, Albert J., Chairman, Department of Psychiatry, Stanford Medical Center, Stanford University, Palo Alto, CA, 2/15/84
92. Vaughan, Warren, Division of Mental Hygiene, Department of Mental Health, Commonwealth of Massachusetts, Boston, MA, 12/16/79

450 Appendix: Informants Interviewed

93. Von Baeyer, Walter Ritter, Professor, Psychiatrische Klinik, Universität Heidelberg, West Germany, 10/30/84
94. Von Felsinger, John H., Psychiatry Service, Massachusetts General Hospital, Boston, MA and Department of Psychology, Boston College, Newton, MA, 9/8/78
95. Von Ferber, Christian, Professor of Sociology, Universität Düsseldorf, West Germany, 10/16/84
96. Wallace, John, Board of Directors, Wellesley Human Relations Service, Wellesley, MA, 12/12/78
97. Wanta, Lorna Doone, Executive Assistant, Psychiatry Service, Massachusetts General Hospital, Boston, MA, 11/16/84
98. Webber, William, psychiatrist, Department of Psychiatry, Stanford Medical Center, Stanford University, Palo Alto, CA, 12/79
99. White, Benjamin, biographer of Stanley Cobb, late Chief, Psychiatric Service, Massachusetts General Hospital, Boston, MA 12/3/79
100. White, Robert W., Department of Social Relations, Harvard University, Cambridge, MA, 11/24/78

Interviewed by Leonard Duhl, M.D.

1. Lindemann, Erich, 6/8,22;7/6,13; 8/6/74
2. Lindemann, Erich; Seeley, John, 7/15/74
3. Lindemann, Erich; Seeley, John; Lindemann, Elizabeth Lindemann, 6/15/74
4. Lindemann, Erich; Lindemann, Elizabeth Lindemann, 7/30/74
5. Duhl, Leonard, former Special Assistant and Director, Special Committee on Social and Physical Environment Variables as Determinants of Mental Health, Office of Planning, National Institute of Mental Health, National Institutes of Health, U.S. Public Health Service, Department of Health, Education and Welfare, Washington, D.C., 6/6/74

Index

Note: Page numbers in *italics* indicate a figure on the corresponding page.

ABCD *see* Action for Boston Community Development (ABCD)
Abdilahi, Hussein 28
Abernethy, George 39, 188
abortion 33, 212, 369, 370
Abrams, Richard 34, 167
Action for Boston Community Development (ABCD) 13, 26
acupuncture 259
Adams, Abigail *see* Eliot, Abigail Adams
Adams, John (MD.) 239
Adler, Gerald 89, 101–104, 107, 109
African Americans 4, 6, 31, 190, 230, 243
Albany Medical Center Community Psychiatry Project 3–4
Albee, George W. 180
Albert Einstein College of Medicine 42–43
alcoholism and alcoholics 55–57, 186; in Berlin 78; Gardner as 188; and Gemeinde Psychiatrie (Community Psychiatry) program 66; Linn's work on 214; treatment unit 80; *see also* Cooperative Commission on the Study of Alcoholism; Public Law 91–616 CMHC Act amended
Alcoholics and Narcotics Addict Rehabilitation Amendments of 1968 (Public Law 90–574) 153
Aliber, Gil 40, 189
Alinsky, Saul 117
Allen, James R. 177, 314–315
Allport, Gordon 346
Almond, Barbara 249, 445
Almond, Richard 115, 188, 239, 248–250, 253, 262–263, 445

Alzheimer's disease 39, 189
American Academy of Arts and Sciences 345
American Academy of Psychoanalysis (AAP) 218
American Federation of State, County, and Municipal Employees (AFSCME) 111
American Friends Service Committee 335
American Independent Movement 118
American Medical Association (AMA) 13
American Mental Health Movement 66
American Philosophical Society xix, xxx
American Psychiatric Association (APA) 12–13, 17, 44, 53, 166, 191, 311, 330; Council 179
American Psychiatric Museum Association 349
American Psychoanalytic Association (APsA) 87–88, 368, 370–372; Standing Committee on Community Psychiatry 88, 212–216, 218; Standing Committee on Social Issues 212
American Psychoanalytic Society 212, 214, 427
American Psychological Association (APA) 330, 344, 353, 369; Board of Trustees 250
American Public Health Association 191, 250, 376
Andrews, Barbara 39, 188
Arden House 100

Index

Aronson, Jason 239, 348
Arvidson, Rolf 100, 103
Astrachan, Boris 111–115, 117–118, 120, 392, 445
asylums 165

Baker and Shulberg Community Mental Health Ideology Scale 17
Baker Guidance Center *see* Judge Baker Guidance Center
Ballantine, Thomas 433
Bandler, Bernard 11–31, 34, 218, 353, 400, 424–425, 445
Bandler, Louise 445
Bangor, Maine, Community Mental Health Program 4
Barber, Floyd 28
Bartholomew, John 108
Barton Road Complex 365
Barton, Walter E. 150, 250, 313
Basaglia, Franco 84–85, 220, 392
Batson, Ruth 16, 19–20, 23–24, 27–28, 30–31, 445
Beecher, Henry 285n117, 308n342
Beers, Clifford 196
Benda, Clemens E. 194, 253, 338
Bergstresser, Sara May 85, 391
Berman, Leo 190
Bernard, Viola 4, 31–34, 112, 368, 445; and American Psychoanalytic Society 212, 214–215; and American Psychological Association 87, 370; Social Issues Committee 372
Bernstein, Norman 60, 83
Berry, George Packer 45, 203, 331, 399, 433, 445
Bethel, Maine 39, 99, 189
Beth Israel Hospital 44, 101, 196–197, 334, 336, 399
Bettelheim, Bruno 255
Bierer, Joshua 224
Binswanger, Ludwig 219
Blaine, Daniel 179
Blum, Henrik 41, 92, 399, 433, 445
Bodarky, Clifford J. 98
Bok, Derek 1, 423
Bond, Douglas 194
Bonner, Frances 369
Bosch, G. 78, 219
Boston Action Center *see* South Boston Action Center
Boston City Hall 26
Boston City Hospital 12, 25

Boston College Department of Psychology 5–11, 190–191, 224, 230, 251
Boston Dispensary 99, 108
Boston Floating Hospital for Children 100, 108
Boston Psycho-Analytic Association 187
Boston Psychoanalytic Society and Institute 20, 101, 187, 217, 243, 346, 352
Boston Psychopathic Hospital/ Massachusetts Mental Health Center 15, 45, 63, 356; *see also* Solomon, Harry
Boston Public Schools 61, 358
Boston Redevelopment Authority 26
Boston State Hospital 24, 58
Boston University 31, 106; Board of Trustees 26; Division of Psychiatry 424
Boston University Community Mental Health Center (BUCMHC) *see* Boston University/Solomon Carter Fuller Mental Health Center
Boston University Medical Center (BUMC) 11, 26, 29
Boston University School of Medicine (BUSM) 11–14, 16; Division of Psychiatry 11–25, 353; *see also* Bandler, Bernard; Cohen, Sanford I.
Boston University School of Social Work 199
Boston University/Solomon Carter Fuller Mental Health Center 11, 15, 25–31, 34
Boston Urban League 8
Bowen, Peter 243
Bradshaw, Walter 373
Bragg, Robert ("Bob") L. 194, 197–199, 357, 359–360, 363, 445; resignation of 202; *see also* Mervyn, Frances
Brewster, Kingman 114
Brines, John K. 445
British Psycho-Analytical Society 187
Brody, Leslie 39–40, 189
Brooke, Edward 205
Brown, Bertram 47, 150, 156, 239; *see also* National Institute of Mental Health (NIMH)
Brown, Burt S. *see* Brown, Bertram
Brown, Jeff 237
Buber, Martin 63, 219, 240

Bunte, Doris 29
Burland, Alex 212, 386n105
Butler, Allen 445

Caplan, Gerald 14, 31, 65, 250; community change, views on 397; and community mental health 366, 412; community psychiatry, views on 403; group sharing common interests, need for 316; and Haylett 94; Jerusalem, move to 352; and Lindemann 65, 70, 81, 208, 210, 228, 342–344, 374, 432; and Pörksen 65; and psychiatry theory 315; resistance to 331; retirement 352
Caplan, Lee 446
Carstairs, Morris 224
Carter, George 11–12, 20
Carter, Jimmy 25, 158, 316
Cath, Stanley 344, 373
Catholic Church 4; *see also* Roman Catholic Church
Caudill, William 224
Chicago Psychoanalytic Institute 212
Chicago West Side Community Mental Health Center 31
Chope (Dr.) 93
Chradini, Irene 368
civil defense 369
civil disobedience 167, 170
civil liberties/libertarians 184–185, 228, 326
civil rights 244; of mental patients 325
civil rights movement 8, 12, 25, 111, 152, 311, 404; activists 116–117, 243; and Community Mental Health 182, 407; in Mississippi 105; and the Vietnam War 171, 241; and War on Poverty 164
civil service 110–111, 197
Civil Service Department 93
Clark, Dean A. 399
Clark, Eleanor 446
Clausen, John 2
Coalition of Concerned Citizens 118
Cobb, Elizabeth *see* Hall, Elizabeth Cobb
Cobb, Stanley 49, 193, 195; Boston roots of 352, 416; and Hackett 374; and Lindemann 347, 434; and Massachusetts General Hospital 243, 335, 343, 352, 357; memorial to 206–207; *see also* Stanley Cobb professorship
Coconut Grove study of grief 332, 334, 338–340, 347–349, 355, 431
Coelho, George 344
Coffey, Franchon 446
Coffey, Hubert 3, 446
Cohen, Donald 372
Cohen, Ed 370
Cohen, Jerome 223
Cohen, Raquel 45, 51, 53, 55, 61
Cohen, Sanford I. 22–25, 29–30, 446; and Bandler 13, 22, 28; and Batson 19–20, 24
Cohen, Ted 212
Cold War 402
Cole, Jean 58
Cole, Jonathan 24
Coleman, Jules 115, 213, 215, 218
Collective Psychotherapy Center 250
Columbia Presbyterian Medical Center-Harlem Hospital 82–84
Commission on Violence 240
Committee on Community Psychiatry *see* American Psychoanalytic Association (APsA)
Committee on Psychoanalysis, Community, and Society 369–372
Committee on Social Issues 368–369
Community Mental Health, and academic psychiatry 350–352
Community Mental Health Centers (CMHC) 1–126; *see also* Bandler, Bernard; Boston University Community Mental Health Center (BUCMHC); Knapp, Peter; Malamud, William I.
Community Mental Health Centers (CMHC) Amendments of 1970 153
Community Mental Health Centers (CMHC) Construction Act Amendments of 1965 153
Conant, James 234
Concord Community Mental Health Center 36–40
Connecticut Mental Health Center (CtMHC) *see* Yale School of Medicine–Connecticut Mental Health Center (CtMHC)
Contra Costa County (California) Public Health Department 40–41
Cooperative Commission on the Study of Alcoholism 332
Cope, Oliver 197, 203, 355, 416, 446

454 *Index*

Coplon, Frederic 39, 188
Cotton, Paul 104
Crockett, David 446
Crowdis (Mr.) 40, 189
CtMHC *see* Yale School of Medicine–Connecticut Mental Health Center (CtMHC)

Daniels, David 227, 230–231, 234, 446; and Almond, Richard 188, 249; at East Palo Alto 41, 242; and Lindemann 239–240, 242; and Ochberg 243
Daniels, R. S. 161
D'Autremont, Chester 37
David C. Wilson Lecture 21
Davis, Elizabeth 82, 213
Dawes, Lydia 399, 446
death 339, 358–359; attitudes towards 369; and depression 341; and dying 232; *see also* Erich Lindemann Symposium; Lindemann, Erich (death of)
Dement, William 227
dementia 39, 188
Democratic Psychiatry (*Psichiatrica Democratica*) 84–85, 392; *see also* Basaglia, Franco
Denham (Dr.) 234
depression (economic) 315, 414, 426
depression (psychological) 56, 72, 223, 341; or grief 355; in rural China 330; social causes of 407; treatment of 187, 332
Detre, Thomas 112, 115
Deutsche Gesellschaft für Soziale Psychiatrie 73, 75, 220–221, 367
Deutsch, Helene 261, 446
Deutschke, Rudy 84
Devlin, Joseph 11
Die Gemeinde Psychiatrie (Community Psychiatry) program *see* Gemeinde Psychiatrie program 66
Dietz, Jean 52, 207
Dohrenwend, Bruce 35
Dorchester Neighborhood Houses 108
Dorn, Robert 369
Dörner, Klaus 220–221, 367, 446
Dorosin, David 231–232, 238, 242, 247–248, 254, 259, 446
Duffy, Mark 446
Duhl, Frederick 575
Duhl, Leonard 1, 40–41, 51, 328, 339, 446, 450; and Community

Mental Health 179; and Lindemann 92, 239, 250, 263, 349, 428; and Ochberg 239
Dukakis, Michael 323, 325
Dumont, Matthew 207, 334
Dziewas, Hartmut 122, 221

East Palo Alto (California) Project 41–42
Eberhard Karls Universität Tübingen 80–81
Ebert, Robert 45, 47, 334
Economic Opportunity Act of 1964 164
Eisenberg, Leon 44, 46, 53, 120, 194–199, 201, 203, 374, 423, 446; and Hackett 353; and Human Relations Service (HRS) of Wellesley 199; and Lindemann 352
Eliot, Abigail Adams 36
Ellinson, Jack 35
Emerson, Eugene 357
Emerson Hospital 37, 39–40, 189
Engel 177, 314
Erich Lindemann Mental Health Center (ELMHC) 43–46, 50–55, 58, 205–212, 331, 334–336, 356–357; and Eisenberg 196–197; and Klerman 60, 208–210, 353, 355; and Massachusetts General Hospital 197; and mental health care 323; and Solomon, Harry 211–212; *see also* Cohen, Raquel; Klerman, Gerald
Erich Lindemann Symposium 334, 340, 354–355
Ervin, Frank 211
Etzioni, Amitai 167
Eulau, Cleo 247–248, 446
Evans, Robert 357–358, 374, 401
Ewalt, Jack 2, 26, 89, 100, 163, 195, 334, 446

Fanon Society 28
Farrah, George 26
Farrell, Jean 195, 205, 268, 446
Fechtenbaum, Leo 114
Felix, Alan 373, 387
Feldman Carol 9
Feldman, Saul 163
Fink, Paul 15
Fischelis, Mary 39, 188
Fisher, Seymour 24

Index 455

Fleck, Stephen 111, 114, 120, 342
Flexner 177, 314
Fogarty International Center 318
Ford Foundation 5, 10, 164
Frankel, Fred 44, 193, 196, 446
Freed, H. 31
Freedman, Daniel 112, 313
Freie Universität Berlin 77–79
Freudian theory and analysis 98, 101
Freud, Sigmund 42, 62, 213, 438n9
Fried, Marc 8, 196, 207, 446
Friedman, Daniel X. 166
Friedman, Henry 103
Friedrich Alexander Universität Erlangen 63
Fromm, Erich 168, 250
Fuller, Ruth 373
Fuller, Solomon Carter see Boston University/Solomon Carter Fuller Mental Health Center

Galdston, Iago xi, 293n184
Gans, Herbert J. 60, 196, 338
Garbarino, Jim 372–373
Gardner, Elmer 92, 97–98, 188
Gardner, George 334
Gaw, Albert 25
Geiger, H. Jack 105, 107, 384
Gemeinde Psychiatrie program 66, 136n165, 138n168, 141n175, 187, 292n175
George Washington University 424
gestalt psychology 75, 178, 427
Gibson, Charles 30
Gibson, Count 105, 236
Gifford, George 447
Gifford, Sanford 352, 447
Gildea (Fr.) 26
Gill, Michael ("Mick") 103–104
Gillen, Chris 243
Glaser, Robert 171, 447
Goethe, Johann Wolfgang von 250, 255, 428
Goldie, Peggy 234
Golovitch, George 241
Gonda, Thomas 226–227, 231, 243, 251, 366, 423, 447
Granatir, Bill 373, 387
Grant Foundation see William T. Grant Foundation
Green (Boston Redevelopment Authority) 26
Greenblatt, Milton 22, 30, 45, 54, 89, 205

Green Party 73
Gregg, Alan 48–49
grief studies see Coconut Grove study of grief
Grinker, Roy 295n187
Group for the Advancement of Psychiatry (GAP) 297n201
Group for Discussion of Problems in Community Mental Health Research 2
Gruenberg, Ernest 2, 35
Gudeman, Jon 324
guru 232, 251, 401, 430–431, 433, 437
Gütersloh (Germany) 62, 219–221
Gütersloh Conference 219

Hackett, Thomas xviii, xx, 51, 109, 198, 247, 352–357, 374, 423, 433, 447; hypnosis, use of 196; and Lindemann, rejection of 352, 354
Häfner, Heinz 63–65, 88, 123, 190, 219–220, 262, 447
Hagopian, Peter B. 194
Hall, Elizabeth Cobb 447
Halleck, Seymour 89–90, 162, 166
Hallen, Philip 160
Hallenbeck, Dorr 39, 188
Hamburg, Beatrix 227, 230–231, 244, 447
Hamburg, David 81, 194, 239–241, 247–249, 251–252, 444, 447; at Stanford Medical Center 227–232, 311, 423, 432
Hämchen (Prof.) 77
Hammett, Val 15
Harbor Mental Health and Mental Retardation Area 55–56, 58, 109
Hargreaves, G. Ronald 415
Harris, Hiawatha 88
Harry C. Solomon Mental Health Center 356–357
Harvard Department of Social Relations (HDSR) 2, 37, 239; see also Parsons, Talcott; White, Robert W.
Harvard Medical School (HMS) 43, 45, 47, 61 187, 190, 204–205; Laboratory of Community Psychiatry 316; and Massachusetts General Hospital 192–203, 263, 374, 396; see also Berman, Leo; Berry, George Packer; Bragg, Robert ("Bob") L.; Caplan, Gerald; Ebert, Robert; Klerman, Gerald;

Lindemann, Erich; Nemiah, John C.; Weisman, Avery
Harvard School of Public Health (HSPH) 2, 61, 90, 187, 198, 204
Harvard University 207, 352
Haylett, Clarice 93–94, 227, 230, 243, 259, 447
Healthy Cities project 329
Heidegger, Martin 219
Heidelberg Clinic *see* Heidelberg Psychiatrische Klinik
Heidelberg Psychiatrische Klinik (Department of Psychiatry) 62, 70, 72; *see also* Sozialistisches Patienten Kollektiv Heidelberg
Hersch, Charles 39
Herzan Helen M. 194, 199
Hilgard, Josephine 227, 230, 238, 248, 253–254, 261, 447
Hippocratic model 315
Hoffmann, Ulrich 125, 447
Hollingshead, August 2, 31
Holmes, Oliver Wendell x, xiii, 404
Hoover, Jackie 25
Hoover, Velma 27–28
Horwitz, Murray 7–8
Howe, Louisa P. 207
Huber, Wolfgang 68, 71
Human Relations Service of Wellesley 5, 64, 80, 108, 197, 261, 400–402, 437; evolution of 357–366; and Lindemann 333, 335–336, 338–339, 343; and Niles, Marion 344; *see also* Klein, Donald C.
Hutcheson, Belenden 194
Huxley, Aldous 1, 121

Ipsen, Johannes 2
India 64, 222–223, 230, 258; philosophy of 428; spiritual environment of 431
Israel 187, 412; *see also* Jerusalem
Italy 83–85

Jacksonian era (United States) 165, 400
Janzarik, Werner 68, 73, *124*, 447
Jaspers, Karl 62, 219
Jeffress, Elizabeth 223
Jerusalem 187, 352, 423
Johnston, Philip 324
Joint Commission on Mental Illness and Health 162, 399; *see also* Ewalt, Jack

Jones, Jen C. 349
Jones, Maxwell 405
Joseph, Ed 369
Judge Baker Guidance Center 358

Kahn, Richard 24
Kaiser Wilhelm II 390
Kaiser Wilhelm Institute, Munich 62
Katchadourian, Herant 231–232, 234, 240–242, 248, 352, 366, 447
Kaufman, Charles 11
Kaufmann, Franz Xavier 447
Keen, Myra 263
Kellam, Sheppard 2
Kellert, Stephen R. 172
Kellner, Harold 8
Kelly, James G. 327, 447
Kennedy administration 100, 183
Kennedy, John F. 12, 25, 139, 160, 405; assassination of 261
Kennedy, Robert 170, 207, 239
Kety, Seymour S. 194
King, Martin Luther, Jr. 166, 170, 239, 436
King, Melvin 6, 8
Kisker, Karl Peter 63, 219
Klein, Donald C. 5, 259, 347, 357, 372–373, 447
Kleinman, Arthur 372–373
Klerman, Gerald 44–45, 50, 52, 54–55, 57, 60–61, 113–120; "Current Evaluative Research in Mental Health Services" 156; deinstitutionalization, views on 183; and Erich Lindemann Mental Health Center (ELMHC) 187, 208–210
Kluckhohn, Clyde 346, 381
Knapp, Peter 11, 15–16, 20, 22–24, 26, 30, 447
Knowles, John 44, 46–49, 54, 399, 416
Kolb, Lawrence C. 32, 34–36, 162
Kornetsky, Conan 24, 29
Kraus, Alfred 73, *123*, 447
Kretz (University of Heidelberg) 68
Krieger, George 223
Kubler-Ross, Elizabeth (Dr.) 341
Kulenkampff, Caspar *125*, 219, 447

Laetrile 259
Lamb (Dr.) 93
Lamb, Richard H. 171, 178, 314
Langee (Dr.) 235

Lazare, Aaron 112, 117, 355
Law 180 of 1978 84
Lebanon 240
Le Carré, John 402
Leighton, Alexander 2, 31, 166, 178, 224, 398
Leopold, Robert 1, 15, 92, 317
Levine, Adeline xiii, 389
Levine, Gig 227, 234
Levine, Howard 212
Levine, Murray xiii
Levinson, Gig 248
Liddell (of United South End Settlements) 26
Lidz, Theodore 22, 111, 115, 117–118, 120
Lieberman, Jeffrey 312
Liebert, Robert S. 34, 167
Liederman, Gloria 227, 255, 448
Liederman, Herbert 234, 248, 448
Lightfoot, Orlando 20, 25
Lincoln Hospital/Albert Einstein College of Medicine 30, 70; Mental Health Center 85–88
Lindau Conference on Psychotherapy 222, 253
Lindau Psychotherapy Group 73, 271, 375, 401, 431
Lindau Psychotherapy Week 221–222
Lindemann, Anna 426
Lindemann, Brenda 258, 374, 376
Lindemann, Elizabeth (Betty) xix, 10–11, 41–42, 60, 81, 94, 225, 243, 247, 250–251, 254–255, 258–262, 269, 376, 448, 450; and Community Mental Health 69, 401; death of 374; and Evans, letter to/from 362–363; and Häfner 67, 69, 73; and Hamburg 229–231; and Jones (Jen) 349; and Lindemann (Anna) 426; and Marsh, letter to 361; and negative attention with the sick 396; obituaries complied by 343, 346; and Pörksen 68, 73; and Stougaard, letter from 340
Lindemann, Erich: books by (reviews of) 346–349; death certificate 274; death of 222, 229, 251, 253–255; illness and personal life of 255–263, 374; legacy of (via obituaries) 331–346; postretirement activities 221–227; see also guru; India; Lindau Psychotherapy Group; Stanford Medical Center

Link (Dr.) 77
Linn, Louis 213
Lodge, Henry Cabot 37
Los Angeles, California Community Mental Health Program 88
Lussier, George 39, 188
Lustman, Seymour 369

Madow, Les 15
Malamud, William I., Jr. 11–15, 19–20, 22–29, 31–32, 448
Malamud, William Sr. 11, 448
Mannheim Clinic see Zentralinstitut für Seelisches Gesundheit
Mannheim, Karl xiii, 413
Marans, Steven 372–373, 387
Marcuse, Herbert 83, 250
Marion, Tovah 39, 189
Martha's Vineyard Mental Health Center 88
Marx, Karl 389
Maryland Mental Health Center 88–89
Mason, Edward 250
Mason, Henry L. 71
Massachusetts General Hospital 352–357; see also Lindemann, Erich
Massachusetts Mental Health Center (MMHC) 89, 113, 115
Masserman 250
Mayo, Clara 93, 448
Mazer, Milton 88
McCance-Katz, Elinore 312
McCourt, William F. 355
McLean, Evelyn 56
McLean Hospital 31, 197, 345
McLennan, B. W. 156
Mead, Margaret 174
Meadow, Harry 46–47
Medicare and Medicaid 183–185, 318
Meers 372–373
Melbin, Nina 189
Mendelsohn, Jack 211
Menninger, Roy 215
Mental Health Planning Committee of Metropolitan Boston 164
Mental Retardation Facilities and Community Mental Health Centers (CMHC) Construction Act of 1963 152
Mental Retardation Facilities and Community Mental Health Centers Construction Act Amendment of 1965 153

458 Index

Merrifield, John 36–38, 188
Mervyn, Frances 357, 360
Mesnikoff, Alvin 36
Meyer, Adolf 196
Meyer (Dr., of Rockefeller Foundation) 222
Meyers, Helen 288n156
Meyersburg 372–373
Meyerson, Arthur 288n156, 291n165
Meyn, M. Christa *125*, 448
Michaels, Joseph 369
Milstein, Robert 39, 189
Mirsky, Alan 22, 24
Mirsky, Henry 39, 189
Moor (Mr., from Human Relations Service of Wellesley) 207
Moore, Burness E. 369
Moos, Rudolf 231, 248, 342
Moosbrucker, Jane 8
Morris, Laura 207, 433, 448
Moynahan (Father) 207
Mt. Sinai School of Medicine, New York 354
Mt. Zion Hospital, San Francisco 2, 94
Mundt, Christoph 68, *124*, 448
Murray, George B. 355
Murray, Henry A. 346
Musto, Angelo 334
Musto, David 151–152, 156
Mutter, Arthur 104
Myerson, David 109
Myerson, Paul 16, 89, 99–105, 108, 372, 448

National Academy of Sciences 228
National Advisory Mental Health Council 201
National Institute of Mental Health (NIMH) 1, 40, 44, 57, 150, 228, 312, 350; budget *155; see also* Brown, Bertram
National Institute on Alcohol Abuse 312
National Institute on Drug Abuse 312
National Mental Health Act 7/3/46 152
National Service Research Act of 1974 321
National Socialism (Nazi Party) (Germany) 62, 219; *see also* Nazi era in Germany

National Training Laboratory (NTL), Bethel, Maine 39, 189
Nazi era in Germany 62–63, 71, 75, 77, 190, 367, 427
Nelson, Duke 26
Nemiah, John C. 46, 94, 195–199, 352–353, 356–357, 399, 433, 448; and Cobb 352; and Lindemann, views of 211, 248, 334, 347; and Solomon 356
Neumann, Ellsworth 448
Newman, Henry 448
Niles, Marion 344
Nixon, Richard 57, 107, 166, 170, 250, 252, 315, 320
Noshpitz, Joseph 373
Nürnberger Neurologischen und Psychiarischen Klinik (Nuremberg Neurological and Psychiatric Hospital) 63
Nuttall, Ronald 8

Ochberg, Frank M. 156, 239, 243
Office of Economic Opportunity (OEO) 3–4, 164, 235
Okin, Robert 51, 107
O'Rourke, Edward J. 2
Osofsky, Joy 372–373, 387

Pacella, Bernard 369
Paolitto, Frank 53
Papanek, George 31
Parans 373
paranoia 10, 41, 227, 417
Parker, Franklin 108, 199, 357, 448
Parker, Franklin (Mrs.) 344
Parker Shelter Central 58, 323
Parsons, Talcott 2, 233, 333, 427, 448
Paul, Benjamin 239, 247, 448
Paul, Lois 259
Pavenstedt, Eleanor 11, 108, 212, 370
Peck, Harris 190, 330
Pepper, Max 113–115, 118
Physicians for Human Rights 105
Physicians for Social Responsibility 105
Pierce, Chester 27–28
Pinderhughes, Charles 25
Pinderhughes, Elaine 27
Pinel, Philippe 438
Pine Street Inn (Boston) 324
Plog, Ursula 78, 220–221, 448
Pollen 372–373
Pörksen, Britta *126*

Index 459

Pörksen, Niels 63–81, *126*, 190–191, 220, 367, 395–396
Poussaint, Alvin 105
Powledge, Fred 116
Presbyterian Hospital, New York 32–34, 36; *see also* Columbia Presbyterian Medical Center-Harlem Hospital
Pribram, Karl 248
Psychiatrische Klinik Häcklingen (Lüneburg) 79–80
Public Law 88–164 152, 162
Public Law 89–105 153
Public Law 90–32 153
Public Law 90–574 153
Public Law 91–211 153
Public Law 91–513 CMHC Act amended 153
Public Law 91–515 CMHC Act amended 153
Public Law 91–616 CMHC Act amended 153
Public Law 92–255 CMHC Act amended 153
Public Law 93–405 CMHC 153
Public Law 94–63 153
Public Law 95–83 CMHC Act amendment 153
Public Law 95–622 CMHC Act amended 153
Public Law 96–32 153
Public Law 96–398 Mental Health Systems Act 153
Public Law 97–35 Omnibus Budget Reconciliation Act 153
Putnam, James Jackson 357
Pynoos, Robert 372–373, 387

Quakers 257, 263, 409, 428
Quarton, Gardner C. 194, 211

racism 2, 6, 21, 23–24, 27, 29, 102, 114, 157, 186, 369; institutional 215; intractable 310; of mental health professionals 316; as risk factor 317
Randolph, Peter 25, 100–106, 449
Raskin, Raymond 212
Reagan, Ronald 166, 185, 400
Redlich, Frederick 2, 31, 64, 111–115, 117–120, 172, 218
Reider, Norman 449
Reiser, Morton 119–120

Rennie, Thomas 2, 31
Ricci, Benjamin 325
Richardson, F.L.W., Jr. 2
Risen, Clay 170
Roberts, Franklin 27
Roberts, L. M. 162
Robinson, Clifford 361
Rogers 250
Rogers versus Okin 107
Rollins, Bryant 8
Roman Catholic Church 26
Rose, Robert 24
Rosenbaum, Milton 42, 227, 241
Rosenberg, Pearl 417
Rosenthal (Dr.) 234–235
Roxbury (Boston) 5–9, 26, 364; Boston College branch 424; Veterans Administration Hospital 355
Roxbury Multi-Service Center 13–14
Rudolph, Paul 51–53, 59
Rubin 218
Ruesch, Jurgen 224
Ryan, William 5–6, 11, 114–117, 211, 344, 395–396, 449

Sabshin, Melvin xiii, 161–162, 242, 413
Sanborn, Charlotte J. 150, 313
Saltonstall, Leverett 37
Saltonstall, William 108
Sargent, Francis W. 37, 45
Sartre, Jean Paul 83
Schachter 373
schizophrenia 44, 68, 78, 99, 168; treatment of 183–184, 332
Schlesinger, Arthur 404
Schmidt, Wolfram 449
Schmitt, Francis O. xix–xx, 345–346, 449
Schneider, Hartmut 74, *125*, 449, 366–367, 449
Schneider, Karl 63
Schneider, Kurt 62, 73, 219
Schwarts, Steven 325
Schwartz, D. A. 162
Schwartz, Jack 198
Schwartz, Jacob 20, 22
Seeley, Jack *see* Seeley, John
Seeley, John R. 2, 168, 344, 413, 449
Semrad, Elvin 115, 334
Settlage, Calvin 369

460 Index

Shader, Richard 89, 101, 108–109, 186, 436, 449
Shapiro, Leon 89, 99–102, 104–105, 107–108, 449
Shore, Miles 101–105, 107–108, 156, 324, 400, 449
Short-Doyle Act for Community Mental Health Service of 1957 94
Siegel, Alberta 51, 240, 247, 449
Sifneos, Peter 196, 334, 433, 449
Sigel, George 103
Sigerist, Henry xi
Simmons, Alvin 200
Simon, Bennett 62, 372–373
Skinner, James 11, 20, 23, 25
Sklarew, Bruce 368, 371, 373
Smith, Brewster 254
Smith College 223
Snyder, Benson 449
social psychiatry, in Germany 219–221
Society of Friends *see* Quakers
Solomon, Brenda 386n105
Solomon, Harry C. 15, 44–45, 63, 100, 207–208, 211; Mental Health Center 356–357
South Boston Action Center 101
South End (Boston) 26, 100
Southern Regional Education Board Meeting (December 13–15, 1966) 171–176
South Shore (Boston) Mental Health Center 179
Sozialistisches Patienten Kollektiv Heidelberg (Socialistic Patients Collective of Heidelberg) 68
Sozial-Medizinischen Institut (Social Medicine Institute), University of Heidelberg 65
Space Cadets 316, 330–331, 401, 431
Special Committee on Social and Physical Environment Variables as Determinants of Mental Health *see* Space Cadets
Spiegel, David 231, 243
Spiegel, John 294n184
Spiegel, R. J. 262
Spinelli, Vic 104
Spock, Benjamin 3
Srole, Leo 31
Stalita, Alberta 369
Stanford Medical Center 366; Department of Psychiatry 228–255;

Lindemann at xiii, 5, 7, 9, 40–41, 51, 54, 191; *see also* Almond, Richard; Daniels, David; Gonda, Thomas; Hamburg, David; Hilgard, Josephine; Moos, Rudolf
Stanley Cobb professorship 197
Stanton, Alfred J. 2, 228
Stein, Arthur 373
Steinhart, Ingmar 122
Steinzor, Bernard 169
Stocking, Myron 104
Stoeckle, John D. 196–197, 355, 449
Stougaard, Elsie 340
Strauss, Anselm xiii, 413
Strauss, Erwin 219
Stunkard, Albert J. ("Mickey") 92, 251–252, 254, 263, 449; and Gonda 366, 423
Supplemental Social Security Income (SSI) 183
Schwartz, Jacob 11, 22, 24
Symposium on Intervention for Children Exposed to Violence and War 372–373

Talbot, Nathan 197, 203
Talbott, John A. 424
Tavistock Clinic 224
Taylor, Donald 16, 27–30
Taylor, Eugene 260
Tegreene, Joseph 186
Thomas, C. S. 57
Thoreau, Henry David 37
Tobin, Ruth 39, 189
Torrey, E. Fuller 9, 234, 323
Trussell, Hugh 35
Trussell, Ray E. 32
Tryst, Eric 224
Tuchman, Barbara 396, 405

Umana, Mario 45
United Community Construction Workers 6
United Community Services of Boston (UCS) 56, 276n24, 277n25
United Nations 329
United South End Settlements 26
United Way 359
University of Heidelberg 60–75; Psychiatrische Polyklinik/ Ambulanz (psychiatric outpatient clinic) 68

Vachon, Louis 22–24
Vaughan, Warren T., Jr. 90, 94, 191, 225, 243, 250, 263, 449
Verein für Fortschritt in Psychiatrie (Association for Progress in Psychiatry) 81
Veterans Administration Hospital (VAH) 107, 239; Bedford, MA 25; Cushing, MA 2; Palo Alto, CA 223, 231, 241, 342; West Haven, CT 111; West Roxbury, MA 355
Victory Village 365
Vietnam War 34, 166–168, 171, 315, 370, 375; agitation 249, 404; anti-Vietnam war stances 152, 164, 241, 244, 375
von Baeyer, Walter Ritter 62–64, 68–69, 71, 73, *124*, 190, 450
Von Bodelschwinghsche Anstalten Bethel, Serepta und Nazareth (Germany) 76
von Felsinger, John Michael 5–7, 9–11, 190, 207, 450
von Ferber, Christian 450
von Gebsattel, Viktor Emil 219
von Weizsäcker, Viktor 62, 427

Wacks, Gerry 39, 189
Walden Clinic 37, 39, 188–189
Wallace, John 450
Wanta, Lorna Doone 281n88, 382n73, 450
Washington Heights Community Mental Health Project 31–36
Webber, William 35, 231, 450
Weick, Karl E. 349
Weil, Gunther 9
Weiner, Jerry M. 424
Weingarten, Randy 305n305
Weisman, Avery 196, 355, 433
Weisz, Al E. 240
welfare: child 368, 370; civic 359; fields 205; law 212; and mental health centers 173; mothers 317; needs 164; programs 111, 190; public 57, 159; social 55, 88, 94, 112, 151, 170, 310, 313
Welfare, Department of 83, 93, 95, 110, 117–118
welfare rights movement 117, 119; New Haven 116

welfare system 29; city 66; county 92, 98; investigators 86; recipients 114; reform 47; state 85
Wellesley Community Chest and Council 344
Wellesley Friendly Aid Society 37, 344
Wellesley Human Relations Service (HRS) *see* Human Relations Service of Wellesley
West End Study (Boston) 59–60, 196, 201, 203, 209, 262, 332–334, 336–338, 340, 435
West Germany 79, 367
Weston, Massachusetts 359–360, 362
West Side program (Chicago) 2
White, Benjamin 194, 260, 450
White Establishment 95
Whitehouse, Jeanne 362
white people in the United States 6–7, 9–10, 20, 26–30, 172; and civil rights 170; liberals 117; racism of 114; rebellion against 190; students 167
White, Robert W. 37, 254
Will, George 152
William T. Grant Foundation 204, 418
Wilmans (professor of psychiatry) 62–63
Wilson Lecture *see* David C. Wilson Lecture
Wilson, Percy 27
Wilson, Woodrow 165
Winant, John Gilbert 186
Windle 163
Wittkower 224
Wohlberg, Gerald 24
Wolfe, Richard J. xix
Wolfe, Tom 165, 369
Worcester (Massachusetts) State Hospital 109–111
Worcester Youth Guidance Center 110
World Health Assembly 329
World Health Organization (WHO) 258, 316–317; Healthy Cities project 329
World War I 341, 390
World War II 63, 164, 182, 186, 313, 402, 405; postwar 219,

235, 241; social problems associated with 415; and social psychiatry 366; veterans of 14, 365
Wren, Christopher (Sir) 336
W. T. Grant Foundation, Inc. *see* William T. Grant Foundation
Wyatt, Gertrud 261
Wynne 224

Yale Medical Center 114
Yale Medical School 22, 212
Yale-New Haven Hospital 111–114
Yale Psychiatric Institute 112
Yale School of Medicine–Connecticut Mental Health Center (CtMHC) 44, 111–120, 187
Yale University 113, 115–118, 187
Yalom, Irving 227, 241, 248
Yolles, Stanley 100, 163, 175

zeitgeist 175, 251
Zentralinstitut für Seelisches Gesundheit 66, 74, *121*, *123*, *125*, 190, 366, 424; *see also* Hafner, Heinz; Schneider, Hartmut
Zusman, Jack 171, 178, 314
Zwerling, Israel 15, 42, 316

Printed in the United States
By Bookmasters